Y0-EKP-314

SHERRY SHINDLER
AN ESCROW MANUAL

ESCROW PRINCIPLES AND PRACTICES

ASHLEY CROWN SYSTEMS, INC.
1998

The publication is designed to provide accurate and current information regarding the subject matter covered. The principles and conclusions presented are subject to local, state and federal laws and regulations, court cases and revisions of same. If legal advice or other expert assistance is required, the reader is urged to consult a competent professional in that field.

Project Manager: Sherry Shindler
Graphic Design: Sherry Shindler
Senior Editor: Cynthia Simone
Legal Reviewer: Joan Thompson

© 1998 by Ashley Crown Systems, Inc.

Published by Ashley Crown Systems, Inc.
22952 Alcalde Drive #130
Laguna Hills, CA 92653-1311

All rights reserved. No part of this book may be reproduced or transmitted in any form or by any means, electronic or mechanical, including photocopying, recording or by any information storage or retrieval system, without prior written permission from the publisher.

Printed in the United States of America.

TABLE OF CONTENTS

Chapter 15 Escrow Review   425

Preface

Whether you are reading this book to increase your knowledge about escrow for the purpose of beginning a new career, using it to satisfy a requirement for your real estate broker's license or simply wanting to learn more, as a consumer, about the fascinating subject of escrow, you will find the information presented in this book to be useful. While the book is written with the beginning student of escrow in mind, inquiring consumers also will find answers to their questions about the subject.

While featuring Northern and Southern California escrow practices and other particular California laws affecting the practice of escrow, practitioners in any state will benefit from the basic information presented here regarding the processing of the transfer of real property by a neutral third party, whether that party is an escrow officer, real estate broker, title insurer or an attorney.

About the Author

Sherry Shindler brings a rich background in real estate and education to the creation and production of this book. Her 20 years in the real estate profession include eight years of specialization in investment properties and residential sales.

A California Community College Real Estate Instructor since 1986, Sherry also has used her experience in the real estate industry as a framework for writing test items for state licensing examinations, authoring *California Real Estate Principles,* reviewing numerous real estate textbooks for major publishers and preparing a series of continuing education courses for private schools. A well-known real estate lecturer and educator, Sherry contributes extensive knowledge to this project.

She holds a bachelor of science degree in education from Long Beach State College, a California Real Estate Broker's License and a California Community College Lifetime Instructor's Credential.

Author's Acknowledgments

Many thanks to the hard working escrow professionals and others who have made contributions to this first edition of *Escrow Principles and Practices*

Pete Meade (SMS)--Thank you, Pete, for supplying all the escrow forms for this book and for being so helpful in sharing information. Your company is fortunate to have such a detail oriented, courteous professional as its representative.

Joan Thompson (San Clemente Escrow)--Your professional judgment as you reviewed the text for the past year has made this project possible, Joan. Thank you for taking the time to be thorough and thoughtful as you journeyed through this book, one chapter at a time.

Cynthia Simone (Simone Communications)--My dear friend and editor Cynthia, how can I thank you enough for helping me get through one more book. Your sense of humor as we negotiated our way through unexpected mine fields and other riddles of textbook character, and your capable, constructive and always unprejudiced suggestions kept me going whenever I wanted to send the whole project to Camp Faraway. Thank you for your tact and wisdom.

Norma Hurlock (retired)--You saved me hours and hours of tedious data entry with your newly learned computer skills. Your cheerful attitude, even when your computer files disappeared before your very eyes, was always a welcome treat. Thanks, Mom.

Jay Achenbach (Ashley Crown Systems)--Thank you, Jay, for your unwavering positive attitude during this entire project and for being such a constant advocate of high standards. Your business and personal philosophy contribute abundantly to real estate education.

GP--Thanks for being my frequent consultant, patron and loyal supporter. You always supplied just the right medicine with plenty of smiles to make each day bright.

chapter **1**

WHAT
IS
ESCROW?

Focus

Pre-Test

The following is a self test to determine how much you know about escrow and title professionals before reading this chapter. Take it without studying, then read the material presented in the text. At the end of the chapter you will find a repeat of this exam. Test your knowledge by answering the questions again, then check your improvement. (The answers are found at the end of the book.) Good luck.

True/False

1. An escrow is a small and short-lived trust arrangement.

2. When there is a conflict between signed instructions and the original agreement, the original contract will prevail.

3. Escrow holds documents, conditionally, until all terms of the escrow are met.

4. A buyer or a seller can change escrow instructions unilaterally.

5. A real estate broker has authority to amend escrow instructions.

6. An escrow agent operates as a dual agent.

7. A beneficiary statement is requested if an existing loan is going to be assumed.

8. Prorations usually include principal and interest.

9. The escrow holder gives closing statements to the buyer and seller at the end of the escrow.

10. The escrow holder must return any funds to buyer or seller if requested to do so by either.

Introduction

For most people, escrow is a mysterious, obscure process. They don't know what "going to escrow" means, nor how you "open an escrow." There is, however, no real mystery about it. An escrow is a time period during which the paperwork required for the sale of real property is processed. An escrow holder, otherwise known as an escrow company, or some other eligible person, acts as a neutral agent of both buyer and seller. Documents and money are collected and distributed by the escrow holder, and escrow instructions are prepared as directed by the principals, insofar as escrow law allows.

The escrow instructions reflect the understanding and agreement of the principals, who may not always be a buyer and seller, because transactions involving the sale of real estate are not the only kind that require the use of an escrow. Any time a neutral third party is needed to handle documents or money, such as in the transfer of real property, loans, sale of trust deeds or bulk sales (business opportunities), an escrow might be required. In this chapter, we will discuss escrow only as it relates to the sale of real estate.

No one is required by law to use an escrow for any of the above transactions, including the sale of real property. However, when a buyer and seller reach an agreement about the sale of property, including terms and price, it is usually advisable to invite a neutral third party to handle the details of completing the agreement.

Misunderstanding, or even criminal or innocent negligence, on the part of the principals could be the cause of loss to one or both parties if the contract is not handled by an outside professional whose business it is to conduct escrows.

After instructions are signed, it is the escrow holder's job to follow them and request all parties involved to observe the terms and conditions of the contract. The escrow holder coordinates communication between the principals, the agents and any other professionals -such as the lender or title company whose services are called for in the instructions.

So an escrow is a small and short-lived trust arrangement. The principals trust that the escrow holder will carry out their wishes, and the escrow holder has a duty to be trustworthy, as the agent of both parties. As a neutral third party, the escrow holder may only operate at the direction of all parties to a transaction. We shall see in this chapter how that is accomplished.

Basic Requirements for a Real Estate Transaction

A real estate transaction usually starts at the time a broker obtains a listing from a property owner. The most common type of listing is an Exclusive Authorization and Right to Sell. With this type of listing, the seller must pay a commission no matter who sells the property--even if the owner makes the sale. The agent promises to use due diligence to find a ready, willing and able buyer under the exact terms of the listing contract, and the seller promises to pay a commission when the agent fulfills the contract.

At some point, either the listing agent or an agent from another brokerage will find a buyer and write an offer. There are certain items the agent must consider carefully when preparing the offer to purchase (also known as a deposit receipt or purchase contract).

The following list of items that must be included in the offer apply only to the most common aspects of a residential purchase. Commercial, industrial, vacant land, farm or ranch development and other types of properties require different treatment by a real estate agent.

<u>Specifically, offers to purchase residential property must address more than two-dozen important items.</u>

1. Date and place the contract is signed by the buyer

2. Correct name and address of the buyer

3. Form of the buyer's deposit: cash, check, cashier's check, promissory note, money order or other

4. Designee to hold the deposit: broker, seller or escrow

5. Purchase price of the property

6. Terms under which the property will be purchased: all cash, refinance, loan assumption or taking title "subject to" the existing loan. Do any of the existing loans contain acceleration clauses or prepayment penalties? If so, has the buyer approved the terms?

Offers to purchase residential property must address: (continued)

7. Amount of time to be allowed for the seller to consider the buyer's offer to purchase, and to complete the transaction. Is time of the essence?

8. Definite termination date stated in the contract.

9. Covenants, Conditions and Restrictions; easements; rights or other conditions of record that affect the property: Are they acceptable to the buyer?

10. Deed of conveyance: Is it to be executed by the seller to contain any exceptions or reservations? Has the buyer approved of this?

11. Are there any stipulations or agreements regarding any tenancies or rights of persons in possession of the property?

12. Roof and electrical wiring inspections: Who pays for inspections and work, and who orders reports?

13. Are there any stipulations or agreements regarding facts a survey would reveal, such as the existence of a common wall, other encroachments or easements?

14. Are there any special or unusual costs or charges to be adjusted through escrow? Who will pay for the title policy, escrow services and other customary charges? Who pays for any unusual charges?

15. Who will select the escrow holder? The parties should reach a mutual agreement on this.

16. Are there any special documents to be drawn in the transaction, and if so, who will prepare them?

Offers to purchase residential property must address: (continued)

17. If prorations are not to be made as of the date escrow closes, what date is to be used?

18. If possession is granted prior to the close of escrow, what type of agreement must be prepared to cover this occupancy and who will prepare it?

19. If structural pest control inspection report and certification are to be furnished, who will pay the cost? Who will pay for any required work? Will multiple reports be required?

20. Are other brokers involved in this transaction? What are their names, addresses and telephone numbers?

21. What is the negotiated sales commission? How and when is it to be paid? If the deposit receipt initially establishes that a commission will be paid, it must contain the commission negotiability statement, which declares that by law all commissions are negotiable.

22. Make sure all parties sign the contract. Check for signatures of all buyers, all sellers and the agents.

23. Every purchase contract prepared or signed by a real estate salesperson must be reviewed, initialed and dated by the salesperson's broker within five working days after preparation or signing by the salesperson or before the close of escrow, whichever occurs first.

Offers to purchase residential property must address: (continued)

24. If the transaction is a residential sale of four-or-fewer units and involves seller-assisted financing, and a licensee is the arranger of such credit, a financing disclosure statement must be prepared and provided to both buyer and seller.

25. A specific written disclosure must be made to prospective buyers of one-to-four dwelling units with facts about the particular piece of property that could materially affect the property's value and desirability.

26. Licensees acting as listing and selling brokers in certain residential real estate transactions must make informational written and oral disclosures concerning who is representing whom.

27. A real estate licensee who acts as the agent for either the buyer or the seller in the sale or transfer of real property, including manufactured housing, must disclose to both parties the form, amount and source of any compensation received or expected to be received from a lender involved in financing related to the transaction.

As soon as possible following the opening of escrow the seller should furnish escrow with the following specifics.

<u>Seller to furnish escrow:</u>

1. Escrow instructions signed by all of the sellers.

2. The latest available tax and assessment bills and any other statements or bills which are to be prorated through escrow.

3. Seller's loan payment books and records.

4. Seller's fire, liability and other insurance policies, if they are to be assigned to the buyer.

5. A beneficiary statement, demand, certificate or offset statement from the holder of any mortgage or trust deed of record on the property; the items that show the amount due on any loan of record; the payment date; the date to which interest is paid; and other important information. Consent to the transfer from lenders of record must be given.

6. Any subordination or other agreement required by the purchase contract, to be approved by the parties through escrow.

7. Certificates or releases showing satisfaction of mechanic's liens, security agreements (chattel mortgages), judgments or mortgages which are to be paid off through escrow.

8. List of tenants' names and the apartments they occupy, together with the amount of rent paid and unpaid, the dates when rents are due, and, if required, an assignment to the buyer of any unpaid rent, as well as details on advance security deposits, if any.

Seller to furnish escrow: (continued)

9. Assignment to buyer of all leases affecting the property.

10. Letters from the seller to tenants instructing them to pay all subsequent rent to the buyer and reaffirming the conditions of the tenancy, including notice of the transfer of the security deposit, if any, to the buyer.

11. The seller's executed and acknowledged deed of conveyance to the buyer or a valid authority to execute the deed of the seller by the seller's attorney-in-fact if the seller is acting through an agent.

12. An executed bill of sale covering any personal property to be conveyed to the buyer, together with an inventory of the items for the buyer's approval.

13. A security agreement (chattel mortgage) for execution by the buyer covering any personal property included in the purchase price but not paid for by the buyer in cash.

14. The deed by which the seller acquired title to the property and the seller's policy of title insurance.

15. Any unrecorded instruments affecting the title.

16. Any other documents or instruments which the seller is to prepare or deliver.

17. Any approvals required for documents the seller is to receive at closing.

18. Information required to be disclosed to the buyer under the seller financing disclosure, if necessary.

As soon as possible after the opening of escrow, the buyer should furnish the escrow holder with certain documents and information, and should review or inspect personally all of the following items.

Buyer to furnish escrow:

1. Review escrow instructions signed by all purchasers.

2. Review the preliminary title report for the subject property to make sure that there are no items of record affecting the property which have not already been approved by the buyer.

3. Review any Conditions, Covenants and Restrictions affecting the property, whether of record or not.

4. Confirm the terms of any mortgages or deeds of trust to be assumed by the buyer or which will remain an encumbrance on the property.

5. Examine any beneficiary statements, fire insurance or liability policies if they are to be assigned to the buyer.

6. Examine offset statements on loans to be assumed, or those under which the buyer is taking title to the property "subject to" existing loan terms; verify the unpaid principal balances owed, the interest rates, dates to which interest is paid and other vital information.

7. Review and approve structural pest control and other reports to be delivered through escrow.

8. Carefully review all new loan documents prior to signing.

9. Compare the terms of the purchase contract, escrow instructions, title report and deed to make sure there are no discrepancies in the transaction documents.

Buyer to furnish escrow: (continued)

10. If tenancies are involved, review the names, addresses and telephone numbers of tenants; the rent amounts, rent due dates, copies of rent agreements or leases, letters from the seller to the tenants verifying the terms of occupancy and notifying the tenants of change of ownership, the assignments of any unpaid rent and leases, details on security deposits if any.

11. Examine the bill of sale and inventory covering the items of personal property to be conveyed to the purchaser.

12. Review copies of any bills to be prorated in escrow.

13. Verify all amounts and prorations on the estimated escrow settlement sheet.

14. Reinspect the property to determine that it is in the same condition as it was when the buyer made the purchase offer. Recheck for any undisclosed items which might affect the use of the property, such as: party walls, access roads to other properties, irrigation canals or ditches, common drives or persons in occupancy or possession of the property, which the county records would not disclose.

15. Deposit sufficient cash or clear funds to cover any balance owed on the purchase contract plus buyer's closing costs and expenses, and approvals as required.

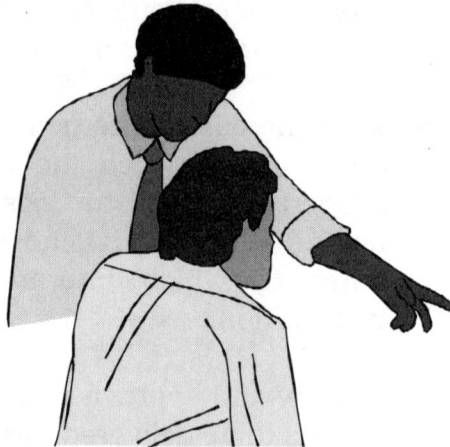

The parties should always keep copies of any documents and instruments they sign, deliver to or receive from any party in the real estate transaction.

Basic Requirements for an Escrow

There must be a binding contract between the parties to an escrow. The binding contract can be a deposit receipt, agreement of sale, exchange agreement, an option, or mutual escrow instructions of the buyer and seller.

The signed instructions become an enforceable contract, binding on all parties to the escrow. However, when there is a conflict between the signed instructions and the original agreement of the principals, the original contract will prevail. Amendments to the escrow instructions can change the original agreement if all parties agree. When all instructions are completed, the escrow closes, the buyer gets a deed and the seller gets the money.

The Clarkes put their home on the market, listing it with a local broker. It was competitively priced, and their broker told them it would probably take about two weeks to sell. One afternoon, an agent with another real estate company showed the house to the Lees, and they loved it. After writing up an offer and later presenting it to the Clarkes, the buyers' agent called them with the good news. The sellers had accepted.

The next day, the agent took the buyers' earnest money (generally about one percent of the purchase price) to the escrow office, gave it to the escrow agent and got a receipt. The escrow holder immediately cashed the check and deposited it in a trust account. The escrow holder then drew up escrow instructions to reflect the terms and

13

conditions of the sale. The sellers signed their copy, the buyers signed theirs, and both were returned to the escrow company. The escrow was now open.

A conditional delivery of transfer documents and funds, the second requirement for a valid escrow, means the seller will deliver a signed grant deed which conveys the title to the buyer, and the buyer and/or the lender will deliver to escrow whatever funds are required for the sale.

Also, the escrow agent will hold the security for any loan (trust deed) conditionally until directed by the terms of the escrow. The escrow agent will keep documents and funds until all other terms of the escrow have been completed, and then distribute them according to the expressed conditions of the escrow.

Sometime before the escrow closes, the seller will be asked to sign a grant deed conveying title to the buyer. Because the seller will sign over the ownership to the buyer before getting the money, the escrow holder is instructed to hold the signed deed until funds from the buyer are deposited in escrow and all other terms of the escrow have been met. Conditional delivery of the grant deed has been made by the seller.

Toward the end of the escrow period, the buyer will be asked to sign a note and trust deed for the loan. The buyer is promising to pay back the money, using the property as security for the loan. Escrow has not closed, and the buyer doesn't own the house yet. Nor has the seller been given the promised money, but the note and trust deed are signed and deposited into escrow, conditionally, until all other terms have been met. Only then will escrow request loan funds.

After the escrow has been completed, the buyer gets a grant deed, after it has been recorded, and the seller gets the money. The escrow is closed.

An Escrow Must Include the Following to be Valid:

- Binding contract between buyer and seller

- Conditional delivery of transfer documents to a third party

---

General Escrow Principles and Rules

Once instructions have been signed by the buyer and seller and returned to the escrow holder, neither party may unilaterally change the escrow instructions. Any changes must be made by mutual agreement between buyer and seller. The escrow agent does not have the authority to make changes in the contract upon the direction of either the buyer or seller, unless both agree to the change, in the form of an amendment.

Also, it should be noted, the broker has no authority whatsoever to amend or change any part of the escrow instructions without the knowledge of the principals. The written consent of both buyer and seller, in the form of an amendment to the original instructions, must be given before any change may be made.

> The Clarkes and the Lees signed escrow
> instructions on June 9. The agreement reflected a
> sales price of $450,000, with $90,000 as a down
> payment. After signing the instructions, however,
> the buyers decided they only wanted to put
> $80,000 down, and told the escrow officer to
> change the instructions. An amendment was
> written for them to sign, and a copy sent to the
> sellers to sign.
>
> The buyers were disappointed when the Clarkes
> did not want to change the contract and refused to
> sign the amendment. When the Lees wanted to
> back out, the escrow officer reminded them that
> they had a mutually binding legal agreement with
> the sellers. Neither side could change any part of
> the agreement, including terminating it, without
> the written agreement of the other.

As agent for both parties to an escrow, the escrow agent is placed in a position of trust. By operating as a dual agent, the escrow holder sits between the buyer and seller as a stakeholder with an obligation to both sides.

As a neutral third party, the escrow officer must observe these rules:

☑ Escrow instructions must be understood by the principals to the escrow and must be mutually binding. Instructions must be carefully written to be very clear about the agreement between the buyer and seller. Each party must understand his or her obligation to carry out the terms of the contract without assuming the escrow holder has any power to force compliance. The escrow holder may not act unless directed by the principals.

✓ The escrow holder does not get personally involved in disagreements between the buyer and seller, nor act as a negotiator for the principals. Escrow instructions make each party's obligations and agreements clear, and it is up to the buyer and seller to keep the promises they each made in their agreement with the other. All parties must know that the escrow agent is not an attorney, and must advise anyone seeking legal advice to get counsel from a professional.

✓ An escrow agent has a limited capacity as agent for buyer and seller, and may only perform acts described in the contents of escrow instructions. While acting as a dual agent, the escrow officer must operate in the best interest of both parties, without special preference to either. The escrow agent serves each principal after escrow closes, in providing them with the documents and/or funds to which they are entitled.

✓ All parties must sign escrow instructions for the contract to be binding. An escrow is officially open when both buyer and seller have signed instructions.

✓ Escrow instructions must be clear and certain in their language.

✓ All documents to be recorded must be sent to the title company in a timely manner (as quickly as possible), and all interested parties should receive copies of recorded documents.

☑ Escrow instructions should specify which documents or funds the escrow holder may accept.

☑ Overdrawn trust accounts (debit balances) are prohibited by law.

☑ Information regarding any transaction is held in trust by the escrow officer and may not be released to anyone without written permission of the principals.

☑ An escrow holder has a duty to disclose to the principals any previously undisclosed information that might affect them. An amendment would be drawn at the direction of the buyer and seller to reflect any change as a result of new disclosures.

☑ A high degree of trust along with good customer service and relations must be provided by an escrow holder.

☑ An escrow holder must remain strictly neutral regarding the buyer's and the seller's interests.

☑ Escrow records and files must be maintained daily. A systematic review of open escrow files will make sure no procedure has been overlooked, or time limit ignored.

☑ Before closing an escrow, all files must be audited carefully.

☑ All checks or drafts must have cleared before any funds may be released to the seller.

☑ Escrow must close in a timely manner, according to the agreement between buyer and seller. A prompt settlement must be made to all principals.

Escrow Procedures

Escrow procedures may vary according to local custom. In some areas, escrow companies or banks conduct escrows. In other areas, title companies do the job. However, there are certain procedures that are followed during the regular course of all escrows.

Open Escrow

The person who usually opens escrow, if there is a real estate agent involved, is the selling agent. That person usually has an earnest money check that must be deposited into escrow or some other trust account no more than one business day after buyer and seller have signed the deposit receipt.

So, at the first opportunity, the real estate agent must take the buyer's check to the escrow officer to put in a trust account. The agent then gives the escrow officer all the information needed to prepare escrow instructions.

Usually within a day or two, computer generated instructions are ready for buyer and seller to sign. The instructions, as you recall, reflect the agreement between the buyer and seller as seen in the offer to purchase (deposit receipt) and usually include all disclosures required by law. Only the seller's set of escrow instructions include the amount of commission to be paid to the broker, unless, as in some cases, the buyer is paying a commission also.

The principals may go to the escrow office if there is no real estate agent involved, and tell the escrow officer to prepare instructions according to their agreement.

Prepare
Escrow Instructions

Usually the escrow holder prepares the instructions on a computer generated form, with details of the particular transaction completed in the blank spaces on the form. All parties sign identical instructions, with the exception of the commission agreement that is prepared for the seller to sign--if the seller in fact is paying the commission. Buyer and seller sign the instructions, which are then returned to the escrow holder who follows the directions in the agreement to complete the escrow.

Imagine you are selling your home. The following probably would be included in your escrow instructions:

1. *Purchase Price*: This is the amount of money the buyer and seller have agreed upon for the sale of the property.

2. *Terms*: The buyer and seller agree on how the buyer will purchase the property: cash, new loan, loan assumption, V.A. or FHA loan, seller to carry a trust deed, trade, or any other special agreements provided in the contract between buyer and seller. This section describes the amount of the down payment and the terms of any loans for which the buyer will apply.

3. *Vesting*: The buyer will take title in one of the following ways: sole ownership, joint tenancy, tenants in common, or tenancy in partnership. How the buyer will take title may be important for tax or inheritance purposes and the escrow holder must be directed how to draw the deed to reflect the wishes of the buyer, but may not give advice regarding vesting.

4. *Matters of Record*: Buyer and seller may agree on a matter of record--some circumstance affecting the property--that is recorded. It may be an easement, an existing street bond or a trust deed. An agreement may be made about who will be responsible for whatever exists as a recorded encumbrance on the title at the time of the sale.

5. *Closing*: Buyer and seller will agree on how long they want the escrow to last. They will mention a specific

length of time for the escrow and instruct the escrow holder accordingly.

6. *Inspections*: Buyer and seller will agree on whether or not to have certain inspections of the property before the close of escrow, such as a pest control inspection; property inspection to identify any plumbing, electrical or structural problems; a soil inspection to check for slippage or unstable compaction. The buyer's approval of the reports will be a contingency of the sale and must be mentioned in the escrow instructions.

7. *Prorations*: The division of expenses and income between the buyer and seller as of the date of closing is known as proration. Some items that are prorated are: taxes, rental deposits or income, insurance premiums. The reason for prorations is that some payments may have been made by the seller for a time period beyond the agreed upon date for escrow to close. Or the seller may be in arrears on taxes. The escrow holder debits or credits the seller or buyer, depending on the escrow closing date.

8. *Possession*: The buyer and seller will have agreed on when the buyer can move into the house, and the escrow instructions must reflect their agreement on the date the buyer will take possession of the property. The close of escrow could be the date of possession, or sometimes the seller will rent the property back from the buyer after the close of escrow. In that case, a lease agreement

should be signed and handled by the parties outside of escrow.

9. *Documents*: The escrow holder will need to know which documents to prepare, have signed by the proper party, and record at the close of escrow. Usually, these will be a grant deed and a trust deed.

10. *Disbursements*: The escrow holder must settle the accounts of the buyer and seller according to the escrow instructions. Also, the escrow holder must provide a closing statement of costs and charges to each party and a final distribution of funds at the close of escrow.

Order Title Search

At the time the buyer and seller reach an agreement about the sale of the property, they also select a title company. One of the jobs of the escrow officer, after escrow has been opened, is to order a title search of the subject property.

The title company prepares a preliminary title report, and searches the records for any encumbrances or liens against the property. The company checks to make sure the seller is the owner of record, and inspects the history of ownership, or chain of title, in the preliminary title search. The purpose is to ensure all transfers of ownership have been recorded correctly, and that there are no unexplained gaps.

The buyer is allowed a certain number of days to approve this preliminary title report. Buyer approval is important to eliminate surprises regarding the title as the escrow progresses. The escrow holder should notify the buyer and seller if there is any difference in the preliminary report and the escrow instruction, by way of an addendum "for information only."

As you recall, the escrow agent is a neutral party and only has the authority to do what is described in the escrow instructions. The escrow officer must wait for instructions about what to do next. The preliminary title report is the foundation for the title insurance policy on the buyer's title as instructed by the buyer and seller in the escrow instructions.

The Clarkes and the Lees had instructed their escrow officer to order a preliminary title search. The Lees had three days to approve the report, as a contingency of the sale. When they examined it, however, they found there was a bond against the property for street repairs. They had not been aware of it.

The bond was a lien in the amount of $3,500. The buyers could not approve the preliminary title report until the issue was cleared up. An agreement about who would pay the bond had to be reached by the buyers and sellers, then new instructions given to the escrow officer, who would prepare an amendment for both parties' signatures.

Request Demands and/or Beneficiary Statements

The escrow officer must also see that existing loans are paid off, or assumed, depending on the agreement of the buyer and seller.

If the existing loan, or the seller's debt, is going to be paid off with proceeds from the sale, a demand from the lender holding the note and trust deed is needed, along with the unpaid principal balance and any other amounts that are due. The escrow officer requests a demand for pay-off of a loan from the lender who holds a loan against the subject property. The exact amount of loans that are to be paid off must be known so the escrow officer's accounting will be correct at the close of escrow.

If an existing loan is going to be assumed, or taken "subject to," a beneficiary statement is requested by the escrow holder from the lender. A statement of the unpaid balance of a loan, the beneficiary statement also describes the condition of the debt.

The escrow agent follows instructions about financing the property, and prepares any documents necessary for completing the escrow at the close. These might be a note and trust deed, or assumption papers.

The buyers are obtaining an adjustable loan in the amount of $360,000. The down payment will be $90,000, to make the purchase price of $450,000. The existing $250,000 loan on the property is held by Union Bank. The existing loan will be paid off when the buyer's new loan is funded, and the seller will get the balance of the purchase price, $200,000, less the seller's costs of selling (commissions, termite work, escrow and title fees, etc.).

Union Bank is notified of the expected pay-off and asked by the escrow officer to send a statement of the unpaid balance and condition of the existing loan. This is known as a request for demand for pay-off.

Other Reports

The parties to an escrow may request any number of reports about the condition of the property. The escrow holder is asked in the instructions to accept any reports submitted into escrow. These may include a structural pest control report (termite report), property inspection report, soil condition report or environmental report. Any approval from the buyer or seller about a report is held in escrow until needed, or given to the appropriate party at the close of escrow.

New Loan Instructions and Documents

Escrow accepts loan documents or instructions about financing the subject property and completes them as directed. The escrow agent gets the buyer's approval of and signature on loan documents, and receives and disburses loan funds as instructed.

Fire Insurance Policies

The parties to an escrow will have agreed on fire insurance policies and will instruct the escrow officer accordingly. The escrow holder will accept, hold and deliver any policies and will follow instructions about transferring them. A lender will require fire insurance, and will expect the escrow holder and the buyer to be accountable for either a new policy or the transfer of an existing one.

Settlement

The escrow holder will be instructed by the buyer and seller about prorations and other accounting to be done at the close of escrow.

<u>Prorations Normally Include:</u>

- Interest

- Premiums on fire insurance

- Security deposits and rents (if the property is a rental)

- Seller's current property taxes

The buyer and seller will have agreed on impound accounts, and the escrow holder will be guided on how to handle the credit and debit. After the escrow agent completes the accounting, the agent tells the buyer to deliver the down payment (usually in the form of a cashier's check), plus other escrow costs, to the escrow office.

At this time, the principals sign the loan documents, and complete any other paperwork required for the financing. If all is in order, the loan is funded and the money sent to the title company to pay off all encumbrances of record. Then the escrow may close.

Audit File

At the close of escrow, the escrow officer must examine each file to make sure all accounting has been accurate, and that escrow instructions have been followed. A cash reconciliation statement is completed by the escrow holder and closing statements are prepared for all principals.

Recording

The escrow holder orders the title company to record all transaction documents as instructed by the buyer and seller. This occurs after a final check of the title company records to be sure nothing has changed since the preliminary title search was done. Then the title company issues a policy of title insurance to insure the buyer's title. Documents that might require recording are the grant deed, trust deed, contract of sale or option.

Balancing the File

The last job of the escrow holder is to close the escrow. The escrow officer gives closing statements to buyer and seller, disburses all money and delivers all documents to the proper parties after making sure all documents have been recorded by the title company. The seller gets a check for the proceeds of the sale minus escrow fees, real estate commissions, or any other costs of selling, and any pertinent documents; and the buyer gets a grant deed.

Termination of an Escrow

The authority to conduct an escrow is given mutually by the buyer and seller in the escrow instructions. Neither party may end the escrow without the agreement of the other, in writing. Also, the escrow officer may not return any funds or documents to either party without agreement from all parties.

During the escrow, the escrow officer is an agent for both buyer and seller, as you recall, and must operate from the original escrow instructions. When they instruct the escrow agent to prepare an amendment canceling the escrow, a buyer and seller mutually end their agreement after they both sign the amendment.

Rights and Obligations of the Parties

A buyer and a seller are known as principals in an escrow. The escrow holder is a neutral third party who is a dual agent for buyer and seller. A real estate agent is not a party to an escrow unless he or she is the buyer or the seller.

A buyer is the party purchasing the property and the one who will receive a deed conveying the title.

A seller is the owner of record who must deliver the title agreed upon in the contract.

An escrow agent is an impartial third party who collects all documents and money, through the escrow, and transfers them to the proper parties at the close of escrow.

An escrow agent may be a bank, savings and loan, title insurance company, attorney, real estate broker or an escrow company. A real estate broker may act as an escrow agent in the course of a regular transaction for which a real estate license is necessary. The broker conducts the escrow as a service only if he or she is the listing or selling broker to the subject sale.

Escrow Companies Incorporated

The Commissioner of Corporations licenses escrow companies, but does not allow individuals to apply. Only a corporation is qualified and must make an application. A $25,000 bond, or more, based upon predicted yearly average transactions and trust fund use must be furnished by an applicant for an escrow office license. A bond must be posted by all parties (officers, directors, trustees and employees) having access to money or securities being held by the escrow company as safety against loss.

Audit

An escrow company must keep accounts and records which can be examined by the Commissioner of Corporations. A yearly inspection prepared by an independent certified public accountant, describing operations, must be delivered to the Commissioner.

Prohibitions

- Referral fees may not be paid by an escrow company to anyone as a reward for sending business to them

- Commissions may not be paid to a real estate broker until the closing of an escrow

- Blank escrow instructions to be filled in after signing are not acceptable. Initials must be placed wherever there is a change or deletion

- Information regarding an escrow may only be provided to parties to the escrow

- Copies of escrow instructions must be provided to anyone signing them

Agency

An escrow agent holds a limited agency, or authority. Any duties to be conducted must be mentioned specifically in escrow instructions or they are not authorized by the buyer and seller. The escrow holder must remain neutral, as the agent of both the buyer and seller, during the course of the escrow. After all conditions of the escrow have been met, the escrow officer is the agent of each of the parties in dealing with their individual needs.

Relationship of the Escrow Agent and the Real Estate Broker

No transaction can be completed without a good relationship between a broker and an escrow agent. The good will, positive guidance and technical knowledge of an escrow officer has helped many brokers get through an escrow, especially those new to the business.

After the real estate broker negotiates the sale, it is the job of the escrow agent to see that the agreements made by the parties are carried out. The broker and the escrow agent must check with each other regularly to make sure information is correct and to inform each other of how the escrow is progressing.

Designating the Escrow Holder

The choice of an escrow agent is always that of the buyer and seller. However, they probably do not have a relationship with an escrow agent, and may rely on the advice of their real estate broker.

Post Test

The following self test repeats the one you took at the beginning of this chapter. Now take the exam again--since you have read all the material-- and check your knowledge of parties, documents and real estate basics.

True/False

1. An escrow is a small and short-lived trust arrangement.

2. When there is a conflict between signed instructions and the original agreement between the principals, the

3. Escrow holds documents, conditionally, until all terms of the escrow are met.

4. A buyer or a seller can change escrow instructions unilaterally.

5. A real estate broker has authority to amend escrow instructions.

6. An escrow agent operates as a dual agent.

7. A beneficiary statement is requested if an existing loan is going to be assumed.

8. Prorations usually include principal and interest.

9. The escrow holder gives closing statements to the buyer and seller at the end of the escrow.

10. The escrow holder must return any funds to buyer or seller if requested to do so by either.

PARTIES, DOCUMENTS, REAL ESTATE BASICS

Focus

- **Introduction**
- **Parties**
- **Types of deeds**
- **Other documents**
- **Real estate basics**
- **Recording system**

Pre-Test

The following is a self test to determine how much you know about parties, documents, and real estate basics before reading this chapter. Take it without studying, then read the material presented in the text. At the end of the chapter you will find a repeat of this exam. Test your knowledge by answering the questions again, then check your improvement. (The answers are found at the end of the book.) Good luck.

True/False

1. A third party who carries out the written provisions of an escrow agreement is known as an escrow holder.

2. Property is usually transferred with a grant deed.

3. A request for notice of default is a way anyone interested in a particular trust deed can make sure of being informed if a notice of default has been recorded.

4. A preliminary change of ownership gives a buyer temporary title.

5. Ownership in severalty is the same as concurrent ownership.

6. An encumbrance is a limitation on ownership to real property.

7. A mechanic's lien is an example of a non-money encumbrance.

8. Property acquired by a husband and wife during a marriage, except for certain separate property, is owned by the wife.

9. An encumbrance that creates a legal obligation to pay is known as a lien.

10. A lis pendens indicates pending litigation on a property.

Introduction

The business of escrow, like many other professions, has a language all its own, as well as sharing much of the vocabulary of the real estate industry. This chapter will introduce and define the terms you will use to open, complete and close an escrow. You also will be introduced to the buyers and the sellers, the borrowers and the lenders, and others, as you journey through this introduction to escrow.

Parties

As an escrow agent, you must be knowledgeable about the parties with whom you are dealing. Following is a list of the likely entities you will meet as you become a practiced escrow professional.

Administrator/Administratrix
A person appointed by the court to handle the affairs of a deceased person when there is no one named in a will to do so

Assignee
The person to whom a claim, benefit or right in property is made

Assignor
The person transferring a claim, benefit or right in property to another

Beneficiary
The lender under a deed of trust

Escrow Holder
An independent third party legally bound to carry out the written provisions of an escrow agreement; a neutral,

bonded third party who is a dual agent for the principals; sometimes called an escrow agent

Executor/Executrix
A person named in a will to handle the affairs of a deceased person

Grantee
The person receiving real property because it has been granted in a deed by another individual

Grantor
The person who executes or signs a document giving title or ownership of real property to another party. A grantor might sign a grant deed, a quitclaim deed or a gift deed

Lessee
Tenant, renter

Lessor
Landlord, owner

Principal
The main party to a transaction

Trustee
Holds bare legal title to property as a neutral third party where there is a deed trust. Only duties are to foreclose or reconvey after a pay-off on a loan

Trustor
The borrower under a trust deed

Types of Deeds

Grant Deed

When property is transferred by private grant the instrument generally used is a grant deed. The parties involved are the grantor, or the person conveying the property, and the grantee, the person or group receiving the property.

A grant deed contains two implied warranties by the grantor. One is that the grantor has not already conveyed title to any other person, and the other is that the estate is free from encumbrances other than those disclosed by the grantor.

The grantor also promises to deed any rights he or she might acquire to the property after conveying it to the grantee. For example, oil or mineral rights might revert to the property at some time in the future, after the present owner has sold the property. "After acquired title" means any benefits that come to the property after a sale must follow the sale and accrue to the new owner. A grant deed must contain certain basics in order to be legally binding.

Requirements for a Valid Grant Deed

- In writing: according to the Statute of Frauds

- Parties identified: the parties to the transfer (grantor and grantee) sufficiently described

- Competent to convey: the grantor must be competent to convey the property (not a minor or incompetent)

Requirements for a Valid Grant Deed (continued)

- Capable of holding title: the grantee must be capable of holding title (must be a real living person, not fictitious)
- Adequately described: the property being conveyed must be adequately described
- Words of granting: words to indicate the act of granting (grant, convey) must be included

- Signed: the deed must be signed by the grantor

- Delivered: the deed must be delivered to and accepted by the grantee

A grant deed is not effective until it is delivered. It must be the intention of the grantor that the deed be delivered during his or her lifetime. For example, a deed would not be valid if signed and put in a safe place until the death of the grantor, and then recorded. Recording a deed is considered the same as delivery.

After a deed has been acknowledged by the grantor, it may be filed with the county recorder, giving constructive notice of the sale. An acknowledgment is a signed statement, made before a notary public, by a named person confirming that the signature on a document is valid and that it was made of free will. A deed does not have to be acknowledged to be valid, but must be acknowledged to be recorded.

The purpose of recording a deed is to protect the chain of title, which is a sequential record of changes in ownership showing the connection from one owner to the next. A complete chain of title is desirable whenever property is transferred and required by title insurance companies if they are writing a policy on a property.

> *Fermina Daza, a single woman, owned the house in which she lived. After marrying Fernando Ariza , she decided to sell the house. Because the chain of title showed that Fermina owned it under her maiden name, she had to sign the deed as "Fermina Ariza (who acquired title as Fermina Daza)" when she sold it.*

The priority of a deed is determined by the date it is recorded. In other words, recording establishes a claim of ownership which has priority over any deeds recorded after it. The first to record a deed is the first in right.

> *Calvin sells his house to Margaret, and--without telling Margaret--also sells it to Anita. Anita records her deed before Margaret has a chance to record hers. Anita is the owner of record and gets the house. Margaret has a definite cause for a lawsuit against Calvin.*

> *Anna sells her house to Victor, who moves in without recording the deed. Anna also sells the house to Alex, telling him to record the deed quickly, making him aware that Victor also has an interest in the property. In this case, Victor gets the house because of Alex's knowledge of the prior sale and also because of Victor's possession of the property (he had moved in), which established his right of ownership.*

A grantee must accept a deed before it is considered effective. Acceptance is automatic if the grantee is an infant or incompetent person. Acceptance may be shown by the acts of the grantee, such as moving onto the property.

The grant deed need not be signed by the grantee. An undated, unrecorded and unacknowledged grant deed may be valid as long as it contains the essential items noted below.

Not Necessary for Valid Grant Deed

- Acknowledgment
- Competent grantee; may be a minor, felon or incompetent
- Date
- Legal description
- Mention of the consideration
- Recording
- Signature of grantee

RECORDING REQUESTED BY
New Land Title Company
AND WHEN RECORDED MAIL
TO:

Name: Robert R. Mullins
Street Address: 2185 Memory Lane
City, State: Costa Mesa, CA 92626
Zip

| REC |
| RCF |
| MICRO |
| RTCF |
| LIEN |
| SMPF |
| PCOR |

Order No. 56748932-SMS

Space Above This Line for Recorder's Use

GRANT DEED

THE UNDERSIGNED GRANTOR(S) DECLARE(S)
City of: <u>Costa Mesa</u>

Conveyance tax is $_____
Parcel No. 123-45-6789

FOR A VALUABLE CONSIDERATION, receipt of which
is hereby acknowledged, Michael L. Horton and Lisa M.
Horton, Husband and Wife as Joint Tenants do (does) hereby
GRANTS to Robert R. Mullins and Margie M. Mullins,
Husband and Wife as Joint Tenants

the following real property in the city of
Costa Mesa
county of Orange, state of California

DOCUMENTARY TRANSFER TAX $_____

☐ Computed on full value of interest of property
conveyed

☐ Full value less value of liens or encumbrances
remaining at the time of sale

Lot 12 in Tract 2316 as recorded in Book 42 pages 5-10 inclusive of Miscellaneous Maps in the office of the County Recorder of the County of Orange, State of California and described as follows: commencing at a point on the Southerly line thereof 450.8 feet West of the Southeast corner thereof, thence North 68 degrees 58 minutes West 100 fee, thence North 23 degrees 02 minutes East 60 feet, thence South 66 degrees 58 minutes East one hundred feet, thence South 23 degrees 02 minutes West 60 feet to the point of beginning.

Dated:_____

STATE OF CALIFORNIA
COUNTY
OF_____

On_____before
me.

a Notary Public in and for said County and State, personally appeared:
_____

_____

Personally known to me (or provided to me on the basis of satisfactory evidence whose name(s) is/are subscribed to the within instrument and acknowledged to me that he/she/they executed the same in his/her/their authorized capacity(ies) and that by his/her/their signature(s) on the instrument the person(s) or the entity upon behalf of which the person(s) acted, executed the instrument.

WITNESS my hand and official seal.

Signature_____

_____
Michael M. Horton

_____
Linda L. Horton

(This area for official notorial seal)

Quitclaim Deed

Another type of deed used to transfer property is a quitclaim deed. This type of deed was commonly used to transfer real property interests between husband and wife.

However, an interspousal grant deed is now used between spouses instead of a quitclaim deed.

A quitclaim deed is often used to clear a cloud on the title; there might be a minor defect in the chain of title which needs to be removed. They may also be used to terminate an easement.

A quitclaim deed is a deed conveyance that operates as a release of whatever interest the grantor has in the property, sometimes called a release of a deed. The quitclaim deed contains similar language to a deed, with the important exception that rather than using the words *grant and release*, it contains language such as *remise, release and quitclaim*. Grantors therefore do not warrant title or possession. Grantors only pass on whatever interest they may have, if any. In effect, a grantor forever quits whatever claim he or she had, if in fact any existed.

The quitclaim deed transfers only whatever right, title and interest the grantor had in the land at the time of the execution of the deed and does not pass to the grantee any title or interest subsequently acquired by the grantor. Thus the grantee cannot claim a right to any "after-acquired title."

Although a quitclaim deed may or may not vest any title in the grantee, it is not inferior to the other types of deeds in what it actually conveys. For example, if a grantor executes and delivers a warranty deed to one person and subsequently executes and delivers a quitclaim deed to the same property to another person, the grantee under the quitclaim deed will prevail over the grantee under the warranty deed, assuming the holder of the quitclaim is first to record the deed.

Depending on local custom, ordinarily a warranty or bargain and sale deed will be used to transfer a fee simple interest (not in California). A quitclaim deed is not commonly used to convey a fee, but is usually restricted to releasing or conveying minor interests in real estate for the purpose of clearing title defects or clouds on title. It may also be used to convey lesser interests such as life estates and to release such interests as a remainder or reversion.

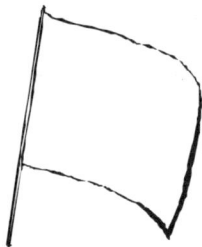

A title searcher will regard a quitclaim deed in the chain of title as a red flag, and most title companies will not guarantee titles derived out of a quitclaim, at least not without further clarification.

Quitclaim deeds also are often used between close relatives, such as when one heir is buying out the other, or where a seller's finances are so troubled that it is inconsequential to the buyer whether he or she is getting any warranties or not.

Executing a quitclaim deed does not carry even an implied warranty as regards ownership, liens, encumbrances or that the grantor has not previously signed a deed to someone else. It does convey ownership of the property to another person.

RECORDING REQUESTED BY
New Land Title Company
AND WHEN RECORDED MAIL
TO:

Name: Robert R. Mullins
Street Address: 2185 Memory Lane
City, State: Costa Mesa, CA 92626
Zip

Order No. 56748932-SMS

| REC |
| RCF |
| MICRO |
| RTCF |
| LIEN |
| SMPF |
| PCOR |

Space Above This Line for Recorder's Use

QUITCLAIM DEED

THE UNDERSIGNED GRANTOR(S) DECLARE(S)
City of: <u>Costa Mesa</u>

Conveyance tax is $_____
Parcel No. 123-45-6789

DOCUMENTARY TRANSFER TAX $_____
☐Computed on full value of interest of property conveyed
☐Full value less value of liens or encumbrances remaining at the time of sale

FOR A VALUABLE CONSIDERATION, receipt of which is hereby acknowledged, Michael L. Horton and Lisa M. Horton, Husband and Wife as Joint Tenants do (does) hereby REMISE, RELEASE AND FOREVER QUITCLAIM to Robert R. Mullins and Margie M. Mullins, Husband and Wife as Joint Tenants
the following real property in the city of Costa Mesa,

County of Orange, State of California

Lot 12 in Tract 2316 as recorded in Book 42 pages 5-10 inclusive of Miscellaneous Maps in the office of the County Recorder of the County of Orange State of California and described as follows: commencing at a point on the Southerly line thereof 450.8 feet West of the Southeast corner thereof, thence North 68 degrees 58 minutes West 100 fee, thence North 23 degrees 02 minutes East 60 feet, thence South 66 degrees 58 minutes East one hundred feet, thence South 23 degrees 02 minutes West 60 feet to the point of beginning.

Dated:_____

STATE OF CALIFORNIA
COUNTY
OF_____

On_____before me.

Michael M. Horton

Linda L. Horton

a Notary Public in and for said County and State, personally appeared:
_____

_____
Personally known to me (or provided to me on the basis of satisfactory evidence) whose name(s) is/are subscribed to the within instrument and acknowledged to me that he/she/they executed the same in his/her/their authorized capacity(ies) and that by his/her/their signature(s) on the instrument the person(s) or the entity upon behalf of which the person(s) acted, executed the instrument.

WITNESS my hand and official seal.

Signature_____

(This area for official notarial seal)

Warranty Deed

A warranty deed is one which contains express covenants of title. In other words, the seller who uses a warranty deed to transfer the property title to a buyer is guaranteeing clear title as well as the right to transfer it. Rarely is it used in California because title companies have taken over the role of insuring title to property.

Trust Deed

A trust deed is a security instrument that conveys title to a trustee to hold as security for the payment of a debt. There are three parties to a trust deed: the borrower (trustor), lender (beneficiary) and a neutral third party called a trustee. The only interest conveyed to the trustee is bare legal title, and the trustee's only obligation is to foreclose if there is a default on the loan, or reconvey the trust deed to the borrower when it is paid in full.

RECORDING REQUESTED BY
SMS SETTLEMENT SERVICES
AND WHEN RECORDED MAIL
TO:

| REC |
| RCF |
| MICRO |
| RTCF |
| LIEN |
| SMPF |
| PCOR |

Name: Robert Trabuco
Street Address: 21128 Rose
City, State: Mission Viejo, CA
Zip: 92691

Order No. 004860-DW

Space Above This Line for

Recorder's Use

DEED OF TRUST WITH ASSIGNMENT OF RENTS

This DEED OF TRUST, made **January 1, 1999**, between **Robert Trabuco and Amelia Trabuco** herein called TRUSTOR,
whose address is **542 Paramount Drive, Chino Hills, CA**

SMS SETTLEMENT SERVICES, a California Corporation, herein called TRUSTEE and **Jim Getz, An Unmarried Man and Mary Anne Getz**, herein called BENEFICIARY, Trustor irrevocably grants, transfers and assigns to Trustee in Trust, with Power of Sale, that property in City of **Mission Viejo,** County of **Los Angeles**, California, described as:

All that tract and parcel of land located on the northwest corner of the subdivision more commonly known as Rainbow Ridge and being more fully described in Deed Book 123, page 891.

Together with the rents, issues and profits thereof, subject, however, to the right, power and authority hereinafter given to and conferred upon Beneficiary to collect and apply such rents, issues and profits. For the Purpose of Securing (1) payment of the sum of $180,000.00 with interest thereon according to the terms of a promissory note or notes of even date herewith made by Trustor, payable to order of Benficiary, and extensions or renewals thereof; (2) the performance of each agreement of Trustor incorporated by reference or contained herein or reciting it is so secured; (3) Payment of additional sums and interest thereon which may hereafter be loaned to Trustor, or his successors or assigns, when evidenced by a promissory note or notes reciting that they are secured by this Deed of Trust.

To protect the security of this Deed of Trust, and with respect to the property above described, Trustor expressly makes each and all of the agreements, and adopts and agrees to perform and be bound by each and all of the terms and provisions set forth in subdivision A of that certain Fictitious Deed of Trust reference herein, and it is mutually agreed that all of the provisions set forth in subdivision B of that certain Fictitious Deed of Trust recorded in the book and page of Official Records in the office of the county recorder of the county where said property is located, noted below opposite the name of such county:

Said agreements, terms and provisions contained in said Subdivision A and B, (identical in all counties are printed on the reverse side hereof) are by the within reference thereto, incorporated herein and made a part of this Deed of Trust for all purposes as fully as if set forth at length herein and Beneficiary may charge for a statement regarding the obligation secured hereby, provided the charge therefor does not exceed the maximum allowed by laws.

The foregoing assignment of rents is absolute unless initiated here, in which case, the assignment serves as additional security.

The undersigned Trustor, requests that a copy of any notice of default and any notice of sale hereunder be mailed to him at this address hereinbefore set forth.

Dated: **January 1, 1999**

STATE OF CALIFORNIA   **Robert Trabuco**
COUNTY
OF_____   _____

                                        Amelia Trabuco
On_____**before**
me.

a Notary Public in and for said County and State, personally appeared:

_____

_____
Personally known to me (or proved to me on the basis of satisfactory evidence whose name(s) is/are subscribed to the within instrument and acknowledged to me that he/she/they executed the same in his/her/their authorized capacity(ies) and that by his/her/their signature(s) on the instrument the person(s) or the entity upon behalf of which the person(s) acted, executed the instrument.

WITNESS my hand and official seal.

Signature_____   **(This area for official notorial seal)**

TO: SMS SETTLEMENT SERVICES COMPANY TRUSTEE

REQUEST FOR FULL RECONVEYANCE

The undersigned is the legal owner and holder of the note or notes, and of all other indebtedness secured by the foregoing Deed of Trust. Said note or notes, together with all other indebtedness secured by said Deed of Trust, have been fully paid and satisfied, and you are hereby requested and directed, on payment to you of any sums owing to you under the terms of said Deed of Trust, to cancel said note or notes above mentioned, and all other evidences of indebtedness secured by said Deed of Trust delivered to you herewith, together with the said Deed of Trust, and to reconvey, withour warranty, to the parties designated by the terms of said Deed of Trust, all the estate now held by you under the same.

Dated_____   _____

_____

_____

SIGNATURE MUST BE NOTARIZED

Please mail Deed of Trust,
Note and Reconveyance to_____

Do not lose or destroy this Deed of Trust OR THE NOTE which it secures. Both must be delivered to the Trustee for cancellation before reconveyance will be made.

Reconveyance Deed

A reconveyance deed conveys title to property from a trustee back to the borrower (trustor) upon payment in full of the debt secured by the trust deed. When the trustor pays off a loan, a request for full reconveyance or a request for partial reconveyance is executed by the beneficiary and given to the trustor along with the original note and deed of trust.

The trustor gives these documents to the trustee, who then issues the deed of reconveyance. Upon recording, it is evidence that the loan has been fully paid and the lien on the trust deed is extinguished.

Following are copies of a request for full reconveyance, the full reconveyance forms, the request for partial reconveyance and the partial reconveyance form. Usually, a partial reconveyance is used with large parcels of property when a portion of the note has been paid and release clauses are part of the trust deed.

The request for full reconveyance generally is found on the back side of a deed of trust (see preceding form). The only time a separate form should be necessary is if the original deed of trust has been lost and a copy is used for reconveyance.

Sheriff's Deed

A sheriff's deed is given to a buyer when property is sold through court action in order to satisfy a judgment for money or foreclosure of a mortgage.

Gift Deed

A gift deed is used to make a gift of property to a grantee, usually a close friend or relative. The consideration in a gift deed is called love and affection.

Deeds

- Grant Deed
- Quitclaim Deed
- Warranty Deed
- Trust Deed
- Reconveyance Deed
- Sheriff's Deed
- Gift Deed

Other Documents

Request for Notice of Default

A request for notice, as it is sometimes called, is a way anyone interested in a particular trust deed can make sure of being informed if a borrower is not making timely payments and a notice of default is recorded. The request for notice must be recorded with the county recorder. Any parties with an interest in knowing whether or not the property is about to be sold at a trustee's sale, if they are on file as requesting notice of an upcoming foreclosure, may then act for their own benefit to protect their interest in the property. The most likely candidate to be harmed by a surprise foreclosure is the holder of a lien junior to the one being foreclosed.

Junior Shrewdmoney sold his home for $200,000 and carried back a second trust deed. At the time of the sale, Junior asked escrow to record a request for notice of default on the first trust deed.

Five years went by before the buyer stopped making payments on the first trust deed. A notice of default was recorded by the holder of the first trust deed, starting foreclosure procedings. During the five years, however, the value of the property had decreased to an amount less than the buyer paid for the property, and in fact, the property was now worth little more than the amount of the first trust deed.

If Junior had not been notified in a timely manner of the trustee's sale, his interest in the property would have been canceled by the sale, with any proceeds going to the foreclosing lender of the first loan. Junior can now file his own notice of default and protect his trust deed by becoming the new owner, subject to bringing current the first trust deed.

A request for notice must contain the recording data applying to the deed of trust and the name and address of the person who wants the information. The recorder will enter this on the record of the deed of trust or mortgage, and if subsequently any notice of default or sale is recorded, the person named in the request will have to be notified. Some trust deeds have the request printed on the deed and it is not necessary to record a separate request for notice.

Substitution of Trustee

The trustee under a deed of trust does not need to formally accept the position of trustee. Forms used by most escrow holders usually name a title company or their own escrow company. Anyone can be a trustee, with the only restriction on naming a trustee under a deed of trust being that it cannot be the borrower (trustor).

Because anyone can be a trustee, it is very easy for a named trustee under a deed of trust to be out of business or out of the state. Who then will start foreclosure, and who will reconvey the property to the trustor when the loan is paid off if the trustee is nowhere to be found?

The beneficiary under a deed of trust has the power to change the trustee of his deed of trust at any time by completing a "substitution of trustee" which deletes the current trustee and names a new one instead.

Request for Notice of Delinquency

Even though a request for notice of default may be filed by the holder of a junior lien (1st, 2nd, 3rd, etc.) , by the time a lender gets around to foreclosure, the borrower may be many months behind in payments. Anyone acquiring the property at a foreclosure sale must bring current all payments and fees for existing senior loans on the property.

By recording a request for notice of delinquency, the junior lien holder filing the request will be notified of the delinquency of four payments and then can decide whether to bring pressure on the borrower in default on the senior loan before the amount becomes unmanageable, or pay the amount in arrears.

Statement of Information

Buyers and sellers must complete a statement of personal information as a necessary and essential part of each escrow opened. The title company needs the correct information regarding places of employment, former residences, former marriages and social security numbers to identify each party to the escrow as just that party and no other.

SMS

Statement of Information
FILL OUT COMPLETELY AND RETURN TO STRATEGIC MORTGAGE SERVICES

ESCROW #00020-SMS   TRACT#   LOT#

Name_____   Social Security   Driver's
____   #_____   License#_____

Date of birth_____   Place of birth_____   Bus. phone_____   Home phone_____

Resided in USA since_____   Resided in California since_____

If you are married, please complete the following: Date Married_____ at_____

Name of Spouse_____   Social Security #_____ Driver's License #_____

Resided in USA since_____   Resided in California since_____

Previous Marriage or Marriages (if no previous marriage, write "None"):
Name of former spouse_____   Deceased___Divorced__Where___When___

Name of former spouse_____   Deceased___Divorced____Where___When___

Children by current or previous Marriages:
Name_____   Born_____   Name_____   Born_____
Name_____   Born_____   Name_____   Born_____

Information covering past 10 years:
Residence: _____

	Number/Street	City	From	To
	Number/Street	City	From	To

Employment _____

	Firm Name	Location
	Firm Name	Location

Spouse Employment: _____

	Firm Name	Location
	Firm Name	Location

Have you or your spouse owned or operated a business?
                                    If so please list
☐Yes   ☐No   names_____

I have never been adjudged, bankrupt, nor are there any unsatisfied judgments or other
matters pending against me which might affect my title to this property except as follows:
_____

The undersigned declare, under penalty of perjury, that the foregoing is true and correct.
Executed on_____   at_____
              date   city
                                        Signature

Preliminary Change of Ownership

This document gives information to the county tax assessor about the property and who now owns it. The assessor can then determine from the sales price the method used to finance the purchase and the reason for the change in ownership, whether or not a change in property tax is required. The following preliminary change of ownership report allows the assessor to place the appropriate tax on the property, starting on the date of conveyance to the next assessment date. The form must be completed before the close of escrow by the buyer, or the county recorder will impose an extra fee for recording the grant deed.

Even then, the buyer must submit the completed form within 60 days after closing escrow or other penalties will be accrued. The tax assessor then gets to revalue the property and increase the taxes due for the time from the close of escrow to when the next tax bill is issued.

PRELIMINARY CHANGE OF OWNERSHIP REPORT

FOR RECORDER'S USE ONLY

To be completed by transferee (buyer) prior to transfer of subject property in accordance with Section 480.03 of the Revenue and Taxation Code. A Preliminary Change of Ownership Report must be filed with each conveyance in the County Recorder's office for the county where the property is located; this particular form may be used in all 58 counties of California.
THIS REPORT IS NOT A PUBLIC DOCUMENT

SELLER/TRANSFEROR: **Michael M. Horton and Linda L. Horton**
BUYER/TRANSFEREE: **Robert R. Mullins and Margie M. Mullins**
ASSESSOR'S PARCEL NUMBER(S) **123-45-6789**
PROPERTY ADDRESS OR LOCATION:

2165 Memory Lane
Santa Ana, CA 92705

MAIL TAX INFORMATION TO:

Name **Robert R. Mullins**
Address **2165 Memory Lane**

Costa Mesa, CA 92626

NOTICE: A lien for property taxes applies to your property on March 1 of each year for the taxes owing in the following fiscal year, July 1 through June 30. One-half of these taxes is due November 1, and one-half is due February 1. The first installment becomes delinquent on December 10, and the second installment becomes delinquent on April 10. One tax bill is mailed before November 1 to the owner of record. **IF THIS TRANSFER OCCURS AFTER MARCH 1 AND ON OR BEFORE DECEMBER 31, YOU MAY BE RESPONSIBLE FOR THE SECOND INSTALLMENT OF TAXES DUE FEBRUARY 1.**

The property which you acquired may be subject to a supplemental assessment in an amount to be determined by the Orange County Assessor. For further information on your supplemental roll obligation, please call the Orange County Assessor at 714-834-2727.

PART I: TRANSFER INFORMATION   Please answer all questions.

YES	NO		
☐	☑	A.	Is this transfer solely between husband and wife (Addition of a spouse, death of a spouse, divorce settlement, etc.)?
☐	☑	B.	Is this transaction only a correction of the name(s) of the person(s) holding title to the property (For example, a name change upon marriage)?
☐	☑	C.	Is this document recorded to create, terminate, or reconvey a lender's interest in the property?
☐	☑	D.	Is this transaction recorded only to create, terminate, or reconvey a security interest (e.g. cosigner)?
☐	☑	E.	Is this document recorded to substitute a trustee under a deed of trust, mortgage, or other similar document?
☐	☑	F.	Did this transfer result in the creation of a joint tenancy in which the seller (transferor) remains as one of the joint tenants?
☐	☑	G.	Does this transfer return property to the person who created the joint tenancy (original transferor)?
		H.	Is this transfer of property:
☐	☑		1. to a trust for the benefit of the grantor, or grantor's spouse?
☐	☑		2. to a trust revocable by the transferor?
☐	☑		3. to a trust from which the property reverts to the grantor within 12 years?
☐	☑	I.	If this property is subject to a lease, is the remaining lease term 35 years or more including written options?
☐	☑	J.	Is this a transfer from parents to children or from children to parents?
☐	☑	K.	Is this transaction to replace a principal residence by a person 55 years of age or older?
☐	☑	L.	Is this transaction to replace a principal residence by a person who is severely disabled as defined by Revenue and Code Section 69.5?

If you checked yes to J, K, or L, an applicable claim form must be filed with the County Assessor.
Please provide any other information that would help the Assessors to understand the nature of the transfer.

IF YOU HAVE ANSWERED "YES" TO ANY OF THE ABOVE QUESTIONS EXCEPT J, K, OR L, PLEASE SIGN AND DATE, OTHERWISE COMPLETE BALANCE OF THE FORM.

PART II: OTHER TRANSFER INFORMATION
A. Date of transfer if other than recording date _____.
B. Type of transfer. Please check appropriate box.
    ☑ Purchase   ☐ Foreclosure   ☐ Gift   ☐ Trade or Exchange   ☐ Merger, Stock, or Partnership Acquisition
    ☐ Contract of Sale - Date of Contract _____
    ☐ Inheritance - Date of Death _____   ☐ Other: Please explain: _____
    ☐ Creation of Lease   ☐ Assignment of a Lease   ☐ Termination of a Lease
    Date lease began _____
    Original term in years (including written options) _____
    Remaining term in years (including written options) _____
C. Was only a partial interest in the property transferred? ☐ Yes ☑ No   If yes, indicate the percentage transferred _____%

PRELIMINARY CHANGE OF OWNERSHIP REPORT

Please answer, to the best of your knowledge, all applicable questions, sign and date. If a question does not apply, indicate with "N/A."

PART III: PURCHASE PRICE AND TERMS OF SALE

A. CASH DOWN PAYMENT OR Value of Trade or Exchange (excluding closing costs) — Amount $5,000.00

B. FIRST DEED OF TRUST @ **7.57**% interest for **30** years. Pymts./Mo.=$**857.00**(Prin. & Int. only) — Amount $80,000.00

- ☐ FHA
- ☑ Conventional
- ☐ VA
- ☐ Cal-Vet
- ☑ Fixed Rate
- ☐ Variable Rate
- ☐ All inclusive D.T. ($ _____ Wrapped)
- ☐ Loan Carried by Seller
- ☑ New Loan
- ☐ Assumed Existing Loan Balance
- ☑ Bank or Savings & Loan
- ☐ Finance Company

Balloon Payment ☐ Yes ☑ No Due Date _____ Amount $ _____

C. SECOND DEED OF TRUST @ _____% interest for _____ years. Pymts./Mo.=$_____ (Prin. & Int. only) — Amount $_____

- ☐ Bank or Savings & Loan
- ☐ Loan Carried by Seller
- ☐ Fixed Rate
- ☐ Variable Rate
- ☐ New Loan
- ☐ Assumed Existing Loan Balance

Balloon Payment ☐ Yes ☐ No Due Date _____ Amount $ _____

D. OTHER FINANCING: Is other financing involved not covered in (b) or (c) above? ☐ Yes ☑ No — Amount $_____

Type _____ @ _____% interest for _____ years. Pymts./Mo.=$_____ (Prin. & Int. only)

- ☐ Bank or Savings & Loan
- ☐ Loan Carried by Seller
- ☐ Fixed Rate
- ☐ Variable Rate
- ☐ New Loan
- ☐ Assumed Existing Loan Balance

Balloon Payment ☐ Yes ☑ No Due Date _____ Amount $ _____

E. IMPROVEMENT BOND ☐ Yes ☑ No Outstanding Balance: Amount $_____

F. TOTAL PURCHASE PRICE (or acquisition price, if traded or exchanged, include real estate commission if paid.)

Total Items A through E $ 100,000.00

G. PROPERTY PURCHASED ☑ Through a broker ☐ Direct from seller ☐ Other (explain)_____

If purchased through a broker, provide broker's name and phone number: **Century One Real Estate (714) 555-7676**

Please explain any special terms or financing and any other information that would help the Assessor understand the purchase price and terms of sale.

_____
_____
_____

PART IV: PROPERTY INFORMATION

A. IS PERSONAL PROPERTY INCLUDED IN PURCHASE PRICE

(other than a mobilehome subject to local property tax)? ☐ Yes ☑ No

If yes, enter the value of the personal property included in the purchase price $_____ (Attach itemized list of personal property).

B. IS THIS PROPERTY INTENDED AS YOUR PRINCIPAL RESIDENCE? ☑ Yes ☐ No

If yes, enter date of occupancy _____ / _____ / _____ or intended occupancy **02/01/1995**

Month Day Year   Month Day Year

C. TYPE OF PROPERTY TRANSFERRED:

- ☑ Single-family residence
- ☐ Multiple-family residence (no. of units: _____)
- ☐ Commercial/Industrial
- ☐ Other (Description: _____)
- ☐ Agricultural
- ☐ Co-op/Own-your-own
- ☐ Condominium
- ☐ Timeshare
- ☐ Mobilehome
- ☐ Unimproved lot

D. DOES THE PROPERTY PRODUCE INCOME? ☐ Yes ☑ No

E. IF THE ANSWER TO QUESTION D IS YES, IS THE INCOME FROM:

☐ Lease/Rent ☐ Contract ☐ Mineral Rights ☐ Other - Explain: _____

F. WHAT WAS THE CONDITION OF PROPERTY AT THE TIME OF SALE?

☑ Good ☐ Average ☐ Fair ☐ Poor

Enter here, or on an attached sheet, any other information that would assist the Assessor in determining the value of the property such as the physical condition of the property, restrictions, etc.

_____
_____
_____

I certify that the foregoing is true, correct and complete to the best of my knowledge and belief.

Signed_____ Dated_____
NEW OWNER/CORPORATE OFFICER

Please Print Name of New Owner/Corporate Officer **Robert R. Mullins and Margie M. Mullins**

Phone Number where you are available from 8:00 a.m. - 5:00 p.m. **(714) 555-2323**

(NOTE: The Assessor may contact you for further information)

If a document evidencing a change of ownership is presented to the recorder for recordation without the concurrent filing of a preliminary change of ownership report, the recorder may charge an additional recording fee of twenty dollars ($20).

Power of Attorney

A power of attorney is used when a principal is not available to sign documents necessary for the conveyance of real property or some other legal act. It is valid for the party named in executing documents, both buying and selling, and has the same force and effect as the principal granting the power would have if he or she signed. The power of attorney must be recorded in the county in which the real property is located.

There are two types of power of attorney you will become familiar with as an escrow officer: specific and general. The specific power is used for a specific function such as the sale of real property. It lists the purpose precisely for what it is intended. The purpose of the general power of attorney is broad and may be used by the person empowered to sign anything the principal giving the power would sign or do.

Some lenders, however, will not allow a person with a power of attorney to sign loan documents or grant deeds, so it may be necessary to check with the title company and the lender to see what is accepted.

Notary Public Jurats

A notary jurat is the form attached (when documents are notarized) that states the person appeared before the notary and proved identity . The form makes a notary responsible for identifying the party whose name is to be notarized, and also makes the notary accountable for that determination. The notary does not necessarily need to see the person sign the document, but simply notarizes the document on the basis of the party appearing in person .and acknowledging the signatures. A notary public jurat is not, as many believe, affirmation of the truth of a document, but of the truth that this person appearing has signed the document.

Real Estate Basics

Ownership of Real Property

All property has an owner--either the government or a private institution or an individual. Title is the evidence that the owner of land is in lawful possession. It is the proof of ownership. Separate ownership and concurrent ownership are the two ways real estate may be owned.

Escrow agents can never tell people how to take title. Parties must consult with their attorney, accountant or anyone they choose and then give the escrow agent instructions regarding vesting.

Separate Ownership

Property owned by one person or entity is known as sole and separate, or ownership in severalty. A corporation is known to hold title in severalty, because it is a sole entity.

Concurrent Ownership

When property is owned by two or more persons or entities at the same time, it is known as concurrent ownership, or co-ownership.

Concurrent ownership comes in several forms such as joint tenancy, tenancy in common, community property and tenancy in partnership.

Four Types of Concurrent Ownership:

- Joint Tenancy
- Tenancy in Common
- Community Property
- Tenancy in Partnership

Joint Tenancy: When two or more parties own real property as co-owners, with the right of survivorship, it is called joint tenancy. The right of survivorship means that if one of the joint tenants dies, the surviving partner automatically becomes sole owner of the property.

The deceased's share does not go to his or her estate or heirs, but becomes the property of the co-tenant without becoming involved in probate. Also, the surviving joint tenant is not liable to creditors of the deceased who hold liens on the joint tenancy property.

John, Paul, George and Edward are joint tenants. Edward dies and his interest automatically goes to John, Paul and George as joint tenants with equal one-third interests.

****

Kelly and Roger own a house as joint tenants. Roger dies and Kelly now owns the house as her sole and separate property without probate. Roger's heirs are not entitled to his share because of the right of survivorship.

In order to have a joint tenancy, there are four things that must be in agreement: time, title, interest and possession.

The Four Unities of Joint Tenancy:

- Time
All parties must become joint tenants at the same time

- Title
All parties must take title on the same deed

- Interest
All parties must have an equal interest in the property

- Possession
All parties have equal right of possession, known as an undivided interest

All four items must occur to have a joint tenancy. If any one of the unities is broken, the joint tenancy is dissolved. Co-owners may sell their interest, give it away or borrow money against it, without consent of the other joint tenants. Because of the right of survivorship, a joint tenant may not will his or her share.

Tenancy in Common: When two or more persons, whose interests are not necessarily equal, are owners of undivided interests in a single estate, a tenancy in common exists. Whenever some other form of ownership or vesting is not mentioned specifically, and there are co-owners, title is assumed to be a tenancy in common.

The only requirement of unity for tenants in common is the equal right of possession or undivided interest--as it is called. That means each owner has a certain equitable interest in the property (such as one-half interest, or one-fourth interest), but has the right to use the whole property. None of the owners may exclude any co-owner from the property, nor claim any portion of the property for exclusive use.

The Four Requirements of Tenants in Common:

- Tenants in common may take title at different times
- Tenants in common may take title on separate deeds
- Tenants in common may have unequal interests
- Tenants in common have an undivided interest or equal right of possession

---

Any tenant in common may sell, encumber or will his or her interest, with heirs simply becoming a tenant in common among the others. A tenant in common must pay a proportionate share of any expenses incurred on the property, including money spent for repairs, taxes, loan payments and insurance. When tenants in common do not agree on matters pertaining to the property, any of the co-owners may file a partition action which asks the court to decide the fate of the investment.

Stacey, Steven, Catherine and Dan are joint tenants. Dan sells his interest to Eva. The joint tenancy has been broken regarding the interest Dan had in the property. The new vesting, after the sale of Dan's interest, is Stacey, Steven and Catherine as joint tenants with equal interests, and the right of survivorship, with Eva as a tenant in common.

Stacey, Steven, Catherine and Eva, in the above property, wish to restore a joint tenancy with each of the four having the right of survivorship. Eva holds a tenancy in common, so she will have to be added to the joint tenancy. Since all joint tenants must take title at the same time, on the same document, Stacey, Steven, Catherine and Eva must sign a new deed that lists Stacey, Steven and Catherine as joint tenants and Eva as a tenant in common. Then the property can be deeded to all four parties as joint tenants. All requirements for a joint tenancy--time, title, interest and possession-- will then be fulfilled.

Community Property: All property acquired by a husband and wife during a valid marriage--except for certain separate property--is called community property. Separate property includes: all property owned before marriage; all property acquired by either of the parties during marriage by gift or inheritance; all income derived from separate property.

If spouses want to maintain the status of their separate property, they must be very careful not to co-mingle it with their community property. Separate property (such as an apartment building with a negative cash flow) may not be supported with community property funds, nor can the income of either spouse be used in any way to maintain separate property. Any income, including wages from either spouse, is considered community property.

Community property can not be sold or encumbered by only one of the partners. Either spouse may <u>buy</u> real or personal property without the consent of the other; both are bound by the contract made by either one, unless the new property is bought specifically as separate property, with funds from a separate property account.

Either party may will one-half of the community property. If there is no will, the surviving spouse inherits all community property. This is important to know, particularly with multiple marriages, for estate planning.

Property may be owned with the intention that it go to one's children, only to learn after the parent's death that children of the first marriage are no longer natural heirs. If there is a subsequent husband or wife and no will has been made, the new spouse will become the natural heir to the real property.

Regarding separate property, if there is no will, the surviving spouse gets one-half and one child gets one-half. If there is more than one child, the surviving spouse gets one-third and the children get two-thirds.

Tenancy in Partnership: Ownership by two or more persons who form a partnership for business purposes is known as tenancy in partnership. Each partner has an equal right of possession for partnership.

Limitations On Real Property

An encumbrance is an interest in real property that is held by someone who is not the owner. Anything that affects the title or the use of the property is an encumbrance. A property is encumbered when it is burdened with legal obligations against the title. Encumbrances fall into two categories: those that affect the title, known as money encumbrances, and those that affect the use of the property, known as non-money encumbrances. The encumbrances that create a legal obligation to pay are known as liens. A lien uses real property as security for the payment of a debt.

Common types of liens are trust deeds and mortgages; mechanic's liens; tax liens; and special assessments, attachments and judgments. Those types of encumbrances that affect the physical use of the property are easements, building restrictions, and zoning requirements and encroachments.

Money Encumbrances (Liens)

A lien is an obligation to pay a money encumbrance that may be voluntary or involuntary. An owner may choose to borrow money, using the property as security for the loan, creating a voluntary lien.

On the other hand, if the owner doesn't pay taxes or the debt owed, a lien may be placed against his or her property without permission, creating an involuntary lien.

A lien may be specific or general. A specific lien is one that is placed against a certain property, while a general lien affects all property of the owner.

Trust deeds and mortgages are both instruments used in real estate financing to create voluntary, specific liens against real property. They will be discussed in detail later.

Tax Liens and Special Assessments: If any government taxes, such as income or property taxes are not paid, they become a lien against the property. Special assessments are levied against property owners to pay for local improvements, such as underground utilities, street repair, or water projects. Payment for the projects is secured by a special assessment which becomes a lien against real property.

Attachments and Judgments: An attachment is the process by which the court holds the property of a defendant pending outcome of a lawsuit. An attachment lien is valid for three years and may be extended in certain cases.

A judgment is the final determination of the rights of parties in a lawsuit by the court. A judgment does not automatically create a lien. A summary of the court decision, known as an abstract of judgment, must be filed with the county recorder. When the abstract is filed, the judgment becomes a general lien on all property owned or acquired by the judgment debtor for 10 years, in the county in which the abstract is filed.

Lis Pendens: A Lis Pendens is recorded notice that indicates pending litigation on a property. It clouds the title preventing the sale or transfer of the property until removed.

Non-Money Encumbrances

A non-money encumbrance is one that affects the use of property such as an easement, a building restriction or an encroachment.

Easements: An easement is the right to use another's land for a specified purpose, sometimes known as a right-of-way.   An interest in an easement is non-possessory.   That means the holder of an easement can use it only for the purpose intended and may not exclude anyone else from using it.

Easements are created in various ways--commonly by express grant or reservation in a grant deed or by a written agreement between owners of adjoining land.   An

easement always should be recorded to assure its continued existence.   It is recorded by the party benefiting from the easement as the "dominant tenement."

Five Ways to Create an Easement:

1. Express Grant: The "servient tenement," or the giver of the easement, grants the easement by deed or express agreement.

2. Express Reservation: The seller of a parcel who owns adjoining land reserves an easement or right-of-way over the former property. It is created at the time of the sale with a deed or express agreement.

3. Implied Grant or Reservation: The existence of an easement is obvious and necessary at the time a property is conveyed, even though no mention is made of it in the deed.

4. Necessity: An easement created when a parcel is completely landlocked and has no access. It is automatically terminated when another way to enter and leave the property becomes available.

5. Prescription: An easement by prescription may be created continuous and uninterrupted use, by a single party, for a period of five years. The owner must know about the use, and the use must be against the owner's wishes (open and notorious). The party wishing to obtain the prescriptive easement must have some reasonable claim to the use of the property, and must have been paying the property taxes for the past five years.

Easements May be Terminated or Extinguished by:

1. <u>Express Release</u>: The only one who can release an easement is the dominant tenement

2. <u>Legal Proceedings</u>: Quiet title action to terminate the easement brought by the servient tenement against the dominant tenement

3. <u>Merger</u>: This joins the dominant tenement and the servient tenement

4. <u>Non-Use</u>: When applied to a prescriptive easement for a period of five years, this terminates the easement

5. <u>Abandonment</u>: Obvious and intentional surrender of the easement

6. <u>Destruction of the Servient Tenement</u>: If the government takes the servient tenement for its use, as in eminent domain, the easement is terminated

7. <u>Adverse Possessions</u>: The owner of the servient tenement may, by his or her own use, prevent the dominant tenement from using the easement for a period of five years, thus terminating the easement

Restrictions: Another type of encumbrance is a restriction, which is a limitation placed on the use of property. It may be placed by a private owner, a developer or the government. It is usually placed on property to assure that land use is consistent and uniform within a certain area.

Restrictions are created in the deed at the time of sale or in the general plan of a subdivision by the developer. For example, a developer may use a height restriction to ensure views from each parcel in a subdivision.

Private restrictions are placed by a present or past owner and affect only a specific property or development, while zoning is an example of government restrictions that benefit the general public.

Restrictions are commonly known as C.C.&R.'s or Covenants, Conditions and Restrictions. A covenant is a promise to do or not do certain things. The penalty for a breach of a covenant is usually money damages. An example of a covenant might be that the tenant agrees to make some repairs, or that a property may be used only for a specific purpose, such as a church or homeless shelter.

A condition is much the same as a covenant, a promise to do or not do something, except the penalty for breaking a condition is return of the property to the grantor. A condition subsequent is a restriction placed in a deed at the time of conveyance on future use of the property. Upon breach of the condition subsequent, the grantor may take back the property. A condition precedent requires that a certain event, or condition, occur before title can pass to the new owner.

Encroachments: The placement of permanent improvements on adjacent property owned by another is known as an encroachment.

Recording System

County Recorders

Each county in the state has a County Recorder's office where documents may be recorded. As you recall, a deed does not have to be recorded to be valid. However, recordation maintains the chain of title necessary to create a history of ownership of real property

Background of Land Title in California

Ownership of land in California began with Spanish explorers who claimed it for the king of Spain in the early 16th Century. Since the king technically owned everything, all land was granted to private parties by the military representatives of Spanish rule. Ownership and transfer of land and property rights were determined by local authorities operating under a strict set of civil laws that were given to them by the Spanish king.

This continued until 1822, when Mexico began colonizing California and governing the territory. Mexican governors totally controlled who received grants of land during this time, and recorded the grants, known as expedientes, in the government archives. Even so, the land descriptions were vague and evidence of title may or may not have been in the actual possession of the owner. This led to many disputes over ownership in later years, after California became as state.

In 1848, the Treaty of Guadalupe Hidalgo ended the war with Mexico, and California became a possession of the United States. Land claims that had been granted by Mexico were honored, and confirmed with patents to the land, by the U.S. government, to those with proven ownership. Even though Spain or Mexico granted ownership, according to the Roman Civil Law they followed, the laws changed after California became a state in 1850. England's Common Law principles now governed the title of real property.

California Adopts a Recording System

In a move that was strictly an American device for safeguarding the ownership of land, the California legislature adopted a system of recording evidence of title or interest. This system meant records could be collected in a convenient and safe public place, so that those purchasing land could be more fully informed about the ownership and condition of the title. Even then, California was a leader in consumer-friendly legislation. Citizens were protected against secret conveyances and liens, and title to real property was freely transferable.

Recording Specifics

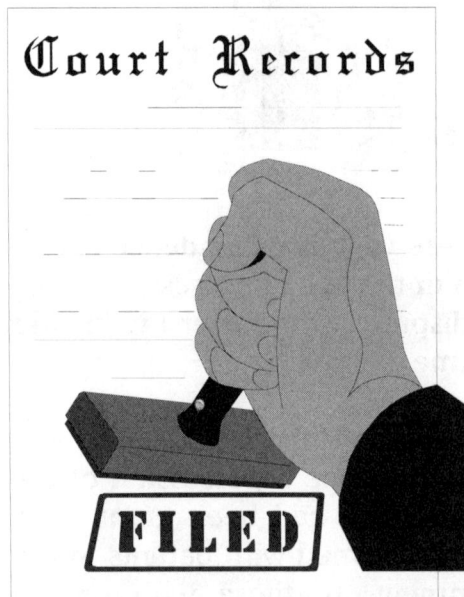

The Recording Act of California provides that, after acknowledgment or being signed before a notary or certain public officials, any instrument or judgment affecting the title to--or possession of--real property may be recorded. Recording permits, rather than requires, the filing of documents that affect title to real property.

The process consists of copying the instrument to be recorded in the proper index, and filing it in alphabetical order, under the names of the parties, without delay. The document must be recorded by the county recorder in the county within which the property is located to be valid there.

When the recorder receives a document to be filed, he or she notes the time and date of filing and at whose request it was filed. After the contents of the document are copied into the record, the original document is marked "filed for record," stamped with the proper time and date of recording, and returned to the person who requested the recording.

The Effect: Public Notice

This process gives constructive notice of the content of any instrument recorded to anyone who cares to look into the records. Recording is considered to be public notice of the information filed there. However, possession is considered actual notice, and a buyer should always check to be sure there is no one living on the property who might have a prior claim to ownership. It is the buyer's duty to conduct proper inquiry before purchasing any property. Failure to do so does not relieve the buyer of that responsibility.

Ann bought a property through her broker, sight unseen. The escrow closed and the deed was recorded. When Ann tried to move into her new home, however, she found George living there. He told her he had bought the property a year ago and had not bothered to record the deed, but had moved in and considered it his home. When she consulted her attorney, Ann found that indeed George--because he was in possession of the property--had given actual notice to anyone who might inquire. Ann had a duty to see for herself, and--failing to do that, or instruct her broker to do it--lost the property.

Priorities in Recording

As we have seen, recording laws are meant to protect citizens against fraud and to give others notification of property ownership. Other information that might influence ownership can be recorded also, such as liens and other encumbrances. To obtain priority through recording, a buyer must be a good faith purchaser, for a valuable consideration, and record the deed first.

Priority means the order in which deeds are recorded. Whether or not it is a grant deed, trust deed or some other evidence of a lien or encumbrance, the priority is determined by the date stamped in the upper right-hand corner of the document by the county recorder at the time it is recorded.

If there are several grant deeds recorded against the property, the one recorded first is valid. In a case where there are several trust deeds recorded against a property, no mention will be made about which one is the first trust deed, which is the second, and so forth.

A person inquiring about the priority of the deeds should look at the time and date the deed was recorded for that information. You will see, as we proceed in our study, the importance of the date and time of recording.

Post Test

The following self test repeats the one you took at the beginning of this chapter. Now take the exam again--since you have read all the material-- and check your knowledge of parties, documents and real estate basics.

True/False

1. A third party who carries out the written provisions of an escrow agreement is known as an escrow holder.

2. Property is usually transferred with a grant deed.

3. A request for notice of default is a way anyone interested in a particular trust deed can make sure of being informed if a notice of default has been recorded.

4. A preliminary change of ownership gives a buyer temporary title.

5. Ownership in severalty is the same as concurrent ownership.

6. An encumbrance is a limitation on ownership to real property.

7. A mechanic's lien is an example of a non-money encumbrance.

8. Property acquired by a husband and wife during a marriage, except for certain separate property, is owned by the wife.

9. An encumbrance that creates a legal obligation to pay is known as a lien.

10. A lis pendens indicates pending litigation on a property.

chapter 3

REAL ESTATE FINANCE

Focus

- Introduction
- How the process works
- Promissory note
- Trust deeds and mortgages
- Transfer of property by the borrower
- Special clauses in financing instruments
- Foreclosure
- Junior trust deeds
- Other types of loans secured by trust deeds
- Unsecured loans
- Alternative financing
- Truth-in-Lending Act (Regulation Z)
- Equal Credit Opportunity Act
- Soldiers' and Sailors' Civil Relief Act

Pre-Test

The following is a self test to determine how much you know about real estate finance before reading this chapter. Take it without studying, then read the material presented in the text. At the end of the chapter you will find a repeat of this exam. Test your knowledge by answering the questions again, then check your improvement. (The answers are found at the end of the book.) Good luck.

True/False

1. Hypothecation is when an owner uses a property as security for a loan, but does not give up possession.

2. A trustee is a neutral third party in a trust deed.

3. In a trust deed, the borrower is the same as the beneficiary.

4. The beneficiary hold bare legal title to a property encumbered by a trust deed.

5. A reconveyance deed is used to deed a property to the trustor after the deed of trust has been paid in full.

6. An "or more" clause allows a borrower to pay off a loan early with no penalty.

7. A holder in due course is someone who buys an existing negotiable note.

8. Foreclosure is the cure for a tenant's default on monthly rental payments.

9. A trustee must sign a reconveyance deed.

10. A land contract and a contract of sale are alike.

Introduction

Imagine buying a house and being required to pay the total price in cash. The sweet pleasure of home ownership probably would belong somewhere in the next century for most of us. With the average price of a single family home being so high, buying a home would be unthinkable without the practical benefit of financing.

By allowing a home buyer to obtain a loan for the difference between the sales price and the down payment, real estate lenders have provided the solution to the problem of how property can be bought and sold without the requirement of an all-cash sale.

What started out as a simple loan by a local bank--with an agreement that the borrower pay it all back in a timely manner--is now a complex subject. Buyers and sellers need to rely on experts to explain all the choices there are on financing the purchase or sale of property. A real estate licensee is probably one of the experts to whom they will turn.

This chapter on real estate finance is organized with each part building on what you have learned in the earlier sections of the chapter. Try to master each subject-- promissory notes, trust deeds, mortgages, special financing clauses, foreclosure, junior trust deeds, other security instruments, miscellaneous provisions of finance and consumer protection--as you come to it. There is a thread that connects everything you are about to study in this chapter. Read with that in mind.

Now that you know real estate finance is nothing more than lenders loaning money so people can buy property, let's start with an examination of the lending process.

How the Process Works

When a loan is made, the borrower signs a promissory note, or note--as it is called, which states that a certain amount of money has been borrowed. The note is the evidence of the debt.

When money is loaned for the purpose of financing real property, some kind of collateral is usually required as well as the promise to pay the money back. That means the lender wants some concrete assurance of getting the money back beyond the borrower's written promise to pay. The property being bought or borrowed against is commonly used as security, or collateral, for the debt. In other words, the lender feels more secure about making the loan if assured of the property ownership in case of default, or nonpayment of the loan. Then the lender can sell it to get the loan money back.

Commonly, financing is secured with a trust deed or mortgage. Under a trust deed, after signing the promissory note, the borrower is required to execute a trust deed at the same time, which is the security guaranteeing loan repayment. This is known as hypothecation, a process which allows a borrower to remain in possession of the property while using it to secure the loan. If the borrower does not make payments per the agreement, he or she then loses the rights of possession and ownership.

The lender holds the trust deed, along with the note, until the loan is repaid.

Note and Trust Deed

The promissory note is *evidence* of the debt, or the money borrowed, and the trust deed is *security* for the debt.

The trust deed allows the lender, in case of loan default, to order the trustee to sell the property described in the deed. (More explanation of this process follows later in the chapter.)

When a buyer obtains a loan to purchase property, he or she is using the lender's money to finance the sale. This is known as leverage. The use of borrowed capital to buy real estate is a process that permits the buyer to use little of one's own money and large amounts of someone else's.

There are several reasons leverage is appealing to both the home buyer and the investor. The main advantage to the home buyer is not having to amass the entire purchase price to become a home owner. The investor can use leverage to control several investments, rather than just one, each purchased with a small amount of personal funds, and a large amount of a lender's money. The investor can then

earn a return on each property, therefore increasing the amount of yield on investment dollars.

Promissory Note

A promissory note is a written promise to pay back a certain sum of money with specified terms at an agreed upon time. Sometimes it is simply called the note. Informally, it could be called an IOU. The maker is the person borrowing the money, or making the note. It is a personal obligation of the borrower and a complete contract in itself, between the borrower and lender. The holder is loaning the money, or the one holding the note.

According to the Uniform Commercial Code, to be valid or enforceable, a promissory note must meet certain requirements.

A Promissory Note is:

1. An unconditional written promise to pay a certain sum

2. Made by one person to another

3. Signed by the maker or borrower

4. Payable at a definite time

5. Paid to bearer or to order

6. Voluntarily delivered by the borrower and accepted by the lender

INSTALLMENT NOTE
(INTEREST INCLUDED)
(THIS NOTE CONTAINS AN ACCELERATION CLAUSE)

$189,000   Mission Viejo   ,California,   1/1/99

In installments and at the times hereinafter stated, for value received, Robert Trabuco and Amelia Trabuco

promise to pay to Jim Getz and Mary Anne Getz

_____ , or order

at 21128 Rose, Rancho Santa Margarita, CA 92626

the principal sum of One Hundred Eighty Thousand   dollars

with interest from January 1, 1999   on the amounts of

principal remaining from time to time unpaid, until said principal sum is paid, at the rate of   8.9   percent

per annum. Principal and interest due in monthly installments of One Thousand Five Hundred Dollars, $1,500, or more on the 15th day of each and every month, beginning on the 15th day of February, 1999.

and continuing until said principal sum has been fully paid. AT ANY TIME, THE PRIVILEGE IS RESERVED TO PAY MORE THAN THE SUM DUE. Should the interest not be so paid, it shall be added to the principal and thereafter bear like interest as the principal, but such unpaid interest so compounded shall not exceed an amount equal to simple interest on the unpaid principal at the maximum rate permitted by law. Should default be made in the payment of any of said installments when due, then the whole sum of principal and interest shall become immediately due and payable at the option of the holder of this note.

If the trustor shall sell, convey, or alienate said property, or any part thereof, or any interest therein, or shall be divested of his title or any interest therein in may manner or way, whether voluntarily or involuntarily, without the written consent of the beneficiary being first had and obtained, beneficiary shall have the right, at its option, to declare any indebtedness or obligations secured hereby, irrespective of the maturity date specified in any note evidencing the same, immediately due and payable.

Should suit be commenced to collect this note or any portion thereof, such sum as the Court may deem reasonable shall be added hereto as attorney's fees. Principal and interest payable for lawful money of the United States of America. This note is secured by a certain DEED OF TRUST to the SMS SETTLEMENT SERVICES, a California corporation, as TRUSTEE.

_____   _____
Robert Trabuco   Amelia Trabuco

A promissory note is a negotiable instrument. The most common type of negotiable instrument is an ordinary bank check. A check is an order to the bank to pay money to the person named. A promissory note is the same thing. It can be transferred by endorsement (signature), just like a check. If correctly prepared, it is the same as cash.

Types of Promissory Notes

Commonly, a promissory note is referred to as "the note." We will follow that practice as we study the basic types of notes in use with a trust deed.

Straight Note

Calls for payment of interest only, or no payments, during the term of the note, with all accrued money (either principal only, or principal and interest if no payments have been made) due and payable on a certain date

Partially Amortized Installment Note

Calls for periodic payments; such payments may or may not include interest; usually demands a balloon payment of unpaid principle and interest at the end of the term to completely pay off debt

Fully Amortized Installment Note

Calls for periodic payments of fixed amounts, to include both interest and principal, which will pay off the debt completely by the end of the term

<u>Adjustable note</u>

The interest rate in the note varies upward or downward over the term of the loan, depending on the money market conditions and an agreed upon index

Conflict in Terms of Note and Trust Deed

As you recall, a note is the evidence of a debt. A trust deed is only an incident of the debt. As we shall see in the next section, a trust deed must have a note to secure it, but a note does not need a trust deed to stand alone. If there is a conflict in the terms of a note and the trust deed used to secure it, the provisions of the note will prevail. If a note is unenforceable, the presence of a trust deed will not make it valid. However, if a note contains an acceleration clause (due on sale), the trust deed must mention it as well for the clause to be enforceable.

Trust Deeds and Mortgages

The term that describes the interest of a creditor (lender) in the property of a debtor (borrower) is security interest.

The security interest allows certain assets of a borrower to be set aside so that a creditor can sell them if the borrower defaults on the loan. Proceeds from the sale of

that property can be taken to pay off the debt. The rights and duties of lenders and borrowers are described in a document called a security instrument. In some statees, trust deeds are the principal instruments used to secure loans on real property.

Mortgages accomplish the same thing as trust deeds, and are used in other states as security for real property loans. You will hear the term mortgage used loosely in trust deed states, as in mortgage company, mortgage broker and mortgage payment--but the mortgage reference here really is a trust deed.

Trust Deeds (Deeds of Trust)

As we mentioned, a trust deed is used to secure a loan on real property. It describes the property being used as security for a debt, and usually includes a power of sale and assignment of rents clause.

Trust Deeds Can Include:

- Power of Sale Clause:
  Gives trustee the right to foreclose, sell and convey ownership to a purchaser of the property if the borrower defaults on the loan

- Assignment of Rents Clause:
  Upon default by the borrower, the lender can take possession of the property and collect any rents being paid

---

The thing to remember about a trust deed is that it is the security for a loan. If the borrower fails to pay, the lender can use the proceeds from sale of the property used as collateral (or secured by the trust deed) for payment.

Foreclosure is the procedure used by the lender who must exercise the right to collect what is owed if the borrower defaults on payments. Under a deed of trust, foreclosure normally takes no more than four months. We will study foreclosure later in this chapter.

A trust deed becomes a lien on a certain described property to secure the repayment of a debt. It does not have to be recorded to be valid, but to insure safety of position and notice to all that a debt is owed. Since trust deeds, and rarely mortgages, are used to secure real property loans in certain states, we will examine the trust deed here.

Title

The most distinguishing feature of a trust deed is the conveyance of title to a trustee by the borrower, until the debt is paid off. When a trust deed is used to secure a loan, even though the borrower technically owns the property, bare legal title is transferred to the trustee by the deed of trust.

The trustee is only given the right to do what is necessary to carry out the terms of the trust. He or she can only foreclose or reconvey, and does not have any other rights relating to the property, such as the right to use or the right to sell. Commonly, the trustee is not even notified until either foreclosure (in case of loan default) or reconveyance (when the loan is paid in full) takes place.

Think of the trustee as a neutral party, holding the title for the borrower until the loan is paid off, and foreclosing for the lender if the borrower defaults. Neither the trustor (borrower) nor the beneficiary (lender) holds the title until all terms of their agreement have been met. Upon payment of the debt in full, the trustee is notified by the beneficiary to sign the reconveyance deed, which states that clear legal title is now vested in the name of the actual property owner.

After being signed by the trustor (borrower), the trust deed--not the note--is recorded in the county where the property is located, then is sent to the lender or trustee to hold for the life of the loan. Recording of the trust deed gives public notice of the lien against the property for anyone interested in searching the title of the property.

The reconveyance deed is also recorded, after being signed by the trustee, to give public notice of the lien payment.

Parties

There are three parties to a trust deed: the trustor, the trustee and the beneficiary.

Three Parties to a Trust Deed:

- Trustor, or borrower; holds equitable title while paying off the loan; conveys bare legal title to trustee by way of the trust deed

- Trustee, or neutral third party; holds bare legal title solely for the purpose of reconveyance or foreclosure; is not involved with the property until asked to reconvey or foreclose

- Beneficiary, or lender; holds the note and trust deed until reconveyance (pay-off of the debt)

Roy and Dale bought a house. They signed a note secured by a deed of trust and were given a grant deed, as proof of conveyance, from the seller. The beneficiary, Bank of America, held the note and trust deed. Commonwealth Land Title Company was named as the trustee. When they signed the trust deed, Roy and Dale granted Commonwealth

Title bare legal title so the company could conduct duties as a trustee. Years went by, and the loan was paid off. Upon notification by Bank of America (the beneficiary), Commonwealth Title (trustee) signed a reconveyance deed, giving clear legal title to Roy and Dale.

Quentin and Kate bought their first house with a 90 percent loan from First Interstate Bank. As trustors, or borrowers, they were given a grant deed by the seller, which conveyed title to them. First Interstate, the beneficiary or lender, held the note Quentin and Kate had signed, promising to pay back the money loaned, and trust deed which secured the loan. Continental Lawyers Title Company was named as the trustee, and held bare legal title until the loan was paid off.

The payments were high, but both Quentin and Kate had good jobs, and were confident they could afford the house. After a few years, Kate was laid off, and they fell behind in their payments. They weren't getting along, and finally Kate left Quentin.

Sadly, he notified the beneficiary (First Interstate) that he could no longer make the payments, and the trustee was notified to start foreclosure procedures. A trustee's sale was held, and the house was sold, with the proceeds going to First Interstate to pay off the debt. Quentin moved to Anchorage tostart over.

Statute of Limitations

The rights of the lender (beneficiary) under a deed of trust do not end when the statute has run out on the note. The trustee has title and can still sell the property to pay off the debt.

Remedy for Default

Under a deed of trust, either a trustee's sale or judicial foreclosure is permitted.

Reinstatement

When a trust deed debtor is in default on a loan, the loan may be reinstated if all delinquencies and fees are paid prior to five business days before the trustee's sale.

Redemption

Under a trust deed with a power of sale, there is no right of redemption after the trustee's sale. The sale is final.

Deficiency Judgment

A deficiency judgment is one against a borrower for the difference between the unpaid amount of the loan, plus interest, costs and fees of the sale, and the amount of the actual proceeds of the foreclosure sale. This means if the property sells for less than what is owed to the lender, the borrower will be personally responsible for repayment after the deficiency judgment is filed.

When a loan is secured by a trust deed and the lender forecloses under a power of sale (trustee's sale), a deficiency judgment is not allowed in most cases. When trust deeds, rather than mortgages, are used to secure loans, the only security for a beneficiary is the property itself. Any other personal assets of the borrower in default are protected from judgment under the trust deed.

> *Edward fell on hard times and lost his house, which was financed with a note secured by a deed of trust, to foreclosure. He owed $250,000 which included the costs of the foreclosure. However, the proceeds of the trustee's sale only amounted to $200,000. The lender lost the deficient $50,000, unable to obtain a deficiency judgment against Edward.*

Satisfaction

Satisfaction, or payment in full of a trust deed, requires that the lender deliver the original note and trust deed to the party making the request.

Benefits of a Trust Deed to a Lender

- In case of default, lender takes possession, collects rents
- Relatively short and simple foreclosure process
- Trustee holds title and can easily grant title to buyer at foreclosure sale
- No redemption after foreclosure
- A trust deed never expires

Benefits of a Trust Deed to a Borrower

- Property is the only security for a loan; no deficiency judgment allowed when loan is a purchase money loan

Mortgages

A mortgage is a financial instrument that is used to secure a property for the payment of a promissory note. It serves the same purpose as a trust deed by acting as the security for a debt. A mortgage is a lien against a described property until payment of the debt.

Do not get confused when you hear the word mortgage to describe some financial transaction. As mentioned earlier, even though mortgages are not commonly used in some states, you will hear reference to home mortgage, mortgage loan broker and mortgage banker. In reality, a trust deed is the instrument used.

A mortgage is held by the lender for the life of a loan, or until the borrower pays it off. There are some similarities to a trust deed, and some differences, as we shall see in the following examination of mortgages.

Parties

In a mortgage there a two parties: a mortgagor and a mortgagee. The mortgagor (borrower) receives a loan from the mortgagee (lender) and signs a promissory note and mortgage. The mortgage becomes a lien in favor of the mortgagee until the debt is paid in full.

The Two Parties to a Mortgage are:

- Mortgagor (borrower)

- Mortgagee (lender)

Title

A mortgage creates a lien on real property. Title is vested in the borrower, unlike a trust deed, where technically a deed of trust gives limited title (bare legal title) to a trustee, even though it is also spoken of as a lien. In both cases, possession of the property remains with the borrower.

Statute of Limitations

The Statute of Limitations runs out on a note secured by a mortgage in four years. This means a lender must sue after four years of nonpayment to get his or her money back, or the mortgage expires.

Remedy

The only remedy for default of a mortgage is judicial foreclosure, or a court action.

Reinstatement

Under a mortgage, a borrower in default may reinstate the loan by paying all delinquencies, plus all costs of the foreclosure action, at any time before the court approves the foreclosure.

Redemption

The right of redemption, or Equity of Redemption as it is known in those states using mortgages rather than trust deeds, allows a borrower in default to redeem the property within three months after foreclosure sale if the proceeds are sufficient to pay off all indebtedness plus any other foreclosure costs. If the sale does not bring enough money to pay off the debt, the mortgagor has one year to redeem the property by paying off the amount owed, plus costs.

Deficiency Judgment

A lender who forecloses against a defaulted mortgage may obtain a deficiency judgment against the debtor. Because a court action is required in order to foreclose against a mortgage, a deficiency judgment is allowed. As you recall, a deficiency judgment may be filed against a borrower for the difference between the unpaid amount of the loan, plus foreclosure costs, and the amount of the proceeds of the foreclosure sale. In that case, the lender may get a personal judgment against the borrower that will be effective for 10 years.

Satisfaction

Satisfaction of a mortgage, or payment in full, requires that the lender deliver the original note and mortgage to the party making the request.

Basic Differences Between Trust Deeds and Mortgages

Parties	Reinstatement
Title	Redemption
Statute of Limitations	Deficiency Judgment
Remedy	Satisfaction

Transfer of Property by the Borrower

A borrower may transfer ownership of the property and responsibility for the debt.

Loan Assumption

When a property is sold, a buyer may assume the existing loan. Usually with the approval of the lender, the buyer takes over primary liability for the loan, with the original borrower secondarily liable if there is a default.

What this means in trust deed states, is that even though the original borrower is secondarily responsible, according to the loan assumption agreement, no actual repayment of the loan may be required of that person. If the new owner defaults, the property is foreclosed, and no deficiency judgment is allowed beyond the amount received at the trustee's sale, even though the original borrower's credit is affected by the foreclosure.

Special Clauses in Financing Instruments

When a borrower signs a note promising to repay a sum, the lender usually will include some specific requirements in the note regarding repayment. These are special clauses meant to protect the lender and his or her interests.

Acceleration Clause

An acceleration clause allows a lender to call the entire note due, on occurrence of a specific event such as default in payment, taxes or insurance, or sale of the property.

Alienation Clause (Due on Sale)

Another clause, known as an alienation or due-on-sale clause, is a kind of acceleration clause. A lender may call the entire note due if there is a transfer in property ownership from the original borrower to someone else. This clause protects the lender from an unqualified, unapproved buyer taking over a loan. Justifiably, the lender fears possible default, with no control over who is making the payments.

Assumption Clause

An assumption clause allows a buyer to assume responsibility for the full payment of the loan with the lenders knowledge and consent.

Subordination Clause

A subordination clause is used to change the priority of a financial instrument. Remember, the priority of a trust deed is fixed by the date it is recorded: the earlier the date, the greater the advantage. When a note and trust deed includes a subordination clause, a new, later loan may be recorded, and because of the subordination clause, assume a higher priority. This clause is used mainly when land is purchased for future purpose construction

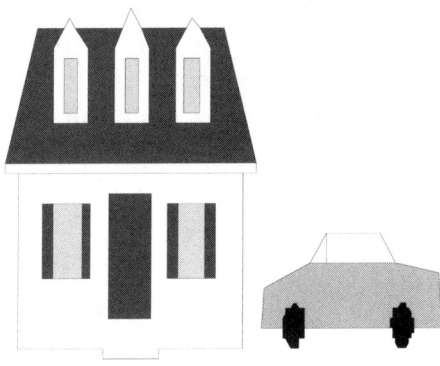

that will require financing. The lender on the new financing would want to be in first position to secure his or her interest, so the trust deed on the land would become subordinate to a new loan on the structure when the new loan was funded and recorded.

Prepayment Clause

Occasionally, a note will include a prepayment clause in case a borrower pays off a loan early. When lenders make loans, they calculate their return, over the term of the loan. If a loan is paid off before that time, the lender gets less interest than planned, thus the return on investment is threatened. So the borrower is required to make it up by paying a penalty. It may not make a lot of sense to us as consumers, but that's the banking business.

Traditionally, a formula that has been used is to charge 20 percent of six month's interest if the loan is less than seven years old. If it is older than seven years, normally a prepayment penalty is not charged. However, most of the new loans currently being made may be paid off at any time without a penalty. Prepayment penalties are rare.

"Or More" Clause
An "or more" clause allows a borrower to pay off a loan early, or make higher payments without penalty.

Foreclosure

Foreclosure is a legal procedure used to terminate the rights and title of mortgagor or trustor in real property by selling the encumbered property and using the sale proceeds to pay off creditors.

Generally, a mortgage can only be foreclosed judicially, or through a court procedure. However, a trust deed containing a power of sale may be foreclosed either judicially or by trustee's sale.

Trustee's Sale

A Trustee's Sale may occur only when there is a power of sale included in the trust deed. This is commonly part of all trust deeds, and a trustee's sale is the most usual way to foreclose against a trust deed in default. In a trustee's sale, as we have seen, normally no deficiency judgments are allowed. Nor does the debtor have any rights of redemption after the sale.

During the statutory reinstatement period, however, the debtor or any other party with a junior lien may reinstate (bring current and restore) the loan in default. After the statutory reinstatement period, the debtor may still redeem the property and stop the foreclosure sale by paying off the entire debt, plus interest, costs and fees, at any time within five business days prior to the date of the sale.

The Procedure

When a borrower is behind in payments, usually a lender will work toward avoiding a foreclosure by allowing a grace period, usually 10 to 15 days. The lender does not want the property, but just wants to get repaid for the loan. At some point, however, the lender must decide to foreclose, notify the trustee of the borrower's failure to pay (default), and deliver the original note and trust deed to the trustee with instructions to prepare and record a notice of default against the debtor.

Notice of Default

The notice of default must be executed by the beneficiary or trustee and must be recorded in the office of the county recorder where the property is located at least three months before notice of sale is given. Within 10 days after recording the notice of default, a copy of the notice must be sent by certified or registered mail to all persons who have filed a request for notice. A copy must also be sent within one month after recording to the specific parties.

Notice of Default must be sent to:

- Successors in interest to the trustor
- Junior lien holders
- Vendee of any contract of sale
- State Controller if there is a tax lien against the property

Anyone interested in a particular deed of trust may record a request for notice of default and notice of sale with the county recorder where the property is located.

Notice of Sale

If the default is not cured by the borrower within the reinstatement period of three months, the trustee issues a notice of trustee's sale, which sets a sale date not sooner than 20 days after the recording date of the notice of trustee's sale.

The trustor and anyone else requesting notice must be notified at least 20 days before the sale, and the notice of sale must be published once a week for a period of 20 days in a local newspaper of general circulation. The notice of sale must be posted publicly in the city of the sale, as well as on a door of the property.

Foreclosure Facts

- Reinstatement period: three months
- Trustee's sale may be held 20 days after notice of sale is issued
- Notice of Sale must be published in local newspaper once weekly for 20 days prior to sale

The Sale

The sale is conducted at public auction by the trustee in the county where the property is located, approximately four months after the Notice of Default is recorded.

Until the auction bidding is over, the debtor or any junior lien holder may still redeem the property by paying off the defaulted loan in full, plus all fees, costs and expenses permitted by law. Reinstatement of the loan by bringing all payments up to date and paying all fees may be made at any time until five business days prior to the date of sale.

Loan Reinstatement:

- Loan may be made current (reinstated) up to five days prior to the foreclosure sale

---

Anyone may bid at the auction, but the first lien holder, or holder of the debt being foreclosed, is the only one who may "credit bid," or bid the amount that is owed the holder on the defaulted loan without actually having to pay the money. All other bids must be in cash or cashier's checks.

The sale is made to the highest bidder, and the buyer receives a Trustee's Deed to the property. The debtor no longer has any interest in, nor right to, redeeming the foreclosed property.

Steps in a Trustee's Sale

1. Beneficiary notifies trustee to foreclose

2. Trustee records notice of default

3. Reinstatement period (three months) is met

4. Notice of trustee's sale posted; date,
   time and place of sale published (three weeks)

5. Sale is held; highest cash bidder wins

6. Trustee's deed is given to buyer (sale is final, borrower
   has no right of redemption)

The sale is subject to certain liens of record that do not get eliminated by a foreclosure sale. That means the new buyer is responsible for payment of those liens.

Liens Not Eliminated by Foreclosure

- Federal tax liens
- Assessments and real property taxes
- Mechanic's liens

The sale of a property at a trustee's sale will extinguish the trust deed lien securing the debt to the beneficiary (lender) and will also extinguish any junior liens. That means the holder of a junior lien (a second, third or fourth trust deed), in order to protect his or her interest, had better make a bid for the property, or possibly lose the right to collect on the loan if the sale amount is not enough for a pay off.

Trustee Applies Foreclosure Sale Proceeds in this Order:

1. Trustee's fees, costs and sale expenses
2. Beneficiary -- to satisfy the full amount of unpaid principal and interest, charges, penalties, costs and expenses
3. Junior lien holders in order of priority
4. Debtor--any money left over

Junior Trust Deeds

Another way to finance a property, either at the time of a sale, or afterward, is by using a Junior Trust Deed, which is any loan recorded after the first trust deed, secured by a second, third or subsequent trust deed. Many times in a sale, where the first trust deed loan plus the buyer's down payment are not enough to meet the purchase price, additional money is needed.

Outside Financing

One way to get the needed financing is for the buyer to obtain a secondary loan through an outside source, such as a mortgage banker, or private investor. At the same time the buyer is applying for a loan secured by a first trust deed from a conventional lender, a second--or junior--loan is arranged to complete the financing.

As you recall, any loan made at the time of a sale, as part of that sale, is known as a purchase money loan. At the close of escrow, then, the loan from the first trust deed is funded and sent to the escrow holder to be given to the seller after all necessary loan documents have been signed by the buyer.

The same is true of the new purchase money loan secured by a second trust deed. That loan is also funded and the money sent to the escrow holder to be given to the seller after all loan documents have been signed by the buyer. At the same time, the escrow holder asks the buyer to bring in the down payment. The proceeds from both the first and the second loan, plus the down payment, are then given to the seller at the close of escrow.

After several weeks of looking for the right home, Tom and Darlene found one that was exactly what they wanted. They only had 10 percent of the purchase price as a down payment, but had excellent credit and felt sure they could qualify to obtain secondary financing.

The house was priced at $200,000. They made a full price offer, with the buyer to qualify for an 80 percent first trust deed, a 10 percent second trust deed and 10 percent as a down payment. Their offer was accepted and the seller was given all cash at the close of escrow.

<u>Tom and Darlene's Offer</u>

New first trust deed	$160,000
New second trust deed	20,000
Down payment	<u>20,000</u>
Sales price	$200,000

Seller Financing

Another common source for secondary financing of a sale is the seller. If the seller is going to be the lender, he or she agrees to "carry back," or act as a banker, and make a loan to the buyer for the needed amount. That loan is secured by a trust deed, in favor of the seller, recorded after the first trust deed.

When a seller "carries the paper" on the sale of his or her home, it is also called a purchase money loan, just like the loan made by an outside lender. If a seller receives a substantial amount from the proceeds of a first loan, plus the buyer's down payment, it may be in the seller's interest to carry a second trust deed--possibly for income or to reduce tax liability by accepting installment payments.

Dominick made an offer on a house owned by Bruno, who accepted an offer of $275,000, with $27,500 as the down payment. The buyer qualified for a new first loan in the amount of $220,000, and asked Bruno to carry a second loan in the amount of $27,500 to complete the purchase price.

When the seller extends credit in the form of a loan secured by a second deed of trust, the note may be written as a straight note, with interest-only payments, or even no payments. Or it could be an installment note with a balloon payment at the end, or Fully Amortized Note with equal payments until it is paid off. The term of the loan is decided by the buyer and seller. The instructions of the buyer and seller regarding the seller financing are usually carried out through escrow.

A trust deed held by the seller may be sold by the seller to an outside party, usually a mortgage broker. The note and trust deed will be discounted, or reduced in value by the mortgage broker, but it is one way a seller can get cash out of a trust deed that was carried back.

Ben and Jerry owned a house together as investors. After several years, they put the house on the market for $350,000 and hoped to get a full-price offer so they could go their separate ways with the profit from the house. After a short time, they did get a full price offer. The buyer offered to put $70,000 down, get a $240,000 new first loan and asked Ben and Jerry to carry $40,000 for five years, as a second trust deed.

Ben and Jerry would have turned the offer down if their agent hadn't suggested they accept and sell the second trust deed after the close of escrow. Even though it would be discounted, it was one way they could get most of the cash out of their investment.

If the second trust deed was sold at a discounted 20 percent, or $8,000, Ben and Jerry would end up with $40,000, less $8,000, or $32,000. In that way they would get the cash out of the sale, though they would be netting less than they originally planned *because of the discount. They followed their agent's suggestion, and were satisfied with the result.*

Disclosures Regarding the Borrower's Credit-Worthiness Needed in Transactions Involving:

- A purchase money loan on one-to-four units
- Seller financing to the purchaser
- "An arranger of credit" (real estate agent)

Whenever there is seller financing in a real estate transaction, the law requires the buyer and seller to complete a Seller Financing Disclosure Statement. It gives both the seller and buyer all the information needed to make an informed decision about using seller financing to complete the sale.

The seller can see from the disclosure whether or not the buyer has the ability to pay off the loan by looking at the buyer's income, and whether or not the buyer has a good credit history. The buyer can see what the existing loans are, as well as such things as due date and payments on existing loans that would be senior to the loan in question.

If there is a real estate agent involved, that agent is known as the arranger of credit. There is a place on the disclosure for the agent to sign, signifying that he or she has complied with thelaw regarding the transaction.

Home Equity Loans

Another way a junior loan can be created is by a home equity loan. Assuming there is enough equity, or the difference between the value of a home and the money that is owed against it, a homeowner can apply for a cash loan for any purpose.

A lender uses strict standards about the amount of equity required in a property before loaning money, and particularly for a junior loan. The reason is simple. All a lender wants is to get his or her money back in a timely manner, along with the calculated return on the investment. Care must be taken, in case of a decrease in the value of the subject property, to make sure there is enough of a margin between the total amount owed and the value of the property. If the lender has to sell the property at a foreclosure sale, he or she will be assured of getting the money back. By only loaning up to 80 percent or 90 percent of the property value, the lender leaves some room for loss.

Michael's home was appraised at $100,000, with a $40,000 first trust deed recorded against it. Michael wants a $40,000 home equity loan. To determine whether or not to make the loan, the lender adds the amount owed to the amount desired in the loan to determine the percentage that would be

encumbered by the existing first trust deed, and the desired second trust deed. If the lender would only loan up to 80 percent of the appraised value of the property, would Michael get his loan?

The priority of the loan will depend on what other instruments are recorded ahead of it, but it will be known as a hard money loan and will be secured by a deed of trust against the property. (Of course Michael does get his loan because the figures work out.)

Alberta, a homeowner, wanted to modernize her home. She owed $50,000 on a first trust deed, and the house was worth about $250,000. She had no trouble obtaining a home equity loan, secured by a second deed of trust, for her improvements.

Balloon Payment Loans

Often, when a lender makes a first trust deed loan or a junior trust deed loan or when a seller takes back a junior purchase money note and trust deed, the monthly installments required do not amortize the loan over the term. The result is a large payment of principal and/or interest (balloon payment), due on the last installment.

In the interest of consumer welfare, the law requires the holder of a balloon note secured by an owner-occupied building of one-to-four units to give 90- to 150-days' warning of the balloon payment due date.

Regarding hard money junior loans negotiated by loan brokers (under $10,000), if payments are made in installments and the term is less than three years, the final payment may not be more than twice the amount of the smallest payment.

The law dealing with balloon payments is for loans other than purchase money loans extended by a seller to help a buyer finance a sale.

Hard Money Loan

- A hard money loan is one made in exchange for cash, as opposed to a loan made to finance a property

---

Other Types of Loans Secured by Trust Deeds

Blanket Loan

A trust deed that covers more than one parcel of property may be secured by a blanket loan. It usually contains a release clause that provides for the release of any particular parcel upon the repayment of a specified part of the loan. Commonly, it is used in connection with housing tracts. or construction loans.

Open-End Loan

An additional amount of money may be loaned to a borrower in the future under the same trust deed. The effect is to preserve the original loan's priority claim against the property.

All Inclusive Deed of Trust

Also known as an all-inclusive trust deed (AITD), or a wrap-around trust deed, this type of wraps an existing trust deed with a new trust deed, and the borrower makes one payment for both. In other words, the new trust deed (the AITD) includes the present encumbrances, such as first, second, third, or more trust deeds, plus the amount to be financed by the seller.

The AITD is subordinate to existing encumbrances because the AITD is created at a later date. This means any existing encumbrances have priority over the AITD, even though they are included, or wrapped, by the new all-inclusive trust deed. At the close of escrow the buyer receives title to the property.

Typically an AITD is used in a transaction between buyer and seller to make the financing attractive to the buyer and beneficial to the seller as well. Instead of the buyer assuming an existing loan and the seller carrying back a second trust deed, the AITD can accomplish the same purpose with greater benefit to both parties in some instances.

AITD's have been popular when interest rates are high and the underlying loans are not adjustable. When interest rates are low and a buyer can obtain a loan from an institution, it does not make sense to wrap an underlying loan, therefore paying a higher rate of interest to the seller than if an outside loan was obtained.

Benefits of an All Inclusive Trust Deed

Seller:
- Usually gets full-price offer
- Higher interest rate on amount carried

Buyer:
- Low down payment
- No qualifying for a loan or payment of loan fees

The AITD does not disturb the existing loan. The seller, as the new lender, keeps making the payments while giving a new increased loan at a higher rate of interest to the borrower. The amount of the AITD includes the unpaid principal balance of the existing (underlying) loan, plus the amount of the new loan being made by the seller. The borrower makes payment on the new larger loan to the seller, who in turn makes payment to the holder of the existing underlying loan. The new loan "wraps around" the existing loan.

A seller usually will carry back a wrap-around trust deed at a higher rate of interest than the underlying trust deed, thereby increasing the yield. The seller continues to pay off the original trust deed from the payments on the wrap-around, while keeping the difference. This type of financing works best when the underlying interest rate is low, and the seller can then charge a higher rate on the wrapped loan.

A wrap-around loan isn't for everyone. If a seller needs to cash out, it won't work. Also, most loans contain a due-on-sale clause, and cannot be wrapped without the lender's knowledge and approval. Depending on the buyer's and seller's motivation, sometimes an AITD will be created, with full knowledge of the risk. This is how the term "creative financing" came into being.

Generally, these payments are collected by the note department of a bank or a professional collection company and sent on to the appropriate parties. This assures the maker (borrower) of the AITD that all underlying payments are being forwarded and are kept current by a neutral party.

Attila wanted to sell his house in San Francisco and return to Asia. He listed it for $100,000. The existing first trust deed was for $50,000 at 8 percent, payable at $377 monthly. He thought about carrying a second trust deed at 10 percent, counting on the income from the note. However, Bonnie, his listing agent, explained he could get a greater return by carrying an all-inclusive trust deed (AITD) instead of just a note and second trust *deed from a buyer. She also told him any offer that included an AITD should be referred to an attorney. Attila, with his attorney's approval, accepted the following offer soon after listing the house:*

<u>Attila's Offer</u>

Sales price

$100,000

Cash by buyer (down payment)

<u>20,000</u>

AITD in favor of Atilla

$80,000

- *Payments on new AITD of $80,000 at 10 percent to be $702 made monthly to Attila*
- *Payments on existing first trust deed of $50,000 at 8 percent, in the amount of $377 monthly, to be paid by Attila to original lender*

AITD payment to Attila

$702

Existing First Trust Deed payment

<u>377</u>

Monthly difference to Attila

$325

In some instances, a "rider" containing additional agreements between a buyer and seller will be attached to an all inclusive deed of trust.

Additions to an AITD

The note will be placed on contract collection with a bank or trust company authorized to do business. Money is collected and disbursed for current installments, payments of taxes and insurance if necessary and any amount then remaining is disbursed to the holder of the note secured by the AITD.

If the trustor (borrower) defaults, beneficiary obligations (lender) will be suspended until the default is cured. If the trustor is delinquent in making any payments due under the note, and the beneficiary incurs any penalties or other expenses on account of the underlying obligations during the period of trustor delinquency, the amount of any penalties and expenses will be added to the amount of the note and will be payable by the trustor with the next payment due under the note.

In the event of foreclosure of the all inclusive deed of trust, the beneficiary agrees that he or she will, at the trustee's sale, bid an amount representing that due under the AITD, less the total balance due on the underlying notes, plus any advances or other disbursements which the beneficiary is allowed by law to include in the bid.

When the note secured by the AITD becomes due or the trustor requests a demand for payoff of the note, the main amount payable to the beneficiary will be reduced by the unpaid balances of the underlying obligations.

If any installment payment under the note secured by the AITD is not paid within 15 days after the due date, a late charge may be incurred by the trustor and be due and payable upon the beneficiary's demand.

Adequate funds for the payment of taxes and fire insurance will be deposited and held by the collection account holder. Monthly, an amount equal to one-twelfth of the annual tax amount and one-twelfth the amount of the annual fire insurance billing will be deposited by the trustor. Taxes and insurance reserves have been provided by the trustor to the beneficiary for the initial reserve fund.

If the trustor makes any additional payments or added increments beyond the required monthly amount, the beneficiary, upon a request by the trustor in writing, will forward any extra funds to the holders of the underlying notes for application to the unpaid principal balances.

Wrap-Around Loans (AITD's)

- Secured by a trust deed that "wraps," or includes existing financing plus the amount to be financed by the seller

Unsecured Loan

The lender receives a promissory note from the borrower, without any assurance of payment. The only recourse is a lengthy court action to force payment. This is truly the traditional IOU.

Alternative Financing

Alternative financing is one way lenders and borrowers can respond to the realities of today's unsteady economy. Because there are different kinds of lenders and different kinds of borrowers who are in need of credit to buy homes, there is no single type of financing that fits everyone.

The changing needs of consumers have caused lenders to respond by offering various solutions to credit demands. In the past, the only way people could buy a home was to use the fixed-rate loan. Today, any number of variable-rate loans are available to serve consumers.

After borrowers began to see the benefits of these "alphabet soup" loans, they realized this was one solution to the uncertainty of a rapidly changing marketplace. It is the job of a real estate agent to help consumers understand these new types of loans and to select the one that best suits their needs.

Graduated Payment Adjustable Mortgage

The loan known as a graduated payment adjustable mortgage (GPAM) has partially deferred payments of principal at the start of the term, increasing as the loan matures. This loan is for the buyer who expects to be earning more after a few years and can make a higher payment at that time. It is also known as a flexible rate mortgage.

Variable or Adjustable Rate Mortgage

The variable rate mortgage (VRM) or adjustable rate mortgage (ARM) loan provides for adjustment of its interest rate as market interest rates change. The interest rate is tied to some reference index that reflects changes in market rates of interest. Changes in the interest rate may be reflected in the changing payment, the term of the loan, or a combination of both.

Shared Appreciation Mortgage

Under a shared appreciation mortgage (SAM), the lender and the borrower agree to share a certain percentage of the appreciation in the market value of the property which is security for the loan. In return for the shared equity, the borrower is offered beneficial loan terms.

Rollover Mortgage

The rollover mortgage (ROM) is a loan where the interest rate and monthly payment are renegotiated, typically every five years.

Reverse Annuity Mortgage

This type of loan--the reverse annuity mortgage (RAM)--is used by older homeowners who have owned their homes for a long time and have a large amount of equity but not much of a monthly income. This loan uses their built-up equity to pay the borrower a fixed annuity, based on a percentage of the property value.

The borrower is not required to repay the loan until a specified event such as death or sale of the property, at which time the loan is paid off. A retired couple can draw on their home equity by increasing their loan balance each month.

Truth-in-Lending Act (Regulation Z)

The Truth-in-Lending Act, known as Regulation Z, requires a lender to inform the borrower how much he or she is paying for credit. The lender must reflect all financing costs as a percentage, called the Annual Percentage Rate (APR).

Equal Credit Opportunity Act

This federal law, the Equal Credit Opportunity Act, protects borrowers from discrimination based on race, sex, color, religion, national origin, age or marital status.

Soldiers' and Sailors' Civil Relief Act

Persons in the military, under this law known as the Soldiers' and Sailors' Civil Relief Act, are protected from foreclosure on their homes while serving time in the military service.

Post Test

The following self test repeats the one you took at the beginning of this chapter. Now take the exam again--since you have read all the material-- and check your knowledge of real estate finance.

True/False

1. Hypothecation is when an owner uses a property as security for a loan, but does not give up possession.

2. A trustee is a neutral third party in a trust deed.

3. In a trust deed, the borrower is the same as the beneficiary.

4. The beneficiary hold bare legal title to a property encumbered by a trust deed.

5. A reconveyance deed is used to deed a property to the trustor after the deed of trust has been paid in full.

6. An "or more" clause allows a borrower to pay off a loan early with no penalty.

7. A holder in due course is someone who buys an existing negotiable note.

8. Foreclosure is the cure for a tenant's default on monthly rental payments.

9. A trustee must sign a reconveyance deed.

10. A land contract and a contract of sale are alike.

chapter 4

ESCROW, TITLE & OTHER PROFESSIONALS

Focus

- **Introduction**
- **Escrow professionals**
- **Title insurance professionals**
- **Escrow associations**
- **Insurers**
- **Real estate brokers**
- **Builders**
- **Attorneys**
- **Independent escrow companies**

Pre-Test

The following is a self test to determine how much you know about escrow and other professionals before reading this chapter. Take it without studying, then read the material presented in the text. At the end of the chapter you will find a repeat of this exam. Test your knowledge by answering the questions again, then check your improvement. (The answers are found at the end of the book.) Good luck.

True/False

1. The job of escrow clerk requires a four year college degree.

2. Mathematical ability is a primary requirement of an escrow officer.

3. A loan escrow officer specializes in loan escrows.

4. An escrow administrator manages a multi-office escrow business.

5. A title clerk is the main person respsonsible for interpretation of the condition of title.

6. A title analyst might deal with tidelands and submerged lands.

7. Another name for a "title rep" is title marketer.

8. In order to conduct escrows, a real estate broker must be licensed by the Real Estate Commissioner.

9. A real estate broker must keep all escrow funds in a personal account.

10. The Corporations Commissioner monitors the escrow activities of lawyers.

Introduction

The jobs of escrow and title officer have developed throughout the years into professions requiring much more than simply searching a title or gathering documents. Both have grown into independent industries, with special designations and codes of ethics which guide their professional conduct, just like those followed by other real estate professionals.

Escrow Professionals

Escrow professionals provide service either as a separate company, as part of a title company, or as a department within banks or other financial institutions. An escrow career track can emphasize sale escrows, loan escrows or a combination of both. Learning the business of escrow requires a personality suited to details, some instructional escrow classes and, most important of all, practical hands-on experience.

Clerk

As an entry level position, the job of clerk, whether it is known as secretary, receptionist or general office worker, is where most escrow professionals start their career. An awareness of office functions as well

129

as word and data processing are basic to being successful. Also, for a beginner in the escrow business, a background in finance or real estate is a valuable asset.

After working in an escrow office for some time, an ambitious escrow secretary may eventually function as a junior escrow officer or escrow officer in training.

Escrow Officer

Escrow officer is the next natural progression after working with escrows and becoming familiar with the many tasks required to complete an escrow.

Duties of an Escrow Officer:

- Gathering information, examining and organizing it into accurate escrow instructions

- Preparing documents for various escrows

- Being aware of aspects which are parallel to escrow, such as title and legal requirements

- Having knowledge of real estate financing to the extent of being able to answer clients' questions and prepare financing documents appropriate to the acquisition and sale of real property

- Being aware of the productivity and its relationship to the cost of doing business as an escrow holder

---

An escrow officer must possess certain personal talents and gifts in order to be successful in the complicated, fast-paced world of escrow. Efficiency, organization and a systematic approach are primary skills an escrow officer must exercise during the orderly process of each unique escrow, to be thorough in processing all details.

Qualifications of an Escrow Officer

Organization is essential in coordinating documents and other instruments. A systematic and logical perception of all processes, as well as the ability to gather information and to produce properly drawn instructions--is a primary qualification.

Because of an escrow's many complicated legal requirements, a background in law is an extra, welcome, qualification. Laws affecting real estate transfers are constantly changing and an escrow officer must be aware of their impact on current escrows.

A competent escrow officer rarely wastes time or money. Mistakes usually cost someone, and an efficient officer can save time and money by conducting business in an orderly, capable manner.

Prorations, closing statements, computation of demands, financial statements and balancing all require mathematical proficiency. An escrow officer must be skillfulwith numbers and have the ability to calculate accurately.

131

A serene, patient personality is well suited to the career of escrow officer. Good judgment and a sense of humor under difficult conditions are basic requirements for a successful career in escrow.

Loan Escrow Officer

A loan escrow professional specializes in closing loan escrows or as a loan underwriter.

An escrow officer and a loan escrow officer have many of the same duties.

Duties of a Loan Escrow Officer

- Supervise the process of closing a loan, from the beginning when the loan committee gives the loan file to the loan officer through the final funding of the loan

- Follow lender directions for supplying support documents, credit requirements, title provisions and other information

- Act as a go-between for lenders and borrowers

- Acknowledge differences in requirements of lenders for loan processing

- Know how loans are structured, from technical provisions of consumer protection laws and requirements of the many regulatory agencies, to the complications of construction loans and income property loans. The loan officer must work closely with the escrow officer to assure all legal aspects are in order for the closing.

Personal Attributes of a Loan Escrow Officer

A loan escrow officer must be capable of adjusting to more changes and having more contact with the customer than a general escrow officer who primarily closes sale escrows.

Outstanding communication skills are necessary when explaining the various steps in the loan escrow process because of the complexities of the lending process. Because of the greater possibility of conflict and surprise in the lending process, a loan officer must be adept at coping with upset and emotional customers.

A loan officer must be skilled at mathematics in order to calculate loan payoffs and payment schedules.

All escrow officers must be efficient and organized, and a loan escrow officer is no different. The use of computer technology has speeded up loan processing and allowed the loan officer greater flexibility and organization in less time than in the past.

Training

Generally, a loan officer has worked in some part of the loan industry before coming to escrow as a professional. Former employment often includes savings banks, commercial banks, mortgage bankers, insurance companies, mortgage brokers, credit unions and finance companies. Formal training is available from professional groups and private schools.

Manager

As an escrow manager, a career professional must possess greater technical knowledge and have more practical experience than an escrow officer.

A manager must be able to coordinate the various concurrent jobs in a timely and efficient way in an escrow office. He or she must balance technical competence with knowledge of how to make a profit for the company. The manager must be profit oriented as well as service oriented.

A successful manager must be able to communicate ideas both written and verbal . The effectiveness of management will be impaired if communication is not free flowing within the organization and between the organization and other real estate professionals. As always, when dealing with fellow workers , respect for their ideas and position is basic to good relations.

The ability to train new escrow professionals is a necessary quality for an escrow manager. Communicating ideas and concepts as well as guiding new workers through the confusing maze of balancing existing escrows while opening new ones is a challenging task for a manager. As we have mentioned before, escrow is learned through doing, and a manager must be able to teach the practical lessons of the business as well as supervise the office.

Another important task for the escrow manager is marketing the business. Customers are necessary if there is to be a business, and constant, aggressive representation in the community of the escrow company is the only way to assure a large market share of the customers.

Finally, an ongoing, objective evaluation of staff workers will allow a manager to identify problemareas and develop training to strengthen weaknesses in the product.

Administrator

All the relationships in a multi-office escrow business are the responsibility of the escrow administrator. The position does require a highly developed technical knowledge of escrow, but most importantly requires excellent management skills.

A complete understanding of the contribution of human resources and how they may be used is basic to the profitability of the company. The administrator is responsible for recognizing the staff's potential and how that potential can be used for a greater return on the company dollar. The major qualification of an administrator is to be skilled at problem solving. Ultimately, all problems will end up with the administrator, whose ability to resolve uncertainty and to settle disputes is essential.

<u>Desirable Traits of an Administrator:</u>

- Exceptional communication skills

- Personal organization

- Ability to delegate tasks

- Fair and unprejudiced dealings with personnel

- Skilled coordination of all aspects of escrow

Title Insurance Professionals

Job descriptions in the business of title insurance go from research and interpretation of title information, to underwriting insurance, to administering and marketing the title company's services.

Searcher

The beginner job position in the title business is as a title searcher. When a title order is opened, the searcher must evaluate the instructions for the type of search required. Normally, tracing the chain of title or history of sales on the property is included in the search. There may also be a request in the instructions for information on loans, ownership of minerals, easements, reversionary rights under a recorded deed restriction, leasehold interest or special title requirements. Particular policy coverages like condemnation, trust deed foreclosure, subdivision and litigation guarantees require special searches. Maps or copies of documents are ordered as requested.

After reviewing the instructions for the title order, the searcher prepares a chain of title, starting from the policy date of the latest title policy issued on the property under search, to the present time. The chain of title includes the types of documents, parties involved and other recorded data on the property in question.

A general index search is the next order of business for the searcher. After the chain of title has been prepared and the title search completed, a search of recorded documents by alphabetical index is done to discover any judgments, divorces, tax liens, bankruptcies, probates, incompetencies and other general matters affecting the parties involved with the property.

Researched documents such as deeds, reconveyances, judgments and other liens are placed on microfilm or microfiche and copies are made for the title search. The job of the searcher is easier in sparsely populated counties where the recordings are few and is more complicated in areas like Los Angeles County where thousands of documents are recorded daily.

Historically, the searcher has had to look through lot books in which documents have been posted by hand and classified by legal description. Today, however, the general index or name search has been automated along with the lot book. Information is now searched from computerized files in a title plant.

After all recorded documents have been found and assembled by date order into a non-interrupted chain of title, the searcher submits the package to the opinion department for legal review. If all is in order, the search is returned to the title department.

Before a sale is recorded, but after the initial or preliminary title search, new documents on the property in question may be recorded. The searcher must complete a final screening by computer or manually before the title order is closed.

The title searcher has a high degree of responsibility for accuracy. Missed documents in the chain of title can cause significant damage to the title company which is guaranteeing that all past title matters have been researched and exposed for examination. It is desirable for a searcher to be detail oriented and to have a high degree of skill in clerical matters.

As the searcher compiles a history of property ownership , decisions must be made about whether a document in the chain should be included and whether, in fact, the document even affects the property. An orderly and logical method must be used to sift through the myriad data found and present it for the issuance of the policy of title insurance.

After entering the title business as a searcher, a capable worker can advance to the position of senior searcher, or long-order searcher. This position requires knowledge and skill in dealing with such complex matters as property resurveys, street abandonments, railroad title reversions, tideland and wetland matters and oil searches.

Examiner

A policy of title insurance is written based upon interpretation. The main person responsible for the interpretation is the title examiner or title officer. The title examiner orders the search and examines the information compiled from the search.

During the course of the title examination, the title officer works closely with the escrow officer who has placed the title order, based on instructions for the transaction in question.

As a result of examination and inquiry, the title examiner submits a written opinion about the clear title of the property, known as a preliminary title report. Also known as an interim binder, this report is a commitment to issue title insurance on the property.

If there is a question about interpretation of the condition of the title of the property in question, the examiner may seek the advise of a title advisor, attorney or reference sources.

Another job of the examiner is to check the accuracy of the preliminary title report regarding the legal description, vesting of title and encumbrances on the land.

All legal documents required by the transaction must be examined by the title officer prior to recording to make sure escrow instructions have been followed and the documentation is adequate for closing.

The most skilled and capable title officers in the company are asked to deal with specialized and complicated title matters where the greatest degree of risk exists for title insurers.

Advisory Title Officers

Many times senior title examiners operate in the capacity of advisor title officers. They solve complicated issues and make underwriting decisions about whether a property is an acceptable insurance risk for the company. A separately staffed underwriting department may exist in the larger title companies.

Title Analyst

The job of title analyst involves research and development, particularly on complex projects. When title insurers are asked to deal with complicated underwriting tasks, the title research analyst complements the work of advisory title officers. The title analyst might deal with questions of Indian lands,

tidelands and submerged lands, lake and river boundaries or land resurvey problems.

Also, a title analyst might develop new underwriting procedures for the company or expand procedures already in place.

Title Marketer

Title companies rely on "title reps" to market their product in specific geographical areas, much like any other sales oriented company. Title representatives call on existing customers and new prospects to promote their title company.

The high tech end of title marketing is usually handled by experienced marketers with technical background in the various fields. Wholesale customers of title insurance might be developers, franchisers or hotel chains.

Branch Manager

The duties of a title company branch manager include staff selection, setting an example, training and development, expanding market share, reporting results and personnel assessment. A manager must be skilled at interviewing, leadership, teaching, sales and communication.

Executive Management

As financial services companies combine their offerings to bring greater opportunity to the public, more administrators are required to manage various locations and to deal with newly developed duties. The title industry requires its executives to develop and understand the big picture as far as planning, market share, future growth and profit.

An executive administrator must possess superior communication skills and be able to project and promote the company image both internally and to the outside business community.

Escrow Associations

The escrow industry, dedicated to professionalism, has advanced various goals through various local and national organizations.

<u>Goals of an escrow association:</u>

"The objects and purposes of an escrow association shall be to promote sound and ethical business practices among its members; to provide for the collection, study and dissemination of information relating to problems of and improvements in land title evidence; to promote and encourage sound legislation affecting land titles; to encourage practices which will best serve the public interest; to educate and inform the public of the integrity and stability of its members and the advantages and desirability of their services."

Under the education arm of state organizations, training programs and continuing education are offered. Seminars, workshops and annual educational conferences are designed to bring escrow professionals current information regarding changes in the industry.

Local and state organizations publish newsletters outlining trends, new legislation, timely topics and recent court decisions. New education opportunities for escrow professionals are provided by *Escrow Update* and *A.E.A. News* (American Escrow Association).

Public recognition and ethical standards of the escrow industry are enhanced by professional organizations. By monitoring laws which impact the industry and advocating legislation which will benefit the industry and the public, escrow organizations educate and strengthen the growth of the industry.

The escrow industry is also empowered by the establishment of career designations for escrow professionals by the CEA, as well as a Code of Ethics.

Professional Escrow Designations:

- Certified Escrow Officer (CEO)

- Certified Senior Escrow Officer (CSEO)

Insurers

Title Companies

Escrow holders use both title insurers and general insurance companies in conducting their business.

There are two kinds of title companies: those directly responsible for their own financial risk, or underwriting, and those indirectly responsible for underwriting policies.

The Insurance Commissioner is the supervisor for title insurers in the state where the home office is located, and is aided by insurance commissioners in states where branch offices are used. The criteria for financial responsibility (bonding and reserve requirements) are regulated by the Insurance Code and are different from those fixed by the Corporations Commissioner, Banking Commissioner and the Real Estate Commissioner.

In some states, many title insurers offer escrow benefits along with their title business. In Northern California most of the sale escrow work is done by title companies. Escrow holders are responsible for most of the escrows in Southern California.

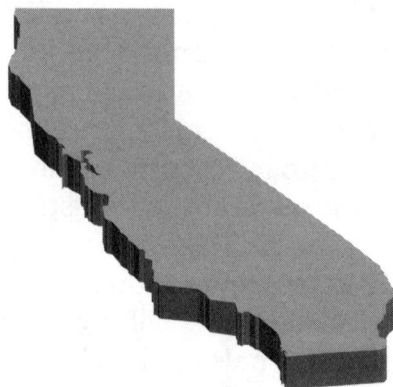

Insurance Companies

In the 1920s and 1930s, insurance companies were major investors in housing. After World War II, the need for housing was so great and the capital to build was so inadequate that insurance companies from the eastern part of the country moved west to fill the need for capital.

Insurance companies became commonplace loan processors and helped maintain the housing boom.

By the 1960s, insurance companies began to move their interest from investing in single family home loans to loans on large, income producing projects. Loan underwriting and escrow practices have had to modify with the changing needs of the insurance industry.

Insurance companies are regulated by the Insurance Commissioner and must conform to the legal and financial requirements and regulations of that department. The Insurance Commissioner is also responsible for audits of financial procedures used by insurance companies.

Commonly, insurance companies make their loans through mortgage bankers or other money brokers. Some companies, however, deal directly with the public and use escrow holders to complete their loans or sales.

Because many insurance companies have large real estate portfolios, they act as principals as well as lenders with real estate as security. In this capacity, they must be very specific about their title insurance needs, usually requiring extended coverage.

Real Estate Brokers

Depending on each situation, real estate brokers can be escrow holders themselves, or customers of escrow services.

A real estate broker operating in the capacity of escrow holder is exempt from the requirements of the Corporations Commissioner and is not under supervision of the Department of Corporations. Any company, broker or agent licensed by the Real Estate Commissioner, while

145

performing acts in the course of or incidental to the real estate business, may hold escrows in connection with any transaction. A broker, however, may not hold escrows for separate individuals or entities, for compensation, unless he or she is representing the buyer or seller or both in a particular transaction.

In order for a broker to advertise escrow services, it must be mentioned in any promotion that the services are only in connection with real estate brokerage. Because the escrow business is so unpredictable, many broker-owned escrows have been converted to independent escrow companies so those businesses can expand their possible markets.

When a broker does act as an escrow holder, he or she must maintain all escrow funds in a trust account. That account, along with all required records, remains subject to inspection by the Real Estate Commissioner's investigative staff and auditors.

The business of escrow holder cannot be taken up as a second job, or sideline. The broker is responsible for accurate record keeping and detailed organization of all aspects of escrow, even though only in-house brokerage transactions are being handled.

As the primary practitioners of the residential resale industry, real estate brokers are the main source of business for escrow holders. One of the jobs of escrow companies is marketing their product. By cooperating and offering special services such as pick up and delivery of documents an escrow company can count certain real estate brokers as steady customers. Other real estate professionals, such as title companies, seek business from brokers directly because of the broker's close association with the escrow company. Hopefully, then, when a title order on a particular transaction is opened, the title company will get the order.

Builders

Many large developers and builders have established their own escrow companies in an effort to control the various parts of their business, and to get a greater return on their investment dollar. These escrow companies are licensed by the Corporations Commissioner, and fall under the guidelines and requirements of that department.

Subdivision escrows are highly specialized and require knowledge of the many different legal requirements. The escrow holder must know about the correct creation of protective restrictions for a development, must make sure that the preliminary public report has been delivered to all prospective purchasers, must be knowledgeable about the formation of homeowners' associations, and must be aware that a legal percentage of parcels in the new development be sold before the first one can close--per legal requirements for subdivisions.

In some states, builders are licensed by the State Contractors Licensing Board, in addition to the Corporations Commissioner overseeing their escrow procedures. Builders are also lightly supervised by the Federal Housing Administration or Veterans Administration or other secondary lenders if they build under government sponsored programs. Developers then may use an escrow company of their choice for the loan processing in connection with their sales.

Many title insurance companies have developed special subdivision departments which have trained personnel to quicken the submission of subdivisions' paperwork throughout the Department of Real Estate. Designated title professionals work specifically with builders and developers to meet their special needs.

Attorneys

The escrow activities of lawyers are monitored by the State Bar Association. Attorneys have the authority to hold escrows for their clients and are exempted from licensing and other requirements as long as the escrow is held in connection with the business of law. Money must be deposited in trust accounts and must be separated by individual files.

Independent Escrow Companies

Closing sale and loan transactions are the principal means of business for independent escrow companies. Additionally, an independent escrow company may act as a corporate trustee on outstanding deeds of trust or as a collection service for customer's accounts as a special service.

Independent escrows are tightly supervised and regulated by the Corporations Commissioner to assure consumer protection. The Commissioner's rules require someone at each escrow company location to have at least five years experience in the escrow field whenever the company is open for business.

An auditing and liaison staff is maintained by the Corporations Commissioner who oversees financial responsibility, ethics and bonding requirements. Frequent audits are held, with the escrow company under examination responsible for the cost of the audit. Each escrow company must maintain orderly files and records in accordance with the Commissioner's rules.

In California, the Escrow Fidelity Corporation (created by the state legislature, governed by industry members and a casualty insurance administrator) provides employee fidelity bonds for independent escrow holders. An annual assessment of $2,250 for each location must be paid by each company as a required member of the fund. The Escrow Fidelity Corporation holds a fidelity bond equal to 1% of the total escrow trust funds on deposit by independent escrows within California. In addition, a trust balance is required of each member escrow company, depending on the amounts of trust funds held.

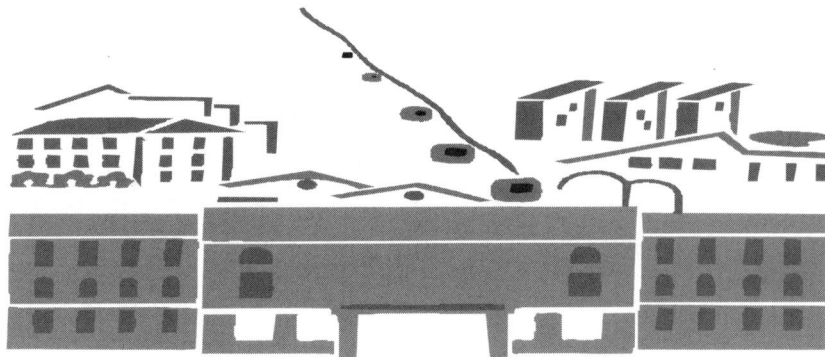

Post Test

The following self test repeats the one you took at the beginning of this chapter. Now take the exam again--since you have read all the material-- and check your knowledge of escrow and title professionals..

True/False

1. The job of escrow clerk requires a four year college degree.

2. Mathematical ability is a primary requirement of an escrow officer.

3. A loan escrow officer specializes in loan escrows.

4. An escrow administrator manages a multi-office escrow business.

5. A title clerk is the main person respsonsible for interpretation of the condition of title.

6. A title analyst might deal with tidelands and submerged lands.

7. Another name for a "title rep" is title marketer.

8. In order to conduct escrows, a real estate broker must be licensed by the Real Estate Commissioner.

9. A real estate broker must keep all escrow funds in a personal account.

10. The Corporations Commissioner monitors the escrow activities of lawyers.

chapter **5**

CONTRACTS

Focus

- **Introduction**
- **Contracts in general**
- **Essential elements of a contract**
- **Statute of Frauds**
- **Performance of contracts**
- **Discharge of contracts**
- **Statute of Limitations**
- **Remedies for breach of contract**
- **Real estate contracts**
- **Liquidated damages**
- **Option**

Pre-Test

The following is a self test to determine how much you know about contracts before reading this chapter. Take it without studying, then read the material presented in the text. At the end of the chapter you will find a repeat of this exam. Test your knowledge by answering the questions again, then check your improvement. (The answers are found at the end of the book.) Good luck.

True/False

1. An option is an example of a unilateral contract.

2. A written contract does not take precedence over oral agreements.

3. A contract is an agreement to do or not to do a certain act.

4. A promise given by one party with the expectation of performance by the other party is known as a bilateral contract.

5. A contract that has been approved is said to be rescinded.

6. Another name for mutual consent is implied agreement.

7. Parties to a contract may be unimancipated minors.

8. Mutual consent is sometimes called a meeting of the minds.

9. In an option, the buyer must perform.

10. The failure to perform a contract is called breach of contract.

Introduction

So far, we have studied the nature of escrow, who needs an escrow, the documents needed with some real estate basics, finance and who the professionals are that carry out escrows. This chapter explains what a contract is and how contracts are used to assure the understanding and approval of all parties to an agreement.

In every real estate transaction, some kind of contract that transfers or indicates an interest in the property is used. It is important that you, as a student of escrow, understand the nature of legal agreements so you are able to prepare instructions which accurately and legally reflect the agreement between the principals.

Contracts in General

A contract is an agreement, enforceable by law, to do or not to do a certain thing. It may be an express contract, where the parties declare the terms and put their intentions in words, either oral or written. A lease or rental agreement, for example, is an express contract. The landlord agrees to allow the tenant to live in the dwelling and the renter agrees to pay rent in return.

An implied contract is one where agreement is shown by act and conduct rather than words. This type of contract is found every day when we go into a restaurant and order food, go to a movie or have a daily newspaper delivered. By showing a desire to use a service, we imply that we will pay for it.

Contracts may be bilateral or unilateral. A bilateral contract is one in which the promise of one party is given in exchange for the promise of the other party. In other words, both parties must keep their agreement for the contract to be completed. An example might be a promise from a would-be aviatrix to pay $2,500 for flying lessons, and a return promise from the instructor to teach her to fly.

A unilateral contract is one where a promise is given by one party with the expectation of performance by the other party. The second party is not bound to act, but if he or she does, the first party is obligated to keep the promise. An example might be a radio station offering $1,000 to the 100th caller. Some lucky person makes the call and the station pays the money.

A contract may be executory or executed. In an executory contract, something remains to be done by one or both parties. An escrow that is not yet closed or a contract not signed by the parties are examples of an executory contract. In an executed contract, all parties have performed completely.

One of the meanings of execute is to sign, or complete in some way. An executed contract may be a sales agreement that has been signed by all parties.

Also, contracts may be void, voidable, unenforceable, or valid.

Types of Contracts

Void contract
No contract at all; lacks legal effect (*example: due to lack of capacity or illegal subject matter*)

Voidable contract
One which is valid and enforceable on its face, but may be rejected by one or more of the parties (*example: induced by fraud, menace or duress, elderly party no longer competent*)

Unenforceable contract
Valid, but for some reason cannot be proved by one or both of the parties (*example: an oral agreement which should be in writing because of Statute of Frauds*)

Valid contract
Binding and enforceable; has all the basic elements required by law

---

Essential Elements of a Contract

For a contract to be legally binding and enforceable, the following requirements must be met:

> ## Essential Elements of a Contract
>
> - Legally competent parties
> - Mutual consent
> - Lawful objective
> - Sufficient consideration
> - Contract in writing (when required by law)

Legally Competent Parties

Parties entering into a contract must have legal capacity to do so. Almost anyone is capable, with a few exceptions. A person must be at least 18 years of age, unless married, in the military or emancipated.

A minor is not capable of appointing an agent, or entering into an agency agreement with a broker to buy or sell. A broker could represent an informed adult in dealing with a minor, but the client must be willing to take a chance that the contract may be voidable. Brokers dealing with minors should proceed cautiously and should seek an attorney's advice.

When it has been determined judicially that a person is not of sound mind, no contract can be made with that incompetent person. Also, if it is obvious that a person is completely without understanding, even without declaration, there can be no contract. In the case of an incompetent, a court appointed guardian would have legal capacity to contract.

Both minors and incompetents may acquire title to real property by gift or inheritance. Any conveyance of acquired property, however, must be court approved. A contract made by a person who is intoxicated or under the influence of legal or illegal drugs may be canceled when the individual sobers up. But it also may be ratified or approved, depending on the parties.

Any person may give another the authority to act on his or her behalf. The document that does this is called a Power of Attorney. The person holding the power of attorney is called an Attorney-in-Fact. When dealing with real property, a power of attorney must be recorded to be valid, and is good for as long as the principal is competent. A power of attorney can be canceled by the principal at any time by recording a revocation and a title company will only honor a power of attorney for one year. After that time, a new one must be signed and recorded. A power of attorney is useful, for example, when a buyer or seller is out of town and has full trust in that agent to operate in his or her behalf.

Mutual Consent

In a valid contract, all parties must mutually agree. Mutual consent, or mutual assent, is sometimes called a meeting of the minds. It is an offer by one party and acceptance by the other party.

Offer

One party must offer and another accept, without condition. An offer shows the contractual intent of the offeror, or the person making the offer, to enter into a contract. That offer must be communicated to the offeree, or the person to whom the offer is being made. Unconditional acceptance of the offer is necessary for all parties to be legally bound. The offer must be definite and certain in its terms, and the agreement must be genuine or the contract may be voidable by one or both parties.

Acceptance

An acceptance is an unqualified agreement to the terms of an offer. The offeree must agree to every item of the offer for the acceptance to be complete. If the original terms are changed in any way in the acceptance, the offer becomes a counteroffer, and the first offer is terminated. The person making the original offer is no longer bound by that offer, and may accept the counteroffer or not. The counteroffer becomes a new offer, made by the original offeree.

Acceptance of an offer must be communicat-ed to the offeror, in the manner specified, before a contract becomes binding between the parties. Silence is not considered to be acceptance.

Termination

An offeror is hopeful that his or her offer will be accepted in a timely manner and a contract will be formed. An offer is specific, however, and an offeror does not have to wait indefinitely for an answer. An offer may be terminated by the following acts.

Termination of an Offer

- Lapse of time: an offer is revoked if the offeree fails to accept it within a prescribed period

- Communication of notice of revocation: this can be done by the offeror anytime before the other party has communicated acceptance

- Failure of offeree to fulfill a condition of acceptance prescribed by the offeror

- A qualified acceptance, or counteroffer by the offeree

- Rejection by the offeree

- Death or insanity of the offeror or offeree

- Unlawful object of the proposed contract

Genuine Assent

A final requirement for mutual consent is that the offer and acceptance be genuine and freely made by all parties. Genuine assent does not exist if there is *fraud, misrepresentation, mistake, duress, menace or undue influence* involved in reaching an agreement.

Fraud is an act meant to deceive in order to get someone to part with something of value. An outright lie, or making a promise with no intention of carrying it out, can be fraud. Lack of disclosure--causing someone to make or accept an offer--is also fraud. For example, failure to tell a prospective buyer who makes an offer to purchase on a sunny day that the roof leaks is fraud. It can make the contract voidable.

Innocent misrepresentation occurs when the person providing the wrong information is not doing it to deceive, but for the purpose of reaching an agreement. Even though no dishonesty is involved, a contract may be rescinded or revoked by the party who feels misled.

Mistake, in contract law, means negotiations were clouded or there was a misunderstanding in the material facts. It does not include ignorance, inability or poor judgment. For example, if you accepted an offer to purchase your home based on what you thought was an all cash offer, and later found that you had agreed to carry a second trust deed, you would be expected to carry through with the agreement. Even though you made a "mistake" in reading the sales contract, you now have a binding agreement.

There are times when you could be credited with a misunderstanding, and ultimately get out of the contract. For instance, what if you were given directions to a friend's beach house, went there on your own and fell in love with it. You immediately made an offer, which was accepted, only to discover you had gone to the wrong house. Because you thought you were purchasing a different property than the one the seller was selling, this could be considered a "major misunderstanding of a material fact," and there would be no mutual agreement, voiding any contract that was signed.

Use of force, known as duress, or menace, which is the threat of violence, may not be used to get agreement. Undue influence or using unfair advantage is also unacceptable. All can cause a contract to be voidable by the injured party.

> ### No Genuine Assent if:
>
> - Fraud
> - Misrepresentation
> - Mistake
> - Duress
> - Menace
> - Undue Influence

Lawful Objective

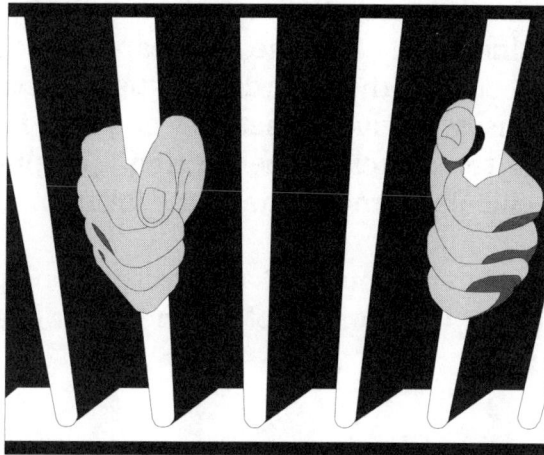

Even though the parties are capable, and mutually agreeable, the object of the contract must be lawful. A contract requiring the performance of an illegal act would not be valid, nor would one where the consideration was stolen.

The contract also must be legal in its formation and operation. For example, a note bearing an interest rate in excess of that allowed by law would be void. Contracts contrary to good morals and general public policy are also unenforceable.

Sufficient Consideration

All contracts require consideration. There are several types of consideration in a contract. Generally, it is something of value such as a promise of future payment, money, property or personal services. For example, there can be an exchange of a promise for a promise, money for a promise, money for property, or goods for services.

Forbearance, or forgiving a debt or obligation, also qualifies as consideration. As a group, the above qualify as valuable consideration. Gifts such as real property based solely on love and affection are considered to be good consideration. They meet the legal requirement that consideration be present in a contract.

In an option, the promise of the offeror is the consideration for the forbearance desired from the offeree. In other words, the person wanting the option promises to give something of value in return for being able to exercise the option to purchase at some specifically named time in the future.

In a bilateral contract, a promise of one party is consideration for the promise of another. For example, in the sale of real property, the buyer promises to pay a certain amount and the seller promises to transfer title. It should be noted that the earnest money given at the time of an offer is *not* the consideration for the sale. It is simply an indication of the buyer's intent to perform the contract, and may be used for damages, even if the buyer backs out of the sale.

Contract In Writing

In California, the Statute of Frauds requires that certain contracts be in writing to prevent fraud in the sale of land, or an interest in land. Included in this are offers, acceptances, loan assumptions, land contracts, deeds, escrows, and options to purchase. Trust deeds, promissory notes, and leases for more than one year also must be in writing to be enforceable.

Statute of Frauds

Most contracts required by law to be in writing are found under the Statute of Frauds. The statute was first adopted in England in 1677, and became part of English common law. Later it was introduced to this country, and is now part of California's law.

The statute's primary purpose is to prevent forgery, perjury and dishonest conduct on the part of scoundrels and crooks against citizens. Thus, it improves the existence and terms of certain important types of contracts.

The law provides that certain contracts are invalid unless they are in writing and signed by either the parties involved or their agents.

Statute of Frauds

- Any agreement where the terms are not to be performed within a year from making the contract

- A special promise to answer for the debt, default or non-performance of another, except in cases covered by the Civil Code

- An agreement made upon the consideration of marriage, other than a mutual promise to marry

- An agreement to lease real property for a period longer than one year, or to sell real property or an interest therein; also, any agreement authorizing an agent to perform the above acts

- An agreement employing an agent, broker or any other person to purchase, sell or lease real estate for one year; or find a buyer, seller, lessee or lessor for more than one year in return for compensation

- An agreement, which by its terms is not to be performed during the lifetime of the promisor, or an agreement that devises or bequeaths any property, or makes provisions for any reason by will

- An agreement by a purchaser of real estate to pay a debt secured by a trust deed or mortgage on the property purchased, unless assumption of that debt by the purchaser is specifically designated in the conveyance of such property

Personal property is also affected by the Statute of Frauds. The sale of personal property with a value of more than $500 must be accompanied by a bill of sale in writing.

Parol Evidence Rule

When two parties make oral promises to each other, and then write and sign a contract promising something different, the written contract will be considered the valid one. When prior oral or written negotiations or agreements of the parties enter into a dispute about a contract, the parol evidence rule is used to settle the disagreement.

This rule prohibits introducing outside evidence to vary or add to the terms of deeds, contracts or other writings once they have been executed. Under the parol evidence rule, when a contract is intended to be the parties' complete and final agreement, no further oral promises are allowed. Occasionally a contract is ambiguous or vague. Then the courts will allow use of prior agreements to clarify an existing disputed contract.

One of a real estate agent's major duties is to make sure all contract language conveys the parties' wishes and agreements. Oral agreements have caused much confusion and bad feelings over the years, particularly in real estate. Even a lease for less than one year should be in writing, though it is not required by the Statute of Frauds. It is easy to forget verbal agreements. A written contract is the most reasonable way to ensure mutual assent.

What about using and changing preprinted real estate forms such as a deposit receipt or a counter offer form? If the parties involved want to make handwritten changes and initial them, those changes control the document.

However, escrow instructions reflect the real estate contract between the parties. If changes are made, they should be in the form of amendments to the escrow instructions after opening the escrow.

Performance of Contracts

A principal has several choices when considering the performance of a contract. One is by the assignment of the contract to an assignee. The effect of assignment is to transfer to the assignee all the interests of the assignor, with the assignee taking over the assignor's rights, remedies, benefits and duties.

For example, the original renter assigns rental interest to a new tenant, who is then responsible for the lease. The assignor is still liable in case the assignee does not perform, but the assignee is now primarily responsible for the contract.

If the assignor wants to be released entirely from any obligation for the contract, it may be done by novation. That is the substitution, by agreement, of a new obligation for an existing one, with the intent to extinguish the original contract. For example, novation occurs when a buyer assumes a seller's loan, and the lender releases the seller from the loan contract by substituting the buyer's name on the loan.

Time is often significant in a contract; indeed, its performance may be measured by the passage of time. Real estate contract and escrow instructions must have closing dates, or they are unenforceable.

Discharge of Contracts

The discharge of a contract occurs when the contract has been terminated. Most contracts are discharged by full performance on the part of the contracting parties in accordance with the agreed-upon terms. Occasionally, the end result is a breach of contract, where someone does not fulfill part of the agreement. In that case, the injured party has several remedies available. Specifically, the following methods may discharge a contract.

Discharge of Contracts

- Acceptance of a breach of the contract
- Agreement between the parties
- Impossibility of performance
- Operation of law
- Part performance
- Release of one or all of the parties
- Substantial performance

Statute of Limitations

Under California law, any person seeking relief for a breach of contract must do so within the guidelines of the Statute of Limitations. This set of laws determines that civil actions can be started only within the time periods prescribed by law. Lawsuits must be brought within the allowed time or the right to do so will expire. Here are some actions of special interest to real estate agents, with the time frames required.

167

Actions Which Must Be Brought Within 90 Days: Civil actions to recover personal property such as suitcases, clothing or jewelry alleged to have been left at a hotel or in an apartment; must begin within 90 days after the owners depart from the personal property.

Actions Which Must Be Brought Within Six Months: An action against an officer to recover property seized in an official capacity--such as by a tax collector.

Actions Which Must Be Brought Within One Year: Libel or slander, injury or death caused by wrongful act, or loss to depositor against a bank for the payment of a forged check.

Actions Which Must Be Brought Within Two Years: Action on a contract, not in writing; action based on a policy of title insurance.

Actions Which Must Be Brought Within Three Years: Action on a liability created by statute; action for trespass on or injury to real property, such as encroachment; action for relief on the grounds of fraud or mistake; attachment.

Actions Which Must Be Brought Within Four Years: An action on any written contract; includes most real estate contracts.

Actions Which Must Be Brought Within 10 Years: Action on a judgment or decree of any court in the United States.

Remedies for Breach of Contract

A breach of contract is a failure to perform on part or all of the terms and conditions of a contract. A person harmed by non-performance can accept the failure to perform, or has a choice of three remedies.

Unilateral rescission is available to a person who enters a contract without genuine assent because of fraud, mistake, duress, menace, undue influence or faulty consideration. Rescission may be used as a means of discharging a contract by agreement, as we have mentioned.

However, once escrow is opened, rescission is not available--no unilateral instruction is acceptable. Once in a while, a buyer may call right after the close of escrow and order the escrow agent to "rescind" the sale. This is not possible except through court order. Some buyers think it's like buying a car where you can change your mind within three days. This is not the case once escrow instructions have been signed, and certainly not so after the escrow closes.

If one of the parties has been wronged by a breach of contract, however, that innocent party can stop performing all obligations as well, therefore unilaterally rescinding the contract. It must be done promptly, restoring to the other party everything of value received as a result of the breached contract, on condition that the other party shall do the same.

When a party is a breach-of-contract victim, a second remedy is a lawsuit for money damages. If damages to an injured party can be reasonably expressed in a dollar amount, the innocent party could sue for money damages to include: the price paid by the buyer, the difference between the contract price and the value of the property, title and document expenses, consequential damages and interest.

A third remedy for breach of contract is a lawsuit for specific performance. This is an action in court by the injured party to force the breaching party to carry out the remainder of the contract according to the precise terms, price and conditions agreed upon. Generally, this remedy is used when money cannot restore an injured party's position. This is often the case in real estate because of the difficulty in finding a similar property.

Real Estate Contracts

Of course, all *real estate contracts* must be in writing, according to the Statute of Frauds, and must be signed by the parties.

Real Estate Contracts Include:

- Contracts for the sale of real property, or of an interest therein

- Agreements authorizing or employing an agent or broker to buy or sell real estate for compensation or commission

- Agreements for leasing realty for more than a year

Liquidated Damages

Parties to a contract may decide in advance the amount of damages to be paid, should either party breach the contract. In fact, the offer to purchase, or sales contract, contains a printed clause that says the seller may keep the deposit as liquidated damages if the buyer backs out without good reason.

Option

An option is a right, given for consideration, to a party (optionee) by a property owner (optionor), to purchase or lease property within a specified time at a specified price and terms. It is a written agreement between the owner of real property and a prospective buyer, stating the right to purchase, a fixed price and time frame. The price and all other terms should be stated clearly, as the option will become the sales agreement when the optionee exercises the right to purchase.

The optionee is the only one who has a choice, once the contract is signed and the consideration given. The option does not bind the optionee to any performance. It merely provides the right to demand performance from the optionor, who must sell if the optionee decides to buy the property during the course of the option. If the optionee decides not to buy the property during the term of the option, the consideration remains with the optionor.

The option may be assigned or sold without permission of the optionor during the course of the term, or the optionee may find another buyer for the property to exercise the option.

Normally, a real estate agent earns commission on an option only when it is exercised.

Post Test

The following self test repeats the one you took at the beginning of this chapter. Now take the exam again--since you have read all the material-- and check your knowledge of contracts.

True/False

1. An option is an example of a unilateral contract.

2. A written contract does not take precedence over oral agreements.

3. A contract is an agreement to do or not to do a certain act.

4. A promise given by one party with the expectation of performance by the other party is known as a bilateral contract.

5. A contract that has been approved is said to be rescinded.

6. Another name for mutual consent is implied agreement.

7. Parties to a contract may be unimancipated minors.

8. Mutual consent is sometimes called a meeting of the minds.

9. In an option, the buyer must perform.

10. The failure to perform a contract is called breach of contract.

chapter 6

LOCAL VARIATIONS

Focus

- Introduction
- Basic regional differences
- General principles
- Southern California escrows
- Northern California escrows

Pre-Test

The following is a self test to determine how much you know about local escrow variations before reading this chapter. Take it without studying, then read the material presented in the text. At the end of the chapter you will find a repeat of this exam. Test your knowledge by answering the questions again, then check your improvement. (The answers are found at the end of the book.) Good luck.

True/False

1. The format for escrow instructions is set by law.

2. Escrow instructions can be bilateral or unilateral.

3. With bilateral instructions, the buyer and seller sign the same set of instructions.

4. Unilateral instructions are used in Northern California.

5. Instructions are drawn at the beginning of the escrow period in Northern California.

6. In Southern California, both parties sign the same set of instructions.

7. One of the main differences between Northern and Southern California escrows is the way duties and responsibilities between the broker and escrow officer are divided.

8. The title insurance process is more closely connected to the escrow procedure in Southern California.

9. In Northern California, the escrow agent begins the escrow process.

10. Unilateral instructions are more complex than bilateral instructions.

Introduction

Every real estate transaction is unique. As a result, escrow instructions differ greatly from transaction to transaction. They all result, however, from the escrow officer's gathering together the purchase agreement and other important information and drawing up instructions in detail to describe how the transaction will be completed. The instructions are the written authorization to the escrow holder or title company to carry out the directions of the parties involved in the transaction.

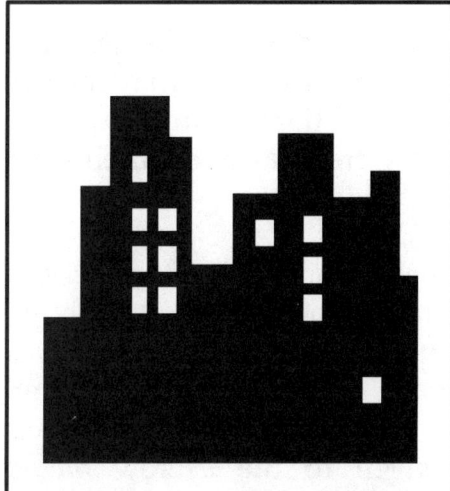

All conditions which must be met before the close of escrow are specifically mentioned in the escrow instructions. Who will pay for what costs, how money is to be disbursed and what documents are to be recorded at the close of escrow are included in the instructions. When an escrow is opened it remains open until it is terminated according to the agreement of the parties.

Escrow instructions must be in writing and signed by all parties involved as principals in the transaction. The instructions are legally binding and are revocable only by mutual consent.

Most escrow companies have standard, computer-generated forms which the escrow officer uses to serve individual transactions. The forms can be altered for different kinds of transactions such as a simple sale of real property or a more complex exchange. If there is an attorney involved, he or she may want to draw up specific escrow instructions to reflect a more complicated transaction.

The format for escrow instructions is not set by law, and as long as all parties approve, escrow officers may receive and follow specially drawn instructions from a qualified outside party just as if they were drawn on their own company forms.

The escrow officer must know all facts of the purchase in order to carry out the expectations of all the parties to the transaction. All agreements between the principals should be made *before* signing escrow instructions, and those agreements must be reflected in the instructions exactly. All information given to the escrow officer should reflect the agreement by the principals in the purchase contract.

Escrow Instructions Should Give the Escrow Holder the Following Information:

- A list of all documents, money or any other items of value to be deposited into escrow and by whom they are to be deposited
- Conditions to be met before the close of escrow, such as financing, pest control work, property inspections or repairs
- A list of all items to be prorated, such as rents, deposits, insurance, interest and property taxes
- An explanation of all fees to be paid by the principals to the escrow

---

If any changes in the original instructions are required, the escrow officer must draw up an amendment for each change. Maybe the seller wants to close later than the original date agreed upon, or maybe the buyer wants to get an adjustable loan rather than a fixed rate as previously stated in the offer to purchase. No matter how small the detail, if it differs from the original agreement, *all* parties to the escrow must agree to the change by signing an amendment.

Escrow instructions are divided into two types. They can be unilateral, where the buyer signs one set of instructions and the seller signs another, or bilateral, where the buyer and seller sign the same set of instructions.

Generally, custom dictates which type is used. In areas which use unilateral instructions, the real estate agent is responsible for getting information to the escrow company and makes sure requirements of the escrow are met where the principal is involved. The instructions are usually drawn after all the information has been given to the escrow officer, just before the escrow is to close.

When the instructions are bilateral, the escrow instructions generally are drawn up and signed when escrow is first opened.

<u>Escrow Instructions Can Be:</u>

Unilateral
Buyer signs one set of instructions and the seller signs another

Bilateral
Buyer and seller sign the same set of instructions

Basic Regional Differences

The forms used for escrow instructions vary almost as much as the number of escrow holders. Each escrow holder (escrow officer) uses the type of instructions that he or she prefers, according to custom. Also, instructions vary widely from one part of the country to another.

However, regardless of geographical area, escrow is interested in gathering the required information and carrying out the closing process in order to transfer real property and provide the accounting to the principals.

General Principles

There are some basic principles that all escrow officers follow, whether they are in Southern, Central or Northern California, or in some other state, in order to complete an escrow.

Prepare Escrow Instruction

The contractual intent and agreement of the parties is stated here. Since escrow is a limited agency, the escrow officer may only perform those duties identified as being necessary to the well being of the escrow and delegated by the parties to the transaction.

An escrow officer is only responsible for carrying out the duties specified in the escrow instructions and is not obligated to fulfill the full disclosure requirement of a general agency.

Gather Documentation

Grant deeds, trust deeds, quitclaim deeds, notes, bills of sale, security agreements, Uniform Commercial Code forms (financing statements, information requests, termination statements, assignments) must all be collected and prepared.

Order Title Report

The title report gives the escrow holder information about liens such as existing trust deeds, unpaid taxes, judgments or tax liens. Generally, the buyer has the right to approve or disapprove the preliminary title report as a contingency of the sale. The preliminary title report gives all the information included in the final title report which is usually insured in favor of the buyer, seller and/or lender.

Complete Escrow Instructions

Escrow instructions are for the purpose of communicating the intentions of the principals in a transaction to the escrow officer. The escrow officer has a stated time period to accomplish all the necessary tasks delegated by the instructions so the escrow will close in a timely manner according to the wishes of the parties. Commissions must be calculated if there is a broker involved, charges must be listed and made to the correct party and all contingencies must be completed.

In Southern California, instructions are likely to be prepared as soon as escrow is opened and amended as

179

ordered by the parties during the escrow. These are known as bilateral instructions.

Unilateral instructions are used in Northern California, with the instructions drawn at the end of the escrow period.

Prepare to Record

Upon completion of all terms of the agreement between the parties, the escrow officer will authorize the recording of documents necessary to the transfer. All documents, signed instructions and amendments have been deposited and are in the possession of the escrow holder. Good funds have been received and are in the possession of the escrow holder. All conditions of the contract have been satisfied.

Recordation

Upon recordation of grant deed, trust deed or other documents required for the transfer, the sale is complete. The seller gets the money, the broker gets the commission and the buyer gets the property, with the grant deed to follow as soon as it is mailed to him or her by the county recorder. Information about the transfer of ownership is forwarded to the fire insurance company and existing lenders or any other interested parties. A closing statement summarizing the disbursement of funds and costs of the escrow is prepared by the escrow officer and given to each of the parties.

The major differences in escrow procedures between Northern and Southern California are the way duties and responsibilities between the real estate agent and the escrow officer are divided, the form of the escrow instructions, the role of bank or title company and the apportionment of fees.

Southern California Escrows

In Southern California the escrow officer gets involved at the very beginning of the transaction, or immediately after the buyer and seller have reached an agreement and have signed the offer to purchase. A connection with the lender begins at the same time as other early stages of the escrow.

The bilateral instructions are more complex than in those drawn in Northern California and are likely to be laden with statements absolving all parties of any innocent wrongdoing or negligent failure to disclose all issues.

Because the instructions are prepared at the beginning of the escrow, they are often much amended. As we have seen, there are basic steps to be taken by the escrow officer. They are taken in somewhat different order than in the north, however. The following looks mainly at the differences between Northern and Southern California.

181

Draw Instructions

In Southern California, the instructions, along with required deeds, purchase money encumbrances and notes are prepared and delivered to the appropriate parties for signatures as soon as possible after opening escrow. Copies of the same document are sent to both buyer and seller (bilateral instructions) or may be delivered by their respective real estate agents. Once the instructions are signed by both sides a valid contract exists and the escrow officer starts preparing the title for closing and following financing instructions.

Review Title

A preliminary title report is ordered from the title company agreed upon by the buyer and seller in the offer to purchase. After reviewing the preliminary report to discover items which must be made to conform with the conditions of the transfer, the escrow officer proceeds to follow the instructions regarding loan payoffs, liens or any other matters necessary to present the title at the closing as agreed upon by the parties.

From the preliminary title report the escrow agent examines any existing liens and reviews taxes to make sure both conform with the agreement of the parties. If instructed to pay off any liens, the escrow agent requests a demand for payment and supportive documents from the holder of the lien. If a new lender has specific requirements regarding taxes, the escrow agent must satisfy those conditions.

When the escrow agent receives any demands for payoff of loans, he or she puts the demands into the open escrow file to be paid at the closing. The payoff amounts shown in the demands must match with the understanding of the parties. Any amounts that seem unreasonable or out of the ordinary, such as a large prepayment penalty, extreme late charges or a surprise principal balance owed, should be questioned by the escrow agent and approved by the party responsible for payment, usually the seller, before the closing.

Financing

At the same time the title review is going on, the escrow agent prepares documents for any assumption of an existing loan on the property or any other special financing, such as an all-inclusive trust deed, contract of sale or any trust deeds required by the escrow. Some of the necessary documents may need to be prepared by an attorney and submitted to the escrow.

If the buyer is to assume an existing loan, a formal agreement, which might change the existing loan terms, must be prepared by the escrow agent and signed by the parties as part of the closing.

In order for a loan to be assumed, the escrow officer requests a beneficiary statement from the lender describing the condition of the loan. Principal, interest rate payment amount, payment status, and any special terms of the loan are specified. If there is a "due on sale" clause in the loan, this request for a beneficiary statement will notify the existing lender of the pending sale, who will then demand the loan be paid in full upon the closing of the escrow. If the loan is assumable, the lender will submit documents and most likely a credit application for the buyer to complete.

183

The escrow agent will determine, from the information provided, if the lender's prior approval of the loan assumption is required before recording the sale. If the lender requests documentation on the sale, the escrow officer will provide what is needed as instructed in the escrow instructions.

While the escrow holder is getting information about existing liens, new financing is being processed. The lender will require cooperation and complete information from the escrow officer in order to give loan approval and fund the loan without unnecessary delays.

If the buyer is applying for a new conventional loan, chances are he or she will complete a Federal Home Loan Mortgage Corporation (Freddie Mac/Fannie Mae) loan application form. VA and FHA forms ask for similar information from the buyer.

After the buyer completes the loan application, the credit history is verified and the property appraised, the loan package is ready to be approved by the loan committee. Once the loan, along with the preliminary title report, is approved, the lender issues a loan commitment letter.

After receiving the lender's approval or qualified

approval, the escrow officer will review the loan terms to make sure they conform with the desires of the buyer as expressed in the escrow instructions. The escrow agent then must get the buyer's approval and acceptance of the terms of the loan, including any lender-required changes in the original terms of the loan.

Kenny and Judi applied for a loan of $250,000 at an interest rate not to exceed 8%, due in 30 years, with points not to exceed 2%. They might be offered only $225,000 because the property did not appraise as high as the buyer expected. At this point they must decide whether to accept the reduced loan and put a larger amount down, renegotiate with the seller or simply cancel the sale because the loan contingency was not met according to the agreement in the offer to purchase.

Review Before Closing

When all conditions of the escrow have been met, all documents have been drawn, are correct and ready for signing by the parties, the escrow officer calculates prorations and other costs as per the closing date.

The required documents such as the grant deed, any trust deeds or other matters to be recorded are sent to the title company for review and recording upon further instructions.

The escrow officer than calls the buyer and asks him or her to come to the escrow office and bring the down payment and other funds necessary to close the escrow.

The buyer signs the loan documents and any disclosures not already signed, and the items are returned to the

185

lender.   The signed trust deed is sent with the other documents to the title company to be recorded.

Funds Requested by Escrow Officer

If all goes smoothly during the review and signing of documents, the escrow agent requests the loan funds from the lender. When the money is received by the escrow holder or the title company the transaction is ready to record.

The differences between Southern and Northern California escrow practices are few from here on. Procedures for auditing, recording, disbursement of funds and closing are conducted by escrow officers in a similar fashion.   Any differences have to do with the fact that procedures in the north combine with the title insurance process to a greater degree, and the escrow officer might perform certain title company functions that would not be required in the south.

Both Northern and Southern California escrow holders conduct competent escrows; neither method is superior to the other.   Bilateral instructions used in Southern California reduce the possibility of disputes between the parties about the terms of the escrow. In the north, since escrow instructions are not drawn until the end of the escrow period, the need for unending amendments is reduced.

Duties of a Southern California Escrow Officer

Broker opens escrow

Prepare escrow instructions and required documents
Obtain signatures of all parties

Order title search
Receive and review preliminary report
Request demands
Request explanation of liens
Review taxes as reported
Receive demands and enter into file

Process financing
Request beneficiary statement
Review terms of transfer and current payment status
Request copy of new loan application
Obtain loan approval
Request loan documents

Review escrow file for:
Completion of all requirements of escrow
Documents correct and ready for signature
Good funds received

Figure prorations and all other costs as of the closing

Request signatures on all remaining documents

Forward documents to title company

Obtain funds from buyer

Return loan documents

Request loan funds sent to title company

Funds received by title company

Order recording

Close file, prepare statements, disburse funds

Close file

187

Northern California Escrows

Three major differences stand out when escrow procedures used in Northern and Southern California are examined.

1. The title insurance process is connected to the escrow procedure much more closely in the north.

2. In the north the escrow agent relies on the real estate broker far more than his or her counterpart in the south.

3. Escrow instructions are prepared by the escrow agent at the end of the escrow period in the north.

4. Unilateral instructions are prepared.

Opening the Order

In Northern California, it is the real estate broker who starts the escrow process. After a buyer and seller have reached an agreement, the title company chosen by the principals is contacted by the real estate broker who orders a preliminary title report.

This is done through the escrow department of the title company.

Before the escrow officer can ask the title department to conduct a title search on the subject property, certain information must be on hand.

Information Required for Title Search:

- Legal description--usually assessor's block and parcel number

- Buyers and sellers complete an identity statement so the title company can obtain complete information about who currently owns the property in question and how title is currently held

- The type of title insurance desired-a standard policy or extended policy

- Name and address of new lender if any

- Any particular information required about copies of C,C&R,s, any special endorsements or inspections requested in the original offer to purchase between the buyer and seller

---

Preliminary Title Report

After receiving a copy of the preliminary title report, the real estate broker carefully reviews it to make sure the title is in the condition it is believed to be in by the buyer and seller as shown in the offer to purchase.

Title/Interests Held

The broker looks at how title is held (joint tenants, community property, tenants in common, and so on), or whether any life estates, leaseholds, easements or other interests affecting title exist.

Current Ownership

Vesting must match the name of the seller on the original offer to purchase. If not, the real estate broker must determine if there has been a misrepresentation by the seller or if some other mistake has occurred. In any case, at this early point vesting must be researched and any discrepancy discovered and corrected.

Parcel Description

The legal description must match the description of the subject property as described in the original offer to purchase document. Measurements of the parcel as shown in the preliminary report are compared with those on the listing to make sure they are accurate.

Exceptions or Encumbrances

The preliminary report will show any money liens, judgments, easements, taxes owed, or any restrictions affecting title or use of the property in question. The lender will then give loan approval based on his or her evaluation of the report. Some items may be named as exceptions to getting the loan, or as items that must be paid prior to the closing.

If an existing loan is to be paid off, a demand for payoff must be sent to the holder of the loan. If the present loan is to be assumed, a beneficiary statement is required from the current lien holder. The real estate broker relays information to the escrow agent regarding financing as agreed upon in the offer to purchase.

Statement of Information

All parties in a transaction are asked by the title company to complete a statement relating to information that might affect their capacity to close the escrow. There are certain matters that might be found in the general index of the recorder's office that must be researched by the escrow officer such as judgments, tax liens, insanities, paroles, attorneys in fact, guardianship proceedings, bankruptcies, probates or other legal matters

relating to the financial responsibility of the principals. Since guarding against forgery is one of the assurances given by the title policy, a signature is required from each of the principals.

Demand

A demand states the balance owed on an existing loan. It is sent to the escrow holder by the lender after a written request is made, asking for a letter disclosing the total amount owed and any supportive documents necessary for the payoff.

After receiving the demand from the lender of record, the escrow officer must verify the payoff information with the

seller to determine its accuracy according to the seller's records. Occasionally, a prepayment penalty of six months' interest on the unpaid balance will be part of the payoff, and the seller must be made aware of the amount and be in agreement.

If there is an alienation (due-on-sale) clause in the existing note, the lender will be notified of the pending sale by the demand for payoff.

Beneficiary Statement

When the buyer wants to assume or take "subject to" an existing loan, a written request for the current status of the loan is made to the lender (beneficiary). Information about the balance of the loan, the terms of payment, any insurance data and requirements of the lender for loan assumption are included in the request.

Some notes simply state that the note is assumable but the lender has the right to approve the buyer, who must submit a loan assumption application. The lender usually has the right to adjust the terms of the loan to the new borrower after giving approval of the assumption.

Neutral Depository

The escrow holder is a neutral party for the forwarding of any bills accumulated as a result of work done to complete the terms of the escrow. Pest controllers, roofers, property inspectors, or any other professionals who have completed work on the property may submit bills to the escrow holder, who will pay them at the closing from the proceeds of the sale, as directed by the principals.

Opening of Escrow

The actual opening of escrow is the main difference between Southern and Northern California escrows. After receiving loan approval and the terms of the loan being approved by the buyer, the documentation is sent to the escrow officer who holds them for the buyer's signature just prior to the closing. Then escrow instructions are drawn and the closing process starts.

Escrow Instructions

Unilateral instructions are prepared for the buyer and seller to sign. Any other documents required by the escrow are prepared at this time also. The seller's instructions show money received and a deed being given. In the buyer's instructions, money is given in return for the deed. Prorations and other fees are charged to the appropriate party and specific terms of the transaction are carried out to close the escrow.

Just prior to recording, the escrow officer conducts a final review of the escrow file to make sure all documents have been properly signed and notarized, and good funds received.

If the file is complete, documents are sent to the title officer who holds them until instructed to record. At the same time, loan funds are requested if there is a new loan involved.

Collecting Funds

The final act of the escrow officer is to collect funds from the buyer and the lender, if a new loan is involved. The buyer is contacted and asked to bring in the remainder of the down payment and the amount needed to close the escrow. After all money is deposited with the escrow officer, including closing costs, the escrow file is reconciled one more time to make sure all conditions have been met.

Closing

After the final audit, documents are ordered to be recorded and final settlement begins. Buyer and seller receive closing statements describing their costs. The buyer gets a deed and the seller gets a check.

Duties of a Northern California Escrow Officer

Broker opens escrow

Request preliminary title report from title department

| Receive and review preliminary report | Order statements of buyer/seller identity |

Order demands
Review, inform client

Order beneficiary statement
Review terms, inform client

Collect bills from pest control company, property inspection, home warranty, contractors, and any other special demands to be paid at closing

Receive loan documents from lender
Prepare buyer/seller instructions and all other required documents
Execute and return buyer/seller instructions and documents

Review escrow file for:
Completion of all requirments of escrow
Documents correctly executed and notarized
Good funds received

Request loan funds from lender

Forward documents to recording desk in title department to be held until recording is ordered

Complete title policy write-up

Receive loan funds

Order recording
Audit escrow

Prepare closing
statements
Disburse funds

Close file

195

Post Test

The following self test repeats the one you took at the beginning of this chapter. Now take the exam again--since you have read all the material-- and check your knowledge of escrow closing procedures.

True/False

1. The format for escrow instructions is set by law.

2. Escrow instructions can be bilateral or unilateral.

3. With bilateral instructions, the buyer and seller sign the same set of instructions.

4. Unilateral instructions are used in Northern California.

5. Instructions are drawn at the beginning of the escrow period in Northern California.

6. In Southern California, both parties sign the same set of instructions.

7. One of the main differences between Northern and Southern California escrows is the way duties and responsibilities between the broker and escrow officer are divided.

8. The title insurance process is more closely connected to the escrow procedure in Southern California.

9. In Northern California, the escrow agent begins the escrow process.

10. Unilateral instructions are more complex than bilateral instructions.

chapter 7

ESCROW INSTRUCTIONS

Focus

- Introduction
- Collecting information
- Preparing for the instructions
- Escrow instructions
- Local variations

Pre-Test

The following is a self test to determine how much you know about escrow instructions before reading this chapter. Take it without studying, then read the material presented in the text. At the end of the chapter you will find a repeat of this exam. Test your knowledge by answering the questions again, then check your improvement. (The answers are found at the end of the book.) Good luck.

True/False

1. A "take sheet" is the framework for the escrow instructions.

2. Collecting the information needed to provide complete escrow instructions is the first step for an escrow agent.

3. The three documents that serve as the heart of a sale escrow are the grant deed, promissory note and bill of sale.

4. A promissory note is the security for a debt.

5. General instructions authorize the escrow holder to carry out general procedures needed to complete the escrow.

6. General instructions are special instructions given by a buyer or seller to the escrow holder.

7. Third party instructions may include a demand or claim from a person not involved in the escrow as a principal.

8. The escrow holder's obligation to the parties starts as soon as escrow instructions are written.

9. Prorations are made on the basis of a 25-day month.

10. If rents are to be prorated, escrow holder should prorate and charge seller and credit buyer with any deposits paid in advance to the seller by tenants.

Introduction

A buyer and seller have come to an agreement and want to complete the sale of real property. To make sure all the items they have agreed upon are carried out or executed, they need a neutral third party to conduct an escrow to carry out their wishes. An escrow agent will probably conduct the escrow.

Escrow instructions are written, as we have seen, from the agreement between the principals. The escrow agent does not direct the transaction; the principals do. The escrow agent reacts to instructions which represent the mutual agreement of the parties.

SALES CONTRACT

The instructions are carefully drawn after the escrow agent gathers all the necessary information from the original agreement and the parties connected with the transaction. It is the escrow instructions that reflect, exactly, the intention of the parties to complete the transaction and describe in detail how that will be accomplished. Once the instructions are prepared, the buyer, seller and real estate agent all get copies either to sign and return to the closing agent, or to be filed and kept as required by law. We shall see here how escrow instructions are assembled.

Collecting Information

Most of the time it is the real estate agent who brings the deposit check from the buyer and is the initial contact for the escrow holder. The process of information gathering takes place before the escrow agent prepares the instructions for the parties to sign.

Deposit receipt

At the first contact with the real estate agent who is opening the escrow, the escrow holder makes a copy of the deposit receipt to keep in the transaction file. It may be used for reference if confusion or conflict arises as the escrow progresses.

Take Sheet

The escrow agent will use a "take sheet" as the framework for the instructions, making sure the escrow contract accurately reflects the understanding and intent of the parties as stated in the original deposit receipt.

This information sheet is used to list the important data without itemizing the terms of the transaction. Each of the conditions of this transaction must be evaluated correctly so the escrow or title agent can reduce them to instructions that satisfy all parties.

Take Sheet

Escrow #_____

Date opened_____

Deposit receipt on file ( )_____
Seller/Lender_____ Buyer/Borrower_____
Mailing address_____ Mailing address_____
Home address_____ Home address_____
Telephone (home)_____ Telephone(home)_____
    (work)_____   (work)_____
Address after close of escrow_____ Address after close of escrow_____
_____ _____

Property address_____ Legal description_____
_____ _____
_____ _____

Buyer will deposit_____ Proration as of close of escrow or:_____
Deposit by buyer_____   Property taxes ( )
Cash to be added_____   Homeowners dues ( )
1st Trust Deed_____   Rents ( )
2nd Trust Deed_____   Interest-1st trust deed ( )
Total consideration_____   Impound account ( )

_____ARM/fixed_____Yearss Points_____
Commission_____%_____Split Close of escrow_____
Seller's agent_____ Buyer's agent_____
Real estate company_____ Real estate company_____
Address_____ Address_____
_____ _____
Telephone_____Fax_____ Telephone_____Fax_____

Title Compnay_____ Credit_____
Address_____ Payoff_____
Telephone_____ Address_____
Title order #_____ Loan #_____
  Payoff_____
  Address_____
  Loan #_____

Subject to buyer/property qualifying for:
( ) All cash
( ) Preliminary title_____days
( ) Homeowner's Protection Plan/seller
( ) Homeowner's Protection plan/buyer
( ) Homeowner's Protection-broker to pay from
   commission
( ) Supplemental taxes
( ) Bonds paid current
( ) HOA transfer paid-buyer/seller
( )Memo items
( )Property inspestion_____days
( ) Condo unit#__Space__Dues____Days_____

( )Escrow instructions signed____days
( )Verbal approval____days
( )Written loan approval____days
( )Walk through____days, not a contingency
( )Possession COE
( )Possession____days after COE
( )Buyer acting as principal
( )Seller acting as principal
( )Geological____days
( )Purchase price includes_____
_____
( ) Buyer to occupy

Gathering the Data

☑ Legal name, current address and telephone number of principals, brokers and lenders must be listed and kept on hand for use during the term of the escrow.

☑ Financial information about the transaction must be collected, such as the sales price, trust deeds to remain and those to be paid off, any new loans to be obtained, or the price of any personal property included.

☑ An accurate legal description is needed to assure that the buyer is getting the right parcel. A street address is also included if there is one.

☑ The type of property (single family residence, income property, etc.) must be noted in case there are local requirements to be met when there is a sale, such as retrofit or zoning limitations.

☑ The seller must provide existing loan information and the buyer or buyer's agent must provide the name of any new lender.

☑ The closing agent must have the proper names of the parties to the transaction (buyer/seller, borrower/lender, vendor/vendee, lessor/lessee).

☑ Exact terms of the escrow must be indicated, including any time limitations and date of closing.

☑ Prorations include such items as interest on existing loans, taxes, assessments, bonds, insurance, homeowner's association dues, maintenance fees and rental deposits. The expectations of the parties regarding prorations must be defined clearly, especially if the principals have agreed mutually on non-traditional proration time frames, such as using an actual "day month" instead of the 30-day month, or have decided not to prorate some normal items.

☑ Identification of the title company indicated by buyer and seller must be noted.

☑ Conditions of fire, liability and lender's insurance must be defined.

☑ Requirements are noted for pest control inspection, time frame for work to be done and an account of who will pay for the inspection and/or any work required.

☑ Distribution of charges is made based on the agreement of the parties to the transaction, as long as the charges are not in conflict with laws or rules regulating legal matters.

☑ Information must be collected, almost always from the listing broker, regarding how commissions are to be paid and how they are to be split between brokers.

☑ Any particular agreements made by the principals must be noted, such as leaseback instructions, an all inclusive trust deed (AITD) agreement to be drawn or instruction for attorney involvement (to be sent copies of all documents, etc.).

Preparing for the Instructions

Collecting the information needed to provide accurate and complete instructions is the first step for an escrow agent, as we have learned. Of major importance is the need to be specific, methodical, well organized and complete in using the information gathered to produce instructions that reflect the agreement of the parties correctly.

In producing complete, error-free instructions, the escrow agent must be sure of the mechanics of the transaction, including the time frame in which the escrow is to be carried out according to the agreement of the principals, the number and types of documents needed, an inclusive description of consideration and other agreements relating to cash, and allocation of charges to the proper parties.

A time line is essential for the smooth progress of the escrow. The escrow holder must be aware of what and when certain actions must be taken on the part of the escrow holder to assure a timely closing. Depending on the locale certain steps are taken at different times during the life of the escrow, as we have seen in Chapter 6.

In any case, the closing agent must proceed steadily and systematically towards the end result, which is the transfer of real or personal property and the hypothecation and/or pledging of real or personal property.

> ### Escrows are Concerned With:
>
> - Title: who owns the property now and to whom and how is it being transferred?
>
> - Consideration: how much is being paid, borrowed, traded or given and how is it to be allocated?

Framework of Transaction

The escrow agent must have a clear understanding of the who are the parties and what do they want to achieve?

An experienced escrow agent will create a summary of the proposed transaction before preparing or ordering any documents.

> ### Transaction Summary
>
> - Amount of deposit
> - Balance of down payment owned
> - Listing of all loan amounts
> - Type of transaction
> - Length of escrow
> - Legal description
>
> - Property address
> - Seller's name
> - Buyer's name
> - Buyer's address
> - Terms of financing
> - Any payoffs
> - Items to be prorated

Transaction Summary

Onofre and Ruby Archuleta are buying a house from Quentin and
Kate Oliver for $400,000. The Archuletas are putting $160,000
down and getting a new first loan in the amount of $240,000.

$ 4,000	Good faith deposit
156,000	Balance of down payment
240,000	New first loan
$400,000	Total consideration

Type of transaction	Sale
Length of escrow	45 days
Legal description	Lot 6, Blk 6, tract 785 City of San Clemente County of Orange Map book page 36, page 12
Property address	305 Avenida Cristobal San Clemente, CA 92672
Seller	Kate/Quentin Oliver 305 Avenida Cristobal San Clemente, CA 92672
Buyer	Ruby/Onofre Archuleta 2234 Monogram Avenue Long Beach, CA 92684
Financing	$240,000 @ 8.5%-new first loan Lender-Home Savings
Payoff	Bank of America $244,000 @ 7.5%-current balance payable monthly @ $1,800 loan #050650
Prorations	$5,000 annually-taxes $1,200 annually-hazard insurance

Documents

An escrow holder generally is able to prepare, or order from the proper source, all documents relating to an escrow. As long as the documents don't include the shaping of a contract requiring legal judgments or other acts that would indicate the escrow holder is practicing law, the services of an attorney usually are not necessary in normal transactions.

There are three documents that serve as the heart of a sale or loan escrow: the grant deed, promissory note and deed of trust. Other documents, such as a quit claim deed, security agreement, financing statement, bill of sale and additional disclosure forms, also may be required by the escrow.

Grant Deed

Deeds may be used to convey any type of interest, burden or encumbrance, as well as fee simple transfers in property.

<u>Deeds Conveying Special Interests</u>

- Rights reserved by the grantor
- General plan restrictions (covenants, conditions and restrictions)
- Rights incidental or appurtenant to the parcel being transferred
- Riparian rights
- Mineral rights
- Stock rights in a mutually owned water company
- Leasehold rights of the grantor created by prior arrangement

When property is transferred by private grant, or by one private party to another, the instrument generally used is a grant deed. The parties involved are the grantor, or the person conveying the property, and the grantee, the person or group receiving the property. At the closing the buyer gets the grant deed, which has been signed by the seller, as evidence of the transfer of ownership. Each time the property transfers from one party to another, a new grant deed must be prepared by the escrow officer.

Requirements for a Valid Grant Deed

- In writing: according to the Statute of Frauds

- Parties identified: the parties to the transfer (grantor and grantee) sufficiently described

- Competent to convey: the grantor must be competent to convey the property (not a minor or incompetent)

- Capable of holding title: the grantee must be capable of holding title (must be a real living person, not fictitious)

- Adequately described: the property being conveyed must be adequately described

- Words of granting: words to indicate the act of granting (grant, convey) must be included

- Signed: the deed must be signed by the grantor

- Delivered: the deed must be delivered to and accepted by the grantee

A grant deed carries with it two specific warrantees: that the grantor has not previously conveyed the same property or an interest in it to someone else, and that the estate is free from encumbrances that have not been disclosed by the grantor.

Also, if a grantor subsequently acquires any title or interest in the property which he or she has granted as a fee simple estate, that after-acquired title passes to the grantee.

A grant deed does not have to be recorded to be valid. In order for the parties' rights to be protected, however, the deed must be recorded. The deed must be acknowledged before it can be recorded.

Each county, upon the transfer of property, may charge a documentary transfer tax. The amount of the transfer tax is stamped in the upper right-hand corner of a recorded deed and sent to the buyer after the closing. The amount of the tax is based on $1.10 per $1,000 or $.55 per $500 of transferred value. The deed is sent to the buyer after the closing by the County Recorder.

How to Calculate Documentary Transfer Tax

- When a sale is all cash, or a new loan is obtained by the buyer, the tax is calculated on the entire sales price.

- When an existing loan is assumed by a buyer, the tax is calculated on the difference between the assumed loan and the sales price.

Promissory Note

A promissory note is a written promise to pay back a certain sum of money with specified terms at an agreed upon time. It is a personal obligation of the borrower and a complete contract in itself, between the borrower and lender.

According to the Uniform Commercial Code, to be valid or enforceable, a promissory note must meet certain requirements.

A Promissory Note is:

- An unconditional written promise to pay a certain sum

- Made by one person to another

- Signed by the maker or borrower

- Payable at a definite time

- Paid to bearer or to order

- Voluntarily delivered by the borrower

Normally, in a transaction where the buyer is financing the sale (borrowing money) through an institutional lender, loan documents which include a promissory note are signed by the buyer/borrower in the presence of the closing agent just before the closing. If the sale is being financed by the seller, loan documents would not be available or necessary and a promissory note is prepared by the closing agent, according to the instructions of the principals.

Types of Promissory Notes

It is useful for a closing agent to be knowledgeable about the types of promissory notes.

Straight Note: Calls for payment of interest only, or no payments, during the term of the note, with all accrued money (either principal only, or principal and interest if no payments have been made) due and payable on a certain date.

Partially Amortized Installment Note: Calls for periodic payments; such payments may or may not include interest; usually demands a balloon payment of unpaid principle and interest at the end of the term to completely pay off debt.

Fully Amortized Installment Note: Calls for periodic payments of fixed amounts, to include both interest and principal, which will pay off the debt completely by the end of the term.

Adjustable Note: The interest rate in the note varies upward or downward over the term of the loan, depending on the money market conditions and an agreed upon index. The escrow holder may not draw this type of note, but must refer the drawing to an attorney.

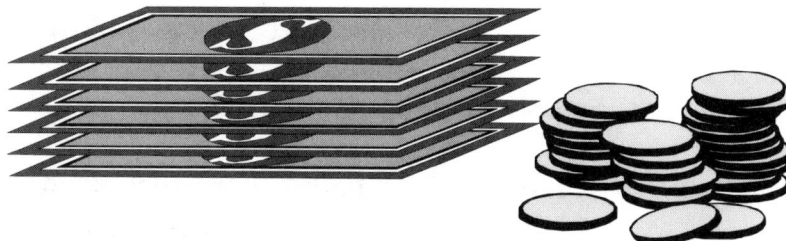

Preparing the Note

There are certain items regarding the note which a closing agent must be aware of and must include in preparing the escrow instructions:

<u>Lender</u>

? Name of lender?

? Institution or individual?

? Is it a loan regulated by the Business and Professions Code involving real estate licensees?

? Is it a loan regulated by the state usury law or is it a purchase money loan to a seller or other private-party loan?

<u>Terms</u>

? Amount borrowed?

? How many notes are required for the principal amount?

? What is the interest rate?

? Is the interest rate fixed or variable? If variable, what is the index, time period for rate changes, how is interest to be treated (deferred or added to principal payment)? Any unusual interest terms?

? How are payments to be made? Are they fixed or variable or a combination of both (graduated payment loans)? If payment does not cover monthly interest, how is deferred interest to be accrued and how are future payments to be applied.

? Is there a balloon payment? Note should be made if the loan is arranged under the Business and Professions Code sections applying to licensee-arranged loans. The regulations specify that no balloon payment is allowed until the 73rd month on a single-family, owner-occupied residence. Holders of notes containing a balloon payment must remind borrowers no sooner than 150 days nor later than 90 days from maturity of when the loan is due.

? Where will payment be made or sent? If the location is outside California, usury laws of that state may apply.

? Will there be late charges?

? Is there a pre-payment penalty?

? If there is a due-on-sale clause it must be contained in both the note and trust deed. The make-up of the acceleration clause usually will be supplied by the lender.

? What type of note is it? Payment should reflect whether the note is a straight note (interest only), installment note (principal amortized) or some other type of note.

? What is the collateral for the note? If more than one property is being used to secure the loan (blanket mortgage), it should be noted that two trust deeds are being utilized for the note.

Special Requirements of the Note:

? Are there restrictions on principal reductions?

? Is there a pre-payment penalty?

? If the transaction deals with a subdivision, is there a partial release clause? Is the subdivision regulated by the Subdivision Map Act and have the proper steps been taken to comply with laws regarding creation of a trust deed dividing an existing lot?

? Will the note specify whether there can be loan advances, extension of the loan, future subordination, renegotiation of rate at any time?

Deed of Trust

As we have mentioned, a trust deed is used to secure a loan on real property. It describes the property being used as security, or collateral, for a debt, and usually includes a power of sale and assignment of rents clause.

Trust Deeds Usually Include:

• Power of Sale Clause:
Gives trustee the right to foreclose, sell and convey ownership to a purchaser of the property if the borrower defaults on the loan

• Assignment of Rents Clause:
Upon default by the borrower, the lender can take possession of the property and collect any rents being paid

---

The process of borrowing money, secured by a trust deed, where the buyer remains in possession of the property during the payoff of the loan or note, is called hypothecation.

A certain uniformity is required by FNMA/FHLMC in trust deeds securing loans bought by those agencies. The following is a list of inclusions necessary to describe the rights and obligations of parties to a trust deed.

Rights and Obligations of Parties to a Trust Deed

1. Payment of principal and interest
2. Payment of taxes and insurance
3. Statement of how payments are to be made relating to the note
4. Charges to be made to borrower (if required to pay taxes and insurance without an impound account by lender) and liens to be placed for non-payment

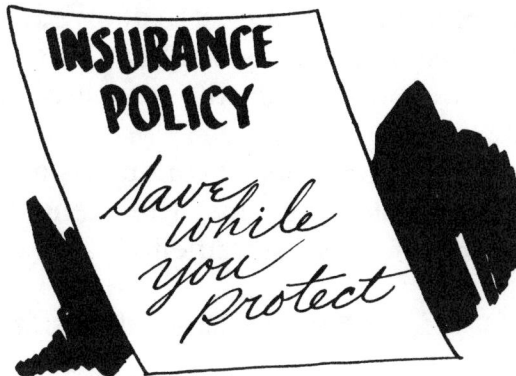

5. Requirements for hazard insurance coverage and application of insurance proceeds
6. Obligations to comply with the provisions of a lease (optional)
7. Statement of lender's right to take action if borrower defaults
8. Property inspection by lender before action is taken upon the default of borrower
9. Settlement agreement in case of eminent domain proceedings

10. Lender's right to give forbearance in certain cases, but no obligation in all cases
11. Description of liability for parties--both joint, several and co-signers, as well as all successors-- of interest.
12. Charges given for the loan
13. Provision for an acceleration clause if all terms are not met
14. Address of borrower and lender listed
15. Copy of document to borrower
16. Requirements of lender with transfer of ownership (due-on-sale, assumption)
17. Methods of curing default
18. Description of lender's right to foreclose upon default of borrower, and of default
19. Rents from property occupants, collected by lender or an appointed receiver, in case of default
20. Conditions for reconveyance after loan paid in full
21. Substitution of trustee allowed
22. Requirement for notification of default to be mailed to borrower at the property address (request for notice)
23. List of any special conditions of the loan
24. Possible fee by the lender for preparing a beneficiary's statement

Trust Deed as a Lien

A trust deed becomes a lien on the real property being conveyed when the buyer borrows money to buy the property. The escrow agent prepares the trust deed and it is then added to the loan document package supplied by the lender for the buyer's signature. The trust deed does not have to be recorded to be valid, but ordering recordation of the signed trust deed is normally part of the closing agent's responsibility.

Quitclaim Deed

Another type of deed that may be prepared by the closing agent is a quitclaim deed. In the past, this type of deed was commonly used to transfer real property interests between husband and wife. However, an inter-spousal grant deed is now used between spouses instead of a quitclaim deed.

A quitclaim deed is a deed of conveyance that operates as a release of whatever interest the grantor has in the property. The quitclaim deed contains similar language to a deed, with the important exception that rather than using the words *grant and release*, it contains language such as *remise, release and quitclaim*. Grantors therefore do not warrant title or possession. Grantors only pass on whatever interest they may have, if any. In effect, a grantor forever quits whatever claim he or she had, if in fact any existed.

Executing a quitclaim deed does not carry even an implied warranty as regards ownership, liens, encumbrances or the possibility that the grantor has not previously signed a deed to someone else. It does convey ownership of the property to another person.

A quitclaim deed is not commonly used to convey a fee, but is usually restricted to releasing or conveying minor interests in real estate for the purpose of clearing title defects or clouds on title. It may also be used to convey lesser interests such as life estates and to release such interests as a remainder or reversion.

Quitclaim deeds also are often used between close relatives, such as when one heir is buying out the other, or where a seller's finances are so troubled that it is inconsequential to the buyer whether he or she is getting any warranties or not.

Although a quitclaim deed may or may not vest any title in the grantee, it is not inferior to the other types of deeds in what it actually conveys. For example, if a grantor executes and delivers a grant deed to one person and subsequently executes and delivers a quitclaim deed to the same property to another person, the grantee under the quitclaim deed will prevail over the grantee under the grant deed, assuming the holder of the quitclaim is first to record the deed.

A title searcher will regard a quitclaim deed in the chain of title as a red flag, and most title companies will not guarantee titles derived out of a quitclaim, at least not without further clarification.

Bill of Sale

A bill of sale is a written agreement by which one person sells, assigns, or transfers to another his or her interest in personal property. A bill of sale sometimes is used by a seller of real estate to show the transfer of personal property, such as when the owner of a store sells the building and includes the store equipment and trade fixtures. The transfer of the personal property can be effected by mentioning in the deed, or more commonly, by a separate bill-of-sale document, which is prepared by the closing agent for signature by the seller.

Security Agreement

A security agreement is a document that creates a lien on personal property, including possessions intended to be attached to land as fixtures after the sale closes. Rather than recording the security agreement to give notice of the lien, however, the law provides for filing a financing statement to perfect the security interest. A closing agent usually will be required to prepare a security agreement in the sale of a business opportunity.

Financing Statement

A financing statement is a written notice (of credit given and ensuing terms in a security agreement) to be filed in the public records. A closing agent will prepare a financing statement and order it to be recorded at the request of a seller who has given credit for the purchase of personal property. The purpose of recording the statement is to establish the creditor's interest in the personal property (separate from the real property being conveyed in the transaction) which is the security for the debt. The financing statement is the document that is recorded to show evidence of a security agreement.

Truth in Lending Documents

The main purpose of the Truth-in-Lending Law or Regulation Z, as it is commonly known, is to assure that borrowers in need of consumer credit are given accurate and meaningful information about the cost of the credit being extended. Most escrow agents are involved in these lender disclosures and will present them to the borrower as required by law.

Real Estate Settlement Procedures Act Disclosures

The Real Estate Settlement Procedures Act (RESPA) is a federal loan disclosure law applicable to first mortgage loans on residential property. It requires certain disclosures to borrowers and provides the consumer with information on loan settlement costs. A special information booklet and good faith estimate of costs must be given to a borrower when he or she applies for a loan. One day before the scheduled closing the borrower has the right under RESPA to inspect the *Uniform Settlement Statement* which gives an itemized account of all fees charged by the lender. Information containing these disclosures usually is provided by the closing agent.

Consideration/Cash Agreements

At the beginning of the printed escrow instructions there is a listing of the consideration included in the transaction. This listing describes the source and use of all funds in the transaction.

Any money required by the transaction is noted, with its source, whether it is a cash deposit or new financing. This amount, plus or minus any fees, adjustments or prorations, represents the true cash that passes through the escrow.

Any other consideration that is not to be given as cash is accounted for in the instructions. Items of value such as personal or other real property to be added to the transaction are listed, as well as the equities to be transferred if the transaction is a tax deferred exchange.

Other Information

Certain basic information must be available to answer questions that may be asked about the escrow instructions, title and transfer documents, new financing being obtained to complete the transfer or any liens being paid off through the transaction. After all necessary information has been gathered and noted in the take sheet, the closing agent is ready to utilize the data in preparing instructions.

Escrow Instructions

Instructions are drawn when the escrow agent has gathered all information specific to the escrow and is ready to proceed with the task of completing the transaction according to the direction given by the principals.

Basic Information

The consideration in dollar amounts, including amount of good faith deposit, additional cash to be added for down payment, any deeds of trust to be recorded, and sales price, term of escrow, title insurance policy liability, legal description of property, street address of property, and vestingare listed at the beginning of the instructions.

Conditions

This section states that the closing and costs allocated to the parties are subject to payment of taxes, liens or other restrictions on financing.

Special Provisions

Preliminary title report approval, home warranty agreement, executed preliminary change of ownership requirement, disclosure of supplemental tax on property, condominium data if applicable, pest control agreement, authorization and instruction for collection and disbursement of funds, and a cancellation agreement are listed in this section.

Costs

Special and general allocation of costs to buyer and seller are mentioned specifically.

Possession

The time and date of property possession by the buyer is listed, even though it may not be essential to the transaction.

Prorations

Items to be prorated as of close of escrow are specified.

General Provisions

By signing the instructions, the buyer and seller agree to the general provisions of the instructions which disclose various elements of the transaction general to most escrows.

Signatures

Instructions are signed by all parties.

Local Differences

As we have seen in Chapter 6, there are differences in the closing practices. There are two main differences between the locales. The first is the timing of the signing of closing documents. The second is the type of instructions prepared for the principals to sign. In the north, the instructions are unilateral, where the buyer and seller sign different sets of instructions. Bilateral instructions where buyer and seller sign an identical set of instructions are used in the southern part of the state.

Third Party Instructions

When third parties are involved in the transaction, such as lenders or other lien holders, special instructions are required giving the escrow holder authority to deal with parties other than the principals. These might include documents, demands or the deposit of funds into escrow.

Parties other than the principals, typically, may execute a third-party instruction to claim or discard a financial interest in the transaction. All parties must accept the additional instruction and sign any amendments affecting a third party.

<u>Third Party Instructions</u>

- For fire insurance authorization
- For commission payment authorization
- For an interspousal transfer grant deed between spouses
- To lender regarding payoff or assumption of an existing loan
- For release of mechanic's and other liens
- For release of a judgment

Local Variations

As we have seen, processing is done differently in the northern and southern parts of the state. In Northern California, an estimated closing statement is issued as part of the instructions, showing, for example, the proceeds going to the seller and the estimated cash needed to close for the buyer. In Southern California, the broker's net sheet serves the same purpose, except the closing statement is provided at the settlement.

General Instructions

The general instructions are usually the pre-printed part of any set of instructions. As important as the contract items of agreement between the buyer and seller, this part of the escrow contract describes the procedures that will be used to accomplish the task required of the escrow officer.

Because different escrow holders have varying ideas regarding the number and extent of protective and disclosure clauses in their general instructions, there are any number of provisions that may be included here. The general instructions also deal with practically every aspect of the escrow, explaining each item of the escrow process.

These instructions authorize the escrow holder to carry out the general procedures needed to complete the escrow.

Deposit of Funds

Escrow holder is authorized and directed to deposit any and all funds placed in this escrow with any state or national bank or savings bank in a trust account in the name of the escrow holder without any liability for interest to be withdrawn by escrow holder and disbursed in accordance with the instructions of the parties.

Disbursements

All disbursements of funds and/or delivery of other documents or instruments concerning this escrow will be mailed to parties entitled thereto by regular first-class mail, postage prepaid to their respective addresses shown on the escrow file.

Instructions Signed

Escrow holder's duty does not commence until mutual escrow instructions signed by all parties are received by escrow holder. Until such time either party may unilaterally revoke these instructions and upon written request delivered to escrow holder, the party may withdraw any funds, instruments, documents or items previously handed to escrow holder by such party.

Prorations

All prorations and adjustments are to be made on the basis of a thirty (30) day month unless otherwise instructed in writing by all parties. For proration purposes, the buyer will have ownership of the real property which is the subject of this escrow for the entire day, regardless of the hour of recording. The "close of escrow" with reference to said prorations and adjustments of all purposes for this escrow shall be the day instruments of conveyance called for are recorded or filed with the county recorder.

Escrow holder is instructed to prorate taxes for the current fiscal year based on the most recent information furnished to you by title insurer herein. Prorations are made on the basis of a 360 day year. In view of the change of ownership of the subject property which will take place on the close of this escrow, it is to be expected that the taxing authorities will re-assess the property and issue a supplemental tax bill. Seller and buyer acknowledge their awareness of the foregoing and hereby release and relieve escrow holder of all liability in connection with same, and escrow holder shall not be further concerned with the above re-assessment in any manner.

Escrow holder is authorized to obtain a Statement of Fees from Homeowners' Association affecting subject property and to charge account of the seller to bring account current, if necessary, and to use said statement to determine amounts required for proration purposes. Seller has furnished or will furnish, prior to close of escrow, to buyer outside of this escrow a copy of CC&R's, By-Laws, Budget and Articles of Incorporation for said Association.

Escrow holder has no duty or responsibility regarding those documents. Escrow holder is instructed to charge to the account of the buyer any transfer fee as charged by the Homeowners' Association and to split any "move-in/move-out" fee 1/2 to seller and 1/2 to buyer.

In the event rents are to be prorated, escrow holder is instructed to prorate and charge seller and credit buyer with any deposits paid in advance on the basis of a statement furnished by seller. Seller represents that he or she will collect all rents which fall due prior to the close of escrow. Escrow holder is to make all adjustments on the basis that all rents are current.

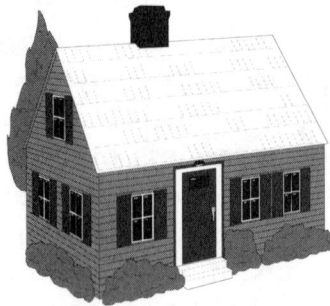

Title Company

Escrow holder is to immediately open an order with title company and request a preliminary title report concerning the subject property, regardless of the consummation of this escrow.

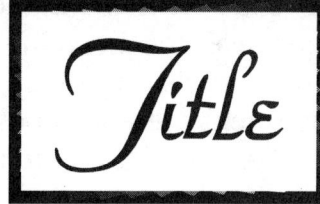

Charges

In addition to other costs and charges set forth in the escrow instructions, seller agrees to pay on demand, whether or not the escrow closes, any and all charges incurred by escrow holder on the seller's behalf, including but not limited to charges for owner's policy of title insurance, beneficiary statements and/or demands, offset statements, documentary transfer tax, preparation of, notarizing and recording of documents necessary on seller's behalf, seller's portion of sub-escrow fee, seller's escrow fee and other costs as charged.

Escrow holder is authorized to deduct from seller's net proceeds or buyer's net proceeds any amount which seller or buyer, as the case may be, may owe in any other matter or transaction. Escrow holder is authorized to charge and the parties agree to pay additional escrow fees for extraordinary services not within the range of customary escrow processing.

Documents

Escrow holder shall not be responsible in any way for the sufficiency or correctness as to form, manner of execution or validity of any documents deposited in this escrow, nor as to the identity, authority or right

227

of any person executing the same, either as to documents of record or those handled in this escrow.

Nor shall escrow holder be responsible in any way whatsoever for the failure of any party to comply with any of the provisions of any agreement, contract or other instrument filed or deposited in the escrow or referred to in the escrow instructions. Escrow holder duties shall be limited to the safekeeping of such money and documents received and for the disposition of the same in accordance with the written instructions.

Escrow holder shall not be required to take any action in connection with the collection, maturity or apparent outlaw of any obligations deposited in this escrow unless otherwise instructed in writing.

Insurance

The closing agent must make arrangements for new fire and hazard coverage or the transfer of coverage from the seller to he buyer. New documents reflecting the change must be gathered or prepared for signature by all parties.

Where the assignment of any insurance policy from seller to buyer is concerned, seller guarantees, as to any insurance policy handed to escrow holder, that each policy is in force, has not been hypothecated and all necessary premiums have been paid. Escrow holder is authorized to execute, on behalf of the parties, assignments of interest in any insurance policy (other than title insurance policies) called for in this escrow. Also to transmit for assignment any insurance policy to the insurance agent requesting that the insurer consent to such assignment and that it attach a loss payee clause or such other endorsement as may be required.

Such policy is to be forwarded to the lender and party entitled to it. Escrow holder shall not be responsible for verifying the acceptance of the request for assignment and the policy of insurance by the insurance company. The parties mutually agree that you will make no attempt to verify the receipt of the request for assignment by the insurance company. The parties are placed on notice that if the insurance company should fail to receive said assignment, the insuring company may deny coverage for any loss suffered by buyer. It is the obligation of the insured or a representative to verify the acceptance of the policy's assignment by the issuing company.

Personal Property Tax

Escrow holder is not responsible in any way for any personal property tax which may be assessed against any former or present owner of the subject property described in these escrow instructions, nor for the corporation or license tax of any corporation as a former or present owner.

Sub-Escrow

In the event it may be necessary, proper or convenient for the completion of this escrow, you are authorized to deposit or have deposited funds or documents or both, handed you under these escrow instructions, with any duly authorized sub-escrow agent. These may include, but are not limited to, any bank, trust company, title insurance company, title company or licensed escrow agent. The above described sub-escrow agent is to be subject to the escrow holder's order at or prior to close of that sub-escrow in the course of carrying out the close of this escrow. Any such deposit shall be considered as one in accordance with the meaning of these escrow instructions.

Subdivision

The parties to this escrow have satisfied themselves outside of escrow that the transaction covered is not in violation of the Subdivision Map Act, any law regulating land division, zoning ordinances or building restrictions. Escrow holder is relieved of all responsibility and/or liability in connection with the above mentioned regulations and is not to be concerned with the enforcement of any laws, restrictions, ordinances or regulations.

Purchase Agreement

In the event any Offer to Purchase, Deposit Receipt or any other form of Purchase Agreement, amendment or supplement is deposited in this escrow, it is understood that such document shall be effective only as between the parties signing the document. Escrow holder is not to be concerned with the terms of such Purchase Agreement and is relieved of all responsibility and/or liability for the enforcement of such terms. The only duty is to comply with the instructions set forth in this escrow.

Escrow holder is not responsible for knowing or interpreting any provisions of any Purchase Agreement on which these instructions may be based. Escrow holder shall not rely on any knowledge or understanding of the Purchase Agreement in performing the duties required by this escrow. In connection with any loan transaction, escrow holder is authorized to deliver a copy of any such Purchase Agreement, along with any supplement or amendment to that document to the lender.

Disclosures

Escrow holder is not to be concerned with the giving of any disclosures required by federal or state law, including, but not limited to, RESPA (Real Estate Settlement Procedures Act), Regulation Z (Truth-In-Lending Disclosures), FIRPTA (Foreign Investment Real Property Tax Act), or other warnings, or any other warranties, expressed or implied.

Escrow holder shall not be responsible in any way and is released from any liability, obligation or responsibility with respect to withholding of funds in response to FIRPTA regulations. Escrow holder is not responsible in determining whether the transferor is a foreign person, or for obtaining a nonforeign affidavit or exemption from withholding under FIRPTA.

Copies Delivered

Escrow holder is authorized to deliver copies of all escrow instructions, supplements and amendments, estimated and final closing statements, preliminary title reports and notices of cancellation, if any, to the real estate broker, real estate agent, lender, lender's agent and/or attorney for the parties, upon their oral or written request. Escrow holder shall not incur any liability in doing so.

Physical Inspection

Escrow holder shall make no physical inspection of the real and/or personal property described in any instrument deposited in this escrow. Escrow holder shall make no representations and/or warranties concerning any such real and/or personal property and is not to be concerned with nor liable for the condition of such properties.

Recording, Delivery of Instruments or Funds

The parties to this escrow authorize the recordation of any instrument necessary or proper for the issuance of the policy of title insurance called for or to effect the closing of this escrow. Funds, instructions or instruments received in this escrow may be delivered to, or deposited with, any title insurance company or title company for the purpose of complying with the terms and conditions of this escrow. Escrow holder is not responsible for the sufficiency, correctness of form or authority of person signing of any documents drawn outside of escrow and deposited with escrow holder.

Pest Control Report

If a structural pest control report and/or notice of work completed are handed to escrow holder, a copy shall be mailed to buyer as soon as is practicable after receipt.

Forms

Escrow holder is to use the usual instrument forms such as notes, deeds or deeds of trust, or the usual forms of any title insurance company. Dates and terms are to be inserted on the usual instruments if they are incomplete in such particulars, provided the insertions comply with the instructions contained in these escrow instructions.

Performance

Escrow holder shall conduct no lien or title search of chattels or personal property in connection with the sale or transfer of same through this escrow.

Usury

Escrow holder shall not be responsible in any way nor concerned with any question of usury in any loan or encumbrance, whether new or of record, which may arise during the processing of this escrow.

Delivery of Documents

The parties agree to deliver to escrow holder all documents, instruments, escrow instructions and funds required to process and close this escrow in accordance with these instructions.

Title

Escrow holder is instructed to clear title to the subject real property according to the beneficiary demands and/or beneficiary statements delivered to escrow holder by the existing lienholders. Escrow holder is not responsible for the correctness of the above. Escrow holder is not required to submit any such beneficiary statement and/or beneficiary demand to the parties for

approval prior to the close of escrow unless expressly instructed to do so, in writing, by the parties.

Terms of New Loan

Escrow holder is not to be responsible in any way nor to be concerned with the terms of any new loan or the content of any loan documents obtained by buyer or seller in connection with the escrow except to order such loan documents into the escrow file and to transmit the same to buyer for execution and transmit the executed loan documents to lender. The parties understand and agree that escrow holder is not involved nor concerned with the processing of any loan and cannot advise or give an opinion regarding the processing of any loan.

Statement of Information

Each principal agrees to immediately deliver to escrow holder a fully completed and executed "Statement of Information", to be delivered to the title company as required. Parties acknowledge that refusal to deliver the "Statement of Information" may be cause for delay in closing.

Tax Information

In connection with the Federal Tax Reform Act of 1986 and the California Revenue and Taxation Code, certain transactions are required to be reported to the Internal Revenue Service and the California State Franchise Tax Board. In those transactions required to be reported, seller will furnish a correct tax identification number to escrow holder for reporting purposes as required by law.

Seller understands that he or she may be subject to civil or criminal penalties for failure to do so.

Third Party Claims

The parties expressly indemnify and hold escrow holder harmless against third party claims for any fees, costs or expenses where escrow holder has acted in good faith, with reasonable care and prudence and/or in compliance with escrow instructions.

Liability for Disclosure

The parties agree that as far as the responsibilities and liabilities of the escrow holder are concerned, this transaction is an escrow, and does not create any other legal relationship except that of an escrow holder upon the terms and conditions expressly set forth in these instructions.

Escrow holder shall have no duty or responsibility to disclose any profit realized by any person, firm or corporation including, but not limited to, any real estate broker, real estate sales agent and/or a party. However, if escrow holder is instructed by any party to this escrow, in writing, to disclose any sale, resale, loan, exchange or other transaction involving any real or personal property described herein or any profit realized by any person, firm or corporation as set forth herein, escrow holder shall do so without incurring any liability to any party.

Escrow holder shall not be liable for any acts or omissions done in good faith nor for any claims, demands, losses or damages made, or claims suffered by any party to this escrow, excepting such as may arise through or be caused by willful neglect or gross misconduct on the part of escrow holder.

Change of Ownership Form

Buyer acknowledges that a Change of Ownership form is required by the county recorder to be completed and affixed to any documents submitted for recording which indicate a conveyance of title. The Change of Ownership form shall be furnished to buyer by escrow holder and buyer is aware that if buyer does not complete the form in full, sign and return to escrow holder prior to closing, a penalty will be assessed by the county recorder.

If the Change of Ownership form is not filed after the close of escrow within the time limits set forth by the county recorder, additional penalties will be assessed against the buyer. For information or assistance in completing the Change of Ownership form, buyer may contact the county assessor's office in the county in which the subject property is located.

Hold Open Fee

Notwithstanding any other provisions contained in escrow instructions, and in addition to such other fees and costs to which escrow holder may be entitled, the parties, jointly and severally, agree that in the event the escrow is not consummated within ninety (90) days of the date set for closing, escrow holder is instructed to withhold the escrow hold open fee of $25.00 per month from the funds on deposit with you regardless of the depositor.

Agency

The agency between the principals to this escrow and the escrow holder shall automatically terminate six (6) months following the date set for the close of escrow. It shall be subject to earlier termination if the parties to the escrow submit mutually executed cancellation instructions.

In the event the conditions of this escrow have not been complied with at the expiration provided, escrow holder is instructed to complete the termination at the earliest possible date, unless any of the parties have made written demand upon the escrow holder for the return of funds and/or instruments deposited by either of the parties.

If there are funds or instruments to be disbursed, escrow holder is instructed to stop proceedings, without liability for interest on funds held, until mutual cancellation instructions are received from the parties. The parties, jointly and severally, agree that in the event of cancellation or other termination of this escrow prior to closing to pay for any expenses which escrow holder has incurred while following these instructions.

The principals agree, if this escrow is mutually terminated prior to the closing date, to pay a reasonable escrow fee for services contracted by them and to deposit such funds into escrow prior to cancellation. Buyer and seller agree that any cancellation charges or fees for services shall be divided fairly between the parties in a manner the escrow holder considers equitable. Escrow holder's decision regarding the distribution of fees will be considered binding and conclusive upon the parties.

Upon receipt of mutual cancellation instructions or a final order or judgment of a court, the escrow holder is instructed to disburse any funds and instruments in accordance with such instructions, order or judgment. This escrow, without further notice, will then be considered terminated and canceled.

Cooperation of Parties

The parties shall cooperate with escrow holder in carrying out the instructions and completing the escrow. In the interest of following the instructions, the parties shall deposit into escrow any additional funds, instruments, documents or authorizations as requested. These additions shall be reasonably necessary to enable escrow holder to comply with demands made by third parties, to secure policies of title insurance, or otherwise carry out the terms of the instructions and close this escrow.

In the event conflicting demands are made upon the escrow holder or controversy arises between the parties or with any third person arising out of this escrow, the escrow holder shall have the absolute right to withhold and stop any further proceedings in the performance of this escrow until receiving written notification of the dispute's settlement.

All parties to this escrow promise to compensate the escrow holder for specific, unexpected costs connected with the escrow. These might be litigation costs, judgments, attorney's fees, expenses, obligations and liabilities of any kind which, in good faith, the escrow holder may incur in connection with carrying out this escrow.

As a safeguard, the escrow holder is given a lien on all rights, titles and interests of parties to this escrow as well as all escrow papers, other property and money deposited in case there is a need for escrow holder to be reimbursed. In the event of failure to pay fees or expenses due escrow holder or for costs and attorneys fees incurred in any litigation or interpleader, the parties agree to pay a reasonable fee for any attorney services which may be required to collect such fees or expenses, whether such attorney's fees are incurred prior to trial, at trial or on appeal.

In Writing

All notices, demands and instructions must be in writing. No notice, demand, instruction, amendment, supplement or modification of these instructions shall be of any effect in this escrow until delivered in writing to the escrow holder. All documents must be executed by all parties affected.

Any purported oral instruction, amendment, supplement, modification, notice or demand deposited with escrow holder by the parties shall be invalid.

Escrow holder is to be concerned only with the directives expressly set forth in the escrow instructions, supplements and amendments. Escrow holder is not to be concerned with nor liable for items designated as "memorandum items" in the escrow instructions.

Counterparts

These instructions may be executed in counterparts, each of which shall be considered an original regardless of the date of its execution and delivery. All such counterparts together shall constitute one and the same document. Together they make up the entire contract.

Dishonored Checks

If any check submitted to the escrow holder is dishonored upon presentment for payment for any reason, escrow holder is authorized to notify all parties to the escrow and/or their respective real estate broker or real estate sales agent.

Oral Instructions

Escrow holder is authorized to accept oral instructions from the parties' real estate broker, real estate agent, lender or lender's agent concerning the preparation of escrow instructions, amendments or supplements. However, escrow holder may not act upon any instruction delivered orally until receiving written authorization signed by all parties to this escrow.

Gender

In these escrow instructions, wherever the context so requires, the masculine includes the feminine and/or neuter and the singular number includes the plural.

Legal Limitations

The parties acknowledge that escrow holder is not authorized to practice law nor to give legal advice. Each of the parties is advised to seek legal or financial counsel and advice concerning the effect of these escrow instructions. Further, the parties acknowledge that no representations are made by escrow holder as to the legal sufficiency, legal consequences, financial effects or tax consequences of this transaction.

Authorization to Dispose of Escrow Paperwork

Escrow holder is authorized to destroy or otherwise dispose of any and all documents, papers, instructions, correspondence and records or other material in this escrow file at any time after five (5) years from the date of close of escrow or cancellation. Escrow holder shall have no liability for disposing of the above without further notice to the parties.

Signatures

The parties' signatures on all escrow instructions and instruments pertaining to this escrow indicate their unconditional acceptance and approval. Escrow holder is entitled to rely on the signatures contained in these instructions.

San Clemente Escrow, Inc.

34932 Calle del Sol, Suite B, Capistrano Beach, CA 92624
(714) 361-1725 telephone-(714) 240-0233 fax

BUYER AND SELLER ESCROW INSTRUCTIONS
Escrow No: 1-4035-J
Joan Thompson: Escrow Officer
Date: January 17, 1997
Page: 1 of 5

THIS COMPANY IS LICENSED BY DEPT. OF CORPORATIONS

BROKER WILL HAND YOU FOR BUYER	$5,000.00
BUYER WILL HAND YOU PRIOR TO CLOSE OF ESCROW	$11,050.00
DEED OF TRUST TO RECORD	$304,950.00
TOTAL SALES PRICE	$321,000.00

Buyer to deliver to you any instruments and/or funds required from Buyer to enable you to comply with these instructions, all of which you are authorized to use and/or deliver on or before March 6, 1997, and when you are in a position to obtain a standard Policy of Title Insurance through CHICAGO TITLE, provided that said policy has a liability of at least the amount of the above total consideration, (new title policy to be delivered to lien holder), covering the following described property in the City of SAN CLEMENTE, County of ORANGE, State of CALIFORNIA:

SEE LEGAL DESCRIPTION ATTACHED HERETO AND MADE A PART HEREOF
AS EXHIBIT "A"
SELLER STATES PROPERTY ADDRESS IS:
310 AVENIDA CRISTOBAL, SAN CLEMENTE, CALIFORNIA 92672
INSURING TITLE VESTED IN:

ONOFRE AND RUBY ARCHULETA, HUSBAND AND WIFE AS COMMUNITY
PROPERTY

SUBJECT ONLY TO:
CURRENT installment(s) of the General and special county, and city (if any) Taxes, including any special district levies, payments which are included therein and collected therewith, for current fiscal year, not delinquent, including taxes for ensuing year, if any, a lien not yet due or payable; personal property taxes, if any; covenants, conditions, reservations (including exceptions of oil, gas, minerals, and hydrocarbons, without right of surface entry), restrictions, rights, rights of way and easements for public utilities, districts, water companies, alley and streets, and any gas and oil leases.

INITIAL HERE: **SELLER (   ) (   )   BUYER (   ) (   )**

San Clemente Escrow, Inc.

34932 Calle del Sol, Suite B, Capistrano Beach, CA 92624
(714) 361-1725 telephone-(714) 240-0233 fax

BUYER AND SELLER ESCROW INSTRUCTIONS
Escrow No: 1-4035-J
Joan Thompson: Escrow Officer
Date: January 17, 1997
Page: 2 of 5

THIS COMPANY IS LICENSED BY DEPT. OF CORPORATIONS

DEED OF TRUST to file, as obtained by the BUYER herein securing a Note in the amount of $304,950.00, in favor of Lender of BUYERS choice. Exact terms of loan to follow with loan documents and BUYERS execution of same shall indicate their full approval of all terms and conditions contained therein. Escrow Holder is authorized and instructed to comply with lenders instructions and requirements.

CLOSE OF ESCROW is subject to BUYER and PROPERTY qualifying for above financing with 6.5% initial adjustable rate with a maximum lifetime interest rate cap of 11% for 30 years, points not to exceed 1%. BUYER to provide verification of down payment funds within 48 hours of 1/17/97.

SELLER agrees to pay a maximum of $6,000.00 towards BUYERS non-recurring closing costs.

CLOSE OF ESCROW subject to Buyers approval of Preliminary Title Report within 7 days of receipt of same. In the event Escrow Holder is not in receipt of written disapproval within time period stated, Escrow Holder shall deem this contingency waived.

Seller to furnish Buyer with a One Year Home Protection Policy issued by SIERRA NATIONAL HOME WARRANTY CO., the cost of which is not to exceed $400.00 and is to be paid from Sellers Net Proceeds upon Close of Escrow.

BUYER shall hand you, prior to the close of escrow, completed, executed preliminary change of ownership to be attached to deed for recording per section 480.30 of revenue and taxation code and in the absence of said report or in the event the recorder deems said report to be incomplete, recorder shall impose $20.00 fee to BUYER.

INITIAL HERE: **SELLER (   )(   )BUYER (   )(   )**

San Clemente Escrow, Inc.

34932 Calle del Sol, Suite B, Capistrano Beach, CA 92624
(714) 361-1725 telephone-(714) 240-0233 fax

BUYER AND SELLER ESCROW INSTRUCTIONS
Escrow No: 1-4035-J
Joan Thompson: Escrow Officer
Date: January 17, 1997
Page: 3 of 5

THIS COMPANY IS LICENSED BY DEPT. OF CORPORATIONS

BUYER is made aware that the tax assessor has the right to impose a supplemental tax on subject property after the close of escrow, and in such event, said tax shall be the BUYER'S responsibility. BROKER, ESCROW HOLDER, and SELLER are relieved of any liability with regard to same. If the SELLER receives a supplemental tax bill prior to the close of escrow, escrow holder is to be notified, and same shall be paid accordingly.

CONDOMINIUM PLAN/P.U.D.: The subject of this transaction is a condominium/planned unit development (P.U.D.) designated as unit specified and specified parking space and an undivided interest in community areas, and _____.
The current monthly assessment charge by the homeowner's association or other governing body is _$43_ approx. As soon as practicable, Seller shall provide Buyer with copies of covenants conditions and restrictions, articles of incorporation, by-laws, current rules and regulations, most current financial statements, and any other documents as required by law. Seller shall disclose in writing any known pending special assessment, claims, or litigation to buyer. Buyer shall be allowed _7_ calendar days from receipt to review these documents. If such documents disclose conditions or information unsatisfactory to Buyer, Buyer may cancel this agreement. BUYER'S FAILURE TO NOTIFY SELLER IN WRITING SHALL CONCLUSIVELY BE CONSIDERED APPROVAL.

BUYER to pay Homeowners Association transfer fee at close of escrow.

A pest control report per item 20 of the Real Estate Purchase Contract and Receipt for Deposit is a requirement of this escrow. Seller to pay for report and any corrective work required for a Notice of Completion. Buyer to pay for work in Section 2, if any.

INITIAL HERE: BUYER( )( )   SELLER( )( )

San Clemente Escrow, Inc.

34932 Calle del Sol, Suite B, Capistrano Beach, CA 92624
(714) 361-1725 telephone-(714) 240-0233 fax

BUYER AND SELLER ESCROW INSTRUCTIONS
Escrow No: 1-4035-J
Joan Thompson: Escrow Officer
Date: January 17, 1997
Page: 4 of 5

THIS COMPANY IS LICENSED BY DEPT. OF CORPORATIONS

ESCROW HOLDER is specifically instructed by the undersigned Buyer and Seller to request that the new loan proceeds be deposited directly in the San Clemente Escrow, Inc. Trust Account for payoff of existing encumbrances and disbursement in accordance with these escrow instructions without the use of the title company subescrow. In the event the new Lender refuses to fund to San Clemente Escrow, Inc. and instead should direct funds to the title company in this transaction, Buyer and Seller herein instruct Escrow Holder to authorize recordation, regardless and agree to hold San Clemente Escrow, Inc. harmless and without liability in connection with funds on deposit with the title company.

CANCELLATION FEE: In the event of cancellation of this escrow, all parties are aware and agree that escrow holders is hereby authorized and instructed to charge a cancellation fee. Said Fee shall be determined upon the stage in the escrow and work done to date.

SELLER, BUYER or BORROWER shall each pay their own respective closing costs, including their own portion of escrow fees, in connection with this transaction, unless otherwise stated herein.

AS A MEMORANDUM ITEM ONLY WITH WHICH ESCROW HOLDER IS NOT TO BE CONCERNED, it is agreed between BUYER AND SELLER outside of escrow that: BUYERS do intend to occupy subject property.

Possession of subject property is to be granted to BUYER 72 hours after close of escrow.

****

In accordance with the manner specified under the "General Provisions" attached hereto, you are authorized and instructed to adjust or prorate the following to CLOSE OF ESCROW: **PROPERTY TAXES AND HOMEOWNERS DUES.**

INITIAL HERE: **BUYER(**   **)(**   **)**   **SELLER(**   **)(**   **)**

San Clemente Escrow, Inc.

34932 Calle del Sol, Suite B, Capistrano Beach, CA 92624
(714) 361-1725 telephone-(714) 240-0233 fax

BUYER AND SELLER ESCROW INSTRUCTIONS
Escrow No: 1-4035-J
Joan Thompson: Escrow Officer
Date: January 17, 1997
Page: 5 of 5

THIS COMPANY IS LICENSED BY DEPT. OF CORPORATIONS

THE FOREGOING TERMS, CONDITIONS AND INSTRUCTIONS, INCLUDING THE "GENERAL PROVISIONS" ATTACHED HERETO, (AS IF FULLY SET FORTH HEREIN), HAVE BEEN READ AND ARE UNDERSTOOD BY EACH OF THE UNDERSIGNED, WHO HEREBY AGREE TO, CONCUR WITH, APPROVE AND ACCEPT THE SAME IN THEIR ENTIRETY.

SELLER'S SIGNATURE: BUYER'S SIGNATURE:

_____   _____
KATE OLIVER   RUBY ARCHULETA

_____   _____
QUENTIN OLIVER   ONOFRE ARCHULETA

Post Test

The following self test repeats the one you took at the beginning of this chapter. Now take the exam again--since you have read all the material-- and check your knowledge of escrow closing procedures.

True/False

1. A "take sheet" is the framework for the escrow instructions.

2. Collecting the information needed to provide complete escrow instructions is the first step for an escrow agent.

3. The three documents that serve as the heart of a sale escrow are the grant deed, promissory note and bill of sale.

4. A promissory note is the security for a debt.

5. General instructions authorize the escrow holder to carry out general procedures needed to complete the escrow.

6. General instructions are special instructions given by a buyer or seller to the escrow holder.

7. Third party instructions may include a demand or claim from a person not involved in the escrow as a principal.

8. The escrow holder's obligation to the parties starts as soon as escrow instructions are written.

9. Prorations are made on the basis of a 25- day month.

10. If rents are to be prorated, escrow holder should prorate and charge seller and credit buyer with any deposits paid in advance to the seller by tenants.

chapter 8

RECORD KEEPING & PRORATIONS

Focus

- **Introduction**
- **Closing statement**
- **Escrow checklist for selling broker**
- **Escrow checklist for listing broker**
- **Prorations**

Pre-Test

The following is a self test to determine how much you know about record keeping and prorations before reading this chapter. Take it without studying, then read the material presented in the text. At the end of the chapter you will find a repeat of this exam. Test your knowledge by answering the questions again, then check your improvement. (The answers are found at the end of the book.) Good luck.

True/False

1. Items that are credits to the seller are debits to the buyer.

2. Taxes, rents and deposits are usually prorated.

3. The day of closing is included for proration purposes.

4. Prorations are based on a 30-day month.

5. Proration of taxes are based on 180 days or six months.

6. The first installment of property tax is due December 1.

7. Supplementary taxes are paid by the seller.

8. The buyer's new taxes are generally calculated on 1% of the purchase price plus part of a percentage for local or county taxes or special assessments.

9. Life insurance is required by most lenders.

10. Property taxes are due twice yearly.

Introduction

If you recall, Onofre and Ruby Archuleta are buying a house from Kate and Quentin Oliver for $400,000. The transaction is due to close and all parties expect to be informed of the costs incurred during the escrow, as well as receive an accounting of the process.

One of the closing agent's main jobs is to represent the obligations of each party in a personalized closing statement. The flow of consideration through escrow is outlined in the closing statement, as well as adjustments and disbursements reflecting the prior agreement of the parties.

Closing Statement

The closing statement is where the accounting for the escrow is set down for the buyer and seller. It is a reflection of the parties' agreements and matches their wishes exactly. Both the seller and buyer are credited and debited for their agreed upon share of costs, ending statement for the transaction.

The debit-credit columns shown on the closing statement are marked *seller/lender* or *buyer/ borrower*, depending on whether it describes a sale or loan escrow. The information from this statement will be used at the closing to conform to the Real Estate Settlement Procedures Act (RESPA).

Seller's Statement

This represents the accounting the Olivers will receive upon the transaction's closing.

Credits

The total consideration in the transaction is $400,000.00 as specified in the escrow instructions. Credit the seller, debit the buyer.

The first installment of taxes for the tax year was paid by the seller. A credit in the amount of $77.34, representing 15 days of prepaid property tax, is given to the seller. Credit the seller, debit the buyer.

The seller has prepaid 15 days of monthly homeowners association dues at the rate of $50.00 per month, or 25.00. Credit the seller, debit the buyer.

Debits

The escrow holder was instructed to calculate rent from 12/16 to 12/31, or $400.00. Debit the seller, credit the buyer.

The payoff on the existing loan plus interest charges is a debit to the seller.

The commission paid to the real estate broker, $24,000, is a debit to the seller.

The seller has agreed to pay for the termite report in the amount of $200.00. Debit the seller.

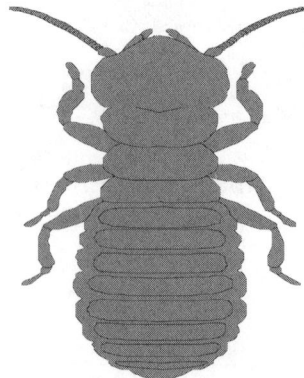

It is the job of the title company to transfer the insured title to the buyer. Seller is debited for the following items:

- Title policy premium $579.00
- Reconveyance fee $60.00
- Documentary transfer tax $440.00
- Recording fee (reconveyance) <u>$3.00</u>
- Total

                                $1,082.00

Balance

This figure represents the proceeds the seller can expect to receive.

Total Debits to Seller

The end debits must balance with the corresponding credits.

Checklist of Seller's Costs and Credits

Seller's Costs

Selling Commission
Title Insurance
Escrow Fee
Legal Fees
Prepayment Penalty
State or Local Transfer Tax
Pest Control Inspection Fee
Pest Control Work
Recording Fee
FHA or VA points

Seller's Costs (continued)

Reconveyance Fees
Notary Fee
Prorated Taxes
Personal Property Tax
Interest if paid in arrears
Prorated Rents
Security Deposits on hand

Seller's Credits

Interest if paid in advance (from recordation to date of next loan payment)
Refund existing Trust Fund (Impound Account), if any
Prorated Taxes (if paid beyond recordation)

Buyer's Statement

This statement represents the accounting the Archuletas will receive upon the closing of the transaction.

Credits

The money deposited by the buyer to open the escrow is noted as a credit to the buyer.

The amount of the new loan, $240,000.00, is a credit to the buyer.

The rental credit of $400, noted as a debit to the seller, is a credit to the buyer (for seller rent back).

The total amount credited to the buyer includes the remainder of the down payment which is due at the closing.

Debits

Items that have been credited to the seller are noted as debits to the buyer, such as the amount of total consideration, tax prorations and association dues.

Charges made by the lender in connection with the new loan may be loan fees or advance collections for taxes or insurance. In this case one month's interest is charged to the buyer. In addition, a tax service charge, credit report, appraisal fee, impound account deposit for taxes, two months' insurance , document fee and mortgage insurance are all listed as debits to the buyer.

Fees related to title company charges are debited to the buyer (lender's title policy premium and recording fees for deed and trust deed).

The end debits must balance with the corresponding credits.

Checklist of Buyers Closing Costs

Non-Recurring Costs

Title Insurance (where payable by buyer)
Escrow Fee
Legal Fees
Loan Fee
Appraisal Fee
Tax Service
Credit Report
Notary Fee
Recording Fee
Pest Control Inspection
Document Preparation Fee
Review Fee

Non-Recurring Costs (continued)

Application Fee
Underwriting Fee
Courier Fee
Verification Fee
Warehousing Fee

Recurring Costs

Hazard Insurance
Trust Fund or Impound Account
Prorated Taxes (if paid beyond recordation)
Prorated Interest (if charged in arrears: to end of month/if charged in advance: to date of first payment?

Credits

Prorated Taxes
Prorated Rents
Security Deposits on hand

Escrow Checklist for Selling Broker

As we have seen, in some areas the real estate broker handles many of the details of collecting information for the escrow and making sure all contingencies are met. In varying degrees, then, the real estate agent is important to the closing process. The following is a list of functions that may be performed by the selling broker.

> ### Selling Broker may:
>
> - Obtain increase of deposit
> - Open the escrow
> - Order credit report on buyer (if required)
> - Order pest control inspection
> - Order other inspections (roof, etc., if required)
> - Check on any contingencies to be eliminated
> - Check occupancy permit
> - Order loan commitment
> - Assist buyer with loan application and submit to lender
> - Arrange for hazard insurance
> - Have closing instructions prepared and signed by buyer

Escrow Checklist for Listing Broker

Once again, in different areas, a real estate agent performs particular duties. The listing broker has a special list of jobs to perform in completing his or her commitment to the seller.

> ### Listing Broker may:
>
> - Notice of sale to multiple listing office
> - Check on increase of deposit
> - Examine preliminary title report and assist in eliminating clouds on the title, of any
> - Check on any contingencies to be eliminated

<u>Listing Broker may (continued)</u>

- Request title company or escrow company to order pay-off demand, or statement of condition and assumption papers from lender
- Check with selling broker on buyer's loan
- If income property, obtain: rent schedule, rent due dates, Security deposits, copies of leases, names and phone numbers of tenants
- Have seller's instructions prepared and signed
- If seller carries a second loan, have escrow holder record a "Request for copy of Notice of Default and subscribe to a tax agency
- Obtain seller's future address and phone

Prorations

Items to be prorated by the closing agent such as taxes and insurance and rents may be calculated using proration tables, financial calculators or software created specifically for that purpose. The closing agent, however, must be aware of the principles used to determine the percentage or dollar figure shown on the proration tables as well as be able to determine simple prorations directly.

The proper time period in which to prorate items must first be established. The day of closing is not included for proration purposes. In completing the prorations for a transaction, time is converted to a day factor, either as an amount per day or as a percentage of the total time period for the transaction. Prorations are typically based on a 30-day month and a 360-day year.

Time Periods for Prorations

Taxes: based on 180 days or six months

Insurance: usually based on a 360-day year

Rents: based on a 30-day month

Taxes

Tax prorations are based on due dates for taxes. Realproperty tax becomes a lien on the property assessed onMarch 1st preceding the tax year for which the taxes are due. As you recall, the tax, or fiscal, year is from July 1 through the following June 30.

Regardless of the time other liens are created, real property taxes have priority over any other liens on the property. The payment of property tax is enforced by the sale of the subject property in a manner dictated by statute.

Taxes are due twice yearly. The first half is due on November 1 and becomes delinquent December 10. The second half is due February 1 and becomes delinquent April 10.

Memory Aid for Tax Due Dates

No--Nov 1
Darn--December 10
Fooling--February 1
Around--April 1

Each year, after April 10, a delinquent roll is prepared showing all property upon which taxes are due.

Also each year, before June 8, a delinquency list of real property taxes is published in local newspapers describing a date upon which the delinquent property will be "sold to the state."

The property is not really "sold to the state," with the state taking possession or ownership. The taxpayer retains legal title to the property and enjoys possession during the five-year redemption period.

The term "sold to the state" refers to a bookkeeping transaction that starts a five-year period during which the owner may pay all delinquent taxes, cost, penalties and interest and return the property to its former lien-free status. At the end of the five-year redemption period, if the delinquency has not been cured, the property is sold at a tax sale, with no recourse by the former owner allowed.

Additional taxes may be levied at the time of a sale to reflect the sales price. These are called supplemental taxes and should be expected by the parties to an escrow. The buyer completes a Preliminary Change of Ownership form which informs the tax assessor of the possible change in value. At that time the tax assessor may levy a supplemental tax for that tax year based on the sales price, and send it to the buyer. This usually occurs outside of escrow and is not a matter for the closing agent.

A supplemental tax may also be assessed if an improvement to the real property is completed during the tax billing period (before November 1). After the improvement has been assessed, the tax collector will calculate the new taxes on a prorated basis, depending on the improvement's date of completion. The new tax generally is based on 1% of the market value or sales price, plus a part of a percentage for local or county taxes or special assessments. The tax is prorated based on the closing date of the transaction.

Taxes on a property may decrease if the value of the property has declined, and the supplemental tax will reflect the change.

Calculation of Prorated Taxes

The close of escrow is 10/25/97 and the unpaid taxes for six months are $980.00. Charge the seller for the unpaid first installment for 1997-98 taxes and charge the buyer for the prorated amount of taxes from 10/25/97 to 1/1/98. Credit that amount to the seller.

To Prorate Taxes:

1. First, calculate the cost of taxes per day for the six-month period in question.

    $980=taxes for 180 days (six months)
    $980 divided by 180=$5.44 daily

2. Count the number of days during the tax period in question when the seller owned the property.

    July 1 to September 30=90 days
    October 1 to October 24=24 days

3. Seller owned the property 114 days of current tax period

    114 x $5.44=$620.16 amount owed by seller

4. After subtracting $620.16 from the total tax charged to the seller, credit the seller and debit the buyer with the difference.

    $980.00 less $620.16=$359.84 (credit seller, debit buyer)

Insurance

Traditionally, the type of insurance required by lenders and expected by buyers was fire insurance. Today, there are several types of policies covering various types of damage, such as earthquake or flood destruction. In any case, the closing agent may prorate some of the policies and some might be done by the insurer. If calculations are required for insurance prorations, the following example will be helpful.

The buyer is taking over a three-year policy with a premium of $1,200, which the seller had prepaid. It was effective May 13, 1997, to be prorated as of the closing, October 25, 1999, using a 30-day month and a 360-day year:

1. Determine number of days to be prorated:

	Year	Month	Day	Total
10/25/99	1999	10	25	
5/13/97	-1997	-5	-13	
	2	5	12	
	x360	x30	x1	
	720	150	12	882

2. Then calculate the cost per day for the term of the policy by dividing $1,200 by 1,080 (the number of days in the three-year policy) to arrive at $1.11.

3. Finally, multiply the total number of days to be prorated, or 882, by $1.11 to arrive at $979.00, or the dollar amount of the premium that has been used.

4. Subtracting $979.00 from the cost of the policy, or $1,200, the seller would be credited $221, and the buyer debited the same amount.

Rents

Normally, a 30-day month is used to prorate rents. The closing agent must be aware that rents are collected in advance and should be prorated accordingly.

A triplex with the following rents is in escrow with the transaction to close on October 25, 1999.

> Apartment A=$780 paid through 11/1/99
> Apartment B=$780 paid through 11/1/99
> Apartment C=$780 paid through 11/1/99

Prorating Rents

1. The closing agent must first calculate the amount of daily interest by dividing the monthly rent of $780 by 30, or $26 a day.

2. The buyer will be taking title on the 25th day of October, and should be credited for 6 days of rent or the number of days between October 25 and November 1.

3. By multiplying 6 x $26 to get $156 per unit for the six days, the closing agent can multiply that amount by 3, to credit the buyer with $468.00.

Also, the seller must provide information about when the rents are collected, amounts of security deposits, cleaning deposits, and any other funds that are to be transferred at the closing. An accounting is done at the closing to reflect funds to be transferred to the buyer or remain with the seller.

Loan Assumptions/Loan Payoffs

The escrow holder must be very careful in calculating the amounts when loans are involved. Terms of a beneficiary statement in the case of a loan assumption, or the demand statement in the case of a loan payoff, must be observed carefully by the closing agent. There are certain items of which the closing agent must be especially aware.

Loan Assumption/Loan Payoff

Payment Date
Most loans are paid monthly. Even though this is usually the case, payments on some loans are due quarterly, semi-annually or annually.

Payment Status
The closing agent must be aware of whether or not all current loan payments are being made in a timely manner. In case the payments are not kept current, any statements of loan condition should not be ordered until the very last part of the escrow period.

Impounds
In the case where existing impounds must be credited to the correct party, the closing agent must receive instructions about the amount and to whom it is entitled.

If the buyer is obtaining a new loan with an impound account, the lender determines the amount of additional funds required from the buyer to establish the account and includes the amount in the loan documents.

Loan Assumption/Loan Payoff (continuedd)

How is the Loan Paid?
Are the payments interest only, partially amortized with a balloon payment or fully amortized?

Calculating Loan Payoff or Assumptions
In the typical loan payoff, the payment is being made in arrears. It also must be determined whether the lender requires payment to the date of closing or to the date the lender receives the payoff funds. Because of this requirement, the money required for closing could change. Interest between buyer and seller must be allocated carefully by the closing agent.

Miscellaneous Prorations

Closing agents should be aware that there may be items to prorate in addition to those normally required. Homeowners association assessments or other items that may have been prepaid by the seller or assumed by the buyer must be calculated and prorated to the close of escrow.

SMS SETTLEMENT SERVICES
SELLER'S ESTIMATED CLOSING STATEMENT

Seller: Jim Getz
    Mary Ann Getz

Escrow No: 004860-999 DW
Close Date: 01-01-1999
Proration Date: 12-31-98
Date Prepared: 11/22/1998

Property: 21128 Rose
    Rancho Santa Margarita, CA 92691

Description	Debit	Credit
TOTAL CONSIDERATION:		189,900
NEW AND EXISTING ENCUMBRANCES:		
County Taxes from 1-20-99 to 1/31-2000		238.33
Based on the annual amount of '$7,800.00		
Assessments f rom 1-01-99 to 1-01-99		100.00
County Taxes 1-01-99 to 3-31-2000	293.33	
Based on the annual amount of $1,200.00		
PAYOFFS:		
Payoff to Bank of America	68,045.63	
67,595.00 Principal balance		
450.63 Interest from 12-01-98 to 1-31-98		
ESCROW AND TITLE CHARGES:		
Settlement/Closing Fee to SMS SETTLEMENT SERVICES	175.00	
Title Examination to SMS SETTLEMENT SERVICES	250.00	
Attorney's Fees to Strachen and Green	85.00	
Title Insurance to SMS SETTLEMENT SERVICES	813.00	
RECORDING FEES:		
City/County Tax Stamps to SMS SETTLEMENT SERVICES	36.00	
COMMISSIONS:	11,394	
5,697.00 to Blue Lagoon Real Estate		
5,697.00 to Grubb & Ellis Company		
Sub Totals	261,184.29	190,238.33
Balance Due from Seller		70,945.96
Totals	261,184.29	261,184.29

_____
Jim Getz, Sr..

Trustor of the Main Street Trust

_____
Mary Ann Getz

267

SMS SETTLEMENT SERVICES
BUYER'S ESTIMATED CLOSING STATEMENT

Buyer: Robert Trabuco
      Amelia Trabuco

Escrow No: 004860-999 DW
Close Date: 01-01-1999
Proration Date: 12-31-98
Date Prepared: 11/22/1998

Property: 21128 Rose
        Rancho Santa Margarita, CA 92691

Description	Debit	Credit
TOTAL CONSIDERATION:		
Total Consideration	189,900	
Deposit/Earnest Money		5,000
NEW AND EXISTING ENCUMBRANCES:		
Existing Loan Amount from Bank of America		180,000
NEW LOAN CHARGES		
Loan Origination Fee to Bank of America	180,000	
Loan Discount to Bank of America	180,000	
Appraisal Fee to Bank of America	350.00	
Credit Report to TRW	15.00	
Servicing/Document Prep. to Bank of America	250.00	
Credit Line to Bank of America	200.00	
Tax Service to Bank of America	68.50	
Underwriting Fee to Bank of America	75.00	
Hazard Insurance Premium to Bank of America	1,200.00	
Hazard Insurance to Bank of America	100.00	
City Property Taxes to Bank of America	600.00	
County Property Taxes to Bank of America	400.00	
PRORATIONS AND ADJUSTMENTS:		
County Taxes from 1-20-99 to 1-31-99	238.33	
Based on annual amount of $7,800.00		
County Taxes 1-01-99 to 3-29-99/		293.33
Based on the annual amount of $1,200.00		
ESCROW AND TITLE CHARGES:		
Settlement/Closing Fee to SMS SETTLEMENT SERVICES	176.00	
Title Insurance to SMS SETTLEMENT SERVICES	60.00	
Creditline Endorsement to SMS SETTLEMENT SERVICES	75.00	
Transfer Fee to SMS SETTLEMENT SERVICES	25.00	
RECORDING FEES		
Recording Fees to SMS SETTLEMENT SERVICES	20.50	
ADDITIONAL CHARGES		
Survey to Anderson Surveying	350.00	
Pest Inspection to D.I. Bruce Exterminating Co.	200.00	
Fed Ex Fee to All Lenders Mortgage	75.00	
Sub Totals	194,727.33	185,386.66
Balance Due From Buyer		9,340.67
Totals	194,727.33	194.727.33

Post Test

The following self test repeats the one you took at the beginning of this chapter. Now take the exam again--since you have read all the material-- and check your knowledge of escrow closing procedures.

True/False

1. Items that are credits to the seller are debits to the buyer.

2. Taxes, rents and deposits are usually prorated.

3. The day of closing is included for proration purposes.

4. Prorations are based on a 30-day month.

5. Proration of taxes are based on 180 days or six months.

6. The first installment of property tax is due December 1.

7. Supplementary taxes are paid by the seller.

8. The buyer's new taxes are generally calculated on 1% of the purchase price plus part of a percentage for local or county taxes or special assessments.

9. Life insurance is required by most lenders.

10. Property taxes are due twice yearly.

chapter 9

PROCESSING & CLOSING

Focus

- **Introduction**
- **Escrow instructions**
- **Requirements for closing**
- **The closing statement**
- **Transfer documents**
- **Financing documents**
- **Other documents needed for closing**
- **Document conveyance**
- **Final closing review**
- **Closing/recording**

Pre-Test

The following is a self test to determine how much you know about processing and closing an escrow before reading this chapter. Take it without studying, then read the material presented in the text. At the end of the chapter you will find a repeat of this exam. Test your knowledge by answering the questions again, then check your improvement. (The answers are found at the end of the book.) Good luck.

True/False

1. Buyers and sellers in Northern California do not sign separate escrow instructions.

2. Unilateral instructions are used in Northern California.

3. Bilateral instructions are used in Southern California.

4. Disclosure clauses limit the closing agent's liability regarding the complication of taxes and conformity to codes and other legal requirements.

5. Both federal and state tax laws are affected by the Foreign Investment in Real Estate Property Tax Act (FIRPTA).

6. Smoke detectors must be installed in all sold residential properties.

7. In most cases, the document of transfer will be a grant deed.

8. Loan documents are usually prepared by the title company.

9. A demand is a statement of loan default.

10. A grant deed does not *have* to be notarized to be recorded.

Introduction

The major commitment of an escrow holder is to complete all the terms of the agreement between the principals. Both in the manner desired and in the time period specified, the escrow holder must perform the appointed tasks. Upon satisfaction of all requirements of the escrow, including loan approval and removal of contingencies, then, and only then, can the escrow close.

One of the major tasks, as the closing nears, is to make sure all requirements of the escrow have been met. As we have seen, the escrow holder has the original take sheet to use as a guide to assure a smooth closing. Each part of the transaction must be evaluated and double checked for accuracy. The following is a list of items which have been ongoing throughout the processing of the escrow. This list can be used as a guide for review just prior to closing.

Items to be Reviewed

- Legal description of property as well as street address if applicable
- Current ownership information
- Any particular conditions or contingencies of the sale, such as the escrow being subject to the sale of the buyer's current home, or subject to loan approval
- Deeds of trust to be created, along with terms, conditions and responsibilities imposed by lender
- Loans to be assumed/impounds involved
- If the loan is current
- If the assumption is subject to lender approval
- Hazard and other insurance provisions
- Charges to buyer and seller
- Commission instructions
- Separate loan escrow instructions required for loans other than purchase money
- Legal name of buyer and method of taking title
- Personal property included in the sale (only personal property for identification purposes)
- Pest control inspection
- Prorations
- Other requirements particular to the transaction

Escrow Instructions

As we discussed in Chapter 6, escrow instructions vary in different states. The differences will affect the documents needed as well as the form of the instructions and the timing of signatures placed on those instructions.

Local Variations

As we have seen, processing is done differently in the northern and southern parts of California. In Northern California, an estimated closing statement is issued as part of the instructions, showing, for example, the proceeds going to the seller and the estimated cash needed to close for the buyer. In Southern California, the broker's net sheet serves the same purpose, except the closing statement is provided at the settlement.

Northern California

Buyers and sellers in Northern California each sign separate instructions at the end of the escrow period. These unilateral instructions represent the end of the transfer process and describe the agreement between the parties to the escrow. The closing agent, however, has been carrying out specific duties, as ordered by the principals, since the opening of the escrow, even though no instructions have been signed. The instructions also apportion closing costs to the appropriate parties. After signing the instructions, all that remains to be completed is the provision of funds from the buyer and the lender.

The contents of the buyer's and seller's instructions differ in requirements for closing. The buyer's instructions call for consideration to be given by the buyer when all documents of title transfer have been signed and the escrow is in a position to close. The seller's instructions provide for the necessary documents of transfer in exchange for consideration, either money or money and debt obligation by the buyer.

A complication that may arise out of having separate instructions is a breakdown of communication between the buyer and seller.

The buyer or seller may have changed some part of the transaction without getting the approval of the other party, and at the closing everyone is surprised. The buyer might decide to change financing arrangements, or one party could change his or her mind about the time of closing or possession. Any number of items could require amendments for all parties to sign before the closing can occur. In northern California, the real estate broker produces the amendments to the purchase contract and gives copies to the closer.

Basically, when buyer and seller sign unilateral escrow instructions they are approving the previously ordered actions of the escrow holder. They are acknowledging that demands have been satisfied, title reports completed, the amount of pest control work determined and any new loans approved.

The unilateral instructions act principally as a closing statement. Closing costs for buyer and seller are disclosed separately in each of their instructions.

Southern California

In the bilateral escrow instructions of the southern part of California, the shared promises of buyer and seller are joined into one document. That instruction contains conditions of the buyer's purchase as well as general (boilerplate) instructions for both parties about requirements of the escrow. The seller agrees to the necessary steps to place title in the name of the buyer.

When bilateral instructions are used, numerous amendments are common as a transaction progresses.

Because escrow instructions are a binding contract between the buyer and seller, any changes in the original instructions require the signature of both buyer and seller on an amendment stating the desired changes. No changes may be made without the agreement of all parties to the escrow.

Requirements for Closing

Certain protective or disclosure clauses may be included in escrow instructions which go beyond the personal, original agreements of the parties. These clauses limit the closing agent's responsibilities and liabilities regarding the complication of taxes and conformity to codes and other legal requirements.

Supplemental Tax Roll: All parties must be made aware that tax bills sent after the closing may increase or decrease the tax level imposed on the property being transferred.

Preliminary Change of Ownership Report: The buyer is required to complete this change of ownership form before closing. The purpose is to inform the county tax assessor of the change in ownership so new taxes can be calculated from the date of closing and the new owner billed appropriately.

FIRPTA: Both federal and state tax laws are affected by the Foreign Investment in Real Property Tax Act (FIRPTA). In both cases the buyer is responsible for making sure either the proper disclosures have been made and/or the proper funds have been set aside. This is the responsibility of the broker, originally, and ultimately, the closing agent. FIRPTA requires that every buyer of real property must deduct and withhold from the seller's proceeds ten percent of the gross sales price unless an exemption applies. Withheld funds must be reported and paid to the IRS within 20 days after the close of escrow.

Transaction is Exempt from FIRPTA Withholding if:

1. Seller's affidavit that he or she is not a "foreign person"

2. "Qualifying statement" from IRS stating no withholding is required

3. The purchase price is not over $300,000 and the buyer intends to live in the property

---

Form 1099-S: The Tax Reform Law of 1986 requires that all real estate transactions be reported to the IRS on the special Form 1099-S. The closing agent must complete this form and return it to the IRS.

Health and Safety Code Provisions

Retrofit Requirements: Smoke detectors must be installed in all sold residential properties and a disclosure must be given to the buyer as a result of state law.

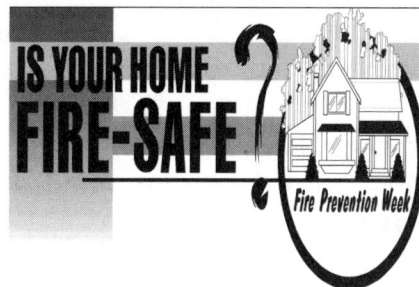

IS YOUR HOME FIRE-SAFE? Fire Prevention Week

The Closing Statement

An escrow has been completed when all documents have been signed, all contingencies have been met, all requirements fulfilled, all money (and other consideration) has been collected and deposited with the closing agent. The closing agent can now request recordation of documents and distribute the proceeds to the proper parties. A closing statement is then prepared by the closing agent for the buyer and seller, explaining the disposition of funds, and credits and debits made to their account.

When all is in order, the closing agent must determine the charges and account for the following items:

Sales price
Was the final sales price the same as it was originally?

Deposits
Have all moneys been disbursed or used according to instructions from all parties?

Trust deeds
Have all trust deeds of record been verified as to balance, interest rate and terms?

Payoff of existing debt
Did the seller approve a payoff of existing debt against the property, including any pre-payment penalty?

Impound account
How are existing impound accounts to be transferred to buyer?

New loan
Are all terms of the new loan agreeable to buyer (amount, interest rate, charges)?

Prorations
Have prorations been made according to instruction regarding interest on any existing debt, homeowners' association fees, taxes, insurance, rents?

Association transfer fee
Were instructions given regarding payment of association transfer fee (who pays it)?

Supplemental tax provisions
How is the supplemental tax bill to be paid?

Commission
Has the seller approved payment of commission to real estate broker?

Fees
Have buyer and seller agreed, in the instructions, to fees incurred during the escrow?

Incidental charges
Have instructions been given by the buyer and seller regarding supplementary charges such as judgments, tax liens, credit card payoffs, private note payments, or purchase of personal property?

Outside of escrow
Are there any special agreements between buyer and seller about money being disbursed outside of escrow?

Remaining balance

There may be a balance due to the seller or a refund to the buyer. If the buyer has not deposited enough money, the escrow is short and may not close.

Transfer Documents

A contract is formed between the parties as soon as the instructions are complete and signed by the principals. At the same time the escrow instructions are being prepared, the escrow holder is preparing documents needed for the transfer of ownership from the seller to the buyer.

In most cases, the document of transfer will be a grant deed. As you recall, a grant deed is a statement granting title, prepared according to written instruction from the parties. It must be signed and notarized by the seller and returned to the escrow holder with the signed escrow instructions.

An important job of the escrow holder at this point, when preparing to close, is to verify that the grant deed and the instructions conform exactly and to make sure the grant deed is completed as required by the county recorder.

The assessor's parcel number (AP number) must be identified correctly on the grant deed in order for the county recorder to accept the document for recording.

The documentary transfer tax must be computed by the escrow holder and the information added to the grant deed in the space provided. As you recall, the transfer tax is calculated based on $1.10 per thousand of the purchase price. It is computed on the consideration or purchase price, or on the consideration or purchase price less remaining encumbrances if the buyer is assuming the existing loan.

The grant deed must be prepared exactly to the specifications of the county recorder or it will be rejected and sent back to the escrow holder . Some common mistakes made by escrow holders, requiring a new deed to be drawn, signed by the seller, notarized and submitted for recording, are:

Common Mistakes in Grant Deeds

- Notary seal unclear or incomplete
- Notarization incorrect or notary commissions expired
- Signatures not clear, missing or questionable
- Legal description of property not clearly visible in photocopy attached to deed
- Property in question in another county

Other documents of transfer might be a patent deed if the transfer is between the government and a private individual, a gift deed or a tax deed.

Financing Documents

When a property is sold, usually some form of financing is involved. Commonly the buyer applies for a new loan, and that, along with the buyer's down payment, constitutes the financing.

Other types of financing may be involved in a sale as well. The seller could carry back a note secured by a deed of trust, seller financing, outside secondary financing could be created, an All Inclusive Trust Deed or Contract of Sale could be used to secure the financing.

Types of Financing

- Note and Trust Deed
- Seller Financing
- Outside Secondary Financing
- All Inclusive Trust Deed
- Contract of Sale

Whatever the case, the escrow holder must be certain that all the documents are in order regarding the financing of the sale before the transaction can close.

The most common document used in a sale is a promissory note. The promissory note is the evidence of the debt created by a loan. It indicates the exact terms of the loan, including any special clauses agreed upon by the borrower and the lender. The note is included for the borrowers signature in the loan documents.

Loan documents are usually prepared by the lender and ordered in a timely manner by the escrow holder when the escrow is ready to close. Commonly, the borrower (buyer) brings in the remainder of the down payment and signs the loan documents, including the note and trust deed in the presence of the escrow holder.

The trust deed is the security for the loan and is also included in the loan documents. This document creates a lien on the buyer's new property once it is recorded. The trust deed includes the name of the borrower, the trustee, the beneficiary (lender), the amount owed, along with the legal description of the property. It does not have to be recorded to be valid, but should be recorded to preserve the lender's priority in case of default. In almost all cases, recording is a requirement of the lender.

Upon the close of the escrow the escrow holder sends the trust deed, along with the grant deed and any other documents requiring filing, to the county recorder's office for recording.

Other Documents Needed for Closing

Escrow instructions are reviewed by the escrow holder to determine what documents other than a grant deed and financing instruments are needed for the closing.

The preliminary title report, which most likely was ordered at the start of the escrow, is reviewed by the escrow holder for liens or other complications or disagreement with the escrow instructions. If any surprises show up, such as a lien for delinquent taxes or a trust deed not previously mentioned by the seller, the escrow holder must contact the principals for direction in the matter. Any changes must be approved, in writing, by all parties.

If any lienholders are to be paid off at the close, a demand must be ordered by the escrow holder. A demand is simply a statement of condition of a loan, including the amount owed along with a request for payment in full.

Document Conveyance

Certain documents require review and processing by the title company issuing the policy of title insurance as well as the tax assessor.

Prior to the close, the deed, properly notarized, is sent to the title insurance company whose title officer examines its acceptability for recording. Correct name and vesting for the buyer are verified, as well as the uninterrupted chain of title..

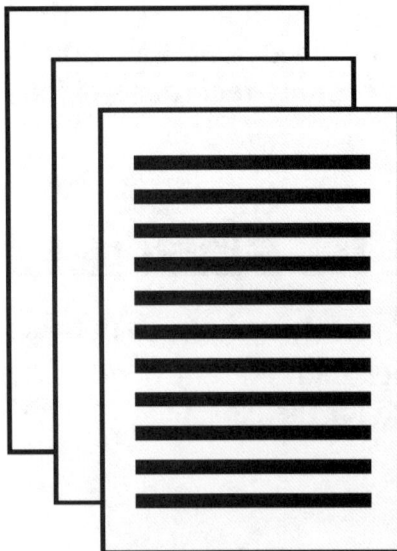

In Northern California, this requires little more than sending the documents to another department within the title company conducting the escrow.

After the notarized trust deed has been signed by the buyer it is sent to the title company for examination and held for further instruction from the escrow holder.

Certain confidential information about the buyer and seller is required by the title company to assure certain identity of the parties. Also, the general index at the title company is checked for judgments against either party that might affect the closing.

A preliminary change of ownership report is required by the tax assessor as a result of the sale. It must be prepared at the closing and sent to the assessor.

Final Closing Review

Most escrow holders will use a check list to make sure all parties have complied with the terms of the instructions. Some will use a checksheet as the escrow progresses, making note as each item is completed. Some of the more important items to be reviewed are emphasized below.

Instructions

Have escrow instructions been signed by all parties and returned to escrow holder? Have all parties with a vested interest in the transaction been included in the instructions?

Supplemental Instructions

Have there been amendments or modifications in the original instructions? Have all changes been reflected in writing and signed by all parties?

Disbursements

Has instruction been given to escrow holder regarding real estate broker commissions, existing loan payoff, loan escrow approval, title fees, pest control work, withholding of funds for work to be performed after the close of escrow, bills to be presented and any other disbursements required by the escrow?

Legal Description

A mistake in the legal description could cause the wrong property to be transferred and incur liability by the parties responsible for the error.

Fire Insurance

Escrow holder must check to make sure the coverage is sufficient and the insurance company approved by the lender.

Correct Names on Documents

The name of the buyer on the preliminary title report must agree with the name of the person taking title to the property. Has the buyer's name and vesting been correctly copied to the appropriate documents?

Sufficient Funds

The escrow file cannot be closed unless there are sufficient funds from the seller and buyer.

Checks Cleared

The buyer or seller should be notified prior to the closing that only cashier's or certified checks may be used to close the escrow. If, in fact, personal checks are used, time must be allowed for them to clear prior to closing.

Taxes

Have all laws relating to tax collection been followed by the escrow holder? Have funds been withheld or exemption filed to comply with the Foreign Investment in Real Property Tax Act (FIRPTA)? If a seller is not a citizen, escrow holder must hold a percentage of the sale proceeds for the IRS in single family residential sales of more than $300,000 and in transactions other than residential of more than $50,000, unless parties qualify for exemption.

Has Form 1099-S been filed by the escrow holder? The IRS requires every seller's name showing the taxidentification number and the amount of consideration passing in the transaction.

Pest Control

Has all required work been completed? If not, has escrow been instructed to withhold funds for work to be completed after the close of escrow?

Closing/Recording

Upon completion of all steps required in the escrow instructions, and after final escrow costs and prorations are computed as of the date of closing, the escrow holder arranges for the buyer to bring in a cashier's check for the amount needed to close the escrow. That would usually include the remainder of the down payment and closing costs.

At that point, depending on the locale of the escrow, the buyer might sign escrow instructions along with loan documents. If escrow instructions have already been signed and returned to escrow, only the promissory note and trust deed still need to be signed by the buyer and notarized.

If the seller has not signed escrow instructions, or the grant deed, he or she must do so before the transaction is complete.

If all is ready, the grant deed, trust deed or deeds and any other documents that need to be recorded are sent to the title company for final examination and recording upon closing.

Upon notification from the escrow holder, funds are sent, by wire, to the title company from the lender with the requirement that the title company insures that the title is clear (all liens have been paid). The title company must have sufficient funds from the lender to pay the loan of record, tax liens, clear up any problems that show up on the preliminary title report and any other necessary payoffs before title insurance is issued.

When the title company has received all the necessary documents and has received the money from the lender, the escrow may close.

Before releasing any funds or recording any documents, the title company pays off all loans, taxes and any recorded liens against the property. The title company is only concerned, however, with paying off matters affecting the title. All other charges relating to the transaction are prorated and/or paid through the sale escrow.

<u>Requirements for Closing</u>

- All contingencies and requirements of escrow met

- Escrow instructions signed by all parties

- Grant deed signed by seller, notarized

- Escrow holder orders loan documents

- Buyer brings in closing funds

- Loan documents signed by borrower and notarized

- Escrow holder sends original signed promissory note and copy of signed trust deed back to lender

- Escrow holder funds to be sent from the lender to the title company

- Title company records original deed, trust deed or deeds in order of priority, as required by the transaction

- Title company pays off all liens and other amounts due to clear the title after a final review of documents

- Any surplus funds are sent to escrow holder for disbursement

After the title company records all documents and pays all existing loans and encumbrances of record, the balance of funds, if there are any, are sent to the escrow holder by the title company for disbursement and proration to the parties according to escrow instructions.

The escrow holder makes all payments, then, to the buyer, seller, real estate agents, termite company, insurance company, construction company and pays another demands on the escrow that may have accumulated.

The escrow holder prepares the closing statements for the buyer and seller, all deposits and other prorations are either debited or credited to the buyer or seller and the seller gets a check for the amount due after selling expenses.

Post Test

The following self test repeats the one you took at the beginning of this chapter. Now take the exam again--since you have read all the material-- and check your knowledge of escrow closing procedures.

True/False

1. Buyers and sellers in Northern California do not sign separate escrow instructions.

2. Unilateral instructions are used in Northern California.

3. Bilateral instructions are used in Southern California.

4. Disclosure clauses limit the closing agent's liability regarding the complication of taxes and conformity to codes and other legal requirements.

5. Both federal and state tax laws are affected by the Foreign Investment in Real Estate Property Tax Act (FIRPTA).

6. Smoke detectors must be installed in all sold residential properties.

7. In most cases, the document of transfer will be a grant deed.

8. Loan documents are usually prepared by the title company.

9. A demand is a statement of loan default.

10. A grant deed does not *have* to be notarized to be recorded.

chapter 10

CONTINGENCIES

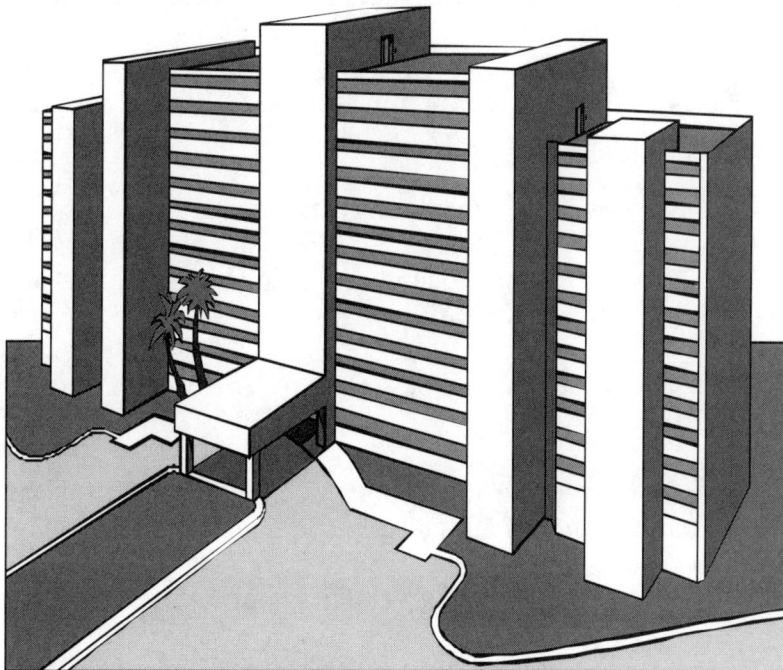

Focus

- **Introduction**
- **Contingencies**
- **Cancellations**
- **Variations on the sale escrow**

Pre-Test

The following is a self test to determine how much you know about contingencies and variations in escrow before reading this chapter. Take it without studying, then read the material presented in the text. At the end of the chapter you will find a repeat of this exam. Test your knowledge by answering the questions again, then check your improvement. (The answers are found at the end of the book.) Good luck.

True/False

1. A contract is binding even though all contingencies have not been met.

2. All principals to an escrow must agree to change contingencies.

3. A deposit receipt is an executory instrument.

4. Time is of the essence means that all parties can take their time in meeting any contingencies.

5. Escrow instructions may be signed by one or all parties to the transaction.

6. Buyers must receive and approve a copy of CC&R's within a certain number of days after receiving them.

7. The sale of the buyer's property may not be a contingency.

8. If parties to an escrow cannot agree about the disposition of funds when an escrow is cancelled, the escrow holder must release them to the seller.

9. Either party may initiate an action for funds, if the escrow is cancelled, through the courts or an arbitrator.

10. A wrap around trust deed is also known as an All Inclusive Trust Deed. (AITD)

Introduction

Escrows are opened, in the majority of cases, with the hopes and expectation that the agreement of the parties will prevail and the transaction will close. That, however, is not always the case. An escrow can fail to close--or "fall-out"--for many reasons. As a matter of fact, it's a miracle so many escrows manage to close considering all the contingencies that must be removed before the contract can be completed.

Along with contingencies, an escrow holder must deal with special types of transactions as well. While most escrows are typical, the escrow holder must be aware of all unusual factors and be able to provide instructions for escrows that vary from those commonly opened by buyers and sellers. We shall see here what an escrow holder can expect when special circumstances prevail. Instructions must reflect any uncommon or unusual meeting of the minds between the parties, as well as the familiar agreements.

Contingencies

A contingency requires the completion of a certain act or the happening of a certain event before a contract is binding. The parties themselves, by imposing contingencies, may cause obstacles to the closing process. In some cases, the contingencies are so abundant that it seems there can never be a meeting of the minds close enough for the transaction to be completed.

As you know, once escrow instructions have been signed by all parties, neither party may unilaterally change the content of the contract. All parties to the escrow may instruct the escrow holder to change the instructions, by mutual agreement.

At the opening of the escrow, the parties already have agreed, in the original deposit receipt, that certain items will be resolved during the process of the escrow. If one party decides that certain contingencies are no longer valid, or wants to add contingencies to the agreement, both must agree.

The problem is, people dislike rethinking decisions. Given another chance to decide, one party may balk at any change. Now we have a situation where someone must renegotiate between the parties or the escrow is at a stalemate. That person is *not* the escrow holder.

The escrow agent is considered a neutral party and is only required to provide written instructions reflecting the mutual thinking of the parties to the escrow. Joining the parties in their controversies or settling them is not part of the job. Keeping the escrow moving along and following the written instructions *is* the job, however.

No matter how carefully everyone tries to escape the possibility of new contingencies being created, it happens more times than not. One of the benefits to the deposit receipt commonly used is that the document includes just about every item buyers and sellers need to agree on at the start of the transaction. Even so, parties to any escrow must confirm or deny their acceptance of contingency removals, according to their prior agreement.

The unilateral instructions used in northern California also offer a benefit: Between the time escrow instructions are drawn and the end of the escrow process, changes have been arranged by the broker as amendments to the original deposit receipt. The escrow holder is presented with the finished agreement in writing.

In the southern part of the state, however, many times amendment after amendment to the escrow instruction is drawn to keep up with the sometimes demanding progression of the escrow. At the end, sometimes the demand overwhelms the ability of the parties to come to a decision and the escrow falls-out.

In reality, then, the deposit receipt is nothing more than an executory contract, with the parties waiting in suspense for the outcome of each contingency removal during the escrow period.

As is stated in the deposit receipt, time is of the essence, especially regarding contingencies. This means each contingency must be met in a timely manner exactly as described in the contract. If the contingency is not accepted or rejected in the manner specified, within the stated restriction of time, the contract is voidable.

There are certain parts of the deposit receipt that contain matters which must be resolved during the escrow and upon which the transaction depends. Escrow instructions will reflect these items also. If all contingencies are not met in a timely manner, the escrow is voidable by the injured party. In other words, the party waiting for satisfaction from the contingency being met has the right to cancel the escrow if the time period is not observed. Once again, the escrow holder must receive signed cancellation orders from all parties for the escrow to be terminated.

Financing

Financing must be obtained, obviously, before the buyer can complete the sale. Terms and conditions of financing are described in the deposit receipt as well as a time period for the buyer and property to qualify for any loans.The escrow also is contingent on agreements about existing and/or seller financing being executed.

Escrow Instructions

Escrow instructions must be signed within the time frame specified in the original deposit receipt.

Condominium

Buyer must receive and approve a copy of CC&R's as well as any pertinent information on the condition of the homeowners association within a certain number of days after receiving them.

Buyer's Investigation of Property Condition

Buyer has the right to inspect and approve of the property within a specified time frame. Seller must be given copies of all reports from inspections.

The buyer is advised to investigate the condition and suitability of all aspects of the property, as well as all matters affecting its value, including the following items:

- Built-in appliances, structural, foundation, roof, plumbing, heating, air conditioning, electrical, mechanical, security, pool/spa systems and components and any personal property included in the sale

- Square footage, room dimensions, lot size and age of improvements to the property

- Property lines and boundaries

- Sewer, septic and well systems and components (Property may not be connected to sewer, and applicable fees may not have been paid. Septic tank may need to be pumped and leach field may need to be inspected.)

- Limitations, restrictions and requirements regarding property use, future development, zoning, building, size, government permits and inspections

- Water and utility availability and use restrictions

- Potential environmental hazards including asbestos, formaldehyde, radon gas, lead-based paint or other lead contamination, fuel or chemical storage tanks, contaminated soil or water

- Geologic/seismic conditions, soil and terrain stability, suitability and drainage

- Neighborhood or property conditions including schools; proximity and adequacy of law enforcement;

proximity to commercial, industrial or agricultural activities; crime statistics; fire protection; other government services; existing and proposed transportation; construction and development; airport noise, noise or odor from any source; other nuisances, hazards or circumstances; and any conditions or influences of significance to certain cultures and/or religions.

Transfer Disclosure Statement

Buyer must approve the TDS (Transfer Disclosure Statement) which has been completed by the seller within three days after delivery. All parties, including the seller, buyer, seller's agent and buyer's agent, must sign the disclosure. Buyer may terminate the agreement if the TDS is not received in a timely manner.

Property Disclosures

When applicable to the property and required by law, the seller shall provide to the buyer, at the seller's expense, the following disclosures and information. The buyer shall then, within the time specified, investigate the disclosures and provide notice of disapproval (Southern California) or written notice of approval (Northern California).

- Geologic/Seismic Hazard Zones Disclosure

- Special Flood Hazard Areas Disclosure

- State Fire Responsibility Areas Disclosure

- Mello-Roos Disclosure

- Earthquake Safety Disclosure

- Smoke Detector Disclosure

- Environmental Hazards Booklet

- Lead Based Paint Disclosure

Governmental Compliance

Seller shall disclose to buyer any improvements, additions, alterations or repairs made without the required permits, final inspections or government approval (local or state). Buyer shall, within the time specified, either disapprove or approve in writing, depending on the custom and requirement of the escrow.

Pest Control

Buyer has the right to disapprove or approve the pest control report within a stated number of days after receiving it.

Sale of Buyer's Property

The escrow may be canceled if the contingency regarding the sale of the buyer's property is not removed in a timely and correct manner. Depending on the agreement between the buyer and seller, several variations on this contingency may be included in the instructions. Seller can continue to market the property or not, by agreement with the buyer. If a new buyer is found, buyer in this escrow has an agreed- upon time period to remove this contingency or the escrow is terminated.

Buyer can continue to market his or her property for a specified time period. If that time period comes and goes, the escrow may be terminated if buyer does not remove the contingency for the sale of his or her property.

Cancellation of Prior Sale/Back-up Offer

The escrow may be contingent on the cancellation of one entered into by the seller, prior to the current buyer's offer. This escrow is contingent on the successful cancellation of the earlier escrow.

Court Confirmation

Court confirmation may be required in a probate, conservatorship, guardianship, receivership, bankruptcy or other proceeding. Buyer understands that the property may continue to be marketed by a broker or others, and that others may represent different competitive bidders

prior to and at the court confirmation. If court confirmation is not obtained by the date shown in the instructions, buyer may cancel this agreement by giving written notice of cancellation to seller.

305

Cancellations

As we have seen, an escrow may be canceled with the mutual consent of all parties. The dissolution of the escrow must be concerned with the mutuality of everyone involved as well as the rights of third parties who are affected by the termination of the escrow.

Often, the parties cannot come to a mutual agreement about cancellation and the disposal of funds on deposit with the escrow holder or fees to be paid to the escrow holder. There are three options for funds being held by the escrow holder:

1. The funds may remain on deposit for three years, after which time they escheat to the state if there are no valid claims.

2. A court may determine the rightful owner of funds on deposit with the escrow holder. Either party may initiate an action for the funds through the court system or an arbitrator.

3. The parties can come to an agreement about the funds and direct escrow to disburse them accordingly.

Variations On the Sale Escrow

As you know, an escrow holder is obligated to produce and follow a set of escrow instructions that exactly mirrors the agreement of the parties in the deposit receipt.

The majority of sale escrows will be either a cash sale, with the buyer to qualify for a new loan sale, or seller financed.

Occasionally, however, certain situations arise where buyer and seller have agreed to a variation on commonly used financing to achieve the desired result.

All Inclusive Deed of Trust

Also known as an all-inclusive trust deed (AITD), or a wrap-around trust deed, this type of loan wraps an existing trust deed with a new trust deed, and the borrower makes one payment for both. In other words, the new trust deed (the AITD) includes the present encumbrances, such as first, second, third or more trust deeds, plus the amount to be financed by the seller.

The AITD is subordinate to existing encumbrances because the AITD is created at a later date. This means any existing encumbrances have priority over the AITD, even though they are included, or wrapped, by the new all-inclusive trust deed. At the close of escrow the buyer receives title to the property.

Typically an AITD is used in a transaction between buyer and seller to make the financing attractive to the buyer and beneficial to the seller as well. Instead of the buyer assuming an existing loan and the seller carrying back a second trust deed, the AITD can accomplish the same purpose with greater benefit to both parties in some instances.

AITD's are popular when interest rates are high and the underlying loans are not adjustable or have a low interest rate. When interest rates are low and a buyer can obtain a loan from an institution, it does not make sense to wrap an underlying loan, therefore paying a higher rate of interest to the seller than if an outside loan were obtained.

Benefits of an All Inclusive Trust Deed

Seller:
- Usually gets full-price offer
- Higher interest rate on amount carried

Buyer:
- Low down payment
- No qualifying for a loan or payment of loan fees

The AITD does not disturb the existing loan. The seller, as the new lender, keeps making the payments while giving a new increased loan at a higher rate of interest to the borrower. The amount of the AITD includes the unpaid principal balance of the existing (underlying) loan, plus the amount of the new loan being made by the seller. The borrower makes payment on the new larger loan to the seller, who in turn makes payment to the holder of the existing underlying loan. The new loan "wraps around" the existing loan.

A seller usually will carry back a wrap-around trust deed at a higher rate of interest than the underlying trust deed, thereby increasing the yield. The seller continues to pay off the original trust deed from the payments on the wrap-around, while keeping the difference. This type of financing works best when the underlying interest rate is low, and the seller can then charge a higher rate on the wrapped loan.

A wrap-around loan isn't for everyone. If a seller needs to cash out, it won't work. Also, most loans contain a due-on-sale clause, and cannot be wrapped without the lender's knowledge and approval. Depending on the buyer's and seller's motivation, sometimes an AITD will be created, with full knowledge of the risk. This is how the term "creative financing" came into being.

Generally, these payments are collected by a professional collection company and sent on to the appropriate parties. This assures the maker (borrower) of the AITD that all underlying payments are being forwarded and are kept current by a neutral party.

In some instances, a "rider" containing additional agreements between a buyer and seller will be attached to an all inclusive deed of trust.

Additions to an AITD

The AITD may be placed on contract collection with a professional collection company authorized to do business. Money is collected and disbursed for current installments, payments of taxes and insurance if necessary. Any amount then remaining is disbursed to the holder of the note secured by the AITD.

If the trustor (borrower) defaults, beneficiary obligations (lender) will be suspended until the default is cured. If the trustor is delinquent in making any payments due under the note, and the beneficiary incurs any penalties or other expenses on account of the underlying obligations during the period of trustor delinquency, the amount of any penalties and expenses will be added to the amount of the note and will be payable by the trustor with the next payment due under the note.

In the event of foreclosure of the all inclusive deed of trust, the beneficiary agrees that he or she will, at the trustee's sale, bid an amount representing that due under the AITD, less the total balance due on the underlying notes, plus any advances or other disbursements which the beneficiary is allowed by law to include in the bid.

When the note secured by the AITD becomes due or the trustor requests a demand for payoff of the note, the main amount payable to the beneficiary will be reduced by the unpaid balances of the underlying obligations.

If any installment payment under the note secured by the AITD is not paid within 15 days after the due date, a late charge may be incurred by the trustor and be due and payable upon the beneficiary's demand.

Adequate funds for the payment of taxes and fire insurance will be deposited and held by the collection account holder. Monthly, an amount equal to one-twelfth of the annual tax amount and one-twelfth the amount of the annual fire insurance billing will be deposited by the trustor. Taxes and insurance reserves have been provided by the trustor to the beneficiary for the initial reserve fund.

If the trustor makes any additional payments or added increments beyond the required monthly amount, the beneficiary, upon a request by the trustor in writing, will forward any extra funds to the holders of the underlying notes for application to the unpaid principal balances.

Wrap-Around Loans (AITD's)

- Secured by a trust deed that "wraps," or includes existing financing plus the amount to be financed by the seller

---

Contract of Sale

The contract of sale is the financing instrument with many names. It may be called an installment sales contract, a contract of sale, an agreement of sale, a conditional sales contract or a land contract.

In this type of agreement, the seller retains legal ownership of the property until the buyer has made the last payment, much like buying a car. This is a contract between a buyer and seller, and can be used during times when usual financing is difficult.

The buyer, or vendee, holds what is known as equitable title. The vendee may enjoy possession and use of the property even though legal title is held by the seller, or vendor. Like the holder of an AITD, the vendor pays off the original financing while receiving payments from the vendee on the contract of sale. Indeed, a contract of sale and an AITD are very similar. The most important distinction is that with the AITD--title passes to the buyer; under a contract of sale--title stays with the seller until the contract is paid off.

Difference Between AITD and Contract of Sale

- AITD: buyer gets title to property

- Contract of Sale: seller keeps title until loan is paid off

---

Contracts of sale are not commonly used except in special circumstances and under the guidance of an attorney, who will draw the document. They were heavily used in the 80s, but fell out of favor because of the risk involved and the difficulty of foreclosure in many cases.

Deed in Lieu of Foreclosure

Normally, when a trustor (borrower) defaults on a loan, the property in question is sold at a trustee's sale or title is conveyed to the beneficiary as a result of the foreclosure. The borrower has a ding on his or her credit as a result of the default and subsequent foreclosure and the lender must pick up any costs accrued by the sale.

Occasionally, however, the lender is willing to forgo the trustee's sale and allow the borrower to deed the property back to them voluntarily. This is most likely to happen if the lender is the former owner. The unpaid debt is then canceled, removing the lien against the property and in the process, saves the borrower's credit. If the beneficiary is an institutional lender, the property would be accepted and become one more unloved and difficult REO (Real Estate Owned) property needing a new owner. This is known as a "deed in lieu of foreclosure."

The escrow holder considers the "deed in lieu" as the principal instrument of conveyance in a transaction where this is the agreement between the parties. The consideration in this sale escrow is the satisfaction of the debt to the lender in return for a deed from the borrower, who executes a grant deed in favor of the beneficiary.

In order to guarantee the insurability of the deed, a disclaimer is added to the deed or a separate affidavit is prepared for the trustor to sign.

The note holder should always get a policy of title insurance with a deed in lieu of foreclosure so that any liens or judgments against the former owner (party in default) will not attach to the note holder.

"Subject to" Sale

A buyer may also purchase a property "subject to" the existing loan. The original borrower remains responsible for the loan, even though the buyer takes title and makes the payments. In this case, also, the property remains the security for the loan. In the case of default, it is sold and the proceeds go to the lender, with no recourse to the original buyer other than the foreclosure going against the buyer's credit.

However, a deficiency judgment is allowed if the loan was not a purchase money loan, or one made specifically upon purchase of the property. If the loan was a hard money loan, or a loan made to get cash, the original borrower could be held personally liable until the loan is paid off.

> *Roberto bought his home 20 years ago, and refinanced it after 10 years for money to add on a room. His first deed of trust was a purchase money loan in the amount of $10,000, and the second loan was a hard money loan, secured by the property.*
>
> *Roberto sold the property to Vicki, who bought the property "subject to" his two loans. When she defaulted on the loans and the property went into foreclosure, Roberto was responsible for the second loan, even though he no longer owned the property.*
>
> *What Roberto should have done, in this case, was to ask the lender, upon sale of the property, for a substitution of liability and agreement to pay (novation), relieving himself of any liability.*

Many times a property will be sold "subject to" existing loans because there is a due-on-sale clause in the present note. It may be the buyer's desire to take over the loan without triggering the due-on-sale clause.

When an escrow holder deals with an existing institutional lender, there is rarely any contact with the lender. Escrow instructions are written to include the appropriate exculpatory language relative to the transfer without compliance with normal lender requirements such as the buyer qualifying for the loan or paying loan fees.

> *"Escrow holder is authorized and instructed not to order a beneficiary statement on existing trust deed of record and both buyer and seller herein release San Clemente Escrow, as escrow holder, from any liability in any manner or way in connection herewith. Seller shall furnish escrow holder with an offset statement and a copy of promissory note setting forth the exact unpaid balance, terms and conditions of said loan for buyer's approval prior to close of escrow. Seller herein shall keep all payments current during the escrow period. In the event offset statement reflects the balance to be more or less than the amount stated herein, escrow holder is instructed to adjust any differences in buyer's cash downpayment.*
>
> *Buyer herein acknowledges that the within loan of record does contain a "due on sale" clause in the note which may cause an acceleration of maturity upon transfer of title. Regardless of this matter, escrow holder is authorized and instructed to close this escrow at the earliest possible date. All parties hold San Clemente Escrow, as escrow holder, from any liability in any manner or way in connection herewith."*

Loan Assumption Sale

When a property is sold, a buyer may assume the existing oan. Usually with the approval of the lender, the

315

buyer takes over primary liability for the loan, with the original borrower secondarily liable if there is a default.

What this means is that even though the original borrower is secondarily responsible, according to the loan assumption agreement, no actual repayment of the loan may be required of that person. If the new owner defaults, the property is foreclosed, and no deficiency judgment is allowed beyond the amount received at the trustee's sale, even though the original borrower's credit is affected by the foreclosure.

An assumption is much like an escrow where the buyer is getting a new loan, as far as the escrow holder is concerned. The escrow is contingent on the buyer qualifying with the existing lender. The buyer completes a loan package and escrow submits it to the lender with a request for a beneficiary statement. When the lender approves, they send the escrow holder a set of assumption documents for the buyer to sign and a beneficiary statement for escrow to follow for closing.

Post Test

The following self test repeats the one you took at the beginning of this chapter. Now take the exam again--since you have read all the material-- and check your knowledge of escrow closing procedures.

True/False

1. A contract is binding even though all contingencies have not been met.

2. All principals to an escrow must agree to change contingencies.

3. A deposit receipt is an executory instrument.

4. Time is of the essence means that all parties can take their time in meeting any contingencies.

5. Escrow instructions may be signed by one or all parties to the transaction.

6. Buyers must receive and approve a copy of CC&R's within a certain number of days after receiving them.

7. The sale of the buyer's property may not be a contingency.

8. If parties to an escrow cannot agree about the disposition of funds when an escrow is cancelled, the escrow holder must release them to the seller.

9. Either party may initiate an action for funds, if the escrow is cancelled, through the courts or an arbitrator.

10. A wrap around trust deed is also known as an All Inclusive Trust Deed. (AITD)

TITLE INSURANCE

Focus

- **Introduction**
- **What is title insurance?**
- **History of title insurance**
- **Types of policies**
- **Policy of title insurance**

Pre-Test

The following is a self test to determine how much you know about title insurance before reading this chapter. Take it without studying, then read the material presented in the text. At the end of the chapter you will find a repeat of this exam. Test your knowledge by answering the questions again, then check your improvement. (The answers are found at the end of the book.) Good luck.

True/False

1. Title insurance is a contract to protect against losses arising through defects in title to real estate.

2. The foundation of real property ownership is title.

3. Title officers today are called conveyancers.

4. Standard coverage insures against matters not of record.

5. A CLTA policy of title insurance is designed primarily for the lender.

6. An extended policy of title insurance protects only against matters of record.

7. A basic policy of title insurance may be expanded or modified by special endorsements.

8. Title insurance covers defects known by the parties prior to the transfer, even though not disclosed.

9. The preliminary title report contains all encumbrances against the property in question.

10. If an untrue statement about the quality of the title to a property is made, the insurance is not valid.

Introduction

The business of title insurance has grown out of increased real estate activity together with the need to process the sale of real property quickly, safely and effectively. Early guarantees of the accuracy of title started with abstractors who established a chain of title by checking land records from the old Spanish and Mexican land grants, along with any records that had been kept from land sales to early settlers.

With the growth of the real estate industry, consumers began making demands for a guarantee of the accuracy of these early searches. Buyers and sellers wanted the title searchers to take responsibility for their comprehensive conclusions about all matters of record. Meeting this demand evolved into the title industry we know today.

What Is Title Insurance?

Title insurance is a contract to protect against losses arising through defects in title to real estate. In other words, the insurer guarantees the title to be free of liens or other encumbrances that would cause title to be unclear or clouded for the new owner. Title insurance is the application of insurance principles to hazards inherent in real estate titles.

Title, as you know, is the foundation of property ownership. It means that the owner has a legal right to possess that property and to use it within the restrictions imposed by authorities or limitations on its use.

No other property has a useful life that compares with the life of land. Owners die, new ones succeed, but land goes on forever. Owners of goods may change their locations at will, but land is immovable. Being both permanent and immovable, it lends itself to the absorption of innumerable rights. Over the ages, this so impressed lawyers and jurists that they formed a separate body of laws for land. These laws, creating many types of rights in land, are so numerous and so complex it is impossible for there to be a mathematical certainty of ownership.

The basic function of a title insurance company is to take positive steps that will minimize the risk that a policy holder will suffer any loss or be subject to any adverse claim, as well as to safeguard his or her ownership of or claim in the property.

The primary purpose of title insurance is to eliminate risks and prevent losses caused by defects in title arising out of events that have happened in the past.

A title defect is anything in the entire history of ownership of a piece of real estate which may encumber the owner's right to the "peaceful enjoyment" of the property or which may cause the owner to lose any portion of the property.

There are many title risks that cannot be revealed by even the most thorough search. Some examples of these risks:

Title Risks

- Mistakes in interpretation of wills or other legal documents
- Impersonation of the real owner
- Forged deeds or reconveyances
- Instruments executed under a fabricated or an expired power of attorney
- Deed delivered after the death of the grantor or grantee or without the consent of the grantor
- Undisclosed or missing heirs
- Wills not probated
- Deeds signed by persons of unsound mind, by minors, or by persons supposedly single but actually married
- Birth or adoption of children after the date of a will
- Mistakes in recording of legal documents
- Want of jurisdiction over persons in judicial proceedings affecting the title
- Errors in indexing of public records
- Falsification of records
- Confusion arising from similarity of names
- Title passing through a foreclosure sale where compliance of the requirements of the applicable foreclosure statutes have not been strictly met

Title insurance, however, is not always used in property transfers. It is not required by law and is usually a matter of agreement between the buyer and seller. A lender's policy usually is required by a lender as a requisite for obtaining new financing.

An abstract of title is one way to research the title to a property and is good as far as it goes. But an abstract is simply a condensed version of the recorded documents affecting title to the property. The limitations on the liability of an abstracter who issues an abstract are the same as those of an attorney who issues an opinion of title.

Sometimes an abstract of title is considered sufficient by the buyer or an attorney will offer an opinion or certificate of title which a purchaser might accept as sufficient protection. There are, however, many title defects which even the most careful title examination will not uncover. Then, chance of recovery in the event of a title loss in this case depends entirely upon the solvency of the attorney examining the title.

The attorney's liability is limited to errors and oversights that would not be made by a diligent attorney. The attorney is not liable for loss caused by hidden defects.

Every attorney knows that there are hazards in real estate title which cannot possibly be discovered with even a diligent search of the public records. For instance, the attorney cannot be sure:

- That the marital rights of all previous owners have been properly relinquished
- That all mortgages, judgments and other liens affecting the property have been properly indexed in the record room
- That all signatures on all recorded documents are genuine
- That no unknown heir of a former owner can appear to assert his or her claim

These are but a few of the matters that can defeat real estate titles. Among others are such circumstances as fraud, duress, insanity or false impersonations.

An attorney is not liable if the buyer should suffer loss because of any of the "hidden defects" in a real estate title. Liability extends only to losses caused by oversights or carelessness in the attorney's work. Then, too, liability is limited by the attorney's ability to pay, as well as by his or her life span.

Title insurance is usually required by a lender before funding a new loan. While the title insurance coverage afforded the lender and owner is somewhat the same, it is also substantially different in important areas. Because of the diminishing debt of the mortgage and the increasing equity of the owner as payments are made, it is apparent that there could be a complete title failure with the lender suffering no loss because of title insurance coverage and the owner suffering substantial loss because he or she had no title insurance.

Many buyers think that the purchase contract they signed makes the sale subject to their getting clear title. While that generally is true, there are cases where the seller cannot be absolutely certain the title is good. The seller knows about the title during his or her property ownership, but what about previous owners? Even a perfect looking title can be seriously unsound because of hidden defects. If anything would happen to defeat the title after escrow has closed

and the buyer is the new owner, the chance of recovery of damages would depend upon finding and suing the seller, winning the suit and, finally, on whether or not the seller was able to pay the judgment. In any event, the attorney's fees and expenses would be the buyer's loss.

Title insurance services are designed to give home owners, lenders and others with interests in real estate the maximum degree of protection from adverse title claims or risks. The financial assurance offered by a title insurance policy--both in satisfying any valid claims against the title as insured and in defraying the expenses of defending against any attacks on the insured title--is, of course, a key aspect of this title protection.

The risk elimination aspects of the title search and examination, performed as a prerequisite to the issuance of a title insurance policy, are equally important, however, since they ensure that all parties have a clear understanding of their interests *before* the transaction is consummated. The parties are enabled, then, to resolve potential title claims before they result in losses.

History of Title Insurance

The need for title insurance arose historically from the fact that traditional methods of conveying real property did not provide adequate safety to the parties involved. Until a century ago, transferring title to real property was handled primarily by conveyancers, who were responsible for all aspects of the transaction. The conveyancer conducted a title search to determine the ownership rights of the seller and any other rights, interest, liens or encumbrances that might exist with respect to the property, and, based on that search, provided a signed abstract (or description) of the status of the title.

Although the conveyancer generally was not a lawyer, he or she was recognized as an authority on real estate law. The origin of title insurance is directly traceable to the limited protection that the work of such a conveyancer provided the buyer of real property.

In 1868, the famous lawsuit of Watson v. Muirhead was filed in Pennsylvania. In that case, Muirhead, a conveyancer, had searched and abstracted a title for Watson, the buyer of a parcel of real estate. In good faith and after consulting an attorney, Muirhead chose to ignore certain recorded judgments and to report the title was good and unencumbered.

On the basis of Muirhead's abstract, Watson went ahead with the purchase, but subsequently was presented with, and required to satisfy, the liens that Muirhead had concluded were not impairments of title. Watson sued Muirhead to recover his losses, but the Pennsylvania

Supreme Court ruled that there was no negligence on the conveyancer's part and dismissed the case. Watson, an innocent buyer who had suffered financial damages because of the encumbrances on his title, had no recourse.

The decision in <u>Watson</u> v. <u>Muirhead</u> showed clearly that the existing conveyancing system could not provide total assurance to purchasers of real property that they would be safe and secure in their ownership. As a result of that decision the Pennsylvania legislature shortly thereafter passed an act "to provide for the incorporation and regulation of title insurance companies." On March 28, 1876, the first land title insurance company, The Real Estate Title Insurance Company, was founded in Philadelphia. During the next few years title insurance companies were organized in other cities throughout the country, including New York, Chicago, Minneapolis, San Francisco and Los Angeles.

The nature and complexity of real estate titles and transfers have increased immeasurably since that time (as a result, in part, of the greater amount of interest and rights that are now recognized in real property). Services provided by title insurance companies also have expanded and adapted to the changing needs of our society. However, the same goals are still sought by title insurance companies today.

Types of Policies

Title requirements vary between transactions, depending on the complexity of the sale, therefore requiring the escrow holder to have a complete understanding of title insurance and the specific coverage that is available with each kind of policy.

In matching the title insurance coverage to the transaction, the elements to be considered are:

- Type of coverage--standard coverage, extended coverage, coverage modified by special endorsements

- Type of estate--fee, leasehold, equitable interest

- Parties insured--owner, lender, lessee, vendee, vendor

Standard Coverage

A Standard Coverage or CLTA (California Land Title Association) policy of title insurance is designed especially for the home buyer. It may be used, however, to insure a lender as well.

The title company insures the buyer, as of the date of the policy, against loss or damage not exceeding the amount of insurance stated in the policy, and any costs, attorneys' fees, and expenses which the title company may be obligated to pay in satisfying the buyer in case of a loss.

The Standard Coverage Policy is limited because it will insure against only those matters which are disclosed in public records and will not cover any defects which are concealed from the title company. Off-record items such as an encroachment, an unrecorded easement, a discrepancy in boundary lines or an interest of parties in possession of the property, which are discovered only by a survey or inspection of the property, are not covered by a CLTA Standard Policy.

The CLTA policy, when issued to insure a lender, provides coverage against a loss suffered because of an invalid trust deed, if the trust deed proved to be in a lessor position than shown or if an assignment in the policy was shown to be invalid.

A CLTA policy may be issued as follows:

- As an owner's policy
- As a lender's policy (either private or institutional)
- As a joint protection policy for both the owner and lender (commonly used when the seller acts as the lender and carries back a trust deed)

If an insured wants coverage against items not included in the standard policy, endorsements may be added to the Standard Coverage policy. Most title companies add an inflation endorsement, at no charge, which requires them, in case of a claim against the title, to cover the appreciated or inflated value of the property rather than the original sales price. Another endorsement usually available is the homeowner's endorsement. This coverage is issued only on owner occupied dwellings with four or less units. It insures against limited off record risks involving certain matters related to access, encroachments, restrictions, zoning, taxes and mechanics' liens.

While a standard title policy offers only limited coverage of off-record matters, an extended policy offers comprehensive protection for a much broader coverage. A standard policy is usually purchased by buyers of single family residences and is normally adequate. In some cases, however, it may not be enough. Some common extensions of standard coverage might be:

- Expanded encroachment coverage
- Expanded access to a public street coverage
- Unrecorded taxes or assessments--limited coverage
- Unrecorded mechanics' liens
- Violation of covenants, conditions and restrictions
- Violation of zoning ordinances
- Damage from a holder of mineral rights searching for or removing minerals from the insured property
- An inflation endorsement which can increase policy coverage up to 150% of the original policy amount

---

Standard Coverage Policy (CLTA)

Risks normally insured against:
- Most matters revealed by public records
- Some off-record risks, such as forgery or incompetence

Risks not normally insured against:
- Matters not disclosed by public records
- Environmental laws, zoning, and laws regarding the use of the property
-
- Defects known to the insured before the property was purchased and not revealed to the title company before the sale

---

Extended Coverage

While a standard title policy offers only limited coverage of off-record matters, an extended policy offers comprehensive protection for much broader coverage.

Extended Coverage Policy (ALTA)

- Matters disclosed by a physical inspection of the property
- Off-record matters disclosed by asking the occupants of the premises
- Matters disclosed by a current survey
- Violations of recorded covenants, conditions and restrictions
- Encroachments of improvements onto existing easements
- Any unrecorded easement rights disclosed by inspection
- The right of other parties, possessory or otherwise
- Unrecorded leases of tenants occupying the land
- Unrecorded assessments and inspection of tax office records
- Unrecorded claims resulting from work performed or materials supplied for improvement of the property

---

In the 1920s the American Title Association, now called the American Land Title Association (ALTA), and lenders from the East formed a partnership which resulted in the ALTA lender's policy of title insurance being offered. The extended coverage, provided at a higher price than standard coverage, protects against many risks which are not a matter of record. A lender's title requirements include any problems that affect the value of the loan security. Today, in almost all transactions where there is a new institutional lender, an ALTA extended coverage policy is required. Some of the risks covered by an ALTA extended coverage lender's policy are listed below.

Extended coverage surveys may reveal information not shown on record, An ordinary survey confirms matters of record and shows where improvements are with regard to lot lines.

An Extended Coverage Survey May Show:

- Shortages or overages in lot dimensions
- Natural watercourses crossing the property
- Unrecorded easements above or below the surface of the property
- Encroachments of existing improvements from adjoining property onto the property to be insured
- Anything existing on the surface or subsurface of the land from which a title claim may arise from other than the owner
- Claims to the title that are not a matter of record by asking the current owner about the occupancy of the land or whether there has been any work done recently on the property

---

Special Endorsements

A basic policy of title insurance may be expanded or modified by special endorsements. Adjustments of coverage requirements are usually made because the parties require special coverage, of the amount of consideration, the type of property being insured, the complexity of the transaction or any title exceptions or encumbrances affecting the property.

Guarantees

Specific limited-use coverages for special situations are called guarantees in the title insurance industry. They may include:

- Subdivision guarantee--When only a *preliminary* subdivision report has been filed with the Real Estate Commissioner on the property in question, this special coverage guarantees a final report will be filed.

- Chain of title guarantee--A chain of title is researched in every transaction and a preliminary title report is produced prior to issuing the policy of title insurance. Occasionally, a chain of title guarantee is required, however. As you know, the preliminary title report contains the legal description of the property to be insured, title vesting and all encumbrances against the property. The encumbrances show what exceptions will be in the title insurance policy desired and will allow the insured to choose what exceptions he or she can live with and which ones will have to be removed before the close of escrow.

No Liability

Title insurance does not cover any defect that was known by the parties prior to the transfer. So, if anyone, such as the real estate broker, escrow agent or seller, lies or knows of an untrue statement that would affect the quality of the title, the insurance is not valid. The title company must prove that the defect was known and mis-stated and is then not liable.

Policy of Title Insurance

LAWYERS TITLE COMPANY
Policy No._____

Subject to the Exclusions from Coverage, the exceptions contained in schedule B and the conditions and stipulations hereof, Lawyers Title Company, a California Corporation, herein called the Company, insures the insured, as of Date of Policy shown in Schedule A, against loss or damage, not exceeding the amount of insurance stated in Schedule A, and costs, attorneys' fee and expenses which the Company may become obligated to pay hereunder, sustained or incurred by said insured by reason of:

1. Title to the estate or interest described in Schedule A being vested other than as stated therein;

2. Any defect in or lien or encumbrance on such title;

3. Unmarketability of such title;

4. Any lack of the ordinary right of any abutting owner for access to at least one physically open street or highway if the land, in fact, abuts upon one or more such street or highway; and in addition, as to an insured lender only:

5. Invalidity of the lien of the insured mortgage upon said estate or interest except to the extent that such invalidity, or claim thereof, arises out of the transaction evidenced by the insured mortgage and is based upon

a. usury, or

b. any consumer credit protection or truth in lending law;

6. Priority of any lien or encumbrance over the lien of the insured mortgage, said mortgage being shown in Schedule B in the order of its priority; or

7. Invalidity of any assignment of the insured mortgage, provided such assignment is shown in Schedule B

IN WITNESS WHEREOF, LAWYERS TITLE COMPANY has caused its corporate name and seal to be hereunto affixed by its duly authorizes officers as of the date shown in Schedule A.

Lawyers Commonwealth Title Company

By:_____
President

Attest:_____

SCOTT SUGAR
UNITED AMERICAN MORTGAGE
2030 MAIN STREET, #120
IRVINE, CALIF. 92714

Dated as of March 6, 1996, at 7:30 AM

In response to the above referenced application for a policy of title insurance ,

CHICAGO TITLE COMPANY

hereby reports that is prepared to issue, or cause to be issued, as of the date hereof, a Policy or Policies of Title Insurance describing the land and the estate or interest therein hereinafter set forth, insuring against loss which may be sustained by reason of any defect, lien or encumbrance not shown or referred to as an Exception in Schedule B or not excluded from coverage pursuant to the printed Schedules, Conditions and Stipulations of said Policy forms.

The printed Exceptions and Exclusions from the coverage of said Policy or Policies are set forth in Exhibit A attached list. Copies of the Policy forms should be read. They are available from the office which issued the report.

Please read the exceptions shown or referred to in Schedule B and the exceptions and exclusions set forth in Exhibit A of this report carefully. The exceptions and exclusions are meant to provide you with notice of matters which are not covered under the terms of the title insurance policy and should be carefully considered.

It is important to note that this preliminary report is not a written representation as to the condition of title and may not list all liens, defects, and encumbrances affecting title to the land.

THIS REPORT (AND ANY SUPPLEMENTS OR AMENDMENTS HERETO) IS ISSUED SOLELY FOR THE PURPOSE OF FACILITATING THE ISSUANCE OF A POLICY OF TITLE INSURANCE AND NO LIABILITY IS ASSUMED HEREBY. IF IT IS DESIRED .THAT LIABILITY BE ASSUMED PRIOR TO THE ISSUANCE OF A POLICY OF TITLE INSURANCE, A BINDER OR COMMITMENT SHOULD BE REQUESTED.

This form of policy of title insurance contemplated by this report is:
A.L.T.A. RESIDENTIAL TITLE INSURANCE POLICY
AMERICAN LAND TITLE ASSOCIATION LOAN EXTENDED COVERAGE POLICY

_____
Title Officer

SAN CLEMENTE ESCROW
34932 CALLE DEL SOL, #B
CAPISTRANO BEACH, CALIF. 92624

Dated as of March 6, 1996, at 7:30 AM

In response to the above referenced application for a policy of title insurance,

CHICAGO TITLE COMPANY

hereby reports that it is prepared to issue, or cause to be issued, as of the date hereof, a Policy or Policies of Title Insurance describing the land and the estate or interest therein hereinafter set forth, insuring against loss which may be sustained by reason of any defect, lien or encumbrance not shown or referred to as an Exception in Schedule B or not excluded from coverage pursuant to the printed Schedules, Conditions and Stipulations of said Policy forms.

The printed Exceptions and Exclusions from the coverage of said Policy or Policies are set forth in Exhibit A attached list. Copies of the Policy forms should be read. They are available from the office which issued the report.

Please read the exceptions sworn or referred to in Schedule B and the exceptions and exclusions set forth in Exhibit A of this report carefully. The exceptions and exclusions are meant to provide you with notice of matters which are not covered under the terms of the title insurance policy and should be carefully considered.

It is important to note that this preliminary report is not a written representation as to the condition of title and may not list all liens, defects, and encumbrances affecting title to the land.

THIS REPORT (AND ANY SUPPLEMENTS OR AMENDMENTS HERETO) IS ISSUED SOLELY FOR THE PURPOSE OF FACILITATING THE ISSUANCE OF A POLICY OF TITLE INSURANCE AND NO LIABILITY IS ASSUMED HEREBY. IF IT IS DESIRED .THAT LIABILITY BE ASSUMED PRIOR TO THE ISSUANCE OF A POLICY OF TITLE INSURANCE, A BINDER OR COMMITMENT SHOULD BE REQUESTED.

The form of policy of title insurance contemplated by this report is:
A.L.T.A RESIDENTIAL TITLE INSURANCE POLICY
AMERICAN LAND TITLE ASSOCIATION LOAN EXTENDED COVERAGE POLICY

Title Officer

SCHEDULE A

Title Order No:6805790

The estate or interest in the land hereinafter described or referred to covered by this report is:

A FEE AS TO PARCEL 1
AN EASEMENT MORE FULLY DESCRIBED BELOW AS TO PARCEL 2

2. Title to said estate or interest at the date hereof is vested in:

LARRY WILD AND NOBUKO WILD, HUSBAND AND WIFE, AS JOINT TENANTS

3. The land referred to in this report is situated in the State of California, County of ORANGE and is described as follows :

PARCEL 1:

LOT 6 OF TRACT NO. 13914, IN THE CITY OF SAN CLEMENTE, COUNTY OF ORANGE, STATE OF CALIFORNIA, AS SHOWN ON A MAP FILED IN BOOK 638, PAGES 45 THROUGH 50, INCLUSIVE OF MISCELLANEOUS MAPS, RECORDS OF ORANGE COUNTY, CALIFORNIA.

EXCEPTING THEREFROM ONTO THE GRANTOR, WITH THE RIGHT TO ASSIGN, TRANSFER OR LEASE TO ANY THIRD PARTY, ALL OIL, GAS AND CASINGHEAD GAS AND OTHER HYDROCARBONS LYING BELOW THE SURFACE OF THE LAND CONVEYED HEREBY, WITHOUT ANY SURFACE ENTRY RIGHTS, AS RESERVED IN THE DEED RECORDED NOVEMBER 1, 1990, AS INSTRUMENT NO. 90-581069, OFFICIAL RECORDS.

PARCEL 2:

A NON-EXCLUSIVE EASEMENT FOR INGRESS AND EGRESS PURPOSES OVER LOTS L, M AND N (THE PRIVATE STREETS) OF TRACT NO. 14682 AS SHOWN ON A MAP IN BOOK 539, PAGES 45 THROUGH 50, INCLUSIVE OF MISCELLANEOUS MAPS, RECORDS OF ORANGE COUNTY, CALIFORNIA.

SCHEDULE B

Title Order No. 6805790

At the date hereof exceptions to coverage in addition to the printed Exceptions and Exclusions in the policy form designated on the face page of this Report would be as follows:

A. 1. PROPERTY TAXES, INCLUDING ANY ASSESSMENTS COLLECTED WITH TAXES, TO BE LEVIED FOR THE FISCAL YEAR 1996-1997 THAT ARE A LIEN NOT YET DUE.

B. 2. PROPERTY TAXES, INCLUDING ANY PERSONAL PROPERTY TAXES AND ANY ASSESSMENTS COLLECTED WITH TAXES, FOR THE FISCAL YEAR 1995-1996

FIRST INSTALLMENT;	$1,749.93 (PAID)
2ND INSTALLMENT;	$1,749.93
PENALTY AND COST;	$184.99 (DUE AFTER APRIL 10)
HOMEOWNERS EXEMPTION;	$7,000.00
CODE AREA	10002
ASSESSMENT NO:	680-561-14

C 3. AN ASSESSMENT BY THE IMPROVEMENT DISTRICT SHOWN BELOW

ASSESSMENT (OR BOND) NO;	829-73
SERIES;	35-1
DISTRICT;	CITY OF SAN CLEMENTE-10
FOR;	30 AMD 85-1
BOND ISSUED;	FEBRUARY 21, 1989
ORIGINAL AMOUNT;	$ NOT SET OUT

SAID ASSESSMENT IS COLLECTED WITH THE COUNTY/CITY PROPERTY TAXES.

D A REPORT ON SAID TAXES AND ASSESSMENTS HAS BEEN ORDERED. WE WILL SEND A TAX SUPPLEMENT WHEN IT IS RECEIVED.

E 4. AN ASSESSMENT BY THE IMPROVEMENT DISTRICT SHOWN BELOW

ASSESSMENT (OR BOND)	NO: 6628
SERIES	95
DISTRICT	CITY OF SAN CLEMENTE-10
FOR	STREET IMPROVEMENTS
BOND ISSUED	JULY 14, 1995
ORIGINAL AMOUNT:	$ NOT SET OUT

SAID ASSESSMENT IS COLLECTED WITH THE COUNTY/CITY PROPERTY TAXES.

SCHEDULE B (CONTINUED)

Title Order No. 6805790

F. A REPORT ON SAID TAXES AND ASSESSMENTS HAS BEEN ORDERED. WE WILL SEND A TAX SUPPLEMENT WHEN IT IS RECEIVED.

G. 5. THE LIEN OF SUPPLEMENTAL OR ESCAPED ASSESSMENTS OF PROPERTY TAXES, IF ANY, MADE PURSUANT TO THE PROVISIONS OF PART 0.5, CHAPTER 3.5 OR PART 2, CHAPTER 3, ARTICLES 3 AND 4 RESPECTIVELY(COMMENCING WITH SECTION 75) OF THE REVENUE AND TAXATION CODE OF THE STATE OF CALIFORNIA AS A RESULT OF THE TRANSFER OF TITLE TO THE VESTEE NAMED IN SCHEDULE A; OR AS A RESULT OF CHANGES IN OWNERSHIP OR NEW CONSTRUCTION OCCURRING PRIOR TO DATE OF POLICY.

H. 6 MATTERS IN VARIOUS INSTRUMENTS OF RECORD WHICH CONTAIN AMONG OTHER THINGS EASEMENTS AND RIGHTS OF WAY IN, ON, OVER AND UNDER THE COMMON AREA FOR THE PURPOSE OF CONSTRUCTING, ERECTING, OPERATING OR MAINTAINING THEREON OR THEREUNDER OVERHEAD OR UNDERGROUND LINES, CABLES, WIRES, CONDUITS, OR OTHER DEVICES FOR ELECTRICITY, TELEPHONE, STORM WATER DRAINS AND PIPES, WATER SYSTEMS, SPRINKLING SYSTEMS, WATER, HEATING AND GAS LINES OR PIPES, AND SIMILAR PUBLIC OR QUASI-PUBLIC IMPROVEMENTS OR FACILITIES.

ALSO THE RIGHT OF USE AND ENJOYMENT IN AND TO AND THROUGHOUT THE COMMON AREA AS WELL AS THE NON-EXCLUSIVE EASEMENTS AND RIGHTS FOR INGRESS, EGRESS TO THE OWNER HEREIN DESCRIBED.

REFERENCE IS HEREBY BEING MADE TO VARIOUS DOCUMENTS AND MAPS OF RECORD FOR FULL AND FURTHER PARTICULARS.

AFFECTS THE COMMON AREA.

I. 7 THE MATTERS SET FORTH IN THE DOCUMENT SHOWN BELOW WHICH, AMONG OTHER THINGS, CONTAINS OR PROVIDES FOR: CERTAIN EASEMENTS; LIENS AND THE SUBORDINATION THEREOF; PROVISIONS RELATING TO PARTITION; RESTRICTIONS ON SEVERABILITY OF COMPONENT PARTS; AND COVENANTS, CONDITIONS AND RESTRICTIONS, (BUT OMITTING THEREFROM ANY COVENANT OR RESTRICTION BASED ON RACE, COLOR, RELIGION, SEX, HANDICAP, FAMILIAL STATUS OR NATIONAL ORIGIN, IF ANY, UNLESS AND ONLY TO THE EXTENT THAT SAID COVENANT (A) IS EXEMPT UNDER CHAPTER 42, SECTION 3607 OF THE UNITED STATES CODE OR (B) RELATES TO HANDICAP BUT DOES NOT DISCRIMINATE AGAINST HANDICAPPED PERSONS).

RECORDED:NOVEMBER 28   1989 AS INSTRUMENTK NO.89-646298, OFFICIAL RECORDS

SCHEDULE B (CONTINUED)

Title Order No..6805790

J. SAID COVENANTS, CONDITIONS AND RESTRICTIONS PROVIDE THAT A VIOLATION THEREOF SHALL NOT DEFEAT THE LIEN OF ANY MORTGAGE OR DEED OF TRUST MADE IN GOOD FAITH AND FOR VALUE.

K. THE PROVISIONS OF SAID COVENANTS, CONDITIONS AND RESTRICTIONS WERE EXTENDED TO INCLUDE THE HEREIN DESCRIBED LAND BY AN INSTRUMENT.

RECORDED   JANUARY 25, 1990 AS INSTRUMENT
                                             NO: 90-045127, OFFICIAL RECORDS

L. 8. THE MATTERS SET FORTH IN THE DOCUMENT SHOWN BELOW WHICH, AMONG OTHER THINGS, CONTAINS OR PROVIDES FOR: CERTAIN BASEMENTS; LIENS AND THE SUBORDINATION THEREOF; PROVISIONS RELATING TO PARTITION; RESTRICTIONS ON SEVERABILITY OF COMPONENT PARTS; AND COVENANTS, CONDITIONS AND RESTRICTIONS (BUT OMITTING THEREFROM ANY COVENANT OR RESTRICTION BASED ON RACE, COLOR, RELIGION, SEX, HANDICAP, FAMILIAL STATUS OR NATIONAL ORIGIN, IF ANY, UNLESS AND ONLY TOTHE EXTENT THAT SAID COVENANT (A) IS EXEMPT UNDER CHAPTER 42, SECTION 3607 OF THE UNITED STATES CODE OR (B) RELATES TO HANDICAP BUT DOES NOT DISCRIMINATE AGAINST HANDICAPPED PERSONS.)

RECORDED   NOVEMBER 28, 1989 AS INSTRUMENT
                                             NO. 89-646299, OFFICIAL RECORDS

M. SAID COVENANTS, CONDITIONS AND RESTRICTIONS PROVIDE THAT A VIOLATION THEREOF SHALL NOT DEFEAT THE LIEN OF ANY MORTGAGE OR DEED OF TRUST MADE IN GOOD FAITH AND FOR VALUE.

N. THE PROVISIONS OF SAID COVENANTS, CONDITIONS AND RESTRICTIONS WERE EXTENDED TO INCLUDE THE HEREIN DESCRIBED LAND BY AN INSTRUMENT.

RECORDED: JANUARY 25, 1990 AS INSTRUMENT
                                             NO. 90-045128, OFFICIAL RECORDS

O. 9. AN EASEMENT FOR THE PURPOSE SHOWN BELOW AND RIGHTS INCIDENTAL THERETO AS SET FORTH IN A DOCUMENT

GRANTED TO: SAN DIEGO GAS & ELECTRIC
PURPOSE: PUBLIC UTILITIES
RECORDED: DECEMBER 1, 1989 AS INSTRUMENT
                                             NO. 89-653629, OFFICIAL RECORDS
AFFECTS: THE NORTHEASTERLY 3 FEET OF
                                             PARCEL 1 AND ALL OF PARCEL 2

SCHEDULE B (CONTINUED)

Title order-No. 6805790

P. 10. AN EASEMENT FOR THE PURPOSE SHOWN BELOW AND RIGHTS INCIDENTAL THERETO AS SET FORTH IN A DOCUMENT GRANTED TO:

GRANTED TO:	RANCHO DEL RIO MASTER ASSOCIATION
PURPOSE:	REASONABLE INGRESS AND EGRESS OVER LOT 16 FOR THE PURPOSES OF MAINTENANCE, REPAIR OR REPLACEMENT OF THE MASONRY WALL, AS SAID WALL IS SHOWN AS "PERIMETER WALL" ON EXHIBIT "A" ATTACHED THERETO AND INCORPORATED THEREIN
RECORDED:	AUGUST 26, 1992 AS INSTRUMENT NO. 92-567937, OFFICIAL RECORDS
AFFECTS:	SAID LAND

Q. 11 A DEED OF TRUST TO SECURE AN INDEBTEDNESS IN THE ORIGINAL AMOUNT SHOWN BELOW:

AMOUNT:	$222,000.00
DATED:	APRIL 21, 1995
TRUSTOR:	LARRY AND NOBUKO WILD
TRUSTEE:	CAL FED SERVICE CORPORATION
BENEFICIARY:	CALIFORNIA REDERAL BANK, FSA
RECORDED:	MAY 1, 1995 AS INSTRUMENT NO. 950184380, OFFICIAL RECORDS
ORIGINAL LOAN NUMBER:	0206470049

R. 12. A DEED OF TRUST TO SECURE AN INDEBTEDNESS IN THE ORIGINAL AMOUNT SHOWN BELOW:

AMOUNT:	$225,500.00
DATED:	JULY 20, 1995
TRUSTOR:	LARRY AND NOBUKO WILD
TRUSTEE:	AMERICAN SECSURITIES COMPANY
BENEFICIARY:	WELLS FARGO BANK
RECORDED:	JULY 19,1995 AS INSTRUMENT NO. 95-0030762, OFFICIAL RECORDS
ORIGINAL LOAN NUMBER:	NOT SHOWN

S. THE ABOVE DEED OF TRUST APPEARS TO SECURE A HOME EQUITY TYPE OF LOAN.IF THIS LOAN IS TO PAID OFF AND RECONVEYED THROUGH THIS
TRANSACTION, CHICAGO TITLE WILL REQUIRE A WRITTEN STATEMENT FROM THE BENEFICIARY THAT A FREEZE IS IN EFFECT ON THE ACCOUNT
AND
THE DEMAND FOR PAY OFF MUST PROVIDE THAT A RECONVEYANCE WILL BE ISSUED UPON PAYMENT OF THE AMOUNTS SHOWN THEREIN.

T. END OF SCHEDULE B

Title Order-No. 6805790

U. NOTE NO.1: IF A 1970 ALTA OWNER'S OR LENDER'S OR 1975 ALTA LEASEHOLD OWNER'S OR LENDER'S POLICY FORM HAS BEEN REQUESTED, WHEN APPROVED FOR ISSUANCE, WILL BE ENDORSED TO ADD THE FOLLOWING TO THE EXCLUSIONS FROM COVERAGE CONTAINED THEREIN:

LOAN POLICY EXCLUSION:

ANY CLAIM, WHICH ARISES OUT OF THE TRANSACTION CREATING THE INTEREST OF THE MORTGAGEE INSURED BY THIS POLICY, BY REASON OF THE OPERATION OF FEDERAL BANKRUPTCY, STATE INSOLVENCY, OR SIMILAR CREDITORS' RIGHTS LAWS.

OWNER'S POLICY EXCLUSION:

ANY CLAIM WHICH ARISES OUT OF THE TRANSACTION VESTING IN THE INSURED, THE ESTATE OF INTEREST INSURED BY THIS POLICY, BY REASON OF THE OPERATION OF FEDERAL BANKRUPTCY, STATE INSOLVENCY OR SIMILAR CREDITOR'S RIGHTS LAWS.

V. NOTE NO. 2: THE CHARGE FOR A POLICY OF TITLE INSURANCE WHEN ISSUED THROUGH THIS TITLE ORDER, WILL BE BASED ON THE SHORT-TERM RATE.

W. NOTE NO. 3: IF THIS COMPANY IS REQUESTED TO DISBURSE FUNDS IN CONNECTION WITH THIS TRANSACTION, CHAPTER 598, STATUES PF 1989 MANDATES HOLD PERIODS FOR CHECKS DEPOSITED TO ESCROW OR SUB-ESCROW ACCOUNTS. THE MANDATORY HOLD PERIOD FOR CASHIER'S CHECKS, CERTIFIED CHECKS AND TELLER'S CHECKS IS ONE BUSINESS DAY AFTER THEDAY DEPOSITED. OTHER CHECKS REQUIRE A HOLD PERIOD OF FROM TWO TO FIVE BUSINESS DAYS AFTER THE DAY DEPOSITED.   IN THE EVENT THAT THE PARTIES TO THE CONTEMPLATED TRANSACTION WISH TO RECORD PRIOR TO THE TIME THAT THE FUNDS ARE AVAILABLE FOR DISBURSEMENT (AND SUBJECT TO COMPANY APPROVAL), THE COMPANY WILL REQUIRE THE PRIOR

WRITTEN CONSENT OF THE PARTIES. UPON REQUEST, A FORM ACCEPTABLE TO THE COMPANY AUTHORIZING SAID EARLY RECORDING MAY BE PROVIDED TO ESCROW FOR EXECUTION.

WIRE TRANSFERS

THERE IS NO MANDATED HOLD PERIOD FOR FUNDS DEPOSITED BY CONFIRMED WIRE TRANSFER. THE COMPANY MAY DISBURSE SUCH FUNDS THE SAME DAY.

CHICAGO TITLE WILL DISBURSE BY WIRE (WIRE-OUT) ONLY COLLECTED FUNDS OR FUNDS RECEIVED BY CONFIRMED WIRE (WIRE-IN). THE FEE FOR EACH WIRE-OUT IS $25.00. THE COMPANY'S WIRE-IN INSTRUCTIONS ARE:

Title Order-No.6805790

WIRE-IN INSTRUCTIONS FOR BANK OF AMERICA:

BANK: BANK OF AMERICA
                                 1811 EL CAMINO REAL
                                 SAN CLEMENTE, CA 92672
BANK ABA: 121000359
ACCOUNT NAME: CHICAGO TITLE COMPANY
title order 6805790   1258972

ACCOUNT NUMBER:

                                 CHICAGO TITLE COMPANY
FOR CREDIT TO: 16969 VAN DARMAN
                                 IRVINE, CA 92714
FURTHER CREDIT TO: ORDER NO: 01689258

X. NOTE NO. 4: THERE ARE NO CONVEYANCES AFFECTING SAID LAND,
        RECORDED WITHIN SIX (6) MONTHS OF THE DATE OF THIS REPORT.

        Y. NOTE NO.5: NONE OF THE ITEMS SHOWN IN THIS REPORT WILL
        CAUSE THECOMPANY TO DECLINE TO ATTACH CLTA INDORSEMENT
        FORM100 TO AN ALTA LOAN POLICY, WHEN ISSUED.

Z. NOTE NO. 6: THERE IS LOCATED ON SAID LAND A SINGLE FAMILY
        RESIDENCE KNOWN AS : 1459 AVENIDA GAVIOTA, IN THE CITY OF
        SANCLEMENTE, COUNTY OF ORANGE, STATE OF CALIFORNIA

PRINTED EXCEPTIONS AND EXCLUSIONS

CALIFORNIA LAND TITLE ASSOCIATION STANDARD COVERAGE POLICY-1990

EXCLUSIONS FROM COVERAGE

The following matters are expressly excluded from the coverage of this policy and the Company will not pay loss or damage, costs, attorney's fees or expenses which arise by reason of:

1.

(a)   Any law, ordinance or governmental regulation (including but not limited to building and zoning laws, ordinances or regulations) restricting, regulating, prohibiting or relating to the occupancy, use or enjoyment of the land; the character, dimensions or location of any improvement now or hereafter erected on the land; a separation in ownership or a change in the dimensions or area of the land or any parcel of which the land is or was a part; or environment protection, or the effect of any violation of these laws, ordinances or governmental regulations, except to the extent that a notice of the enforcement thereof or a notice of a defect, lien or encumbrance resulting from a violation or alleged violation affecting the land has been recorded in the public records at Date of Policy.

(b)   Any governmental police power not excluded by (a) above, except to the extent that a notice of the exercise thereof or a notice of a defect, lien or encumbrance resulting from a violation or alleged violation affecting the land has been recorded in the public records at Date of Policy.

2.

Rights of eminent domain unless notice of the exercise thereof has been recorded in the public records at Date of Policy, but not excluding from coverage any taking which has occurred prior to Date of Policy which would be binding on the rights of a purchaser for value with knowledge,

3.

Defects, liens, encumbrances, adverse claims or other matters:

(a)   whether or not recorded in the public records at Date of Policy, but created, suffered, assumed or agreed to by the insured claimant;

(b)   not known to the Company, not recorded in the public records at Date of Policy, but known to the insured claimant and not disclosed.

(c)   resulting in no loss or damage to the insured claimant;

(d)   attaching or created subsequent to Date of Policy; or

(e)   resulting in loss or damage which would not have been sustained if the insured claimant had paid value for the insured mortgage or the estate or interest insured by this policy.

4.
Unenforceability of the lien of the insured mortgage because of the ability or failure of the insured at Date of Policy, or the inability or failure of any subsequent owner of the indebtedness, to comply with applicable doing business laws of the state in which the land is situated.

5.
Invalidity or unenforceability of the lien of the insured mortgage, or claim thereof, which arises out of the transaction evidenced by the insured mortgage and is based upon usury or any consumer credit protection or truth-in-lending law.

6.
Any claim, which arises out of the transaction vesting in the insured the estate or interest insured by this policy or the transaction creating the interest of the insured lender, by reason of the operation of federal bankruptcy, state insolvency or similar creditor' rights laws.

EXCEPTIONS FROM COVERAGE

This policy does not insure against loss or damage (and the Company will not pay cost, attorneys' fees or expenses) which arise by reason of:

1. Taxes or assessments which are not shown as existing liens by the records of any taxing authority that levies taxes or assessments on real property or by the public records.

2. Proceedings by a public agency which may result in taxes or assessments, or notices of such proceedings, whether or not shown by the records of such agency or by the public records.

3. Any facts, rights, interests or claims which are not shown by the public records but which could be ascertained by an inspection of the land or which may be asserted by persons in possession thereof.

4. Easements, liens, or encumbrances, or claims thereof, which are not shown by the public records.

5. Discrepancies, conflicts in boundary lines, shortage in area, encroachments, or any other facts which a correct survey would disclose, and which are not shown by the public records.

6. (a) Unpatented mining claims; (b) reservations or exceptions in patents or in Acts authorizing the issuance thereof; (c) water rights, claims or title to water, whether or not the matters excepted under (a), (b) or (c) are shown by the public records.

AMERICAN LAND TITLE ASSOCIATION RESIDENTIAL TITLE INSURANCE POLICY

EXCLUSIONS FROM COVERAGE

In addition to the exceptions in Schedule B, you are not insured against loss, costs, attorney's fees and expenses resulting from:

1. Government police power, and the existence or violation of any law or government regulation. This includes building and zoning ordinances and also laws and regulations concerning:

- land use
- improvements on the land
- land division
- environmental protection

This exclusion does not apply to the violations or the enforcement of these matters which appear in the public records at Policy Date. This exclusion does not limit the zoning coverage described in Items 12 and 13 of Covered Title Risks.

2. The right to take the land by condemning it, unless:
- a notice of exercising the right appears in the public records on Policy Date
- the taking happened prior to the Policy Date and is binding on you if you bought the land without knowing of the taking.

3. Title Risks:
- that are created, allowed, or agreed to by you
- that are known to you, but not to us, on the Policy Date unless they appeared in the public records
- that result in no loss to you
- that first affect your title after the Policy Date-this does not limit the labor and material
- lien coverage in item 8 of Covered Title Risks

4. Failure to pay value for your title

5. Lack of a right:
- to any land outside the area specifically described and referred to item 3 of Schedule A, or
- in streets, alleys, or waterways that touch your land

This exclusion does not limit the access coverage in Item 5 of Covered Title Risks

EXCEPTIONS FROM COVERAGE

In addition to the Exceptions, you are not insured against loss, costs, attorneys' fees and expenses resulting from:

1. Someone claiming an interest in your land by reason of:
    A. Easements not shown in the public records
    B. Boundary disputes not shown in the public records
    C. Improvements owned by your neighbor placed on your land

2. If, in addition to a single family residence, your existing structure consists of one or more Additional Dwelling Units, Item 12 of Covered Title Risks does not insure you against loss, costs, attorneys' fees, and expenses resulting from:
   A. The forced removal of any Additional Dwelling Unit, or
   B. The forced conversion of any Additional Dwelling Unit back to its original use.

   If said Additional Dwelling Unit was either constructed or converted to use as a dwelling unit in violation of any law or government regulation

AMERICAN LAND TITLE ASSOCIATION LOAN POLICY WITH ALTA ENDORSEMENT - FORM 1 COVERAGE
and
AMERICAN LAND TITLE ASSOCIATION LEASEHOLD LOAN POLICY WITH ALTA ENDORSEMENT - FORM 1 COVERAGE

EXCLUSIONS FROM COVERAGE

The following matters are expressly excluded from the coverage of this policy and the Company will not pay loss or damage, costs, attorney's fees or expenses which arise by reason of:

1.
(a) Any law, ordinance or governmental regulation (including but not limited to building and zoning laws, ordinances, or regulations) restricting, regulating, prohibiting or relating to (i) the occupancy, use, or enjoyment of the land; (ii) the character, dimensions or location of any improvement now or hereafter erected on the land; (iii) a separation in ownership or a change in the dimensions or area of the land or any parcel of which the land is or was a part; or (iv) environmental protection, or the effect of any violations of these laws, ordinances or governmental regulations, except to the extent that a notice of the enforcement thereof or a notice of a defect, lien or encumbrance resulting from a violation or alleged violation or alleged violation affecting the land has been recorded in the public records at Date of Policy.

(b) Any governmental police power not excluded by (a) above, except to the extent that a notice of the exercise thereof or a notice of a defect, lien or encumbrance resulting from a violation or alleged violation affecting the land has been recorded in the public records at Date of Policy.

2. Rights of eminent domain unless notice of the exercise thereof has been recorded the public records at Date of Policy, but not excluding from coverage any taking which has occurred prior to Date of Policy which would be binding on the rights of a purchaser for value without knowledge.

3. Defects, liens, encumbrances, adverse claims or other matters:
(a) created, suffered, assumed or agreed to by the insured claimant;
(b) not known to the Company, not recorded in the public records at Date of Policy but known to the insured claimant and not disclosed in writing to the Company by the insured claimant prior to the date the insured claimant became an insured under this policy;
(c) resulting in no loss or damage to the insured claimant;
(d) attaching or created subsequent to Date of Policy (except to the extent that this policy insures the priority of the lien of the insured mortgage over any statutory lien for services, labor or material or to the extent insurance is afforded herein as to   assessments for street improvements under construction or completed at Date of Policy);

(e) resulting in loss or damage which would not have been sustained if the insured claimant had paid value for the insured mortgage

4. Unenforceability of the lien of the insured mortgage because of the inability or failure of the insured at Date of Policy, or the inability or failure of any subsequent owner of the indebtedness, to comply with applicable doing business laws of the state in which the land is situated.

5. Invalidity or unenforceability of the lien of the insured mortgage, or claim thereof, which is based upon usury or any consumer credit protection or truth in lending law.

6. Any statutory lien for services, labor or materials (or priority of any statutory lien for services, labor or materials over the lien of the insured mortgage) arising from an improvement or work related to the land which is contracted for and commenced subsequent to Date if Policy and is not financed in whole or in part by proceeds of the indebtedness secured by the insured mortgage which at Date of Policy the insured has advanced or is obligated to advance.

7. Any claim, which arises out of the transaction creating the interest of the mortgagee
insured by this policy, by reason of the operation of federal bankruptcy, state insolvency, or similar creditors' rights laws, that is based on:

(i) the transaction creating the interest of the insured mortgagee being deemed a fraudulent conveyance or fraudulent transfer; or
(ii) the subordination of the interest of the insured mortgagee as a result of the application of the doctrine of equitable subordination; or
(iii) the transaction creating the interest of the insured mortgagee being deemed a referential transfer except where the preferential transfer results from the failure:
(a) to timely record the instrument of transfer; or
(b) of such recordation to impart notice to purchaser for value or a judgment or lien creditor.

The above policy forms be issued to afford either Standard Coverage or Extended Coverage. In addition to the above Exclusions from Coverage, the Exceptions from Coverage in a Standard Coverage policy will also include the following General Exceptions:

EXCEPTIONS FROM COVERAGE

This policy does not insure against loss or damage (and the Company will not pay costs, attorneys' fees or expenses) which arise by reason of:

1. Taxes or assessments which are not shown as existing liens by the records of any taxing authority that levies taxes or assessments on real property or by the public records.

2. Proceedings by a public agency which may result in taxes or assessments, or notices of such proceedings, whether or not shown by the records of such agency or by the public records.

3. Any facts, rights, interests or claims which are not shown by the public records but which could be ascertained by an inspection of the land or by making inquiry of persons in possession thereof.

4. Easements, liens, or encumbrances, or claims thereof, which are not shown by the public records.

5. Discrepancies, conflicts in boundary lines, shortage in area, encroachments, or any other facts which a correct survey would disclose, and which are not shown by public records.

6. (a) Unpatented mining claims; (b) reservations or exceptions in patents or in Acts authorizing the issuance thereof: (c) water rights, claims or title to water, whether or not the matters excepted under (a), (b) or (c) are shown by the public records

AMERICAN LAND TITLE ASSOCIATION OWNER'S POLICY
and
AMERICAN LAND TITLE ASSOCIATION LEASEHOLD OWNER'S POLICY

EXCLUSIONS FROM COVERAGE

The following matters are expressly excluded from the coverage of this policy and the Company will not pay loss or damage, costs, attorney's fees or expenses which arise by reason of:

1.

(a) Any law, ordinance or governmental regulation (including but not limited to building and zoning laws, ordinances or regulations) restricting, regulating, prohibiting or relating to (i) the occupancy, use, or enjoyment of the land; (ii) the character, dimensions or location of any improvement now or hereafter erected on the land; (iii) a separation in ownership or a change in the dimensions or area of the land or any parcel of which the land is or was a part; or (iv) environmental protection, or the effect of any violations of these laws, ordinances or governmental regulations, except to the extent that a notice of the enforcement thereof or a notice of a defect, lien or encumbrance resulting from a violation or alleged violation affecting the land has been recorded in the public records at Date of Policy.

(b) Any governmental police power not excluded by (a) above, except to the extent that a notice of the exercise thereof or a notice of a defect, lien or encumbrance resulting from a violation or alleged violation affecting the land has been recorded in the public records at Date of Policy.

2. Rights of eminent domain unless notice of the exercise thereof has been recorded in the public records at Date ofPolicy, but not excluding from coverage any taking which has occurred prior to Date of Policy which would be binding on the rights of a purchaser for value without knowledge.

3. Defects, liens, encumbrances, adverse claims or other matters:
   (a) created, suffered, assumed or agreed to by the insured claimant;
   (b) not known to the Company, not recorded in the public records at Date of Policy, but known to the insured claimant and not disclosed in writing to the Company by the insured claimant prior to the date the insured claimant became an insured under this policy.
   (c) resulting in no loss or damage to the insured claimant
   (d) attaching or created subsequent to Date of Policy; or
   (e) resulting in loss or damage which would not have been sustained if the insured claimant had paid value for the estate or interest insured by this policy.

352

4. Any claim, which arises out of the transaction vesting in the insured the estate or interest insured by this policy, by reason of the operation of federal bankruptcy, state insolvency, or similar creditors' rights laws, that is based on:
    (i) the transaction creating the estate or interest insured by this policy being deemed a fraudulent conveyance or fraudulent transfer; or
    (ii) the transaction creating the estate or interest insured by this policy being deemed a preferential transfer except where the preferential transfer results from the failure:
    (a) to timely record the instrument of transfer; or
    (b) of such recordation to impart notice to a purchaser for value or a judgment or lien creditor.

The above policy forms may be issued to afford either Standard Coverage or Extended Coverage. In addition to the above Exclusions from Coverage, the Exceptions from Coverage in a Standard Coverage policy will also include the following General Exceptions:

EXCEPTIONS FROM COVERAGE

This policy does not insure against loss or damage (and the Company will not pay costs, attorney's fees or expenses) which arise by reason of:

1. Taxes or assessments which are not shown as existing liens by the records of any taxing authority that levies taxes or assessments on real property or by the public records.
   Proceedings by a public agency which may result in taxes or assessments, or notices of such proceedings, whether or not shown by the records of such agency or by the public records.

2. Any facts, rights, interests or claims which are not shown by the public records but which could be ascertained by an inspection of the land or by making inquiry of persons in possession thereof.

3. Easements, liens, or encumbrances, or claims thereof, which are not shown by the public records.
4. Discrepancies, conflicts in boundary lines, shortage in area, encroachments, or any other facts which a correct survey would disclose, and which are not shown by the public records.
5. (a) Unpatented mining claims; (b) reservations or exceptions in patents or in Acts authorizing the issuance thereof; (c) water rights, claims or title to water, whether or not the matters excepted under (a), (b) or (c) are shown by the public records.

Post Test

The following self test repeats the one you took at the beginning of this chapter. Now take the exam again--since you have read all the material-- and check your knowledge of escrow closing procedures.

True/False

1. Title insurance is a contract to protect against losses arising through defects in title to real estate.

2. The foundation of real property ownership is title.

3. Title officers today are called conveyancers.

4. Standard coverage insures against matters not of record.

5. A CLTA policy of title insurance is designed primarily for the lender.

6. An extended policy of title insurance protects only against matters of record.

7. A basic policy of title insurance may be expanded or modified by special endorsements.

8. Title insurance covers defects known by the parties prior to the transfer, even though not disclosed.

9. The preliminary title report contains all encumbrances against the property in question.

10. If an untrue statement about the quality of the title to a property is made, the insurance is not valid.

chapter 12

COMPUTERIZED ESCROW

Focus

- **Introduction**
- **Computer tasking**
- **Title insurance**
- **Title examination**
- **Automated escrow**

Pre-Test

The following is a self test to determine how much you know about computerized escrows before reading this chapter. Take it without studying, then read the material presented in the text. At the end of the chapter you will find a repeat of this exam. Test your knowledge by answering the questions again, then check your improvement. (The answers are found at the end of the book.) Good luck.

True/False

1. Traditional methods of conducting escrows have been replaced by computer technology.

2. The title industry does not use computer technology.

3. Title research is still done by manual methods.

4. The job of a title searcher is that of recovery of information about a specific property.

5. Legal opinions are sought by title examiners on some matters in the chain of title, rather than getting the information by computer search.

6. Accounting is one of the main uses for computers in escrow offices.

7. A start card places information in a computer at the end of a transaction.

8. An audit trail is created with an escrow receipt which is generated by a computer.

9. Mistakes made when data is entered are corrected with an adjustment slip.

10. A report that keeps track of the balance between the trust bank account and the balance shown in the trust account system is a reconciliation report.

Introduction

Computer technology, for the most part, has replaced traditional methods of conducting escrows. In addition to software which provides conforming forms, word processing programs allow for quick and accurate input of information. Both escrow and title insurance rely heavily on saved information in computers and on reproduction of data.

Computer Tasking

Efficiency and accuracy of the escrow product have been refined as a byproduct of computer technology. In the last decade of the 20th Century, escrow and title officers have learned to use new software capability to create new models for forms and other documents.

Research capabilities also have been extended beyond what was possible before computer memory became available. Word processing software has allowed the timely and consistent storage and retrieval of data as well as faster and more accurate communication between parties to the escrow.

Title Insurance

Computer technology is most often used in the title industry for title searching and title examination. Untold hours have been spent in the past by researchers using archives as their only source to unravel the history of a piece of property. Technology has now supplied those researchers with the tools to make their jobs easier and quicker.

Title Research

The job of a title searcher is mainly to recover nformation about a specific property or parcel. The researcher uses various systems which classify real property by legal description or assessor's parcel number to find data that might affect the title. The information is accessed from computer storage files.

After the title search has been completed, the documents listed in the chain of title are copied for title examination. Computer communications and graphics may be used for this process.

There are certain items-- such as divorce, incompetence, parole proceedings, guardianship, probates, bankruptcy filings, judgments, tax liens, or powers of attorney-- that affect an owner or the property in question. If they cannot be found by legal description of the property in question, the information is gathered using the names of parties involved. These are indexed by grantor and grantee, alphabetically, in computer files.

Unfortunately, all steps necessary to complete a title search do not necessarily lend themselves to automation and the use of technology. Legal opinions still must be sought by the title examiner on matters in the chain of title, such as partition and quiet title actions, orders confirming sale, attachments and executions, divorces, probates and other legal matters.

Many times documents recorded prior to the transaction in question, or other documents in possession of a third party must be obtained. Commonly, copies of CC&R's on a property are required for extended coverage insurance or construction of new improvements.

Title Examination

After the title data is collected by the researcher the information gathered is interpreted by a person who specializes in examining chains of title, and a title report is assembled. This information is then entered into a computer and saved for printing the title report and writing the title policy when the title search process is complete.

At the closing, when the title policy is written, the information may be modified if there have been any new documents recorded, such as reconveyances, deeds of trust or liens, since the title search was completed. The final report is then presented to the insured parties.

Data Processing

Word processing supports the entire course of gathering and interpreting title data for the purpose of issuing title insurance. The speed with which information is input, stored or printed has allowed the title procedures needed to complete a real estate transaction to be much more efficient than in the past, with fewer mistakes or oversights because of human error.

In transactions where there is an institutional lender of record, the title insurer often is involved in a sub-escrow. The lender will send a demand for payoff of a loan to the title company rather than to the escrow holder for payment. Also, if a new loan is being funded, the net proceeds are always sent to the title company instead of to the escrow holder.

The complex task of accounting for all payoff funds, checks for payments to the seller or buyer, or any refunds to the escrow holder or other parties is accomplished by computer. Formerly, hours of the escrow holder's time were spent at accounting, tracking and processing the paperwork.

A special sub-escrow software program may be required to calculate exact figures needed for variations in transactions. Variable interest rate financing, graduated payments and negative amortization, prepayment fees, late charges, or lender fees for producing the demand for pay-off all require special accounting and handling.

Computer calculations are essential to the timely and successful closing of these escrows.

A total data processing system will contain applications for the processing of monetary data for financial statements, investments of surplus cash, maintenance and reconciliations of bank accounts, customer billing and accounting. In addition, a marketing support system of customer profiles, tracking customer activity, analysis of customer volume or other customer related activity supports automated escrow and title procedures.

Automated Escrow

Automated systems for an escrow office must be capable of managing a large extent of accounting and document processing. One of the most important charges to an escrow holder is the protection of money that flows through transactions. Suitable apportionment of charges to the responsible parties, as supported by clear escrow instructions, is an application of that duty.

Accounting Procedures

Each escrow office must decide what kind of accounting system it will use. The system must be appropriate to the size of the escrow operation, the number and type of transactions and the basic management and information requirement of the office.

The escrow office also must decide whether to use manual or automated methods for trust fund accounting and other accounting for which it is responsible.

Manual Accounting

All receipts and disbursements are posted to individual ledger cards by escrow number and then posted and balanced to the office escrow account with the manual bookkeeping method. The main source of information in this process is the ledger card, which is then used to prepare further reports. Manual accounting can be suitable for a small escrow office that keeps a steady but limited volume of business. It is a rare escrow office, however, which manages its accounts without the aid of computerized technology.

Automated Accounting

A small escrow office may use either a small personal computer for accounting or a bank's or title company's mainframe. The types of information and documents or reports generated will be determined by the type, amount and complexity of information put into the computer as well as the adequacy of the accounting software installed for bookkeeping purposes. Each office should assess its accounting needs before making a decision about the extent of automated bookkeeping it will use.

Once an escrow office has committed to using automated accounting rather than the manual method, there are a few basic documents with which to become familiar.

Start Card

The first data for entering a transaction into the system is provided by a start card. Information such as company number, names of buyer and seller, amount of consideration, date escrow opened, legal description or street address of property, type of escrow, escrow officer assigned, designated title company and any other useful information about the transaction is entered.

Escrow Receipt

The escrow receipt acts as an audit trail for money being processed through the computer system. When funds are deposited in the escrow account, a receipt for the amount deposited is generated for this purpose by the accounting program.

Adjustment Slip

If a mistake is made when data is entered into the system, an adjustment slip is used to correct the error.

Escrow Checks

As checks are written against deposited funds in the escrow account, data processing accounts for each individual check debit.

Fee Slips

As work is completed on individual escrow files, payment for services is drawn using a fee slip, and the amount earned is transferred to the bank's fee account.

Periodically, the escrow holder transfers funds, as needed, to its operations account.

Other Reports

Account Control

Report of new escrow
Receipt listing and
adjustments
Disbursement activity and
adjustments
Overdraft report
Fee report
Status reports
Master control and summary
of activity
Closed escrow report
List of missing start cards
Unprocessed and voided checks

Peripheral Data

Indices--cross references by escrow number, buyer, seller, broker, legal description, property address, type of escrow, or other meaningful index for the escrow office.

Trial Balance--monitors escrows open for a prolonged period.

Ledger Card--a permanent file record, produced monthly after final file disbursements.

Reconciliation--a report that keeps track of the balance between the trust bank account and the balance shown in the trust account system, making sure they conform with each other.

Checks Outstanding—a list of checks that are unpaid as yet by the bank.

Purged Escrow Listing—a list of the disbursement of all deposited funds, kept as escrows are removed from the system, either through closing or cancellation.

Roster of Escrow Officers—a list of escrow agents conducting each escrow.

Roster of Business Sources--client list.

Roster of Title Companies--sources most used by the escrow holder.

Audit Confirmation Letter--preprinted and addressed audit letters to the parties who deposit money in escrow to confirm the amounts in the trust account.

Customer Reports--a final file accounting with supporting disbursements.

Marketing Analysis

Escrow Activity--all escrows that have been opened, closed or canceled, listed by date and address.

Income Analysis by Officer—a list of fees earned by each escrow officer, thereby indicating strengths and weaknesses in productivity.

Income Analysis by Source--a marketing tool to indicate where market strengths lie.

Title Business Placement—a list of title orders placed by company.

SMS
STRATEGIC
MORTGAGE
SERVICES

SMS TITLE WORKS

Revolutionize the title business!

SMS Title Works represents a new concept in the title business business--true integration and sharing of information from one department or system to another. This eliminates the need to enter the same information over and over in numerous systems to process a title order.

Imagine entering your new title orders in your computer (just once)! And having that open order information automatically:

- order your title search
- pull the maps, recorded documents and starter file
- create an "Electronic title File" with all necessary paperwork
- prepare the preliminary title report or commitment

Your staff could actually do the examination right on the computer and have the preliminary title report or commitment prepared. All available on the same computer screen, with tracking information about each step. No need to make copies, print documents from the reader printer, or pass the paper file from one desk to another.

SMS Title Works is a suite of application systems offered by SMS including *TITLE/ESCROW/CLOSING production, DMS TITLE PLANT and IMAGE-PRO DOCUMENT IMAGING.* In addition to providing integration between our own systems, we have the ability to interface with competitive products that you may already have in place.

Our goal is to truly automate the process of a title order, from beginning to end. What will this mean to you? Improved productivity, better control, and a competitive advantage that all lead to increased revenue. And the best part...you don't have to radically change the way you currently do business. Simply let SMS Title Works do the work for you!

SMS

COMPANY: NEW

OFFICE: Demo

START CARD

Escrow Number	Opening Date	Officer	Title	Sales Price	Type
1111-Demo	7/8/99	JW	Fatco	$950,000.00	Sale

PROPERTY DESCRIPTION	EST. FEE	EST. COE	STATUS
1907 Elmhurst Costa Mesa, CA 92626	$680.00	9/06/99	

AGENT   **BUYER'S NAME**

Frederick T. McBuyer

BUYER'S ADDRESS (audit letters)

1907 Elmhurst Avenue, Costa Mesa, CA 92626

AGENT   **SELLER'S NAME**

Jonathan J. Sellerman, Jr.

SELLER'S ADDRESS (audit letters)

3445 Avenida de La Carlota, San Joan Capistrano, CA 92222   **BAL. FRWD**

❑YES ❑NO

COMMENTS   **HOLD**

Escrow to close concurrently with E#12341

❑YES ❑NO

FILE COPY

Listing Broker: WimbushRealty
Agent: Frank Allen

Selling Broker: Grubb & Ellis Company
Agent: Mary Allen

Title Company: First American Title Company
123 Marguerite Pkwy, Mission Viejo, CA 92692

Conversation Log

Date: 06-06-99   Page No: 1
Escrow: 1111-DEMO

Officer: Ella Escrowson   Opened: 4-06-99
Property: 8907 elmhurst   Closed: 6-06-99
Avenue
        Costa Mesa, CA 92626

Buyer: Seller:
Frederick McBuyer   Jonathan Sellerman
Josephine Buyertwo   Betty Sellerman

Entry: 06-06-99 2:47 PM By: jjw

This is a sample conversation log which you would use to type
information on this particular escrow, then print a copy and
attach in your escrow file.

Escrow No. 1111-Demo

Date Printed: June 6, 1999
Est. Close Date: June 6, 1999
Actual Close Date: June 6, 1999
Page 1

Reference:
8907 Elmhurst Avenue
Costa Mesa, CA 92626

SELLER:
Jonathan J. Sellerman, Jr.
Betty Jo Sellerman

BUYER:
Frederick T. McBuyere
Josephine P. Buyertwo

CHECK REGISTER

ISSUE DATE	RECEIPT NUMBER	PAYOR	AMOUNT
6/06/99	1234	Deposit: Buyer	2,000.00
6/06/99	01000	Deposit: Frederick T. Mcbuyer	36,700.00
6/06/99	1000	Draft: Fatco	4,311.08

ISSUE DATE	CHECK NUMBER	PAYEE	AMOUNT
6/06/99	1000	Jonathan J. Sellerman Jr.	26,536.97
6/06/99	1001	Frederick T. Mcbuyer	359.93
6/06/99	1002	Wimbush Realty	2,555.00
6/06/99	1003	Frank Allen	2,500.00
6/06/99	1004	Grubb & Ellis Co.	600.00
6/06/99	1005	Mary Allen	4,200.00
6/06/99	1006	Allstate Insurance Company	460.00
6/06/99	1007	ACE Pest Control	50.00
6/06/99	1008	The Elms Homeowners Association	175.00
6/06/99	1009	California Proprty Management	125.00
6/06/99	1010	Home Warranty Company	245.00
6/06/99	1011	Discover Card	2,345.00
6/06/99	1013	Courier Express Services	45.00
6/06/99	1014	Jonathan J. Sellerman	160.27
6/06/99	1015	First American Title Company	1,553.91
6/06/99	1012	SMS	1,000.00

Deposits:		38,700.00
Drafts/Wires: +		4,311.08
Checks: -		43,011.08
Funds Held		.00
Balance		.00

```
Date: 02-20-1999                    Preliminary                         Page 1
                                   Disbursement
                                      Report

Time: 18:30:59              SMS SETTLEMENT SERVICES                User: SMS
```

Escrow No. 004861	Open Date: 01/24/1999
Seller/Buyer: Getz/Trabuco	Closed Date: 02/20/1999

I. RECEIPTS:

1. Bob Trabuco	002381 02/01/1999	$1,750.00.00		
				$1,750.00

A. RECEIPTS IN PROCESS:

Bank of America	002394 02/20/1999	$80,008.13	
Total receipts in process			$80,008.13
Total Receipts			$81,758.13

II. DISBURSEMENTS   0.00

   A. DISBURSEMENTS IN PROCESS:

Total disbursements in process	0.00
	0.00
Total Disbursements	

   B. PRELIMINARY DISBURSEMENTS:

ANDERSON SURVEYING
4475 SOUTHWIND LANE
YORBA LINDA, CA

Survey - Buyer	350.00	
Total Checks		350.00

BLUE LAGOON REAL ESTATE
1590 SOUTH COAST HIGHWAY
LAGUNA BEACH, CA

Commission	5,697.00	
Total Checks		5,697.00

COMMERCIAL CENTER BANK
2900 S. HARBOR BLVD.
SANTA ANA, CA

Interest	450.63	
Principal Balance	67,595.00	
Total Checks		68,045.63

D.L. BRUCE EXTERMINATING CO
100 SANTA ANA BLVD
SANTA ANA, CA

Pest Inspection-Buyer	200.00~	
Total Checks		200.00

Date: 02-20-1999

Preliminary Disbursement Report

Page 2

Time: 18:30:59

SMS SETTLEMENT SERVICES

User: SMS

Escrow No. 004861
Seller/Buyer: Getz/Trabuco

Open Date: 01/24/1999
Closed Date: 02/20/1999

GRUBB & ELLIS CO.
24200 ALICIA PARKWAY
MISSION VIEJO, CA
Commission	5,697.00	
Total Check		5,697.00

MARICOPA COUNTY
RECORDER
Recording Fees-Buyer	20.50	
Recording Fees-Seller	35.00	
Total Check	55.50	

SMS SETTLEMENT
SERVICES
Creditline Endorsement	75.00	
Escrow Fees-Buyer	225.00	
Escrow Fees-Seller	175.00	
Title Examination-seller	250.00	
Title Insurance-Buyer	50.00	
Title Insurance-Seller	813.00	
Transfer Fee	25.00	
Total Check		1613.00

STRACHEN AND GREEN
Attorney's Fees-Seller	85.00	
Total Check		85.00

TRW
Credit Report-Buyer	15.00	
Total Check		15.00

Total Preliminary Disbursements		81,758.13
Total disbursements		81,758.13-
Escrow Balance		0.00

Approved by_____

Approved by_____

Date: 02-20-1999	**Final** **Disbursement** **Report**	Page 1

Time: 18:33:44	SMS SETTLEMENT SERVICES	User: SMS

Escrow No.: 004861   Open Date: 01/24/1999
Seller/Buyer: Getz/Trabuco   Closed Date: 02/20/1999

I. RECEIPTS:

1. Bob Trabuco	002381 02/01/1999	$1,750.00.00	
			$1,750.00

A. RECEIPTS IN PROCESS:

Bank of America	002394 02/20/1999	$80,008.13	
Total receipts in process			<u>$80,008.13</u>

Total Receipts			$81,758.13

II. DISBURSEMENTS			0.00

A. DISBURSEMENTS IN PROCESS:

1. Anderson Surveying	001223 02/20/1999	350.00
2. Blue Lagoon Real Estate	001224 02/20/1999	5,697.00
3. Commercial Center Bank	001225 02/20/1999	68,045.63
4. D.L. Bruce Exterminating	001226 02/20/1999	200.00
5. Grubb & Ellis Company	001227 02/20/1999	5,697.00
6. Maricopa County Recorder	001228 02/20/1999	55.50
7. SMS Settlement Services	001229 02/20/1999	1,613.00
8. Strachen and Green	001230 02/20/1999	85.00
9. TRW	001231 02/20/1999	15.00

Total disbursements in process		81,758.13

Total Disbursements		81,758.13

Escrow Balance		0.00

Approved by:

Lender Summary

Escrow Number	004859	Page 1
Escrow Officer:	Ted D. Gregory	User SMS
Borrower Name	Miller, George	

Lender Name	Bank of America
Type of Loan	New Loan

Amount of Loan	24,750.00
Amount withheld	2,428.50
Amount Due From Lender	122,321.50

Items Withheld From Loan

Description	Amount
Loan Origination Fee	180.00
Loan Discount	180.00
Appraisal Fee	350.00
Credit Line	200.00
Documentation Preparation	250.00
Tax Service	68.50
Hazard Insurance Premium	1,200.00

Post Test

The following self test repeats the one you took at the beginning of this chapter. Now take the exam again--since you have read all the material-- and check your knowledge of escrow closing procedures.

True/False

1. Traditional methods of conducting escrows have been replaced by computer technology.

2. The title industry does not use computer technology.

3. Title research is still done by manual methods.

4. The job of a title searcher is that of recovery of information about a specific property.

5. Legal opinions are sought by title examiners on some matters in the chain of title, rather than getting the information by computer search.

6. Accounting is one of the main uses for computers in escrow offices.

7. A start card places information in a computer at the end of a transaction.

8. An audit trail is created with an escrow receipt which is generated by a computer.

9. Mistakes made when data is entered are corrected with an adjustment slip.

10. A report that keeps track of the balance between the trust bank account and the balance shown in the trust account system is a reconciliation report.

DISCLOSURE
& CONSUMER
PROTECTION

Focus

- **Introduction**
- **Real property disclosures**
- **Subdivision disclosures**
- **Lending disclosures**

Pre-Test

The following is a self test to determine how much you know about disclosure and consumer protection before reading this chapter. Take it without studying, then read the material presented in the text. At the end of the chapter you will find a repeat of this exam. Test your knowledge by answering the questions again, then check your improvement. (The answers are found at the end of the book.) Good luck.

True/False

1. The escrow holder is responsible for making all real estate disclosures.

2. The Transfer Disclosure Statement is an optional disclosure.

3. Required disclosures must be made to the buyer as soon as practicable.

4. The Mello Roos Community Facilities Act is concerned with levying special taxes to finance public facilities.

5. The law requires a structural pest control inspection on all properties in escrow.

6. The Foreign Investment in Real Property Tax Act refers to withholding of taxes when sellers are not citizens.

7. In certain California real estate transactions, the buyer must withhold 3 1/3% of the total sales price as state income tax.

8. RESPA requires disclosure of good credit practice.

9. Truth in Lending Act promotes informed use of consumer credit.

10. Under the Real Property Loan Law, anyone negotiating a loan must have a real estate license.

Introduction

As the business of buying and selling real estate gets more complex, so do the required disclosures. What used to be a matter of a buyer's or seller's word, and simple honesty, is now elevated (or reduced, depending on your point of view) to multiple sworn copies of those same statements, with serious penalties for untruth or misrepresentation.

It is true that most of these disclosures are supplied through the real estate agent. The escrow holder is only concerned with carrying out the requirements of the escrow as they apply to the disclosures. The escrow agent, however, ultimately is the tally keeper, and must be aware of each of the requirements for disclosure as the escrow progresses.

Real Property Disclosures

As an escrow agent, one of your jobs is to guide the parties through the minefield of disclosure. Most of the disclosures are made by the real estate agent, with a small number made by the escrow holder. However, the practical escrow agent will make sure all disclosures have been made and all documents signed by the proper party.

Required Real Estate Disclosures

- Real Estate Transfer Disclosure Statement (TDS)
- Mello-Roos Disclosure
- Smoke Detector Statement of Compliance
- Lead Based Paint Disclosure
- State Responsibility Areas Disclosure
- Geological Hazard Disclosure
- Special Studies Zones Disclosure
- Secured Water Heater Disclosure
- Disclosure of Ordnance Location
- Environmental Hazard Disclosures
- Energy Conservation Retrofit Disclosure
- Flood Zone Disclosure
- City and County Ordinance Disclosure

Required Escrow Disclosures

- Foreign Investment in Real Property Tax Act
- Notice and Disclosure to Buyer of State Tax Withholding
- Controlling Documents and Financial Statement (condo)
- Notice of Advisability of Title Insurance
- Pest Control Inspection Disclosure

Real Estate Transfer Disclosure Statement (TDS)

Many facts about a residential property could materially affect its value and desirability. In the Real Estate Transfer Disclosure Statement, the seller reveals any information that would be important to the buyer regarding condition of the property. The seller states that-to his or her knowledge, everything pertinent, or in other words, anything that would significantly affect the value, has been disclosed. The escrow instructions then reflect the buyer's and seller's agreement about the disclosures.

Required TDS Disclosures

Age, condition and any defects or malfunctions of the structural components and/or plumbing, electrical, heating or other mechanical systems

Easements, common driveways or fences

Room additions, structural alterations, repairs, replacements or other changes, especially those made without required building permits

Flooding, drainage or soils problems on, near or in any way affecting the property

Zoning violations, such as nonconforming uses or insufficient setbacks

Homeowners' association obligations and deed restrictions or common area problems

Citations against the property, or lawsuits against the owner or affecting the property

Location of the property within a known earthquake zone

Major damage to the property from fire, earthquake or landslide

California law requires that a seller of one-to-four dwellings deliver to prospective buyers a Transfer Disclosure Statement about the condition of the property. This requirement extends to any transfer: by sale, exchange, installment land sale contract, lease with an option to purchase, any other option to purchase, or ground lease coupled with improvements.

<u>Exempt from the Obligation to Deliver the Statement are Various Transfers such as:</u>

- A foreclosure sale

- A court-ordered transfer by a fiduciary in the administration of a probate estate or a testamentary trust

- To a spouse or another related person resulting from a judgment of dissolution of marriage or of legal separation or from a property settlement agreement incidental to such a judgment

- From one co-owner to another

- By the state controller for unclaimed property

> ### Exempt from the Obligation to Deliver the Statement are Various Transfers such as:
> #### (continued)
>
> • Result from the failure to pay taxes
>
> • From or to any governmental entity
>
> • The first sale of a residential property within a subdivision

The required disclosure must be made to the prospective buyer, by the real estate agent, as soon as practicable before transfer of title, or in the case of a lease option, sales contract, or ground lease coupled with improvements, before the execution of the contract.

Should any disclosure or amended disclosure be delivered after the required date, the buyer/transferee has three days after delivery in person or five days after delivery by deposit in the U.S. mail to terminate the offer or agreement to purchase. A written notice of termination is the instrument that must reach the seller/transferor or the seller's agent for that purpose.

The obligation to prepare and deliver disclosures is imposed on the seller and the seller's agent and any agent acting in cooperation with them. Should more than one real estate agent be involved in the transaction (unless otherwise instructed by the seller), the agent obtaining the offer is required to deliver the disclosures to the prospective buyer.

Delivery to the prospective buyer of a report or an opinion prepared by a licensed engineer, land surveyor, geologist, structural pest control operator, contractor or other expert (with a specific professional license or expertise) may limit the liability of the seller and the real estate agents when making required disclosures. The overall intention is to provide meaningful disclosures about the condition of the property being transferred. A violation of the law does not invalidate a transfer; however, the seller may be liable for actual damages suffered by the buyer.

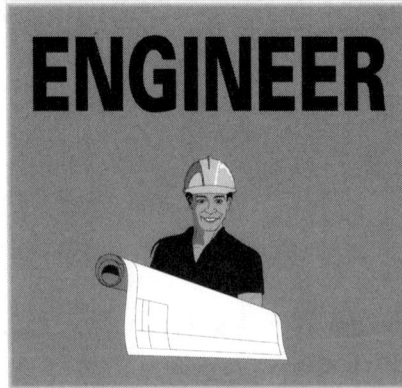

For information about the neighborhood or community, a city or county may require use of a Local Option Transfer Disclosure Statement disclosing special local facts.

Mello-Roos Disclosure

The Mello-Roos Community Facilities Act of 1982 authorizes the formation of community facilities districts, the issuance of bonds and the levying of special taxes which will finance designated public facilities and services. Effective July 1, 1993, the seller of a property consisting of one-to-four dwelling units subject to the lien of a Mello-Roos community facilities district must make a good faith effort to obtain from the district a disclosure notice concerning the special tax and give the notice to a prospective buyer. Exempt from this requirement are the various transfers listed earlier for the Transfer Disclosure Statement.

Smoke Detector Statement of Compliance

Whenever a sale or exchange of a single-family dwelling occurs, the seller must provide the buyer with a written statement representing that the property is in compliance with California law regarding smoke detectors. The state building code mandates that all existing dwelling units must have a smoke detector installed in a central location outside each sleeping area. In a two-story home with bedrooms on both floors, at least two smoke detectors would be required.

New construction, or any additions, alterations or repairs exceeding $1,000 and for which a permit is required, must include a smoke detector installed in each bedroom and also at a point centrally located in a corridor or area outside the bedrooms. This standard applies for the addition of one or more bedrooms, no matter what the cost.

In new home construction, the smoke detector must be hard-wired, with a battery backup. In existing dwellings, the detector may be only battery operated.

Disclosure Regarding Lead-Based Paint Hazards

When an FHA-insured mortgage will be involved in the transfer of a dwelling built before 1978, the prospective buyer/borrower must, prior to signing the offer to purchase, receive and sign a prescribed notice concerning lead-based paint hazards. If this is not done, the buyer/borrower will have to receive and sign the notice and then execute a new offer to purchase. When implementing regulations have been adopted, a

383

similar notice requirement will apply to such transactions when any other federally-related mortgage is involved.

Disclosures Regarding State Responsibility Areas

The Department of Forestry and Fire Protection has produced maps identifying rural lands classified as state responsibility areas. In such a region, the state (as opposed to a local or federal agency) has the primary financial responsibility for the prevention and extinguishing of fires. Maps of these state responsibility areas and any changes (including new maps to be produced every five years) are to be provided to assessors in the affected counties.

Should the seller know his or her real property is located in a state responsibility area, or if the property is included on a map given by the department to the county assessor, the seller must disclose the possibility of substantial fire risk in such wild land area and the fact that the land is subject to certain preventive requirements.

With the department's agreement, and by ordinance, a county may assume responsibility for all fires, including those occurring in state responsibility areas. If there is such an ordinance, the seller of property located in the area must disclose to the buyer that the state is not obligated to provide fire protection services for any building or structure unless such protection is required by a cooperative agreement with a county, city or district.

Disclosure of Ordnance Location

Federal and state agencies have identified certain areas once used for military training and which may contain live ammunition as part of the ordnance--or military supplies--from past activity. A seller of residential property located within one mile of such a hazard must give the buyer written notice as soon as practicable before transfer of title. This obligation depends upon the seller having actual knowledge of the hazard.

Delivery of Structural Pest Control Inspection and Certification Reports

The law does not require that a structural pest control inspection be performed on real property prior to transfer. Should an inspection report and certification be required as a condition of transfer or obtaining financing, however, it must be done as soon as possible. Before transfer of title or before executing a real property sales contract, the seller or the seller's agent (and any agent acting in cooperation) must deliver or have delivered to the buyer a copy of the report. There must also be written certification attesting to the presence or absence of wood-destroying termites in the visible and accessible areas of the property. Such an inspection report and written certification must be prepared and issued by a registered structural pest-control company.

Upon request from the party ordering such a report, the company issuing same must divide it into two categories: one part to identify the portions of the property where existing damage, infection or infestation are noted; and the other to point out areas that may have impending damage, infection or infestation.

Generally, if there is more than one real estate agent in the transaction, the agent who obtained the offer is responsible for delivering the report unless the seller has given written directions regarding delivery to another agent involved. Delivery of the required documents may be in person or by mail to the buyer. In reality, the escrow holder in most cases sends the termite report to all parties. The real estate agent responsible for delivery, however, must retain for three years a complete record of the actions taken to effect delivery.

Disclosure of Geological Hazards and Special Studies Zones

Geologists describe the surface of the earth as always changing. Some of these geological changes are relatively unimportant--not requiring a disclosure. Other changes are apparent by casual inspection--of a nature that a potential buyer should be able to judge the impact of the existing geological condition on the intended property's use.

In some cases, disclosure of a geological condition must be made. This is true of potential hazards from earthquakes, flooding, landslides, erosion and expansive soils. One condition requiring such disclosure is "fault creep," caused by stress and/or earthquake shaking.

Geology in the context of the required disclosures refers to the type of soil and how that soil will respond to earthquakes. Soft sediments tend to amplify shaking, whereas bedrock soils tend to lessen the shaking.

Generally, the closer in location to the fault, the more intense the shaking will be. However, soils types and conditions may be more important than distance from the epicenter.

The state geologist is in the process of identifying areas susceptible to "fault creep," to be shown on maps prepared by the State Division of Mines and Geology. These maps also identify known historic landslides. The seller or the seller's agent and any agent acting in cooperation with such agent usually may rely on the identification of the special studies zones by the state geologist for disclosure purposes. In some instances, additional investigation may be required. Construction on real property of any structure for human occupancy may be subject to the findings and recommendations of a geologic report prepared by a geologist or soils engineer registered in or licensed by the state of California.

A seller of real property situated in a special studies zone, or the agent of the seller and any agent acting in cooperation with such agent, must disclose to the buyer that the property is or may be situated in such a zone as designated under the Alquist-Priolo Special Studies Zones Act.

This disclosure must be made on either the Real Estate Transfer Disclosure Statement or the Local Option Real Estate Transfer Disclosure Statement or in the purchase agreement.

The escrow holder is not responsible for this disclosure, but should be aware of the requirement.

Excluded from Requirements of the Special Studies Zones Act:

- Structures in existence prior to May 4, 1975

- Single family wood-frame or steel-frame dwellings for which geologic reports have been approved, to be built in subdivisions authorized by the Subdivision Map Act

- Single family wood-frame or steel dwellings not over two stories, provided the dwelling is not part of a development of four or more dwellings (includes mobile homes over eight-feet wide)

- Conversions of existing apartments into condominiums, except it must be disclosed that the property is located within a delineated special-studies zone

- Alterations under 50% of the value of the structure

In addition, under the California Legislature's authorization, the Seismic Safety Commission developed a *Homeowner's Guide to Earthquake Safety* for distribution to real estate licensees and the general public. The guide includes information on geologic and seismic hazards for all areas, explanations of related structural and nonstructural hazards, and recommendations for mitigating the hazards of an earthquake.

The guide states that safety or damage prevention cannot be guaranteed with respect to a major earthquake and that only precautions such as retrofitting can be undertaken to reduce the risk of various types of damage.

Should a buyer of real property receive a copy of the Homeowner's Guide, neither the seller nor the agent are required to provide additional information regarding geologic and seismic hazards. Sellers and real estate agents must disclose that the property is in a special studies zone, however, and that there are known hazards affecting the real property being transferred.

Delivery of the *Homeowner's Guide to Earthquake Safety* is required in the following transactions:

- Transfer of any real property with a residential dwelling built prior to January 1, 1960, and consisting of one-to-four units, any of which are of conventional light-frame construction

- Transfer of any masonry building with wood-frame floors or roofs built before January 1, 1975

In a transfer subject to the first item above, the following structural deficiencies and any corrective measures taken that are within the transferor's actual knowledge, are to be disclosed to prospective buyers.

Required Disclosures:

- Absence of foundation anchor bolts
- Unbraced or inappropriately braced perimeter cripple walls
- Unbraced or inappropriately braced first-story wall/walls
- Unreinforced masonry perimeter foundation
- Unreinforced masonry dwelling walls
- Habitable room or rooms above a garage
- Water heater not anchored, strapped or braced

Certain exemptions apply to the obligation to deliver the booklet when transferring either a dwelling of one-to-four units or a reinforced masonry building. These exemptions are essentially the same as those that apply to delivery of the Real Estate Transfer Disclosure Statement described earlier in this section.

The buyer and/or agent may be responsible for making further inquiries of appropriate governmental agencies. The obligation of the buyer and/or agent to make further inquiry does not eliminate the duty of the seller's agent to do the following: make a diligent inquiry to identify the location of the real property in relationship to a defined special studies zone and to determine whether the property is subject to any local ordinance regarding geological and soils conditions. Full and complete disclosure is required of all material facts regarding a special studies zone, local ordinances or known structural deficiencies affecting the property.

Finally, the state geologist is responsible for the long-term project of mapping California's Seismic Hazard Zones, identifying areas susceptible to strong ground shaking, liquefaction, landslides or other ground failure and other seismic hazards caused by earthquakes. The seller's duty to disclose that the property is in a special-studies zone or a seismic-hazard zone may be limited by the availability of the maps at locations specified by local county officials.

Environmental Hazard Disclosures

Numerous federal, state and local laws have been enacted to address the problems created by environmental hazards. Responsible parties, or persons deemed responsible, for the improper disposal of hazardous waste and owners of contaminated property may be held liable for contamination cleanup.

Several disclosure laws relating to the transfer of land affected by hazardous waste contamination also have been enacted.   The California Real Estate Transfer Disclosure Statement now requires sellers to disclose whether they are aware of the presence of hazardous substances, materials or products including--but not limited to--asbestos, formaldehyde, radon gas, lead-based paint, fuel or chemical storage tanks and contaminated soil or water.

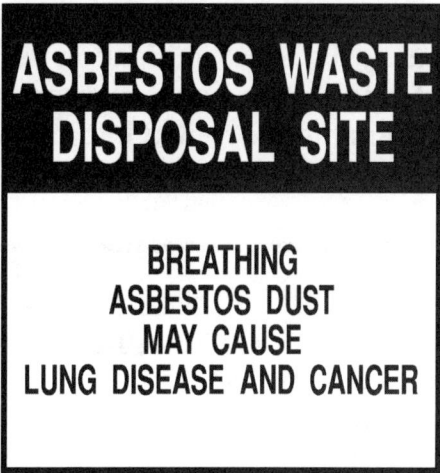

ASBESTOS WASTE DISPOSAL SITE

BREATHING
ASBESTOS DUST
MAY CAUSE
LUNG DISEASE AND CANCER

391

Any owner of nonresidential property who knows or suspects that there has been a release of a hazardous substance or that it may occur on or beneath the property must notify a buyer, lessee or renter of that condition prior to the sale, lease, or rental of that property. Failure to give written notice may subject the owner to actual damages and/or civil penalties.

Under Proposition 65, certain businesses may not knowingly and intentionally expose any individual to a cancer-causing chemical or reproductive toxin without first giving clear, reasonable warning to such individuals. Recently, the law also has imposed extensive asbestos disclosure requirements on owners of commercial buildings constructed prior to January 1, 1979.

The Department of Real Estate and Office of Environmental Health Hazard Assessment have developed a booklet to help educate and inform consumers about environmental hazards that may affect real property. The booklet identifies common environmental hazards, describes the risks involved with each, discusses mitigation techniques and provides lists of publications and sources from which consumers can obtain more detailed information.

Hazards Discussed in the Environmental Hazard Booklet

- Asbestos
- Radon
- Lead
- Formaldehyde

Once the booklet is provided to a prospective buyer of real property, neither the seller nor a real estate agent involved in the sale has a duty to provide further information on such hazards. If the seller or agent has actual knowledge of environmental hazards on or affecting the subject property, that information must be disclosed.

Energy Conservation Retrofit and Thermal Insulation Disclosure

State law prescribes a minimum energy conservation standard for all new construction, without which a building permit may not be issued. Local governments also have ordinances that impose additional energy conservation measures on new and/or existing homes. Some local ordinances impose energy retrofitting as a condition of selling an existing home. The requirements of the various ordinances, as well as who is responsible for compliance, may vary among local jurisdictions. The existence and basic requirements of local energy ordinances should be disclosed to a prospective buyer by the seller and/or the seller's agent and any agent cooperating in the deal.

Federal law requires a "new home" seller to disclose in every sales contract the type, thickness and R-value of the insulation which has been or will be installed in each part of the house, including the ceiling and interior and exterior walls. This law also applies to developers of "new home" subdivisions.

Special Flood Hazard Area Disclosure and Responsibilities of the Federal Emergency Management Agency (FEMA)

Flood Hazard Boundary Maps identify the general flood hazards within a community. They are also used in flood plain management and for flood insurance purposes. These maps, developed by the Federal Emergency Management Agency (FEMA) in conjunction with communities participating in the National Flood Insurance Program (NFIP) show areas within 100-year flood boundary, termed "special flood zone areas." Also identified are areas between 100 and 500-year levels termed "areas of moderate flood hazards" and the remaining areas above the 500-year level termed "areas of minimal risk."

A seller of property located in a special flood hazard area, or the seller's agent and/or any agent cooperating in the deal, must disclose that fact to the buyer and that federal law requires flood insurance as a condition of obtaining financing on most structures located in a special flood hazard area. Since the cost and extent of flood insurance coverage may vary, the buyer should contact an insurance carrier or the intended lender for further information.

Local Requirements Resulting from City and County Ordinances

Residential properties in cities and counties throughout California are typically subject to specific local ordinances on occupancy; zoning and use; building code compliance; fire, health and safety code regulations; and land subdivision descriptions. The various requirements for compliance as well as who and what is affected thereby should be disclosed to the prospective buyer of the

property by the seller or the seller's agent and any agent acting in cooperation with such agent.

Foreign Investment in Real Property Tax Act

Federal law requires that a buyer of real property must withhold and send to the Internal Revenue Service (IRS) 10% of the gross sales price if the seller of the real property is a foreign person.

Primary Grounds for Exemption from this Requirement are:

- Seller's non-foreign affidavit and U.S. taxpayer identification number

- A qualifying statement obtained through the IRS saying arrangements have been made for the collection of or exemption from the tax

- Sales price does not exceed $300,000

- Buyer intends to reside on the property

Because of the number of exemptions and other requirements relating to this law, it is recommended that the IRS be consulted for more detailed information. Sellers and buyers and the real estate agents involved who desire further advice should consult an attorney, CPA or other qualified tax advisor.

Notice and Disclosure to Buyer of State Tax Withholding on Disposition of California Real Property

In certain California real estate sales transactions, the buyer must withhold 3 1/3% of the total sale price as state income tax and deliver the sum withheld to the state Franchise Tax Board. The escrow holder, in applicable transactions, is required by law to notify the buyer of this responsibility.

A buyer's failure to withhold and deliver the required sum may result in penalties. Should the escrow holder fail to notify the buyer, penalties may be levied against the escrow holder.

Transactions Subject to the Law:

- The seller shows an out-of-state address, or sale proceeds are to be disbursed to the seller's financial intermediary

- The sales price exceeds $100,000

- The seller does not certify that he or she is a California resident, or that the property being conveyed is his or her personal residence

---

Furnishing Controlling Documents and a Financial Statement

The owner (other than a subdivider) of a separate legal share in a common interest development (community apartment project, condominium project, planned development or stock cooperative) must provide a prospective buyer with the following:

<u>Required Disclosures:</u>

- A copy of the governing documents of the development

- Should there be an age restriction not consistent with the law, a statement that the age restriction is only enforceable to the extent permitted by law; and applicable provisions of the law

- A copy of the homeowners association's most recent financial statement

- A written statement from the association specifying the amount of current regular and special assessments as well as any unpaid assessment, late charges, interest and costs of collection which are or may become a lien against the property

- Information on any approved change in the assessments or fees not yet due and payable as of the disclosure date

Notice Regarding the Advisability of Title Insurance

In an escrow for a sale (or exchange) of real property where no title insurance is to be issued, the buyer (or both parties to an exchange) must receive and sign the following notice as a separate document in the escrow:

Important:

In a purchase or exchange of real property, it may be advisable to obtain title insurance in connection with the close of escrow where there may be prior recorded liens and encumbrances which affect your interest in the property being acquired. A new policy of title insurance should be obtained in order to ensure your interest in the property that you are acquiring.

While the law does not expressly assign the duty, it is reasonable to assume that the escrow holder is obligated to deliver the notice. A real estate agent conducting an escrow also would be responsible for delivering the notice.

Subdivision Disclosures

A subdivision is the division of land into five or more lots for the purpose of sale, lease or financing. Because of abuses in the early years of development, the division and resale of real property has received significant legislative attention. The escrow officer must be aware of special laws regulating subdivisions and the requirements and time periods involved in the resale of subdivided land.

Subdivision Map Act

This act authorizes city and county governments to enact and carry out subdivision laws according to the regulations set down in the Subdivision Map Act. All division of land into two or more parcels falls under this law.

The main objective of the Subdivision Map Act is to define the rules and procedures for filing maps to create subdivisions. It is directly controlled by local authorities (city and county) and is concerned with the physical aspects of a subdivision--such as building design, streets and environmental impact.

As a result of the Subdivision Map Act, the direct control of the kind and type of subdivisions to be allowed in each community and the physical improvements to be installed are left to local jurisdictions (city and county) within certain general limits specified in the act.

Subdivision Map Act has Two Major Objectives:

1. To coordinate the subdivision plans and planning, including lot design, street patterns, right-of-way for drainage and sewers, etc., with the community pattern and plan, as laid out by the local planning authorities

2. To ensure initial proper improvement of areas dedicated for public purposes by filing subdivision maps, including public streets and other public areas, by the subdivider so that these necessities will not become an undue burden in the future for taxpayers in the community

---

The Subdivision Map Act requires every city and county to adopt a law to regulate subdivisions for which a tentative and final map, or a parcel map, is required. Also, the act allows cities and counties to adopt laws for subdivisions for which no map is required.

State and local requirements for processing subdivision maps must be acknowledged by the escrow agent while working with the title company which will be principally responsible for map processing and recording.

The approval process for a subdivision starts at the preliminary planning stage, moving along to satisfy the requirements of the state, local government, title company and lender

If the transaction includes a map filing, the escrow holder should be practical when calculating the closing time for the escrow. The filing of a parcel map can take six to nine months, and a formal tract map filing process involves 12 to 18 months.

Subdivided Lands Act

In California, the Subdivided Lands Act is administered directly by the Real Estate Commissioner. Its objective is to protect buyers of property in new subdivisions from fraud, misrepresentation or deceit in the marketing of subdivided lots, parcels, units and undivided interests.

The Real Estate Commissioner must issue a subdivision public report before any subdivision can be offered for sale in California. This even applies to lands outside the state, if they are being marketed in California. The public report is a document disclosing all important facts about the marketing and financing of the subdivision.

The public report must show that the subdivider (developer) can complete and maintain all improvements and that the lots or parcels can be used for the purpose for which they are being sold.

Before a developer can sell each lot in the project, he or she must give a copy of the commissioner's final report to the buyer for approval. The buyer signs a receipt for the report stating it has been read. The seller (developer) must keep a copy of the statement for three years.

The public report is valid for five years, with any material changes in the development reported to the commissioner, who then can issue an amendment to the original report.

It can take many months for a developer to get project approval, once all the proper paperwork is submitted to the commissioner. During that time, the developer may want to begin marketing the project while waiting for the final report.

By submitting a minimum application filing package the developer can get a preliminary public report which allows taking reservations for the project, but not accepting any non-refundable money or entering into any binding contracts until receiving the final report from the commissioner.

Lending Disclosures

Along with the need for real property disclosures came a need for consumer protection in lending. Borrowers wanted to know what the real cost of borrowing money was and demanded to be protected from less than honest loan brokers. Thus, disclosures regarding loans and consumer credit and laws governing loan brokers became part of the rapidly growing consumer protection movement.

The Real Estate Settlement Procedures Act (RESPA)

The Real Estate Settlement Procedures Act (RESPA) applies to all federally related mortgage loans. The act requires special disclosures for certain lenders who provide loan funds for transactions involving one-to-four residential units.

Special procedures and forms for settlements (closing costs) must be used for most home mortgage loans, including FHA and VA loans, and those from financial institutions with federally-insured deposits.

The lender must furnish a copy of a Special Information Booklet, together with a Good Faith Estimate of the amount or range of closing costs to every person from whom the lender receives a written application for any federally related loan.

Truth-in-Lending Act (Regulation Z)

The Truth-in-Lending Act became effective July 1, 1969.The main purpose of the law is to promote the informed use of consumer credit by requiring creditors to disclose credit terms so consumers can make comparisons between various credit sources. To accomplish the objectives of the act the Board of

Governors of the Federal Reserve System issued a directive known as Regulation Z.

Later, the Federal Reserve Board adopted model disclosures for closed-end transactions such as the purchase of real property and model language for certain other disclosures. The Federal Reserve Board also announced that its staff would no longer provide written answers to individuals requesting interpretations of Regulation Z, but would issue general statements from time to time to answer questions of interpretation.

Real Property Loan Law

The Real Estate Law requires anyone negotiating a loan to have a real estate license. In the past, abuses have occurred in the form of excessive commissions, inflated costs and expenses, the negotiating of short-term loans with large balloon payments, and misrepresentation or concealment of material facts by licensees negotiating these loans.

As a result of this mistreatment of consumers by corrupt agents, legislation was passed to correct the situation. The Real Property Loan Law now applies to loans secured by first trust deeds under $30,000 and by junior trust deeds under $20,000.

The law requires anyone negotiating a loan to provide a Mortgage Loan Broker's Statement (sometimes called a Mortgage Loan Disclosure Statement) to a prospective borrower, with information concerning all important features of a loan to be negotiated for the borrower.

From time to time, a real estate agent, as part of a transaction, will be involved in negotiating a loan for the borrower. A completed Mortgage Loan Disclosure Statement must be presented to the prospective borrower, and the borrower must sign the statement prior to signing loan documents.

Professionalism and Ethics

Staying informed is probably the most important task left to the escrow agent. Those who make continuing efforts to learn and stay current on real estate industry changes will be the ones to compete successfully in the future.

Increasingly, escrow agents must know what and how to disclose--as well as when, where, why, by and to whom. The uninformed escrow agent is highly vulnerable to court action in our consumer-oriented society.

Post Test

The following self test repeats the one you took at the beginning of this chapter. Now take the exam again--since you have read all the material-- and check your knowledge of escrow closing procedures.

True/False

1. The escrow holder is responsible for making all real estate disclosures.

2. The Transfer Disclosure Statement is an optional disclosure.

3. Required disclosures must be made to the buyer as soon as practicable.

4. The Mello Roos Community Facilities Act is concerned with levying special taxes to finance public facilities.

5. The law requires a structural pest control inspection on all properties in escrow.

6. The Foreign Investment in Real Property Tax Act refers to withholding of taxes when sellers are not citizens.

7. In certain California real estate transactions, the buyer must withhold 3 1/3% of the total sales price as state income tax.

8. RESPA requires disclosure of good credit practice.

9. Truth in Lending Act promotes informed use of consumer credit.

10. Under the Real Property Loan Law, anyone negotiating a loan must have a real estate license.

chapter **14**

OTHER TYPES OF ESCROWS

Focus

- **Introduction**
- **Holding escrow**
- **Loan escrow**
- **Trust deed sale**
- **Subdivision escrow**
- **Leasehold escrow**
- **Mobile home escrow**
- **Bulk transfer**
- **1031 exchange**

Pre-Test

The following is a self test to determine how much you know about other types of escrows before reading this chapter. Take it without studying, then read the material presented in the text. At the end of the chapter you will find a repeat of this exam. Test your knowledge by answering the questions again, then check your improvement. (The answers are found at the end of the book.) Good luck.

True/False

1. Only sale escrows may be conducted by private escrow companies.

2. A loan escrow is used to transfer property which is being sold and funded by a subdivider.

3. A trust deed is sold whenever property transfers ownership.

4. An escrow can be required where fee title is not transferred.

5. Typical leasehold escrows will be a land lease or a space lease.

6. In commercial leasing, title insurance is never used.

7. The primary product in a mobile home escrow is considered personal property.

8. A mobile home never becomes real property.

9. Bulk transfer refers to the sale of a business.

10. Capital gains are deferred when a seller completes a 1031 tax-free exchange.

Introduction

As you have journeyed through this text, the sale escrow has been used as the basic teaching tool for the beginning escrow student. It is desirable, however, for every escrow student to be familiar with other varieties.

Each type of escrow has its own terminology, special requirements and personality. As you read through this chapter you will see the myriad ways escrow serves the real estate industry beyond the common sale escrow.

A description of each type of escrow that may be encountered in the course of a career in escrow follows.

Holding Escrow

The escrow agent, acting in the capacity of a neutral "stake-holder," holds money, documents or something else of value until directed to release them upon performance of conditions specified by the principals.

Subdivision Pre-Sale

Reservations on a subdivision may be taken by a developer who has received a Preliminary Public Report from the Real Estate Commissioner. Parcels may be reserved by placing them in an escrow until the developer is issued a final report, at which time a sale escrow can be opened.

Construction Funding

A builder may receive funds from a construction loan by "draw." The lender deposits the proceeds from the loan in an escrow, with instructions about how the funds are to be released to the builder.

Stock Distribution

When stock representing a majority interest in a corporation is transferred, many times an escrow is required. An escrow agent must be totally familiar with the needs of the parties and the complexity of the process to be involved in these kinds of transactions. The specialized types of documents and procedures along with government regulatory involvement make a stock transfer complicated and demanding for the escrow officer.

Loan Escrow

Separate instructions may be prepared for a loan escrow, depending upon the structure of the sale escrow directions. Typically, a loan escrow would be preparedfor a refinance of an existing loan. In some instances, however, a sub-escrow opened specifically as a loan escrow may be connected to a sale transaction.

In most cases where there is an open sale escrow, the sale instructions include directions for the escrow officer regarding the financing. A separate loan escrow is not commonly opened.

If the lender is a private party, the escrow holder is responsible for preparing the loan documents, usually a promissory note and trust deed. If a transaction requires other types of loan documents, such as a contract of sale or an all inclusive trust deed (AITD), the principals are encouraged to use the services of an attorney to prepare the instruments of finance.

410

If the transaction calls for a loan to be funded by an institutional lender, the loan documents are prepared by the lender and sent to the escrow holder for signing by the borrower. The promissory note and a copy of the trust deed are then returned to the lender. The original notarized trust deed is held by the escrow officer until the escrow is ready to close. When the title company receives the signed, notarized trust deed from the escrow holder, loan funds are released to the escrow officer for disbursement and closing, and the trust deed is recorded.

Trust Deed Sale

A loan may be sold many times during its life, whether it was originated by an institutional lender or a private party. A loan can be bought and sold in the secondary mortgage market or privately, and in the course of the sale, go through an escrow.

The primary instrument in the sale of a loan is the trust deed, just as a grant deed is the primary instrument in the sale of real property. As you recall, the evidence of the debt is the promissory note, with the deed of trust as collateral or security for the loan.

When the holder of a note secured by a deed of trust wants to sell his or her interest, the instrument of transfer is an assignment of trust deed. The buyer may require an escrow and title insurance to confirm clear title to the indebtedness (the trust deed).

SMS - SETTLEMENT SERVICES DIVISION, A CALIFORNIA CORPORATION IS LICENSED AS AN ESCROW AGENT BY THE DEPARTMENT OF CORPORATIONS OF THE STATE OF CALIFORNIA.

LOAN ESCROW INSTRUCTIONS

TO: **SMS - Settlement Services Division**

Date: **July 8, 1999**
Escrow Number: DEMOREFI
Escrow Officer: **Ella Escrowson**
Page 1 of 5

The undersigned Borrower(s) is obtaining a loan on the property hereinafter described and will cause Lender to hand you the proceeds of a new First Trust Deed in the amount of **$171,000.00**, less Lender's normal costs and charges, which you are authorized to use on or before **September 6, 1999**, providing upon recordation of the securing Deed of Trust, you obtain an ALTA Lender's Policy of Title insurance, per Lender's requirements covering real property in the County of **Orange**, State of California, as follows:

Lot 123 of Tract 12345, in the City of Lake Forest, County of Orange as per map recorded in Book 324, Page(s) 12-13, of Miscellaneous Maps in the Office of the County Recorder of said County.

COMMONLY KNOWN AS: **22177 Oakwood Lane, Lake Forest, CA 92222**

The title policy is to show the title to the property to be vested in:

John J. Borrower and Linda K. Borrower, Husband and Wife as Joint Tenants

The policy is to be free of encumbrances except as follows:

(1) Any General and Special Taxes and Special District Levies not due or delinquent; this will include the lien of supplemental taxes, if any, assessed pursuant to Chapter 498, 1983 Statutes of the State of California.
(2) All Taxes, Bonds and Assessments levied or assessed subsequent to the date of these instructions.
(3) Covenants, conditions, reservations (including exceptions of oil, gas minerals, hydrocarbons, and/or lease without right of surface entry), restrictions, right of way, and easements for public utilities, districts, water companies, alleys, and streets.
(4) First Trust Deed to file, securing a note in the principal amount of **$171,000.00** in favor of **Bank of America** at the best prevailing rate and terms per lenders instructions to be deposited into escrow.

DEPOSIT OF FUNDS INTO ESCROW: Each of the undersigned acknowledges and understands that pursuant to State of California Assembly Bill ("Good Funds Legislation") which became effective January 1, 1990, funds deposited into escrow and/or deposited with the Title Company for use in this escrow by the Property Owner, Buyer and New Lender in any form other than a wire transfer may cause a delay in the closing of this escrow and/or disbursement of funds at the time of closing. Each of the undersigned hereby indemnifies and holds SMS - Settlement Services Division and its officers and/or Employees harmless with the respect to any delay in closing and/or disbursement of funds due to compliance with the Provisions of "AB512".

NOTICE REGARDING CLOSING FUNDS: In the event Borrower elects to deposit closing funds by Cashier's Check, said funds MUST be deposited not later than 48 hours prior to the anticipated date of close of escrow, pursuant to AB512 Good Funds Law.

CONDITION OF TITLE: Escrow Holder is authorized and instructed to pay any encumbrance necessary to place title in the condition called for herein and Borrower will hand you any instruments and/or funds as required for such purpose.

LOAN ESCROW INSTRUCTIONS

TO: **SMS - Settlement Services Division**
Date: **July 8, 1999**
Escrow Number: DEMOREFI
Escrow Officer: **Ella Escrowson**
Page 2 of 5

OBTAIN DEMAND: Escrow holder is hereby authorized and instructed to obtain demand from lender(s) of record and to pay for same from Borrower's proceeds at the close of escrow, including prepayment penalties, interest and such other costs, if applicable.

FIRE INSURANCE: Secure for Lender an endorsement on existing insurance policy naming lender as First Trust Deed Holder and providing for replacement cost guarantee, as required by Lender. Charge account of Borrower at close of escrow and pay premiums as may be required for same, per billing to be deposited herein prior to close of escrow.

CLOSING COSTS/CHARGES: Pay escrow charges and proper recording fees, also charges for evidence of title called for above (whether or not this escrow is consummated) and you are authorized to pay off any bonds, assessments and/or taxes, also any encumbrances of record, plus accrued interest, charges and bonus, if any, to show title as called for above and/or necessary to comply with same. Instruct the title company to begin search of title at once.

ADVANCE RELEASE OF DEMAND FEES: In the event the Existing Lienholder(s) requires payment to demand statement fees in advance of issuing their demand statement. Borrower shall deposit sufficient funds as called for by Escrow Holder for payment of same and authorizes Escrow Holder to release said funds to Existing Leinholder(s) prior to close of escrow. Borrower acknowledges and agrees that said funds are NON-REFUNDABLE in the event this escrow is not consummated.

CANCELLATION FEE: Borrower is aware that in the event this escrow is canceled. Borrower shall pay a cancellation fee of $100.00 to Escrow Holder. Said cancellation fee to be deducted from funds on deposit upon written and/or verbal notice of cancellation by Lender or Borrower.

HOLD OPEN FEE: It is agreed that if, for any reason, this escrow is not closed within NINETY (90) days of the established date for closing as shown herein. Escrow Holder may at their option charge a hold-open fee against funds then on deposit in the amount of $25.00 for each month, or fraction thereof, that this escrow remains unclosed.

CLOSE OF ESCROW: The close of escrow shall be the day documents deposited in this escrow are recorded pursuant to these instructions.

EXTENSION OF TIME FOR CLOSING: If the condition of this escrow have not been complied with at the time provided for in these instructions, you are nevertheless to complete this escrow as soon as the conditions (except as to time) have been complied with, unless a written demand for the return of money and/or instruments by a party to his escrow is received by you prior to the recording of any instrument provided for in these instructions.

NECESSITY FOR WRITTEN INSTRUCTIONS: No notice, demand or change or instructions shall be of any effect unless given to you in writing and approved in writing by all parties affected by same.

DEPOSITS AND DISBURSEMENTS: All funds delivered to you by parties to this escrow shall be deposited in any non-interest bearing account designated as a "Trust Account" with any bank or depository authorized by the Federal or State Government, and may be transferred to, and co-mingled with, other such trust accounts. You shall not be obligated to identify or to guarantee the signature of any payee on said checks.

LOAN ESCROW INSTRUCTIONS

TO: **SMS - Settlement Services Division**

Date: **July 8, 1999**
Escrow Number: DEMOREFI
Escrow Officer: **Ella Escrowson**
Page 3 of 5

SUB-ESCROW AGENTS: As you deem reasonably necessary to the closing of this escrow, you may deposit any funds or documents received by you herein, with any bank, title insurance company, savings and loan association, trust company, industrial loan company, credit union, admitted insurer or licensed escrow agent and any such deposit shall be deemed in accordance herewith. In this regard, you are authorized to utilize the services of one or more sub-escrow agents as defined under the California Financial Code and/or documents prior to close of escrow, if reasonable necessary in your discretion.

ADJUSTMENTS AND PRORATIONS: All adjustments shall be made upon the basis of a thirty day month, including, but not necessarily limited to the following: A. Taxes for the current year, based on tax amounts disclosed on last available tax bill; B. Premiums on fire insurance policies as handed you; C. Interest on loans of record, based on statement from the lender.

RECORDING AND TRANSFER FEES: To facilitate the recording of any documents delivered into or through this escrow, you may pay all required fees; all of the costs of which shall be deemed to constitute an authorized expenditure to be paid or charged to the party responsible therefore.

EFFECT OF CONFLICT: If, before or after recording documents, you receive or become aware of any conflicting demands or claims (hereinafter "conflicts") with respect to this escrow, the rights or obligations of any of the parties of any money or property deposited or affected, you shall have the right to discontinue further performance on your part until the conflict is resolved to your satisfaction. In addition, you shall have the right to commence or defend any action or proceeding you deem necessary for the determination of the conflict. A conflict shall be deemed to include, but is not necessarily limited to, your receipt of unilateral instructions or instructions from some, but not all of the escrow. In the event of a conflict, you shall not be liable to take any action of any kind, but may withhold all moneys, securities, documents or other things deposited into escrow, until such conflict has been determined by agreement of the parties or by legal process.

In the event any action is commenced to determine a conflict or otherwise to enforce or declare the provisions of these instructions or to rescind them, including, but not limited to, a suit in inter pleader (whether or not the action is prosecuted to final judgment, voluntarily dismissed or settled, and irrespective of whether you are the prevailing party in any such action) and it becomes necessary or desirable for you to obtain legal advice with respect to a conflict or on account of any matter or thing arising out of or in any way related to these instructions, whether or not suit is actually commenced, the parties to this escrow jointly and severally agree to pay all of your costs, damages, judgments and expenses, including attorney's fees, incurred by you in connection with the same.

PAYMENT OF FEES AND CHARGES: It is understood that the fees agreed to be paid for your services are for ordinary and usual services only, and should there be any extraordinary or unusual services rendered by you, the undersigned agree to pay reasonable compensation to you for such extraordinary or unusual services, together with any costs and expenses which may be incurred by you in connection with same. Upon the close of the escrow, you may retain, on your own behalf, your charges, costs and fees and charge the same in your accounting against the person responsible therefore.

IT IS UNDERSTOOD THAT, IN THE EVENT THIS ESCROW IS CANCELED OR TERMINATED, YOU WILL RECEIVE COMPENSATION FOR SUCH SERVICES AS YOU HAVE RENDERED IN CONNECTION WITH THIS ESCROW.

LOAN ESCROW INSTRUCTIONS

TO: **SMS - Settlement Services Division**

Date: **July 8, 1999**
Escrow Number: DEMOREFI
Escrow Officer: **Ella Escrowson**
Page 4 of 5

LIMITATIONS ON DUTIES AND LIABILITIES: YOU SHALL NOT, IN ANY MANNER OR UNDER ANY THEORY OF LAW OR EQUITY, HAVE ANY RESPONSIBILITY OR LIABILITY FOR ANY OR ALL OF THE FOLLOWING ACTS, EVENTS, KNOWLEDGE OR CIRCUMSTANCES:

1. Determining the sufficiency, genuineness or validity of any document, instrument or writing deposited with you herein or the form of content, or the identity or authority of the person executing or depositing any of the same;

2. Ascertaining the terms, covenants or conditions of any document, instrument or writing deposited with you, or to investigate or examine the circumstances under which it was executed and/or delivered to you;

3. The failure to notify any person, including but not limited to the parties herein, of any sale, resale, loan, exchange or other transaction involving the property or rights that are the subject hereof or incidental thereto, or any profit or advantage to any person, firm or corporation, including by not limited to any broker or agent of any party hereto, regardless of the fact that such other transaction(s) may be directly or indirectly handled by you in connection with the within escrow or any other escrow, or come to your knowledge, in any form whatsoever;

4. The payment, examination as to amount, propriety or validity of any tax, including but not limited to personal property, corporate, business or license tax or any description, assessed against, chargeable or payable by either of the parties hereto;

5. Your failure or refusal to comply with any amendments, supplements and/or notation hereof or hereto which are not signed by all parties hereto and actually delivered to you;

6. Your failure or refusal to terminate or cancel the within escrow, without full and complete compliance, to your satisfaction, with the provisions of paragraph "Necessity for Written Instructions" herein;

7. For any liability predicated upon any relationship other than that of an escrow holder, it being specifically irrevocably and conclusively understood, agreed and deemed no other legal relationship is hereby created or shall be implied, assumed or come into being;

8. For failure of any party to this escrow with any of the provisions of any agreement, contract, or other instrument, contract or other instrument filed or referred to in these instructions;

9. Any duties beyond that of an escrow holder, which are expressly limited to the safekeeping of money, instruments or other document received by escrow holder and for the disposition of them in accordance with the written instructions accepted by you.

10. Your knowledge of matters affecting the property which is the subject hereof shall not, and does not, create any liability or duty in addition to the responsibility of escrow holder under these instructions;

11. You shall not be obligated to make any physical examination of any real or personal property described in any document deposited into this escrow, and the parties agree that you have not made, and will not make, any representations whatsoever regarding said property;

LOAN ESCROW INSTRUCTIONS

TO: **SMS - Settlement Services Division**

Date: **July 8, 1999**
Escrow Number: DEMOREFI
Escrow Officer: **Ella Escrowson**
Page 5 of 5

12. You shall not be concerned with, nor responsible for, the giving of any disclosures required by Federal or State law, including but not limited to, any disclosures required under Regulation Z, pursuant to the Federal Consumer Credit Protection Act, the effect of any zoning laws, ordinances or regulations affecting any other property described in this escrow. The undersigned jointly and severally agree to indemnify and hold you harmless by reason of any misrepresentation of omission by either party or their respective agents, or the failure of the parties to this escrow to comply with the rules and/or regulations of any governmental agency, state, federal, county, municipal or otherwise. Parties to this escrow have satisfied themselves outside of escrow that this transaction is not in violation of the Subdivision Map Act or any other law relating to land division, and you are relieved of all responsibility and/or liability in connection with same, and are not to be concerned with the enforcement of said laws;

13. Any loss that may occur by reasons of (i) forgeries or false representations; (ii) the exercise of your discretion in any particular manner, (iii) for any act, duty requirement or obligation not expressly required of you hereunder or specifically state herein; or, (iv) for any reason whatsoever except your gross neglect or willful misconduct.

AUTHORITY OF BUSINESS ENTITY: As to any corporation, partnership or other entity which may be a party hereto, it shall be conclusively presumed that any document executed by any officer or general partner of such entity was made upon due, full, legal and complete authority of the governing body of such entity, and you shall have no responsibility to independently investigate or verify such authority.

AUTHORITY TO RELEASE INFORMATION: You are authorized and instructed to furnish information from this escrow to lender and/or brokers as may be requested by them, including, but not limited to copies of all instructions and closing statement(s) in this escrow. You are authorized to accept funds deposited to a party's broker or agent without further authorization.

SUCCESSORS AND ASSIGNS: The provisions hereof shall bind each party hereto and his respective heirs, administrators, executors, assigns, trustees, guardians, conservators, receivers and successors in interest.

DESTRUCTION OF DOCUMENTS: You are authorized to destroy or otherwise dispose of all documents, instruments or writings received by you herein and accounting or disbursement records pertaining hereto at the expiration of five ((5) years from and after the initial date hereof, regardless of any subsequent notations thereto or the date of close of escrow, without liability or further notice to any parties hereto.

EFFECT OF EXECUTION: The signatures of the undersigned hereon and on any document(s) and instrument(s) pertaining to this escrow indicates their unconditional acceptance of the same and constitutes acknowledgment of their receipt oa copy of the same.

ESCROW COMPANIES ARE NOT AUTHORIZED TO GIVE LEGAL ADVICE, IF YOU DESIRE LEGAL ADVICE, CONSULT YOUR ATTORNEY BEFORE SIGNING.

We, the undersigned, jointly and severally, acknowledge receipt of a complete copy of the within escrow instructions and by our signature set forth below, acknowledge that we have read, understand and agree to the same in their entirety.

John T. Borrower   Linda K. Borrower

Subdivision Escrow

A subdivision escrow is a specialized subject that is conducted exclusively by certain escrow holders as their sole business.

The subdividing of land parcels by a developer is a time consuming and complex activity. It involves planning and close work between the builder and the escrow holder.

The first step for the builder is acquiring the land and entering into an escrow for the sale of the large parcel to be subdivided.

The next steps require conforming with the regulations of subdivision laws, obtaining approval of a subdivision map, and recording the activity --after the builder receives a final public report from the Real Estate Commissioner. Other state or local requirements may be

417

involved before the developer is allowed to start selling parcels in the subdivision.

At this point, an escrow for the sale of lots in a subdivision involves the basic sale escrow instructions with adaptations to meet specific requirements for the sale of subdivided land.

Leasehold Escrow

An escrow can be required for transactions where fee title is not transferred. In certain instances, a leasehold interest in real property may be transferred from a lessor to a lessee. There are two forms of leases that can be involved in an escrow.

Types of Leaseholds

Land Lease

A land lease conveys the right to use a certain parcel of land and improvements, for a specified number of years, under the terms and conditions described in the lease.

Space Lease

A space lease conveys the right to use a certain suite or unit located on the land. Apartment leases, office space and other commercial uses are common.

In commercial leasing, a large financial investment is usually involved. Because of that, title insurance is particularly important. Leases can be very complex, and determining the validity of a lease can involve many factors. Title insurance is commonly required to protect the investment by assuring the condition of title and providing for a transfer according to the desires of the parties.

Mobile Home Escrow

The primary product in a mobile home escrow is considered personal property. Mobile home escrows can be complicated because of the many regulatory laws and agencies involved in the transfer.

The Mobile Homes Manufactured Housing Act of 1980 is the primary law governing the transfer of mobile homes. It is enforced by the Department of Housing and Community Development.

419

Certain requirements must be met when a mobile home is sold in California to comply with the law.

Requirements for Escrow to Transfer Ownership in a Mobile Home

- In most cases, an escrow must be used
- A notice of escrow opening must be filed with the Housing and Community Development Department
- The legal owner and any junior lien holders must receive a demand for statements of lien release or assumption
- A demand for a tax clearance certificate must be sent to the county tax collector
- If a part of the consideration is for accessories, that part shall not be released until the accessories are actually installed
- The escrow holder may not be an agency under the Department of Corporations in which the mobile home dealer or seller holds more than 5% ownership interest.
- If the mobile home is to be permanently installed on a foundation, it becomes real property. In that case, the registration requirements and other escrow requirements are changed. A document showing delivery and placement on a foundation must be given to the escrow holder for recording upon close of escrow.

Bulk Transfer

The sale of a business, or business opportunity as it is known, is another personal property escrow transaction.

This type of transaction is known as a bulk sale or bulk transfer, subject to regulations in the Uniform Commercial Code.

The primary reason for the regulation of the sale of a business is to protect creditors of the business, so they can submit unpaid bills for payment before the business is sold to a new owner. The sale must be advertised in local publications to notify creditors and give them time to present a final bill.

BULK ESCROW Standard Documents

Opening Documents	Processing Documents	Closing Documents
Instruction: Bulk w/Liquor	Amendment s	Seller Close Letter: Bulk
Instruction: Bulk Sale	Seller Proc Letter	Buyer Close Letter: Bulk
Buyer/Seller Information Form	Seller Misc. Letter: Bulk	New Lender Close Letter
Exhibit "A": Bulk Sec 24074	Buyer Proc Letter: Bulk	Mortgage Broker Close Letter
Exhibit "A": Bulk Sec 6106.2	Buyer Misc. Letter: Bulk	Listing Broker Close Letter
Commission Inst.: Bulk Sale	New Lender Processing Letter	Selling Broker Close Letter
Buyer Open Letter: Bulk Sale	Mortgage Broker Process Letter	Private Lender Close Letter
Buyer Information: Bulk Sale	Private Lender Process Letter	Payoff Close Letter-Institution
Seller Open Letter: Bulk Sale	Payoff Process Letter-Institution	Payoff Close Letter-Private
Seller Information: Bulk Sale	Payoff Process Letter-Private	Existing Lender Close Letter
Inventory Form	Existing Lender Process Letter	Other Disbursement Letter
Landlord Letter	Other Disbursement Letter	
Statement of Information		
Bill of Sale		
Demand Request		
Demand Note		
Demand Note: unsecured		
Demand Note: Sec. Agreement		
Security Agreement		
Security Agreement: Str. Note		
Security Agreement: Inst. Note		
ABC 226: Consideration		
ABC 227: Transfer License		
Assignment of Lease		
Assumption of Lease		
Consent to Lease		
Assign of Lease-Collateral		
Assumption Agreement		
State Board of Equalization		
Notice to Creditors		
Notice to Creditors/Liquor		
Notice to Creditors/Assumption		

1031 Exchanges

Under section 1031 of the Internal Revenue Code, some or all of the profit or gain from the exchange of one property for another may not have to be immediately recognized for tax purposes.

A tax-free exchange is a legal method of deferring capital gains taxes by exchanging one qualified property for another qualified property. When real estate for investment or for production of income is exchanged for like-kind property, and follows strict Internal Revenue Service requirements, a tax-deferred exchange can take place.

In handling a transaction where the properties are involved in a tax deferred exchange, the escrow holder should be a specialist in exchanges. The law is very precise about whether an exchange qualifies as tax deferred, and the instruments used, the timing of recording and myriad other items must be confronted by the escrow holder in a completely accurate manner. A mistake as small as recording a document out of order could cause the exchange to be disqualified, all parties more than irritated and the escrow holder in great need of legal counsel.

Post Test

The following self test repeats the one you took at the beginning of this chapter. Now take the exam again--since you have read all the material-- and check your knowledge of escrow closing procedures.

True/False

1. Only sale escrows may be conducted by private escrow companies.

2. A loan escrow is used to transfer property which is being sold and funded by a subdivider.

3. A trust deed is sold whenever property transfers ownership.

4. An escrow can be required where fee title is not transferred.

5. Typical leasehold escrows will be a land lease or a space lease.

6. In commercial leasing, title insurance is never used.

7. The primary product in a mobilehome escrow is considered personal property.

8. A mobilehome never becomes real property.

9. Bulk transfer refers to the sale of a business.

10. Capital gains are deferred when a seller completes a 1031 tax free exchange.

chapter **15**

ESCROW
REVIEW

Focus

- **Introduction**
- **Procedure**
- **Computerized forms**

Pre-Test

The following is a self test to determine how much you know about conducting an escrow before reading this chapter. Take it without studying, then read the material presented in the text. At the end of the chapter you will find a repeat of this exam. Test your knowledge by answering the questions again, then check your improvement. (The answers are found at the end of the book.) Good luck.

True/False

1. The process of conducting an escrow involves two main steps.

2. There is only one kind of escrow.

3. In opening an escrow, the names of the parties, legal description and selling price, among other information, are collected by the escrow holder.

4. Escrow instructions are prepared to direct the escrow holder.

5. Escrow instructions need to be signed only by the seller to make an escrow valid.

6. The escrow holder never prepares a note and trust deed.

7. Closing costs are calculated before the escrow is opened.

8. The down payment is collected by the escrow holder.

9. The escrow holder coordinates with the lender.

10. Escrow instructions are commonly generated by computer.

Introduction

The process of conducting an escrow, while requiring the services of a highly skilled technician, is basically very simple. As we have seen, it involves three steps; opening the escrow, processing the escrow and finally closing the escrow.

The three basic requirements, however, involve a considerable amount of detail, knowledge, skill and basic understanding of all the elements of each unique escrow. No two escrows are the same, and yet, every escrow can be linked to another by its similarities; opening, processing and closing.

Procedure

This chapter brings together everything you have learned about conducting an escrow. So far, you have seen forms, disclosures and other documents used by the escrow professional as you have studied each part of the escrow process separately. Here you have a summary of procedures as well as samples of documents you will need to conduct an escrow, from the first introductory document to the final closing documents.

Opening the Escrow

The escrow officer obtains basic information about what the principal's agreement requires.

Opening the Escrow

- Names of the parties
- Legal description
- Selling price
- Financing agreements
- Special considerations and conditions for the escrow
- Desired closing date

Once the escrow agent obtains the essential information, instructions are prepared. These basically are written instructions from the principals to the escrow officer, giving clear directions as to what the escrow officer must do in order to process and close the escrow.

Processing the Escrow

The escrow officer must collect and create documents, get signatures and complete all requirements of the escrow.

Processing the Escrow

- Signing escrow instructions
- Gathering loan documents
- Gathering loan funds
- Preparing grant deed
- Completing pest control report
- Preparing trust deed and note
- Making demands for payment of loans of record
- Getting beneficiary statements
- Opening title order
- Getting preliminary title report
- Calculating closing costs
- Collecting buyer's down payment
- Securing signatures of principals on documents

Closing the Escrow

The escrow officer brings all the threads of the transaction together, making sure all requirements are completed, as desired by the principals, for the closing.

Closing the Escrow

- Coordinating with title officer about title insurance
- Coordinating with lenders for existing loan pay-off and funding for new loans
- Balancing the file for accounting to the buyer and seller
- Preparing closing checks and statements for all parties

Closing the Escrow (continued)

- Signed escrow instructions
- Gathering loan documents
- Gathering loan funds
- Preparation of grant deed
- Pest control report
- Preparation of trust deed and note
- Make demands for payment of loans of record
- Get beneficiary statements
- Open title order
- Get preliminary title report
- Calculate closing costs
- Collect buyer's down payment
- Signatures of principals on documents

Computerized Forms

Jonathan J. Sellerman, Jr
Betty Jo Sellerman
8907 Elmhurst Avenue
Costa Mesa, CA 92626

Date: June 6, 1999
Escrow No: 1111-DEMO

Re: **8907 Elmhurst Avenue, Costa Mesa, CA 92626**

Dear Mr. & Mrs. Sellerman:

Thank you for selecting SMS to process your escrow. The enclosed items are required in your escrow, please review and comply as noted below and return to us as soon as possible.

SIGN AND RETURN the enclosed items, retain the copy for your records:
Escrow Instructions
Commission Instructions
Misc sign & return enclosure

COMPLETE IN FULL, SIGN AND RETURN the enclosed items:
CAL-FIRPTA 590 Form and/or Certificate
Statement of Information
Loan Information Sheet
IRS 1099 Reporting Form
Misc complete, sign & return enclosure

SIGN AND ACKNOWLEDGE BEFORE A NOTARY PUBLIC <u>EXACTLY</u> as your name(s) appear on the enclosed items:
Grant Deed
Misc sign before a notary enclosure

Please Furnish the Following:
Misc furnish us with enclosure

All documents should be signed EXACTLY as your name(s) appear. Should your name(s) be misspelled, sign them correctly and advise us in writing when you return these papers.

We appreciate the opportunity to be of service to you in this transaction. Should you have any questions, please call us at the telephone number(s) referenced above.

SMS

Ella Escrowson
Escrow Officer

jjw

Escrow Officer: Debbie Weatherwax
Escrow No: 004860
Date: April 24, 1999

SALE ESCROW INSTRUCTIONS

INITIAL DEPOSIT	**5,000.00**
NEW FIRST TRUST DEED TO FILE	**180,000.00**
ADDIITIONAL CASH THROUGH ESCROW	**8,980.17**
TOTAL CONSIDERATION	**$193,980.17**

I/We will hand you the sum of **$8,980.17**, of which the sum of **$5,000.00** shall be handed escrow as the initial deposit upon opening of this escrow. I/We will further hand you any and all sufficient funds for closing costs, expenses and prorations between Buyer and Seller, prior to the close of this escrow.

I/We will deliver to you any executed instruments and or funds required to enable you to comply with these instructions, all of which you are authorized to use, provided that on or before **01/01/1999** you are in a position to order a standard policy of title insurance with the usual title company exceptions, provided that said policy has a liability of at least the amount of the above total consideration, covering the property described as follows:

All that tract and parcel of land located on the northwest corner of the subdivision more commonly known as Rainbow Ridge and being more fully described in Deed Book 123, page 891.

Commonly known as:

21128 Rose, Rancho Santa Margarita, CA 92691 (not verified by escrow holder)

Showing title vested in: **Robert Trabuco and Amelia Trabuco**

FREE FROM ENCUMBRANCES EXCEPT:
1. First installment(s) of the General and Special County, and City (if any) Taxes for the current fiscal year, not delinquent, and taxes for the ensuing year, if any, a lien not yet payable.
2. All taxes, bonds and assessments levied or assessed subsequent to the date of these instructions.
3. Covenants, conditions, restrictions, reservations, rights, rights of way, easements and the exception or reservation of water, oil, gas, minerals, carbons, hydrocarbons or kindred substances on or under said land, now of record, if any, or in the Deed to file.

**SMS SETTLEMENT SERVICES IS LICENSED BY THE DEPARTMENT OF CORPORATIONS,
STATE OF CALIFORNIA.**

PRORATE OR ADJUST THE FOLLOWING ITEMS AS OF DATE OF CLOSE OF ESCROW:

Taxes (based on latest tax bill)   Homeowners Association Dues

Each party signing these instructions has read the additional escrow conditions, general provisions and instructions on the reverse side hereof and approves, accepts and agrees to be bound thereby as though the reverse side hereof appeared over their signatures.

SELLER: **BUYER:**

Jim Getz   Robert Trabuco

Mary Ann Getz   Amelia Trabuco

Escrow Officer: **Debbie Weatherwax**   Escrow No: **004860**
Date: **April 24, 1999**   **Page 2**

THE CLOSING OF THIS ESCROW IS CONTINGENT UPON:

A. Buyer and property qualifying for new loan set out above. Buyer's execution of loan documents shall constitute Buyer's approval of all terms and conditions contained therein and a satisfaction of this condition.

B. Buyer's approval of a preliminary title report covering the subject property together with any and all exceptions referred to therein, within 5 business days of Buyer's receipt of copies of same from Escrow does not deposit his written disapproval within time limit specified said preliminary title report shall be deemed approved.

INSTRUCTIONS:

1. A new hazard insurance policy to comply with lender's requirements will be delivered to escrow by buyer's agent. The buyer will deposit into his escrow sufficient funds to enable you to pay the premium at close of escrow.

AS A MEMORANDUM AGREEMENT ONLY WITH WHICH ESCROW HOLDER IS NOT TO BE CONCERNED AND/OR LIABLE.

2. All plumbing, electrical, heating and related systems and equipment are to be in working order at the close of escrow.

3. All carpets, drapes, window coverings, attached fixtures and appliances, except any which may be reserved herein, are to remain with subject property at the close of the escrow.

4. Seller herein agrees to maintain subject property in its present condition until possession of subject property is delivered to buyer.

5. Buyers to walk through subject property 7 days prior to close of escrow.

EACH PARTY SIGNING THESE INSTRUCTIONS HAS READ THE ADDITIONAL ESCROW CONDITIONS, GENERAL PROVISIONS AND INSTRUCTIONS ON THE REVERSE SIDE HEREOF AND APPROVES, ACCEPTS AND AGREES TO BE BOUND THEREBY AS THOUGH THE REVERSE SIDE HEREOF APPEARED OVER THEIR SIGNATURES.

SELLER: **BUYER:**

Jim Getz   **Robert Trabuco**

Mary Anne Getz   **Amelia Trabuco**

Escrow Officer: **Debbie Weatherwax** Escrow No: **004860**
Date: **April 24, 1999** **page 3**

BUYER:
SET OUT ON THE FINAL PAGE OF THESE INSTRUCTIONS ARE UNDERSTOOD AND APPROVED IN THEIR ENTIRETY BY EACH OF THE UNDERSIGNED. I AGREE TO PAY ON DEMAND BUYER'S CUSTOMARY COSTS AND CHARGES INCURRED HEREIN, INCLUDING BUT NOT LIMITED TO, RECORDING FEES, DOCUMENT PREPARATION FEES, ONE HALF OF YOUR ESCROW FEE, ANY COSTS INCURRED BY REASON OF ANY FINANCING OBTAINED OR ASSUMED BY ME, ONE-HALF OF ANY TRANSFER FEE CHARGED BY ANY ASSOCIATION COVERING THE SUBJECT PROPERTY, AND ANY OTHER CHARGE INCURRED FOR MY BENEFIT.

SELLER:
THE FOREGOING TERMS, CONDITIONS, PROVISIONS AND INSTRUCTIONS, TOGETHER WITH THE GENERAL PROVISIONS SET OUT ON THE FINAL PAGE OF THESE INSTRUCTIONS ARE UNDERSTOOD, APPROVED AND ACCEPTED IN THEIR
ENTIRETY BY EACH OF THE UNDERSIGNED. I WILL HAND YOU MY EXECUTED GRANT DEED AND/OR OTHER DOCUMENTS OR INSTRUMENTS REQUIRED FROM ME TO CAUSE TITLE TO BE AS SHOWN ABOVE, WHICH YOU ARE AUTHORIZED TO USE AND OR DELIVER WHEN YOU CAN COMPLY WITH THESE INSTRUCTIONS AND WHEN YOU CAN HOLD FOR MY ACCOUNT THE TOTAL CONSIDERATION AS SET FORTH ABOVE (LESS ANY AMOUNT TO BE DEBITED TO MY ACCOUNT SET FORTH BELOW), TOGETHER WITH ANY DOCUMENT(S) EXECUTED IN MY FAVOR.

FROM THE TOTAL CONSIDERATION DUE TO MY ACCOUNT AT THE CLOSE OF ESCROW, YOU ARE AUTHORIZED AND INSTRUCTED TO DEDUCT THE AMOUNT OF ANY REAL ESTATE BROKER'S COMMISSION TO BE PAID BY ME IN ACCORDANCE WITH SEPARATE INSTRUCTIONS, THE AMOUNT OF ANY FUNDS PAID TO ME OUTSIDE OF ESCROW, THE AMOUNT OWING UNDER ANY LIEN OR ENCUMBRANCE TO REMAIN OF RECORD AFTER CLOSE OF ESCROW, THE DEMAND OF ANY LIEN OR ENCUMBRANCE, REQUIRED TO BE PAID TO PLACE TITLE IN THE CONDITION AS CALLED FOR HEREIN, AND SELLER'S CUSTOMARY COSTS AND CHARGES INCURRED HEREIN, INCLUDING, BUT NOT LIMITED TO, THE PREMIUM FOR THE C.L.T.A. OWNER'S POLICY OF TITLE INSURANCE TO BE PROVIDED TO THE BUYER, THE AMOUNT OF ANY DOCUMENTARY TRANSFER TAX OWING ON THE DEED, ONE-HALF OF YOUR ESCROW FEE, RECORDING FEES FOR DOCUMENTS, INSTRUMENTS RECORDED FOR MY BENEFIT, ONE HALF OF ANY TRANSFER FEE CHARGED BY ANY ASSOCIATION COVERING THE SUBJECT PROPERTY, THE COST OF OBTAINING ANY STATEMENT(S) OR DEMAND CONCERNING ANY LIEN OR ENCUMBRANCE OF RECORD, AND ANY OTHER COST OR CHARGE INCURRED FOR MY BENEFIT.

EACH PARTY SIGNING THESE INSTRUCTIONS HAS READ THE ADDITIONAL ESCROW CONDITIONS, GENERAL PROVISIONS AND INSTRUCTIONS ON THE REVERSE SIDE HEREOF AND APPROVES, ACCEPTS AND AGREES TO BE BOUND THEREBY AS THOUGH THE REVERSE SIDE HEREOF APPEARED OVER THEIR SIGNATURES.

SELLER: **BUYER:**

Jim Getz Robert Trabuco

Mary Anne Getz Amelia Trabuco

SMS

DocNet
Standard Documents

SALE ESCROW

OPENING DOCUMENTS:

Instruction: Sale
Instruction: Land contract
Instruction: AITD
CAR Deposit Receipt Phrases
Commission Instruction
Status Sheet: Broker/Lender
Status Sheet: Buyer
Status Sheet: Seller
Seller Open Letter

Buyer Open Letter
Loan Information Sheet
Statement of Information
Fire Insurance Info Form
Cal-FRPTA Notice/Disclosure
California 590-RE Form
PCOR

Vesting Worksheet:
Buyer/Borrower
Vesting Worksheet:
Trust/Corporation
1099 Tax Reporting Form

Listing/Selling Broker Open
Letter
New Lender Open Letter

Mortgage Broker Close Letter

Private Beneficiary Open Letter
Beneficiary Statement Request:
Private
Beneficiary Statement Request:
Institutional
Owner's Offset Statement
Rent Statement
Tenant Estoppel Certificate
Third Party Instruction
FRPTA: Notice to Buyer/Seller
FRPTA: Buyer's Exemption1445
FRPTA: Seller's Affidavit
Nonresident Withholding
Statement
Seller Tax Options
Request for Taxpayer ID Number

PROCESSING DOCUMENTS:

Title Open Transmittal
Preliminary title Report Approval
HOA Demand
Demand Request: Institutional
Demand Request: Private
FHA: 30 Day Notice
Instruction Reminder: Seller
Instruction Reminder: Buyer
Trust Certificate: Probate Section
18100.5
Trust Certification
Seller Amendment Letter
Buyer Amendment Letter
Broker Processing Letter
New Lender Processing Letter
Mortgage Broker Process Letter
Private Beneficiary Process Letter

Payoff Lender Process Letter
Fire Insurance Process Letter
Existing Lender Process Letter
Flood Insurance Process Letter
Earthquake Insurance Process
Letter
Pest Company Process Letter
Septic Company Process Letter
Irrevocable Demand: FROM
Escrow
Irrevocable Demand: TO
Escrow
Cancel Escrow Instructions

CLOSING DOCUMENTS

Request for Insurance
Title Docs Transmittal
Funding Letter: Mortgage
Funding Letter: New Lender
Wire Instructions
Buyer Close Letter
Buyer Title Policy Transmittal
Seller Close Letter
Broker Close Letter
New Lenders Close Letter
Mortgage Broker Close Letter
Private Beneficiary Close Letter
Payoff Lenders Close Letter
Existing Lender Close Letter
HOA Close Letter
Fire Insurance Close Letter
Earthquake Insurance Close
Letter
Pest Company Close Letter
Septic Company Close Letter
Nonresident Withholding
Statement
California 597-A Form
Closing Check List

SMS

AMENDMENT TO ESCROW INSTRUCTIONS

Date: January 18, 1999   Escrow No: 000020

RE: 2165 Memory Lane, Santa Ana, CA 92705

TO: Strategic Mortgage Services

My previous escrow instructions in the above numbered escrow are hereby amended and/or supplemented in the following particulars only:

Type Verbiage or Insert Amendment Clause Here

All other itmes and conditions shall remain the same.

EACH OF THE UNDERSIGNED STATES THAT EACH HAS READ THE FOREGOING INSTRUCTIONS, UNDERSTANDS THEM AND ACKNOWLEDGES RECEIPT OF A COPY OF THESE INSTRUCTIONS.

Michael M. Horton   Robert R. Mullins

Linda L. Horton   Margie M. Mullins

SMS

Date: April 6, 1999

Escrow No. :1111-DEMO

RE: 8907 Elmhurst Avenue, Costa Mesa, CA 92626

Escrow Officer: Ella Escrowson

INSTRUCTIONS TO PAY COMMISSION

Upon close of escrow, from funds received and/or held by you on my behalf you are instructed to pay;

Wimbush Realty
a licensed real estate broker, the sum of $5,300.00

Grubb & Ellis Company
a licensed real estate broker, the sum of $5,300.00

TO COMPLETE A TOTAL $10,600.00
COMMISSION IN THE SUM OF

The employment of said broker(s) to effect the transaction of the above described property described in said escrow is acknowledged by the undersigned, who has agreed to pay sum to said broker(s) as a commission for services rendered pursuant to said employment.

This is an IRREVOCABLE COMMISSION ORDER and cannot be amended or revoked, insofar as it relates to payment of commission, without the prior written consent of broker(s) named herein, who shall be deemed a party to the escrow for the sale and exclusive purpose of receiving said commission.

Jonathan J. Sellerman,   Jr. Betty Jo Sellerman

Please mail payment(s) to address(s) below, unless payment is called for on the day this escrow is closed.

Frank Allen - Wimbush Realty

By:_____
License No. :11111111
Address :890 W. Baker Street, Costa Mesa, CA 92627

Mary Allen - Grubb & Ellis Company

By:_____
License No. :22222222
Address :4000 MacArthur Blvd., Newport Beach, CA 92660

SMS

Statement of Information

FILL OUT COMPLETELY AND RETURN TO STRATEGIC MORTGAGE SERVICES

ESCROW #00020-SMS   TRACT#   LOT#

Name_____ Social Security #_____ Driver's License#_____

Date of Birth_____ Place of Birth_____ Bus. Phone_____ Home Phone_____

Resided in USA since_____ Resided in California since_____

If you are married, please complete the following: Date Married_____at_____

Name of Spouse_____ Social Security #_____ Driver's License #_____

Resided in USA since_____ Resided in California since_____

Previous Marriage or Marriages (if no previous marriage, write "None"):
Name of former spouse_____ Deceased___Divorced____Where_____When____
Name of former spouse_____ Deceased___Divorced____Where_____When____

Children by current or previous Marriages:
Name_____ Born_____ Name_____ Born_____
Name_____ Born_____ Name_____ Born_____

Information covering past 10 years:

Residence: _____

Number/Street	City	From	To

Number/Street	City	From	To

Employment _____

Firm Name	Location

Firm Name	Location

Spouse Employment: _____

Firm Name	Location

Firm Name	Location

Have you or your spouse owned or operated a business?

□Yes   □No   If so please list names_____

I have never been adjudged, bankrupt, nor are there any unsatisfied judgments or other matters pending against me which might affect my title to this property except as follow:

_____

The undersigned declare, under penalty of perjury, that the foregoing is true and correct.
Executed on_____   at_____
                date   city
                                              Signature

SMS SETTLEMENT SERVICES

RECEIPT FOR DEPOSIT

RECEIPT #002392

OFFICE: 999

DATE 02/27/1999   ESCROW **NO.004861-DW**

RECEIVED OF Bank of America

ESCROW NAME Getz/Trabuco

TYPE OF TRANSACTION Loan Proceeds

IN THE AMOUNT OF   IN THE FORM
$80,008.13   OF_____

BY_____

NOTICE OF RIGHT TO EARN INTEREST ON DEPOSITED FUNDS

Interest may be earned on all deposited funds by requesting the Escrow Officer who is handling your transaction to place the escrowed funds into an interest bearing account. The Escrow Officers Agent's charge to set up such an account is $50.00. Your funds will earn interest at the prevailing rate of interest paid by the federally insured financial institution where your funds would be deposited [for example, in a typical transaction, a $1,000.00 deposit for a thirty day (30) period with the prevailing interest rate of 6% per annum would earn $4.93].

(Accounting Copy)

SMS

REQUEST FOR DEMAND

December 29, 1999   Escrow No: **004860**

Attn: Payoff Department
All Lenders Mortgage
1212 N. Main Street
Santa Ana, CA 92705

RE: LOAN NUMBER: 1022290-09
     BORROWER: Jim Getz and Mary Anne Getz

An escrow has been opened with our company by the above reference borrowers and provides for the payment in full of the loan number referenced above. Your loan encumbers the real property described as:

See Exhibit A attached hereto and made a part hereof.

The property is commonly known as **21128 Rose, Rancho Santa Margarita, CA 92691**

We hereby request that you forward your **ORIGINAL DEMAND,** together with either (1) the original Note, Deed of Trust securing same and your executed Request for Full Reconveyance, or (2) your executed Full Reconveyance, to the following title company:

American Title Company
ATTN: Mary Ann Snow
10229 Main Street
Santa Ana, CA 92699
RE: TITLE ORDER No: 4860

Please fax a copy of your DEMAND to our office at (714) 549-0684 with an additional copy in the mail.

We wish to thank you for your cooperation and assistance. Please be sure to call our office if you have any questions concerning this matter.

Sincerely,

Debbie Weatherwax
Escrow Officer

RECORDING REQUESTED BY
SMS SETTLEMENT SERVICES
AND WHEN RECORDED MAIL TO:

REC
RCF
MICRO
RTCF
LIEN
SMPF
PCOR

Name: **Robert Trabuco**
Street Address: **21128 Rose**
City, State: **Mission Viejo, CA**
Zip: **92691**

Order No. **004860-DW**

Space Above This Line for Recorder's Use

DEED OF TRUST WITH ASSIGNMENT OF RENTS

This DEED OF TRUST, made **January 1, 1999**, between **Robert Trabuco and Amelia Trabuco** herein called TRUSTOR,
whose address is **542 Paramount Drive, Chino Hills, CA**

SMS SETTLEMENT SERVICES, a California Corporation, herein called TRUSTEE and **Jim Getz, An Unmarried Man and Mary Anne Getz**, herein called BENEFICIARY, Trustor irrevocably grants, transfers and assigns to Trustee in Trust, with Power of Sale, that property in City of **Mission Viejo,** County of **Los Angeles**, California, described as:

All that tract and parcel of land located on the northwest corner of the subdivision more commonly known as Rainbow Ridge and being more fully described in Deed Book 123, page 891.

Together with the rents, issues and profits thereof, subject, however, to the right, power and authority hereinafter given to and conferred upon Beneficiary to collect and apply such rents, issues and profits. For the Purpose of Securing (1) payment of the sum of $180,000.00 with interest thereon according to the terms of a promissory note or notes of even date herewith made by Trustor, payable to order of Benficiary, and extensions or renewals thereof; (2) the performance of each agreement of Trustor incorporated by reference or contained herein or reciting it is so secured; (3) Payment of additional sums and interest thereon which may hereafter be loaned to Trustor, or his successors or assigns, when evidenced by a promissory note or notes reciting that they are secured by this Deed of Trust.

To protect the security of this Deed of Trust, and with respect to the property above described, Trustor expressly makes each and all of the agreements, and adopts and agrees to perform and be bound by each and all of the terms and provisions set forth in subdivision A of that certain Fictitious Deed of Trust reference herein, and it is mutually agreed that all of the provisions set forth in subdivision B of that certain Fictitious Deed of Trust recorded in the book and page of Official Records in the office of the county recorder of the county where said property is located, noted below opposite the name of such county:

Said agreements, terms and provisions contained in said Subdivision A and B, (identical in all counties are printed on the reverse side hereof) are by the within reference thereto, incorporated herein and made a part of this Deed of Trust for all purposes as fully as if set forth at length herein and Beneficiary may charge for a statement regarding the obligation secured hereby, provided the charge therefor does not exceed the maximum allowed by laws.

The foregoing assignment of rents is absolute unless initiated here, in which case, the assignment serves as additional security.

The undersigned Trustor, requests that a copy of any notice of default and any notice of sale hereunder be mailed to him at this address hereinbefore set forth.

Dated: __January 1, 1999__

STATE OF CALIFORNIA

COUNTY OF_____

                                           Robert Trabuco

                                           Amelia Trabuco

On_____before me.

a Notary Public in and for said County and State, personally appeared:

_____

_____

Personally known to me (or proved to me on the basis of satisfactory evidence whose name(s) is/are subscribed to the within instrument and acknowledged to me that he/she/they executed the same in his/her/their authorized capacity(ies) and that by his/her/their signature(s) on the instrument the person(s) or the entity upon behalf of which the person(s) acted, executed the instrument.

WITNESS my hand and official seal.

Signature_____   (This area for official notorial seal)

The following is a copy of Subdivision A and B of the fictitious Deed of Trust recorded in each county in California as stated in the foregoing Deed of Trust and incorporated by reference is said Deed of Trust as being a part thereof as if set forth at lenght therein.

A. To protect the security of this Deed of Trust, Trustor agrees:

(1) To keep said property in good condition and repair not to remove or demolish any building thereon; to complete or restore promptly and in good and workmanlike manner any building which may be constructed, damaged or destroyed thereon and to pay when due all claims for labor performed and materials furnished therefor; to comply with all laws affecting said property or requiring any alterations or improvements to be made thereon, not to commit or permit waste thereof; not to commit, suffer or permit any act upon said property in violation of law, to cultivate, irrigate, fertilize, fumigate, prune and do all other acts which from the character or use of said property may be reasonably necessary, the specific enumerations herein not excluding the general.

(2) To provide, maintain and deliver to Beneficiary fire insurance satisfactory to and with loss payable to Beneficiary. The amount collected under any fire or other insurance policy may be applied by Beneficiary upon any indebtedness secured hereby and in such order Beneficiary may determine, or at option of Beneficiary the entire amount so collected or any part thereof may be released to Trustor. Such application or release shall not cure or waive any default or notice of default hereunder or invalidate any act done pursuant to such notice.

(3) To appear in and defend any action or proceeding purporting to affect the security hereof or the rights or powers of Beneficiary or Trustee; and to pay all costs and expenses, including cost of evidence of title and attorney's fees in a reasonable sum, in any such action or proceeding in which Beneficiary or Trustee may appear, and in any suit brought by Beneficiary to foreclose this Deed.

(4) To pay: at least ten days before delinquency all taxes and assessments affecting said property, including assessments on appurtent water stock; when due, all incumbrances, charges and liens with interest, on said property or any part thereof, which appear to be prior or superior hereto; all costs, fees and expenses of this Trust.

Should Trustor fail to make any payment or to do any act as herein provided, then Beneficiary or Trustee, but without obligation so to do and without notice to or demand upon Trustor and without releasing Trustor from any obligation hereof, may: make or do the same in such manner and to such extent as either may deem necessary to protect the security hereof, Beneficiary or Trustee being authorized to enter upon said property for such purposes; appear in and defend any action or proceeding purporting to affect the security hereof or the rights or powers of Beneficiary or Trustee; pay, purchase, contest or compromise any incumbrance, charge or lien which in the judgment of either appears to be prior or superior hereto; and, in exercising any such powers, pay necessary expenses, employ counsel and pay his reasonable fees.

(5) To pay immediately and without demand all sums so expended by Beneficiary or Trustee, with interest from date of expenditure at the amount allowed by law in effect at the date hereof, and to pay for any statement provided for by law in effect at the date hereof regarding the obligation secured hereby any amount demanded by the Beneficiary not to exceed the maximum allowed by law at the time when said statement is demanded.

B. It is mutually agreed:

(1) That any award of damages in connection with any condemnation for public use of or injury to said property or any part therof is hereby assigned and shall be paid to Beneficiary who may apply or release such moneys received by him in the same manner and with he same effect as above provided for disposition of proceeds of fire or other insurance.

(2) That by accepting payment of any sum secured hereby after its due date, Beneficiary does not waive his right either to require prompt payment when due of all other sums so secured or to declare default for failure so to pay.

(3)   That at any time or from time to time, without liability therefor and without notice, upon written request of Beneficiary and presentation of this Deed and said note for endorsement, and without affecting the personal liability of any person for payment of the indebtedness secured hereby, Trustee may: reconvey any part of said property, consent to the making of any map or plate thereof; join in granting any easement thereon; or join in any extension agreement or any agreement subordinating the lien or charge hereof.

(4)   That upon written request of beneficiary stating stat all sums secured hereby have been paid, and upon said note to Trustee for cancellation and retention or other disposition as Trustee in its sole discretion may choose and upon payment of its fees; Trustee shall reconvey, without warranty, the property, then hereunder. The recitals in such reconveyance of any matter or facts shall be conclusive proof of the truthfulness thereof. The Grantee in such reconveyance may be described as "the person or persons legally entitled thereto."

(5)   That as additional security, Trustor hereby gives to and confers the right, power and authority, during the continuances of these Trusts, to collect the rents, issues and profits of said property, reserving unto Trustor the right, prior to any default by Trustor in payment of any indebtedness secured hereby or in performance of any agreement hereunder, to collect and retain such rents, issues and profits as they become due and payable. Upon any such default, Beneficiary may at any time without notice, either in person, by agent, or by a receiver to be appointed by a court, and without regard to the adequacy of any security for the indebtedness hereby secured, enter upon and take possession of said property or any part thereof, in his own name sue for or otherwise collect such rents, issues, and profits, including those past due and unpaid, and apply the same, less costs and expenses of operation and collection, including reasonable attorney's fees, upon any indebtedness secure hereby, and in such order as Beneficiary may determine.   The entering upon and taking possession of said property, the collection of such rents, issues and profits and the application therof as aforesaid, shall not cure or waive any default hereunder or invalidate any act done pursuant to such notice.

(6)   That upon default by Trustor in payment of any indebtedness secured hereby or in performance of any agreement hereunder, Beneficiary may declare all sums secured hereby immediately due and payable by delivery to Trustee of written declaration of default and demand for sale and of written notice of default and of election to cause to be sold said property, which notice Trustee shall cause to be filed for record. Beneficiary also shall deposit with Trustee this Deed, said note and all documents evidencing expenditures secured hereby.

After the lapse of such time as may then be rquired by law following the recordation of said notice of default, and notice of sale having been given as then required by law, Trustee, without demand on Trustor, shall sell said property at the time and place fixed by it in said notice of sale, either as a whole or in separate parcels, and in such order as it may determine, at public auction to the highest bidder for cash in lawful money of the United States, payable at time of sale. Trustee may postpone sale of all or any portion of siad property by public announcement at such time and place of sale, and from time to time thereafter may postpone such sale by public announcment at the time fixed by the preceding postponement. Trustee shall deliver to such purchase its deed conveying the property so sold, but without any covenant or warranty, express or implied. The recitals in such deed of any matters or facts shall be conclusive proof of the truthfulness therof. Any person, including Trustor, Trustee, or Beneficiary as hereinafter defined, may purchase at such sale.

After deducting all costs, fees and expenses of Trustee and of this Trust, including cost of evidence of title in connection with sale, Trustee shall apply the proceeds of sale to payment of all sums expended under the terms hereof, not then repaid, with accrued interest at the amount allowed by law in effect at the date hereof; all other sums then secured hereby; and the remainder, if any, to the persons legally entitled thereto.

(7)   Beneficiary, or any successor in ownership of any indebtedness secured hereby, may from time to time, by instrument in writing, substitute a successor or succesors to any Trustee named herein or acting hereunder, which instrument, executed by the Beneficiary and duly acknowledged and recorded in the office of the recorder of the county or counties where said property is situated, shall be conclusive proof of proper substitution of such successor Trustee or Trustees, who shall, without

conveyance from the Trustee predecessor, succeed to all its title, estate, rights, powers and duties. Said instrument must contain the name of the original Trustor, Trustee and Beneficiary hereunder, the book and page where this Deed is recorded and the name and address of the new Trustee.

(8) That this Deed applies to, insures to the benefit of, and binds all parties hereto, their heirs, legatees, devisees, administrators, executors, successors and assigns. The term Beneficiary shall mean the owner and holder, including pledges, of the note secured hereby, whether or not named as Beneficiary herein. In this Deed, whenever the context so requires, the masculine gender includes the feminine and/or neuter, and the singular number includes the plural.

9) That Trustee accepts this Trust when this Deed, duly executed and acknowledged, is made a public record as provided by law. Trustee is not obligated to notify any party hereto of pending sale under any other Deed of Trust or of any action or proceeding in which Trustor, Beneficiary or Trustee shall be a party unless brought by Trustee.

DO NOT RECORD

TO SMS SETTLEMENT SERVICES   **REQUEST FOR FULL RECONVEYANCE**
COMPANY TRUSTEE

The undersigned is the legal owner and holder of the note or notes, and of all other indebtedness secured by the foregoing Deed of Trust. Said note or notes, together with all other indebtedness secured by said Deed of Trust, have been fully paid and satisfied, and you are hereby requested and directed, on payment to you of any sums owing to you under the terms of said Deed of Trust, to cancel said note or notes above mentioned, and all other evidences of indebtedness secured by said Deed of Trust delivered to you herewith, together with the said Deed of Trust, and to reconvey, withour warranty, to the parties designated by the terms of said Deed of Trust, all the estate now held by you under the same.

Dated_____   _____

                                             _____

SIGNATURE MUST BE NOTARIZED

Please mail Deed of Trust,
Note and Reconveyance to_____

Do not lose or destroy this Deed of Trust OR THE NOTE which it secures. Both must be delivered to the Trustee for cancellation before reconveyance will be made.

South County Escrow Co.
8754 W. Camino Capistrano
San Juan Capistrano, CA 92624

1099 ESCROW REPORTING DOCUMENT   **W-9**

Escrow ID_____   **Settlement Date:**_____

Contract Sales Price:$_____

Property Address:_____

City_____   **State**_____   **Zip**_____

Buyer's Name:_____

Address:_____

City_____   **State**_____   **Zip**_____

CERTIFICATION - Under penalties of perjury, I certify that:

(1) The number shown on this form is my correct Taxpayer Identification Number

(2) I am not subject to backup withholding either because I have not been notified by the Internal Revenue Service (IRS) that I am subject to backup withholding as a result of a failure to report all interest or dividends or the IRS has notified me that I am no longer subject to backup withholding.

(3) The value of all cash, property and services I received is equal to my percent of ownership based on contract sales price.

Certification Instructions - You must cross out item (2) above if you have been notified by IRS that you are subject to backup withholding because of under reporting interest or dividends on your tax return. However, if after being notified by IRS that you were subject to backup withholding, you received another notification from IRS that you are no longer subject to backup withholding, do not cross out item (2).

Escrow officer is hereby authorized to forward this information to McGinnis & Zink.

Seller's name	Tax ID or Social Security No.	Percent of Ownership

Forwarding Address		Amount Withheld

City, State and Zip	Seller's Signature	

Seller's name	Tax ID or Social Security No.	Percent of Ownership

Forwarding Address	Amount Withheld	

City, State and Zip	Seller's Signature	

PLEASE COMPLETE, SIGN AND RETURN
501 Parkcenter Drive, Santa Ana, CA 92705 (714) 550-1254
White: McGinnis & Zink Yellow: Branch

TITLE ORDER

December 29, 1999   ESCROW No.: 004860

ATTN; Mary Ann Snow
American Title Company
10229 Main Street
Santa Ana, CA 92699

RE: TITLE ORDER No.: 4860

PLEASE ACCEPT THIS AS OUR REQUEST FOR THE FOLLOWING POLICY(IES):
]CLTA $189,900.00   1,JOINT PROTECTION   ]ALTA $80,000.00

on property described as follows:

All that tract and parcel of land located on the northwest corner of the subdivision more commonly known as Rainbow Ridge and being more fully described in Deed Book 123, page 891.

Subject Property is commonly known as: 21128 Rose, Rancho Santa Margarita, CA 92691

Present Owner's Name: Jim Getz

WE ENCLOSE THE FOLLOWING:
1. Statements of information from Robert Trabuco Amelia Trabuco Jim Getz Mary Ann Getz
2. Grant Deed from Jim Getz, An Unmarried Man and Mary Ann Getz to Robert Trabuco and Amelia Trabuco
3. First Deed of Trust to record in favor of Bank of America, in the amount of $180,000.00
4. Note/Deed of Trust

UPON FURTHER AUTHORIZATION you are to record all instruments without collection when you can issue said form of Policy showing Title vesting in:

Robert Trabuco and Amelia Trabuco

FREE FROM ENCUMBRANCES EXCEPT:
1. ALL general and Special Taxes for the Fiscal Year 1999
2. Covenants, Conditions, Restrictions, Easements and Rights of Way of record.
3. Bonds and assessments not delinquent.
4. Deeds of Trust now of record in the amount of $89,000.90
5. New First Deed of Trust to record in favor of Bank of America

PLEASE ABSTRACT ALL DOCUMENTS AND ADVISE US IMMEDIATELY IF ANY CORRECTIONS ARE NEEDED

Please send the original policy(ies) and/or copies as appropriate to:

Bank of America   SMS SETTLEMENT SERVICES
27571 Trabuco Road   3160 Airway Avenue
Mission Viejo, CA 92674   Costa Mesa, CA 92621

If you have questions, please do not hesitate to contact our office.
Thank you.

Debbie Weatherwax
ESCROW OFFICER

January 17, 1999   Escrow No: 000020

Robert R. Mullins
306 Dublin Lane
Costa Mesa, CA 92626

RE: 2165 Memory Lane, Santa Ana, CA 92705

Dear Robert R. Mullins and Margie M. Mullins:

In connection with the above referenced escrow, we are enclosing the following items:

Please examine the following, and if they meet with your approval, sign and return. Copies are enclosed for your records.

Escrow Instructions
Amendment(s)
FHA/VA Supplemental Instructions
Note
Preliminary Title Report

Please sign the following documents as indicated and return them to our office. Note that each signature on all documents **MUST BE ACKNOWLEDGED BY A NOTARY PUBLIC**. Please be sure to sign your name exactly as it is typed.

Grant Deed
Quitclaim Deed
Corporation Grant Deed
Deed of Trust

Please **complete**, sign and return the following:

Statement of Information
Preliminary Change of Ownership
Loan Information Sheet

Your prompt attention to these items and their return to our office will assist us in the completion of your escrow. We are pleased to have been selected to service your escrow needs. If there is any way we may be of further assistance, please do no hesitate to contact our office.

Sincerely,

System A. User
Escrow Officer

448

December 29, 1999   Escrow NO. 004860

Robert Trabuco
21128 Rose
Rancho Santa Margarita, CA 92691

RE: **21128 Rose, Rancho Santa Margarita, CA 92691**

Dear Robert Trabuco and Amelia Trabuco:

The above referenced escrow closed on 01/01/1999. The following items enclosed for you and your records:

>   **Check in the amount of $102.50**
>   **Closing Statement**
>   **HUD Settlement Statement**
>   **Termite Report and Completion**

Please be advised that we will forward the Policy of Title Insurance to you upon our receipt of same. Any original documents recorded for your benefit will be forwarded to you directly from the County Recorder's office.

TAX INFORMATION

The next installment of property taxes must be paid by June 1, 2000 to avoid penalty. Tax bills are furnished to you as an accommodation of the Tax Assessor's Office, USUALLY by November 1st each year. In the event you do not receive a tax bill for this property at least a month prior to the delinquency date, contact the Tax Assessor's Office to request a duplicate billing. The payment of taxes is your responsibility; if they are not paid prior to the delinquency date, penalties will be assessed.

For any additional taxes which may be due by reason of the change in ownership. Supplemental Tax Bills will be sent to you from the Tax Collector separately from your regular tax bill. You normally must pay these taxes by a delinquency date which is separate from the regualr tax billing. Please read these supplemental tax bills for the particulars concerning same and contact the Tax Assessor's Office with any questions you may have.

It has been a pleasure handling this transaction for you. Please do not hesitate to contact our office if you have any questions regarding this matter.

Sincerely,

Debbie Weatherwax
Escrow Officer

449

SMS

LOAN INFORMATION SHEET

January 18, 1995   Escrow No: 000020

RE: 2165 Memory Lane, Santa Ana, CA 92705

In order to proceed with the above referenced escrow, we need the following information about your property. **PLEASE COMPLETE, SIGN, AND RETURN** this form to our office as soon as possible.

FIRST   Name of Lender _____
LOAN: Address _____
           Loan Number _____ Approximate unpaid balance _____

SECOND Name of Lender _____
LOAN: Address _____
           Loan Number _____ Approximate unpaid balance _____

ADDITIONAL ENCUMBRANCE

Third Trust Deed ☐   Pool Loan ☐   Home Improvement Loan ☐   Lien ☐

Lienholder Name _____
Address _____
Account No_____ Approximate unpaid balance _____

If your property is affected by a Community Association please complete the following:

Name of Association _____
Name of Management Company_____
Address _____
Account No_____

If you have shares of Water Stock please complete the following:

Name of Water Company _____
Address: _____

FORWARDING ADDRESS AFTER CLOSE OF ESCROW:

_____
_____

INSURANCE INFORMATION

Name of Insurance Company_____

Agent's name _____ Phone No. _____
Address _____
Policy Number _____ Expiration Date_____

We, the undersigned, certify that the above information is true and correct to the best of our knowledge.

_____   _____
Michael M. Horton   Linda L. Horton

3160 Airway Ave. Costa Mesa, CA 92626 (714) 549-5700 (714) 549-0684

YEAR		CALIFORNIA FORM

Withholding Exemption Certificate

1995   (For use by Individuals, corporations, partnerships and estates)   **590**

File this form with your withholding agent.

Name
Michael M. Horton and Linda L. Horton

Address (number and street)   Telephone number
2165 Memory Lane

City   State   ZIP code
Santa Ana, CA 92705

Complete the appropriate line: Individuals - Social security no. **545-33-5345** ☑ Married ☐ Single
Corporations - California corporation no. _____ (Issued by Secretary of State)
Partnerships and - F.E.I.N. _____

To **Strategic Mortgage Services** _____
    (Withholding Agent or Payer)

Individuals:

Certificate of Residency
I hereby declare under penalty perjury that I am a resident of California and that I reside at the address shown above.

Signature _____ Date_____

Certificate of Residency of Deceased Person
I hereby certify under penalty of perjury, as executor of the above named person's estate that decedent was a California resident at the time of death.

Name of Executor (type or print)_____ Date_____

Signature _____

Certificate of Principal Residence (Real estate sales only)
I hereby certify under penalty of perjury that the California real property located at **2165 Memory Lane** _____
Santa Ana. CA 92705 was my principal residence within the meaning of IRC Section 1034.

Signature _____ Date_____

Corporations:
I hereby certify the above-named corporation has a permanent place of business in California at the address shown above or is qualified to do business in California.

Signature _____ Date_____

Title of corporate officer_____

Tax Exempt Entities and Non Profit Organizations:
I hereby certify, under penalty of perjury, that the above-named entity is exempt from tax under California or Federal law.

Name and Title _____

Signature _____ Date _____

Trusts:

I hereby certify, under penalty of perjury, that at least one trustee of the above-named trust is a California resident.

Name and Title _____

Signature _____ Date _____

451

PRELIMINARY CHANGE OF OWNERSHIP REPORT

To be completed by transferee (buyer) prior to transfer of subject property in accordance with Section 480.03 of the Revenue and Taxation Code. A Preliminary Change of Ownership Report must be filed with each conveyance in the County Recorder's office for the county where the property is located; this particular form may be used in all 58 counties of California.

THIS REPORT IS NOT A PUBLIC DOCUMENT

FOR RECORDER'S USE ONLY

SELLER/TRANSFEROR: **Michael M. Horton and Linda L. Horton**
BUYER/TRANSFEREE: **Robert R. Mullins and Margie M. Mullins**
ASSESSOR'S PARCEL NUMBER(S) **123-45-6789**
PROPERTY ADDRESS OR LOCATION:

**2165 Memory Lane
Santa Ana, CA 92705**

MAIL TAX INFORMATION TO:

Name   **Robert R. Mullins**
Address **2165 Memory Lane**

Costa Mesa, CA 92626

NOTICE: A lien for property taxes applies to your property on March 1 of each year for the taxes owing in the following fiscal year, July 1 through June 30. One-half of these taxes is due November 1, and one-half is due February 1. The first installment becomes delinquent on December 10, and the second installment becomes delinquent on April 10. One tax bill is mailed before November 1 to the owner of record. **IF THIS TRANSFER OCCURS AFTER MARCH 1 AND ON OR BEFORE DECEMBER 31, YOU MAY BE RESPONSIBLE FOR THE SECOND INSTALLMENT OF TAXES DUE FEBRUARY 1.**

The property which you acquired may be subject to a supplemental assessment in an amount to be determined by the Orange County Assessor. For further information on your supplemental roll obligation, please call the Orange County Assessor at 714-834-2727.

PART I: TRANSFER INFORMATION   Please answer all questions.

YES	NO		
☐	☑	A.	Is this transfer solely between husband and wife (Addition of a spouse, death of a spouse, divorce settlement, etc.)?
☐	☑	B.	Is this transaction only a correction of the name(s) of the person(s) holding title to the property (For example, a name change upon marriage)?
☐	☑	C.	Is this document recorded to create, terminate, or reconvey a lender's interest in the property?
☐	☑	D.	Is this transaction recorded only to create, terminate, or reconvey a security interest (e.g. cosigner)?
☐	☑	E.	Is this document recorded to substitute a trustee under a deed of trust, mortgage, or other similar document?
☐	☑	F.	Did this transfer result in the creation of a joint tenancy in which the seller (transferor) remains as one of the joint tenants?
☐	☑	G.	Does this transfer return property to the person who created the joint tenancy (original transferor)?
		H.	Is this transfer of property:
☐	☑		1. to a trust for the benefit of the grantor, or grantor's spouse?
☐	☑		2. to a trust revocable by the transferor?
☐	☑		3. to a trust from which the property reverts to the grantor within 12 years?
☐	☑	I.	If this property is subject to a lease, is the remaining lease term 35 years or more including written options?
☐	☑	J.	Is this a transfer from parents to children or from children to parents?
☐	☑	K.	Is this transaction to replace a principal residence by a person 55 years of age or older?
☐	☑	L.	Is this transaction to replace a principal residence by a person who is severely disabled as defined by Revenue and Code Section 69.5?

If you checked yes to J, K, or L, an applicable claim form must be filed with the County Assessor.
Please provide any other information that would help the Assessors to understand the nature of the transfer.

IF YOU HAVE ANSWERED "YES" TO ANY OF THE ABOVE QUESTIONS EXCEPT J, K, OR L, PLEASE SIGN AND DATE, OTHERWISE COMPLETE BALANCE OF THE FORM.

PART II: OTHER TRANSFER INFORMATION

A. Date of transfer if other than recording date _____ .
B. Type of transfer. Please check appropriate box.
☑ Purchase   ☐ Foreclosure   ☐ Gift   ☐ Trade or Exchange   ☐ Merger, Stock, or Partnership Acquisition
☐ Contract of Sale - Date of Contract _____
☐ Inheritance - Date of Death _____   ☐ Other: Please explain: _____
☐ Creation of Lease   ☐ Assignment of a Lease   ☐ Termination of a Lease
Date lease began _____
Original term in years (including written options) _____
Remaining term in years (including written options) _____
C. Was only a partial interest in the property transferred? ☐ Yes ☑ No   If yes, indicate the percentage transferred _____%

PRELIMINARY CHANGE OF OWNERSHIP REPORT

Please answer, to the best of your knowledge, all applicable questions, sign and date. If a question does not apply, indicate with "N/A."

PART III: PURCHASE PRICE AND TERMS OF SALE

A. CASH DOWN PAYMENT OR Value of Trade or Exchange (excluding closing costs)   Amount $5,000.00

B. FIRST DEED OF TRUST @ 7.57% interest for 30 years. Pymts/Mo.=$857.00 (Prin. & Int. only)   Amount $80,000.00

- ☐ FHA   ☑ Fixed Rate   ☑ New Loan
- ☑ Conventional   ☐ Variable Rate   ☐ Assumed Existing Loan Balance
- ☐ VA   ☐ All inclusive D.T. ($ _____ Wrapped)   ☑ Bank or Savings & Loan
- ☐ Cal-Vet   ☐ Loan Carried by Seller   ☐ Finance Company
- Balloon Payment ☐ Yes ☑ No   Due Date _____ Amount $ _____

C. SECOND DEED OF TRUST @ _____% interest for _____ years. Pymts/Mo.=$_____(Prin. & Int. only)   Amount $_____

- ☐ Bank or Savings & Loan   ☐ Fixed Rate   ☐ New Loan
- ☐ Loan Carried by Seller   ☐ Variable Rate   ☐ Assumed Existing Loan Balance
- Balloon Payment ☐ Yes ☐ No   Due Date _____ Amount $ _____

D. OTHER FINANCING: Is other financing involved not covered in (b) or (c) above? ☐ Yes ☑ No   Amount $_____

Type _____ @ _____% interest for _____ years. Pymts./Mo.=$_____(Prin. & Int. only)

- ☐ Bank or Savings & Loan   ☐ Fixed Rate   ☐ New Loan
- ☐ Loan Carried by Seller   ☐ Variable Rate   ☐ Assumed Existing Loan Balance
- Balloon Payment ☐ Yes ☑ No   Due Date _____ Amount $ _____

E. IMPROVEMENT BOND ☐ Yes ☑ No   Outstanding Balance: Amount $_____

F. TOTAL PURCHASE PRICE (or acquisition price, if traded or exchanged, include real estate commission if paid.)

Total Items A through E $ 100,000.00

G. PROPERTY PURCHASED ☑ Through a broker ☐ Direct from seller ☐ Other (explain)_____

If purchased through a broker, provide broker's name and phone number: Century One Real Estate (714) 555-7676

Please explain any special terms or financing and any other information that would help the Assessor understand the purchase price and terms of sale.

_____

PART IV: PROPERTY INFORMATION

A. IS PERSONAL PROPERTY INCLUDED IN PURCHASE PRICE

(other than a mobilehome subject to local property tax)? ☐ Yes ☑ No

If yes, enter the value of the personal property included in the purchase price $_____ (Attach itemized list of personal property).

B. IS THIS PROPERTY INTENDED AS YOUR PRINCIPAL RESIDENCE? ☑ Yes ☐ No

If yes, enter date of occupancy ____/____/____ or intended occupancy 02/01/1995

   Month Day Year   Month Day Year

C. TYPE OF PROPERTY TRANSFERRED:

- ☑ Single-family residence   ☐ Agricultural   ☐ Timeshare
- ☐ Multiple-family residence (no. of units: _____)   ☐ Co-op/Own-your-own   ☐ Mobilehome
- ☐ Commercial/Industrial   ☐ Condominium   ☐ Unimproved lot
- ☐ Other (Description: _____)

D. DOES THE PROPERTY PRODUCE INCOME? ☐ Yes ☑ No

E. IF THE ANSWER TO QUESTION D IS YES, IS THE INCOME FROM:

☐ Lease/Rent ☐ Contract ☐ Mineral Rights ☐ Other - Explain: _____

F. WHAT WAS THE CONDITION OF PROPERTY AT THE TIME OF SALE?

☑ Good ☐ Average ☐ Fair ☐ Poor

Enter here, or on an attached sheet, any other information that would assist the Assessor in determining the value of the property such as the physical condition of the property, restrictions, etc.

_____

I certify that the foregoing is true, correct and complete to the best of my knowledge and belief.

Signed_____ Dated_____

NEW OWNER/CORPORATE OFFICER

Please Print Name of New Owner/Corporate Officer Robert R. Mullins and Margie M. Mullins

Phone Number where you are available from 8:00 a.m. - 5:00 p.m. (714) 555-2323

(NOTE: The Assessor may contact you for further information)

If a document evidencing a change of ownership is presented to the recorder for recordation without the concurrent filing of a preliminary change of ownership report, the recorder may charge an additional recording fee of twenty dollars ($20).

1099-S INPUT

IMPORTANT

All areas and data fields
with numbers must be completed
before submissions to SMS.

COMPANY NUMBER	OFFICE NUMBER	TYPE	ORDER/ESCROW FILE NO.	ACTUAL CLOSING DATE
(1)Co#244	(2)Off#1	(3)	(4)5072-J	(5)

SUBJECT PROPERTY INFORMATION

Street Address or Brief Form of Legal Description (for vacant land, use APN, county, state

City	State	Zip Code

TRANSACTION DATA

CONTRACT SALES PRICE (line 401 HUD-1 form If this is an exchange, provide total dollar value of cash, notes and debt relief received by exchangeer.	NO. OF 1099-S forms required for the sale of this property.	2 OR MORE 1099-S FORMS If 2 or more 1099-S forms are required, record the dollar amount for this seller based on the seller's declaration.	BUYERS PART OF REAL ESTATE TAX Show any real estate tax, on a residence, charged to the buyer at settlement.	CONTINGENT TRANSACTION Is this a contingent transaction wherein gross proceeds cannot be determined with certainty at time of closing?	EXCHANGE Was (or will there be) other property or services received?
$321,000.00				yes	yes

SELLER INFORMATION-PLEASE PRINT CLEARLY

Seller's Last Name	Seller's First Name	M.I.
Seller's Forwarding Street Address		
City	State	Zip Code (or country if not USA)
Seller's Social Security Number	or	Seller's Tax Identification Number

You are required by law to provide your closing agent with your correct Taxpayer Identification Number. If you do not' provide your correct Taxpayer Identification Number, you may be subject to civil or criminal penalties imposed by law .

Under penalties of perjury, I certify that the number shown above is my correct Taxpayer Identification Number.

Seller's Signature

SMS

REQUEST FOR DEMAND

January 18, 1995

Escrow No: 000020

Attn: Payoff Department
Bank of the West
6729 Bristol St.
Costa Mesa, CA 92626

RE: LOAN NUMBER: 789123
BORROWER: **Michael M. Horton and Linda L. Horton**

An escrow has been opened with our company by the above referenced borrowers and provides for the payment in full of the loan number referenced above. Your loan encumbers the real property described as:

See Exhibit A attached hereto and made a part hereof.

This property is commonly known as: **2165 Memory Lane, Santa Ana, CA 92705**

We hereby request that you forward your **ORIGINAL DEMAND**, together with either (1) the original Note, Deed of Trust securing same and your executed Request for Full Reconveyance, or (2) your executed Full Reconveyance, to the following title company:

New Land Title
ATTN: Timothy West
114 5th Street
Santa Ana, CA 92705
RE: TITLE ORDER No: 94-8976

Please fax a copy of your DEMAND to our office at (714) 549-0684 with an additional copy in the mail.

We wish to thank you for your cooperation and assistance. Please be sure to call our office if you have any questions concerning this matter.

Sincerely,

System A. User
Escrow Officer

3160 Airway Ave. Costa Mesa, CA 92626 (714) 549-5700 (714) 549-0684

455

AMORTIZATION SCHEDULE
Robert and Amelia Trabuco

Principal Amount:	$180,000.00	Term (Months):	120				
Interest Rate:	8.25	Payment Frequency:	Monthly		Start Date:	03/01/1995	
Payment Amount:	$2,207.75	Loan Start Date:	02/27/1995		End Date:	01/01/2005	

Pmt No.	Due Date	Payment Amount	Interest Paid	Principal Paid	Principal Balance	Unpaid Interest	Balance Due	Modification
1	03/01/95	$2,207.75	$82.50	$2,125.25	$177,874.75		$177,874.75	
2	04/01/95	2,207.75	1,222.89	984.86	176,889.89		176,889.89	
3	05/01/95	2,207.75	1,216.12	991.63	175,898.26		175,898.26	
4	06/01/95	2,207.75	1,209.30	998.45	174,899.81		174,899.81	
5	07/01/95	2,207.75	1,202.44	1,005.31	173,894.50		173,894.50	
6	08/01/95	2,207.75	1,195.52	1,012.23	172,882.27		172,882.27	
7	09/01/95	2,207.75	1,188.57	1,019.18	171,863.09		171,863.09	
8	10/01/95	2,207.75	1,181.56	1,026.19	170,836.90		170,836.90	
9	11/01/95	2,207.75	1,174.50	1,033.25	169,803.65		169,803.65	
10	12/01/95	2,207.75	1,167.40	1,040.35	168,763.30		168,763.30	
	Total Paid For Year		$10,840.80	$11,236.70				
11	01/01/96	2,207.75	1,160.25	1,047.50	167,715.80		167,715.80	
12	02/01/96	2,207.75	1,153.05	1,054.70	166,661.10		166,661.10	
13	03/01/96	2,207.75	1,145.80	1,061.95	165,599.15		165,599.15	
14	04/01/96	2,207.75	1,138.49	1,069.26	164,529.89		164,529.89	
15	05/01/96	2,207.75	1,131.14	1,076.61	163,453.28		163,453.28	
16	06/01/96	2,207.75	1,123.74	1,084.01	162,369.27		162,369.27	
17	07/01/96	2,207.75	1,116.29	1,091.46	161,277.81		161,277.81	
18	08/01/96	2,207.75	1,108.78	1,098.97	160,178.84		160,178.84	
19	09/01/96	2,207.75	1,101.23	1,106.52	159,072.32		159,072.32	
20	10/01/96	2,207.75	1,093.62	1,114.13	157,958.19		157,958.19	
21	11/01/96	2,207.75	1,085.96	1,121.79	156,836.40		156,836.40	
22	12/01/96	2,207.75	1,078.25	1,129.50	155,706.90		155,706.90	
	Total Paid For Year		$13,436.60	$13,056.40				
23	01/01/97	2,207.75	1,070.49	1,137.26	154,569.64		154,569.64	
24	02/01/97	2,207.75	1,062.67	1,145.08	153,424.56		153,424.56	
25	03/01/97	2,207.75	1,054.79	1,152.96	152,271.60		152,271.60	
26	04/01/97	2,207.75	1,046.87	1,160.88	151,110.72		151,110.72	
27	05/01/97	2,207.75	1,038.89	1,168.86	149,941.86		149,941.86	
28	06/01/97	2,207.75	1,030.85	1,176.90	148,764.96		148,764.96	
29	07/01/97	2,207.75	1,022.76	1,184.99	147,579.97		147,579.97	
30	08/01/97	2,207.75	1,014.61	1,193.14	146,386.83		146,386.83	
31	09/01/97	2,207.75	1,006.41	1,201.34	145,185.49		145,185.49	
32	10/01/97	2,207.75	998.15	1,209.60	143,975.89		143,975.89	
33	11/01/97	2,207.75	989.83	1,217.92	142,757.97		142,757.97	
34	12/01/97	2,207.75	981.46	1,226.29	141,531.68		141,531.68	
	Total Paid For Year		$12,317.78	$14,175.22				
35	01/01/98	2,207.75	973.03	1,234.72	140,296.96		140,296.96	
36	02/01/98	2,207.75	964.54	1,243.21	139,053.75		139,053.75	
37	03/01/98	2,207.75	955.99	1,251.76	137,801.99		137,801.99	
38	04/01/98	2,207.75	947.39	1,260.36	136,541.63		136,541.63	
39	05/01/98	2,207.75	938.72	1,269.03	135,272.60		135,272.60	
40	06/01/98	2,207.75	930.00	1,277.75	133,994.85		133,994.85	
41	07/01/98	2,207.75	921.21	1,286.54	132,708.31		132,708.31	
42	08/01/98	2,207.75	912.37	1,295.38	131,412.93		131,412.93	
43	09/01/98	2,207.75	903.46	1,304.29	130,108.64		130,108.64	
44	10/01/98	2,207.75	894.50	1,313.25	128,795.39		128,795.39	
45	11/01/98	2,207.75	885.47	1,322.28	127,473.11		127,473.11	
46	12/01/98	2,207.75	876.38	1,331.37	126,141.74		126,141.74	
	Total Paid For Year		$11,103.06	$15,389.94				
47	01/01/99	2,207.75	867.22	1,340.53	124,801.21		124,801.21	
48	02/01/99	2,207.75	858.01	1,349.74	123,451.47		123,451.47	
49	03/01/99	2,207.75	848.73	1,359.02	122,092.45		122,092.45	
50	04/01/99	2,207.75	839.39	1,368.36	120,724.09		120,724.09	
51	05/01/99	2,207.75	829.98	1,377.77	119,346.32		119,346.32	
52	06/01/99	2,207.75	820.51	1,387.24	117,959.08		117,959.08	
53	07/01/99	2,207.75	810.97	1,396.78	116,562.30		116,562.30	

AMORTIZATION SCHEDULE
Robert and Amelia Trabuco

Principal Amount:	$180,000.00	Term (Months):	120		
Interest Rate:	8.25	Payment Frequency:	Monthly	Start Date:	03/01/1995
Payment Amount:	$2,207.75	Loan Start Date:	02/27/1995	End Date:	01/01/2005

Pmt No.	Due Date	Payment Amount	Interest Paid	Principal Paid	Principal Balance	Unpaid Interest	Balance Due	Modification
54	08/01/99	$2,207.75	$801.37	$1,406.38	$115,155.92		$115,155.92	
55	09/01/99	2,207.75	791.70	1,416.05	113,739.87		113,739.87	
56	10/01/99	2,207.75	781.96	1,425.79	112,314.08		112,314.08	
57	11/01/99	2,207.75	772.16	1,435.59	110,878.49		110,878.49	
58	12/01/99	2,207.75	762.29	1,445.46	109,433.03		109,433.03	
	Total Paid For Year		$9,784.29	$16,708.71				
59	01/01/00	2,207.75	752.35	1,455.40	107,977.63		107,977.63	
60	02/01/00	2,207.75	742.35	1,465.40	106,512.23		106,512.23	
61	03/01/00	2,207.75	732.27	1,475.48	105,036.75		105,036.75	
62	04/01/00	2,207.75	722.13	1,485.62	103,551.13		103,551.13	
63	05/01/00	2,207.75	711.91	1,495.84	102,055.29		102,055.29	
64	06/01/00	2,207.75	701.63	1,506.12	100,549.17		100,549.17	
65	07/01/00	2,207.75	691.28	1,516.47	99,032.70		99,032.70	
66	08/01/00	2,207.75	680.85	1,526.90	97,505.80		97,505.80	
67	09/01/00	2,207.75	670.35	1,537.40	95,968.40		95,968.40	
68	10/01/00	2,207.75	659.78	1,547.97	94,420.43		94,420.43	
69	11/01/00	2,207.75	649.14	1,558.61	92,861.82		92,861.82	
70	12/01/00	2,207.75	638.43	1,569.32	91,292.50		91,292.50	
	Total Paid For Year		$8,352.47	$18,140.53				
71	01/01/01	2,207.75	627.64	1,580.11	89,712.39		89,712.39	
72	02/01/01	2,207.75	616.77	1,590.98	88,121.41		88,121.41	
73	03/01/01	2,207.75	605.83	1,601.92	86,519.49		86,519.49	
74	04/01/01	2,207.75	594.82	1,612.93	84,906.56		84,906.56	
75	05/01/01	2,207.75	583.73	1,624.02	83,282.54		83,282.54	
76	06/01/01	2,207.75	572.57	1,635.18	81,647.36		81,647.36	
77	07/01/01	2,207.75	561.33	1,646.42	80,000.94		80,000.94	
78	08/01/01	2,207.75	550.01	1,657.74	78,343.20		78,343.20	
79	09/01/01	2,207.75	538.61	1,669.14	76,674.06		76,674.06	
80	10/01/01	2,207.75	527.13	1,680.62	74,993.44		74,993.44	
81	11/01/01	2,207.75	515.58	1,692.17	73,301.27		73,301.27	
82	12/01/01	2,207.75	503.95	1,703.80	71,597.47		71,597.47	
	Total Paid For Year		$6,797.97	$19,695.03				
83	01/01/02	2,207.75	492.23	1,715.52	69,881.95		69,881.95	
84	02/01/02	2,207.75	480.44	1,727.31	68,154.64		68,154.64	
85	03/01/02	2,207.75	468.56	1,739.19	66,415.45		66,415.45	
86	04/01/02	2,207.75	456.61	1,751.14	64,664.31		64,664.31	
87	05/01/02	2,207.75	444.57	1,763.18	62,901.13		62,901.13	
88	06/01/02	2,207.75	432.45	1,775.30	61,125.83		61,125.83	
89	07/01/02	2,207.75	420.24	1,787.51	59,338.32		59,338.32	
90	08/01/02	2,207.75	407.95	1,799.80	57,538.52		57,538.52	
91	09/01/02	2,207.75	395.58	1,812.17	55,726.35		55,726.35	
92	10/01/02	2,207.75	383.12	1,824.63	53,901.72		53,901.72	
93	11/01/02	2,207.75	370.57	1,837.18	52,064.54		52,064.54	
94	12/01/02	2,207.75	357.94	1,849.81	50,214.73		50,214.73	
	Total Paid For Year		$5,110.26	$21,382.74				
95	01/01/03	2,207.75	345.23	1,862.52	48,352.21		48,352.21	
96	02/01/03	2,207.75	332.42	1,875.33	46,476.88		46,476.88	
97	03/01/03	2,207.75	319.53	1,888.22	44,588.66		44,588.66	
98	04/01/03	2,207.75	306.55	1,901.20	42,687.46		42,687.46	
99	05/01/03	2,207.75	293.48	1,914.27	40,773.19		40,773.19	
100	06/01/03	2,207.75	280.32	1,927.43	38,845.76		38,845.76	
101	07/01/03	2,207.75	267.06	1,940.69	36,905.07		36,905.07	
102	08/01/03	2,207.75	253.72	1,954.03	34,951.04		34,951.04	
103	09/01/03	2,207.75	240.29	1,967.46	32,983.58		32,983.58	
104	10/01/03	2,207.75	226.76	1,980.99	31,002.59		31,002.59	
105	11/01/03	2,207.75	213.14	1,994.61	29,007.98		29,007.98	
106	12/01/03	2,207.75	199.43	2,008.32	26,999.66		26,999.66	

Page 2

457

AMORTIZATION SCHEDULE
Robert and Amelia Trabuco

Principal Amount:	$180,000.00	Term (Months):	120		
Interest Rate:	8.25	Payment Frequency:	Monthly	Start Date:	03/01/1995
Payment Amount:	$2,207.75	Loan Start Date:	02/27/1995	End Date:	01/01/2005

Pmt No.	Due Date	Payment Amount	Interest Paid	Principal Paid	Principal Balance	Unpaid Interest	Balance Due	Modification
	Total Paid For Year		$3,277.93	$23,215.07				
107	01/01/04	$2,207.75	$185.62	$2,022.13	$24,977.53		$24,977.53	
108	02/01/04	2,207.75	171.72	2,036.03	22,941.50		22,941.50	
109	03/01/04	2,207.75	157.72	2,050.03	20,891.47		20,891.47	
110	04/01/04	2,207.75	143.63	2,064.12	18,827.35		18,827.35	
111	05/01/04	2,207.75	129.44	2,078.31	16,749.04		16,749.04	
112	06/01/04	2,207.75	115.15	2,092.60	14,656.44		14,656.44	
113	07/01/04	2,207.75	100.76	2,106.99	12,549.45		12,549.45	
114	08/01/04	2,207.75	86.28	2,121.47	10,427.98		10,427.98	
115	09/01/04	2,207.75	71.69	2,136.06	8,291.92		8,291.92	
116	10/01/04	2,207.75	57.01	2,150.74	6,141.18		6,141.18	
117	11/01/04	2,207.75	42.22	2,165.53	3,975.65		3,975.65	
118	12/01/04	2,207.75	27.33	2,180.42	1,795.23		1,795.23	
	Total Paid For Year		$1,288.57	$25,204.43				
119	01/01/05	1,807.57	12.34	1,795.23				
	Total Paid For Year		$12.34	$1,795.23				
	Total Paid for Loan		$82,322.07	$180,000.00				

SMS SETTLEMENT SERVICES
SELLER'S ESTIMATED CLOSING STATEMENT

Seller: Jim Getz
      Mary Ann Getz

Escrow No: 004860-999 DW
Close Date: 01-01-1999
Proration Date: 12-31-98
Date Prepared: 11/22/1998

Property: 21128 Rose
      Rancho Santa Margarita, CA 92691

Description	Debit	Credit
TOTAL CONSIDERATION:		189,900
NEW AND EXISTING ENCUMBRANCES:		
County Taxes from 1-20-99 to 1/31-2000		238.33
Based on the annual amount of '$7,800.00		
Assessments from 1-01-99 to 1-01-99		100.00
County Taxes 1-01-99 to 3-31-2000	293.33	
Based on the annual amount of $1,200.00		
PAYOFFS:		
Payoff to Bank of America	68,045.63	
67,595.00 Principal balance		
450.63 Interest from 12-01-98 to 1-31-98		
ESCROW AND TITLE CHARGES:		
Settlement/Closing Fee to SMS SETTLEMENT SERVICES	175.00	
Title Examination to SMS SETTLEMENT SERVICES	250.00	
Attorney's Fees to Strachen and Green	85.00	
Title Insurance to SMS SETTLEMENT SERVICES	813.00	
RECORDING FEES:		
City/County Tax Stamps to SMS SETTLEMENT SERVICES	36.00	
COMMISSIONS:	11,394	
5,697.00 to Blue Lagoon Real Estate		
5,697.00 to Grubb & Ellis Company		
Sub Totals	261,184.29	190,238.33
Balance Due from Seller		70,945.96
Totals	261,184.29	261,184.29

_____

Jim Getz, Sr..

Trustor of the Main Street Trust

_____

Mary Ann Getz

SMS SETTLEMENT SERVICES
SELLER'S CLOSING STATEMENT
FINAL

Seller: Jim Getz
        Mary Ann Getz

Escrow No: 004860-999 DW
Close Date: 01-01-1999
Proration Date: 12-31-98
Date Prepared: 11/22/1998

Property: 21128 Rose
        Rancho Santa Margarita, CA 92691

Description	Debit	Credit
TOTAL CONSIDERATION:		189,900
NEW AND EXISTING ENCUMBRANCES:		
County Taxes from 1-20-99 to 1/31-2000		238.33
Based on the annual amount of '$7,800.00		
Assessments f rom 1-01-99 to 1-01-99		100.00
County Taxes 1-01-99 to 3-31-2000	293.33	
Based on the annual amount of $1,200.00		
PAYOFFS:		
Payoff to Bank of America	68,045.63	
67,595.00 Principal balance		
450.63 Interest from 12-01-98 to 1-31-98		
ESCROW AND TITLE CHARGES:		
Settlement/Closing Fee to SMS SETTLEMENT SERVICES	175.00	
Title Examination to SMS SETTLEMENT SERVICES	250.00	
Attorney's Fees to Strachen and Green	85.00	
Title Insurance to SMS SETTLEMENT SERVICES	813.00	
RECORDING FEES:		
City/County Tax Stamps to SMS SETTLEMENT SERVICES	36.00	
COMMISSIONS:	11,394	
5,697.00 to Blue Lagoon Real Estate		
5,697.00 to Grubb & Ellis Company		
Sub Totals	261,184.29	190,238.33
Balance Due from Seller		70,945.96
Totals	261,184.29	261,184.29

_____

Jim Getz, Sr..

Trustor of the Main Street Trust

_____

Mary Ann Getz

SMS SETTLEMENT SERVICES

BUYER'S ESTIMATED CLOSING STATEMENT

Buyer: Robert Trabuco   Escrow No: 004860-999 DW
     Amelia Trabuco   Close Date: 01-01-1999
     Proration Date: 12-31-98
     Date Prepared: 11/22/1998

Property: 21128 Rose
     Rancho Santa Margarita, CA 92691

Description	Debit	Credit
TOTAL CONSIDERATION:		
Total Consideration	189,900	
Deposit/Earnest Money		5,000
NEW AND EXISTING ENCUMBRANCES:		
Existing Loan Amount from Bank of America		180,000
NEW LOAN CHARGES		
Loan Origination Fee to Bank of America	180,000	
Loan Discount to Bank of America	180,000	
Appraisal Fee to Bank of America	350.00	
Credit Report to TRW	15.00	
Servicing/Document Prep. to Bank of America	250.00	
Credit Line to Bank of America	200.00	
Tax Service to Bank of America	68.50	
Underwriting Fee to Bank of America	75.00	
Hazard Insurance Premium to Bank of America	1,200.00	
Hazard Insurance to Bank of America	100.00	
City Property Taxes to Bank of America	600.00	
County Property Taxes to Bank of America	400.00	
PRORATIONS AND ADJUSTMENTS:		
County Taxes from 1-20-99 to 1-31-99	238.33	
Based on annual amount of $7,800.00		
County Taxes 1-01-99 to 3-29-99/		293.33
Based on the annual amount of $1,200.00		
ESCROW AND TITLE CHARGES:		
Settlement/Closing Fee to SMS SETTLEMENT SERVICES	176.00	
Title Insurance to SMS SETTLEMENT SERVICES	60.00	
Creditline Endorsement to SMS SETTLEMENT SERVICES	75.00	
Transfer Fee to SMS SETTLEMENT SERVICES	25.00	
RECORDING FEES		
Recording Fees to SMS SETTLEMENT SERVICES	20.50	
ADDITIONAL CHARGES		
Survey to Anderson Surveying	350.00	
Pest Inspection to D.I. Bruce Exterminating Co.	200.00	
Fed Ex Fee to All Lenders Mortgage	75.00	
Sub Totals	194,727.33	185,386.66
Balance Due From Buyer		9,340.67
Totals	194,727.33	194,727.33

Robert Trabuco   Amelia Trabuco

SMS SETTLEMENT SERVICES
BUYER'S CLOSING STATEMENT
Final

Buyer: Robert Trabuco
     Amelia Trabuco

Escrow No: 004860-999 DW
Close Date: 01-01-1999
Proration Date: 12-31-98
Date Prepared: 11/22/1998

Property: 21128 Rose
Rancho Santa Margarita, CA 92691

Description	Debit	Credit
TOTAL CONSIDERATION:		
Total Consideration	189,900	
Deposit/Earnest Money		5,000
NEW AND EXISTING ENCUMBRANCES:		
Existing Loan Amount from Bank of America		180,000
NEW LOAN CHARGES		
Loan Origination Fee to Bank of America	180,000	
Loan Discount to Bank of America	180,000	
Appraisal Fee to Bank of America	350.00	
Credit Report to TRW	15.00	
Servicing/Document Prep. to Bank of America	250.00	
Credit Line to Bank of America	200.00	
Tax Service to Bank of America	68.50	
Underwriting Fee to Bank of America	75.00	
Hazard Insurance Premium to Bank of America	1,200.00	
Hazard Insurance to Bank of America	100.00	
City Property Taxes to Bank of America	600.00	
County Property Taxes to Bank of America	400.00	
PRORATIONS AND ADJUSTMENTS:		
County Taxes from 1-20-99 to 1-31-99	238.33	
Based on annual amount of $7,800.00		
County Taxes 1-01-99 to 3-29-99/		293.33
Based on the annual amount of $1,200.00		
ESCROW AND TITLE CHARGES:		
Settlement/Closing Fee to SMS SETTLEMENT SERVICES	176.00	
Title Insurance to SMS SETTLEMENT SERVICES	60.00	
Creditline Endorsement to SMS SETTLEMENT SERVICES	75.00	
Transfer Fee to SMS SETTLEMENT SERVICES	25.00	
RECORDING FEES		
Recording Fees to SMS SETTLEMENT SERVICES	20.50	
ADDITIONAL CHARGES		
Survey to Anderson Surveying	350.00	
Pest Inspection to D.I. Bruce Exterminating Co.	200.00	
Fed Ex Fee to All Lenders Mortgage	75.00	
Sub Totals	194,727.33	185,386.66
Balance Due From Buyer		9,340.67
Totals	194,727.33	194,727.33

Robert Trabuco   Amelia Trabuco

GOOD FAITH ESTIMATE OF SETTLEMENT CHARGES

Borrower:

Creditor:
Westmark Mortgage Corp.
535 Anton boulevard, Suite 500
Costa Mesa, CA 92626

Loan Number: Date:

The information provided below reflects estimates of the charges which you are likely to incur at the settlement of your loan. The fees listed are estimates--the actual charges may be more or less. Your transaction may not involve a fee for every item listed.

The numbers listed beside the estimates generally correspond to the numbered lines contained in the HUD-1 settlement statement which you will be receiving at settlement. The HUD-1 settlement statement will show you the actual cost for items paid at settlement.

LOAN AMOUNT:		$ 118,750.00
ITEMIZATION OF PREPAID FINANCE CHARGES:		
801 Loan Origination Fee 1.25%(Lender)	$ 1,484.38	
810 Tax Servisce	75.00	
811 Processing Fee	200.00	
813 UNDERWRITING	375.00	
814 TAX SERVICE	75.00	
901 Prepaid Interest (5/14/99-6/01/99)	489.78	
1002 Mortgage Insurance Reserves		
TOTAL PREPAID FINANCE CHARGE		$ 2,901.03
AMOUNT FINANCED		115,848.97

OTHER SETTLEMENT CHARGES:

AMOUNTS PAID TO OTHERS ON YOUR BEHALF BY CREDITOR		
803 Appraisal Fee to Truman Bailey	295.00	
804 Credit Report Fee	55.00	
903 Property Insurance to Insurance Co.	400.00	
1001 Property Insurance Reserves (2 mo.)	66.68	
1004 County Tax Reserves (4 mo.)	520.00	
1101 Settlement or Closing Fee	400.00	
1106 Notary Fees to ESCROW COMPANY	10.00	
1108 Title Insurance to TITLE COMPANY	300.00	
1201 Recording Fees	50.00	
TOTAL OTHER SETTLEMENT CHARGES		2,097.52
LOAN PROCEEDS		$ 113,751.45

These estimates are provided pursuant to the Real Estate Settlement Procedures Act of 1974 (RESPA). Additional information can be found in the HUD Special Information booklet, chich is to be provided to you by your mortgage broker or lender.

I (WE) HEREBY ACKNOWLEDGE RECEIVING AND READING A COMPLETEDS COPY OF THIS DISCLOSURE.

_____   _____
Date   Date

Federal Truth-In-Lending Disclosure Statement

Borrower:

Creditor:
WESTMARK MORTGAGE CORP.
535 ANTON BOULEVARD, SUITE 500
COSTA MESA, CA 92626

Loan Number: 2-0111-2457

4/19/99

ANNUAL PERCENTAGE RATE	FINANCE CHARGE	AMOUNT FINANCED	TOTAL OF PAYMENTS
The cost of your credit as a yearly rate.	The dollar amount the credit will cost you.	The amount of credit provided to you or on your behalf.	The amount you will have paid after you have made all payments as scheduled
9.2730%	$229,540.84	$115,848.97	$345,389.81

Your payment schedule will be:

No. of Pmts.	Amt.of Pmts.	Monthly Pmts Begin	No. of Pmts.	Amt. of Pmts.	Monthly Pmts. Begin	No. of Pmts.	Amt. of Pmts.	Monthly Pmts. Begin
359	959.42	7/01/99						
1	958.03	6/01/2029						

INSURANCE: The following insurance is required to obtain credit: *Property
    You may obtain the insurance from anyone that is acceptable to creditor.

SECURITY: You are giving a security interest in the real property being purchased.
    Property Address: 3210 Juniper Court, Hanford, CA 93230

FILING FEES: $50.00

LATE CHARGE: If a payment is more than 15 days late, you will be charged 5% of the payment.

PREPAYMENT: If you pay off your loan early, you will not have to pay a penalty. You will not be entitled to a refund of part of the finance charge.

ASSUMPTION: Someone buying your property cannot assume the remainder of your loan on the original terms.

All dates and numerical disclosures except the late payment disclosures are estimates.

See your contract documents for any additional information about nonpayment, default, any required repayment in full before the scheduled ate, and prepayment refunds and penalties.

Name	Date	Name	Date

INSTALLMENT NOTE
(INTEREST INCLUDED)
(THIS NOTE CONTAINS AN ACCELERATION CLAUSE)

$189,000 _____ Mission Viejo _____ ,California, 1/1/99 _____

In installments and at the times hereinafter stated, for value received, Robert Trabuco and Amelia Trabuco

promise to pay to Jim Getz and Mary Anne Getz _____

_____ , or order

at 21128 Rose, Rancho Santa Margarita, CA 92626 _____

the principal sum of One Hundred Eighty Thousand _____ dollars

with interest from January 1, 1999 _____ on the amounts of

principal remaining from time to time unpaid, until said principal sum is paid, at the rate of 8.9 _____ percent

per annum. Principal and interest due in monthly installments of One Thousand Five Hundred Dollars, $1,500, or more on the 15th day of each and every month, beginning on the 15th day of February, 1999.

and continuing until said principal sum has been fully paid. AT ANY TIME, THE PRIVILEGE IS RESERVED TO PAY MORE THAN THE SUM DUE. Should the interest not be so paid, it shall be added to the principal and thereafter bear like interest as the principal, but such unpaid interest so compounded shall not exceed an amount equal to simple interest on the unpaid principal at the maximum rate permitted by law. Should default be made in the payment of any of said installments when due, then the whole sum of principal and interest shall become immediately due and payable at the option of the holder of this note.

If the trustor shall sell, convey, or alienate said property, or any part thereof, or any interest therein, or shall be divested of his title or any interest therein in may manner or way, whether voluntarily or involuntarily, without the written consent of the beneficiary being first had and obtained, beneficiary shall have the right, at its option, to declare any indebtedness or obligations secured hereby, irrespective of the maturity date specified in any note evidencing the same, immediately due and payable.

Should suit be commenced to collect this note or any portion thereof, such sum as the Court may deem reasonable shall be added hereto as attorney's fees. Principal and interest payable for lawful money of the United States of America. This note is secured by a certain DEED OF TRUST to the SMS SETTLEMENT SERVICES, a California corporation, as TRUSTEE.

_____
Robert Trabuco

_____
Amelia Trabuco

RECORDING REQUESTED BY
New Land Title Company
AND WHEN RECORDED MAIL TO:

Name: Robert R. Mullins
Street Address: 2185 Memory Lane
City, State: Costa Mesa, CA 92626
Zip

REC	
RCF	
MICRO	
RTCF	
LIEN	
SMPF	
PCOR	

Order No. 56748932-SMS

Space Above This Line for Recorder's Use

QUITCLAIM DEED

THE UNDERSIGNED GRANTOR(S) DECLARE(S)
City of: Costa Mesa

Conveyance tax is $_____
Parcel No. 123-45-6789

DOCUMENTARY TRANSFER TAX $_____
☐ Computed on full value of interest of property conveyed
☐ Full value less value of liens or encumbrances remaining at the time of sale

FOR A VALUABLE CONSIDERATION, receipt of which is hereby acknowledged, Michael L. Horton and Lisa M. Horton, Husband and Wife as Joint Tenants do (does) hereby REMISE, RELEASE AND FOREVER QUITCLAIM to Robert R. Mullins and Margie M. Mullins, Husband and Wife as Joint Tenants

the following real property in the city of Costa Mesa county of Orange, state of California

Lot 12 in Tract 2316 as recorded in Book 42 pages 5-10 inclusive of Miscellaneous Maps in the office of the County Recorder of the County of Orange, State of California and described as follows: commencing at a point on the Southerly line thereof 450.8 feet West of the Southeast corner thereof, thence North 68 degrees 58 minutes West 100 fee, thence North 23 degrees 02 minutes East 60 feet, thence South 66 degrees 58 minutes East one hundred feet, thence South 23 degrees 02 minutes West 60 feet to the point of beginning.

Dated:_____

STATE OF CALIFORNIA
COUNTY OF_____

On_____ before me.

a Notary Public in and for said County and State, personally appeared:
_____

_____
Personally known to me (or provided to me on the basis of satisfactory evidence whose name(s) is/are subscribed to the within instrument and acknowledged to me that he/she/they executed the same in his/her/their authorized capacity(ies) and that by his/her/their signature(s) on the instrument the person(s) or the entity upon behalf of which the person(s) acted, executed the instrument.

WITNESS my hand and official seal.

Signature_____

_____
Michael M. Horton

_____
Linda L. Horton

(This area for official notorial seal)

RECORDING REQUESTED BY
New Land Title Company
AND WHEN RECORDED MAIL TO:

Name: Robert R. Mullins
Street Address: 2185 Memory Lane
City, State: Costa Mesa, CA 92626
Zip

REC	
RCF	
MICRO	
RTCF	
LIEN	
SMPF	
PCOR	

Order No. 56748932-SMS

Space Above This Line for Recorder's Use

GRANT DEED

THE UNDERSIGNED GRANTOR(S) DECLARE(S)
City of: <u>Costa Mesa</u>

Conveyance tax is $_____
Parcel No. 123-45-6789

DOCUMENTARY TRANSFER TAX $_____
☐ Computed on full value of interest of property conveyed
☐ Full value less value of liens or encumbrances remaining
at the time of sale

FOR A VALUABLE CONSIDERATION, receipt of which is hereby acknowledged, Michael L. Horton and Lisa M. Horton, Husband and Wife as Joint Tenants do (does) hereby GRANTS to Robert R. Mullins and Margie M. Mullins, Husband and Wife as Joint Tenants

the following real property in the city of Costa Mesa
county of Orange, state of California

Lot 12 in Tract 2316 as recorded in Book 42 pages 5-10 inclusive of Miscellaneous Maps in the office of the County Recorder of the County of Orange State of California and described as follows: commencing at a point on the Southerly line thereof 450.8 feet West of the Southeast corner thereof, thence North 68 degrees 58 minutes West 100 fee, thence North 23 degrees 02 minutes East 60 feet, thence South 66 degrees 58 minutes East one hundred feet, thence South 23 degrees 02 minutes West 60 feet to the point of beginning.

Dated:_____

STATE OF CALIFORNIA
COUNTY OF_____

On_____before me.

a Notary Public in and for said County and State, personally appeared:

_____

_____

Personally known to me (or provided to me on the basis of satisfactory evidence whose name(s) is/are subscribed to the within instrument and acknowledged to me that he/she/they executed the same in his/her/their authorized capacity(ies) and that by his/her/their signature(s) on the instrument the person(s) or the entity upon behalf of which the person(s) acted, executed the instrument.

WITNESS my hand and official seal.

Signature_____

_____
Michael M. Horton

_____
Linda L. Horton

(This area for official notarial seal)

Post Test

The following self test repeats the one you took at the beginning of this chapter. Now take the exam again--since you have read all the material-- and check your knowledge of conducting an escrow.

True/False

1. The process of conducting an escrow involves two main steps.

2. There is only one kind of escrow.

3. In opening an escrow, the names of the parties, legal description, and selling price, among other information, are collected by the escrow holder.

4. Escrow instructions are prepared to direct the escrow holder.

5. Escrow instructions need to be signed only by the seller to make an escrow valid.

6. The escrow holder never prepares a note and trust deed.

7. Closing costs are calculated before the escrow is opened.

8. The down payment is collected by the escrow holder.

9. The escrow holder coordinates with the lender.

10. Escrow instructions are commonly generated by computer.

Glossary of Terms and Phrases

ABSTRACT OF TITLE
A full summary of all consecutive grants, conveyances, wills, records and judicial proceedings affecting title to a specific parcel of real estate.

ACCELERATION CLAUSE
A clause in a loan document describing certain events that would cause the entire loan to be due. In the event the property described herein, or any part hereof, or any interest therein, is sold, conveyed, alienated, assigned or otherwise transferred by the maker, or by the operation of law or otherwise, all obligations secured by this instrument, irrespective of the maturity dates expressed therein, at the option of the payee thereof, and without demand or notice shall immediately become due and payable. This phrase must be placed on note and trust deed, and incorporated into instructions.

ACCESS TO PROPERTY
Seller will provide reasonable access to the property to buyer, inspectors representing buyer, to representatives of lending institutions for appraisal purposes or for any other purpose relating to the sale.

ACCOMMODATION RECORDING
I hand you herewith_____executed by_____to_____which you are authorized to use in connection with the subject escrow. It is agreed that_____shall assume no responsibility in connection with recording of said_____on my behalf as an accommodation to the undersigned. Affix $_____documentary transfer tax (if a Deed) as total consideration is $_____. Charge $_____for transfer tax, if applicable and for recordation of document.

ACKNOWLEDGMENT
A formal declaration to a public official.

ACTUAL NOTICE
Notice given by possession of property.

ADDITIONAL INTEREST DUE/PAYOFFS
The buyer and seller agree that disbursement of any payoffs for encumbrances being paid off at close of escrow must be received by the Lender by a specific date to avoid further accrual of interest. You are instructed to forward payoff funds to the lender and charge the appropriate account any fees at close of escrow. In the event the lender demands additional funds after the close of escrow, buyer or seller agrees to deposit additional funds according to lender's instructions.

ADJUSTABLE RATE MORTGAGE (ARM)
A note whose interest rate is tied to a flexible index.

AGENCY RELATIONSHIP CONFIRMATION
The following agency relationship is hereby confirmed for this transaction: The selling agent is the agent of the buyer exclusively; or seller exclusively; or both the buyer and seller.

AGREEMENT OF SALE
A contract for the sale of real property where the seller gives up possession, but retains the title until the purchase price is paid in full.

ALIENATION CLAUSE
A clause in a loan document that would allow the lender to call the entire loan due upon the sale of the property.

ALL-INCLUSIVE TRUST DEED
A purchase money deed of trust subordinate to–but still including–the original loan.

A.L.T.A. POLICY
American Land Title Association policy of extended title insurance policy, can be purchased by lender or buyer.

AMENDING PREVIOUS INSTRUCTIONS
These instructions supersede and amend any previous instructions in your escrow no._____, relative to the terms set forth These instructions shall be your authority to act as directed in your capacity as escrow agent.

ANNUAL PERCENTAGE RATE (APR)
The relationship of the total finance charge to the total amount to be financed as required under the Truth-in-Lending Act.

APPURTENANCE
Those rights, privileges, and improvements that belong to and pass with the transfer of real property but are not necessarily a part of the actual property.

ASSIGNMENT OF RENTS
An agreement between a property owner and the holder of a trust deed or mortgage by which the holder receives, as security, the right to collect rents from tenants of the property in the event of default by the borrower.

ASSUMPTION CLAUSE
A buyer takes over the existing loan and agrees to be liable for the repayment of the loan.

ATTORNEY FEES
If the buyer, seller, or broker brings an action to enforce his or her rights under this agreement, including an action to recover commissions, the prevailing party shall be entitled to receive from the defaulting party a reasonable attorney fee, to be determined by the court or arbitrator.

BALLOON PAYMENT
Under an installment loan, a final payment that is substantially larger than any other payment and repays the debt in full.

BALLOON PAYMENT CLAUSE
This note provides that the holder of this note shall give written notice to Trustor (borrower) of prescribed information at least 90 and not more than 150 days before any balloon payment is due.

BALLOON PAYMENT DISCLOSURE
All parties agree that they have not received or relied upon any statements or representations made to them by the broker regarding availability of funds, or rate of interest at which funds might be available when buyer is obligated to refinance or pay off the remaining balance of any loan which is part of this agreement.

BASE LINE
A survey line running east and west, used as a reference when mapping land.

BENEFICIARY
The lender under a note and deed of trust.

BILL OF SALE
A written agreement used to transfer ownership in personal property.

BILL OF SALE
Buyer and seller agree to make a joint itemized inventory of all personal items to be conveyed through this escrow and will deposit it with escrow holder. You are to prepare a bill of sale to be executed by the seller, who states that all items being conveyed will be free and clear of encumbrances and/ or liens unless previously disclosed to buyer. You are instructed to include list of the bill of sale being created in escrow instructions.

BLANKET LOAN
A loan secured by several properties.

BONDS OR ASSESSMENTS
If there is a bond or assessment on the subject property, with an outstanding balance and is a lien upon this property, it shall be paid by seller (assumed by b. If the bond or assessment is to be assumed, the obligation shall (not) be credited to buyer at closing. This agreement is conditioned upon all parties verifying and approving in writing the amount of any bond or assessment within ten (10) days of receipt of the preliminary title report. The disapproving party may terminate this escrow, in which case all unused deposits shall be returned to Buyer.

BROKER BUYING AS PRINCIPAL
Seller acknowledges that buyer is a licensed real estate broker (salesperson) acting as a principal, for his or her own account.

BROKER
Listing broker, selling broker, cooperating brokers and all sales persons.

BROKER REPRESENTING BOTH PARTIES
By placing their initials here: b _____ and seller _____ agree that _____, the broker in this transaction, represents all parties, with the consent and knowledge of all parties.

BUSINESS OPPORTUNITY
Any type of business that is for lease or sale.

BULK TRANSFER LAW
The law concerning the transfer in bulk by a retail business (not a sale in the ordinary course of the seller's business).

BUYER'S APPROVAL OF DISCLOSURE STATEMENT
If Transfer Disclosure Statement is delivered to buyer after the execution of this offer, buyer is allowed to terminate this agreement by written notice delivered to seller or his agent within three (3) days from receipt of the Transfer Disclosure Statement. All deposits to be returned, less expenses incurred to date of termination.

CANCELLATION INSTRUCTIONS
The buyer had agreed to purchase, the seller agreed to sell that certain property commonly known as _____. However, buyer and seller mutually agree to cancel the subject escrow and escrow holder is hereby authorized to disburse the deposit you now hold in the sum of $_____ as follows:$_____to_____, $_____to_____ and any charges for title or escrow services $_____to_____. It is also agreed that buyer and seller will hold the broker and escrow holder harmless and free of any liability in connection with the release of funds as directed by the buyer and seller and for the cancellation of the escrow as directed by the principals.

CHAIN OF TITLE
The recorded history of matters such as conveyances, liens and encumbrances affecting title to a parcel of real estate.

CHATTEL
Personal property.

CHATTEL REAL
An item of personal property which is connected to real estate, for example, a lease.

CLOSING COSTS

On or before _____, or within_____ days of acceptance all parties shall deposit with Escrow Holder, all funds and instruments necessary to complete the sale. Escrow fee to be paid by _____, Documentary Transfer Tax, if any, to be paid by _____.

COMMISSION

A commission is to be paid to the broker at the close of escrow as directed by the terms of the commission agreement.

COMMISSION SPLIT

The previously agreed upon division of money between a broker and sales associate when the brokerage has been paid commission from a sale made by the associate.

NEW CONVENTIONAL FIXED RATE LOAN, CASH DOWN PAYMENT

Purchase price payable in cash. Contingent upon buyer obtaining a fixed rate loan, to be secured by the property, in the amount of _____ at_____% of purchase price with equal monthly payments amortized over a period of not less than _____ years, with interest not to exceed _____% per annum. Buyer shall have _____ days from date of acceptance to obtain a loan commitment or waive this condition in writing. Loan fee not to exceed _____%.

CONCURRENT RECORDING

The closing of this escrow is contingent upon the concurrent closing of escrow no_____. Neither escrow may close without the simultaneous closing of the other escrow.

CONDITION PRECEDENT

A condition which requires something to occur before a transaction becomes absolute and enforceable; for example, a sale that is contingent on the buyer obtaining financing.

CONDITION SUBSEQUENT

A condition which, if it occurs at some point in the future, can cause a property to revert to the grantor; for example, a requirement in a grant deed that a buyer must never use the property for anything other than a private residence.

CONSTRUCTIVE NOTICE
Public notice given by recording a document with the county recorder.

CONTINGENCY (WAIVED/SATISFIED)
Escrow holder is instructed that when the condition concerning _____ has been (satisfied/waived), escrow holder is to proceed with the completion of this escrow. If the contingency is waived, all parties should consent, in writing.

CONTRACT OF SALE
A contract for the sale of real property where the seller gives up possession but retains title until the total of the purchase price is paid in full.

CONVEYANCE
The transfer of title to land from one person to another by use of a written instrument.

COPIES
Copies of all documents must be given to buyer and seller at the time of signing.

CORRECTIONS AND DELETIONS
Any corrections and deletions must be approved by all principals.

COURT CONFIRMATION
This escrow is subject to court confirmation. A certified copy of the court order confirming the transfer is to be recorded concurrently with or prior to the recording of other documents of the sale.

DATE OF ACCEPTANCE
Means the date the seller accepts the offer or the buyer accepts the counter offer.

DATE OF CLOSING
Date title is transferred to buyer.

DECLARATION OF HOMESTEAD
The recorded document that protects a homeowner from foreclosure by certain judgment creditors.

DEED OF TRUST - PRIORITY CLAUSE
This Deed of Trust is given to secure a portion of the purchase price of the subject property and is junior to a Deed of Trust in the amount of $_____in favor of _____, recording concurrently.
OR
This Deed of Trust is junior to that certain Deed of Trust for $_____, in favor of _____, which recorded on _____, as Instrument#_____, Official Records of _____County.

DEED OF TRUST SECURING INSTALLMENT NOTE, INTEREST INCLUDED
A_____Deed of Trust to record, executed by buyer, securing an installment note for $_____in favor of _____, payable at _____with interest from _____at the rate of _____percent per annum, principal and interest payable $_____ or more on the _____day of each month, beginning_____and continuing until_____at which time all principal and interest has been paid in full. At close of escrow, escrow holder is instructed to list the interest rate , accrual date, first payment date and maturity date on the reverse of the executed note according to the instructions of the parties.

EASEMENT
The right to use another's land for a specified purpose sometimes known as a right-of-way.

EASEMENT IN GROSS
An easement that is not appurtenant to any one parcel; for example, public utilities.

ENCROACHMENT
The placement of permanent improvements on adjacent property owned by another.

EXTENDED POLICY
An extended title insurance policy.

DEFAULT
Failure to pay a debt or on a contract.

DEFICIENCY JUDGMENT
A judgment against a borrower for the balance of a debt owed when the security for the loan is not sufficient enough to pay the debt.

DEPOSIT INCREASE IN CASH
Initial deposit to be increased to $_____ within _____ days from acceptance of this agreement.

DEPOSITS
Escrow holder should note the form in which the deposit is received: Cash, personal check, certified check, cashier's check.

DOCTRINE OF CORRELATIVE USER
A riparian owner may use only a reasonable amount of the total water supply for his/her beneficial use.

DUE ON SALE DISCLOSURE
If there is a due on sale clause in any existing loan, the lender may demand full payment of the entire loan as a result of this transfer. All parties agree that they are not relying on any representation by the other party or the broker about the enforceability of such a clause in existing notes or deeds of trust to be executed as a result of this sale. All parties have been advised by the broker to seek legal advise.

EMBLEMENTS
Annual crops produced for sale.

EQUAL CREDIT OPPORTUNITY ACT
A Federal law that requires lenders to assure that credit is available with fairness, impartiality and without discrimination.

EQUITABLE TITLE
The interest held by the trustor or vendee.

EQUITY OF REDEMPTION
Also known as the right of redemption; the right of a debtor, before a foreclosure sale, to reclaim property that had been given up due to mortgage default.

ESTATE
A legal interest in land, defines the nature, degree, extent and duration of a person's ownership in land.

ESTATE OF INHERITANCE
A freehold estate that can be passed by descent or by will after the owner's death.

ESTATE IN FEE
The most complete form of ownership of real property, also known as an estate of inheritance.

ETHICS
A set of principles or values by which an individual guides his or her own behavior and judges that of others.

EXCHANGE, RESERVING RIGHT TO
The buyer and seller agree to complete a "like kind" tax deferred exchange under Section 1031 of the Internal Revenue Code, and acknowledge that escrow holder has made no representations as to the sufficiency or effect of this exchange as it relates to Federal and State or Tax law.

EXCHANGE, TAX CONSEQUENCES
Escrow holder has recommended that buyer and seller obtain legal counsel as to the tax consequences and other effects of this transaction. Escrow holder shall be held harmless from any loss which buyer and seller may sustain in the event this transaction is audited and disallowed by the Internal Revenue Service as a tax deferred exchange.

EXCHANGE: AGREE TO COOPERATE
Buyer and seller agree to cooperate with each other in completing all documents required to effect their respective exchange. All parties agree that neither party is to be at any additional expense or liability in connection with the other party's tax deferred exchange.

EXISTING LOANS
Within three (3) days of acceptance of this offer, seller shall provide buyer with all notes and Deeds of Trust to be assumed or taken subject to, and within five (5) days after receiving them, buyer shall give approval or disapproval of the terms of the documents in writing. Seller shall submit a Statement of Condition on the above loan within three (3) days after buyer's acceptance. All loans in the transaction will be current at close of escrow as per seller warranty.

FAX TRANSMISSION
A signed copy of any document sent to the other party or his or her agent by facsimile transmission, followed by faxed acknowledgment of receipt, is considered delivery of the signed document.

FEE
See fee simple, or estate in fee.

FEES
Buyer and seller shall be charged equally for fees and expenses of this escrow, one-half (l/2) each, unless noted elsewhere in escrow instructions.

FEE SIMPLE ABSOLUTE
Also known as fee simple, or fee.

FEE SIMPLE DEFEASIBLE
Also known as fee simple qualified.

FEE SIMPLE QUALIFIED
An estate in which the holder has a fee simple title, subject to return to the grantor if a specified condition occurs.

FEE SIMPLE
The largest, most complete ownership recognized by law, also known as a fee simple absolute, or fee.

FINANCING STATEMENT
A written notice filed with the county recorder by a creditor who has extended credit for the purchase of personal property, establishes the creditor's interests in the personal property which is the security for the debt.

FIRST RIGHT OF REFUSAL

This escrow is contingent upon the sale and close of escrow on buyer's property at _____. Meanwhile, it is agreed that seller shall continue to show subject property to other prospective buyers. In the event that seller should receive a bonafide offer from another buyer, the seller shall immediately notify the buyer in this escrow, in writing. At the time, buyer shall have _____ hours to remove the contingency or withdraw from this transaction in favor of another buyer.

FIXTURE

Personal property that has become affixed to real estate.

FIXTURES AND EQUIPMENT

Seller guarantees that fixtures and equipment shall be in working condition at the time of buyer's possession.

FLOOD HAZARD ZONE

Subject property is located in an area which has special flood hazards and that flood insurance must be purchased by the buyer in order to obtain any loan secured by the property if a federally regulated financial institution is involved. Buyer is aware of this condition.

FORECLOSURE

A legal procedure by which mortgaged property in which there has been default on the part of the borrower is sold to satisfy the debt.

FORECLOSURE SALE

A sale where property is sold to satisfy a debt.

FREEHOLD ESTATE

An estate in real property which continues for an indefinite period of time.

FULLY AMORTIZED NOTE

A note that is fully repaid at maturity by periodic reduction of the principal.

GOODWILL

An intangible, saleable asset arising from the reputation of a business, the expectation of continued public patronage.

GRACE PERIOD
An agreed upon time period after the payment of a debt is past due, during which a party can perform without being considered in default.

GRANT DEED FROM SPOUSES TO CREATE SEPARATE ESTATE
This deed is executed by the husband or wife of the grantee for the sole purpose of giving up any community property interest, He or she may have in the subject property. It is his or her intention to vest the subject property in _____, as his or her sole and separate property.

IMPOUNDS
Escrow holder is instructed to charge buyer and credit seller with the amount shown on Beneficiary Statement as being impounded for future payment of taxes, fire insurance premiums or any other items shown.

HOLDER
The party to whom a promissory note is made payable.

HOME EQUITY LOAN
A cash loan made against the equity in the borrower's home.

INSPECTION
This escrow is contingent upon written notification to escrow holder of buyer's approval of property inspection. Any professional inspector shall be selected and paid for by Buyer.

INSTRUMENT
A written legal document setting forth the rights and liabilities of the parties involved.

INTEREST
The cost of borrowing money.

JUDICIAL FORECLOSURE
Foreclosure by court action.

JUDGMENT
The final legal decision of a judge in a court of law regarding the legal rights of parties to disputes.

JUNIOR TRUST DEED
Any trust deed that is recorded after a first trust deed, whose priority is less than that first trust deed.

LATE CHARGE
Regarding the note created by this escrow; in the event that any installment payment is not received by the holder within_____days of its due date, a late charge of _____may be charged by the holder.

LAND CONTRACT
A contract for the sale of real property where the seller gives up possession, but retains the title until the purchase price is paid in full; also known as a contract of sale.

LEGAL TITLE
Title that is complete and perfect regarding right of ownership; may be held by a trustee under a deed of trust.

LESS-THAN-FREEHOLD ESTATE
A leasehold estate, considered to exist for a definite period of time or successive periods of time until termination.

LICENSE
Permission to use a property which may be revoked at any time.

LIFE ESTATE
An estate that is limited in duration to the life of its owner or the life of some other chosen person.

LINEAR FOOT
A measurement meaning one foot or twelve inches in length as contrasted to a square foot or a cubic foot.

LIS PENDENS
A recorded notice that indicates pending litigation on a property; preventing a conveyance or any other transfer of ownership until the lawsuit is settled and the lis pendens removed.

LITTORAL
Land bordering a lake, ocean, or sea–as opposed to land bordering a stream or river (running water).

MAKER
The borrower who executes a promissory note and becomes primarily liable for payment to the lender.

MANUFACTURED HOUSING
A housing unit primarily constructed in a factory and moved to a permanent site, another name for a mobile home.

MERIDIAN
A survey line running north and south, used as a reference when mapping land.

METES AND BOUNDS
A method of land description in which the dimensions of the property are measured by distance and direction.

MOBILE HOME
A manufactured unit constructed on a chassis and wheels and designed for permanent or semi-attachment to land.

MONUMENT
A fixed landmark used in a metes and bounds land description.

NEGOTIABLE INSTRUMENT
Any written instrument that may be transferred by endorsement or delivery.

NEUTRAL DEPOSITORY
An escrow business conducted by someone who is a licensed escrow holder.

NO BROKERS INVOLVED
Buyer and seller acknowledge that these escrow instructions are the only contract between them and that there are no real estate brokers involved in this transaction. No deposit receipt has been written, and no commissions are to be paid.

NO TAX ADVICE
Buyer and seller acknowledge that they have not received or relied upon any statements or representations by the agent, regarding the effect of this transaction upon their tax liability.

NOVATION
The substitution of a new obligation for an old one.

OPEN END LOAN
A loan where the borrower is given a limit up to which may be borrowed, with each advance secured by the same trust deed.

'OR MORE" CLAUSE
A clause in a promissory note that allows a borrower to pay it off early with no penalty.

PACKAGE LOAN
A loan on real property that can be secured by land, structure, fixtures and other personal property.

PARTITION ACTION
A court action to divide a property held by co-owners.

PARTIALLY AMORTIZED INSTALLMENT NOTE
A promissory note with a repayment schedule that is not sufficient to amortize the loan over its term.

PATENT DEED
Deeds used by the United States government when confirming or transferring ownership to private parties.

PERSONAL PROPERTY INCLUDED IN PRICE
Upon the close of escrow, the following personal property, observed on the property when inspected by buyer, shall be transferred to buyer by a bill of sale. No warranty is implied about the condition of the personal property.

PLEDGE
The transfer of property to a lender to be held as security for repayment of a debt; lender takes possession of property.

POWER OF SALE
A clause in a trust deed or mortgage that gives the holder the right to sell the property in the event of default by the borrower.

PREPAYMENT PENALTY (NONE)
Buyer has the right to pay this note in full or in part at any time prior to its maturity, without penalty.

PROBATE SALE
A court approved sale of the property of a deceased person.

PROMISSORY NOTE
A written promise or order to pay, evidence of a debt.

PROPERTY
Any real or personal property included in the sale.

PRORATIONS
Rents, taxes, interest, payments on bonds and assessments assumed by buyer, homeowners afees, and other expenses of the property are to be prorated as of the close of escrow.

PURCHASE MONEY LOAN
A trust deed created as evidence of a debt at the time of the sale of real property.

RANGE
A land description used in the U.S. Government Survey system consisting of a strip of land located every six miles east and west of each principal meridian.

REAL ESTATE AGENT
Someone licensed by the Department of Real Estate, holding either a broker or salesperson license, who negotiates sales for other people.

REAL ESTATE BROKER
Someone permitted by law to employ persons holding a salesperson license and who may also negotiate sales.

REAL ESTATE LAW
The law that affects the licensing and conduct of real estate agents.

REAL ESTATE SALES ASSOCIATE
The same as a real estate salesperson, holding a real license, employed by a broker.

REAL ESTATE SALESPERSON
Someone holding a real estate license and employed by a real estate broker, for pay, to perform any of the activities of a real estate broker.

REAL PROPERTY
Land, anything affixed to the land, anything appurtenant to the land, anything immovable by law.

RECONVEYANCE DEED
A deed used to transfer title to a property back to the trustor after a trust deed has been paid off.

REINSTATE
Bring current and restore.

RELEASE CLAUSE
A provision found in many blanket loans enabling the borrower to obtain partial release from the loan of specific parcels.

RENT BACK BY SELLER
Buyer and seller agree that seller shall hold possession of subject property for_____days after close of escrow.

REQUEST FOR NOTICE
A notice that is sent, upon request, to any parties interested in a trust deed, informing them of a default.

REVERSE ANNUITY MORTGAGE
A loan that enables elderly homeowners to borrow against the equity in their homes by receiving monthly payments from a lender, that are needed to help meet living costs.

REVOKE
Recall and make void.

RIPARIAN RIGHTS
The rights of a landowner whose land is next to a natural watercourse to reasonable use of whatever water flows past the property.

ROLLOVER MORTGAGE
A loan that allows the rewriting of a new loan at the termination of a prior loan.

SALES TAX
Collected as a percentage of the retail sales of a product, by a retailer, and forwarded to the State Board of Equalization.

SECTION
An area of land, as used in the government survey method of land description; a land area of one square mile, or 640 acres. It is 1/36 of a township.

SELLER'S PERMIT
Allows a retailer to buy his or her product at wholesale prices without paying sales tax. The retailer must then collect the proper sales tax from customers and pay it to the State Board of Equalization.

SEVERALTY
Ownership of real property by one person or entity.

SPECIAL STUDIES ZONE ACT
Buyer is aware that the subject property is located in a Special Studies Zone designated under the Priolo Special Studies Act, and that construction or improvement of any structure may require the submission of a geological report by the buyer, prepared by a registered geologist. Seller or broker have not made any representation about the cost of report or the geological characteristics of the property.

STANDARD POLICY
A policy of title insurance covering only matters of record.

STATUTORY
Regarding laws created by the enactment of legislation as opposed to law created by court decisions.

STRAIGHT NOTE
A promissory note in which payments of interest only are made periodically during the term of the note, with the principal payment due in one lump sum upon maturity; may also be a note with no payments on either principal or interest until the entire sum is due.

'SUBJECT-TO" CLAUSE
A buyer takes over the existing loan payments, but assumes no personal liability for the loan.

SUBORDINATION CLAUSE
A clause in which the holder of a trust deed permits a subsequent loan to take priority.

SUSPEND
Temporarily make ineffective.

TERMINATING THE AGREEMENT
Buyer and seller are relieved of their obligations and all deposits shall be returned to buyer less expenses incurred by or on account of buyer to date of termination.

TITLE
Evidence of ownership of land.

TITLE INSURANCE
An insurance policy that protects the insured against loss or damage due to defects in the property's title.

TOWNSHIP
A land description used in the U.S. Government Survey system consisting of a six-by-six mile area containing 360 sections, each one mile square.

TRADE ASSOCIATION
A voluntary nonprofit organization of independent and competing business units engaged in the same industry or trade, and formed to aid in the industry problems, promote its progress and enhance its service.

TRADE FIXTURE
An article of personal property affixed to leased property by the tenant as a necessary part of business; may be removed by tenant as personal property upon termination of the lease.

TRANSFER TAX NOT TO SHOW ON DEED AT RECORDATION
Title Insurance Company shall be instructed by escrow holder to file grant deed as a separate declaration and not make it a part of the public record.

TRUST DEED
A document where title to property is transferred to a third party trustee as security for a debt owed by the trustor (borrower) to the beneficiary (lender).

TRUSTEE'S DEED
A deed given to a buyer of real property at a trustee's sale.

TRUSTEE'S SALE
The forced sale of real property, by a lender, to satisfy a debt.

TRUSTEE
Holds bare legal title to property as a neutral third party where there is a deed of trust.

TRUST FUNDS
Money received by real estate brokers or salespersons on behalf of others.

TRUSTOR
The borrower under a deed of trust.

UNDIVIDED INTEREST
That interest a co-owner has in property, which carries with it the right to possession and use of the whole property, along with the co-owners.

USURY
The act of charging a rate of interest in excess of that permitted by law.

VENDEE
The buyer under a contract of sale (land contract).

VENDOR
The seller under a contract of sale (land contract).

VESTED
Owned by.

WRAP-AROUND LOAN
A method of financing where a new loan is placed in a secondary position; the new loan includes both the unpaid principal balance of the first loan and whatever sums are loaned by the lender; sometimes called an All-Inclusive Trust Deed (AITD).

INDEX

H

I

J

L

M

N

O

P

ANSWERS TO PRETESTS AND POST TESTS

Chapter1	Chapter2	Chapter3	Chapter4
1.T	1.T	1.T	1.F
2.T	2.T	2.T	2.F
3.T	3.T	3.F	3.T
4.F	4.F	4.F	4.T
5.F	5.F	5.T	5.F
6.T	6.T	6.T	6.T
7.T	7.F	7.T	7.T
8.F	8.F	8.F	8.T
9.T	9.T	9.T	9.F
10.F	10.T	10.T	10.F

Chapter5	Chapter6	Chapter7	Chapter8
1.T	1.F	1.T	1.T
2.F	2.T	2.T	2.T
3.T	3.T	3.F	3.F
4.T	4.T	4.F	4.T
5.F	5.F	5.T	5.T
6.F	6.F	6.F	6.F
7.F	7.T	7.T	7.F
8.T	8.F	8.F	8.T
9.F	9.F	9.F	9.F
10.T	10.F	10.T	10.T

Chapter 9	Chapter 10	Chapter 11	Chapter 12
1.F	1.F	1.T	1.T
2.T	2.T	2.T	2.F
3.T	3.T	3.F	3.F
4.T	4.F	4.F	4.T
5.T	5.F	5.F	5.T
6.T	6.T	6.F	6.T
7.T	7.F	7.T	7.F
8.F	8.F	8.F	8.T
9.F	9.T	9.T	9.T
10.F	10.T	10.T	10.T

Chapter 13	Chapter 14	Chapter 15
1.F	1.F	1.F
2.F	2.F	2.F
3.T	3.F	3.T
4.T	4.T	4.T
5.F	5.T	5.F
6.T	6.F	6.F
7.T	7.T	7.F
8.F	8.F	8.T
9.T	9.T	9.T
10.T	10.T	10T.

Circle International

Logistics Solutions at Work for You

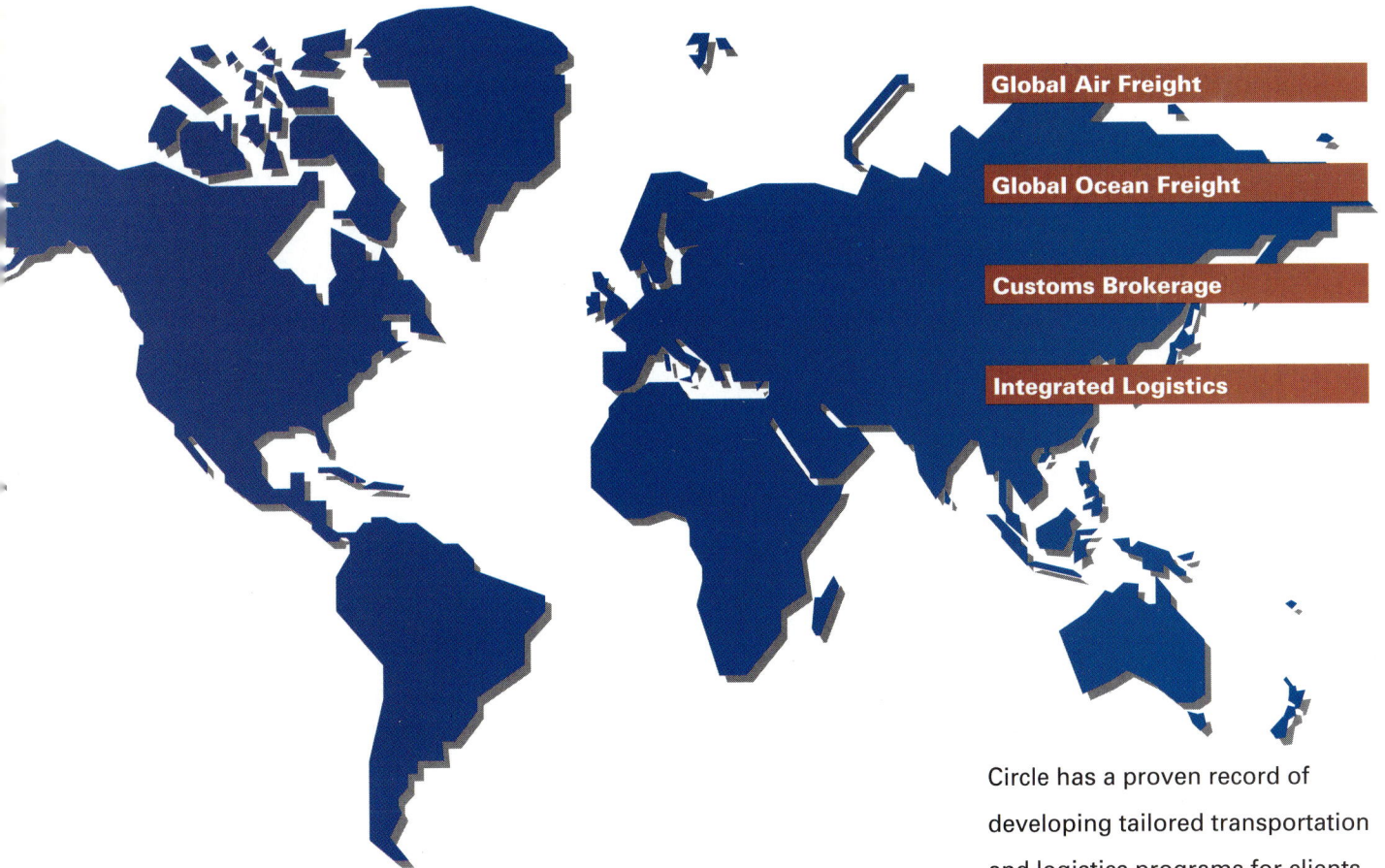

Global Air Freight

Global Ocean Freight

Customs Brokerage

Integrated Logistics

Circle has a proven record of developing tailored transportation and logistics programs for clients around the world. We believe that understanding what is critical to your business is the basis for building a true partnership.

One World.
One Transportation and Logistics Partner.

306 offices in 86 countries

We have worked closely with California-based importers and exporters since 1898.

World Headquarters
260 Townsend Street
San Francisco, California 94107
U.S.A.

National Information Center
1-800-332-4725

Where to find the best rates, from Bedrock™ to Hollyrock.

No matter where you are in the sunny state of California, one of our 80 convenient locations is right around the corner. And that means great rates, quality accommodations, and plenty of Flintstones fun for you and your family. So remember Days Inn on your next trip to California. For reservations, contact your travel agent, or call 1-800-DAYS INN.

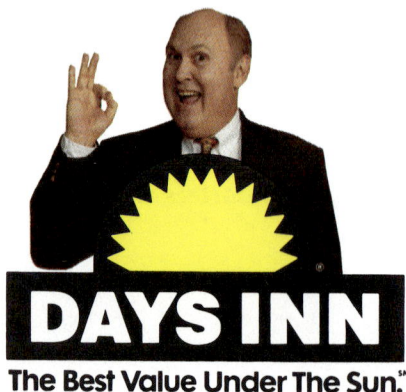

DAYS INN
The Best Value Under The Sun.℠

© 1994 Days Inns of America, Inc. © 1994 Hanna-Barbera Productions, Inc., The Flintstones™ and all related names and likenesses are trademarks of Hanna-Barbera Productions, Inc. All rights reserved.

International Trade Resources Guide

California Trade and Commerce Agency

Pete Wilson
Governor

Julie Meier Wright
Secretary

Brenda Lopes
Deputy Secretary
International Trade and Investment

California Chamber of Commerce

Roger J. Baccigaluppi
Chairman

Kirk West
President

Ezunial Burts
Chairman, International Trade Committee

Susanne T. Stirling
Vice President, International Affairs
California Chamber of Commerce

OFFICE OF THE GOVERNOR
State of California

To California businesses:

International trade is one of the most dynamic sectors of the California economy. More than 15 percent of California workers are employed in jobs related to international trade, and that number will grow as our economy expands and trade opportunities multiply.

As America's leading exporting state -- with more than $100 billion in annual goods and services exported -- California is well-positioned to reap the benefits of an increasingly interdependent global market. Foreign trade is vital to California's economy, and the passage of the North American Free Trade Agreement and the signing of the Uruguay Round of the General Agreement on Tariffs and Trade will help stimulate the economy and usher in thousands of new jobs for Californians.

My administration is committed to doing everything it can to cut red-tape and help California businesses grow and take advantage of job-creating markets. From the creation of the cabinet-level Trade and Commerce Agency and the launching of the California Environmental Technology Partnership to the doubling of the Export Finance Fund and the strengthening of our foreign offices of trade and investment, we've taken the necessary steps to ensure the great California comeback.

This guide to exporting will give you a good start in tapping these services and finding opportunities to expand your businesses in the rapidly approaching 21st century global marketplace.

Good luck and best wishes in your efforts.

Sincerely,

PETE WILSON

CALIFORNIA CHAMBER of COMMERCE

KIRK WEST
PRESIDENT

Dear Reader:

From the state's earliest days in the world spotlight as the destination for pioneers stricken with "gold fever," trade has been an important component of the California economy. Before 1860, in fact, almost every manufactured article used here had to be imported from the East Coast, Europe or China.

Today, California's highly diversified, multibillion-dollar economy ranks among the 10 largest on the globe, and the state is an important supplier of a variety of goods. Trade continues to play a significant role in the state's overall well-being, with international trade offering high potential for further growth.

Lack of information often is the only barrier for the domestic company that wants to expand market opportunities by going abroad. With this in mind, the California Chamber is pleased to produce this ***International Trade Resources Guide*** and its companion volumes, which offer assistance for businesses seeking to begin or expand exporting, identify opportunities with Mexico and Canada, and summarize legal and financial considerations for doing business with nations in the European Community and Europe. These publications, individually and as a set, provide a good starting point for entrepreneurs trying to learn more about doing business on an international scale.

It is our hope that these publications can help businesses to grow and prosper, as well as compete effectively internationally. Their good fortune, in turn, will help create jobs and opportunities for all Californians.

Sincerely,

Kirk West

Kirk West

1201 K Street, 12th Floor P.O. Box 1736 Sacramento, California 95812-1736 Facsimile (916) 444-6685 Telephone (916) 444-6670

ALLIANCE SHIPPERS, INC.
INTERNATIONAL

LARGEST INDEPENDENTLY OWNED INTERMODAL COMPANY

FAR EAST SPECIALIST

- Ocean and Air Freight
- Full Container Load and Consolidation Service
- Customs Clearance ■ Worldwide Service

(213) 437-5702 • LAX OFFICE (310) 536-7010
(800) 783-5702 *(Outside California)* **• FAX (213) 437-5702**

Member

- National Custom House Brokerage Association
- Foreign Trade Association of California
- International NVOC Association

Corporate Office
Oceangate - P200 • Long Beach, CA 90802

About the California Trade and Commerce Agency

Launched on January 1, 1993, the California Trade and Commerce Agency has the lead role in California state government for the coordination of domestic and international economic development efforts. Under the umbrella of the International Trade and Investment Division, the international functions of the agency include the following:

California State World Trade Commission

The California State World Trade Commission, established in 1983, is an advisory body to the Secretary of Trade and Commerce and is comprised of 15 members appointed by the Governor, Speaker of the Assembly and Senate Pro Tempore.

California Export Finance Office

The Export Finance Office provides working capital loan guarantees to financial institutions on behalf of small and medium-sized California companies in support of export transactions. Financial assistance is provided in the form of bank guarantees of up to 90 percent of the loan with a maximum guarantee of $750,000 per transaction. To be eligible, a company must have been in business for one year and total shipments must contain 51 percent California content.

California Export Development Office

- Organizes California group exhibits at leading foreign trade shows.
- Offers the Automated Trade Library Service (ATLS), a free on-line database containing market research, trade leads and other valuable trade information.
- Publishes "made in California" product catalogs and coordinates the development of export directories, such as the California International Trade Register.

California Office of Foreign Investment

The Office of Foreign Investment is the lead office for foreign investment promotion, retention and expansion. Its mission is to promote job-creating, revenue-generating investment.

California State Foreign Trade and Investment Offices

California has six foreign offices operating around the globe promoting state exports, attracting foreign investment to the state, helping California businesses abroad and supporting California's stateside trade and investment programs. The offices are in Tokyo, Hong Kong, London, Frankfurt, Mexico City and Taipei, with a representative in Israel and an office soon to be opened in Sub-Saharan Africa.

Trade activities of the offices include:
- Assisting California exporters with information, advice and appointment setting.
- Responding to trade inquiries.
- Conducting or participating in promotions, trade shows and seminars.
- Assisting California business delegations/trade missions.

Investment activities of the offices include:
- Outreach to targeted overseas investors.
- Responding to investment inquiries.
- Conducting investment seminars.

Office Locations

California Trade and Commerce Agency
Julie Meier Wright, Secretary
Loren Kaye, Undersecretary
Brenda Lopes, Deputy Secretary
  International Trade and Investment
801 K Street, Suite 1700
Sacramento, CA 95814
(916) 322-1394
Fax (916) 322-3524

Office of Foreign Investment
Brenda Lopes, Director
801 K Street, Suite 1700
Sacramento, CA 95814
(916) 322-3518
Fax (916) 322-3401

International Trade and Investment Division/California State World Trade Commission (WTC)
Robert T. Monagan, Chairman
Brenda Lopes, Executive Director, WTC/
  Deputy Secretary, International Trade
  and Investment Division
801 K Street, Suite 1700
Sacramento, CA 95814
(916) 324-5511
Fax (916) 324-5791

California Export Finance Office
James Newton, Acting Director
6 Centerpointe, Suite 760
La Palma, CA 90623
(714) 562-5519
Fax (714) 562-5530

Office of Export Development
R. Sean Randolph, Director
One World Trade Center, Suite 990
Long Beach, CA 90831
(310) 590-5965
Fax (310) 590-5958

About the International Trade Programs of the California Chamber of Commerce

The California Chamber supports expansion of international trade and investment, fair and equitable market access for California products abroad, and elimination of disincentives that impede the international competitiveness of California business.

As part of its ongoing effort to promote international trade and investment opportunities for California businesses, the California Chamber has led missions abroad in conjunction with the opening of the state's trade and investment offices in Tokyo, London, Mexico City, Frankfurt and Hong Kong. More recently, California Chamber Board members traveled to Mexico City with Governor Pete Wilson to discuss the proposed North American Free Trade Agreement. Members also have participated in international trade events at Expo '86 in Vancouver, Expo '88 in Brisbane, Japan, Korea, Taiwan, the People's Republic of China and the World Economic Forum in Davos, Switzerland.

Other international activities include:

- Lobbying and monitoring state and federal legislative issues, as well as bilateral and multilateral trade negotiations of benefit to international business.

- Helping members with general export and import activities. The California Chamber maintains an international library at its offices in Sacramento and distributes written materials to assist member firms in international trade.

- Serving as a clearinghouse for information on international trade.

- Maintaining a liaison with government agencies and private organizations domestically and abroad.

- Supporting international trade events, conferences and educational programs to foster better understanding of international trade.

Contacts: Ezunial Burts
              Chairman, International Trade Committee

              Susanne T. Stirling
              Vice President, International Affairs

              (916) 444-6670
              Fax (916) 444-6685

NATURE'S RECIPE™
INNOVATIVE PET FOODS

Available at your local pet store, feed store and veterinary clinic, including:

B&E FEED, 1414 6th St., Norco • **CLAWS & PAWS,** 1180 W. 6th St., Ste. 104, Corona • **VERLEE'S FANCY PETS,** 1820 Hamner, Norco

© 1995 Nature's Recipe Pet Foods • 341 Bonnie Circle, Corona, CA 91720

International Trade Resources from the California Chamber

International Trade Resources Guide

A comprehensive guide to resources available to the California business community for conducting international trade, including domestic and international chambers of commerce; international trade associations; education contacts; local, state and federal government officials; foreign trade zones; foreign government representatives; resources publications; glossaries; world holidays; metric conversion chart; international telephone calling codes; and world monetary units. The *Guide* lists more than 1,600 resources in the public and private sectors.

Exporting Guide for California

A step-by-step manual to help the California company wishing to become involved in exporting or to expand existing export volumes. Covers organizing for export, identifying markets and distribution avenues, pricing, documentation, shipping and financing. Includes tips on avoiding common pitfalls, plus samples of key documents, including supplier/exporter and distribution agreements. Also highly useful for the person who is new to exporting, but works in a firm that already sells its goods or services in the international market.

European Community and Europe: A Legal Guide to Business Development

Articles by attorneys and accountants from major international law or accounting firms summarize important legal and financial considerations for companies doing business in the European Community and Europe. Includes overview of the creation of the European Economic Community, mergers, joint ventures, distribution and franchising agreements, commercial law, tax considerations, finance, employment law, standards, exporting requirements and other business concerns. Also covers major sectors: public procurement, high technology, environment, telecommunications, pharmaceuticals, energy and utilities. Country-specific chapters highlight requirements unique to individual nations in the EC or Europe.

North American Free Trade Guide

A handbook to help businesses take advantage of the opportunities to be created by the North American Free Trade Agreement (NAFTA), linking the United States with Canada and Mexico, its first and third largest trading partners. NAFTA will create the largest and richest market in the world, with 360 million consumers and $6 trillion in annual output. Focuses on what businesses need to know to gain access to the emerging Mexican market, plus good prospects for expansion in Canada.

Being a good employer has never been easier or more economical...

than it can be when you let Employers Resource handle key employer responsibilities.

You'll no longer need to deal with payroll preparation, tax deposits or

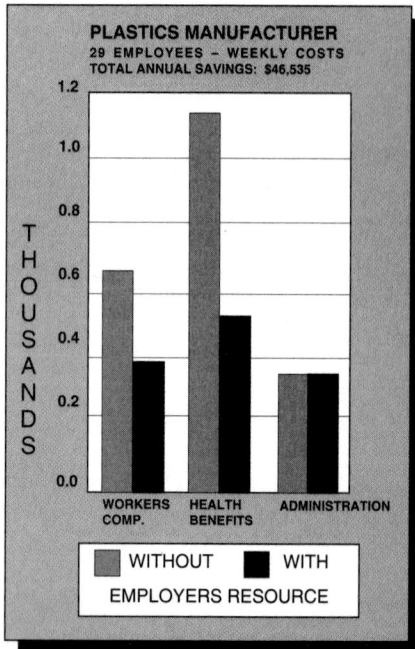

PLASTICS MANUFACTURER
29 EMPLOYEES – WEEKLY COSTS
TOTAL ANNUAL SAVINGS: $46,535

(bar chart, THOUSANDS axis 0.0 to 1.2, categories: WORKERS COMP., HEALTH BENEFITS, ADMINISTRATION)

WITHOUT / WITH
EMPLOYERS RESOURCE

reporting. Even personnel files are maintained by us. The liability for those chores will be ours, even in the eyes of the IRS. That doesn't happen with a payroll service.

Your employees will have the choice of 6 health plans. They'll also have 24-hour accident coverage, a paperless drug card, and life insurance. You can choose to add dental coverage, too.

You'll have workers' compensation coverage that gives you 10% discount with our safety program (a 50% discount is possible). If an injury does occur, your employee will receive the best medical care, personal follow-up, and the earliest return to work that's right for their situation and yours.

All of these matters will be handled by our caring professionals with capable expertise. They've had the experience of working with over 1300 enthusiastic clients since 1985.

Your employer responsibilities will be ones that have a direct impact on the productivity and efficiency of your business. You'll hire the people you want, set their wages, and manage their day-to-day activities. But you won't

Risk Free Guarantee
If, for any reason, we do not live up to your expectations, we will refund your set-up fee and pay the set-up fee for the new service you choose.

have to do it alone. Even for your responsibilities, we'll be there to guide you through all the regulations that affect you as an employer.

"We feel more confident that we are complying with all regulations and are also making our company a better place to work."

If your business has employees in California (or any other state), you owe it to yourself to find out if you can benefit by using the friendly co-employment services of Employers Resource. There's no

better time than now. Call your Employers Resource office today:

1-800-859-8590.

EMPLOYERS
R E S O U R C E

P.S. Be sure to ask for your free copy of Co-Employer Report. It's full of useful information for any employer.

Table of Contents

As long as Americans believe there's nothing they can't do, we'll help them do it.

You were born believing you could do anything.
Be anything. At Bank of America, we're dedicated to affirming this childhood belief. Because all Banking on America really means is that we're banking on you.

BANKING ON AMERICA™

Bank of America

© 1992 BankAmerica Corporation.   Member FDIC.

California Chambers of Commerce
with International Departments

Alhambra Chamber of Commerce
104 South First Street
Alhambra, CA 91801
(818) 282-8481

Anaheim Chamber of Commerce
100 S. Anaheim Boulevard, Suite 300
Anaheim, CA 92805
(714) 758-0222
Fax (714) 758-0468

Calexico Chamber of Commerce
Fred Knechel, Executive Director
1100 Imperial Avenue
P.O. Box 948
Calexico, CA 92231
(619) 357-1166
Fax (619) 357-9043

California Chamber of Commerce
Susanne T. Stirling, Vice President
International Affairs
1201 K Street, 12th Floor
P.O. Box 1736
Sacramento, CA 95814/95812-1736
(916) 444-6670
Fax (916) 444-6685

Camarillo Chamber of Commerce
Executive Director
632 Las Posas Road
Camarillo, CA 93010
(805) 484-4383

Carlsbad Chamber of Commerce
Lee Bohlmann, CCE, Executive Vice President
5411 Avenida Encinas, Suite 100
Carlsbad, CA 92008
(619) 931-8400

Century City Chamber of Commerce
Golda Freedman Epstein, President/Director
2020 Avenue of the Stars, Suite 650
Los Angeles, CA 90067
(310) 553-2222
Fax (310) 553-4623

Greater Chico Chamber of Commerce
Tom Guarino, Public Affairs Director
500 West Main Street
Chico, CA 95928
(916) 891-5556
Fax (916) 891-3613

The Chamber of the Chino Valley
International Trade Group
Jim "J.P." Polhemus, Marketing
13134 Central Avenue
Chino, CA 91710
(909) 627-6177
Fax (909) 627-4180

Chula Vista Chamber of Commerce
Donald Read, Chief Executive Officer
233 Fourth Avenue
Chula Vista, CA 91910
(619) 420-6602
Fax (619) 420-1269

Clovis Chamber of Commerce
Jim Ware, Executive Director
325 Pollasky
Clovis, CA 93612
(209) 299-7273

Conejo Valley Chamber of Commerce
Steve Rubenstein, President & Chief Executive Officer
625 West Hillcrest Drive
Thousand Oaks, CA 91360
(805) 499-1993

Corona Chamber of Commerce
D. David Bolick, Executive Vice President
904 East Sixth Street
Corona, CA 91719
(909) 737-3550
Fax (909) 737-3531

Crescenta Valley Chamber of Commerce
Joyce Thurston, Manager
3131 Foothill Boulevard, Suite M
La Crescenta, CA 91214
(818) 248-4957

Culver City Chamber of Commerce
Steven J. Rose, President
10767 Washington Blvd.
Culver City, CA 90232
(310) 287-3850
Fax (310) 287-1350

El Monte/South El Monte Chamber of Commerce
Ellen Dixon, Executive Director
P.O. Box 5866
El Monte, CA 91734
(818) 443-0180
Fax (818) 443-0463

1

California Chambers with International Departments

Foster City Chamber of Commerce
Executive Vice President
1125 East Hillsdale, Suite 114
Foster City, CA 94404
(415) 573-7600

Fountain Valley Chamber of Commerce
Betty Mignanelli, Executive Director
11100 Warner Avenue, #204
Fountain Valley, CA 92708
(714) 962-4441

Fresno Chamber of Commerce
Stebbins F. Dean, Executive Director
2331 Fresno Street
P.O. Box 1469
Fresno, CA 93716
(209) 495-4800
Fax (same)

Fullerton Chamber of Commerce
Gail Dixon, Executive Vice President
219 E. Commonwealth Avenue
P.O. Box 529
Fullerton, CA 92632
(714) 871-3100
Fax (714) 871-2871

Glendale Chamber of Commerce
Connie Pierce, Executive Vice President
200 South Louise Street
P.O. Box 112
Glendale, CA 91209
(818) 240-7870
Fax (818) 240-2872

Glendora Chamber of Commerce
John Hackney, Executive Director
131 East Foothill Boulevard
Glendora, CA 91741-3336
(818) 963-4128

Goleta Valley Chamber of Commerce
Ann W. Ruhge, Executive Director
5730 Hollister, Suite 1
Goleta, CA 93117
(805) 967-4618
Fax (805) 967-4615

Hanford Chamber of Commerce
Wilda Parks, Executive Director
200 Santa Fe Avenue #D
Hanford, CA 98230
(209) 582-0483
Fax (209) 582-0960

Hollywood Chamber of Commerce
Mary Ann Shemdin, Director and Chair
Small Business Committee
7000 Hollywood Blvd. #1
Hollywood, CA 90028
(213) 469-8311

Humboldt Bay Alliance
Dick Darbo, Executive Director,
2112 Broadway
Eureka, CA 95501
(707) 443-5057
Fax (707) 442-0079

Huntington Beach Chamber of Commerce
Joyce Riddell, President
2100 Main Street #200
Huntington Beach, CA 92648
(714) 536-8888
Fax (714) 960-7654

Huntington Park Chamber of Commerce
Dante D'Eramo, Executive Manager
6330 Pacific Blvd. #208
Huntington Park, CA 90255
(213) 585-1155
Fax (213) 585-2176

Inglewood/Airport Chamber of Commerce
Shannon Howe, Executive Director
330 East Queen Street
Inglewood, CA 90301
(310) 677-1121
Fax (310) 677-0748

Livermore Chamber of Commerce
Patricia Davis Executive Director
2157 First Street
Livermore, CA 94550
(510) 447-1606
Fax (510) 447-1641

Long Beach Area Chamber of Commerce
Randy Gordon, President & Chief Executive Officer
1 World Trade Center, Suite 350
Long Beach, CA 90831
(310) 436-1251
Fax (310) 436-7099

Los Angeles Area Chamber of Commerce
Ray Remy, President
350 South Bixel Street
Los Angeles, CA 90017
(213) 580-7500
Fax (213) 580-7511

2

Mariposa County Chamber of Commerce
Wayne Schulz, Executive Director
P.O. Box 425
Mariposa, CA 95338
(209) 966-2456

Merced Chamber of Commerce
Dorothea Moore, Chief Executive Officer
690 West 16th Street
Merced, CA 95340
(209) 384-3333
Fax (209) 384-8472

Montebello Chamber of Commerce
Andrea Wagg, President
1304 West Beverly Boulevard
Montebello, CA 90640
(310) 721-1153
Fax (310) 721-7946

Monterey Peninsula Chamber of Commerce
Rick Lawrance, Executive Vice President
P.O. Box 1770
Monterey, CA 93942
(408) 648-5360
Fax (408) 649-3502

Mountain View Chamber of Commerce
Liesa Fulton, Executive Director
580 Castro Street
Mountain View, CA 94041
(415) 968-8378
Fax (415) 968-5668

National City Chamber of Commerce
Mary Alice Taliak, Director
P.O. Box 1055
National City, CA 91951
(619) 477-9339
Fax (619) 477-5018

Oakland Chamber of Commerce
Robert L. Toney, President and Chief Executive Officer
475 14th Street
Oakland, CA 94612
(510) 874-4800
Fax (510) 839-8817

Ojai Valley Chamber of Commerce
Margaret Westrom, Executive Director
P.O. Box 1134
Ojai, CA 93024
(805) 646-8126
Fax (805) 646-9762

Orange County Chamber of Commerce
Ken Moore, President & Chief Executive Officer
1 City Boulevard West, Suite 401
Orange, CA 92668
(714) 634-2900
Fax (714) 978-0742

Palo Alto Chamber of Commerce
Susan Frank, Executive Director
325 Forest Avenue
Palo Alto, CA 94301
(415) 324-3121
Fax (415) 324-1215

Pico Rivera Chamber of Commerce
Lawrence Salazar, Executive Director
9122 East Washington Boulevard
Pico Rivera, CA 90660
(310) 949-2473
Fax (310) 949-8320

Pomona Chamber of Commerce
Biff Byrum, Chief Executive Officer
363 South Park Avenue, Suite 104
Pomona, CA 91766
(909) 622-1256

Port Hueneme Chamber of Commerce
Pat Zanuzoski, Executive Director
220 North Market Street
Port Hueneme, CA 93041
(805) 488-2023
Fax (805) 488-6993

Greater Redding Chamber of Commerce
Frank Strazzarino, Jr., Executive Director
747 Auditorium Drive
Redding, CA 96001
(916) 225-4433
Fax (916) 225-4398

Richmond Chamber of Commerce
Judith Morgan, President and Chief Executive Officer
3925 Macdonald Avenue
Richmond, CA 94805
(510) 234-3512
Fax (510) 234-3540

Sacramento Metropolitan Chamber of Commerce
David Orosco, Small Business & Research Management
917 7th Street
Sacramento, CA 95812-1017
(916) 552-6800
Fax (916) 443-2672

California Chambers with International Departments

Salinas Area Chamber of Commerce
Carol Kurtz, Executive Director
P.O. Box 1170
Salinas, CA 93902
(408) 424-7611
Fax (408) 424-8639

Greater San Diego Chamber of Commerce
Angelika Villagrana, Assistant Dir.,/ Gov't Affairs
402 W. Broadway #1000
San Diego, CA 92101
(619) 544-1361

Mid San Fernando Valley Chamber of Commerce
Nancy Hoffman, Executive Vice President
14540 Victory Boulevard, Suite 100
Van Nuys, CA 91411-1618
(818) 989-0300

San Francisco Chamber of Commerce
G. Rhea Serpan, President & Chief Executive Officer
Paul Gormsen, Vice President/Economic Vitality
465 California Street
San Francisco, CA 94104
(415) 392-4511, Ext. 820
Fax (415) 395-0485

San Jose Metropolitan Chamber of Commerce
Jim Tucker, Director
Economic Development
180 South Market Street
San Jose, CA 95113
(408) 291-5250
Fax (408) 286-5019

San Leandro Chamber of Commerce
Mary Lou Eckersley, Executive Vice President
262 Davis Street
San Leandro, CA 94577
(510) 351-1481
Fax (510) 351-6740

San Pedro Peninsula Chamber of Commerce
Dolores Canizales, Executive Director
390 W. 7th Street
San Pedro, CA 90731
(310) 832-7272
Fax (310) 832-0685

Greater Santa Ana Chamber of Commerce
Sara Humphries, Assistant Director
P.O. Box 205
Santa Ana, CA 92702
(714) 541-5353
Fax (714) 541-2238

Santa Barbara Chamber of Commerce
Martin Erickson, Government Affairs Manager
P.O. Box 299
Santa Barbara, CA 93102
(805) 965-3023

Santa Clara Chamber of Commerce
E.A. Betty Hangs, President/General Manager
P.O. Box 387
2200 Laurelwood Road, 2nd Floor
Santa Clara, CA 95052
(408) 970-9825
Fax (408) 970-8864

Santa Cruz Area Chamber of Commerce
Daniel L. Ehrler, Chief Executive Officer
1543 Pacific Avenue
Santa Cruz, CA 95060
(408) 423-1111
Fax (408) 423-1847

Santa Rosa Chamber of Commerce
Keith Woods, President
637 1st Street
Santa Rosa, CA 95404
(707) 545-1414

Scotts Valley Chamber of Commerce
Kate D. Greene, Executive Director
P.O. Box 66928
Scotts Valley, CA 95067-6928
(408) 438-1010
Fax (408) 438-6544

Shingle Springs/Cameron Park Chamber of Commerce
Mimi Escabar, Manager
P.O. Box 341
Shingle Springs, CA 95682
(916) 677-8000
Fax (916) 676-8313

Sonoma Valley Chamber of Commerce
Hal Beck, Executive Director
645 Broadway
Sonoma, CA 95476
(707) 996-1033

Stockton Chamber of Commerce
Paula McCloskey, Chief Executive Officer
445 West Weber, Suite 220
Stockton, CA 95203
(209) 547-2766
Fax (209) 466-5271

Temecula Valley Chamber of Commerce
Leigh Engdahl, General Manager
27459 Ynez Road, #104
Temecula, CA 92591
(909) 676-5090
Fax (909) 694-0201

Torrance Area Chamber of Commerce
Barbara Glennie, Executive Vice President
28924 S. Western Avenue, Suite 104
Rancho Palos Verdes, CA 90275
(310) 519-7153

U.S. Chamber of Commerce
Meg Jacobsen, Executive Director
1901 S. Bascom Avenue, #701
Campbell, CA 95008
(408) 371-6000
Fax (408) 377-1084

Walnut Creek Chamber of Commerce
Jay Hoyer, Executive Director
1501 North Broadway, Suite 110
Walnut Creek, CA 94596
(510) 934-2007
Fax (510) 934-2404

Westchester/LAX Chamber of Commerce
Donald W. Savoie, Executive Director
5930 West Century Boulevard
Los Angeles, CA 90045
(310) 645-5151

West Sacramento Chamber of Commerce
Steven Roberts, Executive Director
1414 Merkley Avenue, Suite 1
West Sacramento, CA 95691
(916) 371-7042
Fax (916) 371-7210

IN THE INTEREST of GLOBAL STANDARDIZATION, ONE WORD CAN NOW *be* USED *for* QUALITY.

Around the world, the word Sunkist always translates into trust, quality and taste. We consistently have the largest supply of fresh citrus in North America. We continually set the highest standards in the industry. And we're always there to help your business keep on growing. You have our word on it.®

——— *Sunkist*® ———

Sunkist Sunkist. and "You have our word on it." are registered trademarks of Sunkist Growers, Inc., ©1994 Sunkist Growers, Inc.

California Chambers of Commerce
Validating Certificates of Origin

Certificates of Origin form #942 can be purchased at local office supply stores or by calling Wolcotts' Legal Forms, Inc. at **1-800-262-1538.**

Alhambra Chamber of Commerce
104 South First Street
Alhambra, CA 91801
(818) 282-8481

Anaheim Chamber of Commerce
100 South Anaheim Boulevard, Suite 300
Anaheim, CA 92805

Calexico Chamber of Commerce
1100 Imperial Avenue
P.O. Box 948
Calexico, CA 92231
(619) 357-1166
Fax (619) 357-9043

Camarillo Chamber of Commerce
632 Las Posas Road
Camarillo, CA 93010
(805) 484-4383

Carlsbad Chamber of Commerce
5411 Avenida Encinas, Suite 100
Carlsbad, CA 92008
(619) 931-8400

Greater Chico Chamber of Commerce
500 Main Street
Chico, CA 95928
(916) 891-5556

The Chamber of the Chino Valley
International Trade Group
13134 Central Avenue
Chino, CA 91710
(909) 627-6177
Fax (909) 627-4180

Chula Vista Chamber of Commerce
233 Fourth Avenue
Chula Vista, CA 91910
(619) 420-6602

Clovis Chamber of Commerce
325 Pollasky
Clovis, CA 93612
(209) 299-7273

Conejo Valley Chamber of Commerce
625 West Hillcrest Drive
Thousand Oaks, CA 91360
(805) 499-1993

Corona Chamber of Commerce
904 East Sixth Street
Corona, CA 91719
(909) 737-3350

Covina Chamber of Commerce
935 W. Badillo Street #100
Covina, CA 91722
(818) 967-4191

Crescenta Valley Chamber of Commerce
3131 Foothill Boulevard, Suite M
La Crescenta, CA 91214
(818) 248-4957

Culver City Chamber of Commerce
10767 Washington Blvd.
Culver City, CA 90232
(310) 287-3850

El Cajon Chamber of Commerce
109 Rea Avenue
El Cajon, CA 92020
(619) 440-6161

El Monte/South El Monte Chamber of Commerce
P.O. Box 5866
El Monte, CA 91734
(818) 443-0180

Escondido Chamber of Commerce
720 North Broadway
Escondido, CA 92025
(619) 745-2125
Fax (619) 745-1183

Fairfield-Suisun Chamber of Commerce
1111 Webster Street
Fairfield, CA 94533
(707) 425-4625

Foster City Chamber of Commerce
1125 East Hillsdale, Suite 114
Foster City, CA 94404
(415) 573-7600

Fountain Valley Chamber of Commerce
1110 Warner Avenue #204
Fountain Valley, CA 92708
(714) 668-0542

Fremont Chamber of Commerce
2201 Walnut Avenue #110
Fremont, CA 94538
(510) 795-2244

Fresno Chamber of Commerce
2331 Fresno Street
Fresno, CA 93721
(209) 495-4800
Fax (209) 495-4811

Fullerton Chamber of Commerce
219 East Commonwealth Avenue
P.O. Box 529
Fullerton, CA 92632
(714) 871-3100

Gardena Valley Chamber of Commerce
1204 West Gardena Boulevard, Suite E
Gardena, CA 90247
(310) 532-9905

Gilroy Chamber of Commerce
7471 Monterey Street
Gilroy, CA 95020
(408) 842-6437

Glendale Chamber of Commerce
200 South Louise Street
P.O. Box 112
Glendale, California 91209
(818) 240-7870

Glendora Chamber of Commerce
131 East Foothill Boulevard
Glendora, CA 91741-3336
(818) 963-4128

Goleta Valley Chamber of Commerce
5730 Hollister, Suite 1
Goleta, CA 93117
(805) 967-4618

Hanford Chamber of Commerce
200 Santa Fe Avenue, Suite D
Hanford, CA 98230
(209) 582-0483

Hawthorne Chamber of Commerce
12427 Hawthorne Boulevard
Hawthorne, CA 90250
(310) 676-1163

Hemet Chamber of Commerce
395 East Latham Avenue
Hemet, CA 92543
(909) 658-3211

Huntington Park Chamber of Commerce
6330 Pacific Blvd #209
Huntington Park, CA 90255
(213) 585-1155

Irvine Chamber of Commerce
17200 Jamboree Road, Suite A
Irvine, CA 92714
(714) 660-9112

La Mesa Chamber of Commerce
8155 University Avenue
La Mesa, CA 91944
(619) 465-7700

Livermore Chamber of Commerce
2157 First Street
Livermore, CA 94550
(510) 447-1606

Long Beach Area Chamber of Commerce
1 World Trade Center, Suite 350
Long Beach, CA 90831
(310) 436-1251

Los Angeles Area Chamber of Commerce
350 South Bixel Street
Los Angeles, CA 90017
(213) 580-7500

Los Gatos Chamber of Commerce
50 University Avenue
Los Gatos, CA 95031
(408) 354-9300

Monrovia Chamber of Commerce
620 South Myrtle Avenue
Monrovia, CA 91016
(818) 358-1159

Monterey Peninsula Chamber of Commerce
P.O. Box 1770
Monterey, CA 93942
(408) 648-5360

Mountain View Chamber of Commerce
580 Castro Street
Mountain View, CA 94041
(415) 968-8378
Fax (415) 968-5668

National City Chamber of Commerce
P.O. Box 1055
National City, CA 91951
(619) 477-9339

Oakland Chamber of Commerce
475 14th Street
Oakland, CA 94612
(510) 874-4800

Ojai Valley Chamber of Commerce
P.O. Box 1134
Ojai, CA 93024
(805) 646-8126

Palo Alto Chamber of Commerce
Susan Frank, Executive Director
325 Forest Avenue
Palo Alto, CA 94301
(415) 324-3121

Petaluma Area Chamber of Commerce
799 Baywood Drive #3
Petaluma, CA 94954
(707) 762-2785

Pico Rivera Chamber of Commerce
P.O. Box 985
Pico Rivera, CA 90660
(213) 949-2473

Port Hueneme Chamber of Commerce
220 North Market Street
Port Hueneme, CA 93041
(805) 488-2023
Fax (805) 488-6993

Greater Redding Chamber of Commerce
747 Auditorium Drive
Redding, CA 96001
(916) 225-4433

Sacramento Metropolitan Chamber of Commerce
917 7th Street
Sacramento, CA 95814
(916) 552-6800

Salinas Area Chamber of Commerce
P.O. Box 1170
Salinas, CA 93902
(408) 424-7611

Greater San Diego Chamber of Commerce
Angelika Villagrana, Assistant Dir., Gov't Affairs
402 W. Broadway #1000
San Diego, CA 92101
(619) 544-1361

San Fernando Chamber of Commerce
519 South Brand Boulevard
San Fernando, CA 91340
(818) 361-1184

Mid San Fernando Valley Chamber of Commerce
14540 Victory Boulevard, Suite 100
Van Nuys, CA 91411-1618
(818) 989-0300

San Francisco Chamber of Commerce
465 California Street
San Francisco, CA 94104
(415) 392-4511

San Jose Metropolitan Chamber of Commerce
180 South Market Street
San Jose, CA 95113
(408) 291-5250

San Marcos Chamber of Commerce
144 West Mission Road
San Marcos, CA 92069
(619) 744-1270

San Pedro Peninsula Chamber of Commerce
390 W. 7th Street
San Pedro, CA 90731
(310) 832-7272
Fax (310) 832-0685

Greater Santa Ana Chamber of Commerce
P.O. Box 205
Santa Ana, CA 92702
(714) 541-5353

Santa Barbara Chamber of Commerce
P.O. Box 299
Santa Barbara, CA 93102
(805) 965-3023

Santa Cruz Area Chamber of Commerce
1543 Pacific Avenue
Santa Cruz, CA 95060
(408) 423-1111

Santa Rosa Chamber of Commerce
637 1st Street
Santa Rosa, CA 95404
(707) 545-1414

California Chambers Validating Certificates of Origin

Scotts Valley Chamber of Commerce
P.O. Box 66928
Scotts Valley, CA 95067-6928
(408) 438-1010

Sonoma Valley Chamber of Commerce
645 Broadway
Sonoma, CA 95476
(707) 996-1033

South Orange County Chamber of Commerce
25431 Cabot Road, Suite 205
Laguna Hills, CA 25431
(714) 837-3000

South San Francisco Chamber of Commerce
P.O. Box 469
South San Francisco, CA 94080-0469
(415) 588-1911

Studio City Chamber of Commerce
12153 Ventura Boulevard, Suite 100
Studio City, CA 91604
(818)769-3213

Temecula Valley Chamber of Commerce
27450 Ynez Road, #104
Temecula, CA 92591
(714) 676-5090

Torrance Area Chamber of Commerce
International Business Committee
28924 S. Western Avenue, Suite 104
Rancho Palos Verdes, CA 90275
(310) 519-7153

Visalia Chamber of Commerce
720 West Mineral King
Visalia, CA 93291
(209) 734-5876

Walnut Creek Chamber of Commerce
1501 North Broadway, Suite 110
Walnut Creek, CA 94596
(510) 934-2007

Westchester/LAX Chamber of Commerce
5930 West Century Boulevard
Los Angeles, CA 90045
(310) 645-5151

Westminister Chamber of Commerce
14491 Beach Boulevard
Westminister, CA 92683
(714) 898-9648

West Sacramento Chamber of Commerce
1414 Merkley Avenue, Suite 1
West Sacramento, CA 95691
(916) 371-7042
Fax (916) 371-7210

Binational Chambers of Commerce and Business Associations in California

ASIA
Asian Business Association
William J. Yang, President
10418 Lower Azusa Road
El Monte, CA 91731
(818) 452-1242

Asian Business League of San Francisco
Julia Hsiao, Executive Director
233 Sansome Street #1102
San Francisco, CA 94104
(415) 788-4664
Fax (415) 788-4756

Center for Asia Pacific Affairs
c/o Asia Foundation
William P. Fuller, President
465 California Street, 14th Floor
San Francisco, CA 94104
(415) 982-4640

AUSTRALIA
Australian-American Chamber of Commerce
Malcolm M. Johns, Executive Director
41 Sutter Street, Suite 621
San Francisco, CA 94104

CANADA
Canada-California Chamber of Commerce
Monika Wegener, Executive Director
P.O. Box 4250
Sunland, CA 91041
(818) 951-2842
(818) 353-5976

Canadian-American Chamber of Commerce
David Roberts President
P.O. Box 2931
San Francisco, CA 94126
(415) 296-0961

CHILE
California-Chile Chamber of Commerce
Richard G. Pascal, President
700 South Flower Street, 11th Floor
Los Angeles, CA 90017
(213) 892-6369
Fax (818) 842-7595

CHINA, PEOPLE'S REPUBLIC OF
Chinese Chamber of Commerce
Ringo Wong, President
730 Sacramento Street
San Francisco, CA 94108
(415) 982-3000

COLOMBIA
California-Colombia Chamber of Commerce
6100 Wilshire Boulevard, Suite 1170
Los Angeles, CA 90048
(213) 938-6755
Fax (213) 965-5029

DENMARK
Danish-American Chamber of Commerce
Jytte Madsen, President
11469 Baird Avenue
Northridge, CA 91324
(818) 360-4802

Danish-American Chamber of Commerce
Jorgen Krejsbol, President
Marion T. Hvidt, Executive Director
1640 Stanley Dollar Drive, 1-A
Walnut Creek, CA 94595
(510) 945-8937

FINLAND
Finnish-American Chamber of Commerce
Krista Yla, President
1900 Avenue of the Stars, Suite 1025
Los Angeles, CA 90067
Fax (310) 203-0301

FRANCE
Califrance Corporation
Nicholas D. Molnar, President
1904 Franklin Street, Suite 501
Oakland, CA 94612
(510) 452-4711
Fax (510) 452-4719

French-American Chamber of Commerce
Barbara Hearn, Managing Director/CEO
6380 Wilshire Boulevard, Suite 1608
Los Angeles, CA 90048
(213) 651-4741
Fax (213) 651-2547

French-American Chamber of Commerce
Jean Ward Jacote, Executive Director
425 Bush Street, Suite 401
San Francisco, CA 94108
(415) 398-2449

GERMANY
German-American Chamber of Commerce
of Los Angeles, Inc.
Bernard B. Clermont, Managing Director
5220 Pacific Concourse Drive, Suite 280
Los Angeles, CA 90045
(310) 297-7979
Fax (310) 297-7966

German-American Chamber of Commerce
of the Western U.S., Inc.
Lawrence A. Walker, Managing Director
465 California Street, Suite 910
San Francisco, CA 94104
(415) 392-2262
Fax (415) 392-1314

GREECE
American-Hellenic Chamber of Commerce
P.O. Box 11116
Beverly Hills, CA 90210
(310) 278-7880
Fax (310) 859-4706

HUNGARY
Hungarian-American Chamber of Commerce
Dr. Eva E. Voisin, President
250A Twin Dolphin Drive
Redwood City, CA 94065
(415) 595-0444
Fax (415) 595-3976

American Chamber of Commerce in Hungary
Nicholas D. Molnar, Regional Director for the Western U.S.
1904 Franklin Street, Suite 501
Oakland, CA 94612
(510) 452-4711
Fax (510) 452-4719

INDIA
United Indian Chamber of Commerce
Dilip Shah, President
P.O. Box 2073
Pioneer Plaza, Suite F
Artesia, CA 90702

INDONESIA
Indonesian Chamber of Commerce of the West
James De Arnuda, President
9111 La Cienega Boulevard, Suite 203
Inglewood, CA 90301
(213) 337-0515

Indonesian Business Society
1801 S. Pritchard Way
Hacienda Heights, CA 91745
(818) 810-4712

ISRAEL
California-Israel Chamber of Commerce
Arthur Stern, President
6505 Wilshire Blvd.
Los Angeles, CA 90048

ITALY
Italy-America Chamber of Commerce West
E. Fontana, President
11520 San Vicente Boulevard, Suite 203
Los Angeles, CA 90049
(310) 826-9898
Fax (310) 826-2876

JAPAN
Japan America Society of Southern California
Mike Mullen, Executive Director
505 South Flower Street, Level C
Los Angeles, CA 90071
(213) 627-6217
Fax (213) 627-1353

Japan Business Association of Southern California
Akira Tsukada, President
Masanori Takeda, Acting Executive Director
345 South Figueroa Street, Suite 206
Los Angeles, CA 90071
(213) 485-0160
Fax (213) 626-5526

Japanese Chamber of Commerce of Northern California
Steven Teraoka, President
300 Montgomery Street, Suite 725
San Francisco, CA 94104
(415) 395-9353
Fax (415) 395-9351

Japanese Chamber of Commerce of Southern California
Hiroshi Kawabe, President
244 South San Pedro Street, Suite 504
Los Angeles, CA 90012
(213) 626-3067
Fax (213) 626-3070

The Japan Society of Northern California
Thomas A. Wilkins, Executive Director
31 Geary Street
San Francisco, CA 94108
(415) 986-4383
Fax (415) 986-5772

The Japan Society of Northern California
Sacramento Valley Chapter
601 University Avenue, Suite 236
Sacramento, CA 95825
(916) 568-1836
Fax (916) 929-2716

KOREA
The Korea Society/Los Angeles
5505 Wilshire Boulevard
Los Angeles, CA 90036
(213) 935-1560
Fax (213) 935-2782

Korea Traders Club of Los Angeles
4801 Wilshire Boulevard, Suite 104
Los Angeles, CA 90010
(213) 954-9500
Fax (213) 954-1707

Korean-American Chamber of Commerce
Walter Knoepfel, President
160 Indian Road
Piedmont, CA 94610
(415) 777-4007

LATIN AMERICA
Pan American Society of California
World Affairs Center
Terry Vog, President
312 Sutter Street
San Francisco, CA 94108
(415) 788-4764

LUXEMBOURG
Board of Economic Development
One Sansome Street, Suite 830
San Francisco, CA 94104
(415) 788-0816

MEXICO
U.S.-Mexico Chamber of Commerce
Pacific Chapter
Leslie Browne-Cazas, Chair
Ronald Pettis, President
Rachel Mullens, Executive Director
555 South Flower Street, 25th Floor
Los Angeles, CA 90071
(213) 623-7725
Fax (213) 623-0032

Camara Nacional de la Industria de Transformacion
(CANACINTRA)
International and Business Office
Julio Jeffrey
1111 Orange Avenue, Suite B
Coronado, CA 92118
(619) 437-6063
Fax (619) 437-0177

MIDDLE EAST
U.S.-Arab Chamber of Commerce
(Pacific), Inc.
89395 Sepulveda Boulevard, Suite 440
Los Angeles, CA 90045
(310) 646-1499
Fax (310) 646-2462

U.S.-Arab Chamber of Commerce
(Pacific), Inc.
D. J. Asfour, Executive Director
Duane McDowell, Public Relations Consultant
One Hallidie Plaza, Suite 504 (94102)
P.O. Box 422218
San Francisco, CA 94142-2218
(415) 398-9200
Fax (415) 398-7111
Telex 278101 USARCUR

NORWAY
Norwegian-American Chamber of Commerce
20 California Street, 6th Floor
San Francisco, CA 94111
(415) 986-0770
Fax (415) 986-6025

Norwegian-American Chamber of Commerce
5750 Wilshire Boulevard, Suite 470
Los Angeles, CA 90036
(213) 933-7717
Fax (213) 933-8711

PAKISTAN
Pakistan American Chamber of Commerce
14461 Shadow Drive
Fontana, CA 92335
(909) 357-3759
Fax (909) 357-8069

POLAND
U.S.-Poland Chamber of Commerce
Southern California
Judith D. Brandon, Chair
P.O. Box 92014
Long Beach, CA 90809-2014
(310) 597-4116-phone/fax

RUSSIA

California-Russia Trade Association
c/o Tim C. Bruinsma
Fulbright and Jaworski
865 South Figueroa, 29th Floor
Los Angeles, CA 90017
(213) 892-9200

Russian-American Pacific Business Council
Gregory Makaron, President
9000 Sunset Blvd., Suite 700
West Hollywood, CA 90069
(310) 858-1990
Fax (310) 858-8103

Russian-American Trade & Commerce, Inc.
George Lavrov, President
P.O. Box 2533
San Francisco, CA 94126-2533
(415) 928-RUSS
Fax (415) 928-7825

Russian Commonwealth Business Forum
Michael Johnson, Executive Director
3 Embarcadero Center, Suite 2210
San Francisco, CA 94111
(415) 989-0536
Fax (415) 391-0759

SINGAPORE

Singapore Trade Development Board
L.A. World Trade Center
350 South Figueroa Street, Suite 909
Los Angeles, CA 90071
(213) 617-7358
Fax (213) 617-7367

SWEDEN

Swedish-American Chamber of Commerce-GLA
10880 Wilshire Boulevard, Suite 914
Los Angeles, CA 90024
(310) 515-7610
Fax (310) 715-2693

Swedish-American Chamber of Commerce
of the Western U.S.
Helena Wahlin, Managing Director
230 California Street, Suite 405
San Francisco, CA 94111-4319
(415) 781-4188
Fax (415) 781-4189

SWITZERLAND

Swiss-American Chamber of Commerce
Edy O. Sennhauser, Chairman
P.O. Box 2269
San Francisco, CA 94126
(415) 433-6679

Swiss-American Chamber of Commerce
California-Los Angeles Chapter
633 W. 5th Street, 64th Floor
Los Angeles, CA 90071
(213) 955-6121
Fax (213) 489-3336

TAIWAN, REPUBLIC OF CHINA

California Taiwan Trade and Investment Council
900 Wilshire Boulevard, Suite 1434
Los Angeles, CA 90017
(213) 627-3442
Fax (213) 627-0398

Far East Trade Service Inc.
Robert Y. Wang, Director
555 Montgomery Street, Suite 603
San Francisco, CA 94111-2564
(415) 788-4304
Fax (415) 788-0468

Kaohsiung Import/Export Association
916 Sierra Vista Avenue
Alhambra, CA 91801
(818) 284-9657

U.S. Liaison Center for the General Chamber of Commerce
of The Republic of China
Douglas T. Hung, Director
870 Market Street, Suite 1046
San Francisco, CA 94102
(415) 981-5387
Fax (415) 362-5404

UNITED KINGDOM

British-American Chamber of Commerce
Peter Gardiner, President
Mostyn Lloyd, Executive Director
41 Sutter Street, Suite 303
San Francisco, CA 94104
(415) 296-8645
Fax (415) 347-1034

*British-American Chamber of Commerce
and Trade Center of Pacific S.W.*
Dennis Storer, Executive Director
1640 5th Street, Suite 203
Santa Monica, CA 90290
(310) 394-4977
Fax (310) 394-0839

*British-American Chamber of Commerce
of Orange County*
Dennis Chant, President
Valerie Blackholly, Executive Director
One Hughes, Suite B404
Irvine, CA 92718
(714) 768-2577
Fax (714) 768-2580

VIETNAM
San Francisco-Vietnam Foundation
Hao Ngyen, President
41 Sutter Street, Suite 1527
San Francisco, CA 94104
(510) 651-1149
Fax (510) 651-1343

...trying to figure out the best way to provide them with insurance.

IF YOUR TRAINING PROGRAM requires individuals to travel outside their home country, you may need to provide accident and medical insurance solutions that these international situations present.

At Seabury & Smith, our Gateway Portfolio is designed to provide comprehensive insurance solutions for just such an occasion. Purchased by individuals, corporations, agencies, and other institutions involved in business, cultural, or academic exchange projects, the Gateway insurance plans are available from 15 days to three years, and offer accident & sickness coverage, medical evacuation and repatriation, and worldwide assistance services, including medical, legal and travel.

For more information about the Gateway Portfolio and/or how we can customize an insurance plan for you, **call Barbara Nenno of Seabury & Smith toll-free at (800) 368-5969 or direct at (202) 457-6822.**

SEABURY & SMITH

Binational Chambers of Commerce and Business Associations in the U.S. (Outside of California)

ARGENTINA
Argentine-American Chamber of Commerce
Carlos E. Alfaro, President
10 Rockefeller Plaza, 10th Floor
New York, NY 10020
(212) 698-2238
Fax (212) 698-2239

ASIA
ASEAN-U.S. Trade Council
40 East 49th Street
New York, NY 10017
(212) 688-2755

The Asia Society
725 Park Avenue
New York, NY 10021
(212) 288-6400

AUSTRIA
U.S.-Austrian Chamber of Commerce
165 West 46th Street, Room 112
New York, NY 10036
(212) 819-0117

BANGLADESH
BJMC Market Promotion Office
820 Mabry Road
Atlanta, GA 30328
Fax (404) 512-8249

BELGIUM
Belgian-American Chamber of Commerce
Southern Chapter
3333 Peachtree Road
Suite 222, South Tower
Atlanta, GA 30326
(404) 231-5985
Fax (404) 233-6828

Belgian-American Chamber of Commerce in the U.S.
350 5th Avenue, Suite 1322
New York, NY 10118
(212) 967-9898
Fax (212) 629-0349

BRAZIL
Brazilian-American Chamber of Commerce, Inc.
801 Brickell
Miami, FL 33131
(305) 377-6700

Brazilian-American Chamber of Commerce
Sueli Cristina Bonaparte, General Manager
22 West 48th Street, Room 404
New York, NY 10036-1886
(212) 575-9030

CHILE
North American-Chile Chamber of Commerce, Inc.
Lester Ziffren, Executive Director
220 East 81st Street
New York, NY 10028
(212) 288-5691
Fax (212) 628-4978

CHINA
Chinese Chamber of Commerce of New York
Confucius Plaza
33 Bowery, Room C202
New York, NY 10002
(212) 226-2795

Chinese Chamber of Commerce of Hawaii
Wen Chung Lin, Executive Vice President
P.O. Box 1975
Honolulu, HI 96805
(808) 533-3181

U.S. Office of China Chamber of International Commerce
4301 Conneticut Avenue, N.W., Suite 136
Washington, D.C. 20008
(202) 244-3244; (202) 362-8462
Fax (202) 244-0478

COLOMBIA
Colombian-American Chamber of Greater Miami
280 Aragon Avenue
Coral Gables, FL 33134
(305) 446-2542
Fax (305) 448-5028

CYPRUS
Cyprus Embassy Trade Center
13 East 40th Street
New York, NY 10016
(212) 213-9100

DENMARK
Danish-American Chamber of Commerce
885 Second Avenue, 18th Floor
1 Dag Hammorskjold Plaza
New York, NY 10017
(212) 980-6240

EGYPT

U.S.-Egypt Chamber of Commerce
28 East Jackson Boulevard, Suite 1204
Chicago, IL 60604
(312) 427-9368

U.S.-Egypt Chamber of Commerce
330 East 39th Street, Suite 32L
New York, NY 10016
(212) 867-2323
Fax (212) 697-0465

U.S.-Egypt Chamber of Commerce
1535 West Loopsouth, Suite 219A
Houston, TX 77027
(713) 993-9650

FINLAND

Finnish-American Chamber of Commerce
P.O. Box 11337
Chicago, IL 60611
(312) 670-4700

Finnish-American Chamber of Commerce
866 U.N. Plaza, Suite 249
New York, NY 10017

FRANCE

French-American Chamber of Commerce in the U.S.
509 Madison Avenue, Suite 1900
New York, NY 10022
(212) 371-4466
Fax (212) 371-5623

GERMANY

German-American Chamber of Commerce
W. Philip Quimby, Marketing Manager
3475 Lenox Road, N.E., Suite 620
Atlanta, GA 30326
(404) 239-9494
Fax (404) 264-1761

German-American Chamber of Commerce of Chicago
Niels Friedrichs, Manager/Director
104 South Michigan Avenue, Suite 600
Chicago, IL 60603-5978
(312) 782-8557
Fax (312) 782-3892

German-American Chamber of Commerce
Werner Walbroel, President
40 West 57th Street, 31st Floor
New York, NY 10019
(212) 974-8830
Fax (212) 974-8867

German-American Chamber of Commerce of Houston
Manfred Dransfeld, Manager Director
5555 San Phillipe
Houston, TX 77056
(713) 877-1114
Fax (713) 877-1602

GREECE

Hellenic-American Chamber of Commerce
960 Avenue of the Americas, Suite 1204
New York, NY 10001
(212) 629-6380

HUNGARY

Hungarian-American Chamber of Commerce of Miami
520 Brickell Key Drive, Suite 2015
Miami, FL 33131
(305) 358-8138
Fax (305) 374-6715

MidAmerica Hungarian Chamber of Commerce
707 Forest Avenue
Evanston, IL 60202
(708) 328-4279
Fax (708) 866-8825

ICELAND

Icelandic-American Chamber of Commerce
370 Lexington Avenue, Suite 505
New York, NY 10017
(212) 686-4100
Fax (212) 532-4138

INDIA

India-America Chamber of Commerce (N.Y)
P.O. Box 873
Grand Central Station
New York, NY 10163
(212) 755-7181
Fax (212) 424-8500

INDONESIA

American-Indonesian Chamber of Commerce
711 3rd Avenue, 17th Floor
New York, NY 10017
(212) 687-4505

IRELAND

Ireland Chamber of Commerce in the U.S.
1305 Post Road
Fairfield, CT 06430
(212) 248-0008
Fax (203) 255-6752

Ireland-U.S. Council for Commerce & Industry, Inc.
460 Park Avenue, 22nd Floor
New York, NY 10022
(212) 751-2660

ISRAEL
American-Israel Chamber of Commerce & Industry
of Metropolitan Chicago
Marlene Greenberg, Executive Vice President
180 North Michigan Avenue, Suite 911
Chicago, IL 60601
(312) 641-2937
Fax (312) 641-2941
E-Mail: NY000975@mail.nyser.net

American-Israel Chamber of Commerce & Industry, Inc.
Ronny Bassan, Executive Vice President
350 Fifth Avenue, Suite 1919
New York, NY 10118-1988
(212) 971-0310
Fax (212) 971-0331

Association of North America-Israel Chambers of
Commerce, Inc.
Howard I. Bernstein, President
180 North Michigan Avenue, Suite 911
Chicago, IL 60601
(800) 645-3433; (312) 641-2944
Fax (312) 641-2941
E-Mail: NY000976@mail.nyser.net

ITALY
Italian Chamber of Commerce of Chicago
Leonora Lipuma, Executive Director
126 West Grand Avenue
Chicago, IL 60610
(312) 661-1336
Fax (312) 767-3299

Italy-American Chamber of Commerce, Inc.
350 Fifth Avenue, Suite 3015
New York, NY 10118
(212) 279-5520
Fax (212) 279-5839
Telex CAMERIT

JAPAN
Honolulu-Japanese Chamber of Commerce
2454 South Beretania Street
Honolulu, HI 96826
(808) 949-5531
Fax (808) 949-3020

Japan Business Association of Houston
14133 Memorial Drive, Suite 3
Houston, TX 77079
(713) 493-1512
Fax (713) 493-2276

Japanese Chamber of Commerce & Industry of Chicago
401 North Michigan Avenue, Room 602
Chicago, IL 60611
(312) 332-6199
Fax (312) 822-9773

Japan Chamber of Commerce & Industry
911 Main Street, Suite 2323
Kansas City, MO 64105
(816) 221-6140

KOREA, REPUBLIC OF (SOUTH KOREA)
U.S.-Korea Society
725 Park Avenue
New York, NY 10021
(212) 517-7730

LATIN AMERICA
Association of American Chambers of Commerce
in Latin America
Keith Miceli, Executive Vice President
1615 H Street, N.W.
Washington, D.C. 20062-2000
(202) 463-5485
Fax (202) 463-3126

Americas Society
Ambassador E.E. Briggs, President
680 Park Avenue
New York, NY 10021
(212) 628-3200
Fax (212) 517-6247

Latin American Chamber of Commerce
P.O. Box 30240
New Orleans, LA 70190
(504) 488-7425

Latin Chamber of Commerce
1417 West Flagler Street
Miami, FL 33135
(305) 642-3870

InterAmerican Chamber of Commerce
510 Bering Drive, Suite 300
Houston, TX 77057
(713) 975-6171

Pan American Society of the U.S.
680 Park Avenue
New York, NY 10021
(212) 249-8950

MEXICO
Americas Society
680 Park Avenue
New York, NY 10021
(212) 249-8950

Mexican Chamber of Commerce of Arizona
Hector Le-Desma, President
6330 North Central Avenue, #5; P.O. Box 626 (85001)
Phoenix, AZ 85012
(602) 252-6448

MIDDLE EAST
Mid-America U.S.-Arab Chamber of Commerce
Douglas Savage, Regional Manager
208 South LaSalle Street, Suite 706
Chicago, IL 60604
(312) 782-0320
Fax (312) 782-7379

National Council on U.S.-Arab Relations
1140 Connecticut Avenue, N.W., Suite 1210
Washington, D.C. 20036
(202) 293-0801
Fax (202) 293-0903

National U.S.-Arab Chamber of Commerce
420 Lexington Avenue, Suite 2739
New York, NY 10170
(212) 986-8024
Fax (212) 986-0216

National U.S.-Arab Chamber of Commerce
1825 K Street, NW, Suite 1107
Washington, DC 20006
(202) 331-8010
Fax (202) 331-8297

National U.S.-Arab Chamber of Commerce
208 South LaSalle Street, Suite 706
Chicago, IL 60604
(312) 782-0320
Fax (312) 782-7379

U.S.-Arab Chamber of Commerce
Mr. J.R. Abinader, President
1825 K Street, N.W., Suite 1107
Washington, D.C. 20006
(202) 331-8010
Fax (202) 331-8297
Telex 9102507574

U.S.-Arab Chamber of Commerce
505 North Belt Drive, Suite 405
Houston, TX 77060
(713) 447-2563

NETHERLANDS
Netherlands Chamber of Commerce in the U.S.
Bram Van Meijl Manager
233 Peachtree Street, N.E., Suite 404
Atlanta, GA 30303
(404) 523-4400
Fax (404) 522-7116

Netherlands Chamber of Commerce in the U.S.
Sandra Vogel, Manager
303 East Wacker Drive, Suite 412
Chicago, IL 60601
(312) 938-9050
Fax (312) 938-8949

Netherlands Chamber of Commerce in the U.S.
Kersen J. de Jong, Manager/Director
One Rockefeller Plaza, 14th Floor
New York, NY 10020
(212) 265-6460
Fax (212) 265-6402

NIGERIA
Nigerian-American Chamber of Commerce, Inc.
828 Second Avenue
New York, NY 10017
(212) 808-0301

NORWAY
Norwegian-American Chamber of Commerce
Upper Midwest Chapter
800 Foshay Tower
Minneapolis, MN 55402
(612) 332-3338

Norwegian-American Chamber of Commerce, Inc.
Inger Tallaksen, General Manager
800 3rd Avenue
New York, NY 10022
(212) 421-9210
Fax (212) 838-0374

PAKISTAN
U.S.-Pakistan Economic Council
c/o Zuckerman and Dunn, PC
1140 Avenue of the Americas
New York, NY 10036
(212) 921-2929

PERU
Peruvian-U.S. Chamber of Commerce
444 Brickell Avenue, Suite M-126
Miami, FL 33131
(305) 375-0885
Fax (305) 375-0884

PHILIPPINES
Filipino Chamber of Commerce-Chicago
Achilles Natividad, Executive Director
2457 West Peterson, Suite 3
Chicago, IL 60659
(312) 271-8008

Philippine-American Chamber of Commerce
711 3rd Avenue, 1702
New York, NY 10017
(212) 972-9326
Fax (212) 867-9882

PORTUGAL
Portugal-U.S. Chamber of Commerce
Executive Director
590 Fifth Avenue, 3rd Floor
New York, NY 10036
(212) 354-4627
Fax (212) 575-4737

PUERTO RICO
Commonwealth of Puerto Rico
304 Park Avenue, South 23rd Street, 5th Floor
New York, NY 10010
(212) 260-3000

SAUDI ARABIA
Saudi Arabian Council of Chamber of Commerce & Industry
c/o Hamed Jared, Representative
Embassy of Saudi Arabia
601 New Hampshire Avenue, N.W.
Washington, D.C. 20037

SINGAPORE
Singapore Trade Development Board
55 E. 59th Street, Suite 21B
New York, NY 10022
(212) 421-2207
Fax (212) 888-2897

SPAIN
Chamber of Commerce of Spain
2655 Le Jeune Road, Suite 1114
Coral Gables, FL 33134
(305) 446-4495

Spain-U.S. Chamber of Commerce
350 5th Avenue, Room 3514
New York, NY 10118
(212) 967-2170
Fax (212) 564-1415

SWEDEN
Swedish-American Chamber of Commerce
Olle Wijkstrom, Executive Secretary
599 Lexington Avenue, 42nd Floor
New York, NY 10022
(212) 838-5530
Fax (212) 755-7953

SWITZERLAND
Swiss-American Chamber of Commerce
New York Chapter
37 West 67th Street
New York, NY 10023
(212) 875-9688
Fax (212) 873-2836

TRINIDAD AND TOBAGO
Trinidad & Tobago Chamber of Commerce of the U.S., Inc.
c/o Trintoc Services Ltd.
400 Madison Avenue, Room 803
New York, NY 10017
(212) 759-3388

UNITED KINGDOM
British-American Chamber of Commerce
52 Vanderbilt Avenue, 20th Floor
New York, NY 10017
(212) 661-4060

VENEZUELA
Venezuela-American Chamber of Commerce of Industry
Antonio Herrera-Vaillant, General Manager
P.O. Box 020010
Miami, FL 33102-0010
(305) 263-0833
Fax (305) 263-1829
Telex 23627 VACCI VC

YUGOSLAVIA
U.S.-Business Council for Southeastern Europe
Gary J. Wolfe, President
P.O. Box 3635
Warrenton, VA 22186
(703) 349-4929
Fax (703) 349-2756

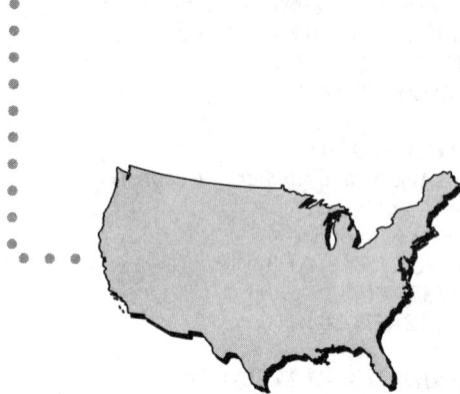

International Trade Quiz:

· · · · You Are Here

You Want To Do
Business Here

Who Do You Call?
Call us — We're everywhere

KPMG Peat Marwick LLP

The Global Leader

Sridar Iyengar (415) 354-1443 • Bryan Isaacs (310) 551-6111

Acquisitions • Customs & Duty Services • Expatriate Compensation & Tax • Export Financing Assistance
Export Strategies • International Financial Services • Market Entry Strategies
Partnerships & Joint Ventures • Accounting & Tax Consulting • Transfer Pricing

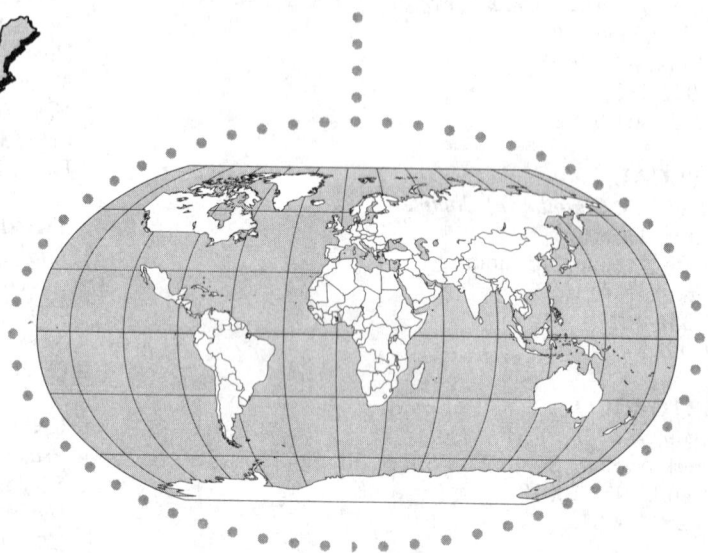

American Chambers of Commerce Abroad

REGIONAL AMCHAM UMBRELLA GROUPS

Association of American Chambers of Commerce in Latin America (AACCLA)

David E. Ivy
c/o Korn/Ferry International Ltd.
Avda. Indianopolis 80
04062 Sao Paulo, Brazil
Telephone 5511-549-7133
Fax 5511-575-0959

David Hirschmann, Executive Vice President

U.S. Chamber of Commerce
1615 H Street, N.W.
Washington, D.C. 20062
(202) 463-5485
Fax (202) 463-3114
Telex 248302 CCUS UR
(This regional group was founded in 1967 to advance human progress in the Western Hemisphere through private enterprise. AACCLA has become a broadly based, closely knit organization of 22 American Chambers of Commerce with seven branches, representing approximately 16,200 firms and individuals of American, host country, and third country nationalities. AACCLA advocates trade and investment between the U.S. and the countries of the region through free trade, free markets and free enterprise. Membership includes: Argentina; Bolivia; Brazil - Rio de Janeiro; Brazil - Sao Paulo; Chile; Colombia; Costa Rica; Dominican Republic; Ecuador - Quito; Ecuador - Guayaquil; El Salvador; Guatemala; Honduras; Jamaica; Mexico; Nicaragua; Panama; Paraguay; Peru; Trinidad & Tobago; Uruguay; and Venezuela.)

European Council of American Chambers of Commerce (ECACC)

Edward Streator, Chairman
32 Phillimore Gardens
London W8 7QF, England
Telephone (44) 71-937-4772
Fax (44) 71-937-3396

William Edgar/Lese Joslyn, Secretariat

2, Enmore Road
London SW15 6LL, England
Telephone (44) 81 789-7891
Fax (44) 81 789-9789
(This regional umbrella organization was formed in 1963 and is made up of American Chambers of Commerce (AmChams) in 16 European nations. The oldest of these was formed in 1894 (France) and the newest in 1991 (Poland). ECACC's purpose is to promote two-way trade and investment between AmCham host countries and the United States. Membership includes: Austria; Belgium; Czech Republic; France; Germany; Greece; Hungary; Israel; Italy; Netherlands; Poland; Portugal; Sweden; Switzerland; Turkey (TABA); and United Kingdom.)

Asia-Pacific Council of American Chambers of Commerce (APCAC)

Douglas C. Henck, Chairman
c/o Aetna International Inc.
3508 One Exchange Square, 8 Connaught Place
Hong Kong
Telephone (852) 523-2053
Fax (882) 810-6775
(Formed in 1968, APCAC represents the interests of about 35,000 businessmen and 6,500 businesses participating in 13 American chambers. The primary role of APCAC is to assist its members in identifying issues of concern to the American business community in the region and to develop and execute a plan of action to influence public policy. APCAC traditionally has supported the international free-trading system. Membership includes: China; Guam; Hong Kong; Korea; Indonesia; Japan; Japan - Okinawa; Malaysia; New Zealand; Philippines; Singapore; Taiwan; and Thailand.)

American Business Council of the Gulf Countries

Lee Eyer, Chairman
Bahrain
Telephone (973) 722-517
Fax (973) 720-256
(This regional group was formed in August 1989 to represent the growing number of American Chambers of Commerce in the Arabian Peninsula. Its primary purpose is to address legal, regulatory and policy barriers to development of U.S. business in the region. Membership includes: Saudi Arabia - Dhahran; Saudi Arabia - Jeddah; Saudi Arabia - Riyadh; and United Arab Emirates-Dubai/N.Emirates.)

Typical AmCham Services include:
- export-import trade leads;
- business and government contacts;
- meetings featuring U.S. and foreign business leaders and officials;
- periodic bulletins and publications;
- clearinghouse of information on trade, investment and commerce; and
- information center for customs duties, tariffs, etc.

ARGENTINA
American Chamber of Commerce in Argentina
Felix Zumelzu, Executive Director
Av. Leandro N. Alem 1110, Piso 13
1001 Buenos Aires
Argentina
Telephone (541) 311-5420/5126
Fax (541) 311-9076

AUSTRALIA
American Chamber of Commerce in Australia
Charles W. Blunt, National Director
Suite 4, Gloucester Walk
88 Cumberland Street
Sydney, N.S.W. 2000, Australia
Telephone (612) 241-1907
Fax (612) 251-5220

American Chamber of Commerce in Australia
Adelaide Branch
Mareylene Williams, State Manager
Level 1, 300 Flinders Street
Adelaide, S.A. 5000
Australia
Telephone (618) 224-0761
Fax (618) 224-0628

American Chamber of Commerce in Australia
Brisbane Branch
Marie Sinclair, State Manager
Level 23, 68 Queen Street
Brisbane, Queensland 4000, Australia
Telephone (617) 221-8542
Fax (617) 221-6313

American Chamber of Commerce in Australia
Melbourne Branch
Frank Bennett, State Manager
Level 1, 123 Lonsdale Street
Melbourne, Victoria 3000
Australia
Telephone (613) 663-2644
Fax (613) 663-2473

American Chamber of Commerce in Australia
Perth Branch
Kate Tudor, State Manager
Level 6, 231 Adelaide Terrace
Perth, W.A. 6000, Australia
Telephone (619) 325-9540
Fax (619) 221-3725

American Chamber of Commerce in Australia
Sydney Branch
Robert Reynolds, State Manager
Level 2, 41 Lower Fort Street
Sydney, NSW, 2000
Australia
Telephone (612) 241-1907
Fax (612) 251-5220

AUSTRIA
American Chamber of Commerce in Austria
Dr. Patricia A. Helletzgruber, Secretary General
Porzellangasse 35
1090 Vienna, Austria
Telephone (43) 1-319-5751
Fax (43) 1-319-5151

BELGIUM
American Chamber of Commerce in Belgium
Jo Ann Broger, General Manager
Avenue des Arts 50, Boite 5
1040 Brussels, Belgium
Telephone (32) 2 513 67 70/9
Fax (32) 2 513 79 28

BOLIVIA
American Chamber of Commerce of Bolivia
Anna Maria Galinda de Paz, General Manager
Casilla 8268, Avda. Arca No. 20171, Oficina 3
La Paz, Bolivia
Telephone (5912) 342-523
Fax (5912) 371-503

BRAZIL
*American Chamber of Commerce for Brazil -
Rio de Janeiro*
Augusto de Moura Diniz, Executive Vice President
C.P. 916, Praca Pio X-15, 5th Floor
20040 Rio de Janeiro, RJ Brazil
Telephone (5521) 203 2477
Fax (5521) 263 4477

American Chamber of Commerce for Brazil
Salvador Branch
Jose Carlos Barretto de Araujo, Executive Director
Rua da Espanha 2, Salas 604-606
40000 Salvador, Bahia, Brazil
Telephone (5571) 242-0077;242-5606
Fax (5571) 243-9986

American Chamber of Commerce for Brazil
Sao Paulo Branch
John Edwin Mein, Executive Vice President
Rua Alexandre Dumas 1976
04717 Sao Paulo, SP, Brazil
Telephone (5511) 246-9199
Fax (5511) 246-9080

CHILE
Chilean-American Chamber of Commerce
M. Isabel Jaramillo, Manager
Av. Americo Vespucio Sur 80, 9 Piso
82 Correo 34
Santiago, Chile
Telephone (562) 208-4140/3451
Fax (562) 206-0911

CHINA, (PRC)
American Chamber of Commerce, PRC
Beijing Branch
Mary Liu, Office Manager
Great Wall Sheraton Hotel, Room 301
North Donghuan Avenue
Beijing 100026, People's Republic of China
Telephone (86-1) 500-5566 ext. 2271
Fax (86-1) 501-8273

American Chamber of Commerce, PRC
Shanghai Branch
Executive Staff
Shanghai Centre, Room 435
1376 Nanjing Road West
Shangai 200040, PRC
Telephone (8621) 279-7119
Fax (8621) 279-8802

COLOMBIA
Colombian-American Chamber of Commerce
Joseph Finnin, Executive Director
Apto. Aereo 8008, Calle 35, No. 6-16
Bogota, Colombia
Telephone (571) 285-7800
Fax (571) 288-6434

Colombian-American Chamber of Commerce
Cali Branch
Leyda Lucia Perez B., Executive Director
Avenida 1N 3N-97
Cali, Colombia
Telephone (5723) 610-162; 672-993
Fax (5723) 672-992

Colombian-American Chamber of Commerce
Cartagena Branch
Jaime Borda Martelo, Executive Director
Avda. San Martin, Of. 309
P.O. Box 15555
Cartagena, Colombia
Telephone (5753) 657-724
Telex (5753) 651-704

Colombian-American Chamber of Commerce
Medellin Branch
Nicolas de Zubiria, Executive Director
Apartado Aereo 66655
Medellin, Colombia
Telephone (574) 268-7491
Fax (574) 268-3198

COSTA RICA
Costa Rican-American Chamber of Commerce
Lynda Solar, Executive Director
P.O. Box 025216, Dept. #1576
Miami, FL 33102-5216
Telephone (506) 220-2200
Fax (506) 220-2300

CZECH REPUBLIC
American Chamber of Commerce in the Czech Republic
Rudolph Barta, Executive Director
Karlovo namesti 24
110 00 Prague 1, Czech Republic
Telephone (42) 2-299-887, 296-778
Fax (42) 2-291-481

DOMINICAN REPUBLIC
American Chamber of Commerce of the Dominican Republic
Arthur E. Valdez, Executive Director
P.O. Box 02-5256
Miami, FL 33102-5256
Telephone (809) 544-2222
Fax (809) 544-0502

ECUADOR
Ecuadorian-American Chamber of Commerce - Quito
Roque Mino, Executive Director
Edificio Multicentro, 4P
La Nina y Avda. 6 de Diciembre
Quito, Ecuador
Telephone (5932) 507-450
Fax (5932) 504-571

Ecuadorian-American Chamber of Commerce - Quito
Ambato Branch
Vicente Villafuerte, Executive Director
Av. Cevallos y Montalvo
3er. Piso, Oficina 301
Ambato, Ecuador
Telephone (5932) 821-073
Fax (5932) 829-561

Ecuadorian-American Chamber of Commerce - Quito
Cuenca Branch
Sra. Yolanda de Gomez, Executive Secretary
Centro Comercial de Parque Industrial
2do. Piso, Oficina 303
Cuenca, Ecuador
Telephone (5937) 861-873
Fax (5937) 806-512

Ecuadorian-American Chamber of Commerce - Quito
Manta Branch
Sr. Horacio Cantos
Edificio Banco del Pichincha
Manta, Ecuador
Telephone (5934) 621-699
Fax (5934) 611-704

Ecuadorian-American Chamber of Commerce - Guayaquil
Dr. Maria Teresa Perez de Ayala, Executive Director
G. Cordova 812, Piso 3, Oficina 1
Edificio Torres de la Merced
Guayaquil, Ecuador
Telephone (5934) 456-6481
Fax (5934) 456-3259

Ecuadorian-American Chamber of Commerce - Guayaquil
Machala Branch
Charlos Chavez, Executive Director
P.O. Box 825
Machala, Ecuador
Telephone (593) 793-0640
Fax (593) 793-0640

EGYPT
American Chamber of Commerce in Egypt
Executive Director
Cairo Marriott Hotel, Suite 1541
P.O. Box 33 Zamalek
Cairo, Egypt
Telephone (20) 2 340-8888
Fax (20) 2 340-6667
Telex 20870 AMCHE UN

EL SALVADOR
American Chamber of Commerce of El Salvador
Patricia Allwood, Executive Director
87 Ave. Norte, No. 720, Apt. A
Col. Escalon
San Salvador, El Salvador
Telephone (503) 23-3292/24-3646/24-6003
Fax (503) 24-6856

FRANCE
American Chamber of Commerce in France
W. Barrett Dower, Executive Director
21 Avenue George V
75008, Paris, France
Telephone (33) 1 47 23 70 28
Fax (33) 1 47 20 18 62

GERMANY
American Chamber of Commerce in Germany
Dierk Muller, General Manager
Rossmarkt 12, Postfach 100 162
60311 Frankfurt am Main 1, Germany
Telephone (49) 69 28 34 01
Fax (49) 69 28 56 32

American Chamber of Commerce in Germany -
Berlin Office
Inka Regler, Assistant Manager
Budapesterstrasse 29
W-1000 Berlin 30, Germany
Telephone (49) 30 261 55 86
Fax (49) 30 262 26 00

GREECE
American-Hellenic Chamber of Commerce
Symeon G. Tsomokos, General Manager
16 Kanari Street, 3rd Floor
Athens 106 74, Greece
Telephone (30) 1 36 18 385/36 36 407
Fax (30) 1 36 10 170

GUAM
Guam Chamber of Commerce
Wayne Brown, Chairman
102 Ada Plaza Center
P.O. Box 283
Agana, Guam 96910
Telephone (671) 472-6311/8001
Telex 7216160 BOOTH GM

GUATAMALA
American Chamber of Commerce in Guatemala
Chuck Chambers, Executive Manager
12 Calle 1-25, Zona 10
Edificio Giminis 10, Torre Norte
12 Nivel, Oficina 1206
Guatamala, Guatamala
Telephone (5022) 353 355
Fax (5022) 353 372

HONDURAS
Honduran-American Chamber of Commerce
Sonia De Aguero, CEO and General Manager
Hotel Honduras Maya, Apartado Postal 1838
Tegucigalpa, Honduras
Telephone (504) 32-7043
Fax (504) 32-2031

Honduran-American Chamber of Commerce
San Pedro Sula Branch
Ingrid Delgado, Office Manager
Centro Bella Aurora
6 Avenida, 13-14 Calles, N.O.
San Pedro Sula, Honduras
Telephone (504) 58-0164
Fax (504) 52-2401

HONG KONG
American Chamber of Commerce in Hong Kong
Frank Martin, President
1030 Swire House, Chater Road
Hong Kong
Telephone (852) 526-0165
Fax (852)-810-1289
Telex 83664 AMCC HX

HUNGARY
American Chamber of Commerce in Hungary
Peter Fath, Executive Director
Dozsa Gyorgy ut 84/A Room 222
1068 Budapest, Hungary
Telephone (361) 142 7518
Fax (361) 269 6016

INDIA
American Chamber of Commerce in India
Alka Kapur, Administrative Executive
Mohan Dev Building, 11th Floor
13 Tolstoy Marg
New Delhi 110 001, India
Telephone (91) 11 332-2723
Fax (91) 11 371-2827

INDONESIA
American Chamber of Commerce in Indonesia
Carol Walker, Executive Director
The Landmark Centre, 22nd Floor, Suite 2204
Jl. Jendral Sudirman
Jakarta, Indonesia
Telephone (62) (21) 571-0800, ext. 2222
Fax (62) (21) 571-0656
Telex 62822 LMARK IA

IRELAND
United States Chamber of Commerce in Ireland
Executive Director
20 College Green
Dublin 2, Ireland
Telephone (353) 1-679-3733
Fax (353) 1 679-3402

ISRAEL
Israel-American Chamber of Commerce and Industry
Nina Admoni, Executive Director
35 Shaul Hamelech Blvd.
64927 Tel Aviv, Israel
Telephone (972) 3 695 2341
Fax (972) 3 695 1272

ITALY
American Chamber of Commerce in Italy
Sergio Minoretti, Managing Director
Via Cantu 1
20123 Milano, Italy
Telephone (39) 2 86 90 661
Fax (39) 2 80 57 737

IVORY COAST
American Chamber of Commerce - Ivory Coast
Margaret Hanson-Muse, Secretary
01 B.P. 3394
Abidjan 01, Ivory Coast
Telephone (225) 21-46-16
Fax (225) 22-24-37
Telex 22435 DAMCI

JAMAICA
American Chamber of Commerce in Jamaica
Dr. Ofe S. Dudley, Executive Director
The Wyndham Hotel
77 Knutsford Blvd.
Kingston 5, Jamaica
Telephone 1 (809) 926-7866/67
Fax 1 (809) 929-8597

American Chambers Abroad

JAPAN
American Chamber of Commerce in Japan
William R. Farrell, Executive Director
Bridgestone Toranomon Bldg., 5/F
3-25-2 Toranomon, Minato-ku
Tokyo 105, Japan
Telephone (8133) 433-5381
Fax (8133) 436-1446

American Chamber of Commerce in Japan - Okinawa
Emi McDaniel, Executive Secretary
P.O. Box 235
Okinawa City 904, Japan
Telephone (819) 889-8935-2684
Telex J79828 SHEROKA

KOREA, REPUBLIC OF (SOUTH KOREA)
American Chamber of Commerce in Korea
William C. Oberlin, Executive Vice President
Room 307, Chosun Hotel
Seoul, Korea
Telephone (822) 753-6471/6516
Fax (822) 755-6577
Telex 23745; 28432 CHOSUN

LATVIA
American Chamber of Commerce in Latvia
Executive Director
Jauniela 24, Room 205
Riga, Republic of Latvia
Telephone 371-2-215-205
Fax 371-882-0090

MALAYSIA
American Malaysian Chamber of Commerce
Amb. John Hawes, Executive Director
15.01 Lev 15th, Amoda/22 Jalan Imbi
55100 Kuala Lumpur, Malaysia
Telephone (603) 248-2407/2540
Fax (603) 242-8540

MEXICO
American Chamber of Commerce of Mexico, A.C.
John M. Bruton, Executive Vice President
P.O. Box 60326, Apdo. 113
Houston, TX 77205-1794
Telephone (525) 724-3800
Fax (525) 703-3908

American Chamber of Commerce of Mexico
Guadalajara Branch
Laura Saucedo, Executive Director
Avda. Moctezuma #442
Col. Jardines del Sol
45050 Zapopan, Jalisco, Mexico
Telephone (5236) 34-6606
Fax (5236) 34-7374

American Chamber of Commerce of Mexico
Monterrey Branch
John K. Barrett, Executive Director
Picachos 760, Despachos 4 y 6
Colonia Obispado
Monterrey, Nuevo Leon, Mexico
Telephone (5283) 48-7141/4749
Fax (5283) 4855-74

MOROCCO
American Chamber of Commerce in Morocco
Ms. Rabea El Alama, Executive Director
18, Rue Colbert
Casablanca 01, Morocco
Telephone (212) 2 31-14-48
Fax (212) 2 31-66-07

NETHERLANDS
American Chamber of Commerce in the Netherlands
Kees Burgersdijk, Executive Officer
Carnegieplein 5
2517 KJ The Hague, The Netherlands
Telephone (31) 70 3 65 98 08
Fax (31) 70 3 64 69 92

NEW ZEALAND
American Chamber of Commerce in New Zealand
John W. Lavelle, Executive Director
P.O. Box 106-002 Downtown
Auckland 1001, New Zealand
Telephone (64) 09 3099140
Fax (64) 09 3091090

NICARAGUA
American Chamber of Commerce of Nicaragua
Susan De Aguerri, Executive Director
Apartado 202
Managua, Nicaragua
Telephone (5052) 67-30-99
Fax (5052) 67-30-98

NORWAY
American Club in Oslo
Sigmund L. Lovold, Secretary General
Ing. Hoels Vei 13, P.O. Box 56
N-1346, Gjettum, Norway
Telephone (47) 67-54-6880
Fax (47) 67-54-6930

PAKISTAN
American Business Council of Pakistan
S. Rafit Ali Hashmi, Secretary
NIC Bldg., 6th Floor
Abbasi Shaheed Road
GPO Box 1322
Karachi 74000, Pakistan
Telephone (92) 21-526 436
Fax (92) 21-568-3935
Telex (952) 23-287 CIGNA PK

PANAMA
American Chamber of Commerce and Industry of Panama
Fred Denton, Executive Director
Apdo. 168, Estafeta Balboa
Panama, Republica de Panama
Telephone (507) 69-3881
Fax (507) 23-3508

PARAGUAY
Paraguayan-American Chamber of Commerce
George Murphy-Lee, Manager
Edif. El Faro International Piso 4
Asuncion, Paraguay
Telephone (595-21) 442-135/136
Fax (595-21) 442-135

PERU
American Chamber of Commerce of Peru
Michael Donovan, General Manager
Av. Ricardo Palma 836, Miraflores
Lima 18, Peru
Telephone (5114) 47-9349
Fax (5114) 47-9352

PHILIPPINES
American Chamber of Commerce of the Philippines
Robert M. Sears, Executive Director
P.O. Box 1578, MCC
Manila, The Philippines
Telephone (632) 818-7911
Fax (632) 816-6359

POLAND
American Chamber of Commerce in Poland
Michael G. Arsenault, Director
36, Swietokrzyska Street, Room 6
00-116 Warsaw, Poland
Telephone (48-22) 209-867
Fax (48-2) 622-5525

PORTUGAL
American Chamber of Commerce in Portugal
Dr. Henrique M. Brito do Rio, Secretary General
Rua de D. Estefania, 155, 5 Esq.
Lisbon P-1000, Portugal
Telephone (351) 1 57 25 61
Fax (351) 1 57 25 80
Telex 42356 AMCHAM P

SAUDI ARABIA
American Businessmen's Association, Eastern Province
John M. McNamara, President
P.O. Box 88
Dhahran, Saudi Arabia 31932
Telephone (966) 3 857-6464
Fax (966) 3 873-8883

American Businessmen of Jeddah
Russ Snyder, President
Hyatt Regency-Jeddah
P.O. Box 8483
Jeddah 21482, Saudi Arabia
Telephone (966) 2-652-1234, ext. 1759
Fax (966) 2-651-6260

American Businessmen's Group of Riyadh
W. T. Ritchie, Chairman
P.O. Box 3050
Riyadh 11471, Saudi Arabia 07045
Telephone (966) 1-477-7341
Fax (966) 1-478-7682
Telex 401950

SINGAPORE
American Business Council of Singapore
Donne Petito, Executive Director
Scotts Road #16-07 Shaw Center
Singapore 0922
Telephone (65) 235-0077
Fax (65) 732-5917

SOUTH AFRICA
American Chamber of Commerce in South Africa
Executive Director
P.O. Box 62280
2107 Marshalltown, South Africa
Telephone (27) 11-788-0265/6
Fax (27) 11-880-1632

SPAIN
American Chamber of Commerce in Spain
Jose A. Manrique, Executive Director
Avda. Diagonal 477
08036 Barcelona, Spain
Telephone (34) 3 405 12 66
Fax (34) 3 405 31 24

American Chamber of Commerce in Spain
Madrid Branch
Maria Nieves Hermida, Assistant Executive Director
Hotel EuroBuilding
Padre Damian 23
28036 Madrid, Spain
Telephone (34) 1 458-65 59
Fax (34) 1 458-65 20

SRI LANKA
American Chamber of Commerce of Sri Lanka
Sarath Devapura, Executive Director
P.O. Box 1000, Lotus Road
Colombo Hilton, 3rd Floor
Colombo 1, Sri Lanka
Telephone (94) 1-54-4644, ext 2318
Fax (94) 1-437-165

SWEDEN
American Chamber of Commerce in Sweden
Marianne Raidna Wali, Executive Director
Box 5512
114 85 Stockholm, Sweden
Telephone (46) 8 666 11 00
Fax (48) 8 662 8884

SWITZERLAND
Swiss-American Chamber of Commerce
Walter H. Diggelmann, Executive Director
Talacker 41
8001 Zurich, Switzerland
Telephone (41) 1 211 24 54
Fax (41) 1 211 95 72
Telex 813448 IPCO CH

TAIWAN, REPUBLIC OF CHINA
American Chamber of Commerce, Kaohsiung
Executive Director
123-3, Ta-Pei Road, 1st Floor, #1-1
Niao Sung Hsiang
Kaohsiung County 83305, Taiwan
Republic of China
Telephone (886) 07 731-3712
Fax (886) 07 731-3712

American Chamber of Commerce, Taipei
Lynn M. Sien, Executive Director
Room 1012-Chia Hsin Building Annex
96 Chung Shan N. Road, Section 2
Taipei, Taiwan
Telephone (886) 02 581-7089
Fax (886) 02 542-3376

THAILAND
American Chamber of Commerce in Thailand
Thomas A. Seale, Executive Director
P.O. Box 1095
140 Wireless Road
7th Floor, Kian Gwan Building I
Bangkok, Thailand
Telephone (662) 251-9266
Fax (662) 255-2454
Telex 82828 KGCOM TH

TRINIDAD/TOBAGO
American Chamber of Commerce on Trinidad & Tobago
June Maharaj, Executive Director
Hilton International, Upper Arcade
Lady Yoiund Road
Port of Spain, Trinidad & Tobago
Telephone (809) 624-3211
Fax (809) 627-8570

TURKEY
Turkish-American Businessmen's Association
Semra Korpe, Manager
Fahri Gizdem Sokak 22/5
80280 Gayrettepe, Istanbul, Turkey
Telephone (901) 274-2824/288-6212
Fax (901) 275-9316

Turkish-American Businessmen's Association
Ankara Branch
Inci Goncuoglu/Fatma Gul Tuncer, Managers
Farabi Sok. 12/8
06680 Cankaya, Anakara, Turkey
Telephone (90) 41 28 06 89 or 67 14 10
Fax (90) 41 67 27 44

Turkish-American Businessmen's Association
Bursa Branch
Jean Karslioglu, Manager
Organize Sanayi Bolgesi
Yesil Cad. No. 21
16080 Bursa, Turkey
Telephone (90) 24 33 12 43 or 30 00 11
Fax (90) 24 43 04 66

Turkish-American Businessmen's Association
Gaziantep Branch
Abdullah Tautak, Secretary General
Ataturk Cad. 49/4
Gaziantep, Turkey
Telephone (90) 85 10 14 14
Fax (90) 85 10 14 16

Turkish-American Businessmen's Association
Izmir Branch
Nese Agaoglu, Manager
Pasaport, Cumhuriyet Blvd. 87/1
35210 Izmir, Turkey
Telephone (90) 51 13 39 75
Fax (90) 51 25 67 27

Turkish-American Businessmen's Association
Izmir Branch
Gures Carkoglu, General Secretary
Altay Is Merkezi 601
Sazir Esref Bulvari No. 18
Izmir 35250, Turkey
Telephone (90) 51 41 40 68/70
Fax (90) 51 41 40 69

Turkish-American Businessmen's Association
Trabzon Branch
Orhan Cakir, Chairman
Siramagazalar 25/2
6110 Trabzon, Turkey
Telephone (90) 31 131-30/137-69
Fax (90) 31 248-07

Turkish-American Businessmen's Association
U.S. Branch (Florida)
Banu Yaylali, Manager
3121 Commodore Plaza, Coconut Grove
Miami, FL 33133
Telephone (305) 445-6344
Fax (305) 445-8559

Turkish-American Businessmen's Association
U.S. Branch (Midwestern Region)
Sabit M. Tairov, Chairman
8501 W. 191 Street
Mokena, IL 60448
Telephone/Fax (815) 469-3071

Turkish-American Businessmen's Association
U.S. Branch (Texas)
Sengul Cakir, Manager
16920 Kuykendahl, Suite 228
Houston, TX 77068
Telephone (713) 583-2900
Fax (713) 585-7600

UKRAINE
American Chamber of Commerce in Ukraine
Ivan Komar, Executive Director
7 Kudriavsky Uzviv, 2nd Floor
Kiev 252053, Ukraine
Telephone (7044) 417-1015
Fax (7044) 416-9841

UNITED ARAB EMIRATES
American Business Council of Dubai/Northern Emirates
Jodie H. Golden, Executive Director
International Trade Center, Suite 1610
P.O. Box 9281
Dubai, United Arab Emirates
Telephone (971) 4 314 735
Fax (971) 4 314 227

UNITED KINGDOM
American Chamber of Commerce of the United Kingdom
Robert E. Brunck, Director General
75 Brook Street
London WIY 2EB, England
Telephone (44) 71 493 03 81
Fax (44) 71 493 23 94
Telex 23675 AMCHAM

URUGUAY
Chamber of Commerce Uruguay - U.S.A.
Carlos Boubet, Manager
Calle Bartolome Mitre 1337
Casilla de Correo 809
Montevideo, Uruguay
Telephone (5982) 95 90 59/48
Fax (5982) 95 90 59

VENEZUELA
Venezuelan-American Chamber of Commerce and Industry
Dr. Antonio Herrera-Vaillant, Vice President and General Manager
Torre Credival, Piso 10
2da Avenida de Campo Alegre
Apartado 5181
Caracas 1010-A, Venezuela
Telephone (582) 263-0833
Fax (582) 263-0586

White (Tiger) International

White Tiger International markets TWO ENVIRONMENTALLY SAFE, ENERGY SAVING technologies worldwide. Target: Construction Projects.

(1) LOW INCOME HOUSING OR STRUCTURES, IN COUNTRY MANUFACTURING: SAVES ENERGY 50%

This high speed, low cost technology is available for licensing agreements for housing, retail and commercial applications. Designed to outperform conventional construction, our systems provide the owners with incredible safety and protection from natures forces. Engineered to resist hurricanes, earthquakes, fires and extreme climates. This system uses NO WOOD. Instead we use recyled materials such as straw, rice, dried garbage, volcanic ash, sugar cane, etc. etc. (The strength engineered into the components exceeds U.S. building codes.)

* Stacks 4 Stories High	* No CFC's	* 50% Less Heating/Cooling
* Resists 200 m.p.h. Winds	* Will Not Mildew	* High Thermal Efficiency
* Build on Any Ground	* Waterproof	* Design Flexibility
* Over Water or Hillsides	* Relocatable	* Insect/Rodent Proof
* Uses Recycled Materials	* Fire Resistant	* Insurable for Hurricanes

Type I system utilizes cement composite materials forming solid panel walls with structural steel studs. Type II system utilizes structural steel studs, fiber cement facings and injected structural polyurethane foam for the ultimate insulation and strength characteristics. Infinite design flexibility from component parts. These designs make our systems ideally suited for large scale development projects and can be finished in any architectural style.

Factories can produce up to 10,000 homes per year.

(2) ENERGY SAVING CERAMIC PAINTS: SAVES ENERGY OR FUEL 25%

An energy-saving, insulating ceramic paint for roofs, interior or exterior walls, pool decking, runways and highways and petroleum tanks. This high performing product is designed for climates of all types. These heat resistant paints and waterproofing systems are also used to reduce heat gain on petroleum tanks and refrigerated trucks. Reduce labor, maintenance and product investment. Costs are returned in savings. Use for residential, commercial, industrial and governmental structures. SUPPORTS THE '94 U.S. ENERGY POLICY ACT and sold in all worldwide markets to distributors interested in product or technology transfer licensing agreements. FAX: SERIOUS INQUIRIES TO 619-453-7335.

* Environmentally Safe	* Low VOC's	* No Cracking
* Elastomeric	* Class A Fire Rating	* No Mildew
* High Performance	* ASTM & FAA Tested	* No Oxidation
* High Emittance	* USDA Approved	* No Yellowing
* High Reflectance	* No Flaking	* No Co-Solvents

Manufactured in White, 150 Colors, Shipped in gallons, five or fifty-five gallon drums or containers. Ten Year Warranty on most products if applied by specifications.

7770 Regents Rd. Suite 113 • San Diego, CA 92122 • 619-457-2585 • Fax: 619-453-7335

International Trade Associations in California

Air Transport Association
Karen Mills-Alston, Director
Government Affairs Office
8939 South Sepulveda Boulevard, Suite 408
Los Angeles, CA 90045
(213) 670-5183

American Electronics Association
Richard J. Iverson, President
P.O. Box 54990
Santa Clara, CA 95056-0990
(408) 987-4200
(408) 970-8565

American Institute for International Steel, Inc.
Pacific Chapter
3808 West Riverside Drive, Suite 600
Burbank, CA 91505-4360
(818) 841-7477
Fax (818) 841-7484

California Central Coast World Trade Center
Thomas Rainey, Executive Director
Shawn Gallegly, Assistant Director
300 Esplanade Drive, Suite 1010
Oxnard, CA 93030
(805) 988-1406
Fax (805) 988-1862

California Council for International Trade
Martina H. Johnson, Executive Director
700 Montgomery Street, Suite 305
San Francisco, CA 94111
(415) 788-4127

California Institute
Jan Denton, Executive Director
419 New Jersey Avenue, S.E.
Washington, D.C. 20003
(202) 546-2390
Fax (202) 546-3700

California-Southeast Asia Business Council
Jeremy Potash, Executive Director
1946 Embarcadero #200
Oakland, CA 94606
(510) 536-1967
Fax (510) 261-9598

Center for the New West
Steve PonTell, Senior Fellow
224 East La Deney Drive
Ontario, CA 91764

The Commonwealth Club of California
James D. Rosenthal, Executive Director
595 Market Street, 2nd Floor
San Francisco, CA 94105
(415) 597-6700

Contra Costa Council
Diane Longshore, Executive Director
1 Annabel Lane, Suite 214
San Ramon, CA 94583
(510) 866-6666

Credit Managers Association of California
Northern California/San Leandro Branch Office
10800 Bigge Street
P.O. Box 1838
San Leandro, CA 94577-9922
(510) 632-7500
Fax (510) 632-9677

Credit Managers Association of Northern California
40 East Verdugo Avenue
Burbank, CA 91502-1931
(818) 972-5300
Fax (818) 972-5301

Customs Brokers and Forwarders Association of Northern California
Jeremy W. Potash, Executive Director
P.O. Box 26269
San Francisco, CA 94126-6269
(510) 536-2233

East Bay SBDC
Selma Taylor, Project Manager
2201 Broadway, Suite 701
Oakland, CA 94612
(510) 893-4117

Export Legal Assistance Network (ELAN)
Los Angeles: Michael R. Doram, (213) 386-1383;
San Francisco: Harry B. Endsley, (415) 296-1141;
San Diego: Harold Pope, (619) 546-2944;
Sacramento: Mark F. Johannsen, (916) 443-5292;
National Coordinator: (202) 778-3080.

Export Managers Association
Laura F. MacLellan, President
110 East 9th Street, Suite A669
Los Angeles, CA 90079
(213) 892-1388
Fax (213) 892-0087

Export Small Business Development Center
of Southern California
Gladys Moreau, Director
110 East 9th Street, Suite A669
Los Angeles, CA 90079
(213) 892-1111
Fax (213) 892-8232

Export Small Business Development Center
Santa Barbara/Ventura Satellite Office
300 Esplanade Drive, Suite 1020
Oxnard, CA 93030
(805) 981-4633
Fax (805) 981-0087

Foreign Trade Association of Southern California
Jay K. Winter, Executive Secretary
900 Wilshire Boulevard, Suite 1434
Los Angeles, CA 90017
(213) 627-0634
Fax (213) 627-0398

Global Trading Center of Sillicon Valley
James Stocker
5201 Great America Parkway, Suite 441
Santa Clara, CA 95054
(408) 562-5717
Fax (408) 562-5704

Harbor Transportation Club
P.O. Box 4250
Sunland, CA 91041
(818) 951-2842
Fax (818) 353-5976

Inland International Trade Association, Inc.
Kelsey Olson, President
c/o Center for International Trade Development
1787 Tribute Road, Suite A
Sacramento, CA 95815
(916) 263-6578
Fax (916) 263-6571

Inland Empire International Business Association
William F. Gavitt, President
12626 Frederick Street, Suite I-5 #276
Moreno Valley, CA 92553
(909) 782-7276
Fax (909) 780-6341

Inland Pacific World Trade Committee
c/o Ontario Chamber of Commerce
421 North Euclid
Ontario, CA 91762
(714) 984-2458
Fax (714) 984-6439

International Business Association
Legislative Committee
Thomas A. Russell, Chair
200 Oceangate, Suite 700
Long Beach, CA 90802-4333
(213) 495-6000
Fax (213) 435-1359

International Business Association of Southern California
c/o Long Beach Chamber of Commerce
Pamela Andrews, Vice President
One World Trade Center, Suite 350
Long Beach, CA 90831-0350
(310) 436-1251
Fax (310) 436-7099

International Business Council
c/o Century City Chamber of Commerce
2049 Century Park East, Suite 460
Los Angeles, CA 90067
(310) 553-2222
Fax (310) 553-4623

International Commerce Council
c/o Los Angeles Area Chamber of Commerce
350 South Bixel Street
Los Angeles, CA 90017
(213) 580-7551
Fax (213) 580-7511

International Trade Club of Southern California
P.O. Box 21286
Long Beach, CA 90801
(213) 380-3770
Fax (213) 380-3987

The International Trade Council
of the Greater Bay Region
465 California Street, 9th Floor
San Francisco, CA 94104
(415) 979-8864

Los Angeles Air Cargo Association
Michael Mastroguisseppe
P.O. Box 90512, Airport Station
Los Angeles, CA 90009
(310) 649-6515

Los Angeles Customs and Freight Brokers Association
Brenda Stringfield, President
Monika Wegener, Executive Director
P.O. Box 4250
Sunland, CA 91041
(818) 951-2842
Fax (818) 253-5976

Los Angeles World Affairs Council
911 Wilshire Blvd., Suite 1730
Los Angeles, CA 90017
(213) 628-2332
Fax (213) 628-1057

Greater Los Angeles World Trade Center Association
Merry A. Tuten, President & CEO
One World Trade Center, Suite 295
Long Beach, CA 90831-0295
(310) 495-7070
Fax (310) 495-7071

Marine Exchange of the San Francisco Bay Region
Terry Hunter, Executive Director
Fort Mason Center, Suite 325
San Francisco, CA 94123
(415) 441-6600

Monterey Bay International Trade Association
Tony Livoti
P.O. Box 523
Santa Cruz, CA 95061
(408) 464-8585
Fax (408) 464-0558

North Bay World Trade Association
P.O. Box 4468
Santa Rosa, CA 95402-4468
(707) 527-2406

Northern California District Export Council (NORCALDEC)
U.S. Department of Commerce
442 Post Street, Suite 800
San Francisco, CA 94102
(415) 433-9084
Fax (415) 421-1697

Oakland World Trade Association
Dan Westerlin, President
475 14th Street
Oakland, CA 94612-1928
(510) 272-1353
Fax (510) 839-3458

Pacific Merchant Shipping Association
1 Kaiser Plaza, Suite 420
Oakland, CA 94612
(510) 839-9560
Fax (510) 839-2980

SRI International
World Business Division
Karen Yorke
333 Ravenswood Avenue
Menlo Park, CA 94025
(415) 326-6200

San Diego District Export Council
c/o U.S. Department of Commerce
Michael Pearlman, Chairman
6363 Greenwich Drive, Suite 230
San Diego, CA 92122
(619) 557-5395
Fax (619) 557-6176

San Diego Economic Development Corporation
Daniel O. Pegg, President
701 B Street, Suite 1850
San Diego, CA 92101
(619) 234-8484
Fax (619) 234-1935

San Francisco International Trade Council
Dana Marak, President
465 California Street
San Francisco, CA 94014
(415) 795-6673
Fax (415) 285-9624

San Francisco Global Trade Council
Harry Orbelian, President & Founder
114 Sansome Street, Suite 1103
San Francisco, CA 94104
(415) 395-9100
Fax (415) 395-9911

San Francisco World Trade Association
c/o San Francisco Chamber of Commerce
Rhea Serpan, President
Anastasia Scourkes, International Program Manager
465 California Street, 9th Floor
San Francisco, CA 94104
(415) 392-4520

San Joaquin Valley International Trade Association
c/o Fresno City College
390 W. Fir Avenue
Clovis, CA 93612
(209) 323-4689

San Mateo County Economic Development Association
Denise de Ville
901 Mariners Island Boulevard, Suite 265
San Mateo, CA 94404
(415) 345-8300
Fax (415) 345-6896

Santa Clara Valley World Trade Association
Tzitza Bozinovich, President
and Chief Executive Officer
P.O. Box 4180
Santa Clara, CA 95056-4180
(408) 986-1406
Fax (408) 988-0150

Semiconductor Equipment and Materials International
Bill Reed, Chief Executive
805 East Middlefield Road
Mountainview, CA 94043
(415) 964-5111
Fax (415) 967-5375

Semiconductor Industry Association
Helen Harris, Director of Trade
4300 Stevens Creek Boulevard, Suite 271
San Jose, CA 95129
(408) 246-2711

Southern California Coordinating Council
c/o Los Angeles Area Chamber of Commerce
350 South Bixel Street
Los Angeles, CA 90017
(213) 580-7551
Fax (213) 580-7511

Southern California District Export Council
Paul Leinenbach, Chair
c/o U.S. Department of Commerce
11000 Wilshire Boulevard, Room 9200
Los Angeles, CA 90024
(310) 235-7115
Fax (310) 235-7220

Steamship Association of Southern California
Maggy Huson, Coordinator
900 Wilshire Boulevard, Suite 1434
Los Angeles, CA 90017
(213) 627-0634

U.S. Council for International Business
Branch Office/ATA Carnet Agents
Tamara Chong, Carnet Clerk
353 Sacramento Street, Suite 700
San Francisco, CA 94111
(415) 433-6464

Valley International Trade Association
P.O. Box 844
Van Nuys, CA 91408
(818) 346-5620

Ventura County Economic Development Association
Nancy Williams, Executive Director
500 Esplanade Drive, Suite 810
Oxnard, CA 93030
(805) 988-1106
Fax (805) 988-1027

Women in International Trade
Northern California
Simone S. Platman, President
P.O. Box 192922
San Francisco, CA 94119-2922
(415) 984-5000 (voice mail)
Fax (415) 661-4320

Women in International Trade
Sacramento
Janice Long, Chair
(916) 985-4871

Women in International Trade
Silicon Valley
Margaret Kahnke, Chair
(408) 452-6545
Darcelle Matsow
(408) 984-5453
Phoenix Technologies
Fax (408) 452-1985

Women in International Trade
San Francisco
Celia Mathews, Chair
(415) 904-8250
Fritz Companies Inc.
Fax (415) 904-8326

Women in World Trade
Orange County
3972 Barranca Parkway, Suite J-200
Irvine, CA 92714
(714) 852-6025

Women in World Trade
San Diego
Karen R. Hennequin, President
4750 70th Street, Suite 51
La Mesa, CA 92041

World Affairs Council
President
312 Sutter Street, Suite 200
San Francisco, CA 94108
(415) 982-2541
Fax (415) 982-5028

World Trade Association of the Inland Empire/Ontario
I. Monte Radlovic, President
427 North Euclid Avenue
Ontario, CA 91762
(714) 983-1615

World Trade Center San Diego
Robert Plotkin, President
6363 Greenwich Drive, Suite 215
San Diego, CA 92122
(619) 453-4605
Fax (619) 453-1907

**World Trade Center Association
of Orange County**
Donald A. Miller, President
Colleen E. Costello, Director of Member Services
One Park Plaza, Suite 150
Irvine, CA 92714
(714) 724-9822
Fax (714) 752-8723

World Trade Center of San Francisco
Stanley Herzstein, President
345 California Street, 7th Floor
San Francisco, CA 94104
(415) 392-2705
Fax (415) 392-1710

World Trade Week
c/o Los Angeles Area Chamber of Commerce
350 South Bixel Street
Los Angeles, CA 90017
(213) 580-7581
Fax (213) 580-7511

California State University Los Angeles

ACLP

Study Intensive English in Southern California

- TOEFL Preparation and Academic Counseling
- University Preparation and "ACCEPTANCE WITH CONDITION"
- Orientation to American Culture
- Field Trips to Southern California Attractions
- Conversational and Business English
- Excellent ESL instruction

I-20s Issued • On Campus Housing Available

"It's the Best" -Yumi Goto

American Culture and Language Program California State University, Los Angeles
5151 State University Dr., Library North B552, Los Angeles, CA 90032-8619
TELEPHONE (213) 343-4840   FAX (213) 343-4954

Certificate in International Business

USD, Continuing Education sponsors a certificate program for professionals interested in gaining a better understanding of the complexities of international business. The series integrates international research, case studies and experience. The certificate requires the completion of 7 one-month courses. Each of these courses include 12-contact hours taught in four 3-hour evening meetings (typically Wednesdays 6:30 to 9:30 p.m.). The courses are taught by faculty from USD and professionals from industry and government.

Some courses offered through the series include:
- ❑ Global Marketing
- ❑ International Finance
- ❑ International Economics
- ❑ Global Decision Making
- ❑ Global Human Resource Management
- ❑ Legal Aspects of International Business
- ❑ Exporting & Importing Strategies
- ❑ Japan/US Comparative Management
- ❑ EC 1992/1993
- ❑ and many more....

USD
University of San Diego

For more information on USD Certificate Programs and Seminars, please call 619-260-4644.

International Programs within California Education
(Public/Private)

Agriculture Business and Trade Center for International
Trade Development
Gordon Spencer, Director
301 West 18th Street, #203
Merced, CA 95340
(209) 384-9268
Fax (209) 384-5892

Cal Poly Pomona Business Education Center
Professor Jerry Rogers, International Business Management
Administration Building, Suite 6
Cal Poly Pomona
3801 West Temple Avenue
Pomona, CA 91768-4083
(714) 869-2425
Fax (714) 869-4353

Ed Net
Ray Raymond, Ph.D., Director, International Trade
5202 Kings Pine Road
Rolling Hills, CA 90274
(310) 373-3098
Fax (310) 375-6343

California State University, Chico
University Center for Economic Development and Planning
Chico, CA 95929-0765
(916) 898-4598
Fax (916) 898-6824

California State University, Fullerton
Department of Marketing & International Business
Dr. Irene Lange
800 North State College Boulevard
Fullerton, CA 92634
(714) 773-2223

California State University, Hayward
School of Business and Economics
International Business
Student Service Center
Hayward, CA 94543
(415) 881-3323

California State University, Long Beach
International program for all state universities
Dr. Richard L. Sulter
400 Golden Shore, Suite 300
Long Beach, CA 90802-4275
(310) 985-2831

California State University, Los Angeles
American Culture and Language Program (ACLP)
Sally Gardner, Director
5151 State University Drive
Los Angeles, CA 90032
(213) 343-4840

California State University, San Francisco
Graduate School of Business
International Business
1600 Holloway Avenue
San Francisco, CA 94132
(415) 338-1279

The Claremont Institute
Asian Studies Center
250 West First Street, Suite 330
Claremont, CA 91711
(909) 621-6825

San Diego State University - BAM 428
Center for International Business Education and Research
(CIBER)
Alvord Branan, Michael Hergert, Co-Directors
5500 Campanile Drive
San Diego, CA 92182-7732
(619) 594-6023
Fax (619) 594-7738

**Community College International Trade Programs
& Resource Centers**
Each Center for International Trade Development **(CITD)**
offers one-on-one couseling, technical assistance in the
areas of management, marketing, financing, regulations and
taxation, information dissemination (trade leads, country
reports and additional overseas market research), resource
and referral services, and basic training workshops, seminars and short courses.

CITD-Citrus College
Ralph Jagodka, Director
375 S. Main Street #101
Pomona, CA 91766
(909) 629-2247
Fax (909) 397-5769

CITD-Coastline Community College
17200 Jamboree Road, Suite W
Irvine, CA 92714
(714) 863-9356
Fax (714) 863-9355

CITD-East Bay SBDC
Selma Taylor, Project Manager
2201 Broadway, Suite 701
Oakland, CA 94612
(510) 893-4117

CITD-Fresno City College
Candy Hansen, Coordinator
390 West Fir Avenue
Clovis, CA 93612

CITD-Merced College
301 West 18th Street #203
Merced, CA 95340
(209) 384-5892
Fax (209) 384-9268

CITD-Oxnard College
Shawn Gallegly, Manager
300 Esplanade Drive, Suite 1020
Oxnard, CA 93030
(805)485-7332
Fax (805) 988-1862

CITD-Riverside Community College
Kathleen Baros, International Trade Specialist
3638 University Avenue, Suite 250
Riverside, CA 92501
(909) 682-2923
Fax (909) 682-2441

CITD-Sacramento City College
Dale Wright, Manager
1787 Tribute Road, Suite A
Sacramento, CA 95815
(916) 263-6578
Fax (916) 263-6571

CITD-Vista Community College
Guadalupe Lucio, Project Director
2020 Milvia Street, Suite 309
Berkeley, CA 94704
(510) 841-8860, ext. 270
Fax (510) 841-7333

Dominican College
Director of MBA Program
International Business
50 Acacia Avenue
San Rafael, CA 94901-8008
(415) 457-4440

Golden Gate University
International Relations Department
536 Mission Street
San Francisco, CA 94105
(415) 442-7840

John F. Kennedy University
MBA Program
International Business
12 Altarinda Road
Orinda, CA 94563
(415) 254-0200

Monterey Institute of International Studies
International MBA
Dean of International Management
425 Van Buren Street
Monterey, CA 93940
(408) 647-4123

Orange County International Marketing Association
Irene Lange, Ph.D., Department Chair
California State University, Fullerton
Department of Marketing/International Business
800 North State College Boulevard
Fullerton, CA 92634
(714) 773-2223

Small Business Development & International Trade Center-
Southwestern College
Mary Wylie, Director
900 Otay Lakes Road, Building 1600
Chula Vista, CA 91910
(619) 482-6375
Fax (619) 482-6402

St. Mary's College of California
Graduate Business Programs
MBA in International Business
P.O. Box 4240
Moraga, CA 94575
(510) 631-4500
(800) 332-4622

Stanford University
The Bechtel International Center
P.O. Box 5816
Stanford, CA 94309
(415) 725-0887
Fax (415) 725-0886
(A service center for foreign graduate and undergraduate
students, and visiting scholars and researchers.)

U.S. International University, San Diego
International MBA
Mink Stavenga, Dean of Business School
10455 Pomerado Road
San Diego, CA 92131
(619) 693-4695

U.S.-Japan Institute
San Francisco State University
College of Business
Mitsuko Saito Duerr, Director
1600 Holloway Avenue
San Francisco, CA 94132
(415) 338-2448
Fax (415) 338-6237

University of California, Berkeley
Berkeley Roundtable on International Economy
Dr. John Zysman, Director
2234 Piedmont Avenue
Berkeley, CA 94720
(510) 642-3067

University of California, Berkeley
International Business Department
UC Extension
Nikki Fuller, Representative
2223 Fulton Street
Berkeley, CA 94720
(510) 642-4231

University of California, San Diego
Graduate School of International Relations
and Pacific Studies
Brian Daley, External Affairs
La Jolla, CA 92093-0519
(619) 534-2777
Fax (619) 534-3939

University of California, Santa Barbara
International program for all Universities of California
6550 Hollister Avenue
Goleta, CA 93117
(805) 893-4139

University of the Pacific
School of International Studies
Dr. Martin Needler, Dean
George Wilson Hall
Stockton, CA 95211
(209) 946-2650

University of San Francisco
MBA/EMBA Global Management
McLaren School of Business
Gary Williams, Dean
Ignatian Heights
San Francisco, CA 94117
(415) 666-6314
Fax (415) 666-2502

University of Southern California
IBEAR Pacific Rim Management Programs
Jack Lewis, Ph.D., Director
John Windler, Associate Director
Graduate School of Business Administration
Los Angeles, CA 90089-1421
(213) 740-7132
Fax (213) 740-9964

University of Southern California
School of International Relations
Linda Cole, Associate Director
Von Klein Smid Center, #330
Los Angeles, CA 90089-0043
(213) 740-2139
Fax (213) 742-0281

University of Southern California
International Business Education and Research Program
Graduate School of Business Administration
Jack Lewis, Associate Director
Los Angeles, CA 90089-1421
(213) 740-7140

Weller International School of Management
114 Sansome Street
San Francisco, CA 94104
(415) 788-5066

Description: State Government International Programs

California Trade and Commerce Agency

Chapter 1364 (SB 1909 Vuich) statutes of 1992 created the California Trade and Commerce Agency transferring the California State World Trade Commission, the Foreign Trade Offices and the Department of Commerce to the agency.

California State Trade and Commerce Agency
Julie Meier Wright, Secretary
Loren Kaye, Undersecretary
John Poimiroo, Deputy Secretary of Tourism
Kathleen Shanahan, Deputy Secretary for Economic
    Development
Brenda Lopes, Deputy Secretary for International
    Trade and Investment
801 K Street, Suite 1700
Sacramento, CA 95814
(916) 322-1394
Fax (916) 322-3524

International Trade and Investment Division
Brenda Lopes, Deputy Secretary
Anne Chadwick, Manager, Agricultural Trade Policy
Paul Oliva, Senior Policy Analyst
Lloyd Day, Trade Analyst
Gabriel Aguilera, Research Analyst
Tami Ele, Executive Secretary
801 K Street, Suite 1700
Sacramento, CA 95814
(916) 324-5511
Fax (916) 324-5791

California State World Trade Commission

The California State World Trade Commission, established in 1983, is an advisory body to the Secretary of the Trade and Commerce Agency.

California State World Trade Commission
California Trade and Commerce Agency
Robert T. Monagan, Chair
Brenda Lopes, Executive Director
801 K Street, Suite 1700
Sacramento, CA 95814
(916) 324-5511
Fax (916) 324-5791

California Export Finance Office

The Export Finance Office provides working capital loan guarantees to financial institutions on behalf of small and medium-sized California companies in support of export transactions. Financial assistance is provided in the form of bank guarantees of up to 90 percent of the loan with a maximum guarantee of $750,000 per transaction. To be eligible, a company must have been in business for one year and total shipments must contain 51 percent California content.

California Export Finance Office
California Trade and Commerce Agency
James Newton, Acting Director
William Jimenez, San Diego Regional Manager
Mark Bertand, Loan Officer
Carolyn Brown, Staff Loan Officer
Michael Stirling, Northern California Regional Manager
Melissa Davis, Assistant Loan Officer
Cheryl Evola, Information Systems Coordinator
Gale Galitz, Executive Assistant
Mounir Ghaly, Staff Loan Officer
6 Centerpointe, Suite 760
La Palma, CA 90623
(714) 562-5519
Fax (714) 562-5530

California Office of Export Development

● Trade Shows. The California Export Development Office organizes California group exhibits at leading foreign trade shows.

● Automated Trade Library Service (ATLS) is a computer-based comprehensive information system available to all California companies. The program allows California exporters immediate access to a network containing market research, trade leads and other valuable information. ATLS has been implemented through a cooperative effort between California's Office of Export Development and the California Agricultural Technology Institute (CATI).

ATLS can be accessed anywhere in the state by using your own computer's modem and dialing a local access number. These access numbers or gateways, are located at 21 campuses of the California State University System and will link your computer to the system's host computer located on the campus of California State University, Fresno. As part of CATI's Advanced Technology Information Network (ATI-NET), ATLS is accessible 24 hours a day, 365 days a year.

Country and industry-specific research, foreign trade leads, announcements of local trade seminars and foreign trade shows, descriptions of government programs and a trade reference index are all available on ATLS. There is no cost to individuals or companies participating in the trade library program — no fees, no monthly charges and no cost for information retrieval. Most users can acess the ATI-NET with just a local, toll-free phone call to a nearby CSU campus.

The ATLS system provides on-line enrollment by dialing any of the remote access points listed on this sheet. The ATLS system operates at either 7,1,E or 8,1,N parameter settings. Your individual communications software may perform better at one of these settings. Registered participants will receive a computer-generated login name and password instantly on their screen. For technical support, please contact:

ATI-NET Office, CSU Fresno
2910 East Barstow Avenue
Fresno, CA 93740-0115
Tel: (209) 278-4872
Fax: (209) 278-4849

Remote Access Instructions:

1. Dial the nearest access point using your modem.
2. At the "please enter CSUnet Access Code" prompt, you should respond by typing: atls.
3. At "login" prompt, tap the RETURN key.
4. At the second "login" prompt, type your login name (in lower case) and hit the RETURN key and then your password at the "password" prompt. If you are a first time user, type public at the "login" prompt. This public login allows you to browse the system for 15 minutes and, as a first time user, will give you on-line registration instructions.
5. As a registered user, you may hang up and login again with your login name and password. Registered users may configure their setup as desired.

Arcata	(707) 822-6205
Bakersfield	(805) 664-0551
Carson	(310) 769-1892
Chico	(916) 894-3033
Fresno (1200)	(209) 278-4265
Fresno (2400)	(209) 278-4615
Fullerton	(714) 526-0334
Hayward	(510) 727-1841
Long Beach	(310) 985-9540
Los Angeles	(213) 225-6028
Mission Viejo	(818) 701-0478
Northridge	(818) 701-0478
Pomona	(909) 595-3779
Rohnert Park	(707) 664-8093
Sacramento	(916) 737-0955
San Bernardino	(909) 880-8833
San Diego	(619) 594-6309
San Francisco	(415) 333-1077
San Jose	(408) 924-1054
San Luis Obispo	(805) 549-9721
San Marcos	(619) 752-7964
Turlock	(209) 632-7522
Ventura	(805) 643-6386

● Publications. The California Export Development Office publishes "made in California" product catalogs and coordinates the development of export directories such as the *California International Trade Register.*

Office of Export Development

Department of International Trade and Investment
California Trade and Commerce Agency
R. Sean Randolph, Director
Gary Lang, Trade Specialist
Larinda Negri, Trade Coordinator
Kimberly Rich, Trade Specialist
Trihn Montrenes, Information Systems Specialist
One World Trade Center, Suite 990
Long Beach, CA 90831
(310) 590-5965
Fax (310) 590-5958

Office of California-Mexico Affairs

The Office of California-Mexico Affairs, established by Chapter 1197 in 1982, consolidated two previous state agencies: the Commission of the Californias and the Southwest Border Regional Conference. Chapter 1197 consolidated the purposes, staff and resources of the two predecessor agencies into two organizational units within the Office.

The primary function of the 18-member Commission of the Californias is the promotion of economic, cultural and educational relations with the regional Mexican government in Baja California and Baja California Sur. The Governor serves as Chairman of the California delegation to the Commission; the Lieutenant Governor serves as Vice Chairman.

The Office of California-Mexico Affairs provides staff support for California's participation in the Southwest Border Regional Conference. The conference is composed of the Governors of California, Texas, Arizona, and New Mexico, and representatives of six Mexican border states. Its purpose is to promote international cooperation in economic, cultural and environmental exchange across the U.S.-Mexican border.

Office of California-Mexico Affairs

California Trade and Commerce Agency
Rudy Fernandez, Director
750 B Street, Suite 1830
San Diego, CA 92101
(619) 645-2660
Fax (619) 645-2663

California Office of Foreign Investment

The Office of Foreign Investment is the lead office for foreign investment promotion, retention and expansion. Its mission is to promote job-creating, revenue-generating investment.

The office focuses on target industries and offers assistance based on a "suitable match" of the needs of individual investors and specific advantages of various California locales. Services include site selection assistance, foreign business advocacy, permit assistance, and technical information and assistance. The marketing strategy is based on direct marketing, advertising, "sales calls" in foreign markets, and inbound investment missions.

Office of Foreign Investment
California Trade and Commerce Agency
Brenda Lopes, Director
Jennifer Stanley, Associate Development Specialist
801 K Street, Suite 1700
Sacramento, CA 95814
(916) 322-3518
Fax (916) 322-3401

California State Foreign Trade and Investment Offices

California has foreign offices operating around the globe promoting state exports, attracting foreign investment to the state, helping California businesses abroad and supporting California's stateside trade and investment programs.

Activities of the offices include:

Trade
- Assisting California exporters with information, advice and appointment setting.
- Responding to trade inquiries.
- Conducting or participating in promotions, trade shows and seminars.
- Assisting California business delegations/trade missions.

Investment
- Outreach to targeted overseas investors.
- Responding to investment inquiries.
- Conducting investment seminars.

Office locations:

Frankfurt
California European Office of Trade and Investment
Trudi Schifter, Director
Bockenheimer Landstrasse 97
60325 Frankfurt am Main
Germany
Telephone (011-49-69) 743-2461
Fax (011-49-69) 745-005

Hong Kong
California Office of Trade and Investment
Elina Lee, Acting Director
Suite 301, St. George's Building
2, Ice House Street
Central, Hong Kong
Telephone (011-852) 2877-3600
Fax (011-852) 2877-2691

Jerusalem
California-Israel Exchange (CIX)
Sherwin Pomerantz, Director
P.O. Box 1671
Jerusalem 91076
Israel
Telephone/Fax (011-972-2) 617-396 or
Telephone/Fax (718) 494-4724 (U.S. Office)

London
California European Office of Trade and Investment
John Cornfield, Deputy Director
27 Dover Street
London W1X 3PA
United Kingdom
Telephone (011-44-71) 629-8211
Fax (011-44-71) 629-8223

Mexico City
California Office of Trade and Investment
Reinhold C. Schrader, Director
c/o U.S. Trade Center
Liverpool #31
Colonia Juarez
06500 Mexico, D.F.
Mexico
Telephone (011-52-5) 546-0199, 546-8697, 546-9092
Fax (011-52-5) 546-0865

After June 1, 1995, the address will be:
California Office of Trade and Investment
Reinhold C. Schrader, Director
Paseo de la Reforma #164
Colonia Juarez
06600 Mexico, D.F.

Sub-Sahara Africa
(Office to be opened)

Taiwan
California Office of Trade and Investment
Chiling Tong, Director
7C04, Taipei World Trade Center
5 Hsinyi Road, Section 5
Taipei 10509
Taiwan
Telephone (011-886-2) 758-6223
Fax (011-886-2) 723-9973

Tokyo
California Office of Trade and Investment
Jon Kaji, Director
Akira Kitagawa, Deputy Director
Kowa 35 Building Annex
1-14-15 Akasaka
Minato-ku, 107
Tokyo, Japan
Telephone (011-81-3) 3583-3140
Fax (011-81-3) 3584-6613

California Office of Tourism

The Office of Tourism plans and directs marketing activities which promote travel to and within California. Mexico, Japan, Canada, the United Kingdom and Germany are the state's primary sources of international visitors. Programs, geared almost exclusively to the travel-trade include: cooperative advertising, brochure distribution, special promotions, trade shows, sales missions, familiarization tours and market research.

California Office of Tourism
California Trade and Commerce Agency
John Poimiroo, Deputy Secretary of Tourism
Caroline Petersen Beteta, Assistant Secretary/Director of
   Tourism Marketing
801 K Street, Suite 1600
Sacramento, CA 95814
(916) 322-2881
Fax (916) 322-3402

Agricultural Export Program

The Agricultural Export Program, operated by the California Department of Food and Agriculture, works to expand California's agricultural exports through:
Trade Development
• Facilitates trade show appearances by California companies and in-store promotions in foreign supermarkets, and conducts California sourcing seminars for overseas buyers.
• Works closely with private industry and commodity organizations to unite widely differing products under a "made in California" grouping.
• Manages federal government resource allocations for the foreign-market promotion of specific California agricultural products
Export Information Resources
The program's on-line database, Agricultural Trade Information Service (ATIS), including auto-fax, alerts California food and agricultural exporters to overseas opportunities by directly matching suppliers with interested buyers. Other services offered are the TRADER database and the Agricultural Export Directory.

Department of Food and Agriculture
Agricultural Export Program
Jim Zion, Program Manager
Fred Klose, Export Specialist
1220 N Street, Room 100
Sacramento, CA 94271-0001
(916) 654-0389
Fax (916) 653-2604

Energy Technology Export Program

The California Energy Commission helps California firms export energy technologies to international markets. The program emphasizes multi-year development projects featuring alternative energy technologies, energy efficiency measures and clean combustion technologies. Developing markets in middle-income nations is the program's primary focus, although market niches exist in Europe, Japan and Canada.

The program's activities include: identifying project opportunities, publishing project trade leads, bringing foreign decisionmakers to California, awarding "seed" funding to California firms for international projects and providing advice to foreign governments on energy policies and programs as a market introduction strategy for California companies.

California Energy Commission
Tim Olson, Program Manager, International
   Programs
1516 9th Street, MS-45
Sacramento, CA 95814-5512
(916) 654-4528
Fax (916) 654-4676

Environmental Technology Export Program

In September 1992, Governor Pete Wilson established the California Environmental Technology Partnership to promote and assist the development, manufacture, use and export of California environmental technologies, products and services. Under the leadership of California's Environmental Protection Agency (Cal/EPA) and the Trade and Commerce Agency, this partnership joins California's public and private sectors to enhance both environmental and economic progress.

A significant component of this partnership is the Environmental Technology Export Program, charged with promoting the export of California's environmental technologies internationally. Promotional activities include:
• Maintaining a directory of California's environmental technology companies interested in exporting (currently more than 1,400 companies);
• Acting as a clearinghouse of environmental technology trade information for domestic sellers and foreign buyers;
• Performing market research studies and soliciting technical advice to identify international market opportunities;
• Participating in technical exchange programs to enhance foreign buyers' awareness and interest in California's environmental technologies;
• Coordinating the activities of domestic and foreign governments to take advantage of trade promotion and financial assistance opportunities to California-based environmental technology companies;
• Leading (or partnering with other agencies on) trade missions and hosting in-bound missions.

Cal/EPA
Environmental Technology Export Program
Jim Graham
Tim Abbott
301 Capitol Mall
P.O. Box 806
Sacramento, CA 95812-0806
(916) 445-2940
Fax (916) 327-4494

California State Government — The Executive Branch

Governor
Pete Wilson

Lieutenant Governor
Gray Davis
445-8994

Secretary of State
Bill Jones
445-6371

Department of Insurance
Chuck Quackenbush
Commissioner
445-5544

State Controller
Kathleen Connell
445-2636

State Treasurer
Matt Fong
653-2894

State Board of Equalization
John Klehs
Chairman
445-4154
Burton W. Oliver
Executive Director
445-6464

Attorney General
Daniel E. Lungren
324-5437

Department of Justice
Daniel E. Lungren
445-9555

Superintendent of Public Instruction
Delaine Eastin
657-5485

Department of Education
657-2451

Governor's Office

Chief of Staff
Bob White 445-2864
Constituent Affairs
Sally McKeag 445-1455
Intergovernmental Affairs
Carol Whiteside 323-5446
Legal Affairs
Daniel Kolkey 445-0873

Deputy Chiefs of Staff
Patricia Clarey 445-8612
George Dunn 445-9947
Kevin Sloat 445-0131

Advance
Fred Bateta 445-6400
Appointments
John Davies 445-1915
Julie Justis
Cabinet
Joe Rodota 445-6131
Communications
Leslie Goodman 445-1682
Emma Suarez 445-1114

Legislative
Kevin Sloat 445-0131
Press
Sean Walsh 445-4571
Special Projects
Alexa Vuksich 445-7097
Scheduling
Margo Reid 445-6533
Trade
Ira Goldman 445-6075

Commission for Economic Development
L.A. (310) 412-6118

California Maritime Academy
(707) 648-4200
Vallejo

Board of Governors, Community Colleges
445-8752

California Board of Education
657-5478

Trustees of State Universities
(310) 985-2500
Long Beach

California Postsecondary Education Commission
445-7933

University of California Board of Regents
(510) 987-9220
Oakland

Agricultural Labor Relations Board
Bruce J. Janigian
Chairman
653-3613

Fair Political Practices Commission
Ravi Mehta
Chairman
322-5660

California Housing Finance Agency
Maureen Higgins
Executive Director
324-4618

California State Lottery
Del Pierce
Interim Director
324-9974

Public Employment Relations Board
Susan Williams-Blair
Chairperson
322-3198

Public Utilities Commission
Daniel W. Fessler
President
S.F. (415) 703-3703

Student Aid Commission
Samuel M. Kipp III
Executive Director
322-1904

State Lands Commission
Robert C. Hight
Executive Officer
322-4105

California Transportation Commission
Robert I. Remen
Executive Director
654-4245

Arts Council
Barbara Pieper
227-2555

Military Department
Tandy Bozeman
Adjutant General
854-3500

State Public Defender
Fern Leathom
322-2676

Secretary of Business, Transportation and Housing Agency
Dean R. Dunphy
323-5401
Jeffrey M. Reid
Undersecretary
323-5410

Secretary of Child Development and Education
Maureen DiMarco
323-0611
Stephen M. Rhoads
Undersecretary
323-0611

Secretary of Environmental Protection Agency
James Strock
445-3846
Jack Pandol, Jr.
Undersecretary
445-3846

Secretary of Health and Welfare Agency
Sandra Smoley
654-3454
Undersecretary
654-3347

Department of Food and Agriculture
Henry J. Voss
Secretary
654-0433
Mike Chrisman
Undersecretary
654-0321

Department of Alcoholic Beverage Control
Jay R. Stroh
Director
263-6900

Department of Corporations
Gary S. Mendoza
Commissioner
L.A. (213) 736-3481

Dept. of Housing & Community Development
Timothy L. Coyle
Director
445-4775

Department of Real Estate
John Liberator
Acting Commissioner
227-0782

Department of Savings and Loan
Keith Bishop
Commissioner
L.A. (213) 897-8202
323-5406

Department of State Banking
Stan Cardenas
Acting Superintendent
322-5966
S.F. (415) 557-3535

California Highway Patrol
Maurice J. Hannigan
Commissioner
657-7152

Department of Motor Vehicles
Frank Zolin
Director
657-6940

Office of Real Estate Appraisers
Bob West
Director
322-0097

Stephen P. Teale Data Center
Chong W. Ha
Director
263-1816

Department of Transportation
James W. van Loben Sels
Director
654-5267

Air Resources Board
John Dunlap
Chairman
322-5840

Office of Environmental Health Hazard Assessment
Carol J. Henry, Ph.D.,
D.A.B.T. Director
324-7572

California Integrated Waste Management Board
Chairman
255-2200

Department of Pesticide Regulation
James W. Wells
Director
445-4000

Department of Toxic Substances Control
Jesse Huff
Director
323-9723

State Water Resources Control Board
John Caffrey
Chairman
657-2399

Department of Aging
Robert P. Martinez
Director
322-5290

Department of Developmental Services
Dennis Amundson
Director
654-1897

Emergency Medical Services Authority
Joseph E. Morales,
M.D.
Director
322-4336

Department of Health Services
Kim Belshe
Director
657-1425

Managed Risk Medical Insurance Board
John Ramey
Executive Director
324-4695

Department of Rehabilitation
Brenda Premo
Director
445-3971

Secretary of Resources Agency
Douglas Wheeler
653-5656
Michael Mantell
Undersecretary
653-5656

Department of Industrial Relations
Lloyd Aubry
Director
S.F. (415) 703-4590
Robert W. Stranberg
Chief Deputy Director
S.F. (415) 703-4590

Department of Alcohol and Drug Programs
Andrew Mecca
Director
445-1943

Department of Economic Opportunity
Michael Micciche
Director
323-8694

Employment Development Department
Thomas Nagle
Director
654-8210

Health and Welfare Data Center
Russ Bohart
Director
739-7700

Department of Mental Health
Stephen W. Mayberg,
Ph.D.
Director
654-2309

Department of Social Services
Eloise Anderson
Director
657-2598

Office of Statewide Health Planning and Development
Dr. David Werdegar
Director, 654-1606

Department of Boating and Waterways
John R. Banuelos
Director
445-6281

California Coastal Commission
Peter Douglas
Executive Director
S.F. (415) 904-5200

Department of Conservation
Michael Byrne
Director
322-1080

California Energy Commission
Charles Imbrecht
Chairman
654-5000

Department of Forestry and Fire Protection
Richard A. Wilson
Director
653-7772

Department of Water Resources
David N. Kennedy
Director
653-7007

Bay Conservation and Development Commission
(510) 286-1015
Alan R. Pendleton
Executive Director
S.F. (415) 557-3686

Colorado River Board of California
Gerald Zimmerman
Executive Director
(818) 543-4676

CA Coastal Conservancy
(510) 286-1015
CA Tahoe Conservancy
(916) 542-5580
Santa Monica Mountains
(310) 456-5046

California Conservation Corps
Al Aramburu
Director
323-6588

Department of Fish and Game
Boyd Gibbons III
Director
653-7667

Department of Parks and Recreation
Donald W. Murphy
Director
653-8380

Office Of Administrative Law
John D. Smith
Director
323-6225

Office of Criminal Justice Planning
Ray Johnson
Executive Director
324-9140

Office Of Emergency Services
Richard Andrews
Director
262-1816

Medical Assistance Commission
Byron Chell
Executive Director
324-2726

Secretary of State and Consumer Services
Joanne C. Kozberg
653-2636
Anne Sheehan
Undersecretary
653-4090

Secretary of Trade and Commerce Agency
Julie M. Wright
322-1394
Loren Kaye
Undersecretary
324-9775

Department of Personnel Administration
David J. Tirapelle
Director
322-5193

Office of Planning and Research
Lee Grissom
Director
322-2318

Secretary of Youth and Adult Correctional Agency
Joe Sandoval
322-6001
Craig L. Brown
Undersecretary
323-6001

California African-American Museum
Director
(213) 744-7432

Fair Employment and Housing Commission
Steve Owyang
Executive Secretary
S.F. (415) 557-0899

Franchise Tax Board
Gerald Goldberg
Executive Officer
369-4543

California Museum of Science and Industry
Jeffrey N. Rudolph
Executive Director
L.A. (213) 744-7484

Teachers' Retirement System
James D. Mosman
Chief Executive Officer
387-3700

Building Standards Commission
Richard T. Conrad
Executive Director
323-6363

Department of Consumer Affairs
Marjorie M. Berte
Interim Director
445-4465

Department of Fair Employment and Housing
Nancy Gutierrez
Director
227-2873

Department of General Services
John Lockwood
Director
445-3441

State Personnel Board
Gloria Harmon
Executive Officer
653-1028

Department of Veterans Affairs
Col. Jay R. Vargas
Director
653-2158

Public Employees' Retirement System
James E. Burton
Executive Officer
326-3829

Office of Fire Marshal
Ronny J. Coleman
262-1883

Board of Corrections
Joe Sandoval
Chairman
445-5073

Department of Corrections
James Gomez
Director
445-7688

Board of Prison Terms
Jim Nielsen
Chairman
322-6366

Department of the Youth Authority
Director
262-1467

Youthful Offender Parole Board
William Pruitt
Chairman
262-1550

Department of Finance
Russell S. Gould
Director
445-4141
Theresa A. Parker
Chief Deputy Director
445-8582
La Fenus Stancell
Chief Deputy Director
445-8610

Referral number for state agencies: 323-0202

California Cities/Local Government International Contacts

BAYTRADE
(A regional export promotion and international trade program in the 12-county San Francisco-Oakland-San Jose- and Monterey Greater Bay Area. BAYTRADE represents a regional partnership among the U.S. Department of Commerce, the State of California, the cities of San Francisco, San Jose and Oakland, and international trade associations and service providers in the 12-county Greater Bay Area. This region extends from Sonoma County in the north to Monterey County in the South. BAYTRADE is a public-private regional partnership dedicated to:

● Expanding international trade and increasing exports for targeted industries in the region.

● Generating new export-related jobs in the region. A primary objective is to facilitate completion of more than 300 new export transactions by the end of the second year, and thereby help mitigate economic impacts resulting from military base closures and defense downsizing.

● Assisting large and small companies to seize the economic opportunities available through international trade.

● Coordinating, integrating and leveraging public and private resources to cost effectively promote exports and expand international trade.

● Developing and deploying a user-friendly electronic communication network, "BayNet," to effectively and efficiently provide prospective exporters with essential information to enter international markets and complete business transactions.
c/o Bay Area Economic Forum
200 Pine Street, Suite 300
San Francisco, CA 94104
(415) 981-7117
Fax (415) 981-6408

Economic Development Board of Sonoma County
Ben G. Stone, Director
401 College Avenue, Suite D
Santa Rosa, CA 95403
(707) 524-7170
Fax (707) 527-1172

City of Los Angeles
Economic Development Office
Office of International Trade
Tina Choi, Director
200 Spring Street, Room 2000
Los Angeles, CA 90012
(213) 847-4409
Fax (213) 237-0893; 247-5606

City of Sacramento
Economic Development Office
Tim Johnson
1231 I Street, Room 300
Sacramento, CA 95814
(916) 264-7223

City of San Diego
International Affairs and Trade Development
Staci Sticht, Director
202 C Street
San Diego, CA 92101
(619) 236-6330

Contra Costa County Redevelopment Agency
James Kennedy, Redevelopment Director
651 Pine Street, 4th Floor, North Wing
Martinez, CA 94553
(510) 646-4076

Economic Development Corporation
County of Los Angeles
Gary Conley, President
6922 Hollywood Boulevard, Suite 415
Los Angeles, CA 90028
(213) 462-5111
Fax (213) 462-2228

Kern County Board of Trade
Ann Gutcher, Manager
P.O. Bin 1312
Bakersfield, CA 93302
(805) 861-2367

Long Beach Export Development Office
Tom Teofilo, Executive Director
1 World Trade Center, Suite 350
Long Beach, CA 90831
(310) 491-0808
Fax (310) 435-0618

Merced County Office of Economic Development
Karen Prentiss, Director
222 M Street
Merced 95340
(209) 385-7312

Office of Commerce and Trade
Mayor's Office of Economic Planning and Development
City and County of San Francisco
City Hall, Room 156
James Fang, Director
400 Van Ness Avenue
San Francisco, CA 94102
(415) 554-6477
Fax (415) 554-6474

San Jose Office of Economic Development
Joseph Hedges, International Program Officer
50 West San Fernando Street, Suite 900
San Jose, CA 95113
(408) 277-5880
Fax (408) 277-3615

California Port/Harbor Contacts

Encinal Terminals
Chengben Wang, President
P.O. Box 2453
Alameda, CA 94501
(510) 523-8800

Oxnard Harbor District
Anthony Taormina, Executive Director
P.O. Box 608
Port Hueneme, CA 93044
(805) 488-3677

Port of Long Beach
Steven R. Dillenbeck, Executive Director
Don Wylie, Trade & Maritime Affairs
P.O. Box 570
Long Beach, CA 90801
(213) 437-0041
Fax (213) 437-3231

Port of Los Angeles/WORLDPORTLA
Ezunial Burts, Executive Director
P.O. Box 151
San Pedro, CA 90733
(310) SEA-PORT
Fax (310) 831-0439

Port of Oakland
Charles Roberts, Executive Director
530 Water Street
Oakland, CA 94607
(510) 272-1100
Fax (510) 839-5104

Port of Redwood City
675 Seaport Boulevard
Redwood City, CA 94063-2794
(415) 365-1613

Port of Richmond
Michael R. Powers
P.O. Box 4046
Richmond, CA 94804
(510) 620-6784

Port of Sacramento
Michael Vernon, Port Director
P.O. Box 815
West Sacramento, CA 95691
(916) 371-8000
Fax (916) 372-4802

Port of San Diego
Don L. Nay, Director
P.O. Box 488
San Diego, CA 92112
(619) 686-6200
Fax (619) 291-0753

Port of San Francisco
Michael P. Huerta, Executive Director
Roger L. Peters, Executive Director
Ferry Building, Suite 3100
San Francisco, CA 94111
(415) 274-0400
Fax (415) 274-0528

Port of Stockton
Alexander Krygsman, Port Director
P.O. Box 2089
Stockton, CA 95201
(209) 946-0246

If you're not exporting, you're missing a world of opportunity.

Does Long Beach, California, offer some of the best exporting opportunities in the nation? Rodney Jones says, you bet!

Vice president of Ameritone Paint, Jones expects to export a half million gallons next year. He credits a Port-sponsored class for the expertise he needed to venture into the export market.

Classes in international trade are one of many assets Long Beach offers businesses engaged in global commerce. Some others? The World Trade Center Association; a U.S. Export Assistance Office; the Port- and City-sponsored Long Beach Export Development Office; an International Business Association; and a California Office of Export Development.

Not to mention the Port of Long Beach—one of the largest containerports in the United States.

Jones now realizes the world is hungry for U.S. products. His sound advice? Get all the help that you can, then wade in. Your next sale may be only a country away.

For further information about the exporting resources available in Long Beach, California, complete this coupon.

Name _____

Title _____

Company _____

Address _____

City,Zip_____ Telephone(____)_____

Clip and return to: Communications Division
Port of Long Beach
P.O. Box 570, Long Beach, CA 90801
Facsimile: (310) 495-4368

ITRG

THE PORT OF LONG BEACH
We Make It Happen.

U.S. Federal Government International Contacts

EXPORT-IMPORT BANK

The U.S. Export-Import Bank (Eximbank) is an independent federal agency that helps finance the sale of U.S. goods and services to creditworthy purchasers in most foreign countries. To qualify for Eximbank assistance, the goods and services must contain at least 50 percent U.S. content and not be intended for military use. In addition, each transaction must be economically viable, offer reasonable assurance of repayment and not adversely affect the U.S. economy. The Eximbank offers four types of programs: loans to overseas buyers, guarantees to commercial lenders, working capital guarantees and export credit insurance.

Export-Import Bank
811 Vermont Avenue, N.W.
Washington, DC 20571
(800) 424-5201
Small Business Hotline: (202) 566-8860
Export Trading Company Assistance: (202) 566-8944
Engineering Division: (202) 566-8802
Advisory Service: (800) 424-5201
Hearing Impaired, TDD: (202) 535-3913

Export-Import Bank

Arthur Obester, West Coast Manager
222 North Sepulveda Boulevard, Suite 1515
El Segundo, CA 90245
(310) 322-1152
Fax (310) 322-2041

OFFICE OF THE U.S. TRADE REPRESENTATIVE

Responsible for policymaking in the trade arena. Provides publications to exporters confronted by foreign barriers to trade and unfair trade practices. Offices are organized according to sectoral responsibilities.

Winder Building
600 17th Street, N.W.
Washington, DC 20506
General Counsel: (202) 395-3150
Private Sector Liaison: (202) 395-6120
Agricultural Affairs & Commodity Policy: (202) 395-6127
The Americas Trade Policy: (202) 395-6135
East-West & Non-Market Economies: (202) 395-4543
Europe & Japan: (202) 395-4620
General Agreement on Tariffs & Trade: (202) 395-6843
Industrial & Energy Trade Policy: (202) 395-7320
Investment Policy: (202) 395-3510
Pacific, Asia, Africa & North-South Trade
Policy: (202) 395-3430

OVERSEAS PRIVATE INVESTMENT CORPORATION

OPIC is a U.S. government agency that assists U.S. investors through three principal programs: project financing, investment insurance and investor services. These programs are available in more than 140 developing nations and emerging economies throughout the world. To qualify for OPIC programs, projects must: be located in a developing or emerging nation where OPIC operates; assist in the social and economic development of the host country; not be opposed by the host country government; be consistent with U.S. economic interests; not adversely affect the U.S. economy or employment; and not have military purposes.

Overseas Private Investment Corporation
1100 New York Avenue, N.W.
Washington, DC 20528
(202) 336-8799
(202) 408-5155

U.S. AGENCY FOR INTERNATIONAL DEVELOPMENT

The U.S. Agency for International Development (AID) is the federal agency that provides health, economic and disaster assistance to eligible developing countries. Through its Office of Investment, AID supports the development of market economies and growth of private sector businesses throughout the world. The Office of Investment's primary development tool is the Private Sector Investment Program, a portfolio of loans, credit guarantees and training created by Congress in 1983. One program of potential interest to U.S. businesses is the Franchise Guarantee Program, which can help U.S. franchisors establish and expand their operations in developing countries.

U.S. Agency for International Development
320 21st Street, N.W.
Washington, DC 20523
(202) 647-3504
Office of Small & Disadvantaged Business Utilization/
Minority Resource Center: (703) 875-1551
(800) USAID4U
Commodities: (703) 875-1590
Technical Assistance Service: (703) 875-1551
Latin America/Caribbean Business Director:
(202) 482-0841, Fax (202) 482-2218

U.S. Agency for International Development

West Coast Business Outreach Office
City Hall
3031 Torrance Boulevard
P.O. Box 13536
Torrance, CA 90503
(310) 533-0770
Fax (310) 533-1325

U.S. DEPARTMENT OF AGRICULTURE

The U.S. Department of Agriculture (USDA) develops U.S. foreign agricultural policy, market analysis and promotion for U.S. agricultural exports, and administers agricultural import regulations. Trade policy issues, market support programs and import-related questions fall under the jurisdiction of the Foreign Agricultural Service (FAS) of the USDA. FAS develops new and expands existing markets for U.S. agriculture, and also assesses and reports on foreign competition and trade barriers, indentifies marketing opportunities, provides input for U.S. trade policy formulation and assists staff trade negotiations.

U.S. Department of Agriculture
Foreign Agricultural Service
14th Street and Independence Avenue, S.W.
Washington, DC 20250
(202) 447-7115
AgExport Services Division: (202) 720-6343,
fax (202) 690-4374.
Commodity and Marketing Programs:
Dairy, Livestock and Poultry: (202) 447-8031
Grain and Feed: (202) 447-6219
Horticultural and Tropical Products: (202) 447-6590
Oilseed and Oilseed Products: (202) 447-7037
Tobacco, Cotton and Seed: (202) 382-9516
Forest Products: (202) 382-8138

Agricultural Cooperative Service

Researches export opportunities for U.S. farmer cooperatives and advises on strategies for exporting.
Tracey Kennedy, International Trade Program:
(202) 690-1428, fax (202) 720-4641.

Agricultural Research Service

Provides exporters with information, research and consultations on a wide array of topics, including shipping, storage, insect control, pesticide residues and market disorders.
Richard Soper, International Activities: (301) 504-5605, fax (301) 504-5298.

U.S. Trade Assistance and Promotion Office (TAPO)

A single contact point within FAS for agricultural exporters seeking foreign market information. The office also counsels firms who believe they have been injured by unfair trade practices.
Homer Sabatini, TAPO: (202) 720-7420,
Fax (202) 690-4374.

U.S. DEPARTMENT OF COMMERCE
Trade Information Center

The Department of Commerce (DOC) promotes and develops the domestic and foreign commerce of the United States. The trade information center is a "one-stop" source for information on all federal export assistance programs. Located in the Department of Commerce, the center is operated by the Trade Promotion Coordinating Committee, an interagency group working to unify federal trade promotion activities. Call for more information on: how to get started in exporting; foreign market research; export financing programs; locating overseas buyers; trade missions and fairs; local export seminars and conferences; and where to find tariff rates and licensing requirements.

U.S. Department of Commerce
Trade Information Center
Tom Cox
14th and Constitution Avenue, N.W.
Room 1800A
Washington, D.C. 20230
(1-800) 872-8723/(1-800) USA-TRADE
Hearing impaired-(9:30 a.m.-5:30 p.m. EST)
(1-800) 833-8723/(1-800) TDD-TRADE

U.S. Export Assistance Centers (USEACs)

USEACs are customer-focused federal export assistance offices. USEACs streamline export marketing and trade finance assistance by integrating in a single location the counselors and services of the U.S. and Foreign Commercial Service of the Department of Commerce, the Export-Import Bank, the Small Business Administration, and in Long Beach, the U.S. Agency for International Development. In addition, through co-location and cooperation with local public and private export service partners, the USEACs will increase the depth and range of export services available to clients and promote a more rational and integrated delivery network. The USEACs will target primarily export-ready businesses, particularly small and medium-sized firms.

The USEACs will provide firms with one-on-one counseling to identify target markets and develop marketing strategies. They also will offer guidance in various areas relating to export finance such as export credit insurance and pre-and post-export financing. The four pilot USEACs are located in Baltimore, Chicago, Long Beach and Miami.

U.S. Export Assistance Center-California

(8 a.m - 4:30 p.m.)
1 World Trade Center, Suite 1670
Long Beach, CA 90831
(310) 980-4550
Fax (310) 980-4561

The International Trade Administration (ITA)

Offers assistance and information to help exporters. ITA units include: domestic and overseas commercial officers; country experts; and industry experts. Each unit promotes products and offers services and programs for the U.S. exporting community.

International Trade Administration

U.S. Department of Commerce
14th and Constitution Avenue, N.W.
Room 1800 A
Washington, DC 20230
(202) 377-5131

International Trade Administration
U.S. Department of Commerce
Western Regional Office
Michael Liikala, Regional Director
250 Montgomery, 14th Floor
San Francisco, CA 94104
(415) 705-2300
Fax (415) 705-2299

International Trade Administration
U.S. Department of Commerce
San Francisco District Office
James Kennedy, Acting Director, San Francisco Office
250 Montgomery, 14th Floor
San Francisco, CA 94104
(415) 705-2300
Fax (415) 705-2297

International Trade Administration
Los Angeles District Office
U.S. Department of Commerce
Steve Arlinghaus, Acting Director
11000 Wilshire Boulevard, Room 9200
Los Angeles, CA 90024
(213) 575-7104
Fax (213) 209-7220

International Trade Administration
Orange County Branch Office
U.S. Department of Commerce
Paul Tambakis, Branch Manager
3300 Irvine Avenue, Suite 345
Newport Beach, CA 92660-3198
(714) 660-0144
Fax (714) 660-9347

International Trade Administration
San Diego District Office
U.S. Department of Commerce
Mary Delmage, Acting San Diego District Director
6363 Greenwich Drive, Suite 230
San Diego, CA 92122
(619) 557-5395
Fax (619) 557-6176

International Trade Administration
Santa Clara Branch Office
James Kennedy, Branch Manager
5201 Great America Parkway, Suite 333
Santa Clara, CA 95054-1127
(408) 291-7625
Fax (408) 291-7625

Bureau of Export Administration:
The Bureau of Export Administration (BXA) is responsible for control of exports for reasons of national security, foreign policy and short supply. Licenses on controlled exports are issued, and seminars on U.S. export regulations are held domestically and overseas. Export license applications may be submitted and issued through computer via the Export License Application and Information Network [ELAIN]. The System for Tracking Export Lincense Applications [STELA] provides instant status updates on license applications by use of a touch-tone telephone. The Export Licensing Voice Information System [ELVIS] is an automated attendant that offers a range of licensing information and emergency handling procedures. Callers may order forms and publications or subscribe to the *Office of Export Licensing* [OEL] *Insider Newsletter,* which provides regulatory updates. While using ELVIS, a caller has the option to speak to a consultant.
Iain Baird, Office of Export Licensing: (202) 482-0436, Fax (202) 482-3322;
ELAIN: (202) 482-4811;
STELA: (202) 482-2752; and
ELVIS: (202) 482-4811.

Bureau of Export Administration
U.S. Department of Commerce
Office of Antiboycott Compliance
14th and Constitution Avenue, N.W.
Room 1099
Washington, DC 20230
(202) 377-4811

Bureau of Export Administration
U.S. Department of Commerce
Office of Export Licensing
14th and Constitution Avenue, N.W.
Room 1099
Washington, DC 20230
(202) 377-4811

Bureau of Export Administration
U.S. Department of Commerce
Western Regional Office
Michael E. Hoffman, Director
3300 Irvine Avenue, Suite 345
Newport Beach, CA 92660-3198
(714) 660-0144
Fax (714) 660-9347

Bureau of Export Administration
U.S. Department of Commerce
Northern California Branch Office
Maureen Dunleavy, Director
5201 Great America Parkway, 4th Floor
Santa Clara, CA 95054-1127
(408) 748-7450
Fax (408) 748-7420

Other:
U.S. DEPARTMENT OF COMMERCE OFFICES

Japan Untied Official Development Assistance Program
A central source for information about how to access procurement through Japan's foreign aid program. In 1990, developing countries benefited from approximately $10 billion in Japanese foreign aid, which includes grant aid, "soft loans" and technical cooperation. About $5 billion was available for procurement by U.S. suppliers.
Robert Lurensky, Office of Energy, Environment and Infrastructure (Trade Development): (202) 482-4002, Fax (202) 482-0316;
Elizabeth Johns, Office of Japan (International Economic Policy): (202) 482-1820, Fax (202) 482-0469.

Minority Business Development Agency
U.S. Department of Commerce
Office of Program Development
Exporter Counseling Division
14th and Constitution Avenue, N.W.
Room 5093
Washington, DC 20230
(202) 377-3237

Office of Business Liason
Information available regarding government services.
U.S. Department of Commerce
14th and Constitution Avenue, N.W.
Room 5898-C
Washington, DC 20230
(202) 377-3176

Office of Domestic Operations
U.S. Department of Commerce
14th and Constitution Avenue, N.W.
Room 3810
Washington, DC 20230
(202) 377-4767

Office of Export Marketing Programs
U.S. Department of Commerce
Office offers tradeshow and trade mission information.
14th and Constitution Avenue, N.W.
Room 2116
Washington, DC 20230
(202) 377-4231

Office of Export Promotion Resources
U.S. Department of Commerce
Office provides information on foreign markets, customers, trade leads, *Commercial News U.S.A.* and other export-related publications.
14th and Constitution Avenue, N.W.
Room 1322
Washington, DC 20230
(202) 377-2432

Office of Export Trading Company Affairs
U.S. Department of Commerce
The office: promotes the formation and use of export trading companies and export management companies; offers information and counseling to businesses and trade associations regarding the U.S. export intermediary industry; and administers the Export Trade Certificate of Review Program, which provides limited antitrust protection to U.S. firms for joint export activities. The office also manages *The Export Yellow Pages,* a directory of U.S. suppliers, banks, service organizations and export trading companies. To register a company in this free directory, contact the local ITA district office.
George Miller
International Trade Administration
14th and Constitution Avenue, N.W.
Room 1800 A
Washington, D.C. 20230
(202) 377-5131
Fax (202) 377-5131

Office of Multilateral Development Bank Operations (MDBO)
The five multilateral development banks (African, Asian, European, Inter-American and World Bank) have a total lending program of approximately $45 billion per year to support economic growth in developing countries. Multilateral bank projects offer excellent opportunities for U.S. companies to supply engineering, construction, and goods and services for manufacturing and investment.

The U.S. Department of Commerce/U.S. and Foreign Commercial Service, Office of Multilateral Development Bank Operations (MBDO) works closely with USAID and other U.S. government agencies (including the U.S. Trade and Development Agency. U.S. Overseas Private Investment Corporation, U.S. Small Business Administration) to assist U.S. firms in formulating strategies and competitive financing packages in pursuit of overseas development projects.

Interested companies can contact the MBDO office in Washington, D.C. for information and guidance on the following:
- approved projects and downstream financing plans;
- procurement and decision-making procedures for each of the five MDBs;
- names of staff contacts handling specific projects;
- strategies for competitive bidding;
- advocacy, including help with procurement disputes;
- electronic media providing current project information;
- future projects under consideration.

Office of Multilateral Development Bank Operations
Brenda L. Ebeling, Director
14th & Constitution Avenue, NW, Room 1107
Washington, D.C. 20230
(202) 482-3399
Fax (202) 273-0927

African Development Bank

Nikki Brajevich, Senior Commercial Oficer
Margaret Hanson-Muse, Commercial Officer
U.S. & Foreign Commercial Service
Ambassade des Etats Unis d'Amerique
5 Rue Jesse Owens
01 B.P. 1712 Abidjan 01, Cote d'Ivoire
(225) 21-46-16
Fax (225) 22-24-37

Alice M. Dear, U.S. Executive Director
Avenue Joseph Anoma
01 B.P 1387 Abidjan 01, Cote d'Ivoire
(225) 20-40-15
Fax (225) 33-14-34

Asian Development Bank

Linda Tsao Yang, U.S. Executive Director
Janet Thomas
Senior Commercial Officer
Office of the U.S. Executive Director
#6 ADB Avenue
1501 Mandaluyong Metro Manila
P.O. Box 789
Manila, 1099, Philippines
(632) 632-6050; (632) 632-6054
Fax (632) 632-4003
or:

U.S. Liaison to the Asian Development Bank/
U.S. and Foreign Commercial Service

Lisa Lumbao, AEP Representative
U.S. Embassy, Manila
APO AP 96-1-10
(632) 813-3248
Fax (632) 816-7684

European Bank for Reconstruction and Development

James Scheuer, U.S. Executive Director
Sarah Shackelton, Commercial Specialist
Office of the U.S. Executive Director
One Exchange Square
London EC2A 2EH
United Kingdom
(44) 71-338-6569; (44) 71-338-6503
(44) 71-338-6487

Inter-American Development Bank

Judith Henderson, Director, Commerce Liaison Office
Michelle Miller, Procurement Liaison Officer
1250 H Street, NW
Washington, D.C. 20005
(202) 942-8260
Fax (202) 942-8275

L. Ronald Scheman, U.S. Executive Director
1300 New York Avenue, NW
Washington, D.C. 20577
(202) 623-1031
(202) 623-3612

World Bank

Jan Piercy, U.S. Executive Director
Thomas Kelsey, Director, Commerce Liaison Office
Janice Mazur, Procurement Liaison Officer
1818 H Street, NW
Washington, D.C. 20433
(202) 458-0118; (202) 458-0110
Fax (202) 477-2967

Export Legal Assistance Network (ELAN)

A corporate program among the Federal Bar Association,
U.S. Department of Commerce and U.S. Small Business
Administration under which lawyers from the Federal Bar
Association and other interested professional associations
volunteer to provide initial legal consultation free of
charge to companies making their first entry into the
export market.
Los Angeles: Michael R. Doram, (213) 386-1383;
San Francisco: Harry B. Endsley, (415) 296-1141;
San Diego: Harold Pope, (619) 546-2944;
Sacramento: Mark F. Johannsen, (916) 443-5292;
National Coordinator: (202) 778-3080.

U.S. POSTAL SERVICE

Provides a full range of delivery services to meet international mailing needs, including hand-delivered fax, express,
advertising mail, business reply, and all types of printed
matter and merchandise shipments.

Postal Business Center

2300 Redondo Avenue
Long Beach, CA 90809
(310) 494-2280
Fax (310) 498-7506

Postal Business Center

7001 S. Central Avenue, Room 264
Los Angeles, CA 90052
(213) 586-1843
Fax (213) 586-1831

Postal Business Center

1675 7th Street, Room 120
Oakland, CA 94615
(510) 874-8600
Fax (510) 832-4024

Postal Business Center
2035 Hurley Way, Suite 200
Sacramento, CA 95825
(916) 923-4357; (1-800) 959-2993
Fax (916) 923-4381

Postal Business Center
11251 Rancho Carmel Drive, Room 266
San Diego, CA 92199
(619) 674-0400
Fax (619) 674-0055

Postal Business Center
3801 3rd Street, #B400
San Francisco, CA 94124
(415) 550-6565
Fax (415) 285-0253

Postal Business Center
1750 Meridian Avenue
San Jose, CA 95101
(408) 723-6262
Fax (same as phone)

Postal Business Center
3101 W. Sunflower Avenue
Santa Ana, CA 92799
(714) 662-6213
Fax (714) 556-1492

Postal Business Center
15701 Sherman Way
Van Nuys, CA 91409
(818) 374-4934
Fax (818) 787-2941

U.S. DEPARTMENT OF STATE
The State Department executes U.S. foreign policy and
promotes the long-range security and well-being of the
United States.
U.S. Department of State
2201 C Street, N.W.
Washington, DC 20520
U.S. Department of State Commerical Coordinators
Bureau of African Affairs: (202) 647-3503
Bureau of Inter-American Affairs: (202) 647-2066
Bureau of East Asian and Pacific Affairs: (202) 647-4835
Bureau of Near Eastern and South Asian
Affairs: (202) 647-9583
Bureau of European and Canadian Affairs: (202) 647-2395

Bureau of Economic and Business Affairs
Formulates and implements policies regarding foreign
economic matters and international trade promotion and
business services. Bureau works with: the Business Council
for International Understanding to arrange business briefings for senior diplomats; the Executive Council on Foreign
Diplomats to arrange briefings by state officials for business
and to place U.S. Foreign Service Officers in long-term
assignments in U.S. industry; and other business groups.
Al White, Director, Office of Commercial, Legislative and
Public Affairs: (202) 647-1942, Fax (202) 647-5713.

Bureau of International Communications and Information Policy
The bureau aims to enhance the competitiveness of the U.S.
communications industry and to secure global market
access for U.S. providers and users of telecommunications,
broadcasting equipment and services.
Doreen McGirr, Office of Development and Satellites:
(202) 647-5231, Fax (202) 647-0158.

U.S. DEPARTMENT OF TRANSPORTATION
Maritime Administration
Provides information and assistance to exporters requring
the use of ocean freight transportation and particularly on
U.S. flag lines. Questions on various aspects of exporting
by sea can be answered directly or by referral to others
having the required expertise
U.S. Department of Transportation
Maritime Administration
Kingdon Dietz
Norma Corwin
501 W. Ocean Blvd., Suite 5100
Long Beach, CA 90802
(310) 980-4111 or 4112

U.S. DEPARTMENT OF THE TREASURY
The Department of the Treasury is responsible for
formulating and regulating U.S. international financial and
tax policy as well as international monetary, economic and
investment matters. Treasury's operations affect every
aspect of U.S. foreign economic relations, including trade
and investment, energy, commodity and monetary policy
and development finance.
U.S. Department of the Treasury
15th Street and Pennsylvania Avenue, N.W.
Washington, DC 20220
U.S. Customs Strategic Investigation Division:
(202) 566-9464

U.S. Customs Office
Custom House
300 South Ferry Street
Terminal Island
Los Angeles, CA 90731
(310) 514-6003
Fax (310) 514-6769

U.S. Customs Office
555 Battery street
P.O. Box 2450
San Francisco, CA 94126
(415) 705-4488

U.S. SMALL BUSINESS ADMINISTRATION
The U.S. Small Business Administration (SBA) is an
independent federal agency created by Congress to aid,
counsel and protect the interests of small businesses. It
provides business development and financial assistance
for exporters.
Small Business Administration
Office of International Trade
409 Third Street S.W., 6th Floor
Washington, DC 20416
(202) 205-6720
(800) 827-5722
Hearing impaired, TDD: (202) 205-7333

Small Business Administration
Western Regional Office
Michael Elkin, Regional International Trade Officer
71 Stevenson Street, 20th Floor
San Francisco, CA 94105
(415) 744-6402
Fax (415) 744-6435

Small Business Administration
Northern California
San Francisco District Office
211 Main Street, 4th Floor
San Francisco, CA 94105-1988
(415) 744-6804

Small Business Administration
Northern California
Fresno District Office
2719 North Air Fresno Drive
Fresno, CA 93727
(209) 487-5189

Small Business Administration
Northern California
Sacramento Branch Office
660 J Street, Suite 215
Sacramento, CA 95814-2413
(916) 551-1426

Small Business Administration
Southern California
Los Angeles District Office
330 North Brand Boulevard, Suite 1200
Glendale, CA 91203-2304
(213) 894-7900

Small Business Administration
Southern California
San Diego Office
880 Front Street, Room 4-S-29
San Diego, CA 92188-0270
(619) 557-7269

Small Business Administration
Southern California
Santa Ana District Office
901 West Civic Center Drive, Suite 160
Santa Ana, CA 92703-2352
(714) 836-2494

**Export Small Business Development Center
of Southern California**
Gladys Moreau, Director
110 East 9th Street, Suite A761
Los Angeles, CA 90079
(213) 892-1111
Fax (213) 892-8232
(A partnership of the U.S. Small Business Administration,
the State of California and Export Managers Association
of California.)

Export Small Business Development Center
Santa Barbara/Ventura Satellite Office
Central Coast World Trade Center
300 Esplanade Drive, Suite 1020
Oxnard, CA 93030
(805) 981-4633
Fax (805) 988-1862

CA Small Business Development Center
CA Department of Commerce
801 K Street, Suite 1700
Sacramento, CA 95814
(916) 324-5068
Fax (916) 322-5084

Listing of International Trade Administration Country Desk Officers, U.S. Department of Commerce

U.S. Department of Commerce, 14th and Constitution Avenue, N.W., Washington, DC 20230, U.S. and Foreign Commercial Service, Office of International Operations, Regional Directors for:
- Africa, Near East and South Asia, Room 1223: (202) 482-4836
- East Asia and Pacific, Room 1223: (202) 482-8422
- Europe, Room 3130: (202) 482-1599
- Western Hemisphere, Room 3130: (202) 482-2736
- Fax (Europe and Western Hemisphere): (202) 482-3159
- Fax (ANESA and EAP): (202) 482-5179

- Single Internal Market 1992 Information Service (SIMIS) on European Community (EC), (202) 482-5276, fax (202) 482-2155. Services provided by SIMIS include a basic packet on EC 1992, *Europe Now* (a quarterly newsletter), sectoral guides to EC legislation, informational seminars and business counseling.

FLASH FACTS: 24-hour automated fax delivery systems (follow instructions and requested information will be faxed to you). Available 24 hours a day, seven days a week for the following offices:

- **Africa, Near East, South Asia:** (202) 482-1064
  For a menu of sub-Saharan Africa documents, request document 3000
  For a menu of North Africa and Near East documents, request document 0100
  For a menu of South Asia documents, request document 4000

- **Russia and the NIS (BISNIS):** (202) 482-3145
  For a menu of investment opportunities and trade information, request document 0001
  For a menu of financing information and country or industry-specific information, request document 0002
  For a menu of all back issues of BISNIS publications, request document 0003

- **Canada:** (202) 482-3101
  For a menu of documents, request document 0100

- **Eastern Europe (EEBIC):** (202) 482-5745
  For a menu of documents, request document 1001

- **Mexico:** (202) 482-4464
  For a menu of documents, request document 0101

- **Pacific Rim:** (202) 482-3875
  For a menu of documents, request document 1000

- **Uruguay Round (GATT):** (800) 872-8723
  For a menu of documents, request document 1000

- Business Information Service for Russia and the Newly Independent States (BISNIS), U.S. Department of Commerce, International Trade Adminstration. U.S. Companies can call BISNIS at (202) 482-3145 to receive information on:
  - ✔ upcoming trade missions;
  - ✔ potential customers and partners;
  - ✔ sources of financing;
  - ✔ trade and investment laws;
  - ✔ market research;
  - ✔ advertising opportunities;
  - ✔ status of trade and investment treaties;
  - ✔ U.S. Government programs supporting trade and investment;
  - ✔ U.S. Department of Commerce-sponsored trade fairs; and
  - ✔ private and voluntary organizations active in the area.

BISNIS will establish an overseas network that will provide the center with continuous updates on local business opportunities and conditions in Russia, Ukraine, Belarus, Moldova, Georgia, Armenia, Azerbaijan, Uzbekistan, Turkmenistan, Tajikistan, Kazakhstan and Kyrgyzstan.

- Eastern Europe Business Information Center (EEBIC), U.S. Department of Commerce, International Trade Administration, Room 6043, Washington, DC 20230, (202) 482-5745, Fax (202) 482-4473. EEBIC serves as a clearinghouse for information on business conditions in Poland, Hungary, Czechoslovakia, the German Democratic Republic, Romania, Bulgaria, Yugoslavia and Albania, and on emerging trade and investment opportunities in those countries. It also serves as a source of information on U.S. Government programs supporting private enterprise, trade and investment in Eastern Europe.
- Office of Mexico, U.S. Department of Commerce, Room H-3026, Washington, D.C. 20230, (202) 482-4464.
- Office of the Pacific Basin: (202) 482-3875 or (202) 482-3646.
- Business Information Service for the Newly Independent States (BISNIS): (202) 482-3145.
- Offices of Africa, Near East and South Asia: (202) 482-1064.
- Office of Canada: (202) 482-3101.

Listing of International Trade Administration Country Desk Officers, U.S. Department of Commerce

Country	Desk Officer	Phone (202) 482-
A		
Afghanistan	Tim Gilman	2954
Albania	EEBIC	2645
Algeria	Claude Clement	5545
	Chris Cerone	1860
Angola	Finn Holm-Olsen	4228
Anguilla	Michelle Brooks	2527
Antigua/Barbuda	Michelle Brooks	2527
Argentina	Randy Mye	1548
Armenia	BISNES	0988
Aruba	Michelle Brooks	2527
ASEAN	Karen Goddin	3877
Australia	Gary Bouck	4958
	George Paine	
Austria	Philip Combs	2920
Azarbaijan	BISNIS	4655
B		
Bahamas	Mark Siegelman	5680
Bahrain	Claude Clement	5545
	Chris Carone	1860
Balkan States (former Yugoslavia Republics)	EEBIC	2645
Bangladesh	John Simmons	2954
Barbados	Michelle Brooks	2527
Belarus	BISNIS	4655
Belgium	Simon Bensimon	5041
Belize	Michelle Brooks	2527
Benin	Debra Henke	5149
Bhutan	Tim Gilman	2954
Bolivia	Rebecca Hunt	2521
Botswana	Finn Holm-Olsen	4228
Brazil	Ted Johnson	3871
Brunei	Edward Oliver	4958
	Raphael Cung	
Bulgaria	EEBIC	2645
Burkina Faso	Philip Michelini	4388
Burma (Myanmar)	Gary Bouck	4958
	Raphael Cung	
Burundi	Philip Michelini	4388
C		
Cambodia	Hong-Phong B. Pho	4958
	Gary Bouck	
Cameroon	Debra Henke	5149
Canada	Jonathan Doh	3103

		Phone (202) 482-
Cape Verde	Philip Michelini	4388
Cayman Islands	Michelle Brooks	2527
Central Africa Republic	Philip Michelini	4388
Chad	Philip Michelini	4388
Chile	Roger Turner	1495
Colombia	Paul Moore	1659
Comoros	Chandra Watkins	4564
Congo	Debra Henke	5149
Costa Rica	Mark Siegelman	5680
Cote d'Ivoire	Philip Michelini	4388
Cuba	Mark Siegelman	5680
Cyprus	Ann Corro	3945
Czech Republic	EEBIC	2645
D		
Denmark	John Larsen	2841
D'Jibouti	Chandra Watkins	4564
Dominica	Michelle Brooks	2527
Domincan Republic	Mark Siegelman	5680
E		
Ecuador	Paul Moore	1659
Egypt	Paul Thanos	1860
	Corey Wright	5506
El Salvador	Helen Lee	2528
Equatorial Guinea	Philip Michelini	4388
Eritrea	Chandra Watkins	4564
Estonia	EEBIC	2645
Ethiopia	Chandra Watkins	4564
European Union	Charles Ludolph	5276
F		
Finland	James Devlin	3254
France	Elena Mikalis	6008
G		
Gabon	Debra Henke	5149
Gambia	Philip Michelini	4388
Georgia	BISNIS	4655
Germany	Brenda Fisher	2435
	John Larsen	2434
Ghana	Debra Henke	5149
Greece	Ann Corro	3945
Grenada	Michelle Brooks	2527
Guatemala	Helen Lee	2528
Guinea	Philip Michelini	4388
Guinea-Bissau	Philip Michelini	4388
Guyana	Michelle Brooks	2527

		Phone (202) 482-
H		
Haiti	Mark Siegelman	5680
Honduras	Helen Lee	2528
Hong Kong	Sheila Baker	4681
Hungary	EEBIC	2645
I		
Iceland	Philip Combs	2920
India	John Simmons	2954
	John Crown	
	Tim Gilman	
Indonesia	Edward Oliver	3877
	Karen Goddin	
Iran	Paul Thanos	1860
	Claude Clement	
Iraq	Thomas Sams	1860
	Corey Wright	5506
Ireland	Boyce Fitzpatrick	2177
Israel	Paul Thanos	1860
	Corey Wright	5506
Italy	Boyce Fitzpatrick	2177
J		
Jamaica	Mark Siegelman	5680
Japan	Eric Kennedy	2425
	Ed Leslie	2425
	Cynthia Campbell	
	Allan Christian	
Jordan	Corey Wright	5506
	Paul Thanos	1860
K		
Kazakhstan	BISNIS	4655
Kenya	Chandra Watkins	4564
Korea	Dan Duvall	4390
	Jeffrey Donius	
	William Golike	
Kuwait	Corey Wright	5506
	Thomas Sams	1860
Kyrgyz Republic	BISNIS	4655
L		
Laos	Hong-Phong Pho	4958
	Gary Bouck	
Latvia	EEBIC	2645
Lebanon	Corey Wright	5506
	Thomas Sams	1860

		Phone **(202) 482-**
Lesotho	Finn Holm-Olsen	4228
Liberia	Philip Michelini	4388
Libya	Christopher Cerone	1860
	Claude Clement	5545
Lithuania	EEBIC	2645
Luxembourg	Simon Bensimon	5401

M

Macau	Sheila Baker	4681
Madagascar	Chandra Watkins	4564
Malawi	Finn Holm-Olsen	4228
Malaysia	Edward Oliver	2522
	Raphael Cung	
Maldives	John Simmons	2954
Mali	Philip Michelini	4388
Malta	Robert McLaughlin	3748
Mauritania	Philip Michelini	4388
Mauritius	Chandra Watkins	4564
Mexico	Shawn Ricks	0300
Moldova	BISNIS	4655
Mongolia	Sheila Baker	4681
Montserrat	Michelle Brooks	2527
Morocco	Claude Clement	5545
	Chris Cerone	1860
Mozambique	Finn Holm-Olsen	4228

N

Nambia	Finn Holm-Olsen	4228
Nepal	Tim Gilman	2954
Netherlands	Simon Bensimon	5401
Netherlands Antilles	Michelle Brooks	2527
New Zealand	Gary Bouck	4958
	George Paine	
Nicaragua	Mark Siegelman	5680
Niger	Philip Michelini	4388
Nigeria	Debra Henke	5149
Norway	James Devlin	4414

O

Oman	Claude Clement	5545
	Christopher Cerone	1860

P

Pacific Islands	George Paine	4958
	Gary Bouck	
Pakistan	Timothy Gilman	2954
Panama	Helen Lee	2528
Paraguay	Randy Mye	1548

		Phone (202) 482-
People's Republic of China	Cheryl McQueen	3932
	Laura McCall	3583
Peru	Rebecca Hunt	2521
Philippines	Edward Oliver	4958
	Jean Kelly	
Poland	EEBIC	2645
Portugal	Mary Beth Double	4508

Q

Qatar	Claude Clement	5545
	Christopher Cerone	1860

R

Romania	EEBIC	2645
Russia	BISNIS	4655
Rwanda	Philip Michelini	4388

S

Sao Tome and Principe	Philip Michelini	4388
Saudi Arabia	Christopher Cerone	1860
	Claude Clement	5545
Senegal	Philip Michelini	4388
Seychelles	Chandra Watkins	4564
Sierra Leone	Philip Michelini	4388
Singapore	Edward Oliver	4958
	Raphael Cung	
Slovak Republic	EEBIC	2645
Somalia	Chandra Watkins	4564
South Africa	Vicky Eicher	5148
Spain	Mary Beth Double	4508
Sri Lanka	John Simmons	2954
St. Kitts-Nevis	Michelle Brooks	2527
St. Lucia	Michelle Brooks	2527
St. Martin	Michelle Brooks	2527
St. Vincent Grenadines	Michelle Brooks	2527
Sudan	Chandra Watkins	4564
Suriname	Michelle Brooks	2527
Swaziland	Finn Holm-Olsen	4228
Sweden	James Devlin	4414
Switzerland	Philip Combs	2920
Syria	Corey Wright	5506
	Thomas Sams	1860

T

Taiwan	Dan Duvall	4390
	Robert Chu	
Tajikistan	BISNIS	4655
Tanzania	Finn Holm-Olsen	4228
Thailand	Edward Oliver	4958
	Jean Kelly	

		Phone **(202) 482-**
Togo	Debra Henke	5149
Trinidad and Tobago	Michelle Brooks	2527
Tunisia	Corey Wright	5506
	Thomas Sams	1860
Turkey	Ann Corro	3945
Turkmanistan	BISNIS	4655
Turks/Caicos Islands	Mark Siegelman	5680

U

Uganda	Chandra Watkins	4564
Ukraine	BISNIS	4655
United Arab Emirates	Claude Clement	5545
	Chris Cerone	1860
United Kingdom	Robert McLaughlin	3748
Uruguay	Roger Turner	1495
Uzbekistan	BISNIS	4655

V

Venezuela	Laura Zeiger-Hatfield	4303
Vietnam	Hong-Phong Pho	4958
	Gary Bouck	
Virgin Islands (UK)	Michelle Brooks	2527

W

West Bank-Gaza Strip	Paul Thanos	1860
	Thomas Sams	

Y

Yemen, Republic of	Christopher Cerone	1860
	Claude Clement	5545

Z

Zaire	Philip Michelini	4388
Zambia	Finn Holm-Olsen	4228
Zimbabwe	Finn Holm-Olsen	4228

Listing of International Trade Administration Industry Desks
U.S. Department of Commerce

● U.S. Department of Commerce, 14th and Constitution Avenue, N.W., Washington, DC 20230, Trade Development, Product/Service Specialists:
  - ✔ Aerospace: (202) 482-2835;
  - ✔ Automotaive Affairs and Consumer Goods, Room 4324: (202) 482-0823;
  - ✔ Basic Industries, Room 4045: (202) 482-0614;
  - ✔ Capital Goods & International Construction, Room 2001B: (202) 482-5023;
  - ✔ Export Trading Company Affairs, Room 1800: (202) 482-5131;
  - ✔ International Major Projects, Room 2015B: (202) 482-5225;
  - ✔ Science and Electronics, Room 1009: (202) 482-3548;
  - ✔ Services, Room 1128A: (202) 482-5261;
  - ✔ Textiles and Apparel, Room 3100: (202) 482-3737;
  - ✔ Trade Information and Analysis, Room 3814B: (202) 482-1316.

Product	Desk Officer	Phone (202) 482-
A		
Abrasives	Graylin Presbury	5158
Accounting	Marc Chittum	0345
Adhesives/Sealants	Raimundo Prat	0128
Advanced Materials	George Driscoll	4431
Advertising	Frederick Elliot	1134
Aerospace Financing Issues	Jeff Jackson	4222
Aerospace Industry Analysis	Walter McDonald	4222
Aerospace Market Development	Tony Largay	2835
Aerospace Trade Policy	Juliet Bender	4222
Aerospace-Space Programs	Clay Mowry	4222
Agricultural Chemicals	Francis Maxey	0128
Agricultural Machinery	Mary Wiening	4708
Air Conditioning Equipment	Patrick Cosslett	0132
Air Couriers	Frederick Elliott	3734
Air Pollution Control Equipment	Loretta Jonkers	0564
Air Traffic Control Eqmt	Audrey Smerkanich	2835
Air Transport Services	Eugene Alford	5071
Air, Gas Compressors	Vacant	0680
Air, Gas Comressors (Trade Promo)	George Zanetakos	0552
Aircraft, Aircraft Engines & Aircraft	Healther Pederson	2835
Aircraft, Aircraft Engines & Aircraft Parts (Industry Analysis)	Walter McDonald	4222
Airlines	Eugene Alford	5071
Airport Equipment	Audrey Smerkanich	2835
Airport Equiment (Trade Promo)	Audrey Smerkanich	2835
Airports (Major Proj.)	Jay Smith	4642
Alcoholic Beverages	Cornelius Kenney	2428
Alum Forgings, Electro	David Cammarota	5157
Alum Sheet, Plate/Foil	David Cammarota	5157
Aluminum, Extruded Alum, Rolling	David Cammarota	5157

		Phone (202) 482-
Analytical Instruments	Marguerite Nealon	3411
Analytical & Scientific Instruments (Trade Promo)	Franc Manzolillo	2991
Antitrust Certificates of Review	Theodore A. Gebhard	5131
Apparel	William Dulka	4058
Apparel (Trade Promo)	Ferenc Molnar	2043
Artificial Intelligence	Shelagh Montgomery	0397
Asbestos/Cement Prod	Charles Pitcher	0132
Audio Visual Services	John Siegmund	4781
Auto Industry Affairs	Stuart Keitz	0554
Auto Industry (Trade Promo)	John White	0671
Auto Industry Affairs	Stuart Keitz	0554
Auto Parts & Supplies	Robert Reck	1418
Avionics (Trade Promo)	Heather Pederson	2835

B

Bakery Products	William Janis	2250
Ball Bearings	Richard Reise	3489
Banking Services	John Shuman	3050
Basic Paper and Board Manufacturing	Gary Stanley	0375
Bauxite, Alumina, Prim Alum	David Cammarota	5157
Beer	Cornelius Kenney	2428
Belting and Hose	Raimundo Prat	0128
Beryllium	Barbara Males	0606
Beverages	Cornelius Kenney	2428
Bicycles	John Vanderwolf	0348
Biomass Energy Eqmt	Les Garden	0556
Biotechnology	Emily Arakaki	0128
Blankbooks and Bookbinding	William S. Lofquist	0379
Boats, Pleasure	John Vanderwolf	0348
Books	William Lofquist	0379
Books (Export Promo)	Edward Kimmel	3640
Breakfast Cereal	William Janis	2250
Brick & Clay Building Products	Charles B. Pitcher	0132
Bridges (Major Proj)	Jay Smith	4642
Broadcasting Eqmt	Theresa Rettig	2952
Brooms and Brushes	John Harris	1178
Building Materials and Construction	Charles Pitcher	0132
Business Forms	Rose Marie Bratland	0380

C

CABEE and CABNIS	Heather Moxon	5004
CAD/CAM/CAE/CASE/CA	Vera Swann	0396
Canned Food Products	William Janis	2250
Carbon Black	Raimundo Prat	0128
Ceiling Boards & Systems	Patrick MacAuley	0132
Cellular Radio Telephone Eqmt	Stephanie McCullough	2872
Cement	Charles Pitcher	0132
Cement Plants (Major Proj)	Max Miles	0679
Chemicals and Allied Products	Michael Kelly	0128
Chinaware	Rose Marie Bratland	0380

		Phone (202) 482-
Civil Aircraft Agreement	Juliet Bender	4222
Civil Aviation Policy	Eugene Alford	5071
Coal Exports	John Rasmussen	1466
Cobalt	Graylin Presbury	5158
Comic Books	Rose Marie Bratland	0380
Commercial Aircraft (Trade Policy)	Juliet Bender	4222
Commercial/Indus Refrig Eqmt	Patrick Cosslett	0132
Commercial Lighting Fixtures	John Bodson	0681
Commercial Printing	William Lofquist	0379
Commercialization of Space (Market)	Clay Mowry	4222
Computer Consulting	Mary C. Inoussa	5820
Computer Networks	Mary A. Davin	0568
Computer Software	Heidi Hijikata	0569
Computer Systems	Timothy Miles	2990
Computer and DP Services	Mary C. Inoussa	5820
Computers (Large Scale)	Sean Iverson	0571
Computers, Personal	Clay Woods	3013
Computers, Portable	Jonathan Streeter	0480
Computers (Trade Promo)	Judy Fogg	4936
Computer (Workstations)	Sean Iverson	1987
Concrete	Charles Pitcher	0132
Confectionary Products	Cornelius Kenney	2428
Consortia of American Bus. (Grant Programs)	Healther Moxon	5004
Construction	Patrick MacAuley	0132
Construction Machinery (Large, Off Road)	Leonard Heimowitz	0558
Consumer Electronics	Howard Fleming	5163
Consumer Goods	Harry Bodansky	5783
Contact Facilitation Svc.	Colleen Ryan	5131
Conveyors/Conveying Equipment	Mary Wiening	4708
Cookware (stamped)	Rose Marie Bratland	0380
Copper	Barbara Males	0606
Cosmetics	Melissa Harrington	0128
Cosmetics (Export Promo)	Edward Kimmel	3640
Countertrade Services	Paula Mitchell	4471
Countertrade Services	Pompiliu Verzariu	4434
Cutlery	Rose Marie Bratland	0380
D		
Dairy Products	William Janis	2250
Data Base Services	Mary Inoussa	5820
Data Processing Services	Mary Inoussa	5820
Dental Equipment	Gregory Rathmell	2794
Dental Equipment	George Keen	2010
Desalination/Water Reuse	Frederica Wheeler	3509
Desalination (Maj. Projects)	Robert Dollison	2733
Direct Marketing	Fred Elliott	1120
Disk Storage	Daniel Valverde	0573
Distilled Spirits	Cornelius Kenney	2428
Dolls	Donald Hodgen	3346
Doors (Wood, Metal, Plastic)	Frank E. Williams	0132

		Phone (202) 482-
Drugs	William Hurt	0128
Durable Consumer Goods	Kevin Ellis	1176
E		
Earthenware	Rose Marie Bratland	0380
Education Facilities (Major Proj)	Wallace Haraguchi	4877
Educational/Training	Achamma Chandersekaran	1316
Electric Industrial Apparatus Nec	John Bodson	0681
Electrical Power Plants (Major Proj)	Robert Dollison	2733
Elec. Power Gen, Transmission & Dist. Eqmt (Trade Promo)	Anthony Kostales	2390
Electrical Test & Measuring Instruments	Paul Barry	2795
Electricity	Vacant	
Electric Components (Trade Promo)	Marlene Ruffin	0570
Electronic Components, Prod & Test Eqmt (Trade Promo)	Marlene Ruffin	0570
Electronic Components	Judee Mussehl-Aziz	0429
Electronic Database Services	Mary Inoussa	5820
ElectroOptical Instruments	Franc Manzulillo	2991
ElectroOptical Instruments	Marguerite Nealon	3411
Elevators, Moving Stairways	Mary Wiening	4708
Energy (Commodities)	Joseph Yancik	1466
Energy, Renewable	Les Garden	0556
Energy Services	Helen Burroughs	1542
Entertainment Industries	John Siegmund	4781
Envelopes	Gary Stanley	0375
Environmental Services	James Walsh	5086
Environment Trade Promotion	Mildred Mack	4152
	Catherine Vial	
Explosives	Francis Maxey	0128
Export Management Companies	Donald C. Stow	5131
Export Trade Certificates of Review (Title III)	Theodore A. Gebhard	5131
Export Trading Companies	Donald C. Stow	5131
F		
Fabricated Metal Construction Materials	Franklin Williams	0132
Factoring & Forfaiting	Elnora Uzzelle	0351
Farm Machinery	May Wiening	4708
Fasteners (Industrial)	Richard Reise	3489
Fats and Oils	William Janis	2250
Fencing (Metal)	Patrick MacAuley	0132
Ferralloys Products	Graylin Presbury	5158
Ferrous Scrap	Charles Bell	0608
Fertilizers	Francis Maxey	0128
Fertilizer Plants (Major Proj)	Max Miles	0679
Fiber Optics	Anthony Mocenigo	2953
Filters/Purifying Equipment	Frederica Wheeler	3509
Flat Panel Displays	Jonathan Streeter	0480
Flexible Mfg Systems	Megan Pilaroscia	0609
Floor Covering, Hard Surfaced	Patrick MacAuley	0132
Flour	William Janis	2250

Phone
(202) 482-

Fluid Power	Edward McDonald	0680
Food Products Machinery	Gene Shaw	3494
Footwear	James Byron	4034
Foreign Sales Corporations	Helen Burroughs	1542
Forest Products	Gary Stanley	0375
Forgings Semifinished Steel	Charles Bell	0608
Foundry Industry	Charles Bell	0608
Frozen Foods Products	William Janis	2250
Fruits (Processed)	William Janis	2250
Fur Goods	James Byron	4034
Furniture	Donald Hodgen	3346

G

Gallium	David Cammarota	5157
Games and Children's Vehicles	Donald Hodgen	3346
Gaskets/Gasketing Materials	Richard Reise	3489
General Aviation Aircraft	Ron Green	4222
Geothermal Energy Eqmt	Les Garden	0556
Germanium	David Cammarota	5157
Giftware (Export Promo)	Regina Beckham	5478
Glass, Flat	Franklin Williams	0132
Glassware (Household)	Rose Marie Bratland	0380
Gloves (Work & Dress)	James Byron	4034
Grain Mill Products	William Janis	2250
Greeting Cards	Rose Marie Bratland	0380
Ground Water Exploration & Development	Frederica Wheeler	3509
Gypsum Board	Charles Pitcher	0132

H

Hand Saws, Saw Blades	Edward Abrahams	0312
Hand/Edge Tools/Saws	Edward Abrahams	0312
Handbags	James Byron	4034
Hardware (Export Promo)	Reginald Beckham	5478
Hardware, Building	Charles Pitcher	0132
Health Care Services	Ernest Plock	4783
Helicopters	Ron Green	4222
Helicopters (Trade Promo)	Heather Pederson	2835
High Tech Trade, U.S. Competitiveness	Victoria Hatter	3895
Highways (Major Proj)	Jay Smith	4642
Hoists, Overhead Cranes	Mary Wiening	4708
Hose and Belting	Raimundo Prat	0128
Hospitals (Major Proj)	Wallace Haraguchi	4877
Hotels and Motels	J. Richard Sousane	4582
Hotel and Restaurants Eqmt (Export Promo)	Edward Kimmel	3640
Household Appliances	John Harris	1178
Household Appliances (Export Promo)	Regina Beckham	5478
Household Furniture	Donald Hodgen	3346
Housewares (Export Promo)	Reginald Beckham	5478
Housing Construction, Domestic	Charles Pitcher	4022
Housing Construction, International	Patrick Cosslett	5125
Hydroelectric Power (Major Proj)	Robert Dollison	2733

		Phone **(202) 482-**
I		
Industrial Controls	John Bodson	0681
Industrial Drives/Gears	Richard Reise	3489
Industrial Organic Chemicals	Michael Kelly	0128
Industrial Robots	Megan Pilaroscia	0609
Industrial Trucks	Mary Wiening	4608
Information Services	Mary Inoussa	5820
Insulation	Patrick MacAuley	0132
Insurance	Bruce McAdam	0346
	S. Cassin Muir	0349
Intellectual Property Rights (Svcs.)	John Siegmund	4781
Irrigation Equipment	Mary Wiening	4608
J		
Jams and Jellies	William Janis	2250
Jewelry	John Harris	1178
Jewelry (Export Promo)	Reginald Beckham	5478
Jute Products	Maria D'Andrea	4058
Juvenile Products	Donald Hodgen	3346
K		
Kitchen Cabinets	Barbara Wise	0375
L		
LNG Plants (Major Proj)	Max Miles	0679
Laboratory Instruments	Marguerite Nealon	3411
Laboratory Instruments (Trade Promo)	Franc Manzolillo	2991
Lasers	Marguerite Nealon	3411
Lasers (Trade Promo)	Frank Manzolillo	2991
Lawn and Garden Equipment	Donald Hodgen	3346
Lead Products	David Larabee	0607
Leasing (Eqmt)	Elnora Uzzelle	0351
Leather Products	James Byron	4034
Leather Tanning	James Byron	4034
Legal Services	Marc Chittum	0345
Local Area Networks	Mary Devin	0568
Logs, Wood	Barbara Wise	0375
Luggage	James Byron	4034
Lumber	Barbara Wise	0375
M		
Machine Tool Accessories	Edward Abrahams	0312
Magazines	Rose Marie Bratland	0380
Magnesium	David Cammarota	5157
Management Consulting	Marc Chittum	0345
Manifold Business Forms	Rose Marie Bratland	0380
Manmade Fiber	William Dulka	4058
Margarine	William Janis	2250
Marine Insurance	William Johnson	5012
Marine Recreational Equipment (Export Promo)	Regina Beckham	5478

		Phone (202) 482-
Maritime Shipping	William Johnson	5012
Mass Transit (Major Proj)	Jay Smith	4642
Mattresses and Bedding	Donald Hodgen	3346
Meat Products	William Janis	2250
Mech Power Transmission Eqmt	Richard Reise	3489
Medical Eqmt (Instruments/Supplies)	Matthew Edwards	0550
Medical Eqmt (Electromedical)	Victoria Kader	4073
Medical Facilities (Major Proj)	Wallace Haraguchi	4877
Medical Instruments and Eqmt	George Keen	2010
Medical/Dental Eqmt (NIS Proj)	Gregory Rathmell	2796
Metal Building Products	Franklin Williams	0132
Metal Cookware	Rose Marie Bretland	0380
Metal Cutting Machine Tools	Megan Pilaroscia	0609
Metal Forming Machine Tools	Megan Pilaroscia	0609
Metal Powders	Barbara Males	0606
Metals, Secondary	David Cammarota	5157
Metalworking	Megan Pilaroscia	0609
Microelectronics	Margaret Donnelly	5466
Microwave Communications	Stuart Sandall	2006
Millwork	Franklin Williams	0132
Mineral Based Construction Materials	Charles Pitcher	0132
Mining Machinery	Leonard Heimowitz	0558
Mining (Major Proj)	Max Miles	0679
Miscellaneous Publishing	William Lofquist	0379
Mobile Homes	Patrick Cosslett	5125
Mobile Radios	Stuart Sandall	2006
Molybdenum	Graylin Presbury	5158
Monorails (Industrial)	Mary Wiening	4708
Motion Pictures	John Siegmund	4781
Motor Vehicles	Albert Warner	0669
Motorcycles	John Vanderwolf	0348
Motors, Electric	John Bodson	0681
Music	John Siegmund	4781
Musical Instruments	John Harris	1178
Mutual Funds	Cassin Muir	0349

N

NATO	Alexis Kemper	1512
Natural Gas	Charles Breckinridge	2374
Natural, Synthetic Rubber	Raimundo Prat	0128
Newspapers	Rose Marie Bratland	0380
Newsprint	Gary Stanley	0375
Nickel Products	Graylin Presbury	5158
Non-Alcoholic Beverages	Cornelius Kenney	2428
Noncurrent Carrying Wiring Devices	John Bodson	0681
Nondurable Consumer Goods	Leslie Simon	0341
Nonferrous Metals	David Cammarota	5157
Nonresidential Construction	Patrick MacAuley	0132
Nuclear Power Plants (Major Proj)	Robert Dollison	2733
Numerical Cntrls, For Mach Tools	Megan Pilaroscia	0609
Nuts, Bolts, Washers	Richard Reise	3489

		Phone (202) 482-
O		
Ocean Shipping	William Johnson	5012
Office Buildings (Major Proj)	Wallace Haraguchi	4877
Office Furniture	Donald Hodgen	3346
Oil & Gas Prod and Ref (Major Proj)	Max Miles	0679
Oil and Gas (Fuels Only)	Charles Breckinridge	2374
Oil/Gas Field Machinery	Edward McDonald	0680
Ophthalmic Goods	Patricia Eyring	2846
Outdoor Lighting Fixtures	John Bodson	0681
Outdoor Power Eqmt	Donald Hodgen	3346
P		
Packaging Machinery	Gene Shaw	3494
Paints/Coatings	Raimundo Prat	0128
Paper	Gary Stanley	0375
Paper and Board Packaging	Gary Stanley	0375
Paper Industries Machinery	Edward Abrahams	0312
Pasta	William Janis	2250
Paving Materials (Asphalt)	Patrick MacAuley	0132
Paving Materials (Concrete)	Charles Pitcher	0132
Pens/Pencils	John Vanderwolf	0348
Periodicals	Rose Marie Bratland	0380
Personal Communications	Linda Gossack	4523
Pet Food	William Janis	2250
Pet Products (Export Promo)	Edward Kimmel	3640
Petrochemicals	Michael Kelly	0128
Petrochemicals Plants (Major Proj)	Max Miles	0679
Petroleum, Crude and Refined Products	Charles Breckinridge	2374
Pharmaceuticals	William Hurt	0128
Photographic Eqmt and Supplies	Joyce Watson	0574
Pipelines (Major Proj)	Max Miles	0679
Plastic Construction Products (Most)	Franklin Williams	0132
Plastic Materials	Raimundo Prat	0128
Plastic Products Machinery	Ray Robinson	0610
Platemaking Services	William Lofquist	0379
Plumbing Fixtures and Fittings	Robert Shaw	0132
Plywood/Panel Products	Kathy Rice	0375
Point-of-Use Water Treatment	Frederica Wheeler	3509
Pollution Control Equipment	Loretta Jonkers	0564
Porcelain Electrical Supplies	John Bodson	0681
Ports, Harbors (Major Proj)	Jay Smith	4642
Potato Chips	William Janis	2250
Pottery	Rose Marie Bratland	0380
Poultry Products	William Janis	2250
Power Generation & Distribution Eqmt (Trade Promo)	Anthony Kostalas	2390
Power Hand Tools	Edward Abrahams	0312
Precious Metal Jewelry	John Harris	1178
Prefabricated Buildings (Wood)	Patrick Cosslett	5125
Prefabricated Buildings (Metal)	Franklin Williams	0132
Prepared Meats	William Janis	2250

		Phone (202) 482-
Pretzels	Willaim Janis	2250
Printing and Publishing	William Lofquist	0379
Printing Trade Services	William Lofquist	0379
Printing Trades Mach/Eqmt	Ray Robinson	0610
Process Control Instruments	Marguerite Nealon	3411
Process Control Instruments (Trade Promo)	Frank Manzolillo	2991
Project Finance	Michael Hinds	5131
Pulp and Paper Mills (Major Proj)	Max Miles	0679
Pulpmills	Gary Stanley	0375
Pumps, Compressors (Trade Promo)	George Zanetakos	0552
Pumps, Pumping Eqmt	Edward McDonald	0680

R

Radio and TV Broadcasting Services	John Siegmund	4781
Radio Communications Eqmt	Linda Gossack	4523
Railroad Services	Richard Sousane	4581
Railroads (Maj Proj)	Jay Smith	4642
Recorded Music	John Siegmund	4781
Recreation Equipment	John Vanderwolf	0348
Recreational Eqmt (Export Promo)	Reginald Beckham	5478
Recycling, Waste Management	Kimberly Copperthite	0560
Refrigeration Eqmt	Patrick Cosslett	0132
Renewable Energy Eqmt	Les Garden	0556
Residential Lighting Fixtures	John Bodson	0681
Retail Trade	James Walsh	5086
	Helen Burroughs	1542
Rice Milling	William Janis	2250
Roads (Major Proj)	Jay Smith	4642
Robots	Megan Pilaroscia	0609
Roller Bearings	Richard Reise	3489
Roofing, Asphalt	Franklin Williams	0132
Rubber & Rubber Products	Raimundo Prat	0128

S

Saddlery and Harness Products	James Byron	4034
Safety and Security Equip (Trade Promo)	Dwight Umstead	2410
Satellite Communications Eqmt	Patricia Cooper	4202
Satellite Communications Services	Patricia Cooper	4202
Satellites and Space Vehicles (Marketing)	Clay Mowry	4222
Science and Electronics (Trade Promo)	Jake Moose	4125
Scientific Instruments	Frank Manzolillo	2991
Scientific Measurement/Control Eqmt	Marguerite Nealon	3411
Screw Machine Products	Richard Reise	3489
Screws, Washers	Richard Reise	3489
Search and Navigation Eqmt	Alexis Kemper	4466
Securities	Cassin Muir	0349
Semiconductors (except Japan)	Robin Roark	3090
Semiconductors, Japan	Robert Scott	3360
Semiconductor Materials	Dorothea Blouin	1333
Semiconductor Prod Eqmt	Paul Barry	2795

		Phone (202) 482-
Services, Data Base Development	Robert Atkins	4781
Services, Telecom	Daniel Edwards	4331
Shingles (Wood)	Barbara Wise	0375
Shipping, Maritime	William Johnson	5012
Shoes	James Byron	4034
Silverware	John Harris	1178
Small Arms, Ammunition	John Vanderwolf	0348
Snack Food	William Janis	2250
Soaps, Detergents, Cleaners	Melissa Herrington	0128
Software	Heidi Hijikata	0569
Software, Custom	Shelagh Montgomery	0397
Software, Packaged	Mary Smolenski	0551
Software (Trade Promo)	Judy Fogg	4936
Solar Cells/Photovoltaic Devices	Les Garden	0556
Solar Eqmt	Les Garden	0556
Soy Products	William Janis	2250
Space Commercialization (Eqmt)	Clay Mowry	4222
Space Policy Development	Clay Mowry	4222
Space Vehicles (Marketing)	Clay Mowry	4222
Speed Changers	Richard Reise	3489
Spirits, Distilled	Cornelius Kenney	2428
Sporting and Athletic Goods	John Vanderwolf	0348
Sporting Goods (Export Promo)	Reginald Beckham	5478
Steel Industry Products	Charles Bell	0608
Steel Mill Products	Charles Bell	0608
Steel Mills (Major Proj)	Max Miles	0679
Stone, Dimension & Crushed	Charles Pitcher	0132
Storage Batteries	David Larrabee	0607
Store Fixtures	Donald Hodgen	3346
Supercomputers	Sean Iverson	1987
Superconductors	Roger Chiarado	0402
Switchgear and Switchboard Apparatus	John Bodson	0681

T

Technology Affairs	Edwin Shykind	4694
Telecommunications (Customer Premises Eqmt)	William Bien	0399
Telecommunications (Major Projects)	Rick Paddock	5235
Telecommunications (Military Comm Eqmt)	Alexis Kemper	1512
Telecommunications (Network Equip)	John Henry	1193
Telecommunication (Services)	Daniel Edwards	4331
Telecommunications (Trade Promo)	Theresa Retting	4523
Telecommunications (Wireless or Radio Eqmt & Svcs)	Linda Gossack	4466
Teletext Services	Mary Inoussa	5820
Textile Production Machinery	John Manger	2732
Textiles	William Dulka	4058
Textiles (Trade Promo)	Ferenc Molnar	2043
Timber Products (Tropical)	Kathy Rice	0375
Tires	Raimundo Prat	0128
Tools/Dies/Jigs/Fixtures	Megan Pilaroscia	0609
Tourism Services	Richard Sousane	4582
Toys	Donald Hodgen	3346

		Phone **(202) 482-**
Toys and Games (Export Promo)	Reginald Beckham	5478
Trade Finance	John Shuman	3050
Transformers	John Bodson	0681
Transportation Industries	William Johnson	5012
Trucking Services	Richard Sousane	4581
Trucks, Trailers, Buses (Trade Promo)	John White	0671
Tungsten Products	David Cammarota	5157
Tunnels (Major Proj)	Jay Smith	4642
Typesetting	William Lofquist	0379

U

Used Reconditioned Eqmt	John Bodson	0681

V

Valves, Pipe Fittings (Except Brass)	Richard Reise	3489
Vegetables	William Janis	2250
Venture Capital	Michael Hinds	5131
Videotex Services	Mary Inoussa	5820
Virtual Reality	Shelagh Montgomery	0397

W

Wallets, Billfords, Flat Goods	James Byron	4034
Warm Air Heating Eqmt	Vacant	3509
Wastepaper	Gary Stanley	0375
Watches	John Harris	1178
Water Resource Eqmt	Frederica Wheeler	3509
Water Supply and Dist	Frederica Wheeler	3509
Water & Sewage Treatment Plants (Maj Proj)	William Holroyd	6168
Welding, Cutting Apparatus	Edward Abrahams	0312
Wholesale Trade	James Walsh	5086
Wind Energy Systems	Les Garden	0556
Windows (wood, metal, plastic)	Franklin Williams	0132
Wine	Cornelius Kenney	2428
Wire and Wire Products	Charles Bell	0608
Wire Cloth, Industrial	Richard Reise	3489
Wire Cloth	Patrick MacAuley	0132
Wood Products	Barbara Wise	0375
Wood Working Machinery	Edward Abrahams	0312
Writing Instruments	John Vanderwolf	0348

Y

Yarn	William Dulka	4058

Z

Zinc	David Larrabee	0607

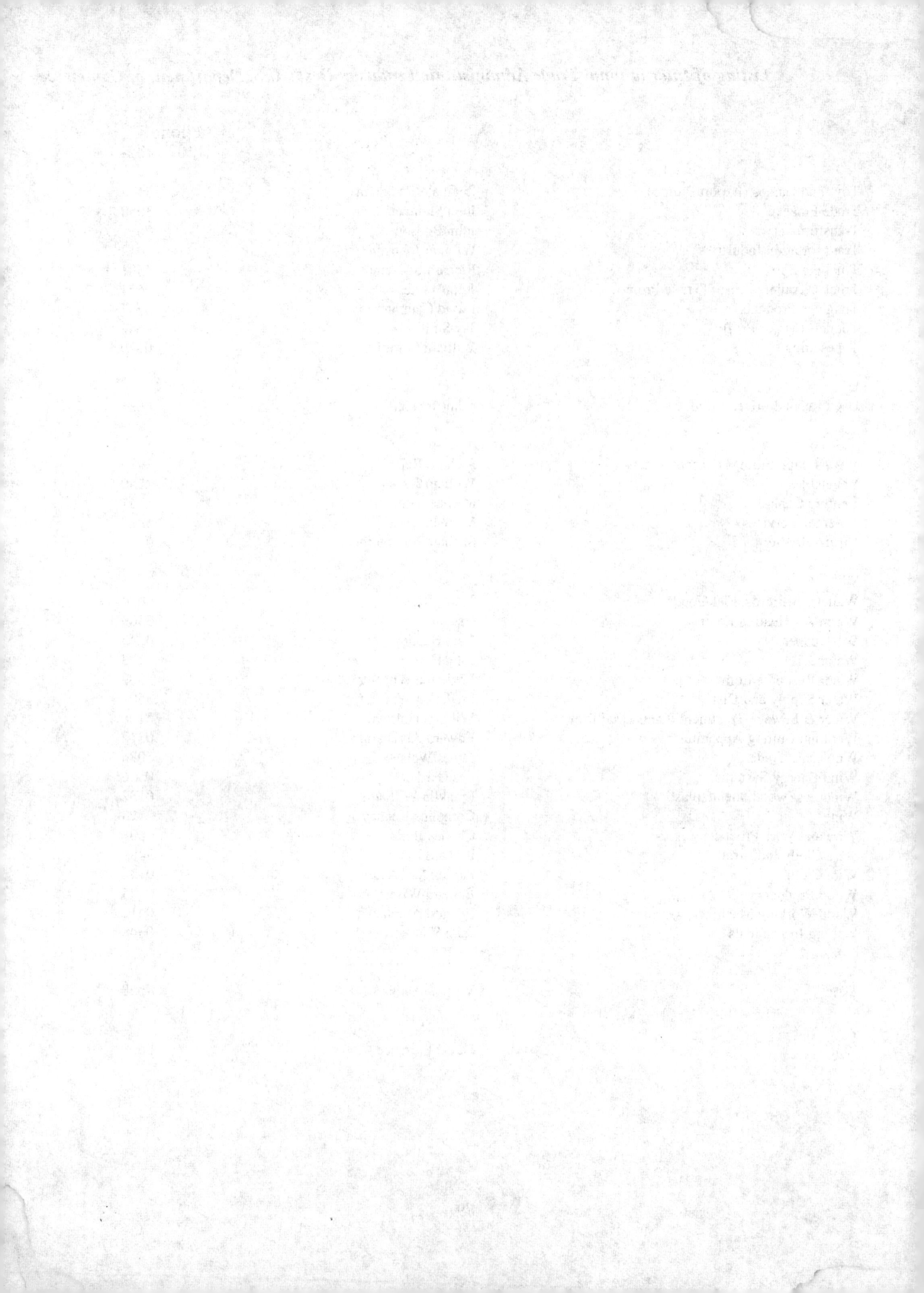

Foreign Trade Zones

A foreign-trade zone (FTZ) is a site within the United States, in or near a U.S. Customs port of entry, where foreign and domestic merchandise is generally considered to be in international commerce. Foreign or domestic merchandise may enter this enclave without a formal customs entry or the payment of custom duties or government excise taxes. Merchandise entering a zone may be:

- stored;
- tested;
- sampled;
- relabeled;
- repackaged;
- displayed;
- repaired;
- manipulated;
- mixed;
- cleaned;
- assembled;
- manufactured;
- salvaged;
- destroyed; or
- processed.

If the final product is exported from the United States, no U.S. Customs duty or excise tax is levied. If, however, the final product is imported into the United States, customs duty and excise taxes are due only at the time of transfer from the foreign-trade zone and formal entry in the U.S. The duty paid is the lower of that appliable to the product itself or its component parts. Thus, zones provide opportunities to realize customs duty savings by zone users. In addition, zone procedures provide one of the most flexible methods of handling domestic and imported merchandise.

In 1934 the U.S. Congress passed the Foreign-Trade Zones Act "to expedite and encourage foreign commerce." The act was designed to stimulate international trade and thereby create jobs and investment in the U.S. At that time zones were envisioned as storage, manipulation and transshipment centers. In 1950, an amendment was passed authorizing manufacturing and exhibition.

On April 21, 1980, an amendment to the U.S. Customs Service Regulations was promulgated which excludes U.S.-sourced processing costs in zones from U.S. Customs duty. The amendment created over 160 new processing operations in the 1980s.

Since the 1980 Customs decision, zones have emerged as an economic development tool that many communities use in order to retain and attract new buisness in their area. Consequently, there has been an unprecedented growth in the number of foreign-trade zones.

Designation as a foreign-trade zone is granted by the Foreign-Trade Zones Board within the U.S. Department of Commerce. The Board consists of the secretary of commerce, the secretary of the treasury and the secretary of the army.

The executive secretariat of the board is located in the U.S. Department of Commerce, Washington, DC 20230.

National Association of Foreign-Trade Zones
1735 I Street, NW, Suite 506
Washington, D.C. 20006
(202) 331-1950
Fax (202) 331-1994

Foreign-Trade Zones in California:

Foreign-Trade Zone #3
Foreign Trade Services, Inc.
Pier 23
San Francisco, CA 94111
(415) 391-0176

Foreign-Trade Zone #18
CCBS Warehousing Services, Inc.
5667 Cinnabar Street
San Jose, CA 95110
(408) 292-9100

Foreign-Trade Zone #50
775 West Manville Street
Rancho Dominguez, CA 90220-5505
(310) 635-7000
Fax (310) 635-7788

Foreign-Trade Zone, Expansion Site #50-1
California Commerce Center
9580 Commerce Center Drive
Rancho Cucamonga, CA 91730
(714) 466-8268
Fax (714) 466-8269

Foreign-Trade Zone, Expansion Site #50-2
20 Civic Center Plaza
P.O. Box 1988, M-35
Santa Ana, CA 92702
(714) 647-6984
Fax (714) 647-6549

Foreign-Trade Zone #56
9401 San Leandro Street
Oakland, CA 94603
(510) 568-8500
Fax (510) 568-4483

Foreign-Trade Zone #143
The Port of Sacramento
2650 Industrial Boulevard
West Sacramento, CA 95691
(916) 372-8322
Fax (916) 372-8389

Foreign-Trade Zone #153
City of San Diego
Economic Development Division
Security Pacific Plaza
1200 3rd Avenue, Suite 1620
San Diego, CA 92101
(619) 236-6550

Foreign-Trade Zone #191
City of Palmdale
Economic Development Department
950 East Palmdale Blvd., Suite E
Palmdale, CA 93550
(805) 267-5125
FAX (805) 267-5155

Foreign Consular Corps, Government Representatives, Trade and Tourism Offices in California (Listed by Country)

ARGENTINA
Consulate General of Argentina
Ambassador Luis Maria Riccheri, Consul General
5055 Wilshire Boulevard, Suite 210
Los Angeles, CA 90036
(213) 954-9155/56/57
Fax (213) 934-9076

Argentine Consulate General
Ambassador Simon N. Arguello, Consul General
Beatriz Graciela Boschi, Deputy Consul General
Luis del Solar-Dorrego, Deputy Consul (Commercial)
Margarita Roldan-Visillac, Attache Adm. Affairs
870 Market Street, Room 1083
San Francisco, CA 94102
(415) 982-3050
Fax (415) 362-8297

Argentine Republic Promotion Office
Ambassador Luis Maria Riccheri, Director General
5055 Wilshire Boulevard, Suite 210
Los Angeles, CA 94036
(213) 954-9233
Fax (213) 934-9076

Argentine Promotion Center
Luis Maria Riccheri, Director
5055 Wilshire Boulevard, Suite 208
Los Angeles, CA 90036
(213) 954-9155
Fax (213) 937-3841

Argentina National Tourist Office
5055 Wilshire Boulevard, Suite 210
Los Angeles, CA 90036
(213) 930-0681

ASIA
Pacific Asia Travel Association
Kane Rufe, Executive Vice President
One Montgomery Street
West Tower, Suite 1750
San Francisco, CA 94104
(415) 986-4646

AUSTRALIA
Consulate General of Australia
Rob O'Donovan, Consul General
611 N. Larchmont Boulevard
Los Angeles, CA 90004-9998
(213) 469-4300

Australian Trade Commission and Consulate General
Paul McCaffrey, Senior Trade Commissioner and
  Consul General
One Bush Street, 7th Floor
San Francisco, CA 94104
(415) 362-6160
Fax (415) 986-5440

Australian Trade Commission
Colin Hook, Trade Commissioner
611 N. Larchmont Boulevard
Los Angeles, CA 90004-9998
(213) 469-4300
Fax (213) 469-9176

Australian Trade Commission
The Concourse, Building Two
224 Airport Parkway
San Jose, CA 95110

Australian Tourist Commission
2121 Avenue of the Stars, Suite 1200
Los Angeles, CA 90067
(310) 552-1988

Victorian Government for Australia
Maurice Keppel, Commissioner
611 N. Larchmont Boulevard, 2nd Floor
Los Angeles, CA 90004
(213) 466-5482
Fax (213) 461-2547

Tourism Victoria
2121 Avenue of the Stars, Suite 1200
Los Angeles, CA 90067
(310) 552-5344
Fax (310) 552-1215

Tourism New South Wales
2121 Avenue of the Stars, Suite 1210
Los Angeles, CA 90067
(310) 552-9566
Fax (310) 277-2263

Australia's Northern Territory Tourist Commission
5855 Green Valley Circle, Suite 204
Culver City, CA 90230
(310) 645-9875
Fax (310) 645-9876

South Australia Tourism Commission
1700 E. Dyer Road, #160
Santa Ana, CA 92705
(714) 852-2270
Fax (714) 852-2277

AUSTRIA
Consulate General of Austria
Dr. Christian Prosl, Consul General
Gerhard Mayer, Deputy Consul General
11859 Wilshire Boulevard, Suite 501
Los Angeles, CA 90025
(310) 444-9310
Fax (310) 477-9897

Honorary Consulate of Austria
Donald Burns, Honorary Consul
41 Sutter Street, Suite 207
San Francisco, CA 94104
(415) 951-8911

Austrian Trade Commission
Hans Kausl, Trade Commissioner
11601 Wilshire Boulevard, Suite 2420
Los Angeles, CA 90025
(310) 477-9988
Fax (310) 477-1643

Austrian National Tourist Office
P.O. Box 491938
Los Angeles, CA 90049
(310) 477-3332
Fax (310) 477-5141

BAHAMAS
Bahamas Tourist Office
3450 Wilshire Boulevard, Suite 208
Los Angeles, CA 90010
(213) 383-3966
Fax (213) 383-3966

BANGLADESH
Consulate of Bangladesh
Nancy C. Bretzfield, Consul General
1564 N. Doheny Drive
Los Angeles, CA 90069
(310) 274-7955
Fax (310) 274-3525

BARBADOS
Barbados Consulate and Trade Offices
Don McCarthy, Vice Consul
3440 Wilshire Boulevard, Suite 1215
Los Angeles, CA 90010
(213) 380-2198
Fax (213) 384-2763

Consulate of Barbados
Jerry Levine, Honorary Consul
442 Post Street, Suite 800
San Francisco, CA 94102
(415) 421-8789
Fax (415) 421-1697

BELGIUM
Consulate General of Belgium
Guy Trouveroy, Consul General
6100 Wilshire Boulevard, Suite 1200
Los Angeles, CA 90048
(213) 857-1244
Fax (213) 936-2564

Consulate General of Belgium
Trade and Economic Representation of Flanders
Willy Robijn, Trade Commissioner
6100 Wilshire Boulevard, Suite 1200
Los Angeles, CA 90048
(213) 857-0842
Fax (213) 938-4024

Honorary Consulate of Belgium
Patrick J. Sebrechts, Honorary Consul
5572 Trinity Way
San Diego, CA 92120
(619) 943-9121
Fax (619) 943-9121

BELIZE
Honorary Consulate of Belize
Ernesto Castillo, Honorary Consul
611 South Wilton Place
Los Angeles, CA 90005
(213) 385-6499

BOLIVIA
Consulate General of Bolivia
870 Market Street, Room 355
San Francisco, CA 94102
(415) 495-5173

BOTSWANA
Consulate of Botswana
William B. Rudell, Consul
333 South Hope Street, 38th Floor
Los Angeles, CA 90071
(213) 626-8484
Fax (213) 626-0078

Consulate of Botswana
Charles Louis Frankel, Honorary Consul
2040 Broadway Street, Suite 402
San Francisco, CA 94104
(415) 346-4435

BRAZIL
Consulate General of Brazil
Ambassador Raul Fernando Leite Ribeiro, Consul General
8484 Wilshire Boulevard, Suite 730
Beverly Hills, CA 90211
(213) 651-2664, ext. 211

Consulate General of Brazil
Joao Almino, Consul General
Carlos Lamback, Deputy Consul
300 Montgomery Street, Suite 1160
San Francisco, CA 94104
(415) 981-8170

Brazil Trade Center
Joao Alberto D. Quintaes, Deputy Consul
8484 Wilshire Boulevard, Suite 730
Beverly Hills, CA 90211
(310) 651-2664
Fax (310) 651-1274

BURKINA FASO
Honorary Consulate General of Burkina Faso
Allan I.Nieman, Honorary Consul General
11755 Wilshire Boulevard, Suite 1310
Los Angeles, CA 90025
(310) 575-5567
Fax (310) 575-5550

CAMEROON
Consulate of Cameroon
Donald Low, Honorary Consul
147 Terra Vista
San Francisco, CA 94115
(415) 921-5372

CANADA
Consulate General of Canada
Dennis Browne, Consul General
Allan S. Poole, Acting Consul General and Senior Trade Comm.
Commercial Division
Douglas Paterson, Consul and Trade Commissioner
Bernard Brandenburg, Commercial Officer
Jeffrey Gray, Commercial Officer
Carl Light, Commercial Officer
Michael Pascal, Commercial Officer
George Simon, Commercial Officer
Deborah Weintraub, Commercial Officer
Investment Division
Matthew H. Fischer, Consul and Senior Investment Advisor
Eric P. Nielsen, Investment Officer
300 South Grand Avenue, 10th Floor
Los Angeles, CA 90071
(213) 346-2700
Fax (213) 620-8827

Consulate of Canada - Trade Office
Robert Logie, Consul and Senior Trade Comissioner
Mark Ritchie, Commercial Officer
Judith Duffy, Tourism Program Manager
Andrew A. Thompson, Public Officers' Officer
50 Fremont Street, Suite 1825
San Francisco, CA 94105
(415) 543-2550
Fax (415) 512-7671

Consulate of Canada - Trade Office
Michael Stinson, Consul and Trade Commissioner
Larry McJannet, Commercial Officer
4370 La Jolla Village Drive, Suite 400
San Diego, CA 92122
(619) 546-4467
Fax (619) 457-2844

Consulate of Canada - Trade Office
Cameron Miller, Consul and Trade Commissioner
Michael Siewecke, Vice Consul/Asst Trade Commissioner
Jeane Weaver, Commercial Officer
333 W. San Carlos Street, Suite 945
San Jose, CA 95110
(408) 289-1157
Fax (408) 289-1168

Government of British Columbia
Peter J. MacLean, Director
2600 Michelson, Suite 1050
Irvine, CA 92715-1550
(714) 852-0201
Fax (714) 852-0168

Quebec Government Office
Marcel Gilbert
11755 Wilshire Boulevard, Suite 2200
Los Angeles, CA 90025
(310) 477-2217
Fax (310) 477-3540

CAYMAN ISLANDS
Cayman Islands Department of Tourism
3440 Wilshire Boulevard, Suite 1202
Los Angeles, CA 90010
(213) 738-1968
(415) 991-1836
Fax (213) 738-1829

CHILE
Consulate General of Chile
Pedro Suckel, Consul General
1900 Avenue of the Stars #2450
Century City, CA 90067
(310) 785-0113
Fax (310) 785-0132

Consulate General of Chile
Jacqueline Jorquera, Consular Officer
Amelia Campos, Visa
870 Market Street, Suite 1058
San Francisco, CA 94102
(415) 982-7662
Fax (415) 982-2384

Consulate of Chile
George L. Gildred, Honorary Consul
550 West C Street, Suite 1820
San Diego, CA 92101
(619) 232-6361
Fax (619) 696-0991

Chilean Government Trade Office
Patricio de Gregorio, Trade Commisioner
1900 Avenue of the Stars, Suite 2470
Los Angeles, CA 90067
(310) 553-4541
Fax (310) 553-6817

CHINA, PEOPLE'S REPUBLIC OF
Consulate General of People's Republic of China
Zhou Wenzhong, Consul General
Liang Bihua, Commercial Consul
443 Shatto Place
Los Angeles, CA 90020
(213) 380-3105
Fax (213) 380-19618
Visa: (213) 380-0372
Commercial Section: (213) 380-0587
Cultural Affairs: (213) 380-1191

Consulate General of People's Republic of China
Ping Mei, Consul General
1450 Laguna Street
San Francisco, CA 94115
(415) 563-4885
Fax (415) 563-0494

Republic of China Tourism Bureau
166 Geary Street, Suite 1605
San Francisco, CA 94108
(415) 989-8677

COLOMBIA
Consulate of Colombia
Maria Helena Cruz, Vice Consul
3580 Wilshire Boulevard, Suite 1450
Los Angeles, CA 90010
(213) 382-1136

Consulate General of Colombia
Miguel Segundo Mazas Alvarez, Consul General
Jose Antonio Solarte, Consul
595 Market Street, Suite 2130
San Francisco, CA 94105
(415) 495-7195/96
(415) 777-3731

Colombian Government Trade Bureau
Douglas Montgomery, Director
6100 Wilshire Boulevard, Suite 1170
Los Angeles, CA 90048
(213) 965-9760/61/62
Fax (213) 965-5029

COSTA RICA
Consulate General of Costa Rica
Ruth Garcia-Corrales, Consul General
3540 Wilshire Boulevard, Suite 404
Los Angeles, CA 90010
(213) 380-7915
Fax (213) 380-5639

Consulate General of Costa Rica
Amelia Barquero Trejos, Consul General
Julian Munoz, Consul Commercial
Peter Surroca, Consul, Culture and
Education
870 Market Street, Suite 546
San Francisco, CA 94102
(415) 392-8488
Fax (415) 398-0361

Consulate General of Costa Rica
Alex Sanchez, Consul General
4007 Camino del Rio South
San Diego, CA 92108
(619) 563-6441
Fax (619) 563-1059

CYPRUS
Honorary Consulate General of Cyprus
Andreas Kyprianides, Honorary Consul General
4219 Coolidge Avenue
Los Angeles, CA 90066
(310) 397-0771

Honorary Consulate General of Cyprus
Anastassios Simonidis, Honorary Consul General
205 Crocker Avenue
Piedmont, CA 94610
(510) 547-5689

DENMARK
Consulate General of Denmark
Leif Reimann, Consul General
Thomas Wilhelmsen, Commercial Counselor
3440 Wilshire Boulevard, Suite 904
Los Angeles, CA 90010-2183
(213) 387-4277
Fax (213) 387-9456

Honorary Consulate of Denmark
Paul E. Bach, Honorary Consul
Inger Bach, Visa
Allan Haugsted, Investment Advisor
601 Montgomery Street, Suite 1440
San Francisco, CA 94111
(415) 391-0100
Fax (415) 391-0181

Honorary Consulate of Denmark
W. Daniel Larsen, Honorary Consul
P.O. Box 80456
San Diego, CA 92138
(619) 224-7640
Fax (619) 223-2376

DOMINICAN REPUBLIC
Consulate of the Dominican Republic
David M. Shaby, Consul Emeritus
12103 West Jefferson Boulevard
Culver City, CA 90230
(310) 827-3873

Consulate General of the Dominican Republic
Miguel Angel Jimenez, Consul General Emeritus
870 Market Street, Suite 915
San Francisco, CA 94102
(415) 982-5144
Fax (415) 391-6924

ECUADOR
Consulate General of Ecuador
Patricio Baca Dabalos, Consul General
548 South Spring Street, Suite 602
Los Angeles, CA 90013
(213) 628-3014

Consulate of Ecuador
Cecilia Acosta, Acting Consul
455 Market Street, Suite 980
San Francisco, CA 94105
(415) 957-5921
Fax (415) 957-5923

EGYPT
Consulate General of Egypt
Ambassador Samir Mokhtar, Consul General
Hamdi Saleh, Consul
Aly Bassoiuay, Consul
3001 Pacific Avenue
San Francisco, CA 94115
(415) 346-9700
Fax (415) 346-9480

Egyptian Tourist Authority
8383 Wilshire Boulevard, Suite 215
Beverly Hills, CA 90211
(213) 653-8815

EL SALVADOR
Consulate General of El Salvador
Gerardo Sol Mixco, Consul General
2412 West 7th Street, 2nd Floor
Los Angeles, CA 90057
(213) 383-5776
Fax (213) 383-8599

Consulate General of El Salvador
Carlos E. Gonzalez, Consul General
870 Market Street, Suite 508
San Francisco, CA 94102
(415) 781-7924
Fax (415) 781-1136

Honorary Consulate of El Salvador
David Porter, Honorary Consul
P.O. Box 81488
San Diego, CA 92138
(619) 661-4000/4001
Fax (619) 661-6339

ESTONIA
Consulate of Estonia
Jaak Treiman, Honorary Consul
21515 Vanowen Street, Suite 211
Canoga Park, CA 91303-2787
(818) 884-5850
Fax (818) 593-2973

FIJI
Fiji Visitors Bureau
5777 West Century Boulevard, Suite 220
Los Angeles, CA 90045
(310) 568-1616
Fax (310) 670-2318

FINLAND
Consulate General of Finland
Tapio Saarela, Consul General
Anette Anas, Deputy Consul General
1900 Avenue of the Stars, Suite 1025
Los Angeles, CA 90067
(310) 203-9903
Fax (310) 203-1986

Honorary Consulate General of Finland
Richard J. Guggenhime, Honorary Consul General
333 Bush Street, 30th Floor
San Francisco, CA 94104
(415) 772-6649
Fax (415) 772-6268

Consulate of Finland
Bert J. Salonen, Honorary Consul
P.O. Box 91368
San Diego, CA 92169
(619) 459-9202
Fax (619) 454-6602

Finnish Tourist Board
1900 Avenue of the Stars, Suite 1070
Los Angeles, CA 90067
(310) 277-5226
Fax (310) 277-4067

FRANCE
Consulate General of France
M. Jean-Maurice Ripert
10990 Wilshire Boulevard, Suite 300
Los Angeles, CA 90024
(310) 479-4426

Consulate General of France
Alain LeGourrierec, Consul General
Chantal Haage, Press Attache
540 Bush Street
San Francisco, CA 94108
(415) 397-4330
Visa: (415) 397-4893
Press Office: (415) 391-4335
Fax (415) 433-8357

Honorary Consular Agency of France
Jean Pierre Paris, Honorary Consul Agent
2230 Fourth Avenue
San Diego, CA 92101
(619) 239-4814
Fax (619) 231-3552

Honorary Consulate of France
Jane R. Wheaton, Honorary Consul
1831 Rockwood Drive
Sacramento, CA 95864
(916) 488-7659

French Trade Office
Francois Alland, Trade Commissioner
1801 Avenue of the Stars, Suite 921
Los Angeles, CA 90067
(310) 843-1700
Fax (310) 843-1701

French Trade Commission
Jean Yves Conte, Trade Commissioner
Thierry Rosset, Agricultural Attache
88 Kearny Street, Suite 1510
San Francisco, CA 94108
(415) 781-0986
Fax (415) 781-4750

French Scientific Mission
Pascal Revel, Scientific Attache
Michele Durand, Scientific Attache
530 Bush Street, 3rd Floor
San Francisco, CA 94108
(415) 397-4440

French Government Tourist Office
9454 Wilshire Boulevard, Suite 715
Beverly Hills, CA 90212-2967
(310) 271-4721

Tahiti Tourist Board
300 N. Continental Boulevard, Suite 180
El Segundo, CA 90245
(310) 414-8484

GAMBIA
Honorary Consulate General of Gambia
Aimee Klaus, Acting Honorary Consul General
10777 Bellagio Road
Los Angeles, CA 90077
(310) 476-0532
Fax (310) 471-7424

GERMANY
Consulate General of Germany
Hans Alard von Rohr, Consul General
Stefan Schlueter, Deputy Consul General
Hendrik Wasserman, Trade and Science Attache
6222 Wilshire Boulevard, Suite 500
Los Angeles, CA 90048-4985
(213) 930-2703
Fax (213) 930-2805

Consulate General of Germany
Ruprecht Henatsch, Consul General
Jens Luetkenherm, Consul, Legal & Cultural Affairs
Heinrich Seitz, Consul, Head of Chancery
Ute Loffler, Vice Consul, Legal Affairs
Paul Harmel, Vice Consul, Visa
1960 Jackson Street
San Francisco, CA 94109
(415) 775-1061
Fax (415) 775-0187
Visa: (415) 775-1851

Honorary Consulate of Germany
Herman Zillgens, Honorary Consul
6215 Ferris Square, Suite 200A
San Diego, CA 92121
(619) 455-1423
Fax (619) 452-0609

German National Tourist Office
11766 Wilshire Boulevard, Suite 750
Los Angeles, CA 90025
(310) 575-9799

GREECE
Consulate General of Greece
Christos Panagapoulos, Consul General
Niki Mavriyanni, Vice Consul
3255 Wilshire Boulevard, Suite 1103
Los Angeles, CA 90010
(213) 385-1447
Fax (213) 385-1976

Consulate General of Greece
Elias Klis, Consul General
Canthi Naisi, Visa, Administrative
2441 Gough Street
San Francisco, CA 94123
(415) 775-2102
Fax (415) 776-6815

Greece Trade Office
Nicholas C. Conteas, Commercial Attache
9555 Van Alden Avenue
Northridge, CA 91324
(818) 993-3477

Greek National Tourism Organization
611 West Sixth Street, Suite 2198
Los Angeles, CA 90017
(213) 626-6696

GUATEMALA
Guatemala Trade Office
German Cerezo, Trade Commissioner
2500 Wilshire Boulevard, Suite 820
Los Angeles, CA 90057
(213) 383-6938
Fax (213) 383-6154

Consulate General of Guatemala
Rafael A. Salazar, Consul General
870 Market Street, Room 667
San Francisco, CA 94102
(415) 788-5651
Fax (415) 788-5653

Honorary Consulate of Guatemala
E.H. Sapper, Honorary Consul
10405 San Diego Mission Road
San Diego, CA 92108
(619) 282-8127
Fax (619) 280-5187

HAITI
Honorary Consulate General of Haiti
Oscar E. Carcelen, Honorary Consul General
David A. Carcelen, Honorary Chancellor
Carlos Duharte, Commercial Attache
48 Ocean Avenue
San Francisco, CA 94112
(415) 334-7930
Fax (415) 469-0201

HONDURAS
Consulate General of Honduras
Ramiro Licona, Consul General
George Chillingar, Honorary Consul
Elvira Quezada, Vice Consul
Astry A. Munoz, Consular Agent
Melba Leiva, Consular Agent
3450 Wilshire Blvd., Suite 230
Los Angeles, CA 90010
(213) 383-9244
Fax (213) 383-9306

Consulate General of Honduras
Mario A. Maldonado, Consul General
870 Market Street, Room 451-453
San Francisco, CA 94102
(415) 392-0076

Honorary Consulate of Honduras
Ella Isabel Flores, Honorary Consul
1477 La Playa Avenue
San Diego, CA 92109
(619) 235-5217
Fax (619) 231-3552

HONG KONG
Hong Kong Trade Development Council
Tohy Wong, Director
350 South Figueroa Street, Suite 282
Los Angeles, CA 90071
(213) 622-3194
Fax (213) 613-1490

Hong Kong Economic and Trade Office
Thomas C.Y. Chan, Director
Patrick Chung, Principal Consultant,
222 Kearny, Suite 402
San Francisco, CA 94108
(415) 397-2215
Fax (415) 421-0646
Industrial Promotion Unit: (415) 956-4560
Trade Development Council: (415) 677-9038
Hong Kong Tourist Association: (415) 421-4582

Hong Kong Tourist Association
10940 Wilshire Boulevard, Suite 1220
Los Angeles, CA 90024
(213) 208-4582

HUNGARY
Consulate of Hungary
Imre Helyes, Acting Consul General
Istvan Vadaszy, Commercial Counselor
11766 Wilshire Boulevard, Suite 410
Los Angeles, CA 90025
(310) 473-9344
Fax (310) 479-6443

Honorary Consulate of the Republic of Hungary
Eva E. Voisin, Honorary Consul
250A Twin Dolphin Drive
Redwood City, CA 94065
(415) 594-2618
Fax (415) 595-3976

ICELAND
Honorary Consulate General of Iceland
Halla Linker, Honorary Consul General
14755 Ventura Boulevard, Suite 1604
Sherman Oaks, CA 91403-3672
(310) 474-8485

INDIA
Consulate of India
All Correspondence:
Barbara Bryant, Director
10940 Wilshire Boulevard, Suite 1220
Los Angeles, CA 90024

Consulate General of India
Sushil Dubey, Consul General
Ravi Thapar, Consul Commercial
R.K. Chhabra, Vice Consul, Visa
540 Arguello Boulevard
San Francisco, CA 94118
(415) 668-0683
Fax (415) 668-2073
Commercial Section: (415) 668-0727

Engineering Export Promotion Council of India
Sampath Ramesh, Resident Director
727 West 7th Street, Suite 658
Los Angeles, CA 90017
(213) 622-8548
Fax (213) 622-0862

India Tourist Office
3550 Wilshire Boulevard, Suite 204
Los Angeles, CA 90010
(213) 380-8855

INDONESIA
Consulate General of Indonesia
Sudjono Haridadi, Consul General
Anwa Santoso, Consul, Economic Affairs
3457 Wilshire Boulevard, 4th Floor
Los Angeles, CA 90010
(213) 383-5126
Fax (213) 487-3971
Telex 674415

Consulate of Indonesia
Ahmad Fauzie Gani, Consul General
Henny Adries da Lopez, Vice Consul, Commercial
Renywati Zulkarnain, Vice Consul, Visa
Hadiono Badjuri, Vice Consul,
Science and Technology, Culture and Education
John Mahakena, Vice Consul, Administration/General
Affairs
1111 Columbus Avenue
San Francisco, CA 94133
(415) 474-9571
Fax (415) 441-4320

Indonesian Trade Promotion Center
Lili Soerojo Danusastro, Director
Djatimoer Damanik, Deputy Director, Trade Promotion
3457 Wilshire Boulevard, Suite 101
Los Angeles, CA 90010
(213) 738-8955
Fax (213) 738-7028

Indonesia Tourist Promotion Office
3457 Wilshire Boulevard, Suite 104
Los Angeles, CA 90010
(213) 387-2078
Fax (213) 380-4876

IRELAND
Consulate General of Ireland
Declan Kelly, Consul General
655 Montgomery Street, Suite 930
San Francisco, CA 94111
(415) 392-4214
Fax (415) 392-0885

Industrial Development Authority of Ireland
Fairmont Plaza
50 W. San Fernando Street, Suite 830
San Jose, CA 95113
(408) 294-9903
Fax (408) 294-9934

Industrial Development Authority of Ireland
1620 26th Street, Suite 480S
Santa Monica, CA 90404
(310) 829-0081
Fax (310) 829-1586

Irish Tourist Board
17875 Von Karman #202
Irvine, CA 92714
(800) 223-6470

ISRAEL
Consulate General of Israel
Yoram Ben Zeev, Consul General
Moshe Benzioni, Deputy Consul General
Jerry Stoch, Consul, Economic Affairs
Tim Plotkin, Deputy Trade Commissioner
6380 Wilshire Boulevard, Suite 1700
Los Angeles, CA 90048
(213) 651-5700
Fax (213) 651-3123
Economic Development: (213) 658-7924
Fax (213) 651-0572
Tourism: (213) 658-7462
Fax (213) 658-6543

Consulate General of Israel
Harry Kney-Tal, Consul General
Anna Azari, Consul
Shlomi Kidron, Consul, Economic Affairs
Rochelle Jaye, Deputy Trade Commissioner
Lea Stist, Information Officer
220 Bush Street, Suite 550
San Francisco, CA 94104
(415) 398-8885
Fax (415) 398-8589
Economic Mission: (415) 434-2450

Israel Government Tourist Office
6380 Wilshire Boulevard, Suite 1700
Los Angeles, CA 90048
(213) 658-7462

Israel Government Tourist Office
Dov Kolani, Director, Northwest U.S.A.
220 Bush Street, Suite 550
San Francisco, CA 94104
(415) 775-5462

ITALY
Consulate General of Italy
Gabriella Meneghello Battistello, Consul General
12400 Wilshire Boulevard, Suite 300
Los Angeles, CA 90025
(310) 826-5998

Consulate General of Italy
Giulio Prigioni, Consul General
Stefania Cassissa, Chancellor
F. Kalmar, Commercial Officer
Antonio Massa, Officer, Visa
2590 Webster Street
San Francisco, CA 94115
(415) 931-4924
Fax (415) 931-7205

Honorary Vice Consulate of Italy
3838 California Street, Suite 412
San Francisco, CA 94118
(415) 668-2626

Honorary Vice Consulate of Italy
751 7th Avenue, Suite 300
San Diego, CA 92101
(619) 231-9111

Honorary Vice Consulate of Italy
Anthony Umberto Virgadamo, Honorary Vice Consul
1420 54th Street, Suite 4
Sacramento, CA 95819
(916) 456-1950

Honorary Vice Consulate of Italy
777 N. First Street, Suite 600D
San Jose, CA 95112
(408) 971-9170

Honorary Vice Consulate of Italy
P.O. Box 1340
Bakersfield, CA 93302
(805) 324-4585
Fax (805) 322-8759

Honorary Vice Consulate of Italy
2409 Merced Street, Suite 3
Fresno, CA 93721
(209) 268-8776
Fax (209) 268-5701

Italian Trade Commission
Pasquale Bova, Trade Commissioner
Marinella Loddo, Deputy Commissioner
1801 Avenue of the Stars, Suite 700
Los Angeles, CA 90067
(213) 879-0950
Fax (310) 203-8335

Italian Government Tourist Board
12400 Wilshire Boulevard, Suite 550
Los Angeles, CA 90025
(310) 820-0098

IVORY COAST
Honorary Consulate General of the Republic
of the Ivory Coast
Edgar D. Osgood, Honorary Consul General
Angela Coppola, Deputy Consul General
Marcella Maza-Schwartz, Visa
Pier 23
San Francisco, CA 94111
(415) 391-0176
Fax (415) 391-0794

JAMAICA
Honorary Consulate of Jamaica
Cleveland O. Neil, Honorary Consul
8730 Wilshire Boulevard, Suite 505
Beverly Hills, CA 90211
(310) 652-0520
Fax (310) 652-4988

Honorary Consulate of Jamaica
22455 Maple Court, Suite 404
Hayward, CA 94541
(415) 882-9865

Jamaica Tourist Board
3440 Wilshire Bouelvard, Suite 1207
Los Angeles, CA 90010
(213) 384-1123
Fax (213) 384-1780

JAPAN
Consulate General of Japan
Seiichiro Noboru, Consul General
Kitagawa, Consul, Economic and Trade Affairs
350 South Grand Avenue, Suite 1700
Los Angeles, CA 90071
(213) 617-6700
Fax (213) 617-6727

Consulate General of Japan
Ryozo Kato, Consul General
Susumu Yamagishi, Deputy Consul General
Susumu Nakazawa, Consul, Visa
Shigeo Natsui, Consul, General Affairs
Hiromichi Aoki, Consul, Commercial
Eiichi Suzuki, Consul, Information and Culture
50 Fremont Street, 23rd Floor
San Francisco, CA 94105
(415) 777-3533
Fax (415) 974-3660

Japan External Trade Organization (JETRO) Los Angeles
Saburo Yuzawa, Chief Executive Director
Harumi Kamekawa, Public Relations Director
725 South Figueroa Street, Suite 1890
Los Angeles, CA 90017
(213) 624-8855
Fax (213) 629-8127

Japan External Trade Organization (JETRO) San Francisco
Fumihiko Kimura, Director General
Yoshifumi Matsudaira, Public Relations Director
235 Pine Street, Suite 1700
San Francisco, CA 94104
(415) 392-1333
Fax (415) 788-6927
Japan Information Service
Hiroshi Furusawa, Director
Takehiko Wajima, Culture and Education
50 Fremont Street, Suite 2200
San Francisco, CA 94105
(415) 777-3533
Fax (415) 777-0518

Hiroshima Representative Office
244 South San Pedro Street, Suite 413
Los Angeles, CA 90012
(213) 617-9704
Fax (213) 626-0906

Nagoya Representative Office
123 Onizuka Street, Suite 101-A
Los Angeles, CA 90012
(213) 620-7980
Fax (213) 620-0174

Japan National Tourist Organization
Yasuyuki Chino, Director
360 Post Street, Suite 601
San Francisco, CA 94108
(415) 989-7140

KENYA
Consulate of Kenya
Kyalo Kasinga, Consul General
9100 Wilshire Boulevard, Suite 111-112
Beverly Hills, CA 90212
(310) 274-6635
Fax (310) 859-7010

Kenya Tourist Office
9150 Wilshire Boulevard, Suite 160
Beverly Hills, CA 90212
(310) 274-6635

KOREA, REPUBLIC OF (SOUTH KOREA)
Consulate General of the Republic of Korea
Taehee Park, Consul General
Seung Kook Byun, Deputy Consul General
3243 Wilshire Boulevard, Suite 1101
Los Angeles, CA 90010
(213) 385-9300
Fax (213) 385-1849

Consulate General of the Republic of Korea
Jung Ha Lee, Consul General
Bae Sang Kil, Deputy Consul General
3500 Clay Street
San Francisco, CA 94118
(415) 921-2251
Fax (415) 931-6330

Korea Trade Center
Y.K. Lee, Director
4801 Wilshire Boulevard, Suite 230
Los Angeles, CA 90010
(213) 954-9500
Telex 674639 LSA
Fax (213) 954-1707

Korea National Tourism Corporation
3435 Wilshire Boulevard, Suite 350
Los Angeles, CA 90010
(213) 382-3435
Fax (213) 480-0483

Korean Cultural Service
5505 Wilshire Boulevard
Los Angeles, CA 90036
(213) 936-7141
Fax (213) 936-5712

LEBANON
Consulate General of Lebanon
Gaby Soufan, Consul General
7060 Hollywood Boulevard, Suite 510
Hollywood, CA 90028
(213) 467-1253
Fax (213) 467-2935

LITHUANIA
Honorary Consulate General of Lithuania
Vytautas Cekanauskas, Honorary Consul General
3959 Franklin Avenue
Los Angeles, CA 90027
(805) 496-5324
Fax (805) 496-7435

LUXEMBOURG
Honorary Consulate General of Luxembourg
Frank Angel, Honory Consul
2961 Valmere Drive
Malibu, CA 90265
(310) 456-8547
Fax (310) 474-7083

Consulate General of Luxembourg
Pierre Gramegna, Consul General
One Sansome Street, Suite 830
San Francisco, CA 94104
(415) 788-0816

MADAGASCAR
Honorary Consulate of Madagascar
James de la Beaujardiere, Honorary Consul
2299 Piedmont Avenue
Berkeley, CA 94720
(800) 856-2721

MALAWI
Honorary Consulate of Malawi
Dr. James F. Clements, Honorary Consul
2001 North Soto Street
Los Angeles, CA 90032
(213) 223-2020
Fax (213) 223-3679

MALAYSIA
Consulate General of Malaysia
Wan Yusof Embong, Consul General
Ismail Iqbal, Consul, Investment
350 South Figueroa, Suite 400
Los Angeles, CA 90071
(213) 621-2991
Fax (213) 485-8617
Trade Office: (213) 617-1000

Malaysian Tourism Promotion Board
818 W. Seventh Street
Los Angeles, CA 90178
(213) 689-9702

MALI

Honorary Consulate of Mali
Dr. William A. Burke, Honorary Consul
11110 West Ohio Avenue, Suite 100
Los Angeles, CA 90025
(310) 274-5825
Fax (310) 573-0152

MALTA

Honorary Consulate of Malta
Dame Dolores Galea, Honorary Consul
419 S. Norton Avenue
P.O. Box 741520
Los Angeles, CA 90020/90004
(213) 939-5011
Fax (213) 939-0316

Honorary Consulate of Malta
Charles J. Vassallo, Honorary Consul General
P.O. Box 34-7001
San Francisco, CA 94134
(415) 468-4321

MAURITIUS

Honorary Consulate of Mauritius
Bruce E. Dizenfeld, Honorary Consul
10100 Santa Monica Boulevard, 8th Floor
Los Angeles, CA 90067
(310) 557-2009
Fax (310) 551-0283; (310) 306-9095

MEXICO

Consulate General of Mexico
Enrique Loaeza Tovar, Consul General
2401 West 6th Street
Los Angeles, CA 90057
(213) 351-6800
Fax (213) 389-9249
Passports: (213) 351-6838
Visa: (213) 351-6828

Consulate General of Mexico
Ambassador Rudolfo Figueroa, Consul General
Alejandro Pescador Castaneda, Deputy Consul General
Elsa Maria Del Carmen Ramirez Morales, Chancellor
Arturo Balderas Rodriguez, Consul, Commercial
Sandra Calderón Barraza, Consul, Culture and Education
870 Market Street, Suite 528
San Francisco, CA 94102
(415) 392-3604
Fax (415) 392-3233

Consulate of Mexico
Eduardo Martinez Curiel, Consul
9812 Old Winery Place, Suite 10
Sacramento, CA 95827
(916) 363-0403
Fax (916) 363-0625

Consulate of Mexico
Ecce Iei Mendoza, Consul
331 W. Second Street
Calexico, CA 92231
(619) 357-3863
Fax (619) 357-6284

Consulate of Mexico
Dr. Gabriel Garcia Perez, Consul General
830 Van Ness Avenue
Fresno, CA 93721
(209) 233-3065
Fax (209) 233-5638

Consulate of Mexico
Luis Humberto Ramirez, Consul
201 E. Fourth Street
Oxnard, CA 93030
(805) 483-4684
Fax (805) 486-9213

Consulate of Mexico
Colmba Calvo Vargas, Consul General
588 W. Sixth Street
San Bernardino, CA 92401
(909) 889-9836
Fax (909) 889-8285

Consulate of Mexico
Arturo Balderas, Consul
380 N. First Street, Suite 102
San Jose, CA 95112
(408) 294-3414
Fax (408) 294-4506

Consulate of Mexico
Felipe Sorea Azuso, General
828 N. Broadway
Santa Ana, CA 92701
(714) 835-3069
Fax (714) 835-3472

State of Baja California, Mexico & Tijuana Convention and
Tourism Bureau, Rosarito Tourism & Convention Bureau
Gina Cord, President
7860 Mission Center Court, Suite 202
San Diego, CA 92108
(619) 299-8518
Fax (619) 294-7366

Mexican Ministry of Fisheries
2550 Fifth Avenue #101
San Diego, CA 92103
(619) 233-4324
Fax (619) 233-0344

MONACO
Consulate of Monaco
7449 Melrose Avenue
Los Angeles, CA 90046
(213) 655-8970
Fax (213) 655-8147

Honorary Consulate General of Monaco
Paula Escher, Honorary Consul General
21 Presidio Avenue
San Francisco, CA 94115
(415) 749-1663

MOROCCO
Honorary Consulate of Morocco
Abdelhak Saoud, Honorary Consul
P.O. Box 80652
San Marino, CA 91118
(818) 570-0318
Fax (818) 308-9061

NEPAL
Honorary Consulate General of Nepal
Richard C. Blum, Honorary Consul General
909 Montgomery Street, Suite 400
San Francisco, CA 94133
(415) 434-1111

THE NETHERLANDS
Consulate General of the Netherlands
Matthieu A. Peters, Consul General
Frank Thijssen, Consul, Commercial Affairs
11766 Wilshire Blvd., Suite 1150
Los Angeles, CA 90025
(310) 268-1598
Fax (310) 312-0989

Honorary Consulate of the Netherlands
Ralph Pais, Consul
1 Maritime Plaza, Room 554
San Francisco, CA 94111
(415) 981-6454

Honorary Vice Consulate of the Netherlands
Theodorus Smit, Vice Consul
540 Laurel Street, 2nd Floor
San Diego, CA 92101
(619) 945-4163
Fax (619) 945-4163

Netherlands Foreign Investment Agency
901 Mariners Island
San Mateo, CA 94404
(415) 349-8848
Fax (415) 349-8201

Netherlands Board of Tourism
9841 Airport Blvd., Suite 102
Los Angeles, CA 90045

NEW ZEALAND
Consulate General of New Zealand
Terry Baker, Consul General
12400 Wilshire Blvd. #1150
Los Angeles, CA 90025
(310) 207-1605
Fax (310) 207-3605

New Zealand Trade Development Board
Ross Graham, Trade Commissioner
10960 Wilshire Boulevard, Suite 1530
Los Angeles, CA 90024
(310) 477-1899
Fax (310) 473-5621

Honorary Consulate of New Zealand
Richard Sears, Honorary Consul
1 Maritime Plaza, Suite 700
San Francisco, CA 94111
(415) 399-1255

New Zealand Tourism Board
501 Santa Monica Boulevard, Suite 300
Santa Monica, CA 90401
(800) 388-5494

New Zealand Tourist Board
10960 Wilshire Boulevard, Suite 1530
Los Angeles, CA 90024
(310) 477-8241

NICARAGUA
Consulate General of Nicaragua
Adan Fletes, Consul General
2500 Wilshire Boulevard, Suite 915
Los Angeles, CA 90057
(213) 252-1170

Consulate General of Nicaragua
870 Market Street, Suite 1050
San Francisco, CA 94102
(415) 765-6821

NORWAY
Consulate General of Norway
Anfin Ullern, Consul General
5750 Wilshire Boulevard, Suite 470
Los Angeles, CA 90036
(213) 933-7717
Fax (213) 933-8711

Consulate General of Norway
Dag Mork-Ulnes, Consul General
Jannicke Jaeger, Vice Consul
Charles Baldwin, Consul, Trade Commissioner
Stein Haukaas, Consul, Technology and Industry Attache
20 California Street
San Francisco, CA 94111
(415) 986-0767
Fax: (415) 986-6025
Trade Commission: (415) 986-0770

Consulate of Norway
Oswald Gilbertson, Consul
6240 Brynwood Court
San Diego, CA 92120
(619) 582-5586
Fax (619) 582-6570

PAKISTAN
Consulate General of Pakistan
Aziz Ahmad Khan, Consul General
10850 Wilshire Boulevard, Suite 1100
Los Angeles, CA 90024
(310) 441-5114
Fax (310) 441-9256

PANAMA
Consulate of Panama
Alfred E. Marohl, Honorary Consul General
435 North Roxsbury Drive, Suite 207
Beverly Hills, CA 90210
(310) 278-6630
Fax (310) 589-1880

Consulate of Panama
Carolina T. Mouritzen, Consul
2552 Chatsworth Boulevard
San Diego, CA 92106
By appointment only
(619) 225-8144
Fax (619) 222-0201

PAPUA NEW GUINEA
Honorary Consulate of Papua New Guinea
Harold Morgan, Honorary Consul
c/o Morgan Equipment Co.
131 Steuart Street, Suite 300
San Francisco, CA 94105
(415) 227-4070

PARAGUAY
Honorary Consulate of Paraguay
Alejandrina V. de Damasco, Honorary Consul
8322 Seaport Drive
Huntington Beach, CA 92646
(714) 969-2955
Fax (714) 969-2760

Honorary Consulate General of Paraguay
Donald M. Haet, Honorary Consul General
David L. Haet, Honorary Vice Consul
450 Magellan Avenue
San Francisco, CA 94116
(415) 759-1874

PERU
Consulate General of Peru
Julio Galindo, Consul General
3460 Wilshire Boulevard, Suite 1005
Los Angeles, CA 90010
(213) 383-9895
Fax (213) 383-9960

Consulate General of Peru
Martha Toledo-Ocampo, Consul General
Oscar Gonzalez, Consul
870 Market Street, Suite 579
San Francisco, CA 94102
(415) 362-7136
Fax (415) 362-2836

THE PHILIPPINES
Consulate General of the Philippines
Victor G. Garcia III, Consul General
3660 Wilshire Boulevard, Suite 900
Los Angeles, CA 90010
(213) 387-5321

Consulate General of the Philippines
Alfredo L. Almendrala, Jr., Consul General
Teresa V. Sapinosa, Consul, Passport/Cultural
Eva G. Betita, Vice Consul, Visa/Trade/Science &
Technology
447 Sutter Street, 6th Floor
San Francisco, CA 94108
(415) 433-6666
Fax (415) 2641
Tourism: (415) 956-4060

Consulate of the Philippines
Gloria Ramos Da Rodda, Consul
600 B Street, Suite 1200
San Diego, CA 92101
(619) 544-9058/9

Philippine Trade Commission
Simeon Hernandez, Jr., Trade Attache
3660 Wilshire Boulevard, Suite 218
Los Angeles, CA 90010
(213) 383-9475
Fax (213) 738-1827
Tourism: (213) 487-4525

Philippine Consulate General
Economic Diplomacy Unit
Consul Isaias F. Begonia, EDU Officer
447 Sutter Street, 6th Floor
San Francisco, CA 94108
(415) 433-6666
Fax (415) 421-2641

Philippine Department of Tourism
447 Sutter Street, Suite 507
San Francisco, CA 94108
(415) 956-4060

POLAND
Consulate General of Poland
Jan Szewc, Consul General
12400 Wilshire Boulevard, Suite 555
Los Angeles, CA 90025
(310) 442-8500
Fax (310) 442-8515

PORTUGAL
Honorary Consulate of Portugal
Edmundo A. Macedo, Honorary Consul
1801 Avenue of the Stars, Suite 400
Los Angeles, CA 90067
(310) 277-1491

Consulate General of Portugal
Joaquin Ferreira da Fonseca, Consul General
Manuela Avila Silveira, Vice Consul
Julia Fung Chin, Chancellor
3298 Washington Street
San Francisco, CA 94115
(415) 346-3400

Macau Tourist Information Bureau
3133 Lake Hollywood Drive
P.O. Box 1860
Los Angeles, CA 90078
(213) 851-3402

PUERTO RICO, COMMONWEALTH OF
Economic Development Administration of Puerto Rico
Henry Ross, Director
650 Town Center Drive, Suite 1340
Costa Mesa, CA 92626
(714) 432-9833
Fax (714) 432-9842

Puerto Rico Office of Tourism
3575 W. Cahuenga Boulevard, Suite 560
Los Angeles, CA 90068
(213) 874-5991
Fax (213) 874-7257

RUSSIA
Consulate General of The Russian Federation
Vladimir S. Kuznetsov, Consul General
2790 Green Street
San Francisco, CA 94123
(415) 202-9800
Fax (415) 929-0306

SAUDI ARABIA
Consulate General of Saudi Arabia
Hassan T. Nazar, Consul General
Ibrahim Ammar, Deputy Consul General
10900 Wilshire Boulevard, Suite 830
Los Angeles, CA 90024
(310) 208-6566
Fax (310) 208-5643

SINGAPORE
Singapore Economic Development Board
C.M. Tan, Center Director
2049 Century Park East, Suite 400
Los Angeles, CA 90067
(310) 553-0199
Fax (310) 557-1044

Singapore Trade Development Board
Francis Tay, Center Director
350 South Figueroa Street, Suite 909
Los Angeles, CA 90071
(213) 617-7358
Fax (213) 617-7367

Singapore Tourist Promotion Board
8484 Wilshire Boulevard, Suite 510
Beverly Hills, CA 90211
(213) 852-1901
(213) 852-0129

Honorary Consul General of Singapore
Ambassador Daryl Arnold
2424 S.E. Bristol Street, Suite 320
Santa Ana Heights, CA 92707
(714) 476-9046
Fax (714) 476-8301

SOUTH AFRICA
Consulate General of South Africa
Frik Schoombee, Consul General
Stefanus Botes, Trade & Economic Consul
50 North La Cienega Boulevard, Suite 300
Beverly Hills, CA 90211
(310) 657-9200
Fax (310) 657-9215

South African Tourism Board
9841 Airport Boulevard, Suite 1524
Los Angeles, CA 90045
(310) 641-8444
(800) 782-9772
Fax (310) 641-5812

SPAIN
Consulate General of Spain
Eduardo Garrigues, Consul General
6300 Wilshire Boulevard, Suite 1630
Los Angeles, CA 90048
(213) 658-6050
Education Department: (213) 852-6997

Consulate General of Spain
Camilo Alonso-Vega, Consul General
Alicia Aranda Auseron, Chancellor
Maria Teresa Perez, Visas
Maria Jose Benito, Administrative Officer
Margarita Baxter, Culture
Gracia Toro, Notarial and Civil Registry
Belen Pardo, Passports
1405 Sutter Street
San Francisco, CA 94109
(415) 922-2995
Fax (415) 931-9706

Commercial Office of Spain
Miguel Comenge, Commercial Consul
350 South Figueroa Street, Suite 498
Los Angeles, CA 90071
(213) 628-1406
Fax (213) 628-1504

Tourist Office of Spain
8383 Wilshire Boulevard, Suite 960
Beverly Hills, CA 90211
(213) 658-7188
Fax (213) 658-1061

SRI LANKA
Honorary Consulate of Sri Lanka
Dr. T. Anthony Don Michael, Honorary Consul
4314 Marina City Drive, Suite 1018
Marina Del Rey, CA 90292
(310) 306-5457
Fax (818) 896-8702

SWEDEN
Consulate General of Sweden
Siri Marie Eliason, Consul General
Sarah Van Zee, Vice Consul
Ulf Corne, Attache, Science and Technology
Ulla Wikander-Reilly, Information Officer
Karin Seeman, Information Officer
120 Montgomery Street, Suite 2175
San Francisco, CA 94104
(415) 788-2631
Office of Science and Technology: (415) 982-7201
Fax (415) 982-7362

Consulate of Sweden
John Norton, Consul
530 Broadway, Suite 1106
San Diego, CA 92101
(619) 233-1106
Fax (619) 233-9890

Swedish Trade Council
10990 Wilshire Boulevard, Suite 1100
Los Angeles, CA 90024
(310) 478-1226
Fax (310) 444-0966

Swedish Technology Office
10880 Wilshire Boulevard, Suite 1105
Los Angeles, CA 90024
(310) 475-0589
Fax (310) 475-2215

Scandinavian Tourist Board
8929 Wilshire Boulevard, Room 212
Beverly Hills, CA 90211
(213) 657-4808

SWITZERLAND
Consulate General of Switzerland
Kurt Welte, Consul General
Anny Cabalzar-Hogquist, Consul and Trade Commissioner
Frank Ustar, Trade Commissioner
11766 Wilshire Boulevard, Suite 1400
Los Angeles, CA 90025
(310) 575-1145
Fax (310) 575-1982

Consulate General of Switzerland
Alfred Baehler, Consul General
Adele Scherrer, Consul, Commercial
456 Montgomery Street, Suite 1500
San Francisco, CA 94104
(415) 788-2272
Fax (415) 788-1402

Swiss National Tourist Office
222 N. Sepulveda, Suite 1570
El Segundo, CA 90245
(310) 335-5980
Fax (310) 335-5982

Swiss National Tourist Office
Joe Lustenberger, Manager
250 Stockton Street
San Francisco, CA 94108
(415) 362-2260
Fax (415) 391-1508

TAIWAN, REPUBLIC OF CHINA
Taipei Economic & Cultural Office (TECO)
Cultural Division
3660 Wilshire Boulevard, Suite 1006
Los Angeles, CA 90010
(213) 385-0512
Fax (213) 385-2197

Taipei Economic & Cultural Office (TECO)
Chinese Culture Center
420 Bernard Street
Los Angeles, CA 90012
(213) 626-7295
Fax (213) 617-7658

Taipei Economic & Cultural Office (TECO)
Science Division
1499 Huntington Drive, Suite 402
South Pasadena, CA 91030
(818) 799-1122
Fax (818) 799-2386

Taipei Economic and Culture Office (TECO)
Jyh Yuan Lo, Director General
Dick Fu, Deputy Director General
Paul Mao, Advisor
Ne Hung, Assistant, Commerce
Elizabeth Chu, Assistant, Visa
Anne Hung, Assistant, Public Relations
555 Montgomery Street, Suite 501
San Francisco, CA 94111
(415) 362-7680

Taipei Economic & Cultural Office (TECO)
Affairs, Cultural Division
Dr. Li Chen-Ching, Director
Clark Cheng, Assistant
Amy Chiang, Assistant
530 Bush Street, Suite 401
San Francisco, CA 94108
(415) 398-4979

Taipei Economic & Cultural Office (TECO)
Affairs, Information Division
555 Montgomery Street, Suite 504
San Francisco, CA 94111
(415) 362-7680

Taipei Economic & Cultural Office (TECO)
Affairs, Travel Division
Chung-Ying Chou, Director
Quentin Shao, Deputy Director
James D. Holland, Consultant
166 Geary Street, Suite 1605
San Francisco, CA 94108
(415) 989-8677

Taipei Economic & Cultural Office (TECO)
Science Division
5201 Great America Parkway, Suite 200
Santa Clara, CA 95054
(408) 986-8686
Fax (408) 986-8066

Taipei Economic & Cultural Office (TECO)
Jui Hsiung Ouyang, Director General
3731 Wilshire Boulevard, Suite 700
Los Angeles, CA 90010
(213) 389-1215
Fax (213) 383-3245

Taipei Economic & Cultural Office (TECO)
Commercial Division
3660 Wilshire Boulevard, Suite 918
Los Angeles, CA 90010
(213) 380-3644
Fax (213) 380-3407

THAILAND
Consulate General of Thailand
Saksit Srisorn, Consul General
Chananta Dhiravibulya, Deputy Consul General
801 North La Brea Avenue
Los Angeles, CA 90038
(213) 937-1894

Thailand Trade Center
Kiartiguna Kitiyakara, Trade Commissioner
3660 Wilshire Boulevard, Suite 230
Los Angeles, CA 90010
(213) 380-5943
Fax (213) 380-6476

Tourism Authority of Thailand
3440 Wilshire Boulevard, Suite 1101
Los Angeles, CA 90010
(213) 382-2353

TONGA
Consulate General of Tonga
S.M. Tuita, Consul General
M.U.S. Tupouniua, Consul
360 Post Street, Suite 604
San Francisco, CA 94108
(415) 781-0365

TUNISIA
Honorary Consulate General of Tunisia
Proctor Jones, Honorary Consul General
3490 Sacramento Street
San Francisco, CA 94118
(415) 922-9222
Fax (415) 922-8837

TURKEY
Consulate General of Turkey
Mehmet Emre, Consul General
4801 Wilshire Boulevard, Suite 310
Los Angeles, CA 90010
(213) 937-0118
Fax (213) 932-0061

UNITED KINGDOM
Consulate General of Great Britain
Merrick Baker-Bates, Consul General
Victor Wallis, Consul (Commercial)
11766 Wilshire Boulevard, Suite 400
Los Angeles, CA 90025
(310) 477-3322
Fax (310) 547-1450

Consulate General of Great Britain
Malcolm Dougal, Consul General
Ray Pringle, Deputy Consul General
Mark Colburn, Vice Consul, Consumer Affairs
Kevin Cook, Vice Consul, Public Affairs
Karen Edge, Vice Consul, Consular/Management Affairs
One Sansome Street, Suite 850
San Francisco, CA 94104
(415) 981-3030

Agency for Development in the North of England
Mark Stoner, Vice President, Business Development
5 Third Street, Suite 1111
San Francisco, CA 94103
(415) 777-2701
Fax (415) 777-2702

British Tourist Authority
350 South Figueroa, Suite 450
Los Angeles, CA 90071
(213) 628-3525

British Virgin Islands Tourist Board
P.O. Box 3574
Culver City, CA
(213) 293-2331
Fax (213) 293-3716

British Virgin Islands Tourist Board
1686 Union Street, Suite 305
San Francisco, CA 94123
(415) 775-0344
(800) 232-7770

URUGUAY
Consulate General of Uruguay
Olga Barbarov, Consul General
Alberto Fajardo, Deputy Consul General
Adriana Stanton, Trade and Promotion Officer
429 Santa Monica Boulevard, Suite 400
Santa Monica, CA 90401
(310) 394-5777
Fax (310) 394-5140

Honorary Consulate General of Uruguay
John Ritchie, Consul
Fernando Sasco, Honorary Vice Consul
564 Market Street, Suite 200
San Francisco, CA 94104
(415) 981-1115
Fax (415) 989-4502

VENEZUELA
Consulate General of Venezuela
Luisana Leoni De Moreno, Consul General
Yudith Romero Marcano, Deputy Consul
Ivan Suros Escalona, Consul
455 Market Street, Suite 220
San Francisco, CA 94105
(415) 512-8340
Fax (415) 512-7693

VIRGIN ISLANDS (U.S.)
U.S. Virgin Islands Division of Tourism
3460 Wilshire Boulevard, Suite 412
Los Angeles, CA 90010
(213) 739-0138
Fax (213) 739-2005

Resource Publications

(The following is a listing, not an endorsement of publications. The cost and availability of these publications are subject to change. Please contact publishers for further information.)

ABC Europ Production (Europe)
$184
Manufacturers' News, Inc.
1633 Central Street
Evanston, IL 60201
(708) 864-7000
Fax (708) 332-1100
(Covers 32 countries; 400,000 entries with 100,000 manufacturing firms; 5,000 pages.)

ACCJ Journal
$64/sea mail
$124/airmail
International Division/Publications
U.S. Chamber of Commerce
1615 H Street, N.W.
Washington, D.C. 20062-2000
(202) 463-5460

ACCJ Membership Directory
$95, plus $24 airmail
International Division/Publications
U.S. Chamber of Commerce
1615 H Street, N.W.
Washington, D.C. 20062-2000
(202) 463-5460

Access to European Union
$80
Euroconfidentiel
rue de Rixensart 18
B-1332 Genval
Belgium
(32 2) 652 02 84
Fax (32 2) 653-01 80
(Latest economic and legislative developments in all major industrial and commercial sectors. Revised annually.)

Access to Social Europe
$320
Euroconfidentiel
rue de Rixensart 18
B-1332 Genval
Belgium
(32 2) 652 02 84
Fax (32 2) 653-01 80

(Essential information for decision makers to promote or defend their interests before the European Union's institutions.)

AID Procurement Information Bulletin
Free of charge
USAID's Office of Small and Disadvantaged Business Utilization/Minority Resource Center
Washington, D.C. 20523-1414
(703) 875-1551

Africa South of the Sahara
$320
International Press Publications Inc.
90 Nolan Court #23
Markham Ontario, Canada L3R 4L9
(905) 946-9588
Fax (905) 946-9590
(800) 666-0220 orders only
(Explores current political, economic and cultural affairs.)

After-Sales Service and Repair, Questions and Answers
$17
National Technical Information Service
5285 Port Royal Road
Springfield, VA 22161
(703) 487-4650
(Explains how services are treated under the U.S.-Canada Free Trade Agreement.)

AgExporter
$17 (annual subscription)
Foreign Agricultural Services-Information Division
U.S. Department of Agriculture
Washington, D.C. 20250
(202) 720-7115
(Monthly publication.)

Agriculture in a North American Free Trade Agreement: Analysis of Liberalizing Trade Between the U.S. and Mexico
$11
S/N 001-000-04591-1
U.S. Government Printing Office
Superintendent of Documents
P.O. Box 371954
Pittsburgh, PA 15250-7954
(202) 783-3238
Fax (202) 512-2250
(Background information and analysis on the agricultural aspects of NAFTA. 176 pages.)

Alternative Finance
$49
Global Training Center, Inc.
Kingsley Building, Suite 102
4124 Linden Avenue
Dayton, OH 45432
(800) 860-5030

American Business in Korea: Guide & Directory
$45
Association of Foreign Traders in Korea
U.S. Trade Center
American Embassy, Unit #15550
APO AP 96205-0001
(202) 377-4957
(Practical tips for doing business in Korea.)

American Electronics
$175
American Electronics Association
5201 Great American Parkway
Santa Clara, CA 95054
(408) 987-4200
Fax (408) 970-8565
(Provides information on more than 3,200 companies that design, manufacture or conduct research in electronics, electronic components and related information technology products.)

American Export Register
$120
Thomas International Publishing
One Penn Plaza
New York, NY 10119
(212) 290-7213
(Two volumes. Forty thousand U.S. manufacturers selling to international markets; carriers, custom house brokers, freight forwarders, banks and packers involved in export and world trade; chamber of commerce officers of other countries in U.S.)

American Subsidiaries of German Firms
$100
German American Chamber of Commerce
40 W. 57th Street, 31st Floor
New York, NY 10019
(212) 974-8830
(250 pages.)

American Wholesalers and Distributors Directory
$150
Gale Researching
Marketing Department
P.O. Box 33477
Detroit, MI 48232-9852
(800) 877-GALE
(313) 961-2242
Fax (313) 961-6083
(Organizes more than 18,000 U.S. wholesalers and distributors of consumer products in a single volume.)

Arthur Andersen North American Business Sourcebook
$150, plus $8.00 shipping/handling
Triumph Books
644 S. Clark Street
Chicago, IL 60605
(312) 939-3330; (800) 626-4330
Fax (312) 663-3557
(An authoritative, all-inclusive reference to the $6.5 trillion Mexican, Canadian and U.S. markets.)

Asian Company Handbook
$65
Toyo Keizai America Inc.
Circulation Services Dept.
c/o PRIMA Circulation & Mailing Services
9401 James Avenue South, Suite 160
Bloomington, MN 55431
(800) 772-3701
(Provides detailed information on more than 1,000 companies in Hong Kong, Indonesia, Malaysia, the Republic of Korea, Singapore, Taiwan and Thailand.)

The Association of Southeast Asian Nations
$150
Oceana Publications, Inc.
75 Main Street
Dobbs Ferry, NY 10522
(914) 693-8100
Fax (914) 693-0402

Associations Canada
$197.50
International Press Publications
90 Nolan Court, Suite 23
Markham, Ontario L3R 4L9
(905) 946-9588
Fax (905) 946-9590
Information on more than 20,000 Canadian associations and
1,200 international organizations active in Canada.)

Atlantic Manufacturers (Canada)
$115.95
Manufacturers' News, Inc.
1633 Central Street
Evanston, IL 60201
(708) 864-7000
Fax (708) 332-1100
(Profiles of approximately 3,000 manufacturers; 422 pages.)

Atlas of Eastern Europe
$16
S/N 041-015-00170-1
U.S. Government Printing Office
Superintendent of Documents
P.O. Box 371954
Pittsburgh, PA 15250-7954
(202) 783-3238
Fax (202) 512-2250
(Two-part publication provides detailed look at the coun-
tries of Eastern Europe, including geography, historical
boundaries, demographics, etc.)

Background Notes
$68/complete set; $20 (annual subscription of 60 notes)
Superintendent of Documents
U.S. Government Printing Office
Washington, D.C. 20402
(202) 783-3238
Fax (202) 512-2233
(Provides economic and trade information on major trading
partners. Published by U.S. Department of State, Bureau of
Public Affairs.)

A Basic Guide to Exporting
$9.50
S/N 003-009-00604-0
Superintendent of Documents
U.S. Government Printing Office
P.O. Box 371954
Pittsburgh, PA 15250-7954
(202) 783-3238
Fax (202) 512-2250
(Explains exporting, financing.)

Bear Hunting with the Politburo
$12.00
Russian Information Services
89 Main Street, Suite 2
Montpelier, VT 95602
(802) 223-4955
Fax (802) 223-6105
(800) 639-4301
(Provides insights into the birth of capitalism in Russia
and gives a realistic view of what private enterprise is
up against in Russia. 270 pages.)

Bergano's Register of International Importers
$95
Bergano Book Company
183 Sherman Street
P.O. Box 190
Fairfield, CT 06430
(203) 254-2054
Fax (203) 255-3817
(Gives information on more than 2,000 importing firms
in more than 75 countries.)

Best in the Business
$120.00
International Press Publications
90 Nolan Court, #23
Markham, ON L3R4L9
Canada
(905) 946-9588
Fax (905) 946-9590
(Includes relevant personal details about Canada's top
business people and their companies.)

Bi-Lateral Study in Private International Law
Oceana Publications, Inc.
75 Main Street
Dobbs Ferry, NY 10522
(914) 693-1320
Fax (914) 693-0402

The Blue Book of Canadian Business
$159.95
Canadian Newspaper Services
65 Overlea Boulevard, Suite 207
Toronto, Ontario M4H1P1
(416) 422-4742
Fax (416) 422-4746
(Overview of Canadian business community gives in-depth
profiled of 100 major companies. Approximately 1,300
pages, published annually.)

BNA's Eastern Europe Reporter
published biweekly
The Bureau of National Affairs, Inc.
1231 25th Street, N.W.
Washington, D.C. 20037
(800) 372-1033

**Border Crossing Procedures Under the United States-
Canada Free Trade Agreement**
$17
National Technical Information Service
5285 Port Royal Road
Springfield, VA 22161
(703) 487-4650

**Bureau of the Census Foreign Trade Report: Annual
U.S. Exports, Harmonized Schedule B Commodity
by Country - FT 477**
$43
Superintendent of Documents
U.S. Government Printing Office
Washington, D.C. 20402
(202) 783-3238

**Bureau of the Census Foreign Trade Report:
Monthly Exports and Imports - SITC Commodity
by Country - FT 925**
$127 (annual subscription)
Superintendent of Documents
U.S. Government Printing Office
Washington, D.C. 20402
(202) 783-3238

Business America
$32 (annual subscription)
Superintendent of Documents
U.S. Government Printing Office
P.O. Box 371954
Pittsburgh, PA 15250-7954
(202) 783-3238
Fax (202) 512-2233
(Monthly publication on trade opportunities.)

**Business and Commercial Laws of Russia:
Translations with Expert Commentary**
$840
Russian Information Services
89 Main Street, Suite 2
Montpelier, VT 95602
(802) 223-4955
Fax (802) 223-6105
(800) 639-4301
(Three-volume set, comprehensive and authoritative
collection of post-Soviet Russian business and commercial
laws. Supplemented six times per year.)

Business Directory of Hong Kong
$180
Current Publications Limited
G.P.O. Box 9848
1503 Enterprise Building, 228 Queen's Road Central
Hong Kong
(852) 543-4702
Fax (852) 815-8396
(First published in 1977, contains more than 12,000 major
and active business firms in Hong Kong, including importers and exporters, financial institutions, manufacturers,
tourism-related industries, professional consulting firms
and general business services. Also included are government departments, trade promotion organizations and
associations.)

Business Directories
Northern California: $595
Southern California:$695
Entire State: $995
American Business Directories
5711 South 86th Circle
Omaha, NE 68127
(402) 593-4600
Fax (402) 331-5481

Business in Germany
$20
German American Chamber of Commerce
40 W. 57th Street, 31st Floor
New York, NY 10019
(212) 974-8830
(55 pages; legal and tax aspects.)

Business in Mexico
$39.95
The Haworth Press, Inc.
10 Alice Street
Binghamton, NY 13904
(800) 342-9678
Fax (607) 722-6362
(Handbook for cross-cultural business dealings. 156 pages.)

Business Opportunities in Atlantic Canada
$17
National Technical Information Service
5285 Port Royal Road
Springfield, VA 22161
(703) 487-4650
(Guide gives an overview of each province.)

Business Services Directory
$10.00
German American Chamber of Commerce
40 W. 57th Street, 31st Floor
New York, NY 10019
(212) 974-8830

Business Start-Up Kits
Sole Proprietorship/Partnership Kit: $30
Corporation Kit: $39
Employer Kit: $34
California Chamber of Commerce
P.O. Box 1736
Sacramento, CA 95812-1736
(916) 856-5200
(Each kit provides state, federal and most local government forms and permits necessary to start a business and instructions on how to fill out forms. Includes date reminder labels and sample letters to government agencies.)

California Agriculture Export Bulletin/Statistical Appendix
$39 (California, include $3.32 tax)
Worldtariff
220 Montgomery Street, Suite 432
San Francisco, CA 94104-3410
(415) 391-7501
Fax (415) 391-7537
(Includes tables on leading California agricultural exports; detailed California and U.S. exports; air, sea, truck/rail value/volumes for California ag shippers; history of export patterns over last 10 years; California exports by product to Canada and Mexico; U.S. government totals by country/by commodity; agriculture trade policy history for 1993; fish and timber products; foreign market destinations.)

California Agriculture Export Directory
$45
Database Publishing Company
P.O. Box 70024
Anaheim, CA 92825-0024
(714) 778-6400
Fax (714) 778-6811
(Listings of more than 1,000 California firms involved in the export of agricultural products.)

California Almanac
$16.95
Pacific Data Resources
P.O. Box 1922
Santa Barbara, CA 93116
(805) 968-2291
Fax (805) 968-8899
(A reference book of facts and statistics concerning California.)

California and the U.S.-Mexico Trade Negotiations
Free (issue paper)
California World Trade Commission
California Trade and Commerce Agency
801 K Street, Suite 1700
Sacramento, CA 95814
(916) 324-5111
Fax (916) 324-5791

California and the World
$12.50
California Institute of Public Affairs
An Affiliate of The Claremont Colleges
P.O. Box 10
Claremont, CA 91711
(916) 442-2472

California Business Directory
$995
American Business Directories
5711 S. 86th Circle
Omaha, NE 68127
(402) 593-4600
Fax (402) 331-5481
(1.2 million businesses listed.)

California Business Register
$285
Database Publishing Company
P.O. Box 70024
Anaheim, CA 92825-0024
(714) 778-6800
Fax (714) 778-6811
(Combines *California Manufacturers and Services*
registers. Contains profiles of more than 60,000 California
manufacturers, wholesalers and service companies.)

California Economic Growth
$195
CCSCE
610 University Avenue
Palo Alto, CA 94301-2019
(415) 321-8550
(Analysis and projections of state and regional economic
trends.)

*California Environmental Technologies and Services
Directory*
Cal/EPA, Toxic Substances Control Department
P.O. Box 806
Sacramento, CA 95812-0806
(916) 322-2822
(Compiled by the California Environmental Technology
Partnership — Environmental Protection Agency, Trade
and Commerce Agency, Department of Toxic Substances
Control and Pollution Prevention and Technology
Development — this directory is a public/private effort to
foster growth, development and exporting of California's
environmental technology industry, and will help users
locate California firms that provide diverse environmental
services and products.)

California International Trade Register
$125
Database Publishing Company
P.O. Box 70024
Anaheim, CA 92825-0024
(714) 778-6400
Fax (714) 778-6811
(Contains updated information on 7,900 California-based
exporters, importers and related service firms.)

California Manufacturers Register
$165
Database Publishing Company
P.O. Box 70024
Anaheim, CA 92825-0024
(714) 778-6400
Fax (714) 778-6811
(28,000 companies. Alphabetical section, addresses,
telephone numbers, Standard Industrial Classification code,
branch offices, number of employees, products, executives,
export/import, year estimates, sales volumes, products
sections.)

California Services Register
$165
Database Publishing Company
P.O. Box 70024
Anaheim, CA 92825-0024
(714) 778-6400
Fax (714) 778-6811
(Industries include: construction; health care; insurance;
finance; communications; transportation; wholesale trade;
commercial real estate; business services; etc.)

California Technology Register
$145
Database Publishing Company
P.O. Box 70024
Anaheim, CA 92825-0024
(714) 778-6400
Fax (714) 778-6811
Focuses on 10,000 companies in California that utilize
medium and high technologies in their operations.)

The Canadian Almanac and Directory
$145
Gale Research Inc.
P.O. Box 33477
Detroit, MI 48232-5477
(800) 877-GALE
Fax (313) 961-6083
(Includes financial institutions, media, transportation
companies, hospitals and public facilities; organizations,
foundations and trade unions; educational boards, universities, community colleges and vocational schools; political
information; municipalities; general information; and
lawyers in Canada.)

Canadian Business Pages
$59.95 (plus $5 shipping/handling)
International Press Publications Inc.
90 Nolan Court #23
Markham Ontario, Canada L3R 4L9
(905) 946-9588
Fax (905) 946-9590
(800) 666-0220 orders only
(Listing of more than 100,000 suppliers; toll-free section
of U.S. 800 numbers accessible in Canada; trade show
directory and dates; government agency contacts.)

Canadian Environmental Directory
$175
Gale Research Inc.
P.O. Box 33477
Detroit, MI 48232-5477
(800) 877-GALE
Fax (313) 961-6083
(1,200 pages.)

Canadian Global Almanac
$14.95
International Press Publications Inc.
90 Nolan Court #23
Markham, Ontario, L3R 4L9
Canada
(905) 946-9588
Fax (905) 946-9590
(Facts about Canada, global information, arts and
entertainment, sports, science and nature.)

Canadian Who's Who
$165
International Press Publications Inc.
90 Nolan Court, #23
Markham, Ontario, L3R 4L9
Canada
(905) 946-9588
Fax (905) 946-9590
(Covers more than 14,000 national figures. 1,200 pages.)

Caribbean Basin Exporter's Guide
$4.75
U.S. Government Printing Office
Superintendent of Documents
P.O. Box 371954
Pittsburgh, PA 15250-7954
(or nearest government bookstore)
Fax (202) 512-2250

**Catalogue of Publications International Bureau of
   Fiscal Documentation**
P.O. Box 20237
1000 HE Amsterdam
The Netherlands
Telephone +31 20 26 77 26
Fax +31 20 20 86 26
Telex 13217 intax nl
Cables Forintax

**Central, East European and Commonwealth of
   Independent States Country Datafiles**
$150/set
International Division/Publications
U.S. Chamber of Commerce
1615 H Street, N.W.
Washington, D.C. 20062-2000
(202) 463-5460

**China Business - The Portable Encyclopedia for
   Doing Business in China**
$24.95
World Trade Press
1505 Fifth Avenue
San Rafael, CA 94901-1827
(800) 833-8586
(415) 454-9934
Fax (415) 453-7980
(Illustrations, color maps, index. 384 pages)

Resource Publications

China Trade Manual: Business, Investment and Regulation
$397
Thompson Publishing Group
P.O. Box 26185
Tampa, FL 33633-0922
(800) 934-1610
Fax (800) 999-2320
(Hands-on information on the business, tax, regulatory, political and cultural aspects of doing business in China.)

Clean Transport Documents
$11.95
ICC Publishing Corporation
156 Fifth Avenue, Suite 820
New York, NY 10010
(212) 206-1150
(Negotiable and non-negotiable documents carried by all modes of transportation.)

Code of Federal Regulations, Title 19, Customs Duties
$35, Parts 1-199, Chapter I
S/N 869-019-00061-5
$11, Part 200-End, Chapter II and III
S/N 869-019-00062-3
U.S. Government Printing Office
Superintendent of Documents
P.O. Box 371954
Pittsburgh, PA 15250-7954
(202) 783-3238
Fax (202) 512-2250

Collection of ICC Arbitral Awards
$125
ICC Publishing Corporation
156 Fifth Avenue, Suite 820
New York, NY 10010
(212) 206-1150
(Excerpts of arbitral awards decided by ICC arbitrators during 1974-1985. Reproduces extracts in original language, accompanied by case notes in English and French.)

Commerce Business Daily
$275 (annually)
Superintendent of Documents
U.S. Government Printing Office
Washington, D.C. 20402
(202) 783-3238

Commercial Arbitration Law in Asia and the Pacific
$75
Oceana Publications, Inc.
75 Main Street
Dobbs Ferry, NY 10522
(914) 693-0402
(Text is organized on the basis of: textual commentary, summarizing legislation, rules and practice, including text of legislation in English, and arbitral awards.)

Competition (Antitrust) and Anti-dumping Laws in the Context of the Canada-U.S. Free Trade Agreement
$49.94
International Division/Publications
U.S. Chamber of Commerce
1615 H Street, N.W.
Washington, D.C. 20062-2000
(202) 463-5460

The Complete Twin Plant Guide (Mexico)
$395
Manufacturers' News, Inc.
1633 Central Street
Evanston, IL 60201
(708) 864-7000
Fax (708) 332-1100
(3-volume set)

Comprehensive Guide: Doing Business with Sovereign Soviet Republics
$250
TAG International
C.I.S. Business Affairs
P.O. Box 1808
Southlake, TX 76099-1808
(800) 728-1360
Fax (817) 481-1361

Comprehensive Guide to International Trade Terms
$36.50
U.S. Department of Commerce
Washington, D.C. 20230
(703) 487-4650

Conditions for Business Activities of Foreign Investors in Czechoslovakia
$42 (Europe)
$50 (outside Europe)
Joint Ventures Club of Czechoslovak
Chamber of Commerce and Industry
Pocernicka 64, 108 00 Praha 10 - Malesice
Czechoslovakia
Telephone and Fax (+42) (2) 77 97 89

Conducting Your Business in Mexico
$24.95
Harbour West Management
11440 West Bernardo Court, #300
San Diego, CA 92127
(619) 674-6678
Fax (619) 672-8963
(Examines what a potential or existing businessperson
needs to know before entering into the Mexican marketplace. Answers questions on how to set up and operate a
business, NAFTA, tax ramifications, how to find a joint
venture partner, law, exporting and importing, markets,
business culture, etc.)

Conducting Your Business in the United States
$24.95
Harbour West Management
11440 West Bernardo Court, #300
San Diego, CA 92127
(619) 674-6678
Fax (619) 672-8963
(Examines what a potential or existing businessperson
needs to know before entering into the U.S. marketplace.
Answers questions on how to set up and operate a business,
NAFTA, tax ramifications, types of corporations, markets,
law, exporting and importing, business culture, etc.)

Congressional Directory
$25
Federal Reprints
P.O. Box 70268
Washington, D.C. 20024
(202) 544-6604
Fax (202) 543-1527

County and City Data Book
$42.50
Federal Reprints
P.O. Box 70268
Washington, D.C. 20024
(202) 544-6604

Country Business Guide Series - "The Portable Encyclopedia for Doing Business Overseas"
$24.95 each
World Trade Press
1505 Fifth Avenue
San Rafael, CA 94901-1827
(800) 833-8586
(415) 454-9934
Fax (415) 453-7980
(Fifty-two guides are planned; each guide covers 25 topics,
including the economy, demographics, foreign investment,
current business and political issues, business culture and
etiquette, business formation and entities, labor, business
law, industry reviews, marketing, trade fairs, foreign trade,
personal taxation, import policy and procedures, export
policy and procedures, currency and foreign exchange,
international payments, opportunities, business travel,
ports and airports, financial institutions, corporate taxation,
business diectionary in local language, 600 to 1,100
important address, and regional, country and city maps in
full color. 310-408 pages.)

Country Marketing Plans
$10 (per country)
U.S. Department of Commerce
International Trade Administration
14th Street and Constitution Avenue, N.W.
Washington, D.C. 20230
(202) 377-4767

Country Studies
$26/Japan; $27/China; $8/Indonesia; $19 & $20/Spain
U.S. Government Printing Office
Superintendent of Documents
P.O. Box 371954
Pittsburgh, PA 15250-7954
(or nearest government bookstore)
Fax (202) 512-2250

County Directories
$75
Database Publishing Company
Database Publishing Company
P.O. Box 70024
Anaheim, CA 92825-0024
(714) 778-6400
Fax (714) 778-6811
(Available for the following counties: Alameda, Contra
Costa, Orange, San Diego, San Francisco, San Mateo
and Santa Clara.)

Craighead's International Executive Travel and Relocation Service
$595
Craighead Publications
P.O. Box 149
Darien, CT 06820
(203) 655-1007
(Reference guide for executives responsible for
international travel and relocation of their organization's
personnel.)

Crawford's Directory of City Connections
$150
St. James Press
835 Penobscot
Detroit, MI 48226
(800) 345-0392
(Provides information on the financial center of the U.K.)

CTIA: European Community Current Document Service
$125/$200, depending on release
Oceana Publications, Inc.
75 Main Street
Dobbs Ferry, NY 10522
(914) 693-1320
(Lists agreements entered into by the European Community
with other countries and international organizations.)

CTIA: United States Current Document Service
$125/release
Oceana Publications, Inc.
75 Main Street
Dobbs Ferry, NY 10522
(914) 693-8100
(Lists agreements entered into by the European Community
with other countries and international organizations.)

Culturgrams
Brigham Young University
David M. Kennedy Center for International Studies
Publication Services
P.O. Box 24538
Provo, UT 84602
(801) 378-6528
(800) 528-6279
(Four-page briefing covering customs, manners, lifestyles,
etc. of over 100 countries. May be purchased as a set or
individually by country of choice.)

Current World Leaders Almanac
$185
International Academy at Santa Barbara
800 Garden Street, Suite D
Santa Barbara, CA 93101-1552
(805) 965-5010
Fax (805) 965-6071
(Three issues provide directory to key officials for more
than 191 independent nations, plus complete listings for
more than 25 colonies and dependent territories.)

Customs Bulletin and Decisions
$99/year
U.S. Government Printing Office
Superintendent of Documents
P.O. Box 371954
Pittsburgh, PA 15250-7954
(202) 783-3238
Fax (202) 512-2233

Customs Law and Administration
$500 (4 binder set)
Oceana Publications, Inc.
75 Main Street
Dobbs Ferry, NY 10522
(914) 693-8100
Fax (914) 693-0402
(Covers experience of the U.S. Court of International Trade
as well as aspects of traditional customs law. Continually
updated publication.)

Customs Tariff Guidebooks
By product, country, sector. Prices depend on country
sector/product
Worldtariff
220 Montgomery Street, Suite 432
San Francisco, CA 94104-3410
(415) 391-7501
Fax (415) 391-7537
(Lists import duties, levies, V.A.T.)

Daily Report for Executives
The Bureau of National Affairs, Inc.
1231 25th Street, N.W.
Washington, D.C. 20037
(800) 372-1033

Destination Japan: A Business Guide for the 90s
$4
S/N 003-009-00602-3
U.S. Government Printing Office
Superintendent of Documents
P.O. Box 371954
Pittsburgh, PA 15250-7954
(202) 783-3238
Fax (202) 512-2250

Dictionary of International Trade
$16.50
World Trade Press
1505 Fifth Avenue
San Rafael, CA 94901-1827
(800) 833-8586
(415) 454-9934
Fax (415) 453-7980
(4,071 entries, including international trade, economic,
banking, legal and shipping terms; plus trade organizations,
addresses, maps and tables. 278 pages)

**Digest of Commercial Laws of the World, Forms of
    Commercial Agreements and State Variations**
$850 (11 binder set)
Oceana Publications, Inc.
75 Main Street
Dobbs Ferry, NY 10522
(914) 693-8100
Fax (914) 693-0402

Direct Marketing for 1992
$4,000
The Direct Marketing and Sales Bureau
14 Floral Street
London, WCZE 9RR, United Kingdom
01-379-7531
Fax 01-836-2810
(Examines direct marketing environment for each of the
12 EC countries.)

Direct Marketing to Canada
$19.95
AT&T
55 Corporate Drive
Bridgewater, NJ 08807
(800) 222-0400

Direct Marketing in Japan
$200
Dodwell Marketing Consultants
Kowa No. 35 Building 14-14, Akasaka 1 chome
Minato-ku, Tokyo 107 JAPAN
Telephone (03) 3589-0207
Fax (03) 5570-7132
Telex J 22274 DODWELL J

Directories for Other States
Price depends on state directory
Database Publishing Company
P.O. Box 70024
Anaheim, CA 92825-0024
(714) 778-6400
Fax (714) 778-6811
(Directories available for 49 states, Canada and Mexico.)

**Directory of American Chambers of Commerce
    Abroad**
$10
International Division/Publications
U.S. Chamber of Commerce
1615 H Street, N.W.
Washington, D.C. 20062-2000
(202) 463-5460
(Names, officers, addresses, telephone and telefax numbers
for the American Chambers Abroad in 56 countries.)

**Directory of American Firms Operating in Foreign
    Countries**
$200
World Trade Academy Press, Inc.
50 East 2nd Street, Suite 509
New York, NY 10017
(212) 697-4999
(Individual country lists available for a smaller charge.)

Directory of California Chambers of Commerce
$20
California Chamber of Commerce
P.O. Box 1736
Sacramento, CA 95814-1736
(916) 444-6670
(Alphabetical listing of chambers of commerce in California with name, address, phone number, chief executive officer, cross referenced by county, updated as changes occur.)

Directory of Chinese Manufacturers With Import and Export Rights
$100
Embassy of China
Commercial Office
2300 Connecticut Avenue, N.W.
Washington, DC 20008
(202) 328-2522
Fax (202) 232-7855
(Contains detailed information on 1,400 production enterprises that were granted rights to handle in import/export by the Ministry of Foreign Trade and Economic Cooperation.)

Directory of Contacts for Central and Eastern Europe and the Soviet Union
$75
International Division/Publications
U.S. Chamber of Commerce
1615 H Street, N.W.
Washington, D.C. 20062-2000
(202) 463-5460

Directory of EC Information Sources
$270
Euroconfidentiel
rue de Rixensart 18
B-1332 Genval
Belgium
(32 2) 652 02 84
Fax (32 2) 653-01 80
(Over 7,000 information sources are covered in this annually revised 1,100-page reference work.)

Directory of European Banking and Financial Associations
$65
St. James Press
835 Penobscot
Detroit, MI 48226
(800) 345-0392

Directory of European Industrial & Trade Associations
$195
Gale Research Company
P.O. Box 33477
Detroit, MI 48232-5477
(800) 877-GALE
(313) 961-2242
Fax (313) 961-6083

Directory of European Retailers
£140
Newman Books, Ltd.
32 Vauxhall Bridge Road
London SW1V 2SS
071 973 6402
Fax 071 233 5056/7
(Over 30,000 retail trade buyers and buying agents.)

Directory of Foreign Firms Operating in the United States
$145
World Trade Academy Press, Inc.
50 East 42nd Street, Suite 509
New York, NY 10017
(212) 697-4999
(Groups 1600 foreign firms by country — some individual county lists are available for a smaller charge.)

Directory of Foreign Manufacturers in the United States, 5th Edition
$195
Georgia State University Business Press
College of Business Administration
University Plaza
Atlanta, GA 30303-3093
(404) 651-4253
Fax (404) 651-4256
(Source of information on foreign investment in manufacturing, mining and petroleum in the United States.)

Directory of Leading U.S. Export Management Companies
Bergano Book Co.
P.O. Box 190
Fairfield, CT 06430
(203) 254-2054

Directory of Local Chambers of Commerce Which Maintain International Trade Services
$5
International Division/Publications
U.S. Chamber of Commerce
1615 H Street, N.W.
Washington, D.C. 20062-2000
(202) 463-5460
(Names and addresses of chambers in the U.S. which provide international trade assistance.)

Directory of Netherlands Subsidiaries in the United States
$125
The Netherlands Chamber of Commerce in the United States
One Rockefeller Plaza, 11th Floor
New York, NY 10020
(202) 265-6460
Fax (202) 265-6402
(Listing of all 850 subsidiaries and branches of Netherlands companies in the U.S.)

Directory of Russian Business Contacts
$199.95
International Press Publications Inc.
90 Nolan Court #23
Markham Ontario, Canada L3R 4L9
(905) 946-9588
(800) 666-0220 orders only
Fax (905) 946-9590
(Complete list of Russian Ministries and government organizations, public companies, state-owned and private enterprises involved in import/export operations.)

Directory of United States Importers and Directory of United States Exporters
$599 both ($399 each)
The Journal of Commerce
445 Marshall Street
Phillipsburg, NJ 08865
(908) 859-1300
(These directories highlight more than 55,000 active U.S. world traders.)

Diskette Package on Monterrey, Nuevo Leon, Mexico
$200
American Chamber of Commerce of Mexico
Picachos 760 Desp. 4, Obispado
64060 Monterrey, N.L.
(48 04) 14 48 47 41
Fax 48-55 74
(Updated information on foreign investment rules and regulations, maquiladoras, economic and industrial profile, employment, export/import capacity, lifestyle, etc.)

Distributorship Agreements in the U.S.
$40
German American Chamber of Commerce
40 W. 57th Street, 31st Floor
New York, NY 10019
(212) 974-8830
(229 pages.)

Doing Business in Australia
$35, plus $10/airmail
American Chamber of Commerce in Australia
Suite 4, Gloucester Walk
88 Cumberland Street
Sydney, NSW
Australia 2000
Telephone +612 241-1907
Fax +612 251-5220
(A guide prepared by legal, accounting and financial experts comparing business reports and practices in Australia and the U.S.)

Doing Business in France
$10.00
French-American Chamber of Commerce
425 Bush Street, Suite 401
San Francisco, CA 94108
(415) 398-2449
(Information on distribution arrangements, agency agreements, incorporation and management. Also includes information on opening an office in France, guidelines for work permits and commercial cards, and information on tax issues and Social Security.)

Doing Business in the Province of Quebec
$17
National Technical Information Service
5285 Port Royal Road
Springfield, VA 22161
(703) 487-4650

113

Doing Business in . . . Series
From $85 to $600 per country
Matthew Bender and Co.
International Division
1275 Broadway
Albany, NY 12204
(800) 424-4200
(518) 487-3542
(Multi-volume manuals for doing business in various
countries.)

Doing Business with Russia, Ukraine & Kazakitstan
$250
TAG Int.
CIS Business Affairs
P.O. Box 1808
Southlake, TX 76099-1808
(800) 653-0489
Fax (817) 481-1361
(Explains rules and regulations for trade and investment.)

Doing Business in Vietnam
$24.95 (Canada $34.95)
Prima Publishing
P.O. Box 1260BK
Rocklin, CA 95677
(916) 632-4400
(Author James Robinson's step-by-step guide to specific
areas of economic opportunity, licenses and trademarks,
Vietnamese business culture, resources and support groups,
special considerations for Vietnamese living overseas. 288
pages.)

Do's and Taboos Around the World
$12.95
The Benjamin Company, Inc.
21 Dupont Avenue
White Plains, NY 10605
(914) 997-0111
Fax (914) 997-7214
(Tips for international business travelers covering
worldwide protocol, customs and etiquette.)

Drawback Made Easy
$49
Global Training Center, Inc.
Kingsley Building, Suite 102
4124 Linden Avenue
Dayton, OH 45432
(800) 860-5030

EC 1992: A Practical Guide for American Business
$27.50
Update #4: $21.00
International Division/Publications
U.S. Chamber of Commerce
1615 H Street, N.W.
Washington, D.C. 20062-2000
(202) 463-5460
(143 pages)

EC Institutions' Yellow Pages
$135
Euroconfidentiel
rue de Rixensart 18
B-1332 Genval
Belgium
(32 2) 652 02 84
Fax (32 2) 653-01 80
(Over 3,000 key personnel in each of the major institution
listed with areas of responsibility, direct telephone number
and address.)

EC Trade & Professional Associations and Their Information
$155
Euroconfidentiel
rue de Rixensart 18
B-1332 Genval
Belgium
(32 2) 652 02 84
Fax (32 2) 653-01 80
(Address, telephone and fax numbers, chairman and contact
person for over 600 EC associations.)

Eastern Europe and the Commonwealth of Independent States
$390
International Press Publications, Inc.
90 Nolan Court #23
Markham Ontario, Canada L3R 4L9
(905) 946-9588
Fax (905) 946-9590
(800) 666-0220 orders only
(Records latest economic, political and cultural
developments.)

Eastern Europe Reporter
The Bureau of National Affairs
1231 25th Street
Washington D.C. 20037
(202) 452-4200
(800) 372-1033
Fax (800) 253-0332
(Annual subscription — biweekly reports.)

Eastern European Business Database CD-ROM
$395
American Directory Corporation
P.O. Box 7426
New York, NY 10116
(718) 797-4311
(Lists 100,000 companies in Eastern Europe and
trade information.)

Economic and Social Progress in Latin America
$16.95
The Johns Hopkins University Press
701 West 40th Street, Suite 275
Baltimore, MD 21211-2190
(800) 537-5487
(Ten-year overview of the Latin American and Caribbean
economies, with country-by-country statistics.)

Economic Bulletin Board
(202) 377-1986
(On-line, PC-board system for accessing the latest government press releases, data files and trade opportunities.)

Economic Reform in India
$20
International Division/Publications
U.S. Chamber of Commerce
1615 H Street, N.W.
Washington, D.C. 20062-2000
(202) 463-5460

Electric Current Abroad
$3
S/N 003-008-00203-0
U.S. Government Printing Office
Superintendent of Documents
P.O. Box 371954
Pittsburgh, PA 15250-7954
(202) 783-3238
Fax (202) 512-2250
(Describes characteristics of electric current
available overseas, types of electric plugs in use.)

Employment Abroad: Facts and Fallacies
$7.50
International Division/Publications
U.S. Chamber of Commerce
1615 H Street, N.W.
Washington, D.C. 20062-2000
(202) 463-5460

**Employment Practices of American Companies
   in Japan**
$40, plus $4 airmail
International Division/Publications
U.S. Chamber of Commerce
1615 H Street, N.W.
Washington, D.C. 20062-2000
(202) 463-5460

Encountering the Chinese, A Guide for Americans
$16.95
Intercultural Press
P.O. Box 700
Yarmouth, Maine 04096
(207) 846-5168
Fax (207) 846-5181

Environmental Auditing
$12.95
ICC Publishing Corporation
156 Fifth Avenue, Suite 820
New York, NY 10010
(212) 206-1150
(International Chamber of Commerce position paper)

Environmental Encyclopedia and Directory
$325
International Press Publications Inc.
90 Nolan Court #23
Markham Ontario, Canada L3R 4L9
(905) 946-9588
Fax (905) 946-9590
(800) 666-0220 orders only

**Establishing a Subsidiary in France of a
   U.S. Company**
$10.00
French-American Chamber of Commerce
425 Bush Street, Suite 401
San Francisco, CA 94108
(415) 398-2449
(Includes practical information, an outline of basic
procedures, data on management and tax issues.)

Europa World Year Book
$610 (2-volume set)
International Press Publications Inc.
90 Nolan Court #23
Markham Ontario, Canada L3R 4L9
(905) 946-9588
Fax (905) 946-9590
(800) 666-0220 orders only
(Contains facts and figures on more than 200 countries and territories.)

European Business Rankings
$160
Gale Researching
Marketing Department
P.O. Box 33477
Detroit, MI 48232-9852
(800) 877-GALE
(313) 961-2242
Fax (313) 961-6083
(Provides 2,250 subject-arranged lists of business statistics and rankings.)

The European Communities Encyclopedia and Directory .
$375
International Press Publications Inc.
90 Nolan Court #23
Markham Ontario, Canada L3R 4L9
(905) 946-9588
Fax (905) 946-9590
(800) 666-0220 orders only
(Examines aspects of the European Communities as they approach the Single Market.)

European Community Company Law
$150
Oceana Publications, Inc.
75 Main Street
Dobbs Ferry, NY 10522
(914) 693-8100
Fax (914) 693-0402

European Community Country Profiles
$40
International Division/Publications
U.S. Chamber of Commerce
1615 H Street, N.W.
Washington, D.C. 20062-2000
(202) 463-5460

European Community: The Single Market
$150
Oceana Publications, Inc.
75 Main Street
Dobbs Ferry, NY 10522
(914) 693-8100
Fax (914) 693-0402

European Community and Europe: A Legal Guide to Business Development
$29.50
California Trade and Commerce Agency
California Chamber of Commerce
3255 Ramos Circle
Sacramento, CA 95827
(800) 331-8877
(Articles by attorneys and accountants from major international law or accounting firms summarize important legal and financial considerations for companies doing business in the European Community and Europe. Includes overview of the creation of the European Economic Community, mergers, joint ventures, distribution and franchising agreements, commercial law, tax considerations, finance, employment law, standards, exporting requirements and other business concerns. Also covers major sectors: public procurement, high technology, environment, telecommunications, pharmaceuticals, energy and utilities. Country-specific chapters highlight requirements unique to individual nations in the EC or Europe. 375 pages.)

European Consultants Directory
$225
Gale Researching
Marketing Department
P.O. Box 33477
Detroit, MI 48232-9852
(800) 877-GALE
(313) 961-2242
Fax (313) 961-6083
(Lists 5,500 European-based consultants.)

European Food Trades Directory
£145
Newman Books, Ltd.
32 Vauxhall Bridge Road
London SW1V 2SS
071 973 6402
Fax 071 233 5056/7
(Instant access to 50,000 key decision-makers, fully indexed and cross-referenced. 1,600 pages.)

The European Monetary System
$45
St. James Press
835 Penobscot
Detroit, MI 48226
(800) 345-0392

European Trade Affairs: A Key to the World for
U.S. Exporters
$5.50
Superintendent of Documents
U.S. Government Printing Office
Washington, D.C. 20402
(202) 783-3238

European Wholesalers and Distributors Directory
$175
Gale Researching
Marketing Department
P.O. Box 33477
Detroit, MI 48232-9852
(800) 877-GALE
(313) 961-2242
Fax (313) 961-6083
(Lists approximately 5,000 wholesalers and distributors of
finished consumer goods and industrial products in Western
and Eastern Europe.)

Expanding Markets Internationally: A Dynamic
and Practical Approach
$30
Instrument Society of America
67 Alexander Drive
P.O. Box 12277
Research Triangle Park, NC 27709
(800) 334-6391
(Explains similarities and points out minor differences
between domestic and international markets.)

Export Administration Regulations
$94
U.S. Government Printing Office
Superintendent of Documents
P.O. Box 371954
Pittsburgh, PA 15250-7954
(202) 783-3238
Fax (202) 512-2233
(Annual subscription includes basic manual and supple-
ments. Includes Department of Commerce field office
addresses, U.S. import certificate and delivery verification
procedures, restrictive trade practices or boycotts, export
licensing procedures, documentation requirements, etc.)

Export and Import Directories
Unz & Co., Inc.
190 Baldwin Avenue
Jersey City, NJ 07306
(800) 631-3098
Fax (201) 795-0695
(Multi-volume set of reference manuals.)

Export Directory of Denmark
$130-surface; $150-airmail
21, Virumgaardsvej
DK-2830 Virum
Copenhagen
Denmark
(45) 4583 4583
Fax (45) 4583 1011
(Lists approximately 3,000 Danish export companies
and valuable information about branches, products,
brands and services.)

Export Documentation and Shipping
$67.50
International Business Strategies, Inc.
10860 Lake Thames Drive
Cincinnati, OH 45242
(513) 489-5469; (800) 245-4300
Fax (513) 489-5469; (800) 622-3036
(Reference material and home study course.)

Export Documentation and Procedures
$65
Global Training Center, Inc.
Kingsley Building, Suite 102
4124 Linden Avenue
Dayton, OH 45432
(800) 860-5030

Export Documentation for Shipments to Canada
$44.50
International Trade Institute
5055 North Main Street
Dayton, OH 45415
(800) 543-2453
Fax (513) 276-5920
(Guide shows how to prepare Candian Customs invoice.)

Resource Publications

Export Guide to Europe
$130
Gale Research Company
P.O. Box 33477
Detroit, MI 48232-5477
(800) 877-GALE
(313) 961-2242
Fax (313) 961-6083

Export Hotline
$50 to be listed in the directory; access to the directory
is free.
800-USA-XPORT
(A nationwide fax retrieval information service offering
more than 4,200 reports on everything from international
trade issues to a country's business rituations, with
information on 78 countries and territories. The 24-hour
hotline operates seven days a week.)

Export-Import Bank of the United States
No Charge
Export-Import Bank of the United States
811 Vermont Avenue, N.W.
Washington, D.C. 20571
(202) 566-2117
(Explains U.S. export financing programs.)

Export/Import Reference Glossary
$65
Global Training Center, Inc.
Kingsley Building, Suite 102
4124 Linden Avenue
Dayton, OH 45432
(800) 860-5030

Export Information Services for U.S. Business Firms
No Charge
Office of Export Development
International Trade Administration
U.S. Department of Commerce
Washington, D.C. 20230
(202) 377-4705
(Describes a wide range of services to assist in export
activities.)

The Export Kit—Window on the World
$25
Community Development Trading Group
50 Washington Square
Newport, RI 02840
(401) 849-7053
(Two-part publication for small businesses designed to
help them assess export potential and enter export markets.)

Export Letters of Credit and Drafts
$67.50
International Business Strategies, Inc.
10860 Lake Thames Drive
Cincinnati, OH 45242
(513) 489-5469; (800) 245-4300
Fax (513) 489-5469; (800) 622-3036
(Reference material and home study course.)

Export Marketing and Sales
$67.50
International Business Strategies, Inc.
10860 Lake Thames Drive
Cincinnati, OH 45242
(513) 489-5469; (800) 245-4300
Fax (513) 489-5469; (800) 622-3036
(Reference material and home study course.)

Export Order Processing
$67.50
International Business Strategies, Inc.
10860 Lake Thames Drive
Cincinnati, OH 45242
(800) 245-4300
(513) 489-5469
Fax (513) 489-3015; (800) 622-3036
(Reference material and home study course.)

Export Reference Glossary
$67.50
International Business Strategies, Inc.
10860 Lake Thames Drive
Cincinnati, OH 45242
(513) 489-5469; (800) 245-4300
Fax (513) 489-5469; (800) 622-3036
(Reference material and home study course.)

Export Reference Manual
$636
Bureau of National Affairs, Inc.
1231 25th Street, NW
Washington, D.C. 20037
(800) 372-1033
Fax (202) 452-7583

Export Sales and Marketing Manual
$295, plus $11.50 s/h (2-day delivery)
$175 Quarterly Updates
Export USA Publications
6901 W. 84th Street, Suite 157
Minneapolis, MN 55438
(800) 876-0624
Fax (612) 943-1535

Export Shipping
$67.50
International Business Strategies, Inc.
10860 Lake Thames Drive
Cincinnati, OH 45242
(513) 489-5469; (800) 245-4300
Fax (513) 489-5469; (800) 622-3036
(Reference material and home study course.)

Export Today
P.O. Box 28189
Washington, D.C. 20038
(202) 737-1060
(Bimonthly magazine.)

Export Trading Company Guidebook
$11
S/N 003-009-00523-0
U.S. Government Printing Office
Superintendent of Documents
P.O. Box 371954
Pittsburgh, PA 15250-7954
(202) 783-3238
Fax (202) 512-2250
(Explains what it takes to export profitably.)

Export Yellow Pages
No Charge
Venture Marketing Corp.
3000 K Street, NW, Suite 690
Washington, D.C. 20007
(202) 337-6300
(Contains information on over 16,000 U.S. companies involved in international business. Copies are available through U.S. Department of Commerce District Offices.)

The Exporter
$144 (annual cost)
34 West 37th Street
New York, NY 10018
(212) 563-2772
(Monthly magazine.)

Exporter's Directory/U.S. Buying Guide
Journal of Commerce
2 World Trade Center, 27th Floor
New York, NY 10048
(212) 837-7000

Exporter's Encyclopedia
$545
Dun's Marketing Services
3 Sylvan Way
Parsippany, NJ 07054-3896
(800) 526-0651
(201) 605-6749
(Annual handbook covers more than 220 world markets.)

Exporter's Resource Directory
$165
Michael Press
180 South Western Avenue, Suite 241
Carpentersville, IL 60110
(708) 428-4126
Fax (708) 428-4131
(Reference book for international traders includes 25,000 entries for 50 states and Washington D.C. and 350 government agencies.)

Exporting Guide for California
$17.50
California Trade and Commerce Agency
California Chamber of Commerce
3255 Ramos Circle
Sacramento, CA 95827
(800) 331-8877
(A step-by-step manual to help the California company wishing to become involved in exporting or to expand existing export volumes. Covers organizing for export, identifying markets and distribution avenues, pricing, documentation, shipping and financing. Includes tips on avoiding common pitfalls, plus samples of key documents, including sample supplier/exporter and distribution agreements. Also highly useful for the person who is new to exporting, but works in a firm that already sells its goods or services in the international market. 145 pages.)

Exporting to Japan
$16, plus $3 airmail
International Division/Publications
U.S. Chamber of Commerce
1615 H Street, N.W.
Washington, D.C. 20062-2000
(202) 463-5460

Exporting: From Start to Finance
$39.95
L. Fargo Wells and Karin D. Dulat
Liberty House
Blue Ridge Summit, PA 17214-9988
(800) 822-8158

Exportise
$49.50
The Small Business Foundation of America
(202) 223-1103
(A 250-page source book.)

F&S Index International/F&S Index Europe
$975/year
Predicasts
10001 Cedar Avenue
Cleveland, OH 44106
(800) 321-6388
(Two-line summaries of business and trade journal articles monthly.)

The Far East and Australasia
$325
International Press Publications Inc.
90 Nolan Court #23
Markham Ontario, Canada L3R 4L9
(905) 946-9588
Fax (905) 946-9590
(800) 666-0220 orders only

Financing and Insuring Exports: A User's Guide to Eximbank and FCIA Programs
$50
Eximbank Public Affairs Office
811 Vermont Avenue, N.W.
Washington, D.C. 20571
(800) 424-5401

Findex: The Directory of Market Research Reports, Studies and Surveys 1988
$285
Cambridge Information Group
7200 Wisconsin Avenue
Bethesda, MD 20814
(800) 227-3052
(301) 961-67509
(Reference guide to commercially-available market and business research.)

Finding a Home in Tokyo
$10, plus $3 airmail
International Division/Publications
U.S. Chamber of Commerce
1615 H Street, N.W.
Washington, D.C. 20062-2000
(202) 463-5460

Foreign Agricultural Trade of the United States
$21/year
U.S. Government Printing Office
Superintendent of Documents
P.O. Box 371954
Pittsburgh, PA 15250-7954
(202) 783-3238
Fax (202) 512-2233
(Bi-monthly publication containing statistics on exports/imports.)

Foreign Agriculture
$18
Foreign Agricultural Service-Information Division
Room 5920-S
U.S. Department of Agriculture
Washington, D.C. 20250-1000
(202) 720-7115
(Annual fact book with agricultural profiles of 90 countries.)

Foreign Chambers of Commerce and Associations in the U.S.
$5
International Division/Publications
U.S. Chamber of Commerce
1615 H Street, N.W.
Washington, D.C. 20062-2000
(202) 463-5460

Foreign Direct Investment in the United States
$13
S/N 003-010-00243-3
U.S. Government Printing Office
Superintendent of Documents
P.O. Box 371954
Pittsburgh, PA 15250-7954
(202) 783-3238
Fax (202) 512-2250
(Detailed data on manufacturing operations of U.S.
affiliates of foreign countries.)

Foreign Government Offices in California:
  A Directory
$15
California Institute of Public Affairs
An Affiliate of The Claremont Colleges
P.O. Box 10
Claremont, CA 91711
(916) 442-2472

Former Soviet Union Marketing, Media &
  Advertising Directory
$432
Russian Information Services
89 Main Street, Suite 2
Montpelier, VT 95602
(802) 223-4955
Fax (802) 223-6105
(800) 639-4301
(Over 3,500 key media listings, 2,000 ad agency and
support services, 2,000 political and commercial contacts.
Includes detailed demographic and market data for each
republic. 660 pages.)

From Nyet to Da
$15.95
Russian Information Services
89 Main Street, Suite 2
Montpelier, VT 95602
(802) 223-4955
Fax (802) 223-6105
(800) 639-4301
(Pertinent reflections on Russian national character and how
understanding it can lead to more effective negotiation and
social/business interaction. 200 pages.)

Geographic and Global Issues Quarterly
$7/year
U.S. Government Printing Office
Superintendent of Documents
P.O. Box 371954
Pittsburgh, PA 15250-7954
(202) 783-3238
Fax (202) 512-2233
(Annual subscription, issued quarterly.)

German American Chamber Membership Directory
$80.00
German American Chamber of Commerce
40 W. 57th Street, 31st Floor
New York, NY 10019
(212) 974-8830

German American Trade
$50/subscription
German American Chamber of Commerce
40 W. 57th Street, 31st Floor
New York, NY 10019
(212) 974-8830

German Commercial Code
$70.00
German American Chamber of Commerce
40 W. 57th Street, 31st Floor
New York, NY 10019
(212) 974-8830

The German Economy — Colossus at the Crossroads
$18.95
German American Chamber of Commerce
40 W. 57th Street, 31st Floor
New York, NY 10019
(212) 974-8830

The Germans — Who Are They Now?
$24.95
German American Chamber of Commerce
40 W. 57th Street, 31st Floor
New York, NY 10019
(212) 974-8830

Germany as a Business Location
$10.00
German American Chamber of Commerce
40 W. 57th Street, 31st Floor
New York, NY 10019
(212) 974-8830

Germany — Buyers' and Sellers' Guide
$127
Manufacturers' News, Inc.
1633 Central Street
Evanston, IL 60201
(708) 864-7000
Fax (708) 332-1100
(9,900 headings with 350,000 sources for buying and selling in Germany; 3,100 pages.)

Germany's Top 300
$95.00
German American Chamber of Commerce
40 W. 57th Street, 31st Floor
New York, NY 10019
(212) 974-8830

Global Marketing
$65
Global Training Center, Inc.
Kingsley Building, Suite 102
4124 Linden Avenue
Dayton, OH 45432
(800) 860-5030

Global Success: International Business Tactics for the 1990s
$25
Global Business and Trade
1385 Don Carlos Court
Chula Vista, CA 91910
(619) 421-5923
(Offers small and medium sized businesses advanced methods to get into the global market.)

Global Trade Magazine
$45 (annual subscription)
North American Publishing Company
401 North Broad Street
Philadelphia, PA 19108
(215) 238-5300
(Monthly magazine.)

Global Trade Talk
$11
U.S. Government Printing Office
Superintendent of Documents
P.O. Box 371954
Pittsburgh, PA 15250-7954
(202) 783-3238
Fax (202) 512-2233
(Bi-monthly U.S. Customs Service journal about international trade issues.)

Global Trade White Pages
$295
Carroll Publishing Company
1058 Thomas Jefferson Street, N.W.
Washington, D.C. 20007
(202) 333-8620
Fax (202) 337-7020

Going International
$34.95
Lennic Copeland and Lewis Griggs
Random House
201 East 50th Street
New York, NY 10022
(800) 733-3000

Government Procurement Opportunities in Canada
$17
National Technical Information Service
5285 Port Royal Road
Springfield, VA 22161
(703) 487-4650

The Greening of World Trade
$14
S/N 055-000-00425-1
U.S. Government Printing Office
Superintendent of Documents
P.O. Box 371954
Pittsburgh, PA 15250-7954
(202) 783-3238
Fax (202) 512-2250
(Comprehensive discussion of the relationship between expanding global markets and increasing concern about the environment. 240 pages.)

Guide to Distributorship Agreements
$25.95
Publication 441
ICC Publishing Corporation
156 Fifth Avenue, Suite 820
New York, NY 10010
(212) 206-1150

Guide to Documentary Credit Operations
$18.95
Publication 415
ICC Publishing Corporation
156 Fifth Avenue, Suite 820
New York, NY 10010
(212) 206-1150

Guide to Doing Business with the Agency for International Development
U.S. Agency for International Development
320 21st Street, N.W.
Washington, D.C. 20523
(202) 647-3504

U.S. Agency for International Development
West Coast Outreach
3031 Torrance Boulevard
P.O. Box 13536
Torrance, CA 90503
(310) 533-0770
Fax (310) 533-1325

Guide to EC Grants and Loans
$265; National supplements $45
Euroconfidentiel
rue de Rixensart 18
B-1332 Genval
Belgium
(32 2) 652 02 84
Fax (32 2) 653-01 80
(Provides detailed information on the 21 billion Ecus
of grants and loans available annually by the European
Communities. 350 pages.)

A Guide to European Financial Centers
$65
St. James Press
835 Penobscot
Detroit, MI 48226
(800) 345-0392

A Guide to Financing Exports
No Charge
Office of Export Development
International Trade Administration
Department of Commerce
Washington, D.C. 20230
(202) 377-4705
(A summary of sources of credit and credit information for
exports. Reviews services offered by Export-Import Bank
of the United States, Foreign Credit Insurance Association,
Overseas Private Investment Corporation and Commodity
Credit Corporation.)

Guide to Foreign Trade Statistics
$16
S/N 003-024-08680-8
U.S. Government Printing Office
Superintendent of Documents
P.O. Box 371954
Pittsburgh, PA 15250-7954
(202) 783-3238
Fax (202) 512-2250
(Loose-leaf list; includes index.)

A Guide to Import Procedures
$67.50
International Trade Institute, Inc.
5055 North Main Street
Dayton, OH 45415
(800) 543-2453
Fax (513) 276-5920
(Includes introduction of parties to an import transaction,
financing imports — methods of payment and application
and agreement for commercial letter of credit.)

The Guide to Incoterms
International Chamber of Commerce Publishing Corp., Inc.
156 Fifth Avenue, Suite 820
New York, NY 10010
(Definitions and interpretations of international commercial
terms.)

Guide to NAFTA Documentation
$67.50
International Business Strategies, Inc.
10860 Lake Thames Drive
Cincinnati, OH 45242
(513) 489-5469; (800) 245-4300
Fax (513) 489-5469; (800) 622-3036
(Reference material and home study course.)

*Guide to Packaging and Labeling Requirements
   in Canada*
$17
National Technical Information Service
5285 Port Royal Road
Springfield, VA 22161
(703) 487-4650

Guide to Penalty Damages
$29.95
ICC Publishing Corporation
156 Fifth Avenue, Suite 820
New York, NY 10010
(212) 206-1150
(Covers main points in major legal systems and draws
attention to rules of mandatory nature. Points out pitfalls to
an uninformed trader.)

A Guidebook on United States Immigration
$24.95
Harbour West Management
11440 West Bernardo Court, #300
San Diego, CA 92127
(619) 674-6678
Fax (619) 672-8963
(Reviews overall structure of the U.S. immigration system
and highlights most important aspects of the Immigration
Act of 1990.)

*A Guidebook on U.S. Taxation of U.S. Taxpayers
   Engaged in Foreign Activities*
$24.95
Harbour West Management
11440 West Bernardo Court, #300
San Diego, CA 92127
(619) 674-6678
Fax (619) 672-8963
(Reviews ramifications and implications of "outbound
investment" — investment made offshore and in any
foreign jurisdiction by a U.S. citizen. Provides strategies
on how to work within the rules that apply to outbound
investment.)

*A Guidebook on U.S. Taxation of Resident Aliens,
   Nonresident Aliens and Foreign Corporations*
$24.95
Harbour West Management
11440 West Bernardo Court, #300
San Diego, CA 92127
(619) 674-6678
Fax (619) 672-8963
(Reviews ramifications of "inward investment" — invest-
ment from outside the U.S. by resident alien, nonresident
alien, and foreign corporations.)

Handbook of Export Controls
$79
International Division/Publications
U.S. Chamber of Commerce
1615 H Street, N.W.
Washington, D.C. 20062-2000
(202) 463-5460

Handbook of GATT Dispute Settlements
$200
Kluwer Law and Tax Publishers
P.O. Box 23
7400 GA DEVENTER
The Netherlands
Telephone (31) 5700 47261
Fax (31) 5700 22244
(Collection of decided cases about and within the institu-
tions of the General Agreement on Tariffs and Trade.)

Health Information for International Travel
$6.50
S/N 017-023-00192-2
U.S. Government Printing Office
Superintendent of Documents
P.O. Box 371954
Pittsburgh, PA 15250-7954
(202) 783-3238
Fax (202) 512-2250

High-Tech Guide
$53.45
Directories of Industry, Inc.
P.O. Box 456
Corona del Mar, CA 92625
(714)729-1090
(National manufacturers, processors, service firms of
electronic, industrial, aerospace equipment, components,
supplies; distributors, representatives, agents, 13 western
states, addresses, phone numbers; product and service
section.)

***Hong Kong Business - The Portable Encyclopedia
for Doing Business in Hong Kong***
$24.95
World Trade Press
1505 Fifth Avenue
San Rafael, CA 94901-1827
(800) 833-8586
(415) 454-9934
Fax (415) 453-7980
(Illustrations, color maps, index. 352 pages)

***How the IRS Views Tax Havens and Offshore
Financial Centres***
$24.95
Harbour West Management
11440 West Bernardo Court, #300
San Diego, CA 92127
(619) 674-6678
Fax (619) 672-8963
(Examines tax havens from the viewpoint of the IRS,
as well as the legal and illegal uses of tax havens.)

***How to Investigate, Own and Operate a Franchise
Successfully***
$24.95
Harbour West Management
11440 West Bernardo Court, #300
San Diego, CA 92127
(619) 674-6678
Fax (619) 672-8963
(Reviews all the concerns of evaluating, purchasing and
then operating a successful franchise. Provides strategies
on how to investigate before making any decisions.)

How to Profit from the Coming Russian Boom
$24.95
Russian Information Services
89 Main Street, Suite 2
Montpelier, VT 95602
(802) 223-4955
Fax (802) 223-6105
(800) 639-4301
(Guide to Russian culture and the Russian mindset as
they relate to business. 350 pages.)

Hungarian Business Book
Free of Charge
Planetwork Ltd.
H-1300 Budapest
P.O.B.. 135
Hungary, Europe
(Includes a review and several offers of Hungarian trading
firms.)

Hungary: The Second Decade of Economic Reform
$25
St. James Press
835 Penobscot
Detroit, MI 48226
(800) 345-0392

ICC Rules of Conciliation and Arbitration
No Charge
ICC Publishing Corporation
156 Fifth Avenue, Suite 820
New York, NY 10010
(212) 206-1150

***Import/Export: How to Get Started in
International Trade***
$14.95
Global Business and Trade
1385 Don Carlos Court
Chula Vista, CA 91910
(619) 421-5923; (800) 822-8138
("How-to" do cross-border business.)

Import Procedures and Documentation
$67.50
International Business Strategies, Inc.
10860 Lake Thames Drive
Cincinnati, OH 45242
(513) 489-5469; (800) 245-4300
Fax (513) 489-5469; (800) 622-3036
(Reference material and home study course.)

Importers Manual USA
$87
World Trade Press
1505 Fifth Avenue
San Rafael, CA 94901-1827
(800) 833-8586
(415) 454-9934
Fax (415) 453-7980
(More than 3,000 addresses, comprehensive index,
212 illustrations, 37 photos, 100 maps. 952 pages.)

Importing to the United States
$10
Federal Reprints
P.O. Box 70268
Washington, D.C. 20024
(202) 544-6604
Fax (202) 543-1527
(Prepared by the U.S. Customs Service.)

Importing into the United States
$4.75
U.S. Government Printing Office
Superintendent of Documents
P.O. Box 371954
Pittsburgh, PA 15250-7954
(or nearest government bookstore)
Fax orders (202) 512-2250
(95 pages.)

Incoterms
$23.95 plus $3 for postage and handling
International Chamber of Commerce Publishing Corp., Inc.
156 Fifth Avenue, Suite 820
New York, NY 10010
(Definitions and interpretations of international
commercial terms.)

Individual Country Practices in International Countertrade
$2.75
Superintendent of Documents
U.S. Government Printing Office
Washington, D.C. 20402
(202) 783-3238

Industrial Goods Distribution in Japan
$750
Dodwell Marketing Consultants
Kowa No. 35 Building 14-14, Akasaka 1 chome
Minato-ku, Tokyo 107 JAPAN
Telephone (03) 3589-0207
Fax (03) 5570-7132
Telex J 22274 DODWELL J

Industrial Groupings in Japan
$800
Dodwell Marketing Consultants
Kowa No. 35 Building 14-14, Akasaka 1 chome
Minato-ku, Tokyo 107 JAPAN
Telephone (03) 3589-0207
Fax (03) 5570-7132
Telex J 22274 DODWELL J

Industry Sector Analysis
$10/report
Commerical Information Management System
(202) 377-4767
(Prepared annually by commerical sections of American
embassies for the U.S. Department of Commerce's U.S.
and Foreign Commercial Service. Covers 67 countries.)

Inside Washington: The International Business Executive's Guide to Government Resources
$49.95
Venture Marketing Corp.
3000 K Street, NW, Suite 690
Washington, D.C. 20007
(800) 288-2582
(202) 337-6300
(Includes case studies on businesses that have profited
from government assistance.)

Intellectual Property in the United States
$24.95
Harbour West Management
11440 West Bernardo Court, #300
San Diego, CA 92127
(619) 674-6678
Fax (619) 672-8963
(Explains the differences between trademark and copyright,
how to patent ideas or products, and the best methods to
protect you or your company.)

Inter-American Commercial Arbitration
$85
Oceana Publications, Inc.
75 Main Street
Dobbs Ferry, NY 10522
(914) 693-8100
Fax (914) 693-0402
(Focuses on 34 countries with overview of historical
development.)

Interbank Funds Transfer
$11.95
ICC Publishing Corporation
156 Fifth Avenue, Suite 820
New York, NY 10010
(212) 206-1150
(Total set of financial institution and banking practices
permitting and facilitating international interbank funds
transfer.)

The International Arbitral Process
$250
Oceana Publications, Inc.
75 Main Street
Dobbs Ferry, NY 10522
(914) 693-8100
Fax (914) 693-0402

International Business Magazine
$48/year
P.O. Box 50286
Boulder, CO 80322
(800) 274-8187

International Chamber of Commerce Arbitration
$100
ICC Publishing Corporation
156 Fifth Avenue, Suite 820
New York, NY 10010
(212) 206-1150
(Deals with arbitral practice and procedures of the ICC
Court.)

International Commercial Arbitration
$400 (4 binder set)
Oceana Publications, Inc.
75 Main Street
Dobbs Ferry, NY 10522
(914) 693-8100
Fax (914) 693-0402
(Made up of collection of international conventions, model
laws, agreements, national legislation, and arbitration rules
of national and international organizations and associations.)

International Corporate 1000 Yellow Book
$125
Monitor Publishing Company
104 Fifth Avenue, 2nd Floor
New York, NY 10011
(212) 627-4140
(Includes complete listing of more than 30,000 chief
executives, managing directors and officers, as well as
subsidiary and division executives.)

*International Countertrade: A Guide for Managers
    and Executives*
$3.75
Superintendent of Documents
U.S. Government Printing Office
Washington, D.C. 20402
(202) 783-3238

International Directories of Company Histories
$130 each
St. James Press
835 Penobscot
Detroit, MI 48226
(800) 345-0392
(250 histories appear in each volume.)

*The International Directory of Business Information
    Agencies and Services*
$75
World Trade Intelligence
Gale Research Company
Book Tower, Dept. 77748
Detroit, MI 48226
(800) 223-4253

International Directory of Corporate Affiliations
$525
National Register Publishing Co.
3004 Glenview Road
Wilmette, IL 60091
(800) 323-6772
(Lists 32,000 companies in the world; key details about
1,000 major foreign parent companies and their 17,000
U.S. and foreign holdings; 1,400 American corporations
and their 13,000 affiliates outside the country.)

The International Directory of Government
$345
IPS/Taylor & Francis
1900 Frost Road, Suite 101
Bristol, PA 19007-1598
(800) 821-8312
(Covers more than 200 countries and 15,000 entries
for government ministries, departments, agencies and
corporations.)

The International Directory of Government
$345
International Press Publications Inc.
90 Nolan Court #23
Markham Ontario, Canada L3R 4L9
(905) 946-9588
Fax (905) 946-9590
(800) 666-0220 orders only
(Contains more than 15,000 entries.)

The International Directory of Importers

$285/Asia/Pacific; $385/Europe; $185/North America;
$185/Middle East; $185/South America; $185/Africa
International Directory of Importers
1741 Kekamek N.W.
Poulsbo, WA 98370
(206) 779-1511
Fax (206) 697-4696
(A key to more than 105,000 importing firms in Europe
[3 volumes], Middle East, North America, South America,
Africa; and the Asia/Pacific Region [2 volumes].)

International Forum: 1992

$60
International Division/Publications
U.S. Chamber of Commerce
1615 H Street, N.W.
Washington, D.C. 20062-2000
(202) 463-5460

International Foundation Directory

$170
International Press Publications Inc.
90 Nolan Court #23
Markham Ontario, Canada L3R 4LR
(905) 946-9588
Fax (905) 946-9590
(800) 666-0220 orders only
(Directory of international foundations, trusts and similar
non-profit institutions.)

The International Legal Framework for Services

$150
Oceana Publications, Inc.
75 Main Street
Dobbs Ferry, NY 10522
(914) 693-8100
Fax (914) 693-0402
(Designed to provide understanding of general agreements
formulated on a global, regional and bilateral basis to
govern international transactions in services.)

International Mail Manual

$17/year
U.S. Government Printing Office
Superintendent of Documents
P.O. Box 371954
Pittsburgh, PA 15250-7954
(202) 783-3238
Fax (202) 512-2233
(Includes international postal rates, prohibitions,
restrictions and information on insurance availability.)

International NewsBreak

No Charge
Candy Hansen
University Export Program
Fresno City College
1101 East University Avenue
Fresno, CA 93747
(209) 442-8295
(The college also provides an international trade library.)

International Organizations: A Dictionary and Directory

$35
St. James Press
835 Penobscot
Detroit, MI 48226
(800) 345-0392

International Shipping

$65
Global Training Center, Inc.
Kingsley Building, Suite 102
4124 Linden Avenue
Dayton, OH 45432
(800) 860-5030

The International Top Company Series

Price depends on volume
Dun's Marketing Services
3 Sylvan Way
Parsippany, NJ 07054
(800) 526-0651
(Four-volume set providing company listings for detailed
international market research and planning.)

International Trade and U.S. Antitrust Law

$115
Clark Boardman Callaghan
155 Pfingsten Road
Deerfield, IL 60015-9917
(800) 221-9428
Fax (708) 948-9340
(Provides guidance on the applicable law, procedure and
other related issues concerning the effects of U.S. antitrust
laws on international trade.)

International Trade Fairs and Conferences Directory
$74.95
International Press Publications
90 Nolan Court #23
Markham Ontario, Canada L3R 4L9
(905) 946-9588
Fax (905) 946-9590
(800) 666-0220 orders only
(Guide to more than 5,000 international shows and
conferences in more than 75 countries.)

International Trade Reporter
$2,607/year
Bureau of National Affairs, Inc.
1231 25th Street, N.W.
Washington, D.C. 20037
(800) 372-1033
Fax (202) 452-7583
(Four sections. Reports give information on trade developments, changing regulations, import and export expansion
opportunities, actions by U.S. trading partners, specific
countries and commodities.)

International Trade Resources Guide
$17.50
California Trade and Commerce Agency
California Chamber of Commerce
3255 Ramos Circle
Sacramento, CA 95827
(800) 331-8877
(A comprehensive guide to resources available to the
California business community for conducting international
trade, including domestic and international chambers of
commerce; international trade associations; education
contacts; local, state and federal government officials;
foreign trade zones; foreign government representatives;
resources publications; glossaries; world holidays; metric
conversion chart; international telephone calling codes;
and world monetary units. The *Guide* lists more than 1,600
resources in the public and private sectors. 180 pages.)

The International Who's Who
$275
International Press Publications Inc.
90 Nolan Court #23
Markham Ontario, Canada L3R 4L9
(905) 946-9588
Fax (905) 946-9590
(800) 666-0220 orders only
(More than 20,000 entries.)

The International Who's Who of Women
$375
International Press Publications Inc.
90 Nolan Court #23
Markham Ontario, Canada L3R 4L9
(905) 946-9588
Fax (905) 946-9590
(800) 666-0220 orders only
(More than 5,000 entries.)

*Investment in the North American Free Trade Area:
Opportunities and Challenges*
$20.00
Edited by Earl H. Fry and Lee H. Radebaugh
Brigham Young University
Publication Services
P.O. Box 24538
Provo, UT 84602
(801) 378-6528
(800) 528-6279
(An analysis of the opportunities and challenges facing
those involved in NAFTA. Includes general information
as well as specific implications of the agreement.)

ISO 9000
$495
Timeplace, Inc.
Department 721
460 Totten Pond Road
Waltham, MA 02154
(800) 544-4023, ext. 721
(617) 890-4636
Fax (617) 890-7274, Dept. 721
(Three-volume source book provides information on the
new European standards, and testing and certification
requirements being implemented as part of the European
Community 92 program legislation.)

*ISO 9000: Handbook of Quality Standards and
Compliance*
$3.95/monthly bulletin
Bureau of Business Practice
Prentice Hall
24 Rope Ferry Road
Waterford, CT 06386
(800) 243-0876
Fax (203) 443-1123
(287 pages.)

J & W Telefax International

$475, plus $55 shipping/handling
Classified section only: $210 plus $55 shipping/handling
Alphabetical section only: $395 plus $55 shipping/handling
International Press Publications
90 Nolan Court #23
Markham Ontario, Canada L3R 4L9
(905) 946-9588
Fax (905) 946-9590
(800) 666-0220 orders only
(International facsimile directory offering immediate access to over 2.7 million listing subscribers worldwide, over 10,000 product/service classificiations; specific country information and international codes; listings of top companies, universities, libraries, government offices and fax bureaus from over 195 countries.)

Japan Auto Abstracts

Dodwell Marketing Consultants
Kowa No. 35 Building 14-14, Akasaka 1 chome
Minato-ku, Tokyo 107 JAPAN
Telephone (03) 5570-7132
Fax 81 (3) 5570-7132
Telex J 22274 DODWELL J

Japan Business - The Portable Encyclopedia for Doing Business in Japan

$24.95
World Trade Press
1505 Fifth Avenue
San Rafael, CA 94901-1827
(800) 833-8586
(415) 454-9934
Fax (415) 453-7980
(Illustrations, color maps, index. 352 pages)

Japan Business Directory

$380
Diamond Lead Co., Ltd.
Diamond Building, 4-2
Kasumigaseki 1-Chome
Chiyoda-Ku, Tokyo
100 Japan
Telephone (81-3) 3504-6790
Telex J-26145 DLED
Fax 81 (3) 3504-6798

Japan Company Handbooks

$110
Toyo Keizai America
Circulation Services Dept.
c/o PRIMA Circulation & Mailing Services
9401 James Avenue South, Suite 160
Bloomington, MN 55431
(800) 772-3701
(Each gives current performance of Japanese companies: first section deals with Blue Chip Japanese companies and second section deals with the country's younger and growing companies.)

The Japan Trade Directory

$335 (1994-1995 edition)
A JETRO Publication
Business Network Corporation
245 Peachtree Center Avenue, Suite 2206
Atlanta, GA 30303
(404) 681-4279
Fax (404) 681-4175
(Provides information on 3,000 Japanese companies and their 24,000 products and services. Also covers Japan's 47 prefectures, highlighting each region and its products, services and attractions.)

Japanese-Affiliated Companies in USA & Canada

$190 (1993-1994)
$260 (1995-1996 revised edition, available February 1995)
$260 (1995-1996 edition available 2/95)
A JETRO Publication
Business Network Corporation
245 Peachtree Center Avenue, Suite 2206
Atlanta, GA 30303
(404) 681-4279
Fax (404) 681-4175
(Lists 9,895 Japanese-affiliated companies with operations in the United States and Canada.)

The Journal of Commerce

$310
San Francisco Office
351 California Street
San Francisco, CA 94104
(415) 982-7642
(Daily newspaper has individual sections devoted to ocean, barge, rail, air and motor transportation, banking and finance, foreign trade, energy, insurance, commodities, chemicals and plastics. Also includes daily import and export trade leads and ship sailing schedules.)

Key Officers of Foreign Service Posts
$5/year
U.S. Government Printing Office
Superintendent of Documents
P.O. Box 371954
Pittsburgh, PA 15250-7954
(202) 783-3238
Fax (202) 512-2233
(Issued three times per year. All U.S. embassies,
missions, consulates general and consulates are listed.)

Keywords in International Trade
Your Language Guide to Business Success
$36.95
ICC Publishing Corporation
156 Fifth Avenue, Suite 820
New York, NY 10010
(212) 206-1150
(Presents more than 1800 business words, terms and
abbreviations in English alphabetical order with corresponding translations in German, Spanish, French
and Italian on facing pages. Complete indexes in each
language.)

Korea Business - The Portable Encyclopedia for
Doing Business in Korea
$24.95
World Trade Press
1505 Fifth Avenue
San Rafael, CA 94901-1827
(800) 833-8586
(415) 454-9934
Fax (415) 453-7980
(Illustrations, color maps, index. 309 pages)

Kuan-Hsi: The Key to American Business Success
in Taiwan
$10
American Institute in Taiwan
Washington, Room 1700
1700 North Moore Street
Arlington, VA 22209-1966
(703) 525-8474

Latin America Country Profiles
$55
International Division/Publications
U.S. Chamber of Commerce
1615 H Street, N.W.
Washington, D.C. 20062-2000
(202) 463-5460

Law and Practice of Transnational Contracts
$85
Oceana Publications, Inc.
75 Main Street
Dobbs Ferry, NY 10522
(914) 693-8100
Fax (914) 693-0402

Law and Practice of United States Regulation of
International Trade
$175
Oceana Publications, Inc.
75 Main Street
Dobbs Ferry, NY 10522
(914) 693-8100
Fax (914) 693-0402

Law and Practice Under the GATT
$450 (3 binder set)
Oceana Publications, Inc.
75 Main Street
Dobbs Ferry, NY 10522
(914) 693-8100
Fax (914) 693-0402
(Includes the European Community and ASEAN binders.)

Legal Services Directory
$10.00
German American Chamber of Commerce
40 W. 57th Street, 31st Floor
New York, NY 10019
(212) 974-8830

Letters of Credit
$65
Global Training Center, Inc.
Kingsley Building, Suite 102
4124 Linden Avenue
Dayton, OH 45432
(800) 860-5030

Licensing Technology and Trademarks in the U.S.
$48
German American Chamber of Commerce
40 W. 57th Street, 31st Floor
New York, NY 10019
(212) 974-8830
(380 pages.)

Living in Japan
$39, plus $13 airmail
International Division/Publications
U.S. Chamber of Commerce
1615 H Street, N.W.
Washington, D.C. 20062-2000
(202) 463-5460
Fax (202) 463-5114

Looking for Employment in Foreign Countries
$16.50
World Trade Academy Press, Inc.
50 East 42nd Street, Suite 509
New York, NY 10017
(212) 697-4999
(Includes information on which countries need particular
job skills, how and where students apply for summer jobs
abroad, 46 country profiles summarizing history and present
economic conditions, and how to obtain a work permit.)

MacRae's Blue Book (United States)
$165
Manufacturers' News, Inc.
1633 Central Street
Evanston, IL 60201
(708) 864-7000
Fax (708) 332-1100
(60,000 leading U.S. manufacturers; 1,314 pages.)

Mail Order Sales to Canada
$17
National Technical Information Service
5285 Port Royal Road
Springfield, VA 22161
(703) 487-4650

Major Companies of Turkey
$135
Poyraz Yayincilik A.S.
Halaskargazi Cad. 309, Sisli 80260
Istanbul, Turkey
(90-212) 248 87 20, 248 43 15
Fax (90-212) 247 91 77
(Lists 5,700 major companies in Turkey, 460 products and
services, names of senior executives of major companies,
profiles of major companies.)

Management in Two Cultures: Bridging the Gap Between U.S. and Mexican Managers
$13.95
Intercultural Press
P.O. Box 700
Yarmouth, Maine 04096
(207) 846-5168
Fax (207) 846-5181

Managing Globally: A Complete Guide to Competing Worldwide
$65.00
Global Business and Trade
1385 Don Carlos Court
Chula Vista, CA 91910
(619) 421-5923; (800) 634-3966
(A do-it-yourself method for screening and analyzing
changing country policies, markets and products.)

Marconi's International Register
$150
Telegraphic Cable & Radio
Registrations, Inc.
19 Dogwood Lane
Larchmont, NY 10538
(914) 632-8171
Alphabetical section includes 40,000 firms in 100 countries
doing business internationally. Each is cross-referenced
throughout 1,500 trade classifications, each product or
service is listed by country under each heading. 100 legal
specialties also by country for each specialty. Published
annually in December.)

Marketing in the U.S.
$45
German American Chamber of Commerce
40 W. 57th Street, 31st Floor
New York, NY 10019
(212) 974-8830
(153 pages.)

Mastering the Harmonized System
$89.95
International Trade Institute
5055 North Main Street
Dayton, OH 45415
(800) 543-2453
Fax (513) 276-5920
(Videotape and accompanying workbook provide principles
of new Harmonized System, affecting importing and
exporting in the United States.)

Medical Device Register
$295
Medical Economics Data
5 Paragon Drive
Montvale, NY 07645
(201) 358-7500
Fax (201) 573-4956
(Directory of 10,650 U.S. manufacturers with key
executives and 30,000 product listings.)

Mexican Business Review Magazine
$36/year
Mexico Information Services, Inc.
P.O. Box 11770
Fort Worth, TX 76110-0770
(817) 924-0746; (800) 446-0746
Fax (817) 924-9687
(A monthly publication covering business information on
Mexico.)

**Mexico Business - The Portable Encyclopedia for
   Doing Business in Mexico**
$24.95
World Trade Press
1505 Fifth Avenue
San Rafael, CA 94901-1827
(800) 833-8586
(415) 454-9934
Fax (415) 453-7980
(Illustrations, color maps, index. 352 pages)

Mexico Documentation and Procedures
$65
Global Training Center, Inc.
Kingsley Building, Suite 102
4124 Linden Avenue
Dayton, OH 45432
(800) 860-5030

Mexico — The New "Land of Opportunity"
$25.00 (2nd edition)
Mexico Information Services
P.O. Box 11770
Fort Worth, TX 76110
(817) 924-0746; (800) 446-0746
Fax (817) 924-9687
(A guide to doing business in Mexico, 330 pages.)

Mexico's Maquiladora Guidebook
87.50
Merchants and Manufacturers Association
P.O. Box 15013
Los Angeles, CA 90015
(213) 748-0421, Extension 336
Fax (213) 742-0301

MEXIS Credit Reports on Mexican Companies
$150-$210 each, depending on location in Mexico
Mexico Information Services
P.O. Box 11770
Fort Worth, TX 76110-0770
(817) 924-0746; (800) 446-0746
Fax (817) 924-9687
(Custom generated credit reports.)

MEXIS Trade Leads
$2/each (minimum $50)
Mexico Information Services
P.O. Box 11770
Fort Worth, TX 76110-0770
(817) 924-0746; (800) 446-0746
Fax (817) 924-9687
(Over 20,000 Mexican companies cataloged based on
products and services sold and bought. Computerized
matching service.)

The Middle East and North Africa
$325
International Press Publications Inc.
90 Nolan Court #23
Markham Ontario, Canada L3R 4L9
(905) 946-9588
Fax (905) 946-9590
(800) 666-0220 orders only

Mineral Industries of Africa
$22
S/N 024-004-02239-6
U.S. Government Printing Office
Superintendent of Documents
P.O. Box 371954
Pittsburgh, PA 15250-7954
(202) 783-3238
Fax (202) 512-2250
(Contains 1991/1992 mineral data for 54 Africal countries.)

Mineral Industries of the Middle East
$10
S/N 024-004-02240-0
U.S. Government Printing Office
Superintendent of Documents
P.O. Box 371954
Pittsburgh, PA 15250-7954
(202) 783-3238
Fax (202) 512-2250
(Contains 1991/1992 mineral data for 15 Middle Eastern
countries.)

Minerals in the World Economy
$4.75
S/N 024-004-02247-7
U.S. Government Printing Office
Superintendent of Documents
P.O. Box 371954
Pittsburgh, PA 15250-7954
(202) 783-3238
Fax (202) 512-2250
(Provides latest available mineral data on more than 150
foreign countries.)

NAFTA Diskettes
$9.95, tax and shipping included
Mexico Information Services
P.O. Box 11770
Fort Worth, TX 76110-0770
(817) 924-0746
(800) 446-0746
Fax (817) 924-9687
(The complete North American Free Trade Agreement and
side agreements on 3.5" or 5.25" diskette.)

NAFTA and the Environment
$14.95 plus $2 shipping and handling
Pacific Research Institute
755 Sansome Street, Suite 450
San Francisco, CA 94111
(415) 989-0833
Fax (415) 989-2411
(120 pages. Collection of papers explores the environmental
issues of liberalized trade. Contrary to the scenarios of
environmentalists, contributors argue that liberalized trade
can lead to enhanced enviromental protection through
increased prosperity and implementation of market-based
environmental policies.)

NAFTA: Expanding U.S. Exports, Jobs and Growth
$1.25
S/N 041-001-00413-1
U.S. Government Printing Office
Superintendent of Documents
P.O. Box 371954
Pittsburgh, PA 15250-7954
(202) 783-3238
Fax (202) 512-2250
(Clinton administration statement on NAFTA. 12 pages.)

NAFTA Impact
$65.95
U.S. Chamber of Commerce
International Division/Publications
1615 H Street, NW
Washington, DC 20062
(202) 463-5460
(Information package customized specially to your
company.)

NAFTA Kit
$34.50
International Business Strategies, Inc.
10860 Lake Thames Drive
Cincinnati, OH 45242
(513) 489-5469; (800) 245-4300
Fax (513) 489-5469; (800) 622-3036
(Reference material.)

*NAFTA, The North American Free Trade
    Agreement: Guide to Customs Procedures*
$3.75
S/N 048-002-00119-2
U.S. Government Printing Office
Superintendent of Documents
P.O. Box 371954
Pittsburgh, PA 15250-7954
(202) 783-3238
Fax (202) 512-2250
(Explains procedural obligations relating to customs
administration. 55 pages.)

The NAFTA: Report on Environmental Issues
$11
S/N 041-001-00414-9
U.S. Government Printing Office
Superintendent of Documents
P.O. Box 371954
Pittsburgh, PA 15250-7954
(202) 783-3238
Fax (202) 512-2250
(Focuses on environmental issues between the U.S. and Mexico. 167 pages.)

National Negotiating Styles
$6
Foreign Service Institute/U.S. Department of State
Government Printing Office Bookstore
1510 H Street, N.W.
Washington, D.C. 20005
(202) 653-5075

The National Trade Data Bank
$360/year
$35/disc
U.S. Department of Commerce
Economics and Statistics Administration
Stat-USA
HCHB Room 4885
Washington, D.C. 20230
(202) 482-1986
(Electronic source for international trade and export information containing more than 160,000 documents including basic export information. Released monthly on CD-ROM and Internet.)

National Trade Estimate Report on Foreign Trade Barriers
Free of charge
U.S. Trade Representative
600 17th Street, N.W.
Washington, D.C. 20506
(202) 395-3230
(Annual publication.)

New American Business System
$49.95
California Chamber of Commerce
P.O. Box 1736
Sacramento, CA 95812-1736
(916) 856-5200
(320-page loose-leaf kit contains more than 80 forms, worksheets and checklists to help small business owners plan and stay organized.)

The New Eurasia: A Guide to the Republics of the Former Soviet Union
$17.95
Russian Information Services
89 Main Street, Suite 2
Montpelier, VT 95602
(802) 223-4955
Fax (802) 223-6105
(800) 639-4301
(Reference book organized by region and country, listing basic data for each nation. Essays examine culture, history, diplomacy, economics and defense. 213 pages.)

The New ICC World Directory of Chambers of Commerce
$420
Gale Research Inc.
P.O. Box 33477
Detroit, MI 48232-5477
(800) 877-GALE
(313) 961-2242
Fax (313) 961-6083
(Published in cooperation with the International Chamber of Commerce in Paris, the directory covers more than 10,000 international business and trade contacts.)

The New Moscow: City Map and Guide
$6.95
Russian Information Services
City Center
89 Main Street, Suite 2
Montpelier, VT 05602
(802) 223-4955
(800) 639-4301
Fax (802) 223-6105

The New St. Petersburg: City Map and Guide
$6.95
Russian Information Services
City Center
89 Main Street, Suite 2
Montpelier, VT 05602
(802) 223-4955
(800) 639-4301
Fax (802) 223-6105

New Zealand Trade Directory
$120
Current Pacific Limited
P.O. Box 36-536
Northcote, Auckland
New Zealand
(64) 09-480-1388
Fax (64) 09-480-1388
(Contains more than 5,000 major and active firms in New Zealand, including importers, distributors, manufacturers, exporters, food processors, financial institutions, tourism-related industries, professional consulting firms and trade-related services. Also includes government departments, trade promotion organizations and associations, and education institutions.)

Nigeria — Who's Who in Business
$30
Mednet Limited
70A Falolu Road
P.O. Box 3418
Surulere
Lagos, Nigeria
(Describes Nigeria business and economy, and lists business leaders and chambers of commerce. Gives information about export/import opportunities, banks, financial operations, government and private companies to help business operations internationally.)

North American Food Processing Directory
$49.95; CD-ROM $199
International Press Publications Inc.
90 Nolan Court #23
Markham, Ontario, L3R 4L9
Canada
(905) 946-9588
Fax (905) 946-9590
(Detailed coverage on Canada, U.S. and Mexico manufacturers, suppliers, retail, wholesale, products, personnel, associations, buyer's guide and comprehensive directory.)

North American Free Trade Agreement
$175
Oceana Publications, Inc.
75 Main Street
Dobbs Ferry, NY 10522
(914) 693-8100
Fax (914) 693-0402
(Covers original bi-lateral trade agreements between U.S., Canada and Mexico through North American Free Trade Agreement.)

North American Free Trade Agreement
$40
S/N 041-001-00407-6
U.S. Government Printing Office
Superintendent of Documents
P.O. Box 371954
Pittsburgh, PA 15250-7954
(202) 783-3238
Fax (202) 512-2250
(Two-volume set presents the agreement objectives and guidelines to interpret the provisions, with applicable rules of international law. 1090 pages.)

North American Free Trade Agreement: Implications
  for California
$4
Governor's Office of Planning and Research
Office of the Governor
State Capitol
Sacramento, CA 95814

North American Free Trade Agreement: Implications
  for U.S. Business
$15.95
International Division/Publications
U.S. Chamber of Commerce
1615 H Street, N.W.
Washington, D.C. 20062-2000
(202) 463-5460

North American Free Trade Agreement: Opportunities for U.S. Industries, NAFTA Industry Sector
  Reports
$24
S/N 003-009-00634-1
U.S. Government Printing Office
Superintendent of Documents
P.O. Box 371954
Pittsburgh, PA 15250-7954
(202) 783-3238
Fax (202) 512-2250
(Statistical data on exports of 36 manufacturing sectors to Mexico, Canada and the world. 396 pages.)

North American Free Trade Agreement Rules of
  Origin and Procedures
$89
Global Training Center, Inc.
Kingsley Building, Suite 102
4124 Linden Avenue
Dayton, OH 45432
(800) 860-5030

North American Free Trade Guide
$19.50
California Trade and Commerce Agency
California Chamber of Commerce
3255 Ramos Circle
Sacramento, CA 95827
(800) 331-8877
(A handbook to help businesses take advantage of the
opportunities to be created by the North American Free
Trade Agreement (NAFTA), linking the United States with
Canada and Mexico, its first and third largest trading
partners. NAFTA will create the largest and richest market
in the world, with 360 million consumers and $6 trillion in
annual output. Focuses on what businesses need to know to
gain access to the emerging Mexican market, plus good
prospects for expansion in Canada. 135 pages.)

Northern California Business Directory
$595
American Business Directories
5711 S. 86th Circle
Omaha, NE 68127
(402) 593-4600
Fax (402) 331-5481
(490,000 businesses listed.)

**Northern California Business Directory and
     Buyers Guide**
$165
Database Publishing Company
P.O. Box 70024
Anaheim, CA 92825-0024
(714) 778-6400
Fax (714) 778-6811
(Provides facts on 29,000 manufacturers, wholesalers,
distributors, finance and service companies in the 45
counties north of San Luis Obispo.)

**Northern California Regional Industrial Buying
     Guide**
$53
Thomas Regional Directory Company, Inc.
Five Penn Plaza
New York, NY 10001
(212) 629-2100
(Industrial products and services, manufacturers, manufac-
turer representatives, distributors and industrial service
companies.)

Official Export Guide
$389
North American Publishing Company
401 North Broad Street
Philadelphia, PA 19108-9988
(800) 777-8074
(Covers entire export process.)

Official Journal of the European Communities
UNIPUB (exclusive U.S. distributor of publications
from the European Communities.)
4611-F Assembly Drive
Lanham, MD 20706-4391
(301) 459-7666
Fax (301) 459-0056
(Gives information and notices of the European
Parliament and Commission.)

**The Omnibus Trade & Competitiveness Act of 1988:
     A Straightforward Guide to Its Impact on U.S. and
     Foreign Business**
$30
International Division/Publications
U.S. Chamber of Commerce
1615 H Street, N.W.
Washington, D.C. 20062-2000
(202) 463-5460

Ontario Manufacturers (Canada)
$215.95
Manufacturers' News, Inc.
1633 Central Street
Evanston, IL 60201
(708) 864-7000
Fax (708) 332-1100
(Information regarding 21,872 manufacturing firms;
1,556 pages.)

Opinions of the ICC Banking Commission
$29.95
ICC Publishing Corporation
156 Fifth Avenue, Suite 820
New York, NY 10010
(212) 206-1150

The Other Europe: A Complete Guide to Business Opportunities in Eastern Europe
$24.95
Russian Information Services
89 Main Street, Suite 2
Montpelier, VT 95602
(802) 223-4955
Fax (802) 223-6105
(800) 639-4301
("How-to" business guide for Eastern Europe and former USSR. 360 pages.)

Overseas Business Report: Marketing in Canada
$19
National Technical Information Service
5285 Port Royal Road
Springfield, VA 22161
(703) 487-4650

Overseas Export Promotion Calendar
$35
Office of Export Development
International Trade Administration
U.S. Department of Commerce
Washington, D.C. 20230
(Designed to help U.S. business firms take advantage of sales opportunities in overseas markets. Booklet contains an 18-month schedule of U.S. Trade Center exhibitions, international trade fairs in which U.S. participation is planned and other overseas promotional activities planned and organized by the U.S. Department of Commerce. Revised quarterly.)

Pacific Bell Northern California Business-to-Business Directory
$26.20
Pacific Bell
(800) 848-8000

Pacific Bell Los Angeles Business-to-Business Directory
$26.20
Pacific Bell
(800) 848-8000

Pacific Bell Orange County - San Diego Business-to-Business Directory
$26.20
Pacific Bell
(800) 848-8000

Pacific Shipper
Pacific Shipper Publishers
562 Mission Street, Suite 601
San Francisco, CA 94105-2919
(800) 221-8633; (415) 546-3946
(Weekly sailing schedules, 2nd editorial updates for international shipping.)

Polish Industrial Directory
$195
Manufacturers' News, Inc.
1633 Central Street
Evanston, IL 60201
(708) 864-7000
Fax (708) 332-1100
(10,000 Polish companies; 863 pages.)

Ports of the World
No Charge
Center for International Trade and Development
(800) 521-4824
(303) 444-4300
(Booklet describes guidelines on export packaging.)

Principal International Businesses
$585
Dun's Marketing Services
3 Sylvania Way
Parsippany, NJ 07054-3896
(800) 526-0651
(Country-by-country directory provides information on top 56,000 international companies located throughout 133 countries.)

Privatization: The U.K. Experience and International Trends
$35
St. James Press
835 Penobscot
Detroit, MI 48226
(800) 345-0392
Fax (312) 787-6448

Profiles of Worldwide Government Leaders
$297
Worldwide Government Directories, Inc.
7979 Old Georgetown Road, Suite 900
Bethesda, MD 20814
(301) 718-8770
Fax (301) 718-8494
(800) 332-3535
(Biographical listings of heads of state and minister
level officials in every country in the world.)

**Profitable Exporting: A Complete Guide to
    Marketing Your Products Abroad**
$35
John Wiley and Sons, Inc.
605 Third Avenue
New York, NY 10158
(800) 225-5945

**Profiting from the Asia-Pacific Dynamo:
    A Corporate Assessment**
$50
International Division/Publications
U.S. Chamber of Commerce
1615 H Street, N.W.
Washington, D.C. 20062-2000
(202) 463-5460

Publishers' International Directory
$215
Gale Research Co.
P.O. Box 33477
Detroit, MI 48232-5477
(800) 877-GALE
(313) 961-2242
Fax (313) 961-6083

Puerto Rico Official Industrial Directory
$120
Manufacturers' News, Inc.
1633 Central Street
Evanston, IL 60201
(708) 864-7000
Fax (708) 332-1100
(8,000 companies; 766 pages.)

Quebec Manufacturers (Canada)
$205.95
Manufacturers' News, Inc.
1633 Central Street
Evanston, IL 60201
(708) 864-7000
Fax (708) 332-1100
(16,600 manufacturers; 1,384 pages.)

Questions and Answers for Export/Import
$44.50
International Trade Institute
5055 North Main Street
Dayton, OH 45415
(800) 543-2453
Fax (513) 276-5920
(Covers documentation, letters of credit, Canada,
shipping and insurance.)

**R&D Activities of Major Japanese Chemical
    Companies**
$550
Dodwell Marketing Consultants
Kowa No. 35 Building 14-14, Akasaka 1 chome
Minato-ku, Tokyo 107 JAPAN
Telephone (03) 3589-0207
Fax (03) 5570-7132
Telex J 22274 DODWELL J

Report on Foreign Trade Barriers
$22.50
Federal Reprints
P.O. Box 70268
Washington, D.C. 20024
(202) 544-6604
Fax (202) 543-1527
(From the office of the U.S. Trade Representative, country
by country descriptions of import policies, export subsidies,
barriers to the protection of intellectual property, service
barriers, investment barriers, government procurement, and
standards for testing, labeling and certification.)

**Resource Guide to Doing Business in Central and
    Eastern Europe**
$1
S/N 044-000-02311-3
U.S. Government Printing Office
Superintendent of Documents
P.O. Box 371954
Pittsburgh, PA 15250-7954
(202) 783-3238
Fax (202) 512-2250

Retail Distribution in Japan
$600
Dodwell Marketing Consultants
Kowa No. 35 Building 14-14, Akasaka 1 chome
Minato-ku, Tokyo 107 JAPAN
Telephone (03) 3589-0207
Fax (03) 5570-7132
Telex J 22274 DODWELL J

Rich's Business Guide to Southern California
$258/two-volume set
Business Guides, Inc.
2973 Harbour Boulevard, Suite 154
Costa Mesa, CA 92626
(800) 333-0509
(Product and company information on nearly 6,000 Southern California companies involved in high-tech industry.)

Rich's High Tech Business Directories
$269
Business Guides, Inc.
2973 Harbour Boulevard, Suite 154
Costa Mesa, CA 92626
(800) 333-0509
(Contains information on 6,000 Silicon Valley and Northern California companies involved in the high-tech industry.)

**The Rocky Mountain and Texas High
  Technology Directories**
$149/$139
Leading Edge Communications, Inc.
1121 Old Siskiyou Highway
Ashland, OR 97520
(503) 482-4990

Russia Survival Guide: Business and Travel
$18.50
Russian Information Services
City Center
89 Main Street, Suite 2
Montpelier, VT 05602
(802) 223-4955
Fax (802) 223-6105
(800) 634-4301
(Guide to doing business and traveling in the new Russia. 214 pages.)

Russian Business Legal Materials
$225/Compendium $68
Russian Information Services
89 Main Street, Suite 2
Montpelier, VT 95602
(802) 223-4955
Fax (802) 223-6105
(800) 639-4301
(Monthly service indexes all Russian laws relating to trade and investment passed or published in preceding month. Legal acts are indexed uner 15 subject headings and numbered chronologically.)

The Russian Privatization Manual
$495
Euromoney Books
Plymbridge Ditributors Ltd.
Estover, Plymouth, Devon PL6 7PZ
United Kingdom
Telephone: +44 (0) 752 695745
Fax: +44 (0) 752 695668
(Produced by the European Bank for Reconstruction and Development and Russian privatisation agency. Financed by the European Community, which explains how the privatization process works in practice.)

A Safe Trip Abroad
$1
S/N 044-000-02392-0
U.S. Government Printing Office
Superintendent of Documents
P.O. Box 371954
Pittsburgh, PA 15250-7954
(202) 783-3238
Fax (202) 512-2250
(General travel information.)

San Francisco Business Resource Guide
$15 ($19.04 delievered)
San Francisco Chamber of Commerce
465 California Street
San Francisco, CA 94104
(415) 392-4511

The Scandinavian Book
$4.50
Royal Norwegian Consulate General
Norway Place
20 California Street, 6th Floor
San Francisco, CA 94111-4803
(415) 986-0766
Fax (415) 986-6025

Selling to the Allies: A Guide for U.S. Firms
$7.50
U.S. Government Printing Office
Superintendent of Documents
P.O. Box 371954
Pittsburgh, PA 15250-7954
(or nearest government bookstore)
Fax orders (202) 512-2250
(134 pages.)

Setting EC Priorities
no price listed yet
Pergamon Press, Inc.
395 Sawmill River Road
Fairview Park
Elmsford, NY 10523
(914) 592-7700
(Counterpart to The Annual Review of European Community
Affairs, the volume assesses past year's policies and makes
recommendations for the future.)

Setting Up an Office in Japan
$28, plus $12 airmail
International Division/Publications
U.S. Chamber of Commerce
1615 H Street, NW
Washington, D.C. 20062-2000
(202) 463-5460
Fax (202) 463-3114

*Singapore Business - The Portable Encyclopedia for
Doing Business in Singapore*
$24.95
World Trade Press
1505 Fifth Avenue
San Rafael, CA 94901-1827
(800) 833-8586
(415) 454-9934
Fax (415) 453-7980
(Illustrations, color maps, index. 352 pages)

Solunet's The Complete Twin Plan Guide
$595
Solunet
The Solutions Network
4150 Pinnacle Street #118
El Paso, TX 79902
(915) 532-1166
Fax (915) 533-3413
(Resource library on the $12 billion maquiladora industry
in Mexico describes the Mexican operation as well as the
American or foreign parent company.)

South America, Central America and the Caribbean
$295
International Press Publications Inc.
90 Nolan Court, #23
Markham, Ontario Canada L3R 4L9
(905) 946-9588
Fax (905) 946-9590
(800) 666-0220 (orders only)
(Provides facts and figures on the countries of Latin
America and the Caribbean.)

Southern California Business Directory
$695
American Business Directories
5711 S. 86th Circle
Omaha, NE 68127
(402) 593-4600
Fax (402) 331-5481
(717,000 businesses listed.)

*Southern California Business Directory and Buyers
Guide*
$165
Database Publishing Company
P.O. Box 70024
Anaheim, CA 92825-0024
(714) 778-6400
Fax (714) 778-6811
(Gives profiles on 29,000 manufacturers, wholesalers and
service businesses in the 13 counties from San Luis Obispo
south to San Diego.)

St. James World Futures and Options Directory
$95
St. James Press
835 Penobscot
Detroit, MI 48226
(800) 345-0392

Standard Trade Index of Japan
$215 (surface mail)
The Japan Chamber of Commerce and Industry
World Trade Center Building, Suite 505
4-1, Hamamatsu-cho 2-chome, Minato-ku
Tokyo 105, Japan
81 (3) 435-4785
Fax 81 (3) 3578-6622

Standby Letters of Credit
$159.95
ICC Publishing Corporation
156 Fifth Avenue, Suite 820
New York, NY 10010
(212) 206-1150
(Presents current uses of standby letters of credit and international guarantees, along with procedures for issuing and reviewing standbys, and for proceeding with presentment when collection is necessary.)

State and Metropolitan Area Data Book 1991
$35
Federal Reprints
P.O. Box 70268
Washington, D.C. 20024
(202) 544-6604

State Export Report
Price depends on data option
Trade Inflo
7311 Grove Road, Suite X
Frederick, MD 21701
(800) 831-4105
(301) 831-4150
Fax (301) 831-4172
(Gives quantitative analysis of state exports by 2-digit SIC code.)

Statistical Abstract of the U.S.
$32.50
Federal Reprints
P.O. Box 70268
Washington, D.C. 20024
(202) 543-1527
Fax (202) 543-1527
(Data and information on the U.S. and its people, institutions, commerce and economy. Covers income, labor, commerce, imports and exports, foreign aid and investments, agriculture and science. Publication is more than 975 pages.)

Statistical Classification of Domestic and Foreign Commodities Exported from the U.S.
$77
U.S. Government Printing Office
Superintendent of Documents
P.O. Box 371954
Pittsburgh, PA 15250-7954
(202) 783-3238
Fax (202) 512-2233
(Contains approximately 40,000 commodity classifications.)

The Structure of the Japanese Auto Parts Industry
$890
Dodwell Marketing Consultants
Kowa No. 35 Building 14-14, Akasaka 1 chome
Minato-ku, Tokyo 107 JAPAN
Telephone 81 (3) 3589-0207
Fax 81 (3) 5570-7132
Telex J 22274 DODWELL J

The Structure of the Japanese Electronics Industry
$700
Dodwell Marketing Consultants
Kowa No. 35 Building 14-14, Akasaka 1 chome
Minato-ku, Tokyo 107 JAPAN
Telephone 81 (3) 3589-0207
Fax 81 (3) 5570-7132
Telex J 22274 DODWELL J

Summary of Provisions of the U.S.-Canada Free Trade Agreement
$17
National Technical Information Service
5285 Port Royal Road
Springfield, VA 22161
(703) 487-4650

Taiwan Business - The Portable Encyclopedia for Doing Business in Taiwan
$24.95
World Trade Press
1505 Fifth Avenue
San Rafael, CA 94901-1827
(800) 833-8586
(415) 454-9934
Fax (415) 453-7980
(Illustrations, color maps, index. 352 pages)

Temporary Importation Provisions for Canada
$17
National Technical Information Service
5285 Port Royal Road
Springfield, VA 22161
(703) 487-4650

Third World Handbook
$45
St. James Press
835 Penobscot
Detroit, MI 48226
(800) 345-0392
(Region-by-region analysis of Third World gives background information as well as updated reference.)

Thomas Register
$210
Thomas Publishing Company
One Penn Plaza
New York, NY 10001
(212) 695-0500
Fax (212) 290-7362
(Directory of American manufacturers by products
and services, company profiles and catalog files.)

The Times Roster of California's Top Companies
$3 annual
Attn: Back Copies
Los Angeles Times
Times Mirror Square
Los Angeles, CA 90058
(213) 626-2323
(California headquartered publicly held companies, ranked
by sales/revenues. Addresses, key executives, description
of products or services, yearly estimates, sales volumes,
income, assets and numbers of employees.)

Tips for Travelers to the Caribbean
$1
S/N 044-000-02390-3
U.S. Government Printing Office
Superintendent of Documents
P.O. Box 371954
Pittsburgh, PA 15250-7954
(202) 783-3238
Fax (202) 512-2250

Tips for Travelers to Mexico
$1
S/N 044-000-02269-9
U.S. Government Printing Office
Superintendent of Documents
P.O. Box 371954
Pittsburgh, PA 15250-7954
(202) 783-3238
Fax (202) 512-2250

Tools of the Trade
A Directory of International Trade Organizations
in Washington State
No Charge
Washington Council on International Trade
2615 Fourth Avenue, Suite 350
Seattle, Washington 98121
(206) 443-3826

Toward a National Export Strategy
$8
S/N 003-009-00632-5
U.S. Government Printing Office
Superintendent of Documents
P.O. Box 371954
Pittsburgh, PA 15250-7954
(202) 783-3238
Fax (202) 512-2250
(Reviews corporative government export promotion policies
and current programs, discusses creative approaches and
relationships, formulates new ideas and recommendations.
124 pages.)

Toxic Substance Control Act: A Guide for Chemical
Importers/Exporters (An Overview)
$2.25
U.S. Government Printing Office
Superintendent of Documents
P.O. Box 371954
Pittsburgh, PA 15250-7954
(or nearest government bookstore)
Fax (202) 512-2250

Trade and Investment in Japan:
The Current Environment
$24, plus $11 airmail
International Division/Publications
U.S. Chamber of Commerce
1615 H Street, N.W.
Washington, D.C. 20062-2000
(202) 463-5460

Trade and Investment Opportunities in the
Persian Gulf
$45
International Division/Publications
U.S. Chamber of Commerce
1615 H Street, N.W.
Washington, D.C. 20062-2000
(202) 463-5460

Trade and Professional Associations in California:
A Directory
$50
CA Institute of Public Affairs
P.O. Box 189040
Sacramento, CA 95818
(916) 442-2472
(Name, address, phone number of over 2,100 statewide
and regional associations)

Trade Inquiry Service
$75 (in advance)
American Chamber of Commerce in Australia
Suite 4, Gloucester Walk
88 Cumberland Street
Sydney, NSW Australia 2000
(612) 241-1907
Fax (612) 251-5220

Trade Policy Review Series
Prices depend on edition/volume
GATT-Publication Services
centre William Rappard - Rue de Luasanne 154 - CH 1211
Geneva 21 - Switzerland
Telephone: 41 (22) 52 08/739 53 08
Telefax: 41 (22) 739 54 58
Telex: 412 324 GATT CH
(Examines the full range of trade policies and practices
of individual countries at regular intervals and indicates
significant developments which have have an impact on
the global trading system.)

**Trade Unions of the World Employers Organizations
of the World**
$130
St. James Press
835 Penobscot
Detroit, MI 48226
(800) 345-0392

Transnational Contracts
$600 (6 binder set)
Oceana Publications, Inc.
75 Main Street
Dobbs Ferry, NY 10522
(914) 693-8100
Fax (914) 693-0402

Transportation Services Directory
Pacific Shipper Publishers
562 Mission Street, Suite 601
San Francisco, CA 94105-2919
(415) 546-3946
(800) 221-8633
(Reference guide to the Pacific Coast transportation
industry. Also, *Pacific Shipper,* weekly sailing schedules
and editorial updates for international shipping.)

The Traveler's Guide to Asian Customs and Manners
Kevin Chambers
Simon and Schuster
1230 Avenue of the Americas
Department MBA
New York, NY 10020

**The Traveler's Guide to European Customs
and Manners**
Nancy L. Braganti and Elizabeth Devine
Simon and Schuster
1230 Avenue of the Americas
Department MBA
New York, NY 10020

The Traveler's Guide to Latin America
$12.95
St. Martin's Press
175 5th Avenue
New York, NY 10010
(212) 674-5151

A Twin Plan/Maquiladora Directory
$125.00
Escalante & Associates International, Inc.
3444 Camino del Rio North, Suite 204
San Diego, CA 92108
(619) 283-7191
Fax (619) 283-7242
(Resource directory on the twin plant/maquiladora industry
in the state of Baja California, Mexico as well as the
American and foreign parent company.)

UN Statistical Yearbook
$110
UN Publications
Two UN Plaza DC2-853
New York, NY 10017
(212) 963-8302
(800) 253-9646
(Provides economic and social data for 220 countries
and territories.)

U.S.-Australia Trade Directory
$285, plus $25 airmail
American Chamber of Commerce in Australia
Suite 4, Gloucester Walk
88 Cumberland Street
Sydney, NSW
Australia 2000
Telephone +61 2 241-1907
Fax +61 2 251-5220
(400 pages. Over 3,000 listings. All chamber members, product references, U.S. affiliates in Australia, Australia affiliates in the U.S.)

U.S.-Canada Free Trade Agreement: Guide to Exporting Procedures
$19
National Technical Information Service
5285 Port Royal Road
Springfield, VA 22161
(703) 487-4650
(Manual for U.S. exporters seeking to benefit from tariff removal. Contains entire legal text of the rules of origin and samples of the certificate of origin.)

U.S.-Canada Free Trade Agreement Publications
U.S. Department of Commerce
National Technical Information Service
5285 Port Royal Road
Springfield, VA 22161
(703) 487-4650
(A series of publications are available.)

U.S.-China Trade: Problems and Prospects
$49.95
Praeger Publishers
88 Post Road West
P.O. Box 5007
Westport, CT 06881
(Step-by-step guide on how to enter and succeed in export marketplace.)

U.S. Department of State Treaties in Force
$29.50
Federal Reprints
P.O. Box 70268
Washington, D.C. 20024
(202) 544-6604

The U.S.-Eastern European Trade Sourcebook
$45
St. James Press
835 Penobscot
Detroit, MI 48226
(800) 345-0392
(Provides country-by-country listings for Bulgaria, Czechoslovakia, Hungary, Poland, Romania and Yugoslavia.)

U.S. Export Competitiveness
$5.50
S/N 003-009-00627-9
U.S. Government Printing Office
Superintendent of Documents
P.O. Box 371954
Pittsburgh, PA 15250-7954
(202) 783-3238
Fax (202) 512-2250
(Assesses U.S. competitiveness in expanding global markets. 80 pages.)

U.S. Export Directory
$179
Reed Information Services
1350 E. Touhy Avenue
P.O. Box 5080
Des Plaines, IL
(800) 347-8743
Fax (708) 390-2850

U.S. Firms in Germany
$100.00
German American Chamber of Commerce
40 W. 57th Street, 31st Floor
New York, NY 10019
(212) 974-8830

U.S. Firms Operating in India
$10
International Division/Publications
U.S. Chamber of Commerce
1615 H Street, N.W.
Washington, D.C. 20062-2000
(202) 463-5460

U.S. German Economic Yearbook
$25
German American Chamber of Commerce
40 W. 57th Street, 31st Floor
New York, NY 10019
(212) 974-8830

U.S. Government Books for Business Professionals Catalog

Free of charge
Free Business Books Catalog
U.S. Government Printing Office
Stop SM
Washington D.C. 20401
(Information regarding books on general business, export/import, patents and trademarks, law, accounting and taxes, labor relations, OSHA and air quality.)

U.S. Imports for Consumption: Harmonized TSUSA Commodity by Country of Origin

$40
S/N 003-024-08692-1
U.S. Government Printing Office
Superintendent of Documents
P.O. Box 371954
Pittsburgh, PA 15250-7954
(202) 783-3238
Fax (202) 512-2250
(U.S. import/export statistics on government and nongovernment shipments of merchandise among the U.S. and foreign countries.)

U.S. Industrial Outlook

$37 (annual subscription)
Superintendent of Documents
U.S. Government Printing Office
Washington, D.C. 20402
(202) 783-3238
(Department of Commerce outlook for more than 350 industries. Historical data, current trends, future prospects, emerging industries and statistical profiles by industry. Trends in world trade, outlook for U.S. manufacturers.)

The U.S.-Mexico Trade Pages

Kara Kent
The Global Source
1511 K Street, NW, Suite 927
Washington, D.C. 20005
(202) 429-5582
Fax (202) 638-1284
(Directory of contacts for doing business in Mexico.)

U.S.-Philippine Business News

Free of charge
International Division/Publications
U.S. Chamber of Commerce
1615 H Street, N.W.
Washington, D.C. 20062-2000
(202) 463-5460

The U.S.A. and Canada

$375
International Press Publications Inc.
90 Nolan Court #23
Markham Ontario, Canada L3R 4L9
(905) 946-9588
Fax (905) 946-9590
(800) 666-0220 orders only

(Reference guide to North American countries and their states and territories.)

Understanding Cultural Differences: Germans, French and Americans

$15.95
Intercultural Press
P.O. Box 700
Yarmouth, Maine 04096
(207) 846-5168
Fax (207) 846-5181

United Nations Publications Catalog

2 UN Plaza, Room DC2-853, Dept. 007C
New York, NY 10017
(212) 963-8302; (800) 253-9646
Fax (212) 963-3489
(A 200-page catalog of all UN publications.)

United States-Canada Free Trade Agreement

Guide to Exporting Procedures
$19
U.S. Department of Commerce
International Trade Administration
14th Street and Constitution Avenue, N.W.
Washington, D.C. 20230
(202) 377-5487

United States Export Controls

$195
John Liebman and Wm. A. Ricot
Prentice Hall Law & Business
910 Sylvan Avenue
Englewood Cliffs, NJ 07632
(800) 223-0231
(Includes U.S. export controls affecting activities outside the territorial limits of the United States.)

United States Importers & Exporters Directories
$599
The Journal of Commerce
445 Marshall Street
Phillipsburg, NJ 08865
(908) 859-1300
(Directories highlight more than 55,000 active U.S. world traders.)

United States International Trade Reports
$525
Oceana Publications, Inc.
75 Main Street
Dobbs Ferry, NY 10522
(914) 693-8100
Fax (914) 693-0402
(Makes available decisions of the Court of International Trade, beginning with 1985, Rules of the Court, and decisions of the Court of Appeals for the Federal Circuit. Seven binder set.)

The Vietnam Business Handbook
$100 includes postage and handling
The Agio Press, Inc.
3384 Peachtree Road, N.W., Suite 302
Atlanta, GA 30326
(404) 365-0892
(800) 925-8217
Fax (404) 261-3954
(Offers 400 pages of business information about Vietnam.)

Vietnam Opportunities: the Official Vietnamese Business Guide
$120
Gracefield Investments Ltd
Box 1888
Edmonton, Alberta, Canada T5J 2P3
(800) 395-7835
Fax (403) 482-2943
(Comprehensive source of Vietnam government-approved contacts in Vietnam. Over 4,000 companies, listing company name, address, telephone number, nature and scope of business.)

Visa and Work Permits for the U.S.
$30
German American Chamber of Commerce
40 W. 57th Street, 31st Floor
New York, NY 10019
(212) 974-8830
(238 pages.)

Welcome to the European Union
$10.00
French-American Chamber of Commerce
425 Bush Street, Suite 401
San Francisco, CA 94108
(415) 398-2449
(A history of the development of the European Union, a profile of the E.U. and information related to community institutions, European law and the European economic arena.)

Western Manufacturers (Canada)
$205.95
Manufacturers' News, Inc.
1633 Central Street
Evanston, IL 60201
(708) 864-7000
Fax (708) 332-1100
(10,000 manufacturing firms, 830 pages.)

Western Europe
$350
International Press Publications Inc.
90 Nolan Court #23
Markham Ontario, Canada L3R 4L9
(905) 946-9588
Fax (905) 946-9590
(800) 666-0220 orders only
(Interlinks text, statistics and directory information in a survey of more than 30 European countries and territories.)

When in Rome . . . A Business Guide to Cultures and Customs in 12 European Countries
$16.95
AMACOM
135 West 50th Street
New York, NY 10020
(212) 586-8100

Where in Moscow
$13.50
Russian Information Services
City Center
89 Main Street, Suite 2
Montpelier, VT 05602
(802) 223-4955
(800) 639-4301
Fax (802) 223-6105

Resource Publications

Where in St. Petersburg
$13.50
Russian Information Services
City Center
89 Main Street, Suite 2
Montpelier, VT 05602
(802) 223-4955
(800) 639-4301
Fax (802) 223-6105

Who's Who in Business and Industry in the U.K.
$250
St. James Press
835 Penobscot
Detroit, MI 48226
(800) 345-0392

Who's Who in Canadian Business
$179.95
International Press Publications Inc.
90 Nolan Court #23
Markham, Ontario, L3R 4L9
Canada
(905) 946-9588
Fax (905) 946-9590
(Detailed biographical reference work on the business
community.)

Who's Who in International Affairs
$295
International Press Publications Inc.
90 Nolan Court #23
Markham Ontario, Canada L3R 4L9
(905) 946-9588
Fax (905) 946-9590
(800) 666-0220 orders only
(Provides information on more than 7,000 key
people involved in international affairs.)

World Aviation Directory
$250
McGraw-Hill, Inc.
1200 G Street, NW
Washington, DC 20005
(202) 383-2485
Fax (202) 383-2440

The World Business Calendar
$13.95
Education Extension Systems
P.O. Box 11048
Cleveland Park Stat.
Washington, DC 20008
(703) 548-1509
(Yearly calendar/manual provides worldwide information
ranging from national holidays to drinking etiquette.)

World Chamber of Commerce Directory
$29
Johnson Publishing Company
P.O. Box 1029
Loveland, CO 80537
(303) 663-3231
Fax (303) 663-6187
(Chambers in the U.S. by city, phone number; foreign
embassies; principal foreign chambers.)

World Development Directory
$85
St. James Press
835 Penobscot
Detroit, MI 48226
(800) 345-0392
(Gives information on more than 1,000 organizations
that provide aid, advice and/or information to rural and
developing countries.)

The World Directory of Diplomatic Representation
$395
International Press Publications Inc.
90 Nolan Court #23
Markham Ontario, Canada L3R 4L9
(905) 946-9588
Fax (905) 946-9590
(800) 666-0220 orders only
(Guide to embassies and other government representation.)

World Fact Book
$31
Federal Reprints
P.O. Box 70268
Washington, D.C. 20024
(202) 544-6604
Fax (202) 543-1527
(Country by country description by U.S. CIA of the
geography, people, government, economy, communications
and defense forces of more than 200 countries. Provides
appendices on the UN and international organizations
with country membership, along with regional maps.)

The World of Learning
$350
International Press Publications Inc.
90 Nolan Court #23
Markham Ontario, Canada L3R 4L9
(905) 946-9588
Fax (905) 946-9590
(800) 666-0220 orders only
(Contains details of more than 26,000 educational,
cultural and scientific institutions.)

**The World is Your Market—An Export Guide for
   Small Business**
Free of Charge
available through local Department
of Commerce and Small Business Administration
district offices

World Trade Exporter/EasyNet Database
$545
U.S. Department of Commerce
National Technical Information Service
Springfield, VA 22161
(703) 487-4630
(A joint venture between U.S. Department of Commerce
and International Systems Development Corporation, the
listing provides information for thousands of industry-
specific products and countries; also provides access to
EasyNet, a collection of more than 900 online databases
from around the world.)

World Trade Resources Guide
$169
Gale Research, Inc.
P.O. Box 33477
Detroit, MI 48232-5477
(800) 877-GALE
(313) 961-2242
Fax (313) 961-6083
(Covers 80 countries.)

Worldcasts
$1,300/complete annual set
$450/volume
Predicasts
11001 Cedar Avenue
Cleveland, OH 44106
(800) 321-6388
(216) 795-3000
(Eight-volume annual series of 60,000 abstracted forecasts
for products and markets outside the United States.)

Worldwide Directory of Defense Authorities
$647
Worldwide Government Directories, Inc.
7979 Old Georgetown Road, Suite 900
Bethesda, MD 20814
(301) 718-8770
Fax (301) 718-8494
(800) 332-3535
(Biographical directory of government defense officials
in every country in the world. Quarterly updates also
available.)

Worldwide Franchise Directory
$129.50
Gale Research, Inc.
P.O. Box 33477
Detroit, MI 48232-5477
(800) 877-GALE
(313) 961-2242
Fax (313) 961-6083
(Information on 1,600 national and international
franchising opportunities.)

Worldwide Government Directory
$347
Worldwide Government Directories, Inc.
7979 Old Georgetown Road, Suite 900
Bethesda, MD 20814
(301) 718-8770
Fax (301) 718-8494
(800) 332-3535
(Biographical directory of national government officials in
every country in the world. Monthly/quarterly updates also
available.

Worldwide Government Directory
$325
Belmont Publications
1454 Belmont Street, N.W.
Washington, D.C. 20009
(202) 232-6334
(Includes names, titles, addresses and phone numbers of
heads of state, ministers, aides, department directors and
cabinet members.)

Worldwide Government Report
$247
Worldwide Government Directories, Inc.
7979 Old Georgetown Road, Suite 900
Bethesda, MD 20814
(301) 718-8770
Fax (301) 718-8494
(800) 332-3535
(Monthly newsletter reporting events affecting government
structure and personnel around the world. Includes reports
on government and military turnover, overview of an
international organization, election updates, country
leader profiles and senior appointments.)

Year in Trade: Operation of the Trade Agreements Program
$18
S/N 049-000-00068-5
U.S. Government Printing Office
Superintendent of Documents
P.O. Box 371954
Pittsburgh, PA 15250-7954
(202) 783-3238
Fax (202) 512-2250
(Historical record of major trade-related activities of the
U.S. 294 pages.)

Yellow Pages Moscow
$45
Russian Information Services
89 Main Street, Suite 2
Montpelier, VT 95602
(802) 223-4955
Fax (802) 223-6105
(800) 639-4301
(Lists over 40,000 Russian and foreign businesses and
government offices in Moscow, complete with 700
subject headings. 650 pages.)

Your Own Import-Export Business: Winning the Trade Game
$79.95 (four-hour video)
Global Business and Trade
1385 Don Carlos Court
Chula Vista, CA 91910
(619) 421-5923
(Explains how to start and operate an import-export
business.

Glossary of International Trade Terms

Ad Valorem Tariff. A tariff calculated as a percentage of the value of goods cleared through customs, e.g., 15 percent ad valorem means 15 percent of the value.

Adjustment Assistance. Financial, training and re-employment technical assistance to workers and technical assistance to firms and industries to help them cope with adjustment difficulties arising from increased import competition. The objective of the assistance usually is to help an industry to become more competitive in the same line of production, or to move into other economic activities. The aid to workers can take the form of training (to qualify the affected individuals for employment in new or expanding industries), relocation allowances (to help them move from areas characterized by high unemployment to areas where employment may be available) or unemployment compensation (to tide them over while they are searching for new jobs). The aid to firms can take the form of technical assistance through Trade Adjustment Assistance Centers located throughout the United States. Industry-wide technical assistance also is available through the Trade Adjustment Assistance program. The benefits of increased trade to an importing country generally exceed the costs of adjustment, but the benefits are widely shared and the adjustment costs are sometimes narrowly-and some would say unfairly-concentrated on a few domestic producers and communities. Both import restraints and adjustment assistance can be designed to reduce these hardships but adjustment assistance-unlike import restraints-allows the economy to enjoy the full benefits of lower-cost imported goods. Adjustment assistance can also be designed to facilitate structural shifts of resources from less productive to more productive industries, contributing further to greater economic efficiency and improved standards of living.

ATA Carnet. An international customs document that is recognized as an international valid guarantee and may be used in lieu of national customs documents and as security for import duties and taxes to cover the temporary admission of goods and sometimes the transit of goods. The ATA ("Admission Temporaire-Temporary Admission") Convention of 1961 authorized the ATA Carnet to replace the ECS ("Echantillons Commerciaux-Commercial Samples") Carnet that was created by a 1956 convention sponsored by the Customs Cooperation Council. ATA Carnets are issued by National Chambers of Commerce affiliated with the International Chambers of Commerce, which also guarantees payment of duties in the event of failure to re-export. A carnet does not replace an export license.

Balance of Payments. A tabulation of a country's credit and debit transactions with other countries and international institutions. These transactions are divided into two broad groups: Current Account and Capital Account. The Current Account includes exports and imports of goods, services (including investment income), and unilateral transfers. The Capital Account includes financial flows related to international direct investment, investment in government and private securities, international bank transactions, and changes in official gold holdings and foreign exchange reserves.

Balance of Trade. A component of the balance of payments, or the surplus or deficit that results from comparing a country's expenditures on merchandise imports and receipts derived from its merchandise exports.

Bankers' Acceptance. A form of credit created when a bank acknowledges in writing on a time draft its obligation to pay the face amount to the holder at a specified time.

Barter. The direct exchange of goods for other goods, without the use of money as a medium of exchange and without the involvement of a third party.

Beggar-Thy-Neighbor Policy. A course of action through which a country tries to reduce unemployment and increase domestic output by raising tariffs and instituting non-tariff barriers that impede imports, or by accomplishing the same objective through competitive devaluation. Countries that pursued such policies in the early 1930s found that other countries retaliated by raising their own barriers against imports, which, by reducing export markets, tended to worsen the economic difficulties that precipitated the initial protectionist action. The Smoot-Hawley Tariff Act of 1930 is often cited as a conspicuous example of this approach.

Beneficiary. The party who receives payment as stipulated in a letter of credit. This party is usually a seller or exporter but also can be a person awarding a contract for services to be performed.

Bid Bond. A financial guarantee to support the bidder's commitment to sign a contract if the bid is successful.

Bilateral Trade Agreement. A formal or informal agreement involving commerce between two countries. Such agreements sometimes list the quantities of specific goods that may be exchanged between participating countries within a given period.

Bill of Lading ("B/L"). This document, issued by an ocean or air carrier, serves multiple purposes. It is a receipt for goods, a contract for their transportation and, in the case of an ocean shipment, may be the document of title to the goods.

Bonded Warehouse. A warehouse authorized by Customs Authorities for storage of goods on which payment of duties is deferred until the goods are removed.

Bounties or Grants. Payments by governments to producers of goods, often to strengthen their competitive position.

Boycott. A refusal to deal commercially or otherwise with a person, firm or country.

CIF. An abbreviation used in some international sales contracts, when the selling price includes all "costs, insurance and freight" for the goods sold ("charge in full"), meaning that the seller arranges and pays for all relevant expenses involved in shipping goods form their point of exportation to a given point of importation. In import statistics, "CIF value" means that all figures are calculated on this basis, regardless of the nature of individual transactions.

Certificate of Origin. Various countries require documentary evidence of the actual origin of the goods that are to enter their boundaries. Exporters usually can obtain these certificates at local chambers of commerce at nominal cost, typically about $15.

Codes of Conduct. International instruments that indicate standards of behavior by nation states or multi-national corporations deemed desirable by the international community. Several codes of conduct were negotiated during the Tokyo Round that liberalized and harmonized domestic measures that might impede trade, and these are considered legally binding for the countries that choose to adhere to them. Each of these codes is monitored by a special committee that meets under the auspices of the General Agreement of Tariffs and Trade (GATT) and encourages consultations and the settlement of disputes arising under the code. Countries that are not Contracting Parties to GATT may adhere to these codes. GATT Articles III through XXIII also contain commercial policy provisions that have been described as GATT's code of good conduct in trade matters. The United Nations has also encouraged the negotiation of several "voluntary" codes of conduct, including one that seeks to specify the rights and obligations of trans-national corporations and of governments.

Collection. In financial transaction in which banks act as intermediaries between two parites, usually buyers and sellers located in different geographic areas.

Commercial Invoice. Describes goods being sold. Very similar to a domestic invoice. The seller, buyer and terms of payment also are identified. The document should always be signed and carry a statement to the effect that the shipment is in conformity with the order, that the goods are of a specified country origin, and that the information listed is true and correct. Customs duties are assessed in many countries on the basis of the invoice.

Commodity. Broadly defined, any article exchanged in trade, but most commonly used to refer to raw materials, including such minerals as tin, copper and manganese, and bulk-produced agricultural products such as coffee, tea and rubber.

Common External Tariff (CXT). A tariff rate uniformly applied by a common market or customs union, such as the European Community, to imports from countries outside the union. For example, the European Common Market is based on the principle of a free internal trade area with a common external tariff (sometimes referred to in French as the Tarif Exterieur Commun-TEC) applied to products imported from non-member countries. "Free trade areas" do not necessarily have common external tariffs.

Confirmed Credit. A letter of credit in which the issuing bank's obligation to pay is backed (confirmed) by a second bank.

Comparative Advantage. A central concept in international trade theory which holds that a country or a region should specialize in the production and export of those goods and services that it can produce relatively more efficiently than other goods and services, and import those goods and services in which it has a comparative disadvantage. This theory was first propounded by David Ricardo in 1817 as a basis for increasing the economic welfare of a population through international trade. The comparative advantage theory normally favors specialized production in a country based on intensive utilization of those factors of production in which the country is relatively well endowed (such as raw materials, fertile land or skilled labor); and perhaps also the accumulation of physical capital and the pace of research.

Consular Invoice. Some countries require that an invoice be prepared on their own forms, supplied via the consul of the country, that they often be in the language of that country, and be officially certified by that consulate in the state or country of export.

Container Freight Station (CFS). The term CFS at loading ports means the location designated by carriers for the receiving of cargo to be packed into containers by the carrier. At discharge ports, the term CFS means the location designated by carriers in the port area for unpacking and delivery of cargo.

Countertrade. A reciprocal trading arrangement. Countertrade transactions include:
a) counterpurchase obligates the foreign supplier to purchase from the buyer goods and services unrelated to the goods and services sold, usually with a one- to five-year period;
b) reverse countertrade contracts require the importer (a US buyer of machine tools from Eastern Europe, for example) to export goods equivalent in value to a specified percent-

age of the value of the imported goods-an obligation that can be sold to an exporter in a third country;

c) buyback arrangements obligate the foreign supplier of plant, machinery, or technology to buy from the importer a portion of the resultant production during a 5-25 year period;

d) clearing agreements between two countries that agree to purchase specific amounts of each other's products over a specified period of time, using a designated "clearing currency" in the transactions;

e) "switch" arrangements that permit the sale of unpaid balances in a clearing account to be sold to a third party, usually at a discount, that may be used for producing goods in the country holding the balance;

f) swap schemes through which products from different locations are traded to save transportation costs; and

g) barter arrangements through which two parties directly exchange goods deemed to be of approximately equivalent value without any flow of money taking place.

Countervailing Duties. Special duties imposed on imports to offset the benefits of subsidies to producers or exporters in the exporting country. GATT Article VI permits the use of such duties. The Executive Branch of the U.S. Government has been legally empowered since the 1890's to impose the countervailing duties in amounts equal to any "bounties" or "grants" reflected in products imported into the United States. Under U.S. law and the Tokyo Round Agreement on Subsidies and Countervailing Duties, a wide range of practices are recognized as constituting subsidies that may be offset through the imposition of countervailing duties. The Trade Agreements Act of 1979, through amendments to the Tariff Act of 1930, established rigorous procedures and deadlines for determining the existence of subsidies in response to petitions filed by interested parties such as domestic producers of competitive products and their workers. In all cases involving subsidized products from countries recognized by the United States as signatories to the Agreement on Subsidies and Countervailing Duties, or countries which have assumed obligations substantially equivalent to those under the Agreement, U.S. law requires that countervailing duties may be imposed only after the U.S. International Trade Commission has determined that the imports are causing or threatening to cause material injury to an industry in the United States.

Current Account. That portion of a country's balance of payments that records current (as opposed to capital) transactions, including visible trade (exports and imports), invisible trade (income and expenditures for services), profits earned from foreign operations, interest and transfer payments.

Customs Broker. An individual or firm licensed to enter and clear goods through Customs on behalf of importers. He/she will advise on technical requirements, prepare and file entry documents, obtain the necessary bonds, deposit

U.S. import duties, secure release of the goods and arrange delivery to the importers warehouse.

Devaluation. The lowering of the value of a national currency in terms of the currency of another nation. Devaluation tends to reduce domestic demand for imports in a country by raising their prices in terms of the devalued currency and to raise foreign demand for the country's exports by reducing their prices in terms of foreign currencies. Devaluation can therefore help to correct a balance of payments deficit and sometimes provide a short-term basis for economic adjustment of a national economy.

Developed Countries. A term used to distinguish the more industrialized nations-including all Organization for Economic Cooperation and Development (OECD) member countries from "developing," or less developed, countries. The developed countries are sometimes collectively designated as the "North," because most of them are in the Northern Hemisphere.

Developing Countries. A broad range of countries that generally lack a high of industrialization, infrastructure and other capital investment, sophisticated technology, widespread literacy, and advanced living standards among their populations as a whole. The developing countries are sometimes collectively designated as the "South," because a large number of them are in the Southern Hemisphere. All the countries of Africa (except South Africa), Asia ad Oceania (except Australia, Japan and New Zealand), Latin America, and the Middle East generally are considered "developing countries," as are a few European countries (Cypress, Malta and Turkey, for example). Some experts differentiate four subcategories of developing countries as having different economic needs and interests: 1) a few relatively wealthy OPEC countries-sometimes referred to as oil exporting developing countries-share a particular interest in a financially sound international economy and open capital markets; 2) Newly Industrializing Countries (NICs) have a growing stake in an open international system; 3) A number of middle income countries-principally commodity exporters-have shown a particular interest in commodity stabilization schemes; and 4) More than 30 very poor countries ("least developed countries") are predominantly agriculture, have sharply limited development prospects during the near future, and tend to be heavily dependent on official development assistance.

Dispute Settlement. Resolution of conflict, usually through a compromise between opposing claims, sometimes facilitated through the efforts of an intermediary. GATT Articles XXII and XXIII set out consultation procedures a Contracting Party may follow to obtain legal redress if it believes its benefits under GATT are impaired.

Distributor. A foreign agent who sells for a supplier directly and maintains an inventory of supplier's products.

Documentary Collection. A collection in which a draft is accompanied by shipping or other documents.

Documentary Credit. A letter of credit that requires documents to accompany the draft or demand for payment.

Domestic International Sales Corporation (Interest Charge DISC). A special U.S. corporation authorized by the U.S. Revenue Act of 1971, as amended by the Tax Reform Act of 1984, to borrow from the U.S. Treasury at the average one-year Treasury bill interest rate to the extent of income tax liable on 94 percent of its annual corporate income. To qualify, the corporation must derive 95 percent of its gross assets, such as working capital, inventories, building and equipment, must be export-related. Such a corporation can buy and sell independently, or can operate as a subsidiary of another corporation. It can maintain sales and service facilities outside the United States to promote and market its goods.

Draft (Bill of Exchange). An instrument, much like an ordinary check in appearance, which is used as a formal demand for payment in a business transaction.

Drawing. Presentation of the draft and documents required by the terms of a letter of credit.

Dumping. Under U.S. law, the sale of an imported commodity in the United States at "less than fair value," usually considered to be a price lower than that at which it is sold within the exporting country or to third countries. "Fair Value" can also be the constructed value of the merchandise which includes a mandatory 8 percent profit margin plus cost of production. Dumping generally is recognized as an unfair trade practice that can disrupt markets and injure producers of competitive products in the importing country. Article VI of GATT permits the imposition of special Anti-Dumping Duties against "dumped" goods equal to the difference between their export price and their normal value in the exporting country. The U.S. Antidumping Law of 1921, as amended, considered dumping as constituting "sales at less than fair value," combined with injury, the likelihood of injury, or the prevention of the establishment of a competitive industry in the United States. The Trade Act of 1974 added a "cost of production" provision, which required that dumping determinations ignore sales in the home market of the exporting country or in third country markets at prices that are too low to "permit recovery of all costs within a reasonable period of time in the normal course of trade." The Trade Agreements Act of 1979 repealed the 1921 act, but re-enacted most of its substance in Title VII of the Tariff Act of 1930.

Drawback. Import duties or taxes repaid by a government, in whole or in part, when the imported goods are re-exported or used in the manufacture of exported goods.

Embargo. A prohibition upon exports or imports, either with respect to specific products or specific countries. Historically, embargoes have been ordered most frequently in time of war, but they also may be applied for political, economic or sanitary purposes. Embargoes imposed against an individual country by the United Nations-or group of nations-in an effort to influence its conduct or its policies are sometimes called "sanctions."

Escape Clause. A provision in bilateral or multilateral commercial agreement permitting a signatory nation to suspend tariff or other concessions when imports threaten serious harm to the producers of competitive domestic goods. GATT Article XIX sanctions such as "safeguard" provisions to help firms and workers adversely affected by a relatively sudden surge of imports adjust to the rising level of import competition. Section 201 of the U.S. Trade Act of 1974 requires the U.S. International Trade Commission to investigate complaints formally known as "petitions" filed by domestic industries or workers claiming that they have been injured or are threatened with injury as a consequence of rapidly rising imports and to complete any such investigation within six months. Section 203 of the Act provides that if the Commission finds that a domestic industry has bene seriously injured or threatened with serious injury, it may recommend that the President grant relief to the industry in the form of adjustment assistance or temporary import restrictions in the form of tariffs, quotas, or tariff quotas. The President must then take action pursuant to the Commission's recommendations within 60 days, but he may accept, modify or reject them, according to his assessment of the national interest. The Congress can, through majority vote in both the Senate and the House of Representatives within 90 legislative days, override a Presidential decision not to implement the Commission's recommendations. The law permits the President to impose import restrictions for an initial period of five years and to extend them for a maximum additional period of three years.

Exchange Controls. The rationing of foreign currencies, bank drafts and other instruments for settling international financial obligations by countries seeking to ameliorate acute balance of payments difficulties. When such measures are imposed, importers must apply for prior authorization from the government to obtain the foreign currency required to bring in designated amounts and types of goods. Since such measures have the effect of restricting imports, they are considered non-tariff barriers to trade.

Exchange Rate. The price (or rate) at which one currency is exchanged for another currency, for gold, or for Special Drawing Rights (SDRs).

Excise Tax. A selective tax-sometimes called a consumption tax-on certain goods produced within or imported into a country.

Export Broker. An individual or firm that brings together buyers and sellers for a fee but does not take part in actual sales transactions.

Export Commission House. An organization which, for a commission, acts as a purchasing agent for a foreign buyer.

Export Management Company. A private firm that serves as the export department for several manufacturers, soliciting and transacting export business on behalf of its clients in return for a commission, salary, or retainer plus commission.

Export Quotas. Specific restrictions or ceilings imposed by an exporting country on the value or volume of certain imports, designed to protect domestic producers and consumers from temporary shortages of the goods affected or to bolster their prices in world markets. Some International Commodity Agreements explicitly indicate when producers should apply such restraints. Export quotas also are often applied in Orderly Marketing Agreements and Voluntary Restraint Agreements, and to promote domestic processing of raw materials in countries that produce them.

Export Restraints. Quantitative restrictions imposed by exporting countries to limit exports to specified foreign markets, usually pursuant to a formal or informal agreement concluded at the request of the importing countries.

Export Subsidies. Government payments or other financially quantifiable benefits provided to domestic producers or exporters contingent on the export of their goods or services. GATT Article XVI recognizes that subsidies in general, and especially export subsidies, distort normal commercial activities and hinder the achievement of GATT objectives. An Agreement on Subsidies and Countervailing Duties negotiated during the Tokyo Round strengthened the GATT rules on export subsidies and provided for an outright prohibition of export subsidies by developed countries for manufactured and semi-manufactured products. The Agreement also established a special committee, serviced by signatories. Under certain conditions, the Agreement allows developing countries to use export subsidies on manufactured and semi-manufactured products, and on primary products as well, provided that the subsidies do not result in more than an equitable share of world exports of the product for the country.

Export Trading Company. A corporation or other business unit organized and operated principally for the purpose of exporting goods and services, or of providing export related services to other companies. The Export Trading Company Act of 1982 exempts authorized trading companies from certain provisions of U.S. anti-trust laws.

FAS. The term "Free Alongside Ship," in international trade, refers to the point of embarkation from which the vessel or plane selected by the buyer will transport the goods. Under this system, the seller is obligated to pay the costs and assume all risks for transporting the goods from his place of business to the FAS point. In trade statistics, "FAS value" means that the import or export figures are calculated on this basis, regardless of the nature of individual transactions reflected in the statistics.

FOB. An abbreviation used in some international sales contracts, when imports are valued at a designated point, as agreed between buyer and seller, that is considered "Free on Board." In such contracts, the seller is obligated to have the goods packaged and ready for shipment from the agreed point, whether his own place of business or some intermediate point, and the buyer normally assumes the burden of all inland transportation costs and risks in the exporting country, as well as all subsequent transportation costs, including the costs of loading the merchandise on the vessel. However, if the contract stipulates "FOB vessel" the seller bears all transportation costs to the vessel named by the buyer, as well as the costs of loading the goods on to that vessel. The same principle applies to the abbreviations "FOR" ("Free on Rail") and "FOT" ("Free on Truck").

Foreign Exchange. The currency of foreign countries and the process of converting the currency of one country to that of a second country.

Foreign Sales Agent. An individual or firm that serves as the foreign representative of a domestic supplier and seeks sales abroad for the supplier.

Foreign Sales Corporation (FSC). A firm incorporated in Guam, the U.S. Virgin Islands, the Commonwealth of the Northern Mariana Islands, American Samoa, or any foreign country that has a satisfactory exchange-of-information agreement with the United States and elects to be taxed as a U.S. corporation, except for the fact that it exempts from taxable income a portion of the combined net income of the FSC and its affiliated supplier on the export of U.S. products.

Forward Transaction. A foreign exchange transaction in which currency is bought or sold for delivery at some specified date in the future, at a rate fixed at the present. Generally, an amount is added or subtracted from the current rate of exchange to account for premium or discount, respectively.

Free Trade. A theoretical concept that assumes international trade unhampered by government measures such as tariffs or non-tariff barriers. The objective of trade liberalization is to achieve "freer trade" rather than "free trade," it being generally recognized among trade policy officials that some restrictions on trade are likely to remain in effect for the foreseeable future.

155

Free Trade Area. A group of two or more countries that have eliminated tariff and most non-tariff barriers affecting trade among themselves, while each participating country applies its own independent schedule of tariffs to imports from countries that are not members. The best known example is the European Free Trade Association (EFTA) - and the free trade area for manufactured goods that has been created through the trade agreements that have been concluded between the European Community and the individual EFTA countries. GATT Article XXIV spells out the meaning of a free trade area in GATT and specifies the applicability of other GATT provisions to free trade areas.

Free Zone. An area within a country (a seaport, airport, warehouse or any designated area) regarded as being outside its customs territory. Importers may therefore bring goods of foreign origin into such an area without paying customs duties and taxes, pending their eventual processing, trans-shipment or re-exportation. Free zones were numerous and prosperous during an earlier period when tariffs were high. Some still exist in capital cities, transport junctions and major seaports, but their number and prominence have declined as tariffs have fallen in recent years. Free zones may also be known as "free ports," "free warehouses," and "foreign trade zones."

Freight Forwarder. Performs international traffic and documentation services on behalf of the exporter, as related to shipments by either airline or seagoing vessel. Also has detailed knowledge of ports and their facilities and can generally orchestrate the entire movement of goods from point of origin to destination in the most efficient and cost-effective manner.

Generalized System of Preferences (GSP). A concept developed within the United Nations Conference on Trade and Development (UNCTAD) to encourage the expansion of manufactured and semimanufactured exports from developing countries by making goods more competitive in developed country markets through tariff preferences. The GSP reflects international agreement, negotiated at UNCTAD-II in New Delhi in 1968, that a temporary and non-reciprocal grant of preferences by developed countries to developing countries would be equitable and, in the long term, mutually beneficial.

Government Procurement Policies and Practices. The means and mechanisms through which official government agencies purchase goods and services. Government procurement policies and practices are non-tariff barriers to trade, if they discriminate in favor of domestic suppliers when competitive imported goods are cheaper or of better quality. The United States pressed for an international agreement during the Tokyo Round to ensure that government purchase of goods entering into international trade should be based on specific published regulations that prescribe open procedures for submitting bids, as had been the traditional practice in the United States. Most governments had traditionally awarded such contracts on the basis of bids solicited from selected domestic suppliers, or through private negotiations with suppliers that involved little, if any, competition. Other countries, including the United States, gave domestic suppliers a specified preferential margin, as compared with foreign suppliers. The Government Procurement Code negotiated during the Tokyo Round sought to reduce, if not eliminate, the "Buy National" bias underlying such practices by improving transparency and equity in national procurement practices and by ensuring effective recourse to dispute settlement procedures. The Code became effective January 1, 1981.

Graduation. The presumption that individual developing countries are capable of assuming greater responsibilities and obligations in the international community-within GATT or the World Bank, for example-as their economies advance, as through industrialization, export development and rising living standards. In this sense, graduation implies that donor countries may remove the more advanced developing countries from eligibility for all or some products under the Generalized System of Preferences. Within the World Bank, graduation moves a country from dependence on concessional grants to non-concessional loans from international financial institutions and private banks.

Harmonized Commodity Coding and Description System. Effective January 1, 1988 the Harmonized System standardizes product classification around the world.

Hedge. A method to limit the risk of possible future loss due to currency fluctuations. This is accomplished by buying or selling foreign currency at a prearranged cost or earnings, such as a forward transaction.

Import Substitution. An attempt by a country to reduce imports (and hence foreign exchange expenditures) by encouraging the development of domestic industries.

Industrial Policy. Encompasses traditional government policies intended to provide a favorable economic climate for the development of industry in general or specific industrial sectors. Instruments of industrial policy may include tax incentives to promote investments or exports, direct or indirect subsidies, special financing arrangements, protection against foreign competition, worker training programs, regional development programs, assistance for research and development, and measures to help small business firms. Historically, the term industrial policy has been associated with at least some degree of centralized economic planning or indicative planning, but this connotation is not always intended by its contemporary advocates.

Infant Industry Argument. The view that "temporary protection" for a new industry or firm in a particular country through tariff and non-tariff barriers to imports can help it to become established and eventually competitive in world markets. Historically, new industries that are soundly based and efficiently operated have experienced declining costs as output expands and production experience is acquired. However, industries that have been established and operated with heavy dependence on direct or indirect government subsidies have sometimes found it difficult to relinquish that support. The rationale underlying the Generalized System of Preferences is comparable to that of the infant industry argument.

Inspection Company. As required, provides special inspection of goods and packing to meet special requirements and specifications called for by buyer and seller.

Intellectual Property. Ownership conferring the right to possess, use, or dispose of products created by human ingenuity, including patents, trademarks and copyrights.

Investment Performance Requirements. Special conditions imposed on direct foreign investment by recipient governments sometimes requiring commitments to export a certain percentage of the output, to purchase given supplies locally, or to ensure the employment of a specified percentage of local labor and management.

Invisible Trade. Items such as freight, insurance, and financial services that are included in a country's balance of payments accounts (in the "current" account), even though they are not recorded as physically visible exports and imports.

Irrevocable Credit. A letter of credit that cannot be changed or cancelled without the consent of all parties involved.

Joint Venture. A form of business partnership involving joint management and the sharing of risks and profits as between enterprises based in different countries. If joint ownership of capital is involved the partnership is known as an equity joint venture.

Least Developed Countries (LDCs). Some 36 of the world's poorest countries, considered by the United Nations to be the least developed of the less developed countries. Most of them are small in terms of area and population, and some are land-locked or small island countries. They generally are characterized by low per capita incomes, literacy levels, and medical standards; subsistence agriculture; and a lack of exploitable minerals and competitive industries. Many suffer from aridity, floods, hurricanes, and excessive animal and plant pests, and most are situated in the zone 10 to 30 degrees north latitude. These countries have little prospect of rapid economic development in the foreseeable future and are likely to remain heavily dependent upon official development assistance for many years. Most are in Africa, but a few, such as Bangladesh, Afghanistan, Laos, and Nepal, are in Asia. Haiti is the only country in the Western Hemisphere classified by the United Nations as "least developed." See developing countries.

Letter of Credit. An instrument issued by a bank upon request by a customer that states the bank will pay an obligation of its customers to a third party, usually when certain stated conditions have been met. The two most frequently used letters of credit are the commercial letter of credit, which is used to finance the buying and selling of merchandise, and the standby letter of credit, which is used to support a customer's obligations to perform.

Liberal. When referring to trade policy, "liberal" usually means relatively free of import controls or restraints and/or a preference for reducing existing barriers to trade, often contrasted with the protectionist preference for retraining or raising selected barriers to imports.

LIBOR. An acronym for the London Interbank Offered Rate. The interest rate at which banks in London place Eurocurrency/Eurodollar deposits with each other for a specific period of time.

Mixed Credits. Exceptionally liberal financing terms for an export sale, ostensibly provided for a foreign aid purpose.

Mercantilism. A prominent economic philosophy in the 16th and 17th centuries that equated the accumulation and possession of gold and other international monetary assets, such as foreign currency reserves, with national wealth. Although this point of view generally is discredited among 20th century economists and trade policy experts, some contemporary politicians still favor policies designed to create trade "surpluses," such as import substitution and tariff protection for domestic industries, as essential to national economic strength.

Most-Favored-Nation Treatment (MFN). The policy of non-discrimination in trade policy that provides to all trading partners the same customs and tariff treatment given to the so-called "Most-Favored-Nation." This fundamental principle was a feature of U.S. trade policy as early as 1778. Since 1923 the United States has incorporated an "unconditional" Most-Favored-Nation clause in its trade agreements, binding the contracting governments to confer upon each other all the most favorable trade concessions that either may grant to any other country subsequent to the signing of the agreement. The United States now applies this provision to its trade with all of its trading partners except for those specifically excluded by law. The MFN principle has also provided the foundation of the world trading system since the end of World War II. All Contracting Parties to GATT apply MFN treatment to one another under Article 1 of GATT.

157

Multi-Fiber Arrangement Regarding International Trade in Textiles (MFA). An international compact under GATT that allows an importing signatory country to apply quantitative restrictions on textiles imports when it considers them necessary to prevent market disruption. The MFA provides a framework for regulating international trade in textiles and apparel with the objectives of achieving "orderly marketing" of such products, and of avoiding "market disruption" in importing countries. It provides a basis on which major importers, such as the United States and the European Community, may negotiate bilateral agreements or, if necessary, impose restraints on imports from low-wage producing countries. It provides, among other things, standards for determining market disruption, minimum levels of import restraints, and annual growth of imports. Since an importing country may impose such quotas unilaterally to restrict rapidly rising textiles imports, many important textiles-exporting countries consider it advantageous to enter into bilateral agreements with the principal textiles-importing countries. The MFA went into effect on January 1, 1974, was renewed in December 1977, in December 1981, and again in July 1986, for five years. It succeeded the Long-term Agreement on International Trade in Cotton Textiles (The "LTA"), which had been in effect since 1962. Whereas the LTA applied only to cotton textiles, the MFA now applies to wool, man-made (synthetic) fiber, silk blend and other vegetable fiber textiles and apparel.

Multilateral Agreement. An international compact involving three or more parties. For example, GATT has been, since its establishment in 1947, seeking to promote trade liberalization through multilateral negotiations.

Multilateral Trade Negotiations (MTN). Seven Rounds of "Multilateral Trade Negotiations" have been held under the auspices of GATT since 1947. Each Round represented a discrete and lengthy series of interacting bargaining sessions among the participating Contracting parties in search of mutually beneficial agreements looking toward the reduction of barriers to world trade. The agreements ultimately reached at the conclusion of each Round became new GATT commitments and thus amounted to an important step in the evolution of the world trading system.

Negotiate (letter of credit). To verify that the documents presented under a letter of credit conform to requirements and then, if the documents are in order, to pay the seller of goods.

Newly Industrializing Countries (NICs). Relatively advanced developing countries whose industrial production and exports have grown rapidly in recent years. Examples include Brazil, Hong Kong, Korea, Mexico, Singapore, and Taiwan.

Non-Market Economy. A national economy or a country in which the government seeks to determine economic activity largely through a mechanism of central planning, as in the Soviet Union, in contrast to a market economy that depends heavily upon market forces to allocate productive resources. In a "non-market" economy, production targets ,prices, costs, investment allocations, raw materials, labor, international trade, and most other economic aggregates are manipulated within a national economic plan drawn up by a central planning authority, and hence the public sector makes the major decisions affecting demand and supply within the national economy.

Non-Tariff Barriers (NTBs). Government measures other than tariffs that restrict imports. Such measures have become relatively more conspicuous impediments to trade as tariffs have been reduced during the period since World War II.

Non-Vessel Operating Common Carrier (NVOCC). A cargo consolidator of small shipments in ocean trade, generally soliciting business and arranging for or performing containerization functions at or near the port.

Opening Bank. The bank that issues the letter of credit and that makes payment according to the conditions stipulated (also known as Issuing Bank).

Orderly Marketing Agreements (OMAs). International agreements negotiated between two or more governments, in which the trading partners agree to restrain the growth of trade in specified "sensitive" products, usually through the imposition of import quotas. Orderly Marketing Agreements are intended to ensure that future trade increases will not disrupt, threaten or impair competitive industries or their workers in importing countries.

Paris Club. A popular designation for meetings between representatives of a developing country that wishes to renegotiate its "official" debt (normally excluding debts owned by and to the private sector without official guarantees) and representatives of the relevant creditor governments and international institutions. Such meetings normally take place at the initiative of a debtor country that wishes to consolidate all or part of its debt service payments falling due over a specified period. The meetings traditionally are chaired by a senior official of the French Treasury Department. Comparable meetings occasionally take place in London and in New York for countries that which to renegotiate repayment terms for their debts to private banks. Such meetings sometimes are called "creditors clubs."

Par Value. The official fixed exchange rate between two currencies or between a currency and a specific weight of gold or a basket of currencies.

Performance Bond. A bond issued at the request of a contractor to protect the purchaser against loss in the event of default on a contract.

Peril Point. A hypothetical limit beyond which a reduction in tariff protection would cause serious injury to a domestic industry. U.S. legislation in 1949 that extended the Trade Agreements Act of 1934 required the Tariff Commission to establish such "peril points" for U.S. industries, and for the President to submit specific reasons to Congress if and when any U.S. tariff was reduced below those levels. This requirement, which was an import constraint on U.S. negotiating positions in early GATT tariff-cutting Rounds, was eliminated by the Trade Expansion Act of 1962.

Protectionism. The deliberate use or encouragement of restrictions on imports to enable relatively inefficient domestic producers to compete successfully with foreign producers.

Purchasing Agent. An agent who purchases goods in his or her own country on behalf of foreign importers such as government agencies and large private concerns.

Quantitative Restrictions (QRs). Explicit limits, or quotas, on the physical amounts of particular commodities that can be imported or exported during a specified time period, usually measured by volume but sometimes by value. The quota may be applied on a "selective" basis, with varying limits set according to the country of origin, or on a quantitative global basis that only specifies the total limit and thus tends to benefit more efficient suppliers. Quotas are frequently administered through a system of licensing. GATT Article XI generally prohibits the use of quantitative restrictions, except under conditions specified by other GATT articles; Article XIX permits quotas to safeguard certain industries from damage by rapidly rising imports; Articles XII and XVIII provide that quotas may be imposed for balance of payments reasons under circumstances laid out in Article XV; Article XX permits special measures to apply to public health, gold stocks, items of archeological or historic interest, and several other categories of goods; and Article XXI recognizes the overriding importance of national security. Article XII provides that quantitative restrictions, whenever applied, should be non-discriminatory.

Reciprocity. The practice by which governments extend similar concessions to each other, as when one government lowers its tariffs or other barriers impeding its imports in exchange for equivalent concessions from a trading partner on barriers affecting its exports (a "balance of concessions"). Reciprocity traditionally has been a principal objective of negotiators in GATT "Rounds." Reciprocity also is defined as "mutuality of benefits," "quid pro quo," and "equivalence" of advantages. GATT Part IV (especially GATT Article XXXVI) and the "Enabling Clause" of the Tokyo Round "Framework Agreement" exempt developing countries from the rigorous application of reciprocity in their negotiations with developed countries.

Retaliation. Action taken by a country to restrain its imports from a country that has increased a tariff or imposed other measures that adversely affect its exports in a manner inconsistent with GATT. The GATT, in certain circumstances, permits such reprisal, although this has very rarely been practiced. The value of trade affected by such retaliatory measures should, in theory, approximately equal the value affected by the initial import restriction.

Round of Trade Negotiations. A cycle of multilateral trade negotiations under the aegis of GATT, culminating in simultaneous trade agreements among participating countries to reduce tariff and non-tariff barriers to trade. Seven "Rounds" have been completed thus far: Geneva, 1947-48; Annecy, France, 1949; Torquay, England, 1950-51; Geneva, 1956; Geneva, 1960-62 (the Dillon Round); Geneva, 1963-67 (the Kennedy Round); and Geneva, 1973-79 (the Tokyo Round).

Section 301 (of the Trade At of 1974). Provision of U.S. law that enables the President to withdraw concessions or restrict imports from countries that discirinate against U.S. exports, subsidize their own exports to the United States, or engage in other unjustifiable or unreasonable practices that burden or discriminate against U.S. trade.

Services. Economic activities-such as transportation, banking, insurance, tourism, space launching telecommunications, advertising, entertainment, data processing, consulting and the licensing of intellectual property-that are usually of an intangible character and often consumed as they are produced. Service industries have become increasingly important since the 1920s. Services now account for more than two-thirds of the economic activity of the United States and about 25 percent of world trade. Traditional GATT rules have not applied to trade in services.

Shipper's Export Declaration (SED). Used to control exports and compile trade statistics. Must be prepared and submitted to the U.S. customs agent for shipments by means other than mail valued at more than $2,500 per harmonized system (U.S. schedule "B") classification; it also must be prepared for all shipments covered by an individually validated license in any amount or to a destination that is not "free world."

Sight Credit. A letter of credit under which drafts are payable immediately upon presentation or on demand if the documents meet the terms and conditions of the letter of credit.

Smoot-Hawley Tariff Act of 1930. U.S. protectionist legislation that raised tariff rates on most articles imported by the United States, triggering comparable tariff increases by U.S. trading partners. The Tariff At of 1930 is also known as the Smoot-Hawley Tariff.

Special Drawing Rights (SDRs). Created in 1969 by the International Monetary Fund as a supplemental international monetary reserve asset. SDRs are available to governments through the Fund and may be used in transactions between the Fund and member governments. IMF member countries have agreed to regard SDRs as complementary to gold and reserve currencies in settling their international accounts. The unit value of an SDR reflects the foreign exchange value of a "basket" of currencies of several major trading countries (the U.S. dollar, the German mark, the French franc, the Japanese yen, and the British pound). The SDR has become the unit of account used by the Fund and several national currencies are pegged to it. Some commercial banks accept deposits denominated in SDRs (although they are unofficial and not the same units transacted among governments and the fund).

Spot Transaction. A foreign exchange transaction in which foreign currency is bought at a rate of exchange and delivered within two business days after the transaction date.

State Trading Nations. Countries such as the People's Republic of China, and nations that rely heavily on government entities, instead of the private sector, to conduct trade with other countries. Some of these countries (e.g., Cuba) have long been Contracting Parties to GATT, whereas others became Contracting Parties later under special Protocols of Acession. The different terms and conditions under which these countries acceded to GATT were designed in each case to ensure steady expansion of the country's trade with other GATT countries, taking into account the relative insignificance of tariffs on imports into state trading nations.

Steamship Agency. Represents a steamship company that does not have an office in the particular port being considered for shipment of goods. Performs services to maintain steamship operations on behalf of vessel owners.

Steamship Line. A company that owns a fleet of vessels and is usually composed of the following departments: vessel operations, container operations, tariff and documentation departments, booking, outbound rates, inward rates and sales.

Stevedoring Company. Contracts with shipowner or operator to provide labor, i.e., stevedores/longshoremen, to perform services related to loading or unloading the ship in port.

Subsidy. An economic benefit granted by a government to producers of goods, often to strengthen their competitive position. The subsidy may be direct (a cash grant) or indirect (low-interest export credits guaranteed by a government agency, for example).

Tariff. A duty (or tax) levied upon goods transported from one customs area to another. Tariffs raise the prices of imported goods, thus making them less competitive within the market of the importing country. After seven "Rounds" of GATT trade negotiations that focused heavily on tariff reductions, tariffs are less important measures of protection than they used to be. The term "tariff" often refers to a comprehensive list or "schedule" of merchandise with the rate of duty to be paid to the government for importing products listed.

Terms of Trade. The volume of exports that can be traded for a given volume of imports. Changes in the terms of trade generally are measured by comparing changes in the ratio of export prices to import prices. The terms of trade are considered to have improved when a given volume of exports can be exchanged for a larger volume of imports. Some economists have discerned an overall deteriorating trend in this ratio for developing countries as a whole. Other economists maintain that whereas the terms of trade may have become less favorable for certain countries during certain periods-and even for all developing countries during some periods-the same terms of trade have improved for other developing countries in the same periods and perhaps for most developing countries during other periods.

Tied Loan. A loan made by a government agency that requires a foreign borrower to spend the proceeds in the lender's country.

Trade Acceptance. A draft by the seller of goods on the buyer and accepted by the buyer for payment at a specified future date.

Trade Policy Committee (TPC). A senior inter-agency committee of the U.S. Government, chaired by the U.S. Trade Representative, that provides broad guidance to the President on trade policy issues. Members include the Secretaries of Commerce, State Treasury, Agriculture, and Labor.

Trading Company. Assists exporters and importers in selling products abroad and locating sources of supply. Arranges for non-monetary exchange of goods by matching buyers and sellers of merchandise.

Transfer of Technology. The movement of modern or scientific methods of production or distribution from one enterprise, institution or country to another, as through foreign investment, international trade licensing of patent rights, technical assistance or training.

Transparency. Visibility and clarity of laws and regulations. Some of the codes of conduct negotiated during the Tokyo Round sought to increase the transparency of non-tariff barriers that impede trade.

Trigger Price Mechanism (TPM). A U.S. system for monitoring imported steel to identify imports that are possibly being "dumped" in the United States or subsidized by the governments of exporting countries. The minimum price under this system is based on the estimated landed cost at a U.S. port of entry of steel produced by the world's most efficient producers. Imported steel entering the United States below that price may "trigger" formal anti-dumping investigations by the Department of Commerce and the U.S. International Trade Commission. The TPM was in effect between early 1978 and march 1980. It was reinstated in October 1980 and suspended for all products except for stainless steel wire in January 1982.

Trucking Company. Provides delivery services to and from port to airport. Can also serve as container freight station and perform warehouse and distribution services.

Turnkey Contract. A compact under which the contractor assumes responsibility to the client for constructing productive installations and ensuring that they operate effectively before turning them over to the client. By centering responsibility for the contributions of all participants in the project in his own hands, the contractor often is able to arrange more favorable financing terms than the client could. The responsibility of the contractor ends when he hands the completed installation over to the client.

Unfair Trade Practices. Unusual government support to firms-such as export subsidies-or certain anti-competitive practices by firms themselves-such as dumping, boycotts or discriminatory shipping arrangements-that result in competitive advantages for the benefiting firms in international trade.

Uniform Customs and Practice for Documentary Credits. The publication issued by the International Chamber of Commerce (publication #400, 1983 revision) which outlines the rules and guidelines agreed to for documentary credit transactions effective October 1, 1984. These provisions are followed by most banks, unless there is an express agreement otherwise.

Usance (Time) Credit. A letter of credit that specifies payment against drafts payable at a future date, generally six months or less.

Valuation. The appraisal of the worth of imported goods by customs officials for the purpose of determining the amount of duty payable in the importing country. The GATT Customs Valuation Code obligates governments that sign it to use the "transaction value" of imported goods-or the price actually paid or payable for them-as the principal basis for valuing the goods for customs purposes.

Value Added Tax (VAT). An indirect tax on consumption that is levied at each discrete point in the chain of production and distribution, from the raw material stage to final consumption. Each processor or merchant pays a tax proportional to the amount by which he increases the value of the goods he purchases for resale after making his own contribution. The Value Added Tax is imposed throughout the European Community and EFTA countries.

Voluntary Restraint Agreements (VRAs). Informal arrangements through which exporters voluntarily restrain certain exports, usually through export quotas, to avoid economic dislocation in an importing country, and to avert the possible imposition of mandatory import restrictions. Such arrangements normally do not entail "compensation" for the exporting country.

Wharfinger. A group, agency or individual that oversees the use of waterfront facilities and collects revenue for the owner. Literally translated "wharf master."

Glossary of International Trade Acronyms

A

ABC	American Business Center
ACDA	Arms Control and Disarmanent Agency
ACTPN	Advisory Committee on Trade Policy Negotiations
Ad Val	Ad Valorem Tariff Rate
AD	Anti-Dumping
ADB	Asian Development Bank
A/DS	Agent Distributor Service (Commerce Department)
AECA	Arms Export Control Act
AFDB	African Develpment Bank
AID	Agency for International Development
ANDEAN	Andean Pact Countries
APCAC	Asia-Pacific Council of American Chambers of Commerce
APEC	Asian-Pacific Economic Cooperation
APTA	Automotive Products Trade Act
ASEAN	Association of Southeast Asian Nations
ATACs	Agricultural Technical Advisory Committee
ATCA	Agreement on Trade in Civil Aircraft
ATPI	Andean Trade Preference Initiative
AUI	ASEAN-U.S. Initiative
AVE	AD Valorem Equivalent

B

BEA	Bureau of Economic Analysis (U.S. Commerce Department)
BFC	Business Facilitation Center (U.S. Commerce Department)
BISNIS	Business Information Service for the Newly Independent States
BITS	Bilateral Investment Treaties
BNC	Binational Commission
BOND	Business Outreach to New Democracies Program
BOP	Balance of Payments
BSP	Business Sponsored or Between Show Promotion
BXA	Bureau of Export Administration (U.S. Commerce Department)

C

C&F	Cartage & Freight
CABEE	Consortia of American Businesses in Eastern Europe
CABNIS	Consortia of American Businesses in the Newly Independent States
CACM	Central America Common Market
CAD/CAM	Computer Aided Design/Computer Aided Manufacturing
CAP	Country Action Plan or Common Agricultural Policy (EC)

CARIBCAN	Canadian-Caribbean Basin Intiative
CARICOM	Caribbean Common Market
CASE	Council of American States in Europe
CBERA	Caribbean Basin Economic Recovery Act
CBI	Caribbean Basin Initiative
CCC	Commodity Cooperation Council or Commodity Credit Corp.
CCCN	Customs Cooperation Council Nomenclature
CCL	Commodity Control List
CCNA	Coordination Council for North American Affairs
CCPIT	China Counsel for the Promotion of International Trade
CEO	Cultural Exchange Officer of Chief Executive Officer
CET	Common External Tariff
CFIUS	Committee on Foreign Investment in the U.S.
CG	Consul General, Consulate General
CG-18	Consultative Group of Eighteen (GATT)
CHG	Charge d'Affaires
CIME	Committee on International Investment & Multinational Enterprises
CIMS	Commercial Information Management System (U.S. Commerce Department)
CIS	Commonwealth of Independent States
CIT	Court of International Trade
CITA	Committee for the Implementation of Textile Agreement
CITIC	China International Trust and Investment Corp.
CMP	Country Marketing Plan
CNUSA	Commercial News USA (U.S. Commerce Department)
COCOM	Coordination Committee on Multilateral Export Controls
COE	Council of Europe
CON	Consul, Consular Section
COP	Cost of Production
CPAC	Commodity Policy Advisory Committee
CSCE	Conference on Security and Cooperation in Europe
CSIS	Center for Strategic & International Studies
CSS	Comparison Shopping Service (Commerce Department)
CTA	Committee on Trade in Agriculture (GATT)
CTF	Certified Trade Fair (U.S. Commerce Department)
CV	Constructed Value
CVD	Countervailing Duty

D

DAC	Development Assistance Committee
DCs	Developed Countries
DEC	District Export Council
DF	Duty Free
DISC	Domestic International Sales Corp.
DO	District Office (U.S. Commerce Department)
DOC	US Department of Commerce
DPACT	Defense Policy Advisory Committee on Trade
DRAM	Dynamic Random Access Memory

E

EAA	Export Administration Act
EBRD	European Bank for Reconstruction and Development
EC	European Community
ECE	Economic Commission for Europe
ECLS	Export Contact List Services (U.S. Commerce Department)
ECO/COM	Economic/Commercial Section
EDA	Economic Development Administration (U.S. Commerce Department)
EDO	Export Development Officer
EEA	European Economic Area
EEBIC	Eastern Europe Business Information Center (U.S. Commerce Department)
EEC	European Economic Committee
EFTA	European Free Trade Assocation
EMS	European Monetary System
EMU	European Monetary Unit
EOD	Entrance on Duty
EPC	Economic Policy Council
EPROM	Electronically Programmable Read-Only Memory
EPS	Export Promotion Services
ESA	European Space Agency
ESCMIA	Education, Scientific & Cultural Material Import Act
ETC	Export Trading Company
ETSI	European Telecommunications Standards Institute
EU	European Union
EXIM BANK	Export-Import Bank of the U.S.

F

FAM	Foreign Affairs Manual
FAS	Foreign Agriculture Service (U.S. Agriculture Department)
FBP	Foreign Buyer Program (U.S. Commerce Department)
FCIA	Foreign Credit Insurance Association
FCO	Foreign Commonwealth Office
FCPA	Foreign Corrupt Practices Act
FCS	Foreign Commercial Service (U.S. Commerce Department)

FDIUS	Foreign Direct Investment in the US
FET	Foreign Economics Trends Report (U.S. Commerce Department)
FIRA	Foreign Investment Review Corporation
FMC	Federal Maritime Commission
FMS	Foreign Military Sales
FMSCR	Foreign Military Sales Credit
FMV	Foreign Market Value
FOB	Free on Board
FOGS	Functioning of the GATT System
FOIA	Freedom of Information Act
FR	Federal Register
FSC	Foreign Sales Corporation
FSN	Foreign Service National
FSO	Foreign Service Officer
FTA	Free Trade Area or Free Trade Agreement
FTS	Federal Telecommunications System
FTZ	Foreign Trade Zone
FTZ-board	Federal Trade Zones Board
FTZ-SZ	FTZ-Subzone
FUPDOL	Foreign Unit Price in Dollars
FV	Fair Value
FX	Foreign Exchange Service

G

GATT	General Agreement on Tariffs & Trade
GDP	Gross Domestic Product
GNG	Group of Negotiations on Goods
GNP	Gross National Product
GNS	Group of Negotiations on Services
GP-zones	General Purpose FTZs
GSP	Generalized System of Preferences

H

HM	Home Market
HTS	Harmonized Tariff Schedule Nomenclature

I

IA	Import Administration (U.S. Department of Commerce)
IC	Integrated Circuit or Industry Committee of the OECD
ICA	International Coffee Agreement or International Cocoa Agreement
ICAO	International Civil Aviation Organization
ICB	International Commodity Bodies
ICC	International Chamber of Commerce
ICO	International Coffee Organization
IDA	International Development Association
IDB	Inter-American Development Bank
IDCA	International Development Bank
IEP	International Economic Policy (U.S. Commerce Department)
IEPG	Independent European Program Group
IESC	International Executive Service Corps.
IFA	International Franchise Association

IFAC	Industry Functional Advisory Committee
IFC	International Finance Corporation
IFI	International Finance Institution
IMF	International Monetary Fund
INR	Initial Negotiating Right
INRA	International Natural Rubber Agreement
INRO	International Natural Rubber Organization
INTELSAT	International Telecommunication Satellite Organization
IOGA	Industry-Organized Government-Approved
IOS	International Organization for Standardization
IPAC	Industry Policy Advisory Committee
IPC	Integrated Program for Commodities
IPR	Intellectual Property Rights
ISA	International Sugar Agreement
ISAC	Industry Sector Advisory Committee
ISO	International Standards Organization
ITA	International Trade Administration (U.S. Commerce Department)
ITA	International Tin Agreement
ITC	International Trade Commission

J

JCCT	(U.S.-Mexico) Joint Commission on Commerce & Trade
JCP	Japan Corporate Program
JETRO	Japan External Trade Organization

L

LAFTA	Latin America Free Trade Area
LC	Letter of Credit
LDC	Less Developed Country
LDDC	Least (or Lesser) Developed Countries
LTA	Long-Term Agreement
LTFV	Less Than Fair Value

M

MDB	Multilateral Development Banks
MFA	Multi-Fiber Arrangement
MFN	Most Favored Nation
MITI	Ministry of International Trade & Industry (Japan)
MKR	Matchmaker Program (U.S. Commerce Department)
MNC	Multinational Corporation
MOCP	Market Oriented Cooperation Plan
MOFERT	Ministry of Foreign Economic Relations & Trade (PRC)
MOSS	Market-Oriented Sector-Selective (U.S.-Japan)
MOU	Memorandum of Understanding
MPT	Ministry of Post & Telecommunication
MT	Metric Tons
MTN	Multilateral Trade Negotiations

N

NAFTA	North American Free Trade Agreement
NCUSCT	National Council for U.S.-China Trade
NIC	Newly Industrialized Country
NIS	Newly Independent States
NME	Non-Market Economy
NOAA	National Oceanic & Atmospheric Administration (U.S. Commerce Department)
NP	Nairobi Protocol
NPIS	New Product Information Services
NSC	National Security Council
NTB	No-Tariff Barrier
NTDB	National Trade Data Bank
NTE	New to Export
NTIA	National Telecommunications & Information Administration (U.S. Commerce Department)
NTIS	National Technical Information Service (U.S. Commerce Department)
NTM	New to Market
NTM	Non-Tariff Measure
NTS	Non-Traffic Sensitive Costs
NTT	Nippon Telephone & Telegraph Co.

O

OAS	Organization of American States
OBR	Overseas Business Report (U.S. Commerce Department)
OECD	Organization for Economic Cooperation & Development
OEM	Original Equipment Manufacturers
OMA	Orderly Marketing Agreement
OPIC	Overseas Private Investment Corporation
OTA	Office of Technology Assessment (Congress)
OTCA	Omnibus Trade & Competitiveness Act of 1988

P

P.L. 480	Public Law-Agricultural Trade & Assistance
PAS	Paris Air Show
PEC	President's Export council
PL	Public Law
PRC	People's Republic of China
PSI	Pre-Shipment Inspection

Q

QR	Quantitative Restriction

R

R&D	Research & Development
RBP	Restrictive Business Practices
REDO	Regional Export Development Office

S

SB	Surveillance Body
SBA	Small Business Administration
SCO	Senior Commercial Officer
SDR	Special Drawing Rights
SEED	Support for East European Democracy
SFO	Solo Fair, Washington-recruited
SHAPE	Supreme Headquarters Allied Powers Europe
SIC	Standard Industrial Classification
SII	Structural Impediments Initiative
SIMIS	Single Internal Market Information Systems
SIMS	Single Internal Market Service
SIPS	Statutory Import Program Staff (U.S. Commerce Department)
SITC	Standard International Trade Classification
SM	Seminar Mission (U.S. Commerce Department)
SOGA	State-Organized Government-Approved
SP	Exporter Sales Price
STC	Security Trade Control
STE	State Trading Enterprises

T

TAA	Trade Adjustment Assistance Program
TAAC	Trade Adjustment Assistance Centers
TBAG	Technical Business Assistance Working Group
TD	Trade Development (U.S. Commerce Department)
TDP	Trade and Development Program
TELMEX	Telefono de Mexico
TF	Trade Fair Certification
TFO	Trade Fair, Overseas-recruited
TFW	Trade Fair, Washington-recruited
TIMS	Textiles Information Management System
TM	Trade Mission
TNC	Trade Negotiations Committee
TOP	Trade Opportunity Program (Commerce Department)
TPC	Trade Policy Committee
TPCC	Trade Promotion Coordinating Committee
TPIS	Trade Policy Information System
TPM	Trigger Price Mechanism
TPRG	Trade Policy Review Group
TPRM	Trade Policy Review Mechanism
TPSC	Trade Policy Staff Committee or Trade Policy Subcommittee
TRA	Trade Adjustment Allowance
TRIM	Trade-Related Investment Measure
TRIP	Trade-Related Aspects of Intellectual Property Rights

TS	Trade Specialist
TSB	Textile Surveillance Body
TSUS	Tariff Schedule of the U.S.
TWA	Trade-Weighted Average

U

UNCTAD	United Nations Conference on Trade and Development
UNCTC	United Nations Centre on Transnational Corporations
UNEP	United Nations Environment Program
UNESCO	United Nations Educational, Scientific & Cultural Organization
UNIDO	United Nations Industrial Development Organization
USDIA	U.S. Direct Investment Abroad
US&FCS	U.S. & Foreign Commercial Service (U.S. Department of Commerce)
USC	U.S. Code
USCITCA	U.S.-China Industrial Technological Cooperation Accord
USCJCCT	U.S.-China Joint Commission on Commerce & Trade
USDOC	U.S. Department of Commerce
USEC	US Mission to European Communities
USITC	U.S. International Trade Commission
USKJCC	U.S.-Korea Joint Committee on Commercial Cooperation
USOECD	U.S. Mission to the Organization for Economic Cooperation & Development
USP	United States Price
USTCC	U.S.-Thailand Commercial Commission
USTR	United States Trade Representative
USTTA	United States Travel & Tourism Administration (U.S. Commerce Department)
USUN	U.S. Mission to the United Nations

V

VARs	Value-Added Resellers
VAT	Value-Added Tax
VC	Video Catalog Show (U.S. Commerce Department)
VER	Voluntary Export Restraint
VRA	Voluntary Restraint Agreement

W

WEPZA	World Export Processing Zones Association
WIPO	World Intellectual Property Organization
WTDR	World Traders Data Report
WTO	World Trade Organization

World Commercial Holidays

Many commercial holidays occur on a different calendar date from year to year. Holidays and even weekends often vary from country to country, and from region to region.

In cases where holidays fall on Saturday or Sunday, commercial establishments may be closed the preceding Friday or following Monday.

For many countries, such as those in the Moslem world, holiday dates can be only approximated because the holidays are based on actual lunar observation and exact dates are announced only shortly before they occur. Note that references to the Moslem holidays often vary in spelling and dates, and that businesses in many Moslem countries are closed on Fridays.

This calendar is intended as a working guide only. Corroboration of dates is suggested in final business travel planning.

Algeria

January 1	New Year's
March/April	Aid-El-Fitr
May 1	Labor Day
May/June	Aid-El-Adha
June 19	Revolutionary Recovery Day
June/July	Awal Mouharrem
June/July	Achoura
July 5	Independence Day
August/September	El-Mawlid-En-Nabaoui
November 1	Revolution Day

Angola

January 1	New Year's
February 4	Beginning of Liberation
March 27	Victory or Carnival Day
May 1	Workers' Day
September 17	Memorial Day for A. Neto
November 11	Independence Day
December 10	MPLA Day
December 25	Family Day

Antigua

January 1	New Year's
March/April	Good Friday
March/April	Easter Monday
May 3	Labor Day
May/June	Whit Monday
July 5	Caricom Day
August 2-3	Carnival
November 1	Independence Day
December 25	Christmas
December 26	Boxing Day

Argentina

January 1	New Year's
March/April	Good Friday
May 1	Labor Day
May 25	Revolution Day
June	Sovereignty Day
June	Flag Day
July 9	Independence Day
August 16 or 17	Death of San Martin
October 12	Columbus Day
December 25	Christmas

Australia

January 1	New Year's
March/April	Good Friday
March/April	Easter Monday
April	ANZAC Day
June	Queen's Birthday
December 25	Christmas
December 26	Boxing Day

Austria

January 1	New Year's
January 6	Epiphany
March/April	Easter Monday
May 1	Labor Day
May	Ascension
May/June	Whit Monday
May/June	Corpus Christi
August 15	Assumption
October 26	Flag Day
November 1	All Saints
December 8	Immaculate Conception
December 25	Christmas
December 26	St. Stephen's Day

Bahamas

January 1	New Year's
March/April	Good Friday
March/April	Easter Monday
June 5	Labor Day
May/June	Whit Monday
July 10	Independence Day
August	Emancipation Day
October 12	Discovery Day
December 25	Christmas
December 26	Boxing Day

Bahrain

January 1	New Year's
March/April	Eid Al Fitr
May/June	Eid Al Adha
July	Islamic New Year

June/July	Ashura
September	Prophet's Birthday
December 16	National Day

Bangladesh

February/March	Shab-E-Barat
February 21	Martyrs' Day
March/April	Shab-E-Qdr
March/April	Jumat-Ul-Wida
March/April	Eid-Ul-Fitr
April	Bengali New Year's
April	Buddha Purnima
May 1	May Day
June	Eid-Ul-Azha
July	Muharram
September	Eid-E-Miladdun Nabi
September/October	Durgah Puja
November 7	National Indegrity Day
December 16	Victory Day
December 25	Christmas

Barbados

January 1	New Year's
January 21	Errol Barrow's Birthday
March/April	Good Friday
March/April	Easter Monday
May 1	Labor Day
May/June	Whit Monday
August 2	Kadooment Day
October 4	United Nations Day
November 30	Independence Day
December 25	Christmas
December 27	Boxing Day

Belgium

January 1	New Year's
March/April	Easter Monday
May 1	Belgian Labor Day
May	Ascension
May/June	Whit Monday
July	Belgian Independence Day
August	Assumption
November	All Stants
November 11	Veterans' Day
December 25	Christmas
Regional Holidays:	
July	Flanders region
September	Wallonia region

Belize

January 1	New Year's
March	Baron Bliss Day
March/April	Good Friday
March/April	Easter Monday
May 1	Labor Day
May	Commonwealth Day
September 10	Battle of St. George's Caye
September 21	Independence Day
October	PanAmerican Day
November	Garifuna Settlement Day
December 25	Christmas
December 26	Boxing Day

Bolivia

January 1	New Year's
February/March	Carnival
March/April	Good Friday
May 1	Bolivian Labor Day
May/June	Corpus Christi
August 6	Bolivian Independence Day
November	All Saints
December 25	Christmas
Regional Holidays:	
February 10	Oruro's Local Day
April 5	Tarija's Local Day
May 25	Chuquisaca's Local Day
July 16	La Paz' Local Day
September 24	Santa Cruz' & Pando's Local Day
November 10	Potosi's Local Day
November 18	Beni's Local Day

Botswana

January 1	New Year's
January 2	Public Holiday
March/April	Good Friday
March/April	Public Holiday
March/April	Easter Monday
May	Ascension
July	President's Day
July	Public Holiday
September 30	Botswana Day
October 1	Public Holiday
December 25	Christmas
December 26	Boxing Day

Brazil

January 1	New Year's
January 20	San Sebastian Day
February/March	Carnival
February/March	Ash Wednesday
March/April	Good Friday
March/April	Tiradentes' Day
May 1	Labor Day
May/June	Corpus Christi
June 24	St. John's Day
July 2	Bahia Independence Day
July 16	N.S. Do Carmo Receife
September 7	Independence Day
October 12	N. Sra. Aparecida
November 2	All Souls
December 8	Immaculate Conception
December 25	Christmas

Bulgaria

January 1	New Year's
March 3	Liberation Day from the Ottomon Yoke Day
May 1	Labor Day
May	Cyril & Methodius Day
September	Liberation from Fascism
December 25	Christmas

Burma

January 4	Independence Day
February 12	Union Day
March 2	Peasants' Day
February/March	Full Moon of Tabaung
March 27	Armed Forces Day
April	Thingyan-Water Festival
April	Burmese New Year
May 1	Workers' Day
May	Full Moon of Kason
July 19	Martyrs' Day
July/August	Full Moon of Waso
October	Full Moon of Thadingyut
November/December	National Day
December 25	Christmas

Cameroon

January 1	New Year's
February	Youth Day
March/April	Good Friday
March/April	End of Ramadan
May 1	Labor Day
May	Ascension
May 20	National Day
70 days after End of Ramdan	Fete du Moutan
August 15	Assumption
December 25	Christmas

Canada

January 1	New Year's
March/April	Good Friday
March/April	Easter Monday
May	Victoria Day— most businesses in the province of Quebec are open.
July 1	Canada Day
September	Labor Day
October	Thanksgiving Day
November 11	Remembrance Day— all businesses closed until 11:00 am.
December 25	Christmas
December 26	Boxing Day

In the Province of Quence, commercial businesses are open after 1 p.m. on holidays. In Canada, national holidays are established by federal statute, which provides that when a holiday falls on a Saturday or Sunday, it is observed on the following Monday.

Chad

January 1	New Year's
March/April	Aid-El-Fitr
March/April	Easter Monday
May 1	Labor Day
May/June	African Liberation Day
May/June	Aid-El-Adha
August 11	Chad Independence Day
September	Maouloud-El-Nebi
November 28	Proclamation of the Republic
December	Freedom/Democracy Day
December 25	Christmas

Chile

January 1	New Year's
March/April	Good Friday
May 1	Labor Day
May 21	Combate Naval de Iquique
May/June	Corpus Christi
June 29	Saints Peter & Paul
August 15	Assumption
September 11	Official Holiday
September 18	Independence Day
September 19	Armed Forces Day
October 12	Columbus Day
November 1	All Saints
December 25	Christmas

China, People's Republic of

January 1	New Year's
January/February	Spring Festival
May 1	International Labor Day
October 1-2	National Day

Columbia

January 1	New Year's
January 6	Epiphany
March	St. Joseph's Day
March/April	Holy Thursday
March/April	Good Friday
May 1	Labor Day
May	Ascension
May/June	Corpus Christi
June	Feast of the Sacred Heart
June/July	Saints Peter & Paul
August 7	Battle of Boyaca
August	Assumption
October	Columbus Day
November	All Saints
November	Independence of Cartegena
December 25	Christmas

From December 26 through January 1 (Folklore Festival), offices are open only from 8:00 a.m. to 1:00 p.m.

Regional Holidays:

February/March	Carnival, Barranquilla

Congo

January 1	New Year's
March/April	Easter
May 1	Labor Day
May	Ascension
May 31	Pentecost
June 10	Independence Day
August 15	National Day
November 1	All Saints
December 24	Christmas

Costa Rica

January 1	New Year's
March 19	St. Joseph's Day
April 11	Juan Santamaria
March/April	Holy Thursday
March/April	Good Friday
May 1	Labor Day
May/June	Corpus Christi
June 29	Saints Peter & Paul
September 25	Independence Day
October 12	Columbus Day
December 25	Christmas

Cyprus

January 1	New Year's
January 6	Epiphany
February/March	Clean Monday-start of Lent
March 25	Greek Independence Day
April 1	Eoka Day
March/April	Good Friday
March/April	Holy Saturday
March/April	Easter Monday
May 1	Labor Day
August 3	Makarios Memorial Day
August 15	Assumption
October 1	Cyprus Independence Day
October 28	OHI Day
December 24	Christmas Eve
December 25	Christmas
December 26	Boxing Day

Czech Republic

January 1	New Year's
March/April	Easter Monday
May 1	Labor Day
May	Liberation Day
July 5	Cyril & Methodius Day
July 6	Jam Bus
October 28	Republic Day
December 24-26	Christmas

Denmark

January 1	New Year's
March/April	Maundy Thursday
March/April	Good Friday
March/April	Easter Monday
April/May	Prayer Day
May	Ascension
May/June	Whit Monday
June 5 half-day	Constitution Day
December 25	Christmas
December 26	Second Christmas Day

June 4 (Constitution Day), December 24 and 31 are traditional half-day holidays and most businesses and banks will be closed.

Dominican Republic

January 1	New Year's
January 6	Epiphany
January 21	Nuestra Sra. de la Altagracia
February 27	Dominicar Independence Day
March/April	Good Friday
May 1	Dominical Labor Day
May/June	Corpus Christi
September 24	Dia de Ntra. Sra de Las Mercedes
December 25	Christmas

Ecuador

January 1	New Year's
February/March	Carnival
March/April	Good Friday
May 1	Labor Day
July	Bolivar's Birthday
August 10	Independence Day
October	Independence of Guayaquil
October 12	Columbus Day
November 2	All Souls
November 3	Independence of Cuenca
December 25	Christmas

Egypt

January 1	New Year's
March/April	Sham El Nessim
April	Ramadan Bairam
April 25	Sinai Liberation Day
May 1	Labor Day
June/July	Kurban Bairam
July 23	National Day
October 6	Armed Forces Day

El Salvador

January 1	New Year's
March/April	Holy Thursday
March/April	Good Friday

May 1	Labor Day
August 3-6	San Salvador Feasts
September 15	Independence Day
October 12	Columbus Day
November 2	All Souls
November 5	Anniversary of First Cry of Independence
December 25	Christmas

Ethiopia

January 7	Ethiopian Christmas
January	Ethiopian Epiphany
March 2	Victory of Adwa
March/April	Easter Sunday
March/April	Good Friday
March/April	Id Al-Fitr
April 6	Victory Day
May 1	International Labor Day
May/June	Id Al-Adha
September	Ethiopian New Year
September/October	Birthday of Mohammed

Fiji

January 1	New Year's
March/April	Good Friday
March/April	Easter Saturday
March/April	Easter Monday
June 2	Ratu Sir Lala Sukuna
June 15	Queen's Birthday
July 27	Constitution Day
September/October	Prophet Mohammed's Birthday
October 12	Fiji Day
October 26	Diwali
November 16	Prince Charles' Birthday
December 25	Christmas
December 26	Boxing Day

Finland

January 1	New Year's
January 6	Epiphany
March/April	Good Friday
March/April	Easter Monday
May 1	May Day
May	Ascension
May/June	Whitsun Eve
June	Midsummer's Eve
June	Midsummer's Day
October/November	All Saints
December 6	Independence Day
December 24	Christmas Eve
December 25	Christmas
December 26	Second Christmas Day

France

January 1	New Year's
March/April	EasterMonday
May 1	Labor Day
May 8	Veteran's Day-World War II
May	Ascension
May/June	Whit/Pentecost Monday
July 14	Bastille Day/French National Day
August 15	Assumption
November 1	All Saints
November 11	Armistice Day-World War I
December 25	Christmas

Gabon

January 1	New Year's
March/April	Easter Monday
May 1	Labor Day
May 31	Pentecost Monday
August	Assumption
August 17	Independence Day
November 1	All Saints
December 25	Christmas

Germany

January 1	New Year's
March/April	Good Friday
March/April	Easter Monday
May 1	Labor Day
May	Ascension
May/June	Whit Monday
October 3	Day of German Unity
November	Repentance Day
December 25	Christmas
December 26	Second Day of Christmas

Ghana

January 1	New Year's
March 6	Independence Day
March/April	Good Friday
March/April	Easter Monday
May 1	Labor/May Day
June 4	Uprising Day
July 1	Republic Day
December 25	Christmas
December 26	Boxing Day
December 31	Revolution Day

Greece

January 1	New Year's
January 6	Epiphany
February/March	Clean Monday
March 25	Greek Independence Day
March/April	Good Friday
March/April	Easter Sunday
March/April	Easter Monday
May 1	May Day
August 15	Assumption
October 28	OXI Day
December 25	Christmas
December 26	Boxing Day

Grenada

January 1	New Year's
February 7	Independence Day
March/April	Good Friday
March/April	Easter Monday
May 1	Labor Day
May/June	Whit Monday
May/June	Corpus Christi
August 5-6	Emancipation Day
October 25	Thanksgiving Day
December 25	Christmas
December 26	Boxing Day

Guatemala

January 1	New Year's
March/April	Holy Thursday
March/April	Good Friday
March/April	Holy Saturday
March/April	Easter
May 1	Labor Day
June 30	Army Day
August 15	Assumption
September 15	Independence Day
October 20	Revolution Day
November 1	All Saints
December 24-from noon	Christmas Eve
December 25	Christmas
December 31-from noon	New Year's Eve

When an official holiday falls on a Sunday, the following Monday is observed by several labor unions, the banking system and government agencies.

Guinea

January 1	New Year's
April 3	Declaration of Second Republic
March/April	End of Ramadan
May 1	Labor Day
Mid-June	Tabaski
August 15	Assumption
October 2	Independence Day
September	Prophet Mohammed's Birthday
December 25	Christmas

Guyana

January 1	New Year's
February	Republic Anniversary
March	Phagwah
March/April	Good Friday
March/April	Easter Monday
May 1	Labor Day
May/June	Eid-Ul-Azah
July	Caribbean Day
August	Freedom Day
August/September	Youm-Un-Nabi
Fall	Deepavali

December 25	Christmas
December 26	Boxing Day

Haiti

January 1-2	New Year's and Independence Day
February/March	Lundi Gras
February/March	Mardi Gras
March/April	Good Friday
May 18	Flag Day
May	Ascension
June 10	Corpus Christi
November 2	All Souls
November 18	Battle of Vertieres
December 25	Christmas
December 31	New Year's Eve

Honduras

January 1	New Year's
March/April	Holy Thursday
March/April	Good Friday
April 14	Pan American Day
May 1	Labor Day
September	Independence Day
October 3	General Francisco Morazan's Day
October 12	Columbus Day
October 21	Armed Forces Day
December 25	Christmas

Hong Kong

January 1	New Year's
January/February	Lunar New Year's Holiday
March/April	Good Friday
March/April	Easter Monday
June	Dragon Boat Festival
June	Queen's Birthday
August 31	Liberation Day
October	Day following Chung Yeung Festival
December 25	Christmas

Hungary

January 1	New Year's
March 15	1848 Revolution Day
March/April	Easter Monday
May 1	Labor Day
August 20	St. Stephen's Day
October 23	Republic Day
December 25	Christmas
December 26	Boxing Day

Iceland

January 1	New Year's
March/April	Maundy Thursday
March/April	Good Friday
March/April	Easter Monday

April	First Day of Summer
May 1	Labor Day
May	Ascension
May/June	Whit Monday
June 17	Icelandic National Day
August	Bank Holiday
December 24	Christmas Eve
December 25	Christmas
December 31	New Year's Eve

India

January 1	New Year's
January 26	Republic Day
March	Maha Shivratri
March	Holi
March/April	Idu'l Fitr
April	Mahavir Jayanti
March/April	Good Friday
May	Buddha Purnima
June	Idu'l Zuha-Bakrid
July 11	Muharram
August 15	Independence Day
August	Janmashtami
September 10	Milad-Un-Nabi
October 2	Mahatma Gandhi's Birthday
October 5	Dussehra
October 25	Diwali
November	Guru Nanak's Birthday
December 25	Christmas

Indonesia

January 1	New Year's
January/February	Ascension of Mohammed
March	Saka New Year Hindu, Bali
March/April	Idul Fitri
March/April	Good Friday
May	aisak-Buddha, Bali
May	Ascension of Christ
June	Idul Adha Haj New Year
June/July	1st Muharam-Moslem New Year
August 17	Independence Day
September	Mohammed's Birthday
December 25	Christmas

Ireland

January 1	New Year's
March 17	St. Patrick's Day
March/April	Good Friday
March/April	Easter Monday
June	June Bank Holiday
August	August Bank Holiday
October	October Bank Holiday
December 25	Christmas
December 26	St. Stephen's Day

Israel

March/April	Passover-first day
March/April	Passover-last day
April/May	Independence Day
May/June	Pentecost-Shavuot
September	Rosh Hashana-Jewish New Year
September/October	Yom Kippur-Day of Atonement
September/October	Succot-Feast of Tabernacles
September/October	Simhat Tora-Rejoicing of the Law
December	Hanukkah

Italy

January 1	New Year's
January 6	Epiphany
March/April	Easter Monday
April 25	Anniversary of the Liberation
May 1	Labor Day
August 15	Assumption
December 25	Christmas
December 26	St. Stephen's Day

Jamaica

January 1	New Year's
February/March	Ash Wednesday
March/April	Good Friday
May	Labor Day
August	Independence Day
October	National Heroes' Day
December 25	Christmas
December 26	Boxing Day

Japan

January 1	New Year's
January 15	Adults' Day
February 11	National Foundation Day
March	Vernal Equinox Day
April 29	Greenery Day
May 3	Constitution Day
May 5	Children's Day
September 15	Respect for the Aged Day
October	Sports Day
November 3	Culture Day
November 23	Labor Thanksgiving Day
December 23	Emperor's Birthday

In addition to government holidays, most Japanese companies and government offices traditionally close for several days during the New Year's holiday season.

Jordan

January/February	Prophet Mohammad's Ascension Day
March/April	Easter
March/April	Id Al-Fitr

May 25	Independence Day
May/June	Id Al-Adha
June 10	Great Arab Revolt & Army Day
June	Islamic New Year
August 11	King Hussein's Accession to the Throne
September	Prophet Mohammad's Birthday
November 14	King Hussein's Birthday

Kenya

January 1	New Year's
March/April	Good Friday
March/April	Easter Monday
May 1	Labor Day
June 1	Madaraka Day
October	Kenyatta Day
December 25	Christmas

Korea

January 1-2	New Year's
January/February	Lunar New Year's
March 1	Independence Movement Day
March/April	Arbor Day
May 5	Children's Day
June 6	Memorial Day
July 17	Constitution Day
August 15	Independence Day
September	Korean Thanksgiving Days
October 3	National Foundation Day
December 25	Christmas

Kuwait

January 1-3	New Year's
January/February	Ascension
February 25	National Day
February 26-27	Liberation Holiday
March/April	Eid Al-Fitr
May/June	Eid Al-Adha
June	Waqfa
July	Islamic New Year
September	Prophet's Birthday

Lebanon

January 1	New Year's
February 9	St. Maron's Day
April	Feast of Ramadan-Al Fitr
March/April	Good Friday-Western
March/April	Easter Monday-Western
March/April	Good Friday-Eastern
March/April	Easter Monday-Eastern
May 1	Lebanese Labor Day
May/June	Feast of Al-Adha
July	Moslem New Year-Al Hijra

July	Feast of Al-Ashura
August 15	Assumption
September	Prophet's Birthday
November 1	All Saints
November 22	Independence Day
December 25	Christmas

Liberia

January 1	New Year's
February 11	Armed Forces Day
March	Decoration Day
March 15	JJ Roberts' Birthday
April 12	National Redemption Day
March/April	Good Friday
May 14	Unification Day
July 26	Independence Day
August	Flag Day
November	Thanksgiving Day
November 29	William VS Tubman's Birthday
December 25	Christmas

Luxembourg

January 1	New Year's
February/March	Shrove Monday
March/April	Easter Monday
May 1	Luxembourg Labor Day
May	Ascension
May/June	Whit Monday
June 23	Grand Duke's Birthday
August 15	Assumption
November 1	All Saints
November 2	All Souls
December 25	Christmas
December 26	Second Day of Christmas

Madagascar

January 1	New Year's
March 29	Day Commemorating the Martyrs of the Malagasy Revolution
March/April	Easter Monday
May 1	Labor Day
May	Ascension
May/June	Whit Monday
June 26	Independence Day
August 15	Assumption
November 1	All Saints
December 25	Christmas

Malawi

January 1	New Year's
March 3	Martyrs Day
March/April	Good Friday
March/April	Easter Monday
May 14	Kamuzu Day
July 6	Republic Day
October 18	Mother's Day

December 21	Tree Planting Day
December 25	Christmas
December 26	Boxing Day

Malaysia

January 1	New Year's
February 1	Kuala Lumpur City Day
February	Chinese New Year's
March/April	Hari Raya Ruasa
May 1	Malaysian Labor Day
May	Wesak Day
June 5	King's Birthday
June	Hari Raya Haji
June/July	Awal Muharram
August 31	Malaysian National Day
September	Prophet Mohammad's Birthday
October/November	Deepavali
December 25	Christmas

Malta

January 1	New Year's
February 10	St. Paul
March 19	St. Joseph
March 31	Freedom Day
March/April	Good Friday
June 7	Sette Giugno
June 29	Saints Peter and Paul
September 8	Victory Day
September 21	Independence Day
December 8	Immaculate Conception
December 13	Republic Day
December 25	Christmas

Mauritania

January 1	New Year's
March 8	Women's Day
March/April	Id El-Fitr, End of Ramadan
May 1	Labor Day
May 25	Africa Day
May/June	Id-ElAdha, Tabaski
July	Muslim New Year
July 10	Armed Forces Day
September	Id El Maouloud El Nabi
November 28	Mauritian Independence Day
December 12	Anniversary of the Restructuring of CMSN

Mexico

January 1	New Year's
February 5	Anniversary of Mexican Constitution
March 21	Benito Juarez' Birthday
March/April	Holy Thursday
March/April	Good Friday
May 1	Mexican Labor Day
May 5	Anniversary of the Battle of Puebla
September 16	Mexican Independence Day
October 12	Dia de la Raza & Columbus Day
November 2	All Souls
November 20	Anniversary of the Mexican Revolution
December 25	Christmas

Morocco

January 1	New Year's
January 11	National Day
March 3	Feast of the Throne
March/April	Aid El Fitr
May 1	Labor Day
May 23	National Day
May/June	Aid El Adha
June/July	Moslem New Year
July 9	King's Birthday
August 14	Ouad Eddahab Day
August 20	National Day
September	Prophet's Birthday
November 6	Green March Day
November 18	Independence Day

Mozambique

January 1	New Year's
February 3	Day of Mozambican Heroes
April 7	Womens' Day
May 1	Workers' Day
June 25	Independence Day
September 7	Lusaka Agreement
September 25	Revolution Day
November 10	Maputo City Day
December 25	Christmas

Nepal

January	Martyrs' Day
February	National Democracy Day
February/March	Shivaratri
March 8	Women's Day (half-holiday for women only)
March/April	Ramnavami
April	New Year's Day
April/May	Mothers' Day
July	Teachers' Day
August	Janai Purnima
August/September	Krishnashtami
August/September	Fathers' Day
August/September	Teej (for women only)
September	Rishi Panchami (for women only)
September/October	Ghatasthapana
October	Dasain Festival
October/November	Tihar Festival
December 29	King Birendra's Birthday

World Commercial Holidays

Netherlands

January 1	New Year's
March/April	Good Friday
March/April	Easter Monday
April 30	Queen's Birthday
May 5	Liberation Day
May	Ascension
May/June	Whit Monday
December 25	Christmas
December 26	Boxing Day

Netherlands, Antilles & Aruba

January 1	New Year's
February/March	Carnival Monday
March/April	Good Friday
March/April	Easter Monday
April 30	Queen's Birthday
May 1	Labor Day
May	Ascension
December 25	Christmas
December 26	Boxing Day

New Zealand

January 1-2	New Year's
February 6	Waitangi Day
March/April	Good Friday
March/April	Easter Monday
April 25	ANZAC Day
June	Queen's Birthday
October	Labor Day
December 25	Christmas
December 26	Boxing Day

Nicaragua

January 1	New Year's
March/April	Holy Thursday
March/April	Good Friday
May 1	Labor Day
July 19	Sandinista Revolution Anniversary
August 1	Festival of Santo Domingo
September 14	Battle of San Jacinto
September 15	Independence Day
December 8	Immaculate Conception
December 24	Christmas Eve
December 25	Christmas

Niger

January 1	New Year's
March 23	Ramadan
March/April	Easter Monday
May 1	Niger Labor Day
May/June	Aid-al Adha
August 3	National Independence Day
August 28	Mouloud
December 18	Niger Republic Day
December 25	Christmas

The exact dates of the religious holidays are tentative, to be determined based on lunar sightings.

Nigeria

January 1	New Year's
March/April	Good Friday
March/April	Easter Monday
April	Eid-el-Fitr
May 1	Workers' Day
October 1	National Day
December 25	Christmas
December 26	Boxing Day

Norway

January 1	New Year's
March/April	Holy Thursday
March/April	Good Friday
March/April	Easter Monday
May 1	Labor Day
May 17	Constitution Day
May	Ascension
May/June	Whit Monday
December 25	Christmas
December 26	Second Christmas Day

Oman

January	New Year's
January/February	Ascension
March/April	Eid Al-Fitr
May/June	Eid Al-Adha
June/July	Islamic New Year
September	Birth of the Prophet
November	National Day
December	Christmas

Pakistan

March	Pakistan Day
March/April	Eid-Ul-Fitr
May 1	May Day
May/June/July	Eid-Ul-Azha
June/July	9th & 10th of Moharram
August 14	Independence Day
September 6	Defense of Pakistan Day
August/September	Eid-I-Milad-Un-Nabi
September 11	Death Anniversary of the Quaid-E-Azam
November 9	Iqbal Day
December 25	Birthday of Quaid-E-Azam

Panama

January 1	New Year's
January 9	Mourning Day
February/March	Carnival
March/April	Good Friday
May 1	Labor Day
November 3	Independence Day-Panama from Columbia
November 10	Uprising of Los Santos
November 28	Independence Day-Panama from Spain
December 8	Mothers' Day
December 25	Christmas

Paraguay

January 1	New Year's
February 3	St. Plas, Patron of Paraguay
March 1	Heroes' Day
March/April	Holy Thursday
March/April	Good Friday
May 1	Labor Day
May 15	Independence Day
June 12	Chaco Armistice
August 15	Founding of City of Asuncion
December 8	Virgin of Caacupe
December 25	Christmas

Peru

January 1	New Year's
March/April	Holy Thursday
March/April	Good Friday
May 1	Labor Day
June 24-afternoon	Countryman's Day
June 29	Saints Peter & Paul
August 30	St. Rose of Lima
October 8	Battle of Angamos
November 1	All Saints
December 8	Immaculate Conception
December 25	Christmas

Philippines

January 1	New Year's
April 9	Heroism Day
March/April	Maundy Thursday
March/April	Good Friday
May 1	Labor Day
June 12	Independence Day
August	National Heroes' Day
November 1	All Saints
November 30	Bonifacio Day
December 25	Christmas
December 30	Rizal Day

Regional holidays: June 24 (Manila Day), August 19 (Quezon City Day).

Poland

January 1	New Year's
March/April	Easter Monday
May 1	Labor Day
May 3	Constitution Day
May/June	Corpus Christi
August 15	Assumption
November 1	All Saints
November 11	National Independence Day
December 25	Christmas
December 26	Boxing Day

Portugal

January 1	New Year's
February/March	Carnival
March/April	Good Friday
April 25	Liberty Day
May 1	May Day
June 10	Portugal Day
June 13	St. Anthony's Day
May/June	Corpus Christi
August 15	Assumption
October 5	Portuguese Republic Day
November 1	All Saints
December 1	Portuguese Independence Day
December 8	Immaculate Conception
December 25	Christmas

Romania

January 1-2	New Year's
May 1	Labor Day
December 1	National Day
December 25	Christmas

Russia

January 1	New Year's
March 8	International Women's Day
May 1-2	International Labor Day
May 9	Victory Day-WWII

The Republics that have comprised the USSR will legislate different holidays than those celebrated under communism. Holidays on the preceding list are those that the US Embassy in Moscow believes might continue to exist in at least some of the Republics. 1991 was the last year for October 7 (Revolution Day) and November 7-8 (October Revolution Day).

Saudi Arabia

March/April	Id-Al-Fitr/Ramadan
May/June	Id-Al-Adha/Hajj or Pilgrimage to Mecca

Senegal

January 1	New Year's
April 4	Senegalese Independence Day
March/April	Easter Monday or Paques
May 1	Senegalese Labor Day
May	Ascension
May/June	Whit Monday or Pentecost
June	Tabaski or Eid-Ul Kabir
June/July	Tamxarit/Yawmal Achoura/Muslim New Year's
August 15	Assumption
September	Maouloud/Birth of the Prophet
November 1	All Saints
December 25	Christmas

177

Sierra Leone

January 1	New Year's
March/April	Eid Ul Fitri
March/April	Good Friday
March/April	Easter Monday
April 27	Independence Day
May/June	Eid Ul-Adha
September	Moulid Um Nabi
December 25	Christmas
December 26	Boxing Day

Singapore

January 1	New Year's
January/February	Chinese New Year's
March/April	Good Friday
March/April	Hari Raya Puasa
March/April	Good Friday
May 1	Singapore Labor Day
May	Vesak Day
June	Hari Raya Haji
August 10	Singapore National Day
October/November	Deepavali
December 25	Christmas

Slovak Republic

January 1	New Year's
March/April	Easter Monday
May 1	Labor Day
November 1	Reconciliation Day
December 24-26	Christmas

Slovenia

January 1-2	New Year's
February 8	Day of Preseren—Slovene Cultural Holiday
March/April	Easter Monday
April 27	Resistance Day
May 1-2	Labor Day
June 25	Slovene State Day
August 15	Assumption
October 31	Reformation Day
November 1	All Saints
December 25	Christmas
December 26	Independence Day

South Africa

January 1	New Year's
April 6	Founder's Day
March/April	Good Friday
April	Family Day
May 1	Workers' Day
May	Ascension
May	Republic Day
October 10	Kruger Day
December 16	Day of the Vow
December 25	Christmas
December 26	Day of Goodwill

Spain

January 1	New Year's
January 6	Epiphany
March/April	Good Friday
May 1	Labor Day
August 15	Assumption
October 12	National Day
December 8	Immaculate Conception
December 25	Christmas

Sri Lanka

January	Tamil Thai Pongal Day
January	Duruthu Full Moon Pova Day
February 4	National Day
February	Navam Full Moon Poya Day
February/March	Maha Sivarathri Day
February/March	Medin Full Moon Poya Day
April	Ramazan Festival Day
April	Day prior to Sinhala & Tamil New Year's
April	Sinhala & Tamil New Year's
April 16	Bak Full Moon Poya Day
March/April	Good Friday
May 1	May Day
April/May	Wesak Full Moon Poya Day
April/May	Day following Full Moon Poya Day
May 22	National Heroes' Day
June	Hadji Festival Day
June	Poson Full Moon Poya Day
June 30	Special Bank Holiday
July	Escala Esala Full Moon Poya Day
August	Nikini Full Moon Poya Day
September	Holy Prophet's Birthday
September	Binara Full Moon Poya Day
October	Vap Full Moon Poya Day
October	Deepavali Festival
November	Il Full Moon Poya Day
December	Unduvap Full Moon Poya Day
December 25	Christmas
December 31	Special Bank Holiday

Suriname

January 1	New Year's
March 19	Holi Phagwa
March/April	Id-Al-Fitr
March/April	Good Friday

March/April	Easter Monday
May 1	Labor Day
July 1	Emancipation Day
November 25	Independence Day
December 24	Christmas
December 31	New Year's

The dates for Holi Phagwa and Id-Al-Fitr are determined by lunar sightings and the dates may vary slightly from those given.

Swaziland

January 1	New Year's
March/April	Good Friday
March/April	Easter Monday
April 19	King Mswati III's Birthday
April 25	National Flag Day
May	Ascension
July 22	Public Holiday
August/September	Reed Dance
December 25	Christmas
December 26	Boxing Day
December/January	Incwala

Sweden

January 1	New Year's
January 6	13th Day of Christmas
March/April	Good Friday
March/April	Easter Monday
May 1	First of May
May	Ascension
May/June	Whitsun
June	Midsummer
October	All Saints
December 25	Christmas
December 26	Boxing Day

Switzerland

January 1-2	New Year's & Baerzelistag Days
March/April	Good Friday
March/April	Easter Monday
May	Ascension
May/June	Whit Monday
August 1	Swiss National Day
December 25	Christmas
December 26	Boxing Day

Syria

January 1	New Year's
March 8	Revolution Day
March 21	Mother's Day
March/April	Al-Fitr
April 17	Independence Day
May 1	Labor Day
May 6	Martyrs' Day

May/June	Al-Adha
July	Moslem New Year
September	Prophet's Birthday
October 6	Tishreen War
December 25	Christmas

Taiwan, Republic of China

January 1-2	New Year's
February	New Year's Eve & Spring Festival
March 29	Youth Day
April 4	Women's & Children's Day
April 5	Festival of Sweeping of the Tombs
June	Dragon Boat Festival
September 11	Mid-Autumn Festival
September 28	Confucius' Birthday
October 10	Double Ten Day
October 25	Taiwan Restoration Day
October 31	President Chiang Kai-Shek's Birthday
November 12	Dr. Sun Yat-Sen's Birthday
December 25	Constitution Day

Thailand

January 1	New Year's
February	Magha Puja Day
April 6	King Rama I Memorial & Chakri Day
April	Songkran Day
May 5	Coronation Day
May	Plowing Ceremony Day
May	Visakha Puja Day
July	Aslha Puja Day
July	Buddhist Lent
August 12	Her Majesty the Queen's Birthday
October 23	Chulalongkorn Day
December 5	His Majesty the King's Birthday
December 10	Constitution Day
December 31	New Year's Eve

Togo

January 1	New Year's
January 13	National Liberation Day
January 24	Economic Liberation Day
March/April	Easter Monday
April 27	Independence Day
May 1	Labor Day
May	Ascension
June 8	Pentecost
June 21	Martyrs' Day
August 15	Assumption
November 1	All Saints
December 25	Christmas

Trinidad & Tobago

January 1	New Year's
March/April	Good Friday
March/April	Easter Monday
May/June	Whit Monday
June	Corpus Christi
June 19	Labor Day
August 1	Emancipation Day
August 31	Independence Day
September 24	Republic Day
December 25	Christmas
December 26	Boxing Day

Tunisia

January 1	New Year's
March 20	Independence Day
March	Youth Day
March/April	Aid Esseghir El-Fitr
April	Martyrs' Day
May 1	Labor Day
May/June	Aid El-Kebir-El Idha
July	Ras El Am El Hijri
July 25	Republic Day
August 13	Women's Day
September 9	Mouled
November 7	Memorial

Turkey

January 1	New Year's
March/April	Sugar Holiday
April 23	National Sovereignty & Children's Day
May 19	National Sovereignty & Children's Day
June	Sacrifice Holiday
August 30	Victory Day
October 28-29	Turkish Independence Day

Uganda

January 1	New Year's
January 26	Liberation Day
March/April	Good Friday
March/April	Easter Monday
March/April	Idd-El-Fitr
May 1	Labor Day
June	Martyrs' Day
July 3	Independence Day
October 9	Independence Day
December 25	Christmas
December 26	Boxing Day

Ukraine

January 1	New Year's
January 7	Orthodox Christmas
March 8	International Women's Day
May 1 and 2	Days of International Solidarity
May 9	Victory Day
August 24	Ukrainian Independence Day
November 7-8	Revolution Days

United Arab Emirates

January 1	New Year's
January/February	Ascension
March/April	Eid Al-Fitr
June	Waqfa Arafat
May/June	Eid Al-Adha
July	Islamic New Year
August	Sh. Zayed Accession Day
September	Prophet's Birthday
December 2-3	National Day
December 25	Christmas

United Kingdom

January 1	New Year's
March/April	Good Friday
March/April	Easter Bank Monday
May	May Day
May	Spring Holiday
August	Summer Bank Holiday
December 25	Christmas
December 26	Boxing Day

United States

January 1	New Year's
January 18	Martin Luther King, Jr. Day
February	Ash Wednesday
February 12	Lincoln's Birthday
February 14	Valentine's Day
February 19	Washington's Birthday, or President's Day, or Washington-Lincoln Day
March 17	St. Patrick's Day
March/April	Good Friday
March/April	Easter
April	Palm Sunday
May	Memorial Day or Decoration Day
May	Mother's Day
June	Father's Day
June 14	Flag Day
July 4	Independence Day
September	Labor Day
October	Columbus Day, or Discovers' Day, or Pioneers' Day
October 31	Halloween
November	Election Day
November 11	Veterans' Day
November 25	Thanksgiving Day
December 8-9	Hanukkah
December 25	Christmas

World Commercial Holidays

Uruguay

January 1	New Year's
January 6	Ephiphany
February/March	Carnival
March/April	Holy Week
May 1	Uruguayan Labor Day
May 18	Battle of Las Piedras
June 19	Birthday of Artigas
August 25	Uruguayan Independence Day
October 12	Columbus Day
November 2	Dia de Los Difuntos
December 25	Christmas

Venezuela

January 1	New Year's
January 6	Epiphany
March	Carnival
March	St. Joseph
March/April	Maundy Thursday
March/April	Good Friday
May 1	Labor Day
May/June	Ascension
June	Corpus Christi
June 24	Battle of Carabobo
June 29	Saints Peter & Paul
July 24	Bolivar's Birthday
October 12	Columbus Day
November	All Saints
December	Immaculate Conception
December 25	Christmas

Yemen

January 1	New Year's
February	Prophet's Ascent to Heaven in the month of Rajab
March/April	Eid Al-Fitr
May 1	Labor Day
May 22	Unification Day
May/June	Eid Al-Adha
July	Islamic New Year
September	Prophet's Birthday
September 26	Former North Yemen Revolution Day
October 14	Former South Yemen Revolution Day
November 30	Former South Yemen Independence Day

Yugoslavia

January 1-2	New Year's
May 1-2	May Day
July 4	Fighters' Day
November 29-Dec. 1	Day of the Republic

Regional holidays observed in respective republics:

January 7	Orthodox Christmas, Serbia and perhaps Macedonia
March 28	Serbian State Day
April 27	Slovenian Liberation Day
July 7	Serbian Uprising Day
July 13	Montenegrin Uprising Day
July 22	Slovenian Uprising Day
July 27	Croatian & Bosnian Uprising Day
August 2	Macedonian Uprising Day
October 11	Macedonian Uprising Day
November 1	Slovenian & Coatian Day of the Dead
November 25	Bosnian State Day

Zaire

January 1	New Year's
January 4	Day of the Martyrs for Independence
May 1	Labor Day
June 24	Anniversary of New Constitution
June 30	Independence Day
August 1	Parents' Day
October 14	Youth Day/President's Birthday
November 17	Armed Forces Day
November 24	Anniversary of the Regime
December 25	Christmas

Zambia

January 1	New Year's
March 12	Youth Day
March/April	Good Friday
March/April	Holy Saturday
May 1	Labor Day
May 25	African Freedom Day
July 6	Heroes' Day
July 7	Unity Day
August 3	Farmers' Day
October 24	Independence Day
December 25	Christmas

Zimbabwe

January 1	New Year's
March/April	Good Friday
March/April	Easter Monday
April 18	Independence Day
May 1	Workers' Day
May 25	Africa Day
August 11	Heroes' Day
August 12	Defense Forces Day
December 25	Christmas
December 26	Boxing Day

World Monetary Units

Country	Monetary Unit	Country	Monetary Unit
Afgahnistan	Afghani	Finland	Markka
Albania	Lek	France	Franc
Algeria	Dinar	Germany	Deutsche Mark
Argentine Republic	Peso	Ghana	Cedi
Australia	Dollar (Aust.)	Great Britain	Pound Sterling
Austria	Schilling	Greece	Drachma
Bahamas	Dollar (B.sh)	Guatemala	Quetzal
Belgium	Franc	Haiti	Gourde
Bolivia	Peso	Honduras	Lempira
Brazil	Real	Hungary	Forint
Bulgaria	Lev	Iceland	Krona
Burma	Kyat	India	Rupee
Canada	Dollar	Indonesia	Rupiah
Chad	Franc	Iran	Rial
Chile	Peso	Iraq	Dinar
China	Yuan	Ireland	Pound
Colombia	Peso	Israel	Shekel
Cosa Rica	Colon	Italy	Lira
Cuba	Peso	Japan	Yen
Czech, Republic of	Koruna	Kenya	Schilling
Denmark	Krone	Korea	Won
Dominican Republic	Peso	Kuwait	Dinar
Ecuador	Sucre	Latvia	Latvian Ruble/Lats
Egypt	Pound	Lebanon	Pound
El Salvador	Colon	Liberia	Dollar
Estonia	Kroons	Libya	Dinar
Ethiopia	Birr	Liechtenstein	Swiss Franc

Country	Monetary Unit	Country	Monetary Unit
Lithuania	Litas	Swaziland	Lilangeni
Luxembourg	Franc	Sweden	Krona
Malaysia	Ringgita	Switzerland	Franc
Mexico	Peso	Syria	Pound
Monaco	French Franc	Taiwan (Republic of China)	Dollar
Morrocco	Dirham	Thailand	Baht
Netherlands	Guilder	Turkey	Lira
New Zealand	Dollar (N.Z.)	United Arab Emirates	Dirham
Nicaragua	Cordoba	United States	Dollar
Nigeria	Naira	Uruguay	Peso
Norway	Krone	Venezuela	Bolivar
Pakistan	Rupee	Vietnam	Dong
Panama	Balboa	Yemen	Dinar
Paraguay	Guarani	Yugoslavia	Dinar
Peru	Sol	Zaire	Zaire
Phillipines	Peso	Zambia	Kwacha
Poland	Zloty		
Portugal	Escudo		
Romania	Leu		
Russia	Ruble		
Saudi Arabia	Riyal		
Singapore	Dollar		
Slovakia, Republic of	Koruna		
South Africa	Rand		
Spain	Peseta		
Sri Lanka	Rupee		

International Telephone Calling Codes

*To dial direct abroad from the United States, dial 011 + country code + city code + local number. To charge to a certain number or credit card, dial 01 + country code + city code + local number. *Dial 1 + 809 + local number.*

Algeria 213

American Samoa 684

Andorra 33
All points 628

Anguilla 809*

Antigua 809*
(including Barbuda)

Argentina 54
Buenos Aires 1
Cordoba 51

Armenia 7

Aruba 297
All points 8

Ascension Island 247

Australia 61
Brisbane 7
Canberra 62
Melbourne 3
Perth 9
Sydney 2

Austria 43
Graz 316
Innsbruck 512
Salzburg 662
Vienna 1 or 222

Bahamas 809

Bahrain 973

Bangladesh, Peoples Republic of 880
Dhaka 2

Barbados 809*

Belgium 32
Antwerp 3
Brussels 2
Ghent 91

Belize 501

Benin, People's Republic of 229

Bermuda 809*

Bolivia 591
La Paz 2
Santa Cruz 33

Botswana 267
Gaborone 31

Brazil 55
Brasila 61
Porto Alegre 512
Recife 81
Rio de Janeiro 21
Sao Paulo 11

British Virgin Island 809*

Brunei 673
Bandar Seri Begawan 2

Bulgaria 359
Sofia 2

Burkina Faso (upper volta) 226

Cambodia 855

Camerron, United Republic of 237

Canada (dial 1 + area code + local number)

Cape Verde Islands 238

Cayman Islands 809*

Chile 56
Santiago 2
Valparaiso 32

China, PRC 86
Beijing (Peking) 1
Ghuangzhou (Canton) 20
Shanghai 21

Colombia 57
   Barranguilla 5
   Bogota 1
   Cali 23

Cook Islands 682

Costa Rica 506

Croatia 38

Cyprus 357
   Nicosia 2

Czech, Republic of 42
   Bratislava 7
   Prague (Praha) 2

Denmark 45
   Aalborg 8
   Aarhus 6
   Copenhagen 1
     (suburbs) 2
   Odense 7

Djibouti, Republic of 253

Dominica 809

Dominican Republic 809*

Ecuador 593
   Cuenca 7
   Guayaquil 4
   Quito 2

Egypt, Arab Republic 20
   Alexandria 3
   Cairo 2

El Salavador 503

Ethiopia 251
   Addis Ababa 1

Faeroe Islands 298

Fiji Islands 679

Finland 358
   Helsinki 0

France 33
   Bordeaux 56
   Marseille 91
   Nice 93
   Paris 1

French Antilles 596

French Guiana 594

French Polynesia 689
   (including Moorea & Tahiti)

Gabon Republic 241

Gambia 220

Germany 49
   Berlin 30
   Bonn 228
   Cologne 221
   Dresden 51
   Frankfurt 69
   Hamburg 40
   Leipzig 41
   Munich 89
   Stuttgart 711

Ghana 233
   Accra 21

Gibraltar 350

Greece 30
   Athens (Athinai) 1
   Rodos 241

Greenland 299
   Godthaab 2
   Soendre Stroemfjord 11
   Thule 50

Grenada 809
   (including Carriacou)

Guadeloupe 590

Guam 671

Guantanamo Bay (U.S. Naval Base) 5399

Guatemala 502
   Guatemala City 2
   All other cities 9

Guinea, Peoples Republic of 224
   Conakry 4

Guyana 592
   Georgetown 2

Haiti 509
   Port Au Prince 1

Honduras 504

Hong Kong 852
Hong Kong 5
Kowloon 3

Hungary 36
Budapest 1

Iceland 354
Reykjavik 1

India 91
Bombay 22
Culcutta 33
New Delhi 11

Indonesia 62
Jakarta 21

Iran 98
Tehran 21

Iraq 964
Baghdad 1

Ireland 353
Cork 21
Dublin 1
Galway 91
Killarney 64

Israel 972
Haifa 4
Jerusalem 2
Tel Aviv 3

Italy 39
Florence 55
Naples 81
Rome 6
Venice 41

Ivory Coast, Republic 225

Jamaica 809

Japan (including Okinawa) 81
Hiroshima 82
Kobe 78
Kyoto 75
Nagasaki 958
Osaka 6
Tokyo 3
Yokohama 45

Jordan 962
Amman 6

Kenya, Republic of 254
Nairobi 2

Kiribati 686

Korea, Republic of 82
Pusan (Busan) 51
Seoul 2

Kuwait 965

Lebanon 961

Lesotho 266

Liberia 231

Libyan Arab People's Soc. Jamahiriya 218
Tripoli 21

Liechtenstein 41
All points 75

Lithuania 7

Luxembourg 352

Macao 853

Malawi 265

Malaysia 60
Kuala Lumpur 3

Maldives, Republic of 960

Mali Republic 223

Malta 356

Marshall Islands 692

Mauritius 230

Mexico 52
Acapulco 748
Cancun 988
Guadalajara 36
Mexico City 5
Monterrey 83
Tijuana 66

Micronesia, Fed. States 691

Monaco 33
All points 93

Montserrat 809

Morocco 212
  Casablanca (no city code)
  Marrakech 4
  Tanger (Tangiers) 9

Namibia 264
  Windhoek 61

Nepal 977

Netherlands 31
  Amsterdam 20
  The Hague 70

Netherlands Antilles 599
  Curacao 9

Nevis 809*

New Caledonia 687

New Zealand 64
  (including Chatham Island)
  Auckland 9
  Christchurch 3
  Wellington 4

Nicaragua 505
  Managua 2

Niger Republic 227

Nigeria, Fed. Republic of 234
  Lagos 1

Norway 47
  (including Svalbard)
  Bergen 5
  Oslo 2

Oman 968

Pakistan 92
  Islamabad 51
  Karachi 21

Panama, Republic of 507

Papua New Guinea 675
  (including Admiralty Islands, Bougainville, New Britian
  & New Ireland)

Paraguay 595
  Asuncion 21

Peru 51
  Arequipa 54
  Lima 14

Philippines 63
  Cebu City 32
  Dagupan 75
  Manila 2

Poland 48
  Crakow 12
  Gdansk 58
  Warsaw 22

Portugal 351
  (including Azores & Madeira Islands)
  Lisbon 1
  Ponta Del Gada 96

Qatar 974

Reunion Island 262

Romania 40
  Bucharest 0

Russia 7
  Moscow 095
  St. Petersburg 812

Rwanda 250

St. Kitts 809*

St. Lucia 809*

St. Pierre and Miquelon 508

St. Vicent & the Grenadines 809*
  (including Bequia, Mustique, Palm Island, Union Island)

Saipan 670

San Marino 39
  All points 549

Saudia Arabia 966
  Dhahran (Aramco) 3
  Jeddah 2
  Medina 4
  Riyadh 1

Senegal Republic 221

Seychelles Islands 248

Sierra Leone 232
  Freetown 22
  All other points 232

Singapore, Republic of 65

Slovakia, Republic of 42
Bratislava 7

South Africa, Republic of 27
Cape Town 21
Durban 31
Johannesburg 11
Pretoria 12

Spain 34
(including Balearic Islands, Canary Islands, Ceuta, Melilla)
Barcelona 3
Bilbao 4
Las Palmas de Gran Canaria 28
Madrid 1
Seville 54

Sri Lanka, Dem. Soc. Republic of 94
Colombo Central 1

Suriname, Republic of 597

Swaziland 268

Sweden 46
Goteborg 31
Stockholm 8

Switzerland 41
Berne 31
Geneva 22
Lucerne 41
Zurich 1

Taiwan, Republic of China 886
Taipei 2

Tanzania 255
Dar Es Salaam 51

Thailand 66
Bangkok 2
Chieng Mai 53

Togo, Republic of 228

Tonga Islands 676

Trinidad & Tobago, Dem. Republic of 809*

Tunisia 216
Tunis 1

Turkey 90
Ankara 41
Istanbul 1

Turks & Caicos Islands 809*

Uganda 256
Kampala 41

United Arab Emirates 971
Abu Dhabi 2

United Kingdom 44
(including the Channel Islands, England, Isle of Man, Northern Ireland, Scotland and Wales)
Belfast 232
Cardiff 222
Edinburgh 31
Glasgow 41
Liverpool 51
Inner London 71
Outer London 81

United States 1
New York City (Manhattan) 212
Chicago 312
Los Angeles 213/310
Washington, D.C. 202
San Francisco 415
Dallas 214

Uruguay 598
Canelones 332
Mercedes 532
Montevido 2

Vatican City 39
All points 6

Venezuela 58
Caracas 2
Maracaibo 61
Maracay 43

Western Samoa 685

Yemen Arab Republic 967
Sanaa 2

Yugoslavia 38
Belgrade (Beograd) 11

Zaire, Republic of 243
Kinshasa 12

Zambia 260
Lusaka 1

Zimbabwe 263
Harare 4

Metric Conversion Chart

English to Metric

To Convert	Into	Multiply By
Acres	Hectares	0.4047
Bushels	Cubic Meters	0.03524
Cubic Feet	Cubic Meters	0.02832
Cubic Inches	Cubic Centimeters	16.39
Feet	Meters	0.3048
Gallons	Liters	3.785
Inches	Centimeters	2.540
Inches	Millimeters	25.40
Miles	Kilometers	1.609
Ounces	Grams	28.3495
Ounces (fluid)	Liters	0.02957
Pints	Liters	0.4732
Pounds	Kilograms	0.4536
Square Feet	Square Meters	0.0929
Square Inches	Square Centimeters	6.452
Square Miles	Square Kilometers	2.590
Square Yards	Square Meters	0.8361
Tons (short)	Tons (metric)	0.9078
Yards	Meters	0.9144

Metric Information

For information about metric transition and requirements, companies can contact the U.S. Metric Association, Inc., 10245 Andasol Avenue, Northridge, CA 91325, (310) 832-3763. U.S. Government assistance is available to firms interested in changing to the metric system. Contact the U.S. Department of Commerce Metric Program at (301) 975-3690 to get advice on steps industry might take in dealing with the opportunities of metric transition. The Commerce Department's Single Internal Market Information Service (SIMIS) can answer questions on the EC's new standards program and its effects on U.S. exporters. Contact SIMIS at (202) 482-5276.

Metric to English

To Convert	Into	Multiply By
Centiliters	Ounces (fluid)	0.3382
Centimeters	Inches	0.3937
Cubic Centimeters	Cubic Inches	0.06102
Cubic Meters	Bushels	28.37
Cubic Meters	Cubic Feet	35.31
Grams	Ounces	0.03527
Hectares	Acres	2.471
Kilograms	Pounds	2.205
Kilometers	Miles	0.6214
Liters	Gallons	0.2642
Liters	Pints	2.113
Millimeters	Inches	0.03937
Meters	Feet	3.281
Meters	Yards	1.094
Square Centimeters	Square Inches	0.1550
Square Kilometers	Square Miles	0.3861
Square Meters	Square Feet	10.76
Square Meters	Square Yards	1.196
Tons (Metric)	Tons (Short)	1.10156

Temperature

To convert from Centigrade to Fahrenheit, multiply by 9/5 and then add 32.
To convert from Fahrenheit to Centigrade, subtract 32 and then multiply by 5/9.

CLASSIFICATION OF ADVERTISERS

AIR HORNS

GROVER PRODUCTS CO.
Automotive - Marine - Industrial
3504 East Olympic Blvd.
Los Angeles 90023 ... (213) 263-9981
FAX: .... (213) 268-8555

ARBITRATION

AMERICAN ARBITRATION ASSOCIATION
417 Montgomery St., 5th Floor
San Francisco 92104.(415) 981-3901
FAX: .... (415) 362-6226

ATTORNEYS

BAKER & MCKENZIE
101 West Broadway, 12th Floor
San Diego 92101 .... (619) 236-1441
FAX: .... (619) 236-0429
See Our Ad on this page

ROSS & ASSOCIATES
SUSAN KOHN ROSS
Attorney at Law
Licensed Customs Broker

**CUSTOMS, INTERNATIONAL TRADE
and TRANSPORTATION LAW
MANAGEMENT and LEGISLATIVE
CONSULTING SERVICES**

5777 West Century Boulevard, Suite 520
Los Angeles, California 90045-5659
Tel: (310) 410-4414 • Fax (310) 410-1017

ATTORNEYS - IMMIGRATION

HIRSON, KAPLAN & PERL
8910 University Center Lane
Suite 300
San Diego 92122 .... (619) 452-5700
FAX: .... (619) 452-1911

JOHN A. QUINN, ATTORNEY AT LAW
1420 Kettner Blvd., Suite 502
San Diego 92101 .... (619) 233-6661
FAX: .... (619) 238-5544
See Our Ad on the next page

LAW OFFICES OF BETTY A. JAMGOTCHIAN
100 N. Brand Blvd., Suite 200
Glendale 91203 .... (818) 246-7422
FAX: .... (818) 240-3041

ATTORNEYS - INTERNATIONAL

RICHARD I. FINE & ASSOCIATES
10100 Santa Monica Blvd., Ste. 1000
Los Angeles 90067 ... (310) 277-5833
FAX: .... (310) 277-1543
See Our Ad on the next page

ATTORNEYS - INTERNATIONAL TRADE

MORRISON & FOERSTER
345 California St.
San Francisco 94104.(415) 677-7000
FAX: .... (415) 677-7521
See Our Ad on the next page

Worldwide Since 1949:

Amsterdam	Bangkok
Barcelona	Beijing
Berlin	Bogota
Brussels	Budapest
Buenos Aires	Cairo
Caracas	Chicago
Dallas	Frankfurt
Geneva	Hanoi
HoChi Min City	Hong Kong
Juarez	Kiev
London	Madrid
Manila	Melbourne
Mexico City	Miami
Milan	Monterrey
Moscow	New York
Palo Alto	Paris
Rio de Janeiro	Riyadh
Rome	**San Diego**
San Francisco	Sao Paulo
Singapore	St. Petersburg
Stockholm	Sydney
Taipei	Tijuana
Tokyo	Toronto
Valencia	Warsaw
Washington, D.C.	Zurich

San Diego Office:
101 West Broadway
Twelfth Floor
San Diego, CA 92101
(619) 236-1441

Is your law firm promising you the world when it hasn't even left the country?

Decades before the Berlin Wall fell, Perestroika and NAFTA, Baker & McKenzie was helping its clients enter new markets around the globe.

Today Baker & McKenzie knows the law, the people, and the culture in more than 27 countries. We represent clients in virtually every kind of business transaction in every corner of the world. Our 1600 attorneys in more than 50 Baker & McKenzie offices worldwide support clients at home, within their region, and internationally.

No other law firm combines the local expertise and international presence of Baker & McKenzie. No other law firm is better positioned to help its clients compete in today's global market.

So if your law firm is suggesting it can represent your interests abroad, maybe you ought to ask where in the world it's planning to start. Or, call Baker & McKenzie at (619) 236-1441. We're already there.

BAKER & MᶜKENZIE

ATTORNEYS AT LAW

SERVING THE LEGAL NEEDS OF SAN DIEGO'S
BUSINESS COMMUNITY AT HOME AND ABROAD

Solving the Problems of International Human Resources

Certified Immigration & Nationality Specialists
Board of Legal Specialization of the California State Bar

Representation of companies and individuals before the U.S. Immigration & Naturalization Service and related agencies. Practice coordinating all aspects of immigration and nationality law, including visa petitions, employer sanctions and other defense.

Bejar Hurwitz & Quinn

(619) 233-6661 • Fax: (619) 238-5544 • In LA. Call: (818) 507-5017
1420 KETTNER BOULEVARD, SUITE 502

U.S. BANK
- Full Range of International Banking Services.
- Global Information Network.
- Financing Under Exim Bank Programs.

980 9th Street, Suite 1100
Sacramento, CA 95814 (916) 552-5698

WELLS FARGO BANK

Global Experience That Delivers™

We can help you do business around the world in 800 ways.

525 Market Street, San Francisco, CA 94105

I-800-479-2858

BANKS

BANK OF AMERICA
1 South Van Ness
San Francisco 94103. (415) 241-4924
FAX: .... (415) 241-3648
See Our Ad on page xvi

COMERICA BANK - CALIFORNIA
International Banking Department
333 W. Santa Clara St.
San Jose 95113 .... (408) 556-5211
FAX: .... (408) 556-5216
See Our Ad on the next page

FIRST INTERSTATE BANK
Judith Blakeney
Southern California ... (714) 253-4268
FAX: .... (714) 253-4337
See Our Ad on the next page

FIRST INTERSTATE BANK
Patrick Carman
Northern California ... (510) 891-2037
FAX: .... (510) 891-2007
See Our Ad on page

CAR RENTALS - SACRAMENTO

SUBURBAN FORD
4625 Madison Ave.
Sacramento 95841..... (916) 349-3338
FAX: .... (916) 331-0749
See Our Ad on page 196

Unique solutions to international trade legal issues.

Our professional staff specialize in global and United States legal issues requiring uniquely creative strategies and execution. Our resume includes precedent-setting solutions to cases involving major multi-national corporations and trade associations.

Telephone: (310) 277-5833
Fax: (310) 277-1543

The Law Offices of
Richard I. Fine & Associates
A Professional Corporation

10100 Santa Monica Blvd. Suite 1000
Los Angeles, CA 90067-4090

Helping Decision Makers Decide

Morrison & Foerster

INTERNATIONAL LEGAL SERVICES

MERGERS & ACQUISITIONS · JOINT VENTURES AND STRATEGIC ALLIANCES

INTERNATIONAL SECURITIES · INTERNATIONAL TRADE · PROJECT FINANCE

INTELLECTUAL PROPERTY · ENVIRONMENTAL LAW · BANKING AND FINANCIAL SERVICES

REAL ESTATE · INTERNATIONAL TAX · DISPUTE RESOLUTION

For more information on the firm's international practice, contact Carl E. Anduri at (415) 677-7000 or write him at 345 California Street, San Francisco, California 94104-2675

MORRISON & FOERSTER

SAN FRANCISCO · LOS ANGELES · NEW YORK · WASHINGTON DC · BRUSSELS · HONG KONG · TOKYO
SACRAMENTO · PALO ALTO · WALNUT CREEK · ORANGE COUNTY · DENVER · SEATTLE

CITRUS PRODUCTS

SUNKIST GROWERS, INC.
ATTN: Export Sales
14130 Riverside Drive
Sherman Oaks CA ..... (818) 986-4800
See Our Ad on page 6

CO-EMPLOYMENT SERVICES

EMPLOYERS RESOURCE
2404 Bank Dr., Suite 305
Boise ID 83705........... (208) 345-7500
FAX:............................ (208) 336-4623
See Our Ad on page xiv

CONSULTANTS - BUSINESS

STELLAR GROUP
Business Management &
Development
405 W. Washington St., Suite 176
San Diego 92103 .... (619) 294-7642
FAX:............................ (619) 294-6593
EMail:hartness@cerfnet.com

CONSULTANTS - JAPAN

VENTURE LINK USA, INC.
13101 Washington Blvd., Suite 242
Los Angeles 90066 .... (310) 822-7234
FAX:............................ (310) 822-2175
See Our Ad on the next page

CONSULTANTS - MEXICO

ALFA SOUTHWEST CORPORATION
1031 Bay Blvd., Suite M
Chula Vista 91911...... (619) 476-9238
FAX:............................ (619) 476-9241
See Our Ad on this page

ComericA
WE LISTEN. WE UNDERSTAND.
WE MAKE IT WORK.℠

For information regarding our
International Trade Services
please call 408-556-5211

Comerica Bank-California   Member FDIC

MAKING IT IN MEXICO!

OPPORTUNITIES CONTINUE TO EXPAND, UNDER NAFTA AND IN THE MAQUILADORA INDUSTRY.

With experience since 1969, Alfa Southwest Corp., based in San Diego, offers the best option to relocate labor intensive production to Mexico, **with our foreign subsidiary, starting in just a few weeks, using Alfa's Mexican business and labor,** while you keep control of the Production area, assuring your productivity and quality.

TO START MAKING IT IN MEXICO, CALL ALFA TODAY, AT 619-476-9238, FAX. 476-9241

We're in the business of taking small business international.

First Interstate Bank is committed to taking small business worldwide... With government guaranteed loan programs designed to help the small business exporter do just that. So call the First Interstate Bank contact listed below. We'll help match the right loan program to your business's need to grow beyond its borders.

Export loan programs:

California Export Finance Office Program (CEFO) -
Supports working capital needs arising from the export of goods, commodities or services with more than 50% of their value created in California with the use of a 90% loan guarantee.

SBA Export Working Capitol Program -
Provides pre-export and post-shipment working capital financing for the manufacture or purchase of goods or services for export with a 90% loan guarantee.

Ex-Im Bank Programs -
Offers a variety of programs including the new Working Capital Guarantee Program and Export Credit Insurance for exporters. Also guarantees and provides loans to foreign buyers who are purchasing goods with at least 50% U.S. content from U.S. exporters.

Northern California Patrick Carman (510) 891-2037

Southern California Judith Blakeney (714) 253-4268

First Interstate Bank

Member FDIC   EQUAL HOUSING LENDER

Rent A Ford, Passenger Vans, Trucks or 4x4 Units

Rent by a day, week or month
Free customer pickup available
Rates include insurance

The Regional Ford Center
Suburban Ford

Located in service/parts area Date Avenue
(916) 349-3338 • (916) 349-3391

Discover New Business Opportunities in Japan.

Venture Link USA is the source for a complete range of services that give global thinking companies a vital edge in the markets of Japan.

- MATCH MAKING • EXPORT REPRESENTATION
- DIRECT MARKETING • MARKET RESEARCH
- CONSULTING • TRANSLATION • INTERPRETATION
- TRADE SHOW REPRESENTATION • ADVERTISING

•NEW BUSINESS CREATOR
VENTURE LINK USA, INC.

13101 WASHINGTON BLVD., LOS ANGELES, CA 90066 310-822-7234 FAX: 310-822-2175

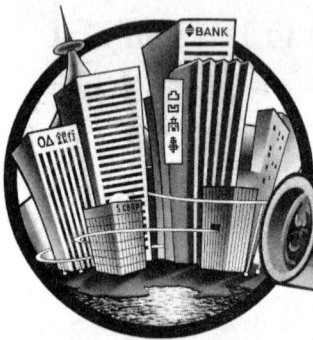

CONSULTING - WATER RESOURCES

NRCE, INC.
Colorado Office
11 Old Town Square, Suite 250
Fort Collins CO 80524 (303) 224-1851
FAX: .... (303) 224-1885
See Our Ad on the next page

NRCE, INC.
East Africa Office
P.O. Box 5260/RAS Dashen St., #5
Phone 011-291-1-120574
FAX: 011-291-1-120629
Asmara, Eritrea
See Our Ad on the next page

NRCE, INC.
Main Office
1250 Addison St., Suite 204
Berkeley 94702 .... (510) 841-7814
FAX: .... (510) 841-3728
See Our Ad on the next page

COUNTERTRADE

AMERICAN COUNTERTRADE ASSOCIATION
121 S. Meramec Ave., Suite 1102
St. Louis MO 63105 ... (314) 727-5522
FAX: .... (314) 727-8171
See Our Ad on the next page

CUSTOMS BROKERS

INTERNATIONAL AUTOMATED BROKERS
Warehouse & Freight Forwarding
9051 Siempre Viva Rd., Suite J
San Diego 92173 .... (619) 661-6464
FAX: .... (619) 661-6491

ABI Certified Customs Brokers
■
Fast, Reliable Service at Border Since 1962

ROMERO AND McNALLY
COMPANY, INCORPORATED

- Complete U.S. and International Distribution Services
- 25,000 sq. ft. Transloading Border Terminal
- Twin Plan (9802) and NAFTA Specialists

Main Office at Otay Mesa Crossing
9465 Customhouse Plaza, Suite G
San Diego, CA 92173
Fax (619) 661-6950

(619) 661-6944

CUSTOMS BROKERS (cont)

PAXTON, SHREVE & HAYS, INC.
2191 Main St.
San Diego 92101 .... (619) 232-8941
FAX: .... (619) 232-3006

PORTER INTERNATIONAL, INC.
9295 Siempre Viva Rd.
San Diego 92173 .... (619) 661-4000
FAX: .... (619) 661-6339
See Our Ad on this page

CUSTOMS BROKERS - SAN DIEGO

CASAS INTERNATIONAL

CALIFORNIA'S #1 FULL SERVICE BORDER BROKER

Main Office:
10030 Marconi Dr., Otay Mesa,
San Diego, CA 92173-3255 .... (619) 661-6162
Fax .... (619) 661-6800

Calexico/Mexicali .... (619) 357-5911
Fax .... (619) 357-5912

ROMERO & MCNALLY
9465 Customhouse Plaza, Suite G
San Diego 92173 .... (619) 661-6944
FAX: .... (619) 661-6950
See Our Ad on the previous page

DELIVERY SERVICES

U.S. POSTAL SERVICE
1-800-THE-USPS Ext. 1128
See Our Ad on Inside Front Cover

DENTAL, PHARMACEUTICAL & MEDICAL PRODUCTS

PROFESSIONAL PRODUCTS CO.
P.O. Box 1628
San Diego 92112 .... (619) 231-1951
FAX: .... (619) 231-0804

DISTRIBUTION & WAREHOUSING

CASAS INTERNATIONAL BROKERAGE INC.
10030 Marconi Drive
Otay Mesa CA 92173 (619) 661-6162
FAX: .... (619) 661-6800
See Our Ad on this page

DISTRIBUTORSHIPS AVAILABLE

WHITE TIGER INTERNATIONAL
7770 Regents Rd., Suite 113
San Diego 92122 .... (619) 457-2585
FAX: .... (619) 453-7335
See Our Ad on page 32

DRIED FRUITS

MARIANI PACKING CO., INC.
320 Jackson St.
San Jose 95112 .... (408) 288-8300
FAX: .... (408) 280-5219

DRY GROCERIES

CERTIFIED GROCERS OF CALIFORNIA - CERGRO INTERNATIONAL
P.O. Box 3396 Terminal Annex
Los Angeles 90051 .... (213) 723-7476
FAX: .... (213) 264-7070
See Our Ad under Grocery Products

NRCE

NATURAL RESOURCES CONSULTING ENGINEERS, INC.

Civil, Environmental, and Water Resources Consultants

Technical Services
• Water Resources Evaluation
• Hydraulic Design and Study
• Water Quality
• Environmental Studies and Investigations
• Sedimentation Studies
• Irrigation and Drainage Systems Design and Management
• Construction Management
• Numerical and Computer Model Studies
• Expert Witness Testimony

Qualifications
• International reputation for excellence
• Highly experienced
• Multi-disciplinary staff
• Certified through the U.S. Small Business Administration 8(a) Program
• Registered professional engineers and scientists
• Successfully providing professional services to federal, commercial, and international clients

Main Office
1250 Addison Street, Suite 204
Berkeley, CA 94702
510-841-7814/Fax 510-841-3728

East Africa Office
P.O. Box 5260/Ras Dashen Street, #5
Asmara, Eritrea
011-291-1-120574/Fax 011-291-1-120629

Colorado Office
11 Old Town Square, Suite 250
Fort Collins, CO 80524
303-224-1851/Fax 303-224-1885

aca

An organization for the COUNTERTRADE PROFESSIONAL which is dedicated to EDUCATION and NETWORKING

The American Countertrade Association

121 S. Meramec Avenue #1102
St. Louis, MO 63105-1725
Tel: 314 727-5522
Fax: 314 727-8171

PORTER INTERNATIONAL INCORPORATED

FMC-1296-R

Customs Brokers
Int'l Freight Forwarders
IATA Agents (#05-8-1199)

Offices at:
San Diego / Otay Mesa
Los Angeles Int'l Airport

Calexico (Mexicali)

• 619-661-4000 • FAX: 619-661-6339
• 310-646-4803 • 800-640-4803
• FAX: 310-642-0561
• 619-357-6411 • FAX: 619-357-7014

DISCOVER THE RICHES BRAWLEY HAS TO OFFER.

LABOR
Wages 25% lower than the California average. Put our work force to work for you.

POWER
At a flat rate of $.066 per Kilowatt, you can see why moving to Brawley is a bright idea.

LAND
Industrial zoned land starting at $5,000 an acre, you can't go wrong planting roots here.

WATER
At only $58 an acre foot (326,000 gallons), your company won't get soaked.

FINANCING
With tax exempt bond financing for business. It makes dollars and sense to locate in Brawley.

TRADE
Only minutes from Mexico. Put your products on the NAFTA trade route.

BRAWLEY
ECONOMIC DEVELOPMENT
COMMISSION
Designated a "Federal Enterprise Community"
(619) 344-3160
204 S. Imperial Ave. • Brawley, CA 92227
FAX (619) 344-7611

AMERICA, THE BEAUTIFUL BEZJIAN DYE-CHEM, THE COLORFUL
EXPORT

BEZJIAN DYE-CHEM, ONE OF THE LARGEST INDEPENDENT SUPPLIERS OF TOP QUALITY DYES MADE IN U.S.A.

- Greatest selection of polyester colors
- Top Quality
- Over 40 years of experience
- Fast & efficient service
- Competitive prices

MARKETING TOP QUALITY DYES

BEZJIAN DYE-CHEM, INC.
DYESTUFF SPECIALISTS Since 1954

PRODUCERS, WHOLESALERS AND EXPORTERS OF INDUSTRIAL COLORS AND CHEMICALS
1020 AIR WAY, GLENDALE, CA 91201 • FAX: (213) 461-4713

DYESTUFFS FOR EXPORT

BEZJIAN DYE-CHEM, INC.
1020 Air Way
Glendale CA 91201
FAX:............................ (213) 461-4713
See Our Ad on this page

ECONOMIC DEVELOPMENT

BRAWLEY ECONOMIC DEVELOPMENT COMMISSION
P.O. Box 218
Brawley 92227........... (619) 344-3160
FAX:........................... (619) 344-7611
See Our Ad on this page

CITY OF UNION CITY
"The most culturally diverse and business friendly City in the San Francisco Bay Area"
CENTRAL LOCATION
BUILDINGS AND SITES AVAILABLE
Contact: Mark Leonard, Development Director
510-471-3232

ENGINEERING - CIVIL/ENVIRONMENTAL

NRCE, INC.
Colorado Office
11 Old Town Square, Suite 250
Fort Collins CO 80524(303) 224-1851
FAX:........................... (303) 224-1885
See Our Ad on the previous page

NRCE, INC.
East Africa Office
P.O. Box 5260/RAS Dashen St., #5
Phone 011-291-1-120574
FAX:....................... 011-291-1-120629
Asmara, Eritrea
See Our Ad on the previous page

NRCE, INC.
Main Office
1250 Addison St., Suite 204
Berkeley 94702 .... (510) 841-7814
FAX:........................... (510) 841-3728
See Our Ad on the previous page

EXPORTER - FRESH PRODUCE

MISSION PRODUCE INC.
P.O. Box 2888
Oxnard 93034 .... (805) 986-3736
FAX:........................... (805) 488-6196

EXPORTER - LIQUID FERTILIZER

LIQUINOX
221 W. Meats Ave.
Orange 92665............. (714) 637-6300
FAX:........................... (714) 637-6302

EXPORTING

INTERPORT INTERNATIONAL, INC.
1111 Bayside Drive, Suite 250
Corona Del Mar
92625.......................... (714) 760-3100
FAX:........................... (714) 760-3180
See Our Ad on the next page

INTERPORT • INTERNATIONAL, INC.

Co-awarded the coveted "E Award" with Interstate Engineering for continued superior performance in export sales by the President of the United States.

Continuing its expansion into the Pacific Rim, Central, and South America, INTERPORT INTERNATIONAL offers unprecedented success for clients and products it represents. Domestic and foreign companies, large and small, often lack the resources necessary to engage successfully in international trade and business. Differing cultures, languages, and business practices in foreign markets present themselves as barriers, rendering investments of time and money unproductive. With offices in Japan, Taiwan, and Korea, and subsidiary corporations representing Latin America, INTERPORT INTERNATIONAL has the resources necessary to ensure that your product or business venture has a good start and life in the very competitive Asian/Latin American markets. In addition, Interport International has a film and television division producing corporate & merchandise infomercials in any language. INTERPORT currently represents Interstate Engineering's entire vacuum cleaner line, Bio-Therapeutic Computers' micro-current technology, Boyer Ford's heavy trucks, as well as various cosmetic and health-related products.

1111 Bayside Drive, Suite 250 • Corona del Mar, CA 92625
Telephone: (714) 760-3100 • Fax: (714) 760-3180

FOOD - DRIED FRUIT

SUN-MAID GROWERS OF CALIFORNIA

Sun-Maid, the world's largest processor of raisins, can meet your needs with a wide selection of retail packs and customized high spec. industrial products on a world-wide basis. Other dried fruit also readily available.

13525 S. Bethel Avenue
Kingsburg, CA 93621-9232 U.S.A. .... (209) 896-8000
Fax .... (209) 897-2362

FOOD - PROCESSED PERSIMMONS AND KUMQUATS

LA VIGNE ENTERPRISES, INC.

Organically grown foods

Our kumquat and persimmon purées, conserves and sauces are preferred by discriminating chefs. Our sliced dried persimmons are great too.

LA VIGNE ENTERPRISES, INC.

3320 Reche Rd., Fallbrook 92028
Tel: (619) 728-9007   Fax: (619) 728-2710

FOREIGN SALES CORPORATIONS

EXPORT FSC INTERNATIONAL, LTD.
11200 Montgomery Blvd., Suite 8
Albuquerque
NM 87111 .... (800) 243-1372
FAX: .... (505) 821-0597
See Our Ad on this page

US VIRGIN ISLANDS
461 Park Ave. S., 12th Floor
New York NY 10001 .. (212) 725-0707
FAX: .... (212) 725-2254
See Our Ad on the next page

FREIGHT FORWARDERS

ALLIANCE SHIPPERS INTERNATIONAL
100 Oceangate, P-200
Long Beach 90802 ..... (310) 437-5702
FAX: .... (310) 437-0363
See Our Ad on page viii

CIRCLE INTERNATIONAL, INC.
Logistics Solutions at Work for You
See Our Ad on page i and on the next page

PANALPINA, INC.
9020 Activity Rd., Suite E-2
San Diego 92126 .... (619) 689-8333
FAX: .... (619) 689-8353
See Our Ad on the next page

Export FSC International, Ltd.

EXPORT SUBSIDY!
FOREIGN SALES CORPORATIONS

Exports in excess of $500k eligible for 15% to 30% Tax Exemption.

Specialists in IRA owned FSCs for "S" exporters. Nationwide Network of IRA/FSC Custodians.

FSCs formed in 24 hours!

Free 1995 FSC Booklet now available.
Robert J. Thornton, CPA

800-243-1372

Albuquerque Boston Saipan St. Thomas

An FSC Management Company

RIGHT NOW, YOU'RE PAYING 15% TO 30% MORE TAXES ON YOUR EXPORT INCOME THAN YOU NEED TO.

HERE'S WHAT TO DO ABOUT IT.

Set up a Foreign Sales Corporation in the U. S. Virgin Islands. An FSC is an off-shore instrument created by Congress that allows a U. S. company to lop as much as 15% to 30% off the taxes on its export-derived income.

A U. S. Virgin Islands FSC is easy to set up and inexpensive to maintain. It requires no staffing or facilities, just a "postal" relationship with an FSC management company and a nominal fee to the government.

Oh, there is one catch to saving all this money. You may have to mix business with pleasure by visiting our lovely islands. But we find most executives are willing to make that sacrifice.

For more information on money-saving FSC's, call 212-725-0707, fax this coupon to 212-725-2254, or mail it to U. S. Virgin Islands, 461 Park Avenue South, New York, NY 10016.

Name_____
Title_____
Company_____
Address_____
City_____ State_____ Zip_____
Telephone_____
Product_____

FULL SERVICE FREIGHT FORWARDING

31 U.S. LOCATIONS - OVER 200 WORLDWIDE

ROUND-THE-CLOCK EDP SURVEILLANCE

EXPORT · INSURANCE · DUTY DRAWBACKS · CONSOLIDATION

IMPORT · CONTAINERIZATION · CUSTOM BROKERS · AIR/OCEAN/INTERMODAL

WAREHOUSING/STORAGE/PACKING/DISTRIBUTION

The world's most sensitive INTERNATIONAL FREIGHT FORWARDER

Actually, we're thick-skinned when coping with shipper's problems, but sensitive to the understanding of the shipper's problems.

Air or ocean, export and import, customs, insurance, duty drawback, bulk charters, warehousing, intermodal handling are only part of our full service operation. Our 30 U.S. offices are linked by satellite to our 202 locations overseas. EDP software can link your operation to our sensitive system network. Call any Panalpina local office, or the locations listed below.

Panalpina offices in 30 major U.S. cities – over 200 locations worldwide

PANALPINA on 6 continents

California Offices
Los Angeles   (310) 338-1100
San Francisco   (415) 873-1390
San Diego   (619) 689-8333

FREIGHT FORWARDERS - INTERNATIONAL

AIR MARINE TRANSPORT INC.
Air/Ocean Freight -
Cargo Insurance
Personalized Service To
Customers
1499 Bayshore Hwy., Suite 133
Burlingame 94010 .... (415) 692-6971
FAX:............................. (415) 692-6974

COURIER LINK INTERNATIONAL
452 Oak St.
Inglewood 90302 ...... (310) 671-1200
FAX:............................. (310) 674-3826

NIPPON EXPRESS U.S.A., INC.
435 Valley Drive
Brisbane 94005 .... (415) 467-0100
FAX: .... (415) 467-0300
See Our Ad on the next page

FREIGHT FORWARDERS - NORTHERN CALIFORNIA

J.E. LOWDEN & CO.
1 Embarcadero Center, Suite 1950
San Francisco 94111. (415) 781-7040
FAX:............................. (415) 392-3970

FROZEN FOODS

CERTIFIED GROCERS OF CALIFORNIA - CERGRO INTERNATIONAL
P.O. Box 3396 Terminal Annex
Los Angeles 90051 .... (213) 723-7476
FAX: .... (213) 264-7070
See Our Ad under Grocery Products

One World. One Global Partner.

Comprehensive Transportation and Logistics Solutions.

306 Offices in 86 Countries

• Global Air Freight
• Global Ocean Freight
• Customs Brokerage
• Warehousing & Distribution
• Global Communication
• Sophisticated Information Systems

National Information Center
1-800-332-4725

Circle International
Logistics Solutions at Work for You

GOVERNMENT TRADE MISSION

HONG KONG ECONOMIC & TRADE OFFICE
222 Kearny St., Suite 402
San Francisco 94108. (415) 397-2215
FAX: .... (415) 421-0646

GROCERY PRODUCTS

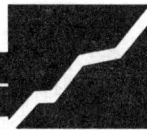

MARKET WHOLESALE EXPORT
P.O. Box 1087
Santa Rosa 95402 ..... (707) 542-5848
FAX: .... (707) 544-2744
See Our Ad on this page

CERGRO INTERNATIONAL
❑ Private Label (Springfield)
❑ Health & Beauty Aids
❑ Grocery Products
❑ Dry Groceries
❑ Frozen Foods
❑ Housewares
P.O. BOX 3396, Terminal Annex
Los Angeles, CA 90051
FAX (213) 264-7070 • 264-9320
(213) 723-7476 Ext. 7120

HEALTH, BEAUTY AIDS & HOUSEWARES

CERTIFIED GROCERS OF CALIFORNIA - CERGRO INTERNATIONAL
P.O. Box 3396 Terminal Annex
Los Angeles 90051 .... (213) 723-7476
FAX: .... (213) 264-7070
See Our Ad on this page

HOTELS

DAYS INNS OF AMERICA
3838 E. Van Buren
Phoenix AZ 85008.......(602) 389-3800
FAX: .... (602) 389-3959
See Our Ad on page iv

PARK MANOR SUITES HOTEL
525 Spruce St.
San Diego 92103 .... (619) 291-0999
.... (800) 874-2649
FAX: .... (619) 291-8844

HOTELS - SACRAMENTO

LA QUINTA INN - DOWNTOWN
200 Jibboom St.
Sacramento 98525..... (916) 448-8100
FAX: .... (916) 447-3621
See Our Ad on the next page

HOTELS - SOUTHERN CALIFORNIA

DEL CORONADO CROWN MOTEL
330 N. Imperial Ave.
El Centro 92243 .... (800) 653-3226
FAX: .... (619) 353-0415
See Our Ad on the next page

IMPORT/EXPORT

BMK IMPORT/EXPORT
2555 Pacheco Blvd., Suite 3
Martinez 94553........... (510) 229-0333

CALRICAN INTERNATIONAL
710 Rimpau Ave., Suite 202
Corona 91719 .... (909) 340-0347
FAX: .... (909) 340-0340
See Our Ad on this page

QUALITY SERVICE FROM U.S.A. TO ASIA
Japan • Singapore • Hong Kong • Malaysia • Taiwan • Thailand

Nippon Express U.S.A., Inc.

Specializing in priority service for many Asian countries and backed by our experienced staff. We are equipped to handle full container load (FCL), as well as less-than-container load (LCL) cargo from San Francisco.

CONTACT LOCATIONS
San Francisco Ocean Cargo Branch: 435 Valley Drive, Brisbane, CA 94005 Tel: (415)467-0100 Fax: (415)467-0300
Singapore Branch Tel: 565-5585 Fax: 560-6535 Hong Kong Branch Tel: 408-1177 Fax: 408-1212
Malaysia Branch Tel: (3)376-2194 Fax: (3)376-2198 Taiwan Branch Tel: (2)702-1161 Fax: (2)701-3221
Thailand Branch Tel: (2)513-9449 Fax: (2)513-9472

Market Wholesale Export
The Export Experts

■ **Market Wholesale** epitomizes trust and superior customer service
• Trust built on honesty, integrity and fair play
• Reliable and dependable service since 1925

■ **Market Wholesale** distributes fresh, high-quality products
• All major national brands
• Top quality Home & Garden® private label items

■ **Market Wholesale** provides extraordinary variety
• Dry grocery, frozen and deli
• Approximately 13,000 national brand items
• 700 high-quality Home & Garden® items
• 130 value-priced Better Buy® private label items

■ **Market Wholesale** offers competitive prices
• No hidden charges
• Discounts for large quantities
• 21-day terms with approved credit

Santa Rosa Division – Export
P.O. Box 1087 • Santa Rosa, CA 95402-1087
(707) 542-5848 • FAX (707) 544-2744

CALRICAN INTERNATIONAL
(A Division of Nyrican Corp.)

CALRICAN INTERNATIONAL
710 Rimpau Ave., #202
Corona, CA 91719 U.S.A.
PHONE: (909) 340-0347
FAX: (909) 340-0340

An Export Management Company which specializes in providing service to Central and South American Countries.

La Quinta Inn

Cut Expenses Overnight.

10% OFF Rack Rate
2/1/95 thru 1/31/96

Sacramento
Two Locations

NORTH • 916-348-0900
4604 Madison near I-80

DOWNTOWN • 916-448-8100
200 Jibboom at I-5 & Richards

Guest Services: ■ Free continental breakfast ■ Free local telephone calls ■ Free satellite TV with sports and movie channels ■ Over 50% non-smoking rooms ■ And more.

10% discount off rack rate of standard room. For King Plus room, add $5. Valid at La Quinta Inns-Sacramento only. Discount is not valid with other discounts/promotions or during special events. Room availability may be limited.

SACAD1

PRESENT AD AT CHECK-IN

Reservations/Information
1-800-531-5900

Over 225 Nationwide Locations

©1995, La Quinta Inns, Inc.

DEL CORONADO CROWN MOTEL

CONVENIENTLY LOCATED
IN
SOUTHERN CALIFORNIA'S
IMPERIAL VALLEY

Only 15 Miles to
Mexicali, Baja California

Direct Dial International
Phone Services

FAX

Multi-Lingual Staff

330 N. Imperial, El Centro, CA
800 / 653-3226 or 619 / 353-0030

INDUSTRIAL COLORS - EXPORT

BEZJIAN DYE-CHEM, INC.
1020 Air Way
Glendale 91201
FAX:..................... **(213) 461-4713**
See Our Ad on page 198

INSURANCE

SEABURY & SMITH
1255 23rd St. NW
Washington DC
20037 .... **(202) 457-6822**
FAX: .... **(202) 457-6877**
See Our Ad on page 16

INSURANCE - FINANCIAL SERVICE

THE BERKSHIRE GROUP
Bill Colosimo - CFP
3545 Camino Del Rio S., Suite A
San Diego 92108....... **(619) 281-1100**
FAX:........................... **(619) 621-1656**

INTERPRETING & TRANSLATIONS

TRANSLATING SOURCES, INC.
P.O. Box 2038
Cypress 90630 .... **(800) 300-4010**
FAX: .... **(714) 527-4501**
See Our Ad on this page

LAUNDRY EQUIPMENT

SPEED QUEEN COMPANY
P.O. Box 990, Shepard St.
Ripon WI 54971.......... **(414) 748-1672**
FAX: .... **(414) 748-4564**
See Our Ad on the next page

Translating Sources, Inc.

*Serving
Fortune 500 Companies
for over 25 Years...*

65 Languages

Expert Translations

Business	Science
Technical	Law
Engineering	Petro-Chemical
Manuals	Other

Consecutive & Simultaneous Interpreting

Negotiations	Teleconferences
Conferences	Video-Conferences

(Interpretation services for traveling executives.)

Cross-Cultural Training

Call or fax for a free quote and consultation

Corporate Headquarters:
P.O. Box 2038 • Cypress, CA 90630-1538

Tel: (714) 527-5252 or (800) 300-4010
Fax:(714) 527-4501 or (800) 300-8812

Providing Effective Communication for Effective Results...

Capturing International Markets

Today, unlike in the past, non-English speaking countries are demanding product and service information be provided to them in their own native language. This is true with government agencies as well as with the business sector.

Communicating effectively with your international clients in their own language and culture will go a long way to helping you get and keep their business.

Carlos Jimenez, President
Translating Sources, Inc.

INTERNATIONAL SERVICE GROUP

Customs Brokers - Freight Forwarders

International - Domestic

**1571 Grandview Drive
South San Francisco, CA 94080
Tel: (415) 871-1420 Fax: (415) 871-7359
(800) 486-4741**

LIMOUSINE SERVICE

ENCORE LIMOUSINE COMPANY
P.O. Box 38665
Hollywood 90038........ (213) 938-6711
FAX: .... (213) 938-5708

JOJO'S - A PRIVATE LIMOUSINE SERVICE
TCP 5528P
West Hollywood
90046........................... (213) 935-5656
.... (213) 650-4274

LIMOUSINES

ENCORE LIMOUSINE COMPANY
P.O. Box 38665
Hollywood 90038........ (213) 938-6711
FAX: .... (213) 938-5708

FLEETWOOD LIMOUSINE & TRANSPORTATION SERVICE, LTD.
Serving All Of Southern California
Nationwide Network... (800) 283-5893
FAX: .... (310) 572-1302
Limousines/Sedans/Passenger Vans

LOGISTICS - DOMESTIC & INTERNATIONAL

INTERNATIONAL SERVICE GROUP
1571 Grandview Drive
San Francisco 94080. (800) 486-4741
FAX: .... (415) 871-7359
See Our Ad on this page

We do the world's laundry.

In 89 countries worldwide, Speed Queen is the world laundry specialist. The name Speed Queen always means reliable and durable large-capacity laundry equipment for home, commercial and on-premise laundries.

To find out what Speed Queen can do for you, contact Speed Queen, International Sales, Ripon, WI 54971-0990 USA.
Phone: 1 414 748-4443.
Or Fax: 1 414 748-4456.

Speed Queen
A **Raytheon** Company

THE WHOLE WORLD IS TURNING TO

KYOLIC®

ODORLESS AGED GARLIC EXTRACT™

**WORLD'S BEST SELLING
GUARANTEED ODORLESS
AGED GARLIC PREPARATIONS
IN VARIOUS FORMULAS**

PRODUCTS INFORMATION AND OFFER
AVAILABLE UPON REQUEST,
FOR MANUFACTURERS/DISTRIBUTORS
WHO HAVE NATIONAL SALES NETWORKS
ON PHARMACEUTICAL AND
NUTRITIONAL PRODUCTS

★ ★ ★

**WAKUNAGA OF AMERICA CO., LTD.
23501 MADERO
MISSION VIEJO, CA 92691 - U.S.A.
(714) 855-2776 & FAX # (714) 458-2764**

A SUBSIDIARY OF
WAKUNAGA PHARMACEUTICAL CO., LTD.

COBE
Laboratories

CONTRACT PACKAGING - PRIVATE LABELING

- THIGH CREAM
- SKIN & HAIR CARE PRODUCTS
- PEELING PROD (GLYCOLIC/AHA)
- ETHNIC PRODUCTS
- ALOE VERA & NATURAL ROSE
  HIP OIL PRODUCTS
- HERBAL PRODUCTS
- ALOE DRINKS
- PHARMACEUTICAL
- SUNSCREENS
- ALL PRODUCTS AVAILABLE
  FOR EXPORT
- CUSTOM FORMULATIONS
- LARGE OR SMALL ORDERS

SE
HABLA
ESPAÑOL

FDA
LICENSE

(213) 587-3604

**TOLL FREE: 800-359-3223
FAX: (213) 585-1265**

5729 Maywood Ave., Maywood, CA 90270 - USA

BASIC®

YOUR QUALITY SOURCE FOR VEGETABLE INGREDIENTS

BASIC VEGETABLE PRODUCTS
P.O. Box 599 • Vacaville, CA 95696
(800) 358-9145
(707) 864-4550 (International)
(707) 864-4505 FAX

MANAGEMENT & INVESTMENT SERVICES

CRIVELLO CORPORATION

**MANAGEMENT
& INVESTMENT SERVICES**

501 West Broadway, Suite 1220
San Diego, CA 92101
Contact: David J. Hartness
Tel: (619) 544-9049 • Fax: (619) 544-9618

MANUFACTURER - FOOD INGREDIENTS

SHADE FOODS, INC.
400 Prairie Village Drive
Industrial Airport
KS 66031 .... (913) 780-1212
FAX: .... (913) 780-1720

MANUFACTURER - FOOD SUPPLEMENTS

WAKUNAGA OF AMERICA CO., INC.
23501 Madero
Mission Viejo 92691 .. (714) 855-2776
FAX: .... (714) 458-2764
See Our Ad on this page

MANUFACTURER - HIGH - PERFORMANCE AUTOMOTIVE & MARINE PARTS

MOONEYES

MOON

10820 S. NORWALK BLVD.
SANTA FE SPRINGS, CA 90670
(310) 944-6311
Fax: (310) 946-2961

MANUFACTURER OF WORLD FAMOUS
MOON DISCS, MOON TANKS,
VALVE COVERS, MANIFOLD AND OTHER
SPEED AND MARINE EQUIPMENT

*Also Distributor Of All Automotive
AFTER Market Automotive Parts & Accessories*

MANUFACTURER - UTILITY TRAILERS

UTILITY TRAILER MANUFACTURING CO.
P.O. Box 1299
City Of Industry
91749 .... (818) 965-1541
FAX: .... (818) 965-2790

MANUFACTURER - VALVES

PACIFIC VALVES
3201 Walnut Ave.
Long Beach 90807 ..... (310) 426-2531
FAX: .... (310) 595-9717

MANUFACTURER AND EXPORTER OF PREMIUM PET FOOD

NATURE'S RECIPE PET FOODS
341 Bonnie Circle
Corona 91720 .... (909) 278-4280
FAX: .... (909) 278-9729
See Our Ad on page xii

MANUFACTURER AND EXPORTER OF VEGETABLE INGREDIENTS

BASIC VEGETABLE PRODUCTS
P.O. Box 599
Vacaville 95696 .... (707) 864-4550
FAX: .... (707) 864-4505
See Our Ad on this page

MANUFACTURER/BROKER- VITAMINS SNACKS NON-FOOD

CASEY SALES CO., INC.
P.O. Box 961
San Leandro 94577 ... (510) 632-2357
FAX: .... (510) 632-5505

MANUFACTURER/EXPORTER

METROTECH CORPORATION
670 National Ave.
Mountain View 94043 800-200-Metro
FAX: .... (415) 962-9527

MANUFACTURER/EXPORTER HEALTH & BEAUTY PRODUCTS

COBE LABORATORIES
5729 Maywood Ave.
Maywood 90270 .... (213) 587-3604
FAX: .... (213) 585-1265
See Our Ad on this page

MANUFACTURER - TEST EQUIPMENT

PACIFIC WESTERN SYSTEMS, INC.
505 E. Evelyn Ave.
Mountain View 94041 (415) 961-8855
FAX: .... (415) 965-2661

MANUFACTURERS

PREMIER SPRING WATER
Pumps & Filters For Swimming
Pools, Spas, Fountains, Irrigation
13280 Paxton St.
Pacoima 91331 .... (818) 899-7373
FAX: .... (818) 899-8005

MEDICAL COORDINATION

INTERNATIONAL MEDICAL CARE
11901 Santa Monica Blvd., Ste.484
Los Angeles 90025... (310) 659-9565
FAX: .... (310) 854-4961

MEDICAL EQUIPMENT - REFURBISHED

AMERICAN EXPORT COMPANY
P.O. Box 28123
Fresno 93729.............. (209) 323-7972
FAX: .... (209) 323-7972
See Our Ad on this page

MEETING FACILITIES

**CALIFORNIA STATE UNIVERSITY -
DOMINGUEZ HILLS**
1000 E. Victoria St.
Carson 90747 .... (310) 516-3830
FAX: .... (310) 516-4418
See Our Ad on page 208

METAL POWDERS MANUFACTURER

VALIMET, INC.
431 Sperry Rd.
Stockton 95206 .... (209) 982-4870
FAX: .... (209) 982-1365

MOLD MAKERS - PLASTIC INJECTION

CACO PACIFIC CORPORATION

One of America's largest and most respected moldmakers, CACO PACIFIC has molds operating in 29 countries on five continents. Industries served include: Medical/Food and Beverage Packaging/ Closures/Magnetic Media/Home Entertainment/ Shaving and Personal Care/Writing Instruments/Optics & Reflectors/Electronics/Quality Packaging & Display Boxes.

FAX: (818) 966-4219

813 N. Cummings Road
Covina, CA 91724 ....(818) 331-3361

NURSERY - STRAWBERRY PLANTS

LASSEN CANYON NURSERY
1300 Salmon Creek Rd.
Redding 96003 .... (916) 223-1075
FAX: .... (916) 223-6754

PLASTICS - MOLD MAKERS

CACO PACIFIC CORPORATION
813 N. Cummings Rd.
Covina 91724.............. (818) 331-3361
FAX: .... (818) 996-4219
See Our Ad on this page

PORTS

PORT OF LONG BEACH
P.O. Box 570
Long Beach 90801 ..... (310) 437-0041
FAX: .... (310) 491-0237
See Our Ad on page 52

PRIVATE LABEL (SPRINGFIELD)

**CERTIFIED GROCERS OF CALIFORNIA
- CERGRO INTERNATIONAL**
P.O. Box 3396 Terminal Annex
Los Angeles 90051 .... (213) 723-7476
FAX: .... (213) 264-7070
See Our Ad under Grocery Products

PROFESSIONAL SERVICES

KPMG PEAT MARWICK
Sridar Iyengar, Partner
3460 W. Bayshore Rd.
Palo Alto 94303.......... (415) 354-1443
FAX: .... (415) 493-4978
See Our Ad on page 22

KPMG PEAT MARWICK
Bryan Isaacs, Partner
1999 Ave. Of The Stars, Suite 1100
Los Angeles 90067 .... (310) 551-6111
FAX: .... (310) 551-6150
See Our Ad on page 22

PRUNES

MARIANI PACKING CO., INC.
320 Jackson St.
San Jose 95112 .... (408) 288-8300
FAX: .... (408) 280-5219

PUBLISHER - COOKBOOKS

MARCUS KIMBERLY PUBLISHING
2701 Watt Ave.
Sacramento 95821..... (916) 488-1830
FAX: .... (916) 488-1863

RAISINS

MARIANI PACKING CO., INC.
320 Jackson St.
San Jose 95112 .... (408) 288-8300
FAX: .... (408) 280-5219

REAL ESTATE

AZTECA PROPERTY INVESTMENTS
317 W. Las Tunas Drive, Suite 208
San Gabriel 91776..... (818) 576-1737
FAX: .... (818) 576-1175

American Export Company
"Worldwide Export Management & Consulting."

Specializing In:
Refurbished Medical Equipment
i.e. Portable X-Ray
C.T. Scanner - M.R. 1 Unit
Also New Supplies -
HIV test kits, sutures, etc.

Contact:
Brian Gladden - President

P.O. Box 28123
Fresno, California 93729

(209) 323-7972
Fax Also: (209) 323-7972

REAL ESTATE - COMMERCIAL PROPERTY MANAGEMENT

Eli Rodriguez
Realtor
ER REALTY   REALTOR

Property Management
Resident and Light Commercial
Sales of Home and Income Property
Mobile Notary Public

1446 Front St., Suite 201   (619) 696-7423
San Diego, CA 92101   Fax: (619) 234-7433

The University of the State of New York

Regents College   7 Columbia Circle, Albany, NY 12203
518-464-8500

The College that Works for Adults

Fully accredited. 26 degree programs in Liberal Arts, Business, Nursing, and Technology. No residency requirement. Enroll all year around. Advisors to help you plan. Complete your degree at your own pace. Use college-level credit from the widest array of sources.

an affirmative action/equal opportunity institution

Join 64,000 graduates who found Regents College the best option.

IUA
SAN FRANCISCO

INTERNATIONAL UNIVERSITY OF AMERICA
The Link Between Continents

AN EMPHASIS IN INTERNATIONAL BUSINESS

IUA
SAN FRANCISCO

The University located in the San Francisco Financial District offers:

DBA
Doctorate of Business Administration for International Management
- 12-month full-time residential program in San Francisco, followed by a 2-year non-residential dissertation period.
- Minimum admission criteria: Master's Degree or equivalent; significant professional experience.

MBA
Master of Business Administration for International Management
- 12-month intensive, full-time program in San Francisco.
- Rigorous academic program including a thesis.
- Minimum admission criteria: 4 years university education or its equivalent; professional experience.

BBA
Bachelor of Business Administration for International Management
- Undergraduate program, 18 months in San Francisco.
- Minimum admission criteria: 2 year university or its equivalent.

FOR FURTHER INFORMATION CONTACT:

Admissions Office
International
University of America

114 Sansome St.
San Francisco
California, 94104
U.S.A.
Tel: (415) 397-2000
Fax: (415) 397-2052

OR

Main European
Information Center

17-25 rue de Chaillot
75116 Paris France
Tel: (1) 40 70 10 00
Fax: (1) 40 70 10 10

OR

Your local
representative

California State Approved - W.A.U.C. Accredited - Member A.C.B.S.P. - Member Better Business Bureau

UNIVERSITY OF CALIFORNIA AT BERKELEY, UNIVERSITY EXTENSION

4-MONTH DAYTIME CERTIFICATE PROGRAMS

Business Administration   *Marketing*   *Tourism Management*

- Seven credit courses in four months
- Sessions: March-June and September-December
- Assistance with visa and housing

- Admission: TOEFL score of 550, IELTS of 6.5, Cambridge Proficiency Test or Certificate of Advanced English.

Coming in summer 1996:
International Business Program

For information and an application contact:
Director, Four-Month Certificate Programs
Dept. TCS, 2223 Fulton Street, Berkeley, CA 94720, U.S.A.
Telephone: (510) 642-2564 Fax: (510) 643-0216

Earn an MBA in International Business in the San Francisco Bay Area.

Saint Mary's College of California offers an international MBA program that is designed to integrate a global perspective on business with a conceptually rigorous exposure to the analytical skills and functional knowledge typical of MBA programs. This challenging, full-time 72 unit program is offered in an accelerated 13 month format. The program commences on October 2, 1995.

Founded in 1863, Saint Mary's College has been rated among the top ten regional universities in the western United States by *U.S. News* and *World Report.* The College enrolls 4,000 students and is located on a beautiful 425 acre campus 21 miles from San Francisco and 10 miles from Berkeley.

To receive an application and a catalog, mail your name and address to: Saint Mary's College, Graduate Business Programs, P.O. Box 4240, Moraga, California, 94575 USA. Or, FAX to 1(510)376-6521. Telephone:1(510)631-4500.

SAINT MARY'S COLLEGE OF CALIFORNIA

✝USF
UNIVERSITY of SAN FRANCISCO

MANAGEMENT EDUCATION OPPORTUNITIES

Executive Programs
• Custom Designed Programs for Individuals or Companies
• English Certification
• Internship Opportunities
• Seminars and Mgmt. Certificate Programs
• Short Term and Extended Programs

Executive M.B.A.
• Accredited 21-Month Program
• Meets Alternating Fridays and Saturdays
• International Management Course Taught Off-Campus
• Management Experience Required
• Executives From Around the World Encouraged to Apply

For information, contact:
Executive Education, University of San Francisco McLaren Graduate School of Management
2130 Fulton St., San Francisco, CA 94117 USA
(415) 666-2511
Fax: (415) 666-2502
Internet: chanw@usfca.edu

SCHOOLS - COLLEGES & UNIVERSITIES

CALIFORNIA STATE UNIVERSITY - DOMINGUEZ HILLS
1000 E. Victoria St.
Carson 90747 .... (310) 516-3741
FAX: .... (310) 516-3971
See Our Ad on this page

CALIFORNIA STATE UNIVERSITY LOS ANGELES
5151 State University Drive
Library North B552
Los Angeles 90032 .... (213) 343-4840
FAX: .... (213) 343-4954
See Our Ad on page 38

INTERNATIONAL UNIVERSITY OF AMERICA
114 Sansome St.
San Francisco 94104. (415) 397-2000
FAX: .... (415) 397-2052
See Our Ad on the previous page

REGENTS COLLEGE
The University Of The State Of New York
7 Columbia Circle
Albany NY 12203 .... (518) 464-8500
FAX: .... (518) 464-8777
See Our Ad on page 205

ST. MARY'S COLLEGE OF CALIFORNIA
P.O. Box 4240
Moraga 94575..............(510) 631-4500
FAX: .... (510) 376-6521
See Our Ad on this page

Tailoring programs for the needs of International Business

California State University Dominguez Hills in Carson (just south of Los Angeles) can offer your organization degree & certificate programs plus seminars designed to enhance skills on campus, on site or through distance learning technologies.

Distance Learning offers MBA programs, MA in Negotiation & Conflict Management, other degree & certificate programs – available over Satellite, broadcast TV, 2-Way Interactive television and other distance learning formats

Joint Institute for Intercultural Enterprise & Development offers programs to help you develop plans for doing business in a multicultural arena, including programs on NAFTA

American Language and Culture Program offers Intensive ESL classes plus business writing, speaking and American Culture classes

Many other programs for career enhancement or college credit are available. Call for more information today!

(310) 516-3741

California State University
Dominguez Hills
DIVISION OF EXTENDED EDUCATION

Our MBA Comes With A Lifetime Guarantee.

Graduates of our Executive and Fully Employed MBA Programs can count on a lifetime relationship that includes ongoing education and valuable business networks, from local to global.

More reasons to choose an

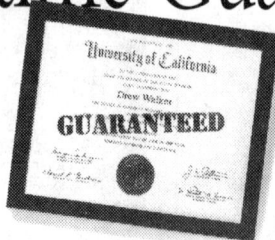

MBA from UCI include national accreditation from the AACSB and a computer lab ranked among the top five in the country.

See for yourself why it's hard to beat a lifetime relationship at one of our upcoming information sessions.

UNIVERSITY OF CALIFORNIA, IRVINE
Executive and Fully Employed MBA Programs, Graduate School of Management

---

SCHOOLS - COLLEGES & UNIVERSITIES (cont)

UNIVERSITY OF CALIFORNIA AT BERKELEY, UNIVERSITY EXTENSION
Four-Month Certificate Programs
Dept. TCS, 2223 Fulton St.
Berkeley 94720 .... (510) 642-2564
FAX: .... (510) 643-0216
See Our Ad on page 206

UNIVERSITY OF CALIFORNIA, IRVINE
Executive And Fully Employed
MBA Programs
Graduate School Of Management,
Room 202
Irvine 92717 .... (714) 856-5374
FAX: .... (714) 725-2944
See Our Ad on this page

UNIVERSITY OF SAN DIEGO
School Of Continuing Education
5998 Alcala Park
San Diego 92110 .... (619) 260-4644
FAX: .... (619) 260-2961
See Our Ad on page 38

UNIVERSITY OF SAN FRANCISCO
McLaren Graduate School
Of Management
2130 Fulton St.
San Francisco 94117. (415) 666-2511
FAX: .... (415) 666-2502
See Our Ad on the previous page

SCHOOLS - ENGLISH AS SECOND LANGUAGE

California State University, Dominguez Hills
American Language & Culture Program

Offering intensive English as a Second Language Programs plus classes designed to assist the international businessman in business writing, speaking and American Culture.

INFO: (310) 516-3830 FAX: (310) 516-4418
1000 E. Victoria, Carson, CA 90747

SCRAP METAL - EXPORT

LOS ANGELES SCRAP IRON & METAL CORP.
1910 E. Olympic Blvd.
Los Angeles 90021 .... (213) 622-5744
FAX: .... (213) 622-8501

SMALL BUSINESS LENDING

THE MONEY STORE INVESTMENT CORP.
9255 Towne Centre Drive, Suite 250
San Diego 92121 .... (619) 550-1700
FAX: .... (619) 550-1707

SOLAR ELECTRIC DISTRIBUTOR

Electricity from the Sun   20 Years of Solar Service

WM. LAMB CORP.
Distributor of Siemens Solar Modules

In California   Fax
1-800-310-5262   (818) 980-0856

10615 Chandler Boulevard
North Hollywood, CA 91601 .... (818) 980-6248

SOUPS AND SAUCES (ALL FROZEN)

TODD'S FROZEN SOUPS & SAUCES
1722 Kettering St.
Irvine 92714 .... (714) 250-4080
FAX: .... (714) 724-1338

TEMPERATURE MEASURING EQUIPMENT

REOTEMP INSTRUMENT CORP.
11568 Sorrento Valley Rd., Suite 10
San Diego 92121 .... (619) 481-7737
FAX: .... (619) 481-7150

THERMOMETERS - BIMETAL

REOTEMP INSTRUMENT CORP.
11568 Sorrento Valley Rd., Suite 10
San Diego 92121 .... (619) 481-7737
FAX: .... (619) 481-7150

TOURS

FLEETWOOD LIMOUSINE & TRANSPORTATION SERVICES, LTD.
Serving All Of Southern California
Nationwide Network... (800) 283-5893
FAX: .... (310) 572-1302
Limousines/Sedans/Passenger Vans

TRADE DEVELOPMENT US/MEXICO

IRVINE WORLD TRADE CORPORATION
SPECIALIZING IN MEXICO/U.S. TRADE

REPRESENTING MEXICAN AND AMERICAN COMPANIES
EDUARDO TREVIÑO, PRESIDENT

PHONE: (714) 651-0704
FAX: (714) 651-9092

7 POSSUM RUN
IRVINE, CALIFORNIA 92714

TRANSLATION & INTERPRETATION

FREE REFERRALS
1-800-992-0367

Cut costs by working directly with highly qualified independent translators and interpreters. All major languages.

The Translators and Interpreters Guild

TRANSLATION SERVICES

INTERNATIONAL CONTACT, INC.
1970 Broadway, Suite 315
Oakland 94612 .... (510) 836-1180
FAX: .... (510) 835-1314
See Our Ad on this page

TRANSPORTATION

ENCORE LIMOUSINE COMPANY
P.O. Box 38665
Hollywood 90038........ (213) 938-6711
FAX: .... (213) 938-5708

**FLEETWOOD LIMOUSINE &
TRANSPORTATION SERVICES, LTD.**
Serving All Of Southern California
Nationwide Network... (800) 283-5893
FAX: .... (310) 572-1302
Limousines/Sedans/Passenger Vans

TRANSPORTATION - TRUCKING

CASAS INTERNATIONAL

U.S. - MEXICO TRANSPORTATION SPECIALISTS

(619) 661-1491

FAX: (619) 661-2581

TRANSLATION SERVICES
Your Passport to Multi-Language Communication

• Original Production
• Translation and Adaptation
• Terminology Standardization
• Typesetting and Graphics
• Lip Synch • Subtitling • Narration

The International Contact for
print, audio and video... in *any* language.
Over 12 years experience.

1970 BROADWAY,
SUITE 315
OAKLAND, CA 94612

Tel: (510) 836-1180   **Fax:** (510) 835-1314   **E-Mail:** (510) 444-4184

UNDERGROUND UTILITY LOCATING INSTRUMENTS

METROTECH CORPORATION
670 National Ave.
Mountain View 94043   800-200-Metro
FAX: .... (415) 962-9527

VANS/BUSES

**FLEETWOOD LIMOUSINE &
TRANSPORTATION SERVICES, LTD.**
Serving All Of Southern California
Nationwide Network... (800) 283-5893
FAX: .... (310) 572-1302
Limousines/Sedans/Passenger Vans

VITAMIN AND MINERAL MANUFACTURER

**NION LABORATORIES (NATIONAL
INSTITUTE OF NUTRITION)**
15501 First St.
Irwindale 91706 .... (818) 969-1932
FAX: .... (818) 969-4915

WINDOWS

HEHR INTERNATIONAL INC.
Van, RV, Bus, Heavy Truck, Truck
Cap
3333 Casitas Ave.
Los Angeles 90037 .... (213) 663-1261
FAX: .... (213) 666-3204

X-RAY SPECTROMETERS

FISONS INSTRUMENTS/KEVEX
24911 Avenue Stanford
Valencia 91355........... (805) 295-0019
FAX: .... (805) 295-8714

ADVERTISERS INDEX

California Chamber of Commerce
BUSINESS SURVIVAL GUIDES

Survival Guides to the Labor Law Jungle

■ **1995 Labor Law Survival Kit — *Plus Update Newsletter***

Save $98. Includes *California Labor Law Digest,* Volumes 1 & 2, a one-year subscription to the *Labor Law Update* newsletter ($109 value), *Exempt Versus Non-Exempt: How to Classify California Employees,* and the *1995 Employer Poster Set.* A two-book set. See description below. *($169-Order #LK1)*

■ **1995 Labor Law Survival Kit**

Save $39. Includes all items listed above except the newsletter. See descriptions below. *($119-Order #LK2)*

■ **California Labor Law Digest, Volumes 1 and 2**

The books explain in lay terms how to comply with complex state and federal labor laws. Both books have a single combined index listed in each book, making topics easier to locate. Includes special sections on how to calculate overtime, vacations, holidays and leaves of absence, employee benefit plans and sexual harassment. Revised annually to reflect new laws, expanded advice on topics that cause employers the most trouble. (Part of the *Labor Law Survival Kit*-not sold separately)

■ **1995 Employer Posters**

All 12 posters required by the government, attractively printed on two 24" x 36" posters. Avoid the hassle of contacting seven different state agencies to get them. One set is FREE if you buy a *Labor Law Survival Kit.* *($10-English: Order #PSE; Spanish: Order #PSS)*

■ **Exempt v. Non-Exempt: A Guide for California Employers**

One of the most confusing issues for employers is how to determine whether your employees are exempt or non-exempt. Also, once the employee's status has been determined, you must follow the rules and treat employees properly to avoid paying back wages for overtime and to avoid lawsuits. This helpful guide will teach you everything you need to know about exempt and non-exempt employees. It shows you how to follow the rules and includes checklists and sample forms to copy and use. The guide is FREE if you buy a *Labor Law Survival Kit.* *($29-Order #EXE)*

■ **Unemployment Insurance/State Disability Insurance Pamphlets**

A revision to the Unemployment Insurance (UI) Code clarified a long-standing requirement that you must give every employee who is terminated, laid off or given a leave of absence a pamphlet about UI and SDI. You also must give a pamphlet on SDI to every new employee and anyone leaving on disability. *($10 - English: Order #UIE; Spanish: Order #UIS)*

■ **Labor Law Update Newsletter**

This monthly newsletter keeps you posted on fast-changing labor laws and court cases. Get timely advice on how to handle problems many employers experience, such as wage garnishment, reference checks, severance pay, job posting, English only rules and preparing for administrative hearings.

You also will get a quarterly index of past issues in 1995 with references to the *Labor Law Update Newsletters* themselves and a binder to keep them in. You can order the newsletter with the Labor Law Survival Kit (see above) or you can purchase it separately. *($109-Order #LLN)*

■ **Sexual Harassment Compliance Packet**

The packet contains 25 copies of a thoughtfully designed "information sheet." It satisfies the spirit and letter of the law, yet minimizes the likelihood that the information might trigger complaints against your firm. It also includes a sample written sexual harassment complaint and investigation procedure.
(1-3 packets: $10/packet; 4-19 packets: $8/packet; 20+ packets: $7.50/packet - English: Order #SHP; Spanish: Order #SHS)

■ **Classic Poster Frames**

Protect your posters from being damaged with our attractive *Classic Poster Frames.* Even when your posters go out of date, all you have to do is order new posters and use the frames over and over again. The frames are durable and crystal clear. The black thin-line edges create an attractive border for our colorful posters. You may want an extra single frame to post additional miscellaneous notices (such as the Family/Medical Leave Poster, OSHA Log 200 and IWC wage orders, which are included in the poster set). *(2 frames - $39.95, single frame - 19.95; Order #FRA)*

Hiring and Termination Kit

■ **Complete Hiring and Termination Kit**

Save $34. Includes *California Hiring and Termination Guide, Update Service* (see descriptions below), and *UI/SDI Pamphlets* and *Sexual Harassment Information Sheets* (see descriptions under **Survival Guides to the Labor Law Jungle**). *($95 - Order #HFK)*

■ **California Hiring and Termination Guide**

This useful *Guide* is designed to take you through the maze of forms and requirements in each step of the employment relationship. Its step-by-step approach helps employers be sure they are complying with complex California labor laws while avoiding costly litigation. The guidebook combines practical advice with 36 forms and brochures that are required by law or recommended for good business practices. Includes sample forms filled out as examples along with blank forms to copy and use. Clear explanations accompany each form. *($79 - Order #HFG)*

■ **California Hiring and Termination Guide Update Service**

Our annual *Update Service* will keep you current with rapidly changing forms and accepted employment practices. Throughout the year, we'll keep track of new laws and court cases that will change the forms and procedures covered in the *Guide.* We'll send you any new forms or changed procedures when they're available. *($30 - Order #HFU)*

Prices subject to change.

To Order Call 1-800-331-8877

Cal/OSHA Kit

■ **Cal/OSHA Kit**

Save $21. Includes *Cal/OSHA Handbook, SB 198 Handbook, Hazard Communication Handbook* and *Cal/OSHA Organizer.* See descriptions below. *($129 - Order #OSK)*

■ **Cal/OSHA Handbook**

The *Cal/OSHA Handbook* is written for businesspeople who aren't safety experts. It tells how to find the regulations which apply to your firm. Then it gives step-by-step instructions to satisfy the regulations that apply to every firm, and also the most costly rules that apply to most industries. Know what to do when the inspector arrives, your rights, when to appeal a citation and how to do it. *($45 - Order #CAL)*

■ **SB 198 Handbook**

SB 198 requires every employer to have a formal, written injury and illness prevention program. The *Handbook* is written with the premise that most employers can comply on a do-it-yourself basis. It contains legal requirements, sample plans to follow for various industries, fill-in-the-blank forms and step-by-step instructions. *($45 - Order #SB)*

■ **Hazard Communication Handbook**

Hazard communication standards apply to every firm where employees may be exposed to chemicals. If you receive an MSDS (Material Safety Data Sheet) from a supplier then you need a hazard communication program. The *Hazard Communication Handbook* gives clear guidelines on how to write your own program. *($35 - Order #HAZ)*

■ **Cal/OSHA Organizer**

The *Organizer* is a guide for the safety novice to comply with Cal/OSHA. Follow the steps in the *Organizer.* It refers to sections in the three companion handbooks where you'll get clear, detailed instructions on what you need to do, and cookbook-like steps on how to do it. Then file your safety programs and records right in the *Organizer.* *($25 - Order #ORG)*

Cal/OSHA Tools

■ **Cal/OSHA: Beyond the Basics**

This new book covers the hottest and newest Cal/OSHA regulations: bloodborne pathogens ● process safety management ● lead ● HAZWOPER ● asbestos ● confined spaces ● cadmium ● formaldehyde ● respiratory protection. Includes overview of the latest trends and developments and what they really mean to employers. A step-by-step guide on how to comply with many new regulations, complete with sample plans and procedures. Get a preview of draft regulations with a major impact on your business: tuberculosis ● ergonomics ● smoking in the workplace ● Federal OSHA reform ● SB 198 changes. *($69 - Order #COB)*

■ **Cal/OSHA Update Service**

You'll keep in compliance with that steady stream of Cal/OSHA regulations with our quarterly *Update Service.* Each quarter you will receive new and revised chapters for your *Cal/OSHA: Beyond the Basics* handbook. BONUS: *Cal/OSHA Insider Newsletter* — in just 15 minutes each quarter you can review this highly condensed newsletter and learn about the new Cal/OSHA standards that apply to your business. *($120/year - Order #COS))*

■ **SB 198 Software**

The California Chamber's *SB 198 Software* is made to be used with our *SB 198 Handbook.* It helps you write your SB 198 program and much more. The software is an ongoing recordkeeping system that will save you tremendous amounts of time. Organizes your records of training, accidents and injuries. Allows you to "batch" in updates instead of making single, time-consuming entries. Reminds you to do inspections and training. (IBM PC-AT compatible — *not* XT) *($195 - 3.5" diskette - Order #SB3; 5.25" diskette - Order #SB5)*

■ **SB 198 Video Safety Set**

Two-tape set makes it easy for you to initially train employees and managers about your injury/illness prevention program then annually review important information. One video lets your employees know safety is their responsibility and very important to your company. It offers common sense instruction about safe work procedures (12 minutes). The second video tells your supervisors and managers how other companies are making their safety programs work and emphasizes the importance of training, hazard identification and inspections (16 minutes). Employee training video also available in Spanish. *(English set $75 - Order #SVE; Spanish tape $45 - Order #SVS)*

■ **Hazard Communication Training Video**

Comply with Cal/OSHA's second most-cited regulation — hazard communication. This standard requires that the employer have a written hazard communication plan, identify and label all chemicals and train employees by communicating information on Material Safety Data Sheets (MSDSs). This video emphasizes proper procedures to store and handle chemicals, reading an MSDS, and maintaining a workplace free from chemical hazards. (13 minutes) *($45 or $25 if you purchase the Safety Training Series Video set - see below - English: Order #HCV; Spanish: Order #HCS)*

■ **Safety Training Video Series**

Save $39. A complete video safety training program at an incredibly low price. You get 12 separate training sessions, each with a quality 8-17 minute video. A quiz at the end of each video keeps employees involved, increases retention and documents your training for Cal/OSHA. Videos will open discussion to unique safety issues at your company. The helpful leader's guide makes your role as safety instructor easy. The program comes on two cassettes, each with six training sessions. *(Buy both cassettes for $199. English order #ST1; Spanish order #ST2.)*

Cassette #1, *Safety for All Employers,* covers the most important safety topics common to every business: reporting to work ● back injury prevention ● office safety ● fire prevention ● ergonomics ● bloodborne pathogens. *($119 - English Order #SEV; Spanish Order #SES)*

Cassette #2, *Safety for Industrial Employers,* is for the more industrial workplaces with machinery and chemicals: personal protective equipment ● electrical safety ● flammables/combustibles ● machine guarding — lockout/tagout ● material handling equipment ● the environment. *($119 - English Order #SIV; Spanish Order #SIS)*

(BONUS! Buy both cassettes for only $199 and get the *Hazard Communication Training Video* (13 minutes) for only $25 — Save $59.)

Prices subject to change.

To Order Call 1-800-331-8877

Environmental Library

■ **Complete Environmental Compliance Library**

Save $69. Includes *California Environmental Compliance Handbook, Proposition 65 Compliance, Community Right-to-Know, Hazardous Waste Management, Environmental Organizer* and a one-year subscription to *California Regwatch*. ($219 - Order #EVK)

■ **California Environmental Update Service**

Save $29. Includes *California Environmental Compliance Handbook* and a one-year subscription to *California Regwatch*. ($95 - Order #EK2)

■ **California Environmental Compliance Handbook**

Overall guide to California's unique and far-reaching environmental programs. Gives an overview of more than 20 of the most significant environmental programs, along with the essential steps to take for compliance. Provides concise descriptions of numerous additional, but less frequently encountered federal, state and local regulations that have an impact on business and local public facilities. The guide is your checklist and roadmap through California's maze of environmental regulations. *($49 - Order #ENV)*

■ **Proposition 65 Compliance**

This complex and confusing initiative imposes many requirements on businesses that use or distribute chemicals and products which contain ingredients known to the state to cause cancer or reproductive toxicity. More than 300 substances are subject to the law. The proposition provides for government prosecutions, as well as "bounty hunter" rewards for informants and citizen plaintiffs. The handbook is your best explanation of the law and how to comply. *($40 - Order #PRO)*

■ **Community Right-to-Know**

For firms that store, sell or use any of thousands of common materials or chemicals that are regulated by local governments under the concept of community right-to-know. Step-by-step instructions explain how to: determine if your firm handles hazardous materials, qualify for business plan exemptions, immediately report releases and develop a business plan in five easy steps. *($45 - Order #HMH)*

■ **Hazardous Waste Management**

For any business that uses or handles chemicals. Tells how to determine if your business generates hazardous waste, what permits are needed, how to manage hazardous waste, how to ship and dispose of waste and how to determine where permits can be required for certain hazardous waste activities. This handbook explains how to comply with this complicated and stringently enforced area of environmental law. *($49 - Order #HWH)*

■ **California Regwatch**

The *Regwatch* is your early warning system for California's ever-changing environmental laws. Each month you'll receive this brief update on new and proposed regulations that may affect your business. One-year subscription FREE with purchase of *Complete Environmental Compliance Library* or *Environmental Update Service*. FREE to California Chamber members. Cannot be purchased separately.

■ **Environmental Organizer**

This tool organizes your many environmental programs and recordkeeping to demonstrate compliance. Divider sections in the *Organizer* provide brief descriptions of each environmental program and how to comply, with references to the companion handbooks for details. *($30 - Order #EMO)*

■ **Hazardous Waste Management Supplement: Forms and Instructions**

Many businesses have paid thousands of dollars or devoted hundreds of hours to prepare hazardous waste documentation because the Title 22 regulations do not make clear what is required. Let the *Hazardous Waste Management Supplement* guide your efforts. The *Supplement* is a forms and document management system that will allow the typical generator of hazardous wastes to meet the highly complicated documentation requirements of Title 22. *($49 - Order #HWS. Sold separately — not included with the Environmental Library.)*

Employee Handbook

■ **Employee Handbook Kit**

Save $29. Includes *Employee Handbook, Software* and *Update Service*. See descriptions below. *(English: $129/kit - Order #EMK; Bilingual: $164/kit - Order #EM2)*

■ **Employee Handbook: How to Write One for Your Company**

Explains why you should have a personnel policy, then gives step-by-step instructions for writing one. Contains sample policies and a sample handbook, that will enable any company to develop its own written employee handbook with a minimum of time and confusion. Protect your business and avoid unnecessary costly litigation by having your personnel policy in writing. *($59 - Order # EMP)*

■ **Employee Handbook Update Service**

Be confident your new *Employee Handbook* will not go out of date because you were too busy to keep track of new laws and court cases. All you need to do is receive the changes we send to you and decide whether to include them in your employee handbook. Simply type the new policy changes into your computer. *(Includes English and Spanish for one low price of $30-Order #EA6)*

■ **Employee Handbook Software**

Makes writing and updating your employee handbook even easier. Select or modify the policies you need, push a button and print your customized, formatted employee handbook. *Bilingual* software lets you select pre-written policies in English, then print your handbook in both Spanish and English. Purchase of *Employee Handbook* is required so you will have the legal reasoning and requirements behind the policies you select. (IBM PC-AT compatible — *not* XT) *(English: $79 - 3.5" diskette - Order #EM3; 5.25" diskette - Order #EM5) (Bilingual: $99 - 3.5" diskette - Order #BE3; 5.25" diskette - Order #BE5)*

■ **Employee Handbook Training Videos**

Two-tape set helps you introduce your employee handbook. One video shows managers how to introduce the employee handbook to workers to ensure the least resistance and best results (10 minutes). The second video explains the purpose and benefits of your employee handbook to employees (6 minutes). English and Spanish version on the same tape. *($75 - Order #EMV)*

Prices subject to change.

To Order Call 1-800-331-8877

International Trade Resources

■ **International Trade Library**

Save $25. Includes *International Trade Resources Guide, Exporting Guide for California, North American Free Trade Guide* and *European Community and Europe.* See descriptions below. *($59 - Order #INK)*

■ **International Trade Resources Guide**

A comprehensive guide to resources available to the California business community for conducting international trade, including domestic and international chambers of commerce; international trade associations; education contacts; local, state and federal government officials; foreign trade zones; foreign government representatives; resources publications; glossaries; world holidays; metric conversion chart; international telephone calling codes; and world monetary units. The *Guide* lists more than 1,600 resources in the public and private sectors. (FREE with purchase of all three guides; half-price with purchase of any other international trade book.) *($17.50 - Order #ITG)*

■ **Exporting Guide for California**

A step-by-step manual to help the California company wishing to become involved in exporting or to expand existing export volumes. Covers organizing for export, identifying markets and distribution avenues, pricing, documentation, shipping and financing. Includes tips on avoiding common pitfalls, plus samples of key documents, including supplier/exporter and distribution agreements. Also highly useful for the person who is new to exporting, but works in a firm that already sells its goods or services in the international market. *($17.50 - Order #EGC)*

■ **European Community and Europe: A Legal Guide to Business Development**

Articles by attorneys and accountants from major international firms summarize important legal and financial considerations for companies doing business in the European Community and Europe. Includes overview of the creation of the European Economic Community, mergers, joint ventures, distribution and franchising agreements, commercial law, tax consider-ations, finance, employment law, standards, exporting requirements and other business concerns. Also covers major sectors: public procurement, high technology, environment, telecommunications, pharmaceuticals, energy and utilities. Country-specific chapters highlight requirements unique to individual nations in the EC or Europe. *($29.50 - Order #ECB)*

■ **North American Free Trade Guide**

A handbook to help businesses take advantage of opportunities to be created by the North American Free Trade Agreement (NAFTA), linking the United States with Canada and Mexico, its first and third largest trading partners. NAFTA will create the largest and richest market in the world, with 360 million consumers and $6 trillion in annual output. Focuses on what businesses need to know to gain access to the emerging Mexican market, plus good prospects for expansion in Canada. *($19.50 - Order #NAF)*

Recycling for Business

■ **Recycling Kit**

Save $15. Includes *Recycling Handbook for Business, Employee Training Video* and *Recycling Organizer.* See descriptions below. *($80 - Order #RCK)*

■ **Recycling Handbook for Business**

Save time and confusion by starting your recycling and waste reduction program in an organized manner. The business person's guide to a cost-efficient waste reduction program. Follow the logical steps, fill out worksheets and refer to checklists. Model plans to follow for six industries — retail, wholesale, offices, manufacturers, construction and restaurants. *($35 - Order #REC)*

■ **Employee Training Video**

Help build employee enthusiasm, pride and support in every aspect of your business with *Reduce...Reuse...Recycle... The Bottom Line.* This video demonstrates techniques that small and large companies are using and which can be adapted readily by smaller and medium-sized firms in nearly every industry. It's an ideal way to launch your recycling program (21 minutes). *($35 - Order #REV)*

■ **Recycling Organizer**

The *Recycling Organizer* will save you time, keep your program on track and document your waste reduction. It's a guide for the recycling novice and has easy-to-follow steps to document your recycling program. This well-planned system is a place to file your initial waste assessment, your waste reduction plan, vendor contracts and records of diverted waste. When the regulator calls, the *Organizer* documents your program and proves you're reducing solid waste. *($25 - Order #REO)*

For the New Small Business

■ **Business Start-Up Kits**

Provides every state, federal and most local government forms and permits necessary to start a business. Tells you what forms are necessary for your business and provides you with the forms, along with lay instructions on how to fill them out. Includes date reminder labels so you don't forget to file forms, and sample letters to government agencies. Three kits are available:

● **Sole Proprietorship/Partnership Kit** (18 forms) *($30 - Order #SBP)*
● **Corporation Kit** (28 forms) *($39 - Order #SBC)*
● **Employer Kit** (23 forms) *($34 - Order #SBE)*
● **Limited Liability Kit** (30 forms) *($39 - Order #SBL)*
(No member discount available)

■ **Which Business Structure Is Best For You?**
Overview of Corporations, Limited Liability Companies and Sole/ Proprietor/Partnerships

If you are just starting a new business, one of the most important decisions you must make is the form of business you are going to be. This *Guide* will provide you with a description and comparison of the most common business organizations in California. To make sure you choose the business form that's best for you, order this helpful *Guide* for only $15. Also, when you purchase the *Guide,* you'll get a coupon to receive $5 off of the *Business Start-Up Kit* that you decide to order.

■ **New American Business System**

Helps new small businesses succeed by helping you plan and stay organized. It's also your consultant with specific help on top problems new small businesses face: raising money, a business plan, a marketing plan, insurance, legal contracts, copyrights and trademarks, personnel, recordkeeping, accounting and budgeting, and 71 other essential topics. This 320-page loose-leaf kit also contains more than 80 forms, worksheets and checklists to help you plan and stay organized. *($49.95 - Order #AMB)* (No member discount available)

■ **BizPlan Builder**

BizPlan Builder is a working business plan on diskette. Stuffed with more than 90 pages, it's already typed and formatted into 33 word processing and spreadsheet files. Avoid starting from scratch or having to first learn how to write a business plan. *BizPlan Builder* is a complete business plan outline that follows the most popular format used. Fill in the blanks by following the outline headings and built-in tutorials. Prompts ask questions and make suggestions. You can easily edit and reformat any of the text or layout. Create a business plan with a minimum of time and confusion. *($99 - IBM Order #BZD; Macintosh Order #BZM)*

Prices subject to change.

To Order Call 1-800-331-8877

Survival Guides to Avoid the Hidden Traps

■ **Set of Survival Guides to Avoid the Hidden Traps**

Save $20. Includes *Independent Contractors: A Manager's Guide and Audit Reference, Unemployment Insurance: A Cost You Can Cut* and *Employer's Survival Guide to Workers' Compensation.* See descriptions below. *($90 - Order #CRK)*

■ **Independent Contractors: A Manager's Guide and Audit Reference**

Survive the IRS and state audit war against employers that misclassify workers as independent contractors. A single mistake can cost an employer $15,000 per worker per year. The guide details what factors the IRS looks for, explains special rules for over 300 industries and fatal flaws other companies have made. Contains a sample legal contract, pre-hire worksheet and required government forms. *($40 - Order #ICK)*

■ **Unemployment Insurance: A Cost You Can Cut**

Unemployment insurance benefit increases of 39 percent started in 1990, meaning wrongful claims and errors by the state and your firm will cost much more. The sweeping reform law that went into effect in 1990 provides protections to employers who know how the system works. Learn how to protest claims and how to audit every unemployment insurance form just like your firm audits any invoice. *($35 - Order #UIH)*

■ **Employer's Survival Guide to Workers' Compensation**

Explains California's complex workers' compensation system, including how to avoid unnecessary costs and litigation. Explains anti-fraud provisions and limits on stress claims. Chapter on stress teaches you how to avoid and manage stress claims. New information on experience modification and workers' comp and the Americans with Disabilities Act. Includes *Workers' Comp Fraud Kit ($35 - Order #WCH)*

■ **Workers' Comp Fraud Kit**

Stop fraudulent workers' comp claims with the help of this kit designed to meet the requirements of the workers' comp fraud prevention law. Contains: posters warning your employees that filing a phony workers' comp claim is a felony; stickers that you affix to workers' comp claim forms warning that fraud is a felony (meets your legal duty); checklist on how to spot fraud and what to do about it. Get one FREE when you order *Employer's Survival Guide to Workers' Compensation. ($5 - English Order #AFE; Spanish Order #AFS)*

■ **Workers' Comp Videos**

Two-tape video set begins with a strong statement that workers' comp fraud is a felony and that employees don't need a lawyer to get workers' comp benefits. These two videos target a major cause of skyrocketing workers' comp premiums: lawyers. The first video helps educate your employees about how the system works (6 minutes). A second and very similar video is to be shown to your injured workers. It reassures them their medical bills will be paid, they'll get cash benefits while out, and that you want them back on the job (5 minutes). *($39.95 - English Order #WVE; Spanish Order #WVS)*

■ **Family Leave Laws: A Guide for California Employers**

Explains the interaction of the federal and state family/medical leave acts. Helps end confusion with a step-by-step explanation of how to comply. Includes: a checklist of the records you must keep to protect against future complaints by employees; a sample Family/Medical Leave Act poster; family/medical leave fact sheet; sample forms; and a sample family leave policy that you can copy and use. *($29 - Order #FAM)*

ADA Compliance

■ **ADA Kit**

Save $15. Includes *ADA: 10 Steps to Compliance, ADA Software, ADA Video Set* (see descriptions below) and *Employer Poster Set* (see description under **Survival Guides to the Labor Law Jungle**). *($199 - Order #ADK)*

■ **ADA: 10 Steps to Compliance**

Easy-to-use, comprehensive guide shows you how to determine what you need to do to comply with the Americans with Disabilities Act (ADA), the most complex, sweeping labor law in years. Includes examples, worksheets, checklists, sample forms. Explains key terms, such as "essential functions," "reasonable accommodation," "direct threat," "undue hardship." *($40 - Order #ADA)*

■ **ADA Software**

Job descriptions identifying "essential job functions" are the best way to document your compliance with the ADA. This quality "graphical interface software" helps you write customized ADA-ready job descriptions quickly. Select from 1,300 sample complete job descriptions, then modify, combine, cut 'n' paste or add your own words. (IBM PC, XT, AT, PS/2-compatible with 640K RAM, DOS 2.11 or later. 3MB hard disk capacity.) *($99 - 3.5" diskette - Order #AD3; 5.25" diskette - Order #AD5)*

■ **ADA Video Set**

Two-tape set saves you time and gives you the assurance that everyone who oversees or interviews other people will have the knowledge to keep your company out of trouble. One video gives your managers an overview of the ADA (15 minutes). The other shows a manager in action trying to prepare for an interview (22 minutes). *($75 - Order #AVE)*

Sexual Harassment Prevention

■ **Sexual Harassment Compliance Kit**

Save $39. Includes *Stopping Sexual Harassment: An Employer's Guide, Stopping Sexual Harassment Videos,* and FREE *Sexual Harassment Compliance Packet* and FREE *Employer Poster Set.* See descriptions below. *($149 - Order #SHK)*

■ **Stopping Sexual Harassment: An Employer's Guide**

Clear, thorough handbook teaches you how to prevent, investigate and resolve sexual harassment complaints within your company. The handbook is written in lay terms and is easy to use. *($39 - Order #SXE)*

■ **Stopping Sexual Harassment Videos**

Three-part video explains to your employees what sexual harassment is and how to prevent it from happening at your company. Part 1 trains your employees about what behavior constitutes sexual harassment, what to do if it should happen to them, and encourages them to resolve the complaint within your company (7 minutes). Part 2 trains your managers and supervisors on the importance of taking sexual harassment complaints seriously. They're told that your company, and in some cases, they personally, are liable for tremendous penalties if they were aware of and did not respond promptly to a complaint (10 minutes). Part 3 teaches the investigator how to plan and conduct the investigation. Checklists also are provided to ensure the investigation is thorough and well-documented (10 minutes). *($129 - Order #SHV)*

FREE BONUS: *Sexual Harassment Compliance Packet* and *Employer Poster Set* (see description under **Survival Guides to Labor Law Jungle**).

Prices subject to change.

To Order Call 1-800-331-8877

Notes